FIFTH EDITION

Geology and the Environment

About the Authors

DR. BERNARD W. PIPKIN is Professor Emeritus at the University of Southern California. He received his doctorate from the University of Arizona and is a licensed geologist and certified engineering geologist in the state of California. After graduation he worked for the U.S. Army Corps of Engineers on a variety of military and civil projects, from large dams to pioneer roads in rough terrain for microwave sites. He has been a consulting engineering geologist as well as a university teacher since 1965.

Dr. Pipkin is past president of the National Association of Geology Teachers and is a Fellow in the Geological Society of America. He hosted the PBS 30-part program Oceanus that won a local Emmy for Best Educational Television Series. He recently shared the Clare Holdredge Award (1995) with Richard Proctor from the Association of Engineering Geologists for their book *Engineering Geology Practice* in Southern California. Dr. Pipkin is a private pilot with a flight instructor's rating; he took many of the aerial photos in the book. He and his wife Faye have three grown children and live south of Los Angeles in Palos Verdes.

DR. D. D. "DEE" TRENT has been working at, or teaching, geology since 1955. After graduating from college he worked in the petroleum industry where his geologic skills were sharpened with projects in Utah, Arizona, California, and Alaska. When the company decided to send him to Libya he decided it was time to become a college geology teacher. He has taught for for 28 years at Citrus Community College in Glendora, California, and along the way has worked for the National Park Service, done field research on glaciers in Alaska and California, visited numerous mines in the United States and Germany, picked up a Ph. D. from the University of Arizona, appeared in several episodes of the PBS telecourse, The Earth Revealed, and served as an adjunct faulty member at the University of Southern California, where he taught field geology. He and his wife raised two children in Claremont, California and when not involved with geology he's either skiing or playing banjo in a dixieland band.

RICHARD W. HAZLETT teaches environmental geology, introduction to environmental studies and a course in agroecology at Pomona College in southern California. He is a physical volcanologist by training, with research experience in the Pacific Northwest, Central America, Italy, New Zealand, the Aleutian Islands, Iceland, and Mongolia. He is three time winner of the Pomona College Wig Award for outstanding teaching, and a National Park Service media award winner for his publications *Puuhonua-o-Honaunau Discovery Book* and *Joshua Tree National Park Geology* (the latter co-written with Dee Trent). Other books he has written include *Roadside Geology of Hawaii* and *Field Geology of Kilauea Volcano*.

DR. PAUL BIERMAN is a professor of Geology at the University of Vermont where he engages people of all ages in the study of how Earth's surface works. For more than 15 years, he's done research in Vermont and many other places around the world including far northern Canada, central Australia, southern Africa, Israel and the American southwest. His latest efforts use historic imagery to document the impact of people on the Vermont landscapes and the impact of landscape events on people and societies. Paul earned his BA from Williams College in 1985 and his MS and PhD from the University of Washington, the latter in 1993. He has been at the University of Vermont ever since then with appointments in Geology and the School of Natural Resources. In 1996, Paul was awarded the Donath medal as the outstanding young scientist of the year by the Geological Society of America; he has since received a CAREER award from the National Science Foundation specifically for integrating scientific education and research. In 2005, Paul was awarded the National Science Foundation's Distinguished Teaching Scholar award in recognition of his on-going attempts to integrate these two strands of his academic life. Together, Paul, his graduate and undergraduate students, and collaborators have 50 publications in refereed journals and books.

Geology and the Environment

BERNARD W. PIPKIN
Emeritus, University of Southern California

D. D. TRENT
Citrus College

RICHARD HAZLETT
Pomona College

PAUL BIERMAN
University of Vermont

THOMSON
BROOKS/COLE

Australia • Brazil • Canada • Mexico • Singapore • Spain • United Kingdom • United States

THOMSON
★
BROOKS/COLE

Executive Editor: Peter Adams
Development Editor: Melinda Newfarmer
Assistant Editor: Alex Brady
Marketing Manager: Joseph Rogove
Marketing Communications Manager: Bryan Vann
Project Manager, Editorial Production: Belinda Krohmer
Creative Director: Rob Hugel
Art Director: Vernon Boes
Print Buyer: Doreen Suruki
Permissions Editor: Roberta Broyer

Production Service: Ben Kolstad, ITC
Text Designer: Lisa Buckley
Photo Researcher: Terri Wright
Copy Editor: Anthony Green
Illustrator: Precision Graphics
Cover Designer: Roger Knox
Cover Image: Daryl Benson/Masterfile
Cover Printer: Courier Kendallville
Compositor: International Typesetting and Composition
Printer: Courier Kendallville

For more information about our products, contact us at:
Thomson Learning Academic Resource Center
1-800-423-0563
For permission to use material from this text or product,
submit a request online at *http://www.thomsonrights.com.*
Any additional questions about permissions can be
submitted by e-mail to thomsonrights@thomson.com.

Thomson Higher Education
10 Davis Drive
Belmont, CA 94002-3098
USA

Library of Congress Control Number: 2007920035

ISBN-13: 978-0-495-11305-8
ISBN-10: 0-495-11305-0

Brooks/Cole—Thomson Learning
10 Davis Drive
Belmont, CA 94002
USA

Asia
Thomson Learning
5 Shenton Way #01-01
UIC Building
Singapore 068808

Australia/New Zealand
Thomson Learning
102 Dodds Street
Southbank, Victoria 3006
Australia

Canada
Nelson
1120 Birchmount Road
Toronto, Ontario M1K 5G4
Canada

Europe/Middle East/Africa
Thomson Learning
High Holborn House
50/51 Bedford Row
London WC1R 4LR
United Kingdom

Latin America
Thomson Learning
Seneca, 53
Colonia Polanco
11560 Mexico D.F.
Mexico

Spain/Portugal
Paraninfo
Calle Magallanes, 25
28015 Madrid, Spain

Brief Contents

Chapter 1
Humans, Geology, and the Environment 1

Chapter 2
Getting Around in Geology 15

Chapter 3
Plate Tectonics 45

Chapter 4
Earthquakes and Human Activities 70

Chapter 5
Volcanoes 109

Chapter 6
Soils, Weathering, and Erosion 148

Chapter 7
Mass Wasting and Subsidence 178

Chapter 8
Fresh-Water Resources 213

Chapter 9
Hydrologic Hazards at the Earth's Surface 246

Chapter 10
Coastal Environments and Humans 276

Chapter 11
Glaciation and Long-Term Climate Change 311

Chapter 12
Arid Lands and Desertification 351

Chapter 13
Mineral Resources and Society 370

Chapter 14
Energy and the Environment 412

Chapter 15
Waste Management and Geology 447

Appendix 1   Periodic Table of the Elements 474
Appendix 2   Some Important Minerals 475
Appendix 3   Planes in Space: Dip and Strike 477
Appendix 4   Modified Mercalli Scale 478
Glossary 479
Credits 491
Index 494

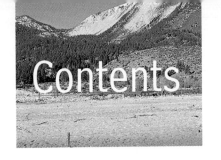

Contents

Chapter 1

Humans, Geology, and the Environment   1

What Is Environmental Geology?   2
   Humans and the Geological Environment   3
   IPAT   3
   Carrying Capacity   5
   Putting Ourselves At Risk   7
   The Environmental Geologist   8
   Tools of the Trade   9

Some Case Histories   10

Case Study 1.1 EXPONENTIAL GROWTH, WEALTH, POVERTY, AND POPULATION   11

Gallery   *Overpopulation Problems*   12

Summary   13
Key Terms   13
Study Questions   13
For Further Information   14

Chapter 2

Getting Around in Geology   15

The Earth System   16

Earth Materials   18
   Elements, Atoms, and Atomic Structure   18
   Minerals   19
   Rock-Forming Silicates   20
   Mineral Identification   20
   Rocks   23
   Rock Defects   29

Geologic Time   30

Age of Earth   34

Case Study 2.1 MINERALS, CANCER, AND OSHA—FACT AND FICTION   37
Case Study 2.2 A GIRL'S BEST FRIEND AND OTHER GEMS   38
Case Study 2.3 MINERALS, CATS, AND THE LITTER BELT   40

Gallery   *A Rock Collection*   41

Summary   43
Key Terms   43
Study Questions   44
For Further Information   44

Chapter 3

Plate Tectonics   45

Continental Drift   47
   Wegener Vindicated   48

Plate Tectonics   51
   How Fast Do the Plates Move?   56
   What's Causing All This Restlessness?   56
   The Dance of the Continents   58

Plate Tectonics and the Rock Cycle   61
   Hot Spots   61

Plate Tectonics and the Environment   61
   Plate Tectonics and the Human Environment   61

Case Study 3.1 EXOTIC TERRANES—A CONTINENTAL MOSAIC   64

Gallery   *Visions of How the Earth Works*   66

Summary   68
Key Terms   68
Study Questions   69
For Further Information   69

Chapter 4

Earthquakes and Human
Activities 70

The Nature of Earthquakes 71
    Locating the Epicenter 74
    Earthquake Measurement 75

Fault Creep, the "Nonearthquake" 79
    Forensic Use of Seismic Records 79

Seismic Design Considerations 79
    Ground Shaking 79
    Landslides 82
    Ground or Foundation Failure 82
    Ground Rupture and Changes in Ground
        Level 83
    Fires 84
    Tsunamis 84

Five Earthquakes That Make a Point 84
    Gujarat, India, 2001 85
    Alaska, 2002 86
    Colima, Mexico, 2003 86
    Sumatra, 2004 87
    Northridge, California, 1994 88
    What We Can Learn 90
    Does Earthquake Country Include Idaho, Missouri,
        and New York? 91
    The Pacific Northwest 93

Prediction 94
    Forecasts 95
    Statistical Approach 95
    Geological Methods 95

Mitigation 97
    Survival Tips 99

Case Study 4.1 EARTHQUAKES, LANDSLIDES, AND DISEASE 101
Case Study 4.2 PREDICTABLE "FUTURE SHOCKS" 101
Case Study 4.3 RX FOR FAILED FREEWAYS 102
Case Study 4.4 DEPRESSED TIGERS, RESTLESS TURTLES, AND
    EARTHQUAKES! 104

Gallery Earthquakes Are Hard on Cars 105

Summary 107
Key Terms 107
Study Questions 108
For Further Information 108

Chapter 5

Volcanoes 109

Who Should Worry 111

The Nature of the Problem 113

Types of Eruptions and Volcanic Cones 115
    Effusive Eruptions 115
    Explosive Eruptions 119

Benefits of Volcanic Action 122
    Geothermal Energy 122

Volcanic Hazards 123
    Lava Flows 123
    Ash Falls 124
    Pyroclastic Flows 125
    Lahars 127
    Tsunamis 127
    Weather and Climate 128
    Gases 129

Mitigation and Prediction 130
    Diversion 130
    Volcano Hazard Zones and Risk 130
    Eruption Forecasting 131
    What to Do When an Eruption Occurs 134

Case Study 5.1 NEW ZEALAND'S BLAST IN THE PAST,
    A SKIFIELD, AND FLUIDIZATION 135
Case Study 5.2 MONTSERRAT, PARADISE LOST 138
Case Study 5.3 CARBON DIOXIDE, EARTHQUAKES, AND THE
    LOS ANGELES WATER SUPPLY 139
Case Study 5.4 VOLCANIC CO_2 AND FOUNTAINING LAKES 141

Gallery Volcanic Wonders 143

Summary 145
Key Terms 146
Study Questions 146
For Further Information 146

Chapter 6

Soils, Weathering, and Erosion   148

Weathering   149
  Physical Weathering   150
  Chemical Weathering   151
  The Rate of Weathering   153
  Geologic Features of Weathering   154

Soils   155
  Soil Genesis   155
  Soil Profile   155
  Soil Color and Texture   157
  Soil Classification   159

Soil Problems   161
  Soil Erosion   161
  The Impact of Cropland Loss on Humans   164
  Expansive Soils   166
  Permafrost   166
  Settlement   169
  Other Soil Problems   170

Case Study 6.1 SALINIZATION AND WATERLOGGING   172
Case Study 6.2 GENERAL PATTON'S SOILS DECADES LATER   172
Case Study 6.3 RX FOR CONTAMINATED SOILS   174

Gallery   *Soils as an Album of History*   175

Summary   176
Key Terms   177
Study Questions   177
For Further Information   177

Chapter 7

Mass Wasting and Subsidence   178

Classifying Mass Movements   179

Flows   180
  Types of Flows   180
  Causes, Behavior, and Prediction of Debris Flows   180

Landslides That Move as a Unit   184
  Types   184
  Falls   186
  Lateral Spreading   187
  The Mechanics of Slides: a Matter of Balance   188

Reducing Losses from Mass Wasting   190
  Landslide Hazard Zonation   190
  Building Codes and Regulations   191

Control and Stabilization   192
  Water Drainage and Control   192
  Excavation and Redistribution   192
  Retaining Devices   193
  Mitigating Debris Flows   194
  Snow Avalanches   195

Subsidence   197
  Human-Induced Subsidence   197
  Natural Subsidence   197

A Classification of Subsidence   198
  Deep Subsidence   198
  Shallow Subsidence   199

Mitigation   200

Case Study 7.1 DYNAMIC REAL ESTATE IN OREGON   201
Case Study 7.2 COLORADO'S SLUMGULLION LANDSLIDE—A MOVING STORY 300 YEARS OLD   202
Case Study 7.3 A RESCUE PLAN FOR THE MERCHANTS OF VENICE   204
Case Study 7.4 WATER, WATER EVERYWHERE   205
Case Study 7.5 WHEN THE TREES COME DOWN, SO DO THE HILLS   206

Gallery   *Slip, Slide, and Fall*   208

Summary   210
Key Terms   211
Study Questions   211
For Further Information   212

Chapter 8

Fresh-Water Resources   213

Water as a Resource   215

Fresh Water at Earth's Surface   216
  Rivers   216
  Lakes   216

Fresh Water Underground   218

Groundwater Supply 219

Location and Distribution 220
Static Water Table 220
Pressurized Underground Water 223

Groundwater Storage and Management 224
Groundwater Mining 226
Groundwater–Saltwater Interaction 227
Groundwater–Surface Water Interaction and Usage
Trends 228
Geologic Work by Underground Water 229

Water Quality 230
Dissolved Substances 230
Groundwater Pollutants 232

Conservation and Alternative Sources 234

Case Study 8.1 WHO SHRUNK THE ARAL SEA? 235
Case Study 8.2 FLUID FLOW IN POROUS ROCKS 237
Case Study 8.3 GROUNDWATER LAW 238
Case Study 8.4 THE EDWARDS AQUIFER, A TEXAS
BONANZA 239
Case Study 8.5 LONG ISLAND, NEW YORK—SALTWATER OR
FRESH WATER FOR THE FUTURE? 240

Gallery   *Groundwater Wonders* 242

Summary 243
Key Terms 244
Study Questions 245
For Further Information 245

Chapter 9
Hydrologic Hazards at the Earth's Surface 246

Weather and Climate 248

Types of Floods 250

Impacts of Floods 252
River Systems 252
Stream Features 254

When There Is Too Much Water 257
Flood Measurement 258
Flood Frequency 258

Mitigation 261
Options 261

Case Study 9.1 THE NILE RIVER—THREE CUBITS BETWEEN
SECURITY AND DISASTER 264
Case Study 9.2 NEW ORLEANS, THE FLOOD HAPPENS 265
Case Study 9.3 WHEN ICE MELTS AND MOVES 266
Case Study 9.4 DAMS—"IN" OR "OUT" 268
Case Study 9.5 A VERY WET FALL 269
Case Study 9.6 THE IMPERMEABLE FLOOD 270

Gallery   *Going . . . Going . . . Gone! Dam Failure* 272

Summary 274
Key Terms 275
Study Questions 275
For Further Information 275

Chapter 10
Coastal Environments and Humans 276

Wind Waves 277
Waves in Deep Water and at
the Shore 277
Wave Refraction 279

Impulsively Generated Waves 281
Tsunamis 281

Shorelines 286
Beaches 286
Beach Accumulation and Erosion—The River of
Sand 288
Hurricanes, Nor'easters, and Coastal Effects 293

Case Study 10.1 DISTANT TSUNAMIS—THE SILENT THREAT
301
Case Study 10.2 A MOVING EXPERIENCE 302
Case Study 10.3 KATRINA—HOW COULD IT BE SO BAD? 304
Case Study 10.4 TSUNAMI—A QUARTER MILLION PERISH 305

Gallery   *Reminders of Nature's Force* 307

Summary 308
Key Terms 309
Study Questions 309
For Further Information 309

Chapter 11
Glaciation and Long-Term Climate Change 311

Glaciation 312
Origin and Distribution of
Glaciers 313
Glacier Budget 313
Glacial Features 314

The Effects of Glaciation 316
    Distribution of Soils 317
    Groundwater Resources 317
    Sea-Level Changes 317
    Isostatic Rebound 318
    Human Transportation Routes 318
    Pleistocene Lakes 319
    Glaciation and Climate Change 322

Climate 323
    Factors That Control Climate 323

Causes of Climate Change 326
    Variations in Earth's Orbit 326
    Breaking the Ice: Evidence of Climate Change 330

Today's Global Warming 332
    Evidence of Global Warming 332
    Consequences of Global warming 336
    Causes of Today's Global Warming 337
    Living with Uncertainty 338

Implications for the Future 338
    What Individuals Can Do 340
    What Industry and Governments Can Do 340

Case Study 11.1 A SUMMER ON ICE: RESEARCH ON THE
                 GREENLAND ICE SHEET 341
Case Study 11.2 CLIMATE DATA ON ICE: THE NATIONAL ICE
                 CORE LABORATORY 344
Case Study 11.3 WHERE ARE THE WILD THINGS? 345

Gallery Wonders of Glaciation 347

Summary 348
Key Terms 349
Study Questions 349
For Further Information 349

Chapter 12

Arid Lands and Desertification 351

Wind as a Geologic Agent
in Deserts 352

Arid Regions, Winds, and Human Health 352

Deserts 354
    Kinds of Deserts 355

Desertification 356

Case Study 12.1 IS DESERTIFICATION SWALLOWING
                 CHINA? 363

Case Study 12.2 ARROYO CUTTING AND ENVIRONMENTAL
                 CHANGE IN THE WESTERN UNITED STATES:
                 CLIMATE OR OVERGRAZING? 365

Gallery Desert Oddities 367

Summary 368
Key Terms 368
Study Questions 368
For Further Information 368

Chapter 13

Mineral Resources and Society 370

Mineral Abundances
and Distribution 372
    Economic Mineral
        Concentration 372
    Factors That Change Reserves 373
    Distribution of Mineral Resources 375

Origins of Mineral Deposits 375
    Igneous Processes 375
    Sedimentary Processes 377
    Weathering Processes 380
    Metamorphic Processes 381
    Metallic Mineral Reserves 382
    Nonmetallic Mineral Reserves 382

Mineral Resources for the Future 384

Mining and Its Environmental Impacts 386
    Impacts of Coal Mining 388
    Impacts of Underground Mining 389
    Impacts of Surface Mining 391
    Impacts of Mineral Processing 393

Mine-Land Reclamation 396
    Surface- and Groundwater Protection 396
    Mill and Smelter Waste Contamination 397
    Revegetation and Wildlife Restoration 398

The Future of Mining 398
    Mining Legislation in the United States 399

Case Study 13.1 ACID MINE DRAINAGE AND EARTH SYSTEMS
                 400
Case Study 13.2 CLEANING UP A CENTURY OF HARDROCK
                 MINING: THE ABANDONED MINE LANDS
                 INITIATIVE 401
Case Study 13.3 RECLAMATION OF OPEN PIT COAL MINES 404
Case Study 13.4 A WOUNDED MOUNTAIN SPEWS POISON 405

Gallery The Legacy of Mines and Mining 407

Summary 409
Key Terms 410
Study Questions 410
For Further Information 411

Chapter 14
Energy and the Environment 412

Petroleum 414
  Origin and Accumulation of Hydrocarbon Deposits
    415
  Geologic Traps—Oil and Gas Stop Here 416
  Oil Production 417
  Quality and Price 419
  Reserves and the Future for Oil 419
  Energy Gases and the Future 422

Coal 423
  Coalification and Rank 424
  Reserves and Production 425

Nonconventional Fossil Fuels 426
  Tar Sands 426
  Oil Shales 426

Problems of Fossil Fuel Combustion 427
  Air Pollution 427
  Mine Collapse 429

Energy for the Future 429
  Beyond Petroleum—Alternatives for the Future 430
  Direct Solar Energy 430
  Indirect Solar Energy 431
  Geothermal Energy 433

Nuclear Energy 434
  Geological Considerations 435

Energy from the Sea 436
  Ocean Thermal Energy Conversion 436
  Wave Energy 436
  Tidal Currents 436

Case Study 14.1 ROCK OIL AND THE COLONEL 438
Case Study 14.2 INDUSTRY CRACKS OPEN A NEW OIL SOURCE
    IN THE GULF OF MEXICO 439
Case Study 14.3 BAKING SODA, VINEGAR, AND ACID RAIN 440

Gallery *Energy Is Where You Find It* 442

Summary 444
Key Terms 445
Study Questions 445
For Further Information 445

Chapter 15
Waste Management and Geology 447

Municipal Waste Disposal 449
  Municipal Waste Disposal
    Methods 449
  Problems of Municipal Waste
    Isolation 453

The Completed Landfill 455
  Recycling 455
  Multiple Land-Use Strategies 458

Hazardous Waste Disposal 459
  Hazardous-Waste Disposal Methods 459
  Superfund 459

Nuclear Waste Disposal 460
  Types of Nuclear Waste 461
  Isolation of Nuclear Waste 462
  Health and Safety Standards for Nuclear Waste 464
  Is There a Future for Nuclear Energy? 464

Private Sewage Disposal 465

Case Study 15.1 THE SOCIOLOGY OF WASTE DISPOSAL 466
Case Study 15.2 THE HIGHEST POINT BETWEEN MAINE AND
    FLORIDA 466
Case Study 15.3 DEEP-WELL INJECTION AND HUMAN-CAUSED
    EARTHQUAKES 467
Case Study 15.4 LOVE CANAL—A PRECEDENT IN HUMAN-
    CAUSED ENVIRONMENTAL POLLUTION 468
Case Study 15.5 RADON AND INDOOR AIR POLLUTION 469

Gallery *Waste Disposal Then and Now* 471

Summary 472
Key Terms 472
Study Questions 473
For Further Information 473

Appendix 1 *Periodic Table of the Elements* 474
Appendix 2 *Some Important Minerals* 475
Appendix 3 *Planes in Space: Dip and Strike* 477
Appendix 4 *Modified Mercalli Scale* 478
Glossary 479
Credits 491
Index 494

Preface

Our Changing Planet

Environmental geology is the study of the relationship between humans and their geologic environment. An underlying assumption is that this relationship is interactive. Not only do naturally occurring geologic phenomena affect the lives of people each day, but also human activities affect geological processes, sometimes with tragic consequences. Renowned historian Will Durant noted that our physical environment "exists by geological consent, subject to change without notice." In the face of skyrocketing levels of atmospheric CO_2, and the potential for abrupt global and regional climate change, this statement is more true today than it has ever been. We may regard this as the historian's assurance that during our lifetimes, we will probably be subject to an earthquake, a flood, a landslide, volcanic activity, or some other significant geologic hazard. No one is truly educated until she or he knows about our geological environment and these hazards.

This book deals with the geology of now, not some distant past. The reader will find that the seismic chapter deals with earthquakes as recent as 2005 and emphasizes that earthquakes don't kill people; the collapse of human-built structures is the danger that seismic hazards present to our existence. The devastating magnitude-7.7 earthquake near Gujarat, India in 2001 that killed close to 20,000 people is the example presented of the danger that poorly constructed buildings present to humans. An earthquake in the central United States in 2003 reminds us also that the most widely felt and perhaps the strongest earthquake in U.S. history was centered near New Madrid, Missouri, which has a geologic setting similar to Gujarat, India. Gujarat is worthy of study for this reason; the U.S. Geological Survey believes the Gujarat earthquake to be an important event that can expand our understanding of mid-continent seismicity. The human misery and economic impact of natural disasters is difficult to evaluate, but the book emphasizes that practically no area is free from geologic hazards.

Fresh water is now thought to be the limiting factor to man's existence on earth, and this and the hydrologic hazards presented by too much water are emphasized. In late 2003 a group of young people were camped at the foot of the mountains in southern California that had been subject to an intense forest fire several months earlier. A debris flow caught them by surprise and took many lives. It is the sincere hope of the authors that the students who take this course and read this book will be more aware of the hazard that denuded slopes present during the rainy season. The same might be said of rip currents (erroneously called rip tides) in the surf zone discussed in the chapter on coastal environments. Less dramatic, but in the long term just as important are the decisions we make every day, such as whether we park on a lawn and reduce the ability of rainwater to infiltrate or whether we choose to manage our forests wisely, given the link between clearcutting and erosion. Awareness of your geologic surroundings will lead to a safer existence in an increasingly complex world, and has the added benefit of being intellectually satisfying.

In a society where science and technology are interwoven with economics and political action, an understanding of the sciences is increasingly important. The National Science Foundation, the National Center for Earth Science Education, and several other prestigious earth science organizations are promoting earth science literacy in the United States for students from elementary school through college. The hope is that through education, today's students will become better stewards of our planet than their predecessors have been. How long can civilization sustain itself if it continues to harvest Earth's natural resources at the current rate? How much responsibility should we as individuals take for maintaining the planet that we share, and how much can we accomplish as individuals? Earth science literacy opens our minds to such questions and allows us to give them better answers. It helps us to appreciate Earth's beauty, but also to recognize its limitations.

One thing is certain: the planet can sustain just so much life, and it is now being pushed to the limit. The fragility of Earth was described very eloquently by *Apollo 14* astronaut Edgar Mitchell:

> It is so incredibly impressive when you look back at our planet from out there in space and you realize so forcibly that it's a closed system—that we don't have unlimited resources, that there's only so much air and so much water. You get out there in space and you say to yourself "That's home. That's the only home we have, and the only one we're going to have for a long time." We had better take care of it. We don't get a second chance.

About This Book

In this new edition, we are pleased to welcome our longtime friend and professional colleague, Paul Bierman, to the author team. All of us have drawn upon our many field studies in the writing of this text. One of us (Pipkin) has specialized in the study of geologic hazards and their mitigation—more specifically, in the safe siting of engineering works ranging from dams and tunnels to single-family dwellings. Dee Trent has focused on geologic fieldwork, exploration for natural resources, and glacier studies. Rick Hazlett, formerly a ranger at Hawaii Volcanoes National Park, has maintained his interest and his research on volcanoes and is active in environmental studies. Paul Bierman's areas of expertise include understanding how humans and landscapes interact. He is particularly interested in the impact of humans on the built and natural landscape. As colleagues in the teaching profession, it seemed natural for us to combine our past experiences and mutual interests in teaching and environmental protection in a textbook.

Geology and the Environment, Fifth Edition, is intended to fulfill the needs of a one-semester college course for students with little or no science background. It examines geologic principles, processes, and phenomena and relates them to human activities. What you learn in this course will be useful to you throughout your life. It will serve you as you form opinions about environmental issues, select a home site, or evaluate property in a business venture. At the very least, when you understand how Earth "works," any fears you have about such things as earthquakes, hurricanes, and volcanic eruptions should be lessened.

This books presents geology that can be applied to improving the human endeavor. Chapter 1 presents an overview of the underlying cause of many of our present environmental problems. The stress of overpopulation on the environment has resulted in water and air pollution, land degradation, occupation of lands subject to geological hazards, and uncontrolled extraction of resources. The impact of overpopulation and the relatively new awareness of the environment are reasons that colleges are adding "environmental" courses such as environmental geology to their curricula.

Because this book is intended for students who are not (yet!) geology majors, Chapters 2 and 3 offer some basic information useful for "getting around in geology." Chapter 2 presents information that is needed for the book's subsequent examinations of geological hazards and processes, mineral resources, and so on. The emphasis is that the earth is an interacting "system." Students will see that one cannot divorce atmospheric and oceanic processes from processes that occur on the solid earth surface, nor moving tectonic plates (Chapter 3) from volcanic and seismic activity.

Following these groundwork chapters, the focus shifts to various types of geologic processes and hazards. Earthquakes and volcanoes are two of the most spectacular expressions of the energy contained *within* the planet, and Chapters 4 and 5

examine how this energy is transferred to Earth's surface—where we live—and how we can learn to recognize the signals that "something's up" and work to minimize the damage when the inevitable occurs.

The next two chapters focus on geologic processes that occur on or very near the surface of Earth. Much of the soil that we build our homes on and grow our food in today is bedrock of the far distant past that has been chemically and physically altered through weathering processes (Chapter 6). Present-day rocks and soils continue to undergo these processes, in some cases assisted by human activities such as construction, mining, and extraction of water from underground. The results—mass wasting (landslides) and ground subsidence and collapse—cause deaths and millions of dollars of damage each year. These ground-failure problems are examined in detail in Chapter 7.

Earth is sometimes described as the water planet, and the presence or absence of water is essential in defining the geological and biological environments in which we live. Chapter 8 deals with fresh-water resources, with the emphasis on underground water and how we can protect and conserve this most essential resource. Streams, rivers, and lakes are also vital water and esthetic resources. They sustain life along their banks, and some of them are important means of transportation. They also pose hazards, most notably floods, to people who live along them. These hazards are the subject of Chapter 9.

In Chapter 10 we look at the effects of the largest bodies of water on Earth, the oceans, on life. Coastal geologic processes, waves, beaches, and hurricanes—the most life-threatening of all natural hazards—are examined. Because oceans play an important role in global climate, the phenomenon known as El Niño is discussed.

Glaciers and glaciation and their impacts on humans are the subject of Chapter 11. This chapter logically includes a discussion of long-term climate change, which leads naturally to the consideration of the potential for global warming that is so much on people's minds today. The theme of climate extremes continues in Chapter 12, which deals with arid environments and the consequences of human-induced desertification.

Geology and the Environment, Fifth Edition, closes with a look at mineral resources—their origins, limits, extraction, and processing—and at the potential health hazards to humans from mining and smelting activities (Chapter 13). All sources of energy that can be utilized by humans, their geology and limitations, are considered in Chapter 14. The geology of disposing of waste materials generated by affluent, energy-rich societies is discussed in the final chapter.

Distinctive Features of the Book

At most schools, the course for which this book is used is a component of the general education curriculum. General education broadens and enriches students' lives and minds beyond the specialization of their major interest. To this end, **Galleries** of photos at the end of each chapter illustrate many geologic wonders and some oddities. For example, at the end of Chapter 5 (Volcanoes), there are photographs of often-visited scenic volcanic features with explanations of how they formed. In addition, we also show some jarring images highlighting the often catastrophic collision of humans with the volcanic environment. The Galleries are intended to stimulate students' curiosity and appreciation for natural geologic wonders.

Case Studies at the end of each chapter highlight the relevance of the text discussion. These cover a broad spectrum of subjects and geographic areas, but many of them focus on the causes and aftereffects of bad environmental and geological planning. Also within each chapter are several provocative **Consider This** questions. These questions require students to apply the information just presented in the text and, thus, reinforce their learning. The questions will stimulate classroom discussion as well.

At the end of each chapter is a list of **Key Terms** introduced in the chapter, a **Summary** of the chapter in outline form, **Study Questions** geared to test understanding of the chapter's key concepts, and a list of related books and articles (**For Further Information**).

The Fifth Edition

- In this fifth edition of *Geology and the Environment,* we have attempted to incorporate as many of the reviewers' suggestions as possible. Understanding that students might read the Case Studies more closely than the text, we have incorporated more critical information into each case and in many chapters we have replaced or updated case studies. We continue to strive for figures that can be found close to their discussions in the text.

- The new edition has been significantly enhanced with the introduction of a powerful new interactive media program called ThomsonNOW, which has been seamlessly integrated with the text, enhancing students' understanding of important geologic processes. It brings geology alive with animated figures based directly on figures in the text (Active Figures), media-enhanced activities, tutorials, and personalized learning plans. Like other features in our new edition, it encourages students to be curious, to think about geology in new ways, and to connect with their new-found knowledge of the world around them.

- In chapter 6, new case studies have been added to consider the effects of soil compaction on and near college campuses, desert soils and the effects of military maneuvers. Soil classification schemes have been updated to reflect current professional usage. New,

cutting edge dating and erosion monitoring techniques are explained in terms that students can understand.

- In chapter 7, mass movement and avalanche sections have been updated and expanded providing valuable information for skiers and climbers. Links between physical, biological and hydrological processes are now explicitly made. A new case study links clear cutting and erosion.

- In chapter 8, water quality standards have been updated to reflect changes in federal statutes and sections of sustainability of water resources, mining fossil water, have been expanded. Examples of medical geology, tied to public health—for example, how fluoride was found to prevent tooth decay—have been expanded.

- Chapter 9 has been revised extensively, with several new sections describing weather phenomena that drive floods, flood types, and the impacts of floods. All case studies have been revised and several new case studies added including ones that significantly broaden the geographic coverage of the chapter. New case studies include ice jam flooding, nor'easter flooding, the flooding from hurricane Katrina, and the hydrologic effects of development.

- In chapter 10, the hurricane section has been updated and expanded to consider in more depth the physical processes driving these monster storms and the effects of warming climate on their intensity and duration. Nor'easters, their genesis and effects, are now covered. The tsunami section has been greatly expanded to consider waves striking eastern North America. Two new case studies have been added: The first tells how hurricane Katrina caused such a disaster. The second is about the Indonesian tsunami in 2004.

- The text continues to emphasize remediation and prevention, an outgrowth of the authors' professional geological experiences. All of the chapters on geological hazards have dedicated sections on mitigation options, and resource and pollution issues are considered both in terms of the problems we face and of the potential ways to help forestall or lessen the impacts of these problems.

- We also continue to employ the systems approach in this edition—the idea that all of the earth's reservoirs (atmosphere, hydrosphere, solid earth, biosphere, and extraterrestrial) and the processes acting within them are interconnected.

- Environmental legal issues are discussed in the text where they are applicable, rather than placed in a separate chapter near the end of the text.

- All chapters have been updated in terms of data (where available), art, and photos.

Supplements
ThomsonNOW for Environmental Geology

As described above, we now have a powerful new interactive media program called ThomsonNOW, which has been seamlessly integrated with the text, enhancing students' understanding of important geologic principles. It brings geology alive with animated figures, media-enhanced activities, tutorials, and personalized learning plans. This student tutorial system is available using the access codes available with the text.

Thomson Brooks/Cole Earth Science Resource Center

This full-service Web site offers an array of teaching and learning resources. It contains discussion forums, interactive field trips, links to mapping activities, and many more features to make your course an interactive experience.

InfoTrac® College Edition

InfoTrac can be packaged free with each copy of the text and is an online library offering the full text of articles from hundreds of scholarly and popular publications. It is updated daily, and adopters and their students receive unlimited access for one academic term (four months).

Acknowledgments

We gratefully acknowledge the thoughtful and helpful reviews by the following individuals, some of whom have also reviewed for earlier editions. We also acknowledge the contributions of other reviewers and those who have generously contributed published and unpublished materials and photographs as this book evolved to its Fifth Edition. These have truly helped us build this book. The list is long and our thanks to many:

Dan Cayan, *U.S. Geological Survey*
Terry DeVoe, *Hecla Mining Company*
Raymond C. Harris, *Arizona Geological Survey*
Earl Francis
Lloyd Olson
Peter Kresan, *Univiersity of Arizona*
Joe Kirschvink, *California Institute of Technology*
Kevin Lamb
Rick Lozinski, *Fullerton College*
John Maurer, *CIRES, University of Colorado*
Lisa McKeon, *U.S. Geological Survey*
Kerry Sieh, *California Institute of Technology*
Konrad Steffen, *CIRES, University of Colorado*
Dean Stiffarm, Environmental Control Officer, Fort Belknap Reservation
Todd Wilkinson

Ning Zing, *University of Maryland*
Richard M. Allen, *University of Wisconsin-Madison*
Elizabeth Catlos, *Oklahoma State University*
Kevin Cornwell, *California State University-Sacramento*
James Cotter, *University of Minnesota, Morris*
Larry Fegel, *Grand Valley State University*
George H.Myer, *Temple University*
Jennifer Shosa, *Colby College*
Edward Shuster, *Rensselaer Polytechnical Institute*
Neptune Srimal, *Florida International University*
Peter J. Thompson, *University of New Hampshire*
Thomas B. Anderson, *Sonoma State University*
Robert Boutilier, *Bridgewater State College*
Kathleen M. Bower, *Eastern Illinois University*
David Bowers, *Montana Dept. of Environmental Quality*
Christopher Cirmo, *State University of New York, Cortland*
Rachael Craig, *Kent State University*
Charles DeMets, *University of Wisconsin, Madison*
John Field, *Western Washington University*
Josef Garvin, *Eden Foundation, Falkenberg, Sweden*
Tark S. Hamilton, *Consultant*
Gilbert Hanson, *State University of New York, Stony Brook*
Douglas W. Haywick, *University of South Alabama*
David D. Jackson, *UCLA*
Hobart King, *Mansfield University*
Robert Kuhlman, *Montgomery County Community College*
Kenneth A. LaSota, *Robert Morris College*
Berry Lyons, *University of Alabama*
Harmon Maher, *University of Nebraska, Omaha*
William Mode, *University of Wisconsin, Oshkosh*
Robert Sanford, *University of Southern Maine*
Steven Schafersman, *Miami University*
Hongbing Sun, *Rider University*
Terry Swanson, *University of Washington*
Glenn D. Thackray, *Idaho State University*
James L. Baer, *Brigham Young University*
William B. N. Berry, *University of California, Berkeley*
Lynn A. Brant, *University of Northern Iowa*
Don W. Byerly, *University of Tennessee, Knoxville*
Susan M. Cashman, *Humboldt State University*
Robert D. Cody, *Iowa State University*
Mark W. Evans, *Emory University*
Robert B. Furlong, *Wayne State University*
Bryan Gregor, *Wright State University*
Roger D. Hoggan, *Ricks College*
Alan C. Hurt, *San Bernardino Valley College*
Michael Lyle, *Tidewater Community College*
Lawrence Lundgren, *University of Rochester*
Garry McKenzie, *Ohio State University*
Robert Meade, *California State University, Los Angeles*
Marie Morisawa, *State University of New York, Binghamton*
William J. Neal, *Grand Valley State University*
Michael J. Nelson, *University of Alabama, Birmingham*
June A. Oberdorfer, *San Jose State University*
Charles Rovey, *Southwest Missouri State University*

Susan C. Slaymaker, *California State University, Sacramento*
Frederick M. Soster, *DePauw University*
Douglas J. Lathwell, *Cornell University*
Jack A. Muncy, *Tennessee Valley Authority*
T. K. Buntzen, *Alaska Department of Natural Resources*
Chuck Meyers, *U.S. Dept. of the Interior, Surface Mining Reclamation and Enforcement*
Ed Nuhfer, *University of Colorado, Denver*
Peter W. Weigand, *California State University, Northridge*
Joe Snowden, *University of Southeastern Missouri*
James L. Schrack, *Arco, Anaconda, Montana*
Marcie Kerner, *Arco, Anaconda, Montana*
Herbert G. Adams, *California State University, Northridge*
Lisa DuBois, *San Diego State University*
Edward B. Evenson, *Lehigh University*
Raymond W. Grant, *Mesa Community College*
Roger D. Hoggan, *Ricks College*
Steve Kenaga, *Grand Valley State University*
Barbara Hill, *Onondaga Community College*
Rita Leafgren, *University of Northern Colorado*
Joan Licari, *Cerritos College*
Larry Mayer, *Miami University*
David McConnell, *University of Akron*
James Neiheisel, *George Mason University*
Geoffrey Seltzer, *Syracuse University*
Albert J. Robb, III, *Mobil Exploration and Producing U.S., Inc., Liberal, Kansas*
Joan Van Velsor, *California Department of Transportation*

Lydia K. Fox, *University of the Pacific*
Bill Kane, *University of the Pacific*
Randall Jibson, *U.S.G.S.*
John E. Gray, *U.S.G.S.*
Edwin Harp, *U.S.G.S.*
Lynn Highland, *U.S.G.S.*
Robert Schuster, *U.S.G.S.*
Pam Irvine, *California Division of Mines and Geology*
Siang Tan, *California Division of Mines and Geology*
John Gamble and Ed Belcher, *Wellington, New Zealand*
Rick Giardino, *Texas A&M University*
Kenneth Ashton, *West Virginia Geological Survey*
Peter Martini, *University of Guelph*
Ward Chesworth, *University of Guelph*
Marion M. Gallant, *Colorado Department of Public Health and Environment*
Simon Young, *Montserrat Volcano Observatory*

Special thanks are due to Ben Kolstad of ITC who managed the production of this edition and Melinda Newfarmer who rode herd over four authors, and to Keith Dodson and Peter Adams, Science Editors at Thomson Brooks/Cole, who encouraged Paul Bierman to become one of our authors.

BERNARD W. PIPKIN
D. D. TRENT
RICHARD HAZLETT
PAUL BIERMAN

Humans, Geology, and the Environment

During the past few years, people have become increasingly aware of human vulnerability to nature's power: a giant tsunami drowned nearly a quarter of a million people in the Indian Ocean Basin in just a few terrible hours in late December of 2004; eight months later a major hurricane, Katrina, slammed into the city of New Orleans, causing the greatest urban disaster in American history since the great San Francisco earthquake and fire of 1906; meanwhile hurricane Wilma, the strongest Atlantic storm in history, forced evacuations in Mexico's Yucatan Peninsula a few weeks later. Suddenly the topic of global warming became a part of everyday conversation, together with concerns about Peak Oil, organic versus industrial farming, water depletion in the American midwest, and a possible "supervolcanic" eruption in Yellowstone National Park. To borrow a phrase from the well-known environmentalist David Orr, we now have "Earth in mind," and many of us have grown uneasy about the environmental future.

> The science of the environment is just the classic natural science of the past century in the context of modern environmental issues. It is Thoreau with a computer rather than a pen.
>
> Professor Richard Turco,
> University of California at
> Los Angeles

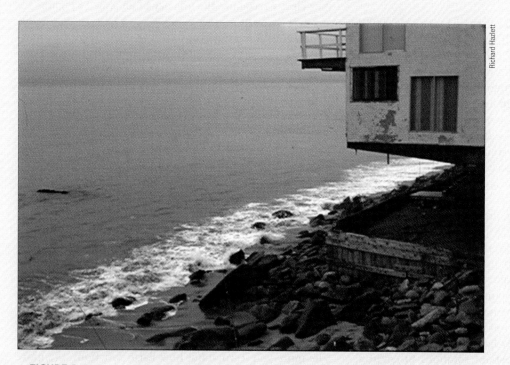

Richard Hazlett

◆ **FIGURE 1** Home versus the ocean (Malibu, California)—Hmmm, what a view! What's it like in a storm, though?

Disasters and environmental changes cannot always be prevented, of course, though some *are* avoidable given foresight and planning. In fact, the perils posed by unleashed natural forces and seemingly inexorable environmental change are largely the fault of people making bad choices, failure to heed warnings signs, and inadvertent or deliberate placement in harm's way.

Each of the concerns above pertains to our relationship with planet Earth on a grand scale. But even at a modest level, you are likely to face questions in your own life that deal with issues of humans in nature: "What do I do if someday I have to buy a house in an area where there might be landslides?" "What becomes of the waste I'm washing down the sink, and is my tap water safe to drink?" "Is it really bad to be opening a mine in my local forest, as the Sierra Club says? Or are they exaggerating the problems?"

This book will take you on a journey to build your awareness of the ultimate environment—the physical Earth—helping put great events in more practical perspective. It will also help you evaluate such questions as the ones above in ways that someday might prove to be personally meaningful.

What Is Environmental Geology?

In his play *As You Like It*, William Shakespeare (1564–1616) writes "All the world's a stage, and all men and women merely players. They have their exits and their entrances, and one man in his time plays many parts . . ." This is one of The Bard's best-loved and most-quoted lines.

Starting with that metaphor, this book takes a close look at Shakespeare's "stage" and how its changing scenery can affect the many exits, entrances, and parts that we play on it. The stage, of course, is meant to be Earth itself, together with its retinue of ever-changing societies and civilizations—the "background" for our individual human stories. The technical term for the study of the physical Earth is *geology,* a word unknown in Shakespeare's day.

An earlier British author, Geoffrey Chaucer (1343–1400), first introduced to the English language another word we also use in our book title: *environment.* The word originally appeared in early medieval France as *environnement,* meaning "surroundings." Chaucer found "environment" a clever choice for building rhymes, and he composed many lines of poetic verse describing people in nature.

Today the news is abuzz with references to "environmental problems" and "environmentalism" in general. Although we can clearly appreciate an environmental problem when we see it—smog, for instance, or a startlingly red trickle of fish-killing mine water—the meaning of the term "environmentalist" is less clear. Just *who* or *what* is an environmentalist?

If such a person is someone who believes that it's important we strive to keep our physical environment from deteriorating to the point of harming people and wiping out wildlife, then who among us is *not,* on at least rare occasions, an environmentalist? No one (rationally speaking at least) wakes up in the morning thinking it would be a fine day to destroy Earth. Unfortunately, years of hard politicking to bring about solutions to environmental problems has given the term a somewhat pejorative overtone. And many of us have become dependent upon jobs that, quite frankly, *do* end up destroying at least small parts of the natural world each day, creating conflicting values and awkward intellectual compromises within our own minds. Some opponents of environmentalism regard green activists not only as protectors of nature, but also as attackers of livelihoods and even of an entire national way of life.

But when we begin to face problems on a global scale that we all agree need to be tackled—the deterioration of the ozone, the impacts of global warming, the ecological destruction of the world ocean—then political divisiveness and dissonance almost magically disappear. People are often great at finding solutions in a mutually agreeable way once they clearly recognize the urgency of an issue (◆Figures 1.1 and 1.2).

Environmental geology is the study of how the natural workings of the physical Earth apply to the problems that we face in dealing with our environment. Virtually all of these problems have arisen because people have not appreciated how the natural world works. We are inventive creatures, to say the least, and introducing a new technology, such as synthetic fertilizer or the internal combustion engine for the modern car brings with it an almost childlike excitement—the thrill of playing with a new toy. But history shows that we tend to "leap" before we "look," unable or unwilling to assess the potential impacts of new inventions upon the natural world, and ultimately upon ourselves, too. Those consequences, ranging from water to air pollution and worse, often come back to haunt us, because we live in a finite world where everything is physically and chemically interlinked. Only so many resources and so much land exist, after all, and everything is connected in a remarkably self-sustaining natural system—one that has functioned spontaneously to support life, according to radiometric dating, for approximately 4 billion years. The more you learn about how Earth functions, the more wonderful and interlinked it all seems. To eliminate further

1) Only one person drives a hybrid electric vehicle...

The 16 cars above are producing 90-95 tons of atmospheric CO_2/year (average U.S. driving).

2) Only one person doesn't drive a hybrid electric vehicle...

The 16 cars above are producing 35-50 tons of atmospheric CO_2/year (average U.S. driving).

◆ **FIGURE 1.1** Collective behavior can change the global-scale environment, while lone behavior usually counts for little.

unintended consequences in the future it is important to understand our planet's behavior well.

That is the spirit of this book; it is not only a vehicle to give some of you general elective college credit, but we hope a stimulant for building new lifelong insight, appreciation, and sensibility for interacting with Earth in this day and age. Harking back to Shakespeare, it is our time to appear on stage. Let's make our act a good one!

Humans and the Geological Environment

Throughout most of our history, we have liked to think of ourselves as somehow apart from nature. This, it turns out, is a painful delusion, reinforced in the past by ignorance and religious traditions. Moreover, we have liked to think of Earth as a comfortably Big Place. We can throw something away, say by flushing it down the toilet or by tossing it out the car window, and it will simply disappear into the eternal vastness of the environment—out of sight, out of mind. When there were few of us on the planet and individual possessions were minor, throw-away behavior had no significant impact on the world. But now there are over 6 billion people, and within your lifetime you'll likely see the world become even more pressingly crowded. According to the United Nations, there will be nearly 9 billion people by 2050, even factoring in the declining birth rates that have appeared since the 1960s.

IPAT

The **IPAT equation** is a measure of human environmental impact: $I = P + A + T$; I = impact, P = population, A = affluence (standard of living), T = technology. It is a qualitative expression; no one can really put exact numbers to its factors, but it is important to bear in mind as a conceptual framework when we talk about how we relate to the geological environment.

The IPAT equation tells us that wealthy developed states with a lot of available technology (e.g., computers per household) and affluence (disposable incomes) have enormous environmental impacts. In a typical lifetime, for instance, an American will consume over 35 times the resources of an average citizen of India, whose country is much less economically developed. One of the conveniences of globalization and export-import trade economies is that we in the developed world *rarely see our personal environmental impacts;* they take place indirectly thousands of kilometers away, often on different continents.

A case in point concerns wood products. Prior to World War I (1914–1918) the wood we used in the United States was harvested domestically, but by 1900 the nation's forests had been so severely cut back that people began to worry about an American timber famine, rather like we worry about the energy crisis today. President Theodore Roosevelt and his Chief Forester, Gifford Pinchot, established the National Forest Service to help address this concern. They believed that with the loss of its forests, the economy of the United States would falter, and with that, the country's national power. Although conservation imposed by the federal government helped save America's forests, the real salvation came in the forms of introducing new technologies, developing new resources, and building a global economy. The first petrochemical plant in the world opened in Bayonne, New Jersey in 1923, and soon we were mass producing new construction materials such as plastics, which could substitute for wood in many manufactured products. Likewise, following World War II, we no longer needed to satisfy our demand for wood from an exclusively domestic market. Lumber could now be imported in tremendous quantity from tropical countries such as Brazil and Indonesia, thanks to the low cost of fuel. By the year 2000 more land was under forest cover in the United States than a century before. Denuded landscapes had recovered with secondary forest growth in many parts of the country, especially in the south and east.

A. GLOBAL-SCALE ENVIRONMENTAL CHANGE CAN IMPACT INDIVIDUAL BEHAVIOR...

Large ◄──── Hierarchy of Scales ────► Small

1. GLOBAL CLIMATE CHANGE

2. AT THE REGIONAL LEVEL
Onset of persistent drought dries out land and annual snow pack dwindles.

3. AT THE LOCAL LEVEL
Diminished water supply means higher water bills, and rationing.

4. IN YOUR HOME
You respond by purchasing water-conserving appliances, putting drought-tolerant plants in your garden, and taking shorter, fewer showers.

B. INDIVIDUAL BEHAVIOR CAN CHANGE THE GLOBAL-SCALE ENVIRONMENT

Small ◄──── Hierarchy of Scales ────► Large

INTENDED (Good)

UNINTENDED CONSEQUENCES (Not so good)

1. Fritz Haber fixes nitrogen, enabling development of artificial fertilizers and other commercial nitrates.

2a. Farm yields boosted worldwide.

2b. Cheap manufacture of military ordnance enabled (World War I, II).

2c. Waterways and shallow seas worldwide suffer oxygen depletion, causing dead zones.

2d. Nitrous oxide global air pollution worsens.

◆ **FIGURE 1.2** Human–Earth interaction is a two-way street.

But over the same interval of time the American per capita demand for wood actually *rose*. In fact, world demand for forest products grew three fold between 1975 and 2005, after more than doubling in the previous 70 years.

At present the minimum average annual consumption of paper believed required per person for basic communication and literacy is about 30–40 kilos (81–120 lbs). In the United States, each of us uses a staggering 330 kilos (890 lbs) of paper averaged per annum—much of it in the form of throw-away commercial packaging. Contrast this with sub-Saharan Africa, a large region where poverty and hunger are almost overwhelming; there the average consumption of paper is only about 15 kilos (47 lbs) per person each year.

The clear-cutting of forests for paper, pulp for plywood, and roundwood for construction creates many geological problems, including landslides, soil erosion, and the silting up of streams and waterways. By transferring our demand for wood products overseas, we in effect transfer environmental problems to other countries as well, where in fact standards and regulations may be much less strict and the ensuing environmental damage much greater.

In lesser developed counties, the I = P + A + T equation must be reformulated, given that there is often little technology or affluence to take into consideration. I = P means not only that numbers of people correlate more closely with actual environmental impacts but also that the problems that develop tend to be closer to home because resources usually must be collected and used locally. There is much less "out of sight, out of mind" warping personal perspectives. Farmers can see their land eroding away as a result of windstorms blowing across their freshly plowed fields (⁎ Table 1.1), and household refuse is not hauled away to some sanitary landfill kilometers away but accumulates in the backyard or in the streambed behind it. In fact, at least one-sixth of the world's population—over a billion people—suffer malnutrition on a daily basis, most in what we'd regard as environmentally squalid conditions. When we speak about the world suffering from *overpopulation*, we must also speak of *overconsumption* and *resource inequities.* The characteristics and remoteness of the stresses we put on Earth are related directly to the society and economy in which we live.

*TABLE 1.1	Estimated World Soil Degradation, 1945–1990		
Region	Degraded Land Area as a Percentage of Vegetated Land		
	Total	Light Erosion*	Moderate to Extreme Erosion**
World	17	7	10
Asia	20	7	13
South America	14	6	8
Europe	23	6	17
Africa	22	8	14
North America (U.S., Canada)	5	1	4
Central America, Mexico	25	1	24

*Light: crop yields reduced less than 10 percent.
**Moderate: crop yields reduced 10–50 percent. Severe: crop yields reduced more than 50 percent. Extreme: no crop growth possible. About 9 million hectares worldwide exhibit extreme erosion, less than 0.5 percent of all degraded lands.
Source: Various sources compiled by World Resources Institute and the United Nations, World Resources 1992–93 (New York: Oxford University Press, 1992).

Carrying Capacity

One of the most famous passages from all of environmental literature comes from Aldo Leopold (◆Figure 1.3) an ecologist who was a forest ranger in New Mexico assigned to shoot wolves for the then-new National Forest Service.

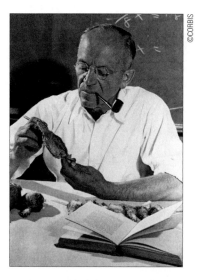

◆ **FIGURE 1.3** Aldo Leopold (1887–1948) is widely regarded as the father of ecology. His book, *A Sand County Almanac,* is a classic in the environmental literature.

The wolves threatened livestock that ranchers were allowed to let graze on public forestland by permit from the Federal Government. Leopold wrote an essay called "Thinking Like a Mountain" (1948) about what his experience taught him. Read this excerpt carefully and reflect about how it pertains to geology and the natural environment:

Only the mountain has lived long enough to listen objectively to the howl of a wolf . . . My own conviction on this score dates from the day I saw a wolf die. We were eating lunch on high rimrock, at the foot of which a turbulent river elbowed its way. We saw what we thought was a doe fording the torrent, her breast awash in white water. When she climbed the bank toward us and shook her tail, we realized our error: it was a wolf. A half-dozen others, evidently grown pups, sprang from the willows and all joined in a welcoming melee of wagging tails and playful maulings. What was literally a pile of wolves writhed and tumbled in the center of an open flat at the foot of our rimrock. In those days we had never heard of passing up a chance to kill a wolf. In a second we were pumping lead into the pack, but with more excitement than accuracy . . . When our rifles were empty, the old wolf was down, and the pup was dragging a leg into impassible slide-rocks. We reached the old wolf in time to watch a fierce green fire dying in her eyes. I was young then, and full of trigger-itch; I thought that because fewer wolves meant more deer, that no wolves would mean a hunters' paradise. But after seeing the green fire die, I sensed that neither the wolf nor the mountain agreed with such a view . . ."

Since then I have lived to see state after state extirpate its wolves. I have watched the face of many a newly wolf-less mountain and then seen the south-facing slopes wrinkle with a maze of new deer trails. I have seen every edible tree defoliated to the height of a saddlehorn. Such a mountain looks as if someone had given God a new pruning shears, and forbidden Him all other exercise. In the end the starved bones of the deer herd, dead of its own "too much," bleach [in the sun] with . . . the dead sage, or molder under the high-lined junipers. I now suspect that just as a deer herd lives in mortal fear of its wolves, so does a mountain live in mortal fear of its deer. And perhaps with better cause, for while a buck pulled down by wolves can be replaced in two or three years, a range pulled down by too many deer may fail of replacement in as many decades. So also with cows. The cowman who cleans his range of wolves does not realize that he is taking over the wolf's job of trimming the herd to fit the range. He has not learned to think like a mountain. Hence we have dustbowls, and rivers washing the future into the sea [through soil erosion].

Leopold's essay illustrates the reason why "out of sight, out of mind" can be such a destructive attitude. It also highlights the meaning of **carrying capacity**—the maximum size to which a population can grow and be maintained indefinitely given an existing resource base. In the case of the

◆ **FIGURE 1.4** Populations of predator and prey are dependent upon natural carrying-capacity limits.

◆ **FIGURE 1.5** Two hundred years ago, Thomas Malthus used a detailed economic argument to explore the concept of human carrying capacity.

wolves, the carrying capacity under natural conditions is determined by the size of the deer herd (◆Figure 1.4). In the case of the deer, it is the amount of edible forest vegetation. The wolves actually hold the deer in check by preying on them, so that the actual deer population in a forest with predators is less than the carrying capacity would allow. On the other hand, as Leopold saw, the removal of the predators allowed the deer population to grow without bounds, and it soon exceeded the capacity of the forest to support it, consuming the food supply base so intensively that the herd eventually starved and collapsed. The exceeding of carrying capacity with destructive consequence is termed **ecological overshoot.**

If it is true that we are not apart from nature, that we are beholden like every other species to a specific carrying-capacity resource base, then what is *our* resource base? For wolves and deer, it is defined by food supply, and the same is true for us as well. The size of our population is limited by the productiveness of our fisheries and agricultural lands—by the amount of food that we can grow.

As a case in point, consider this thumbnail history of modern farming. In the late nineteenth century scientists grew worried as global population exceeded one billion people; they were concerned that the world could not feed all the newborns coming into it, coupled with the fact that improved health care was keeping more and more people alive into old age. Surely we would soon enter a time of global famine and societal breakdown, as Thomas Malthus (◆Figure 1.5) warned in his influential *An Essay on The Principle of Population as it Affects the Future Improvements of Society* in 1798. In fact, if the scale and method of growing food had not improved, then this "Malthusian" prediction might well have come to pass; by 1950, with 2.5 billion people in the world, we would have exceeded our **human carrying capacity** and would be suffering from global ecological overshoot. But several key developments kept this catastrophe from taking place.

In 1912 Fritz Haber, a German chemist, learned how to fix nitrogen from the atmosphere in the form of ammonia compounds to make synthetic fertilizer (◆Figure 1.6). Suddenly we could fertilize farmlands to greatly increase crop yields. Haber had no way of understanding at the time that this would eventually lead to almost apocalyptic global water pollution problems, about which you'll learn more later in the book. But at the time he was hailed, and rightly so, as a savior of the human condition. It is hardly hyperbole to say that Fritz Haber is one of the least known and most important people who ever lived. Artificial fertilizer had suddenly boosted the planet's carrying capacity to sustain people—by billions.

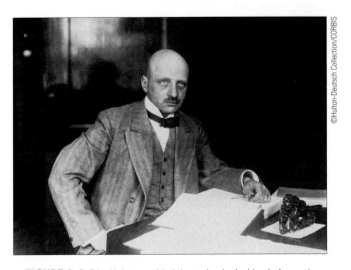

◆ **FIGURE 1.6** Fritz Haber provided the technological basis for modern farming through his research on artificial nitrogen fixation. He greatly expanded the limit of human carrying capacity.

Haber's success was followed soon after World War II with the intensive genetic modification of grains and other crops, and the application on a regular basis of new and powerful strains of pesticide and herbicide, including DDT and other compounds related to nerve gas (orthophosphates) and nicotine (neonicotinoids). These innovations led to the industrial scale farming we see all around us in the present world (◆Figure 1.7). Coupled with further improvements in modern medicine and sanitation, the human population surged. Since 1950, for the first time ever, some people have lived to see population more than double in a lifetime, and some have lived long enough to see it triple. This is economically challenging and socially disorienting (especially for us older folks), but even more staggering is the general level of improved well-being for most of the world's population. The lesson seems to be clear: human ingenuity has rendered irrelevant the warnings of Thomas Malthus. We do not have to worry about carrying capacity like the species found in Leopold's quaintly wild nature.

Or is this dangerous and delusional thinking? The world's most important commercial fertilizers depend upon fossil fuels for production—especially natural gas and petroleum. These are finite resources, and we have good reason to believe that we are approaching the peak of our ability to exploit them, right at a time when the population is continuing to grow and become more prosperous, especially in the lesser-developed world. Likewise, intensive cultivation has led to further extensive deforestation, especially in tropical countries such as Brazil, where soybeans now cover thousands of square miles, much of which was virginal forest until just a few years ago. Soil erosion continues unabated. Since 1950 about a third of all U.S. cropland has been abandoned due to erosion, and some 90 percent is losing soil faster than it can naturally replenish. If there is no soil, there is no farming, and certainly then *no food*. Many experts believe an even more urgent concern is the depletion of vital groundwater supplies needed for irrigation, which may become even more important as the world experiences possibly severe climate shocks from the buildup of industrial CO_2 in the atmosphere in coming decades. So, there is reason indeed to believe that the technologically supported human carrying capacity we presently enjoy may not be *sustainable*, that in the end it may turn out to be a "false" carrying capacity.

For the purposes of this book, it is worth keeping in mind how the topical material of some of the chapters you'll be reading relates to human carrying capacity. Any good stewardship of carrying capacity resources will require an understanding of related geological processes. It may well be, after all, that the famous baseball catcher Yogi Berra was right when he said, "Nature bats last, and Nature owns the stadium."

Putting Ourselves At Risk

The upswing in human population over the past 50 years is wholly without precedent in human history. During World War II, there were some 15 persons/km^2 on average across the world's land surface. At present, mean population density stands around 45 persons/km^2 and by 2050, even with declining birth rates, this will increase to 65 persons/km^2. Because only about 10% of Earth's land surface can be farmed, most of this population is crowded close to or directly upon precious agricultural areas, and at present nearly half the world's population is living in cities (75% in developed countries, 40% in lesser-developed countries). Most of the world's urban population lives under arguably wretched conditions; ghettos, barrios, slums, and shantytowns (◆Figure 1.8). (The names vary according to the part of the

◆ **FIGURE 1.7** Agricultural pests and diseases reduce human carrying capacity. Pesticides, herbicides, fungicides, and other chemical applications help boost yields from farmlands, hence expanding carrying capacity for people, but often causing serious environmental problems.

◆ **FIGURE 1.8** The fastest-growing segment of human population in recent decades has been poor and urban. Vulnerability to natural disasters and environmental problems is high for this part of humanity.

world you are visiting, but no matter, each term evokes human misery to which most readers of this book are unaccustomed.)

A greater number of people means that there are more people at risk from geological processes that otherwise might not inflict much damage and loss of life. These include earthquakes, volcanic eruptions, landslides, and floods—all vital components of the Earth system responsible for creating new lands, revitalizing soils, and developing some of the most strikingly beautiful scenery. A part of environmental geology, therefore, deals with how we can learn to reduce losses while living in greater numbers with these powerful, necessary, and unavoidable forces of nature. Especially important is the recognition of how we can actually worsen conditions and increase risk through foolish land-use decisions. (Building atop a fault could add new meaning to the term "split level home!")

The Environmental Geologist

Like other scientists, an environmental geologist employs the time-honored *scientific method* to learn more about a particular situation involving people and the physical environment, and to achieve conclusions that will be useful, either to a client who has hired the geologist, or to the scientific community at large.

Many famous detectives from fiction, including Sherlock Holmes, employ the scientific method in their investigations (◆Figure 1.9). This approach is multi-step, straightforward, and often leads to fascinating discoveries:

1. At the beginning, a geologist poses a question—perhaps simply indulging some personal curiosity about nature or perhaps addressing a problem presented by someone who needs authoritative assistance. Examples of typical questions include: "How did the water in this stream come to have so much arsenic?" and "Will the land surface subside destructively if we continue to pump water from beneath this neighborhood?"

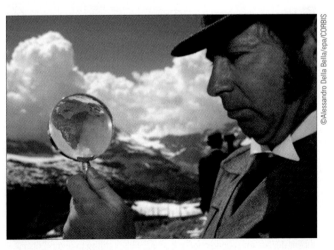

◆ **FIGURE 1.9** Detectives are scientists, and scientists are detectives.

2. Next the geologist goes into the field to gather preliminary information through direct observation or from the collection of samples to be analyzed later in a laboratory. The integrity of an entire scientific study depends largely upon the effectiveness of this step. A good geologist would like to leave "no stone unturned," employing a useful pun, but limited time, stamina, and budgeting require that only so much data can be collected. The investigator must make a judgment call in the field about whether sufficient information has been gathered. In other words, thoughtful selectivity and a certain amount of serendipity enter the early stage of every scientific investigation.

3. The geologist then considers the data carefully, formulating a *hypothesis*—an idea about what is going on—that now must be tested with an additional visit to the field. The process of formulating a hypothesis gives the geologist a better idea of what data need to be collected next. Like a good detective homing in on the culprit, the geologist begins to feel in control of the situation. An answer is shaping up, even if several hypotheses must be tested and discarded in succession. An example of a geological hypothesis might be a statement such as the following: "The groundwater has a large amount of perchlorate in it because there was once a fireworks company located upslope. The company must have been leaking or dumping wastewater." Note that this statement is not yet a *conclusion*.

4. Finally, once a hypothesis is verified, the geologist is at last in a position to develop and announce conclusions. These need not be definite. Sometimes scientists are left able to say only that something is "probably this" or "probably that"—and in the legal cases in which environmental geologists frequently provide testimony, it may be up to a jury to decide whether the scientific argument is persuasive or not. In the case of the above sample hypothesis, the geologist might conclude "The *most likely source* of pollution was a fireworks company located upslope." The public and political system often find routine scientific uncertainties such as this frustrating, but science is commonly an iterative process in which many people are engaged over long periods of time; and as different scientists assemble their own independently collected data to confirm the conclusions of their peers, certainties of vast importance do emerge (e.g., Earth revolves around the Sun, the tectonic plates move, etc.). In fact, the act of independent scientific verification is a necessary part of scientific culture. A scientist can well feel honored to have his or her work under scrutiny by other scientists; this generally means that one's work is considered "relevant and important."

A theory is a cause-and-effect relationship regarded by scientists as certain or nearly certain. It is a hard and fast, widely accepted scientific conclusion. Hypotheses are far more readily modified and overturned than theories. In Chapter 3, you'll see how a number of hypotheses, some of which were erroneous, eventually led to the revolutionary theory of plate tectonics.

Tools of the Trade

Environmental geologists work with a wide range of maps, tables, and diagrams, which they may in fact play a direct role in preparing. *Topographic maps* (also known as "contour" or "elevation" maps) illustrate the roughness of Earth's land surface (◆Figure 1.10a). The standard topographic maps used by wilderness backpackers might be useful, but quite often maps have to be made of much smaller areas than the ones represented in standard topographic formats.

Using a topographic base, the geologist may draw in, through accurate and precise surveying, the locations of special features, such as the boundaries between different rock bodies (known as "geologic contacts"), and the locations of faults, springs, seeps, and landslide scarps. The angle of rock layers in various locations may be depicted using special "strike and dip" map symbols. Different soil types and soil thicknesses or depths to water tables beneath the surface as

(a)

(b)

(USGS)

(c)

◆ **FIGURE 1.10** (a) A topographic map shows the roughness and vegetative cover of a landscape, using lines of equal elevation called contours, and colors to represent vegetation, clear areas, and water bodies. (b) A geologic map uses a topographic contour base to show where different kinds of bedrock are distributed in a landscape. (c) A derivative map takes data collected from various research studies to show information of use for a particular purpose, in this case seismic hazards in the central San Francisco Bay area.

measured in wells might also be shown. In any event, these *geologic maps* are pictures of reality—readily understood visual representations of the vital data (◆Figure 1.10b).

The geologist may use compasses, clinometers, measuring tapes, and other surveying tools, such as laser theodolites in the field to gather additional information. Quite often environmental geologists employ highly sensitive **Global Positioning Systems (GPS)** to pinpoint locations using satellites (◆Figure 1.11).

In some cases, the data may already have been collected by someone else and entered into a computer-based format that can be tapped and analyzed numerically to make *derivative maps*—maps derived for a special application, such as illustrating for an insurance company the susceptibility of ground in a particular region to intensive shaking during earthquakes (Figure 1.11). The on-line data sets and their processing by high-speed computers constitute the **Geographic Information System (GIS).**

GIS technology has refined and improved the power of traditional mapping by facilitating production of cross-sections and three-dimensional images of buried geologic features. Being able to ascertain what lies underground is of vital importance to environmental geologists. The practice of environmental geology is very visual, requiring a

◆ **FIGURE 1.11** A typical GPS (Global Positioning System) installation. GPS has become an important tool for monitoring environmental and geological changes, using satellite telemetry to precisely locate positions on Earth's surface. Changes in position then are useful in forecasting phenomena like volcanic eruptions, earthquakes, and landslides. The gray dome in the background houses the GPS unit proper, and the open cabinet under the solar panel contains the electronics.

keen understanding of the structure of the shallow crust and of how fluids move through it. An ability to work three-dimensionally is one reason that many students with artistic inclinations often make very fine geologists.

Some Case Histories

Some examples of the kinds of projects environmental geologists undertake are hinted at above. More specifically, an environmental geologist might be called upon to

- investigate the pollution caused by mining operations, golf courses, industries, culverts, or waste-storage ponds;
- assess the risk of land destabilization from extraction of groundwater, oil, or gas, or from the construction of structures on slopes;
- evaluate the risk from natural disasters, such as flooding, earthquake activity, or volcanic eruptions, and help governments formulate zoning or regulatory restrictions to reduce costly impacts;
- locate future dam sites or investigate the reasons dams have failed;
- study the quality and erosive potential of soils being considered for agricultural use or suffering from faulty farming practices;
- deal with coastal erosion and storm-related issues;
- track the movement of contamination plumes underground;
- determine the best way to store solid and liquid wastes coming from an urban area or a radiation source such as a hospital, college laboratory, or government establishment. Plus many other applications.

Implicit in the above is the need for environmental geologists to work extensively with engineers, ecologists and microbiologists, chemists, legal and civil officials, and other specialists. There is rarely a dull moment in such work, though data collecting can sometimes seem tedious before answers begin to emerge. And no two environmental projects are alike.

Whether or not you seek a career path in environmental geology, however, it is worth grasping the perspectives that guide this profession. To a certain extent, as explained above, each of us may find reason to apply practical lessons from this field at one time or another in our own lives.

CASE STUDY 1.1

Exponential Growth, Wealth, Poverty, and Population

The growth of any population of anything—is easy to quantify using a *compound growth equation*. The equation simply states that Future Quantity of Something = Present Quantity of Something multiplied by (e)^{kt}, where "e" is the exponential growth rate constant or *natural log* 2.71828, "k" is the rate of change in amount of whatever is being studied (usually measured as an *annual* change and expressed as a decimal, so a growth rate of 10 percent equates to 0.1; of 20 percent, 0.2, etc.), and "t" is the number of years during which the growth takes place.

The symbol "N" is commonly associated with "Future Quantity," and "N_0" with "Present Quantity"; hence the formal expression of the equation is

$$N = N_0 \times e^{kt}$$

Consider the following example, which you may want to crank out with a pocket calculator for confirmation: In June of 2000 the world's total population was 6.1 billion. Given a global population growth rate that *holds steady* at 1.25 percent, this means that 7.8 billion people will live in the world 20 years hence, or mathematically put

$$7.8 \text{ billion} = 6.1 \text{ billion} \times (2.71828)^{1.25(20)}$$

The vital point to note here is that the rate of increase seems almost trivial to most people (1.25%), but this small number applied to a big quantity (6.1 billion) means an enormous growth in population. In other words, we tend to be lulled into a sense of false security by the exponential aspect of the compound growth equation, and to underestimate its often staggering consequences or sometimes unrealistic implications. For example, the huge boom in global population that has altered the world's environment so significantly over the past 50 years was fueled by a growth rate that peaked at a "mere" 1.99 percent in 1965 (⚹ Table 1.2).

Since 1965 the global population growth rate has declined to 1.22 percent, but this of course does not mean that the world is losing total population—merely that the total is not growing quite so fast. A rough estimate of how long it takes for a population to double may be made by dividing the number 70 by the percent age of rate increase. In other words, the present population would double in (70/1.22) years or 57 years time, if the growth rate remained at 1.22 percent. This calculation is called the **doubling time** (⚹ Table 1.3).

The rate of growth varies according to the wealth of countries; it is correlated directly with the IPAT equation. With few exceptions, those countries that have the greatest environmental impacts have the lowest growth rates in population. Immigration from poorer to richer countries can radically offset this trend of course, as in the case of the United States, which has the seventh-fastest-growing population on Earth, exceeded only by India, China, Pakistan, Bangladesh, and Nigeria.

The current annual increase in population is only 0.25 percent in wealthier regions, while in poor countries it is six times faster—1.46 percent, and in the 49 poorest nations, home to nearly 700 million people, it is 2.41 percent (2006 data).

What accounts for these differences? There are many social and economic factors involved. In poor countries lacking welfare, health care, and institutional care for the elderly, many children ensure that parents will be cared for in old age or times of unemployment. Contraceptives and family planning are lacking. Children are cheap to have and to rear, because expensive educational systems, clothes, toys, and other items we take for granted as part of an ordinary childhood in the United States are simply unavailable to most people. Women, who might take an active role in earning family incomes and reducing family size if professionally trained and employed, have little incentive not to stay at home and bear more children. Indeed, the United Nations regards the education and professional empowerment of women as one of the most powerful tools we have to combat overpopulation, and with it, many of the related environmental problems we'll explore further in this book.

⚹TABLE 1.2   World Population and Growth Rate, 1950–2002

Year	Population, Billions	Growth Rate, %*
1950	2.52	
1955	2.75	1.77
1960	3.03	1.95
1965	3.34	1.99
1970	3.77	1.90
1975	4.08	1.84
1980	4.45	1.81
1985	4.85	1.75
1990	5.30	1.70
1995	5.76	1.68
2002	6.26	1.56

*Average annual rate for the previous five-year period.
Sources: Estimates in United Nations, *Demographics Yearbooks* for 1985 and 1990, and in *World Resources, 1994–95* (New York: Oxford University Press).

⚹TABLE 1.3   How Populations Grow

Growth Rate, %	Doubling Time, Years*
1.0	70.0
2.0	35.0
3.0	23.3
4.0	17.5
5.0	14.0
6.0	11.7
7.0	10.0

*Calculated by using the formula 70 ÷ growth rate (%), which yields a close approximation up to a growth rate of 10%.

Overpopulation Problems

As emphasized in this chapter, overpopulation is responsible for environmental damage, societal problems, and human suffering. In some countries population growth is utterly out of control. In other countries—China, for instance—measures and incentives are in place for curbing the growth and achieving a sustainable population. This photo gallery highlights the dilemma.

◆ **FIGURE 1** Coney Island beach in the 1930s, when the U.S. population was a fraction of what it is today. Imagine this beach on a summer weekend today.

B. Pipkin

Owen Frankyn/Sygma/CORBIS

(a)

Owen Frankyn/Sygma/CORBIS

(b)

◆ **FIGURE 2** Deforestation near the city of Manaus in Amazonia, Brazil's largest state. (a) False-color satellite photo of the confluence of the Rio Negro (*black*) and the sediment-laden Amazon River (*light green*). Healthy rain forest is shown in red, and deforested areas appear in light colors. Manaus is on the point of land that extends into the Rio Negro. The waters of the Rio Negro are recognizable for more than 80 kilometers (48 mi) downstream in the Amazon. (b) Adjacent rain forests have been removed as the population of the area has grown. Manaus's population is now more than a million people, and the city is rapidly expanding into areas that were once sparsely populated.

◆ **FIGURE 3** A model Chinese family in front of a billboard encouraging the one-child family; Beijing. Although the People's Republic of China is pushing population control, its population of more than a billion people makes continued growth inevitable.

Summary

Environmental Geology

Defined

The study of how humans interact with the geological part of the natural environment.

Utilizes

Most of the traditional geological specialties including petrology, engineering geology, geophysics, geochemistry, structural geology, and hydrology. Tools used by environmental geologists include precision surveying instruments, maps, and computerized data bases.

Areas of Interest

Geologic hazards such as volcanism, earthquakes, and flooding; mineral and water resources; and land-use planning–should I build my house on this hillside? Environmental geologists are concerned not only with what is happening at Earth's surface, but underground as well. They are "three-dimensional" thinkers and interact intensively with many other kinds of professionals.

Goals

To predict, anticipate, and solve geologic problems by collecting data in the field and analyzing it in the laboratory. Data may be portrayed on special-use (derivative) maps and utilized by planners and public officials.

Methods

Environmental geologists follow the scientific method of:

1. posing a question
2. collecting initial data and framing a hypothesis
3. testing the hypothesis
4. reaching a conclusion based upon the results of their testing, which might include the development of a new theory.

Humans and the Geologic Environment

The IPAT Equation

I = PAT defines the human factors causing environmental impacts (I). Those factors include population (P), affluence (A), and technology (T). In very poor countries, the equation reduces to I = P.

Out of Sight, Out of Mind

In wealthy countries, environmental impacts tend to be "out of sight, out of mind," whereas impacts are more direct and local in lesser-developed countries.

Carrying Capacity

Carrying capacity is the population that can be supported in a stable, long-term manner by the natural environment. The most important factor in carrying capacity is food supply. Human ability to grow food and support carrying capacity has increased in recent decades owing to the introduction of commercial fertilizers, pest and disease control, and genetic modification of crops.

Ecological Overshoot

Ecological overshoot occurs when a population exceeds its carrying capacity. This can cause great environmental problems, including many of a geological nature (soil erosion, land subsidence, etc.).

Rural to Urban Transformation

The greatest transformation in human population over the past century has been from rural to urban growth. Larger concentrations and numbers of people mean greater vulnerability to natural disasters such as earthquakes and floods, topics of great importance in environmental geology.

Key Terms

Anthropocene	doubling time	environmental geology	human carrying capacity
carrying capacity	ecological overshoot	GIS	hypothesis
compound growth equation	environment	GPS	IPAT Equation

Study Questions

1. Do you consider yourself an environmentalist? Why or why not? How has reading this chapter changed your view of environmental issues, if at all?
2. Think of one good example of an "out of sight, out of mind" environmental impact that you have caused or are presently causing on a routine basis. Was (is) this impact avoidable? Why or why not?
3. Aldo Leopold asks that we "think like a mountain." This is a metaphor for changing our attitudes and broadening our perspectives, but in what way(s)? Do you think that it is practical to "think like a mountain?"
4. Do you agree with the assertion that "We do not have to worry about carrying capacity like . . . wild species" of animals? Are you much concerned with the possibility of "human ecological overshoot?" What is the evidence for your answer to these questions?
5. Given the importance of farmlands, do you think that the continuing growth of huge cities in or upon agricultural areas

is such a bad thing? Why or why not? What other information would you like to know in order to answer this question?

6. Distinguish between a *hypothesis* and a *theory*. Cite an example of a hypothesis you have yourself formulated in the past, even to solve a simple problem at home or at school. How would a society in which hypotheses were not expected to be tested differ from one in which they are routinely tested?

7. Can you think of ways we can reconcile the reality of probability and much uncertainty in science with the absolute certainties required by our political-economic and legal systems? Can you think of a great scientific question today that has caused heated debate because it has not been definitely, concretely answered?

8. The United States has a growth rate of 0.7 percent. At this rate how much time is required for the national population to double? Discuss the impact of a doubling of your community's population in that length of time.

9. What will the population of the world be in the year 2100 if a steady growth rate of 1.22% is maintained?

10. How does the education and training of women in lesser-developed countries relate to geological problems like soil erosion and flooding?

11. The IPAT formulation implies that technology and affluence always have negative environmental impacts. Can you think, though, of situations in which impacts have been reduced, or actually reversed, by technology and affluence? Do you think that the IPAT relationship is too simple to be useful?

For Further Information

Brown, L. 2001. *Eco-economy—building the economy for the Earth.* Norton Publishing.

Easton, T. 2005. *Taking sides: clashing views on controversial environmental issues,* 11th ed. McGraw-Hill Publishing.

Goudie, A. 2005. *The human impact on the natural environment: past, present, and future,* 6th Edition. Blackwell Publishing.

Hertsgaard, M. 1999. *Earth odyssey; around the world in search of our environmental future.* Broadway Books.

Kennedy, D. and the editors of Science. *Science Magazine's state of the planet 2006–2007.* Island Press.

McNeill, J.R. and P. Kennedy 2001. *Something new under the sun: an environmental history of the twentieth-century world.* Norton Publishing.

Zwingle, E. 2002. *Cities.* National Geographic Magazine. November issue.

Getting Around in Geology

About five billion years ago an interstellar cloud of gas and dust began to collapse, probably under the force of its own gravity. As it shrank it started spinning, which caused the cloud to flatten into a disc shape. Eventually, the compression accompanying the collapse created temperatures and pressures in the center of the cloud sufficient to initiate nuclear reactions. Hydrogen atoms fused, forming helium and releasing enormous energy. Our primordial sun began to shine. Around the sun a cooler disc, the solar nebula, contained the elemental leftovers of the solar implosion that eventually would form the planets. Low-boiling-point compounds such as methane, ammonia, and various ices condensed in the cold far reaches of the nebula to form the outer planets, the very large *Jovian planets*. Closer to the sun, metallic and rocky substances with high melting points condensed and collided to form the four dense inner planets, the *terrestrial planets*. Of that group, the third and fourth planets from the sun are most interesting to geologists.

On January 3 and January 24, 2004 two spacecraft landed on the surface of Mars, each carrying a remote-controlled vehicle, the Martian Exploration Rovers "Opportunity" and "Spirit." Directed remotely by scientists at Cornell University and California's Jet Propulsion Laboratory, few thought that the vehicles would last much longer than the three months they were designed

◆ **FIGURE 1** Panorama taken by Spirit Rover on April 18, 2006 looking toward Husband Hill on the horizon. The smooth patch in the middle distance in front of Husband Hill is Home Plate. Note the Rover's vehicle tracks closer by. The Rover was positioned in its winter station at this time, patiently recharging its solar batteries in the low light of the long Martian winter.

NASA/JPL/Cornell

to survive under the harsh conditions of the Martian surface. But over two years later they are still operating and have become one of the most successful space missions ever undertaken. Each of these robotic "mechanical geologists" has traveled over 7 km (4.2 mi) across the planet's stony desert landscape, with special attention given to outcrops of *sedimentary rock*—layered rock formed by deposition of eroded debris carried by wind and water or by evaporation and biologic activity. The controllers of Opportunity and Spirit are looking for definite evidence that Mars once had persistent bodies of water, such as we find on Earth today. Where there was once standing water, there once was likely to have been life—a tantalizing possibility!

Navigating the Martian landscape has required the naming of numerous geographical features, including "Home Plate," a patch of level ground that looks like part of a giant baseball diamond from Mars orbit (◆ Figure 1). Following up on the baseball theme, scientists have named the most spectacular outcrops near Home Plate after famous African-American baseball players including David Barnhill, a former pitcher for the New York Cubans, and "Bullet Joe" Rogan. These outcrops consist of layers formed by falling ash and jagged blocks of ejected rock tossed through the air. They indicate that an ancient volcanic eruption or large meteorite strike occurred nearby.

The evidence looks strong that Mars once had lakes, streams, even small seas. At Erebus Crater, Opportunity discovered sandstone showing cross-beds and drying (desiccation) cracks. From research on Earth we know that such sedimentary features indicate the presence of an ancient water body big enough to have had a current flowing through it. The water body later evaporated.

Elsewhere, Spirit has plowed up Martian soil in two places rich in crystals of iron sulfate, a salt mineral, which would most easily have accumulated by evaporation of salty water (◆ Figure 2). Many of the sedimentary rocks seen so far also contain tiny granules of iron, which probably formed as water soaked through the rocks. The most abundant form of iron is the mineral hematite, which crystallizes under oxygen-rich conditions.

The emerging picture provided by careful examination of rocks and minerals is that Mars once was a much warmer world with lots of violent geological processes and a much denser atmosphere. Water was abundant in many places; but then the Martian air thinned out and grew cold and dry. Where did all of the water go? What became of any life that might have existed? The environmental history of Mars is a story of extreme climate change taking place on a world in some ways once very similar to our own.

To answer all of the questions raised will require future geologic study of our neighbor by explorations yet to be planned. It is likely that we'll develop a clearer understanding of Earth's own long history in the process.

◆ **FIGURE 2** A bed of iron-rich salt accidentally trenched up beneath a thin layer of red, wind-blown Martian dust by Spirit Rover on January 20, 2006. The trench is about 30 cm wide

The Earth System

Earth functions like a finely tuned machine, a natural, self-maintaining spaceship for its inhabitants, constantly rotating about its polar axis at 1670 km/hr and revolving around the Sun at 107,000 km/hr. Just as the elements of human physiological systems are connected and interdependent, so on Earth are there linkages and interactions between its surface of rock and soil (*lithosphere*), the air (*atmosphere*), bodies of water and ice (*hydrosphere*), and its living realm (*biosphere*). Just as a healthy human body depends upon the proper circulation of blood and other fluids and solids within, so does a "healthy Earth"—one habitable for life at least—depend upon a proper circulation of matter and energy between each of its major natural components; lithosphere, atmosphere, hydrosphere, and biosphere.

One example of an important but little-appreciated interconnection is the one that exists between dust storms in the Gobi and Takla Makan deserts in China, life in the North Pacific Ocean, and Earth's climate. Airborne silt from those deserts is seasonally carried all the way to the North Pacific where it increases the nutrient content and fertility of this otherwise barren stretch of ocean. The blooming of marine plankton in response to the dust fertilization subtracts a large amount of carbon dioxide from the atmosphere, thanks to photosynthesis, which in turn keeps the air from getting as warm as it might, because carbon dioxide is a greenhouse gas. Average atmospheric temperature has a significant impact on climate worldwide, and it turns out that floating microscopic marine life such as plankton is important for making our climate comfortable.

A *system* is simply a set of components or parts that work together to perform a particular function. And all systems, including the Earth System, require energy to operate. The human body acquires its energy from eating food. An automobile requires fuel, or electricity to function. A transportation system—the network of streets and interchanges required to move automotive traffic around a city—requires routine street maintenance and the power for traffic signals to work.

The Earth System needs energy to work as well, and this comes from two sources: one *internal,* the other *external* (◆Figure 2.1). Inside the planet's deep interior, uranium, thorium, and to a lesser extent potassium atoms are continuously decaying into more stable, lighter-weight elements. A by-product of this *radiogenic decay* is heat, which gradually escapes to Earth's surface. We see manifestations of this escaping internal heat directly expressed as volcanoes and hot springs. Some of this heat converts to mechanical energy, causing earthquakes, mountain building, and the slow shifting of massive tectonic plates (see Chapter 3).

By far more noticeable to us at the surface, however, is the energy coming from Earth's external heat source—the Sun. Without the daily input of solar radiation, our planet would be a frozen, stony ice ball, despite all of the heat slowly escaping from its interior. There would be no wind, rainfall, or circulating surface water (see Chapter 8). Since the biosphere critically depends upon sunlight for photosynthesis and various other vital processes, so too most life as we know it would be nonexistent.

The interface between the external and internal sources of energy is Earth's surface (◆Figure 2.2). Soil—an essential factor in human carrying capacity—is a result of the conflicting processes, one set internally driven, the other set externally driven, which come together at the surface. Wind, rain, ice, snow, and chemical corrosion break down the land that

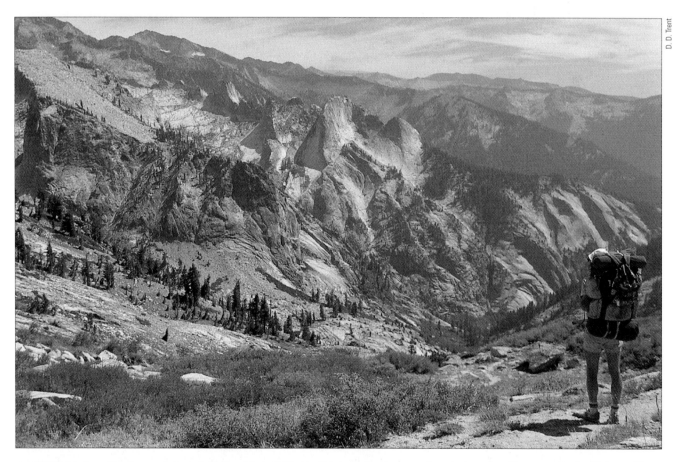

◆ **FIGURE 2.1** Lone Pine Canyon in Sequoia National Park, California. This landscape is the product of mountain uplift powered by Earth's internal heat engine, interacting with erosion by glaciers, weathering, and running water powered by Earth's external heat engine, the Sun. Contrast this image with Figure 2.1. How generally do these landscapes differ? (Mars has a less active internal heat engine than Earth, is farther from the Sun, and as far as we know, has no life.)

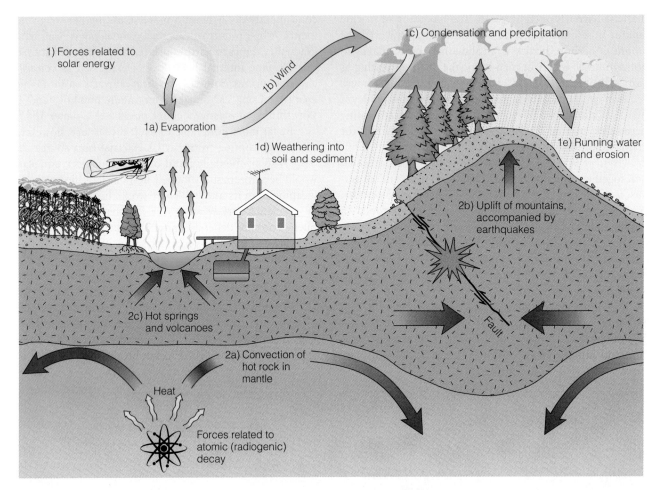

◆ **FIGURE 2.2** Earth's surface is a resolution of two sets of forces, modified by the activity of life.

earthquakes, volcanic eruptions, sedimentation, and mountain building gradually construct. The form of the landscape on which we live may be thought of as a compromise in the never-ending tug-of-war of opposing forces. Biological activity modifies the ways in which these forces operate. For example, a dense cover of vegetation will inhibit erosion and sedimentation, while a landscape denuded by logging and overgrazing quickly wears way, as Aldo Leopold observed (see Chapter 1).

In this chapter we're going to take a close look at the raw material that makes up Earth's lithosphere. This is essential background for all the chapters to follow, and will provide some insight into the framework of knowledge all geologists hold in common. As the Martian example above illustrates, rocks and minerals can tell us much about a planet's changing environment. Moreover, particular kinds of rocks and minerals can provide us great environmental benefits in some cases while causing great harm in others. We begin by looking at the smallest building blocks of the Earth System: atoms, ions, and isotopes. Then we'll progress to higher states of organization and put it all together in discussing Earth's age.

Earth Materials
Elements, Atoms, and Atomic Structure

Elements are substances that cannot be changed into other substances by normal chemical methods. They are composed of infinitesimal particles called **atoms.** In 1870 Lothar Meyer published a table of the 57 then-known elements arranged in the order of their atomic weights. Meyer left blank spaces in the table wherever elements of particular weights were not known. About the same time Dmitry Mendeleyev developed a similar table, but his table was based upon the similar chemical properties of the particular known elements. Where an element's placement based on weight did not group it with elements of similar properties, Mendeleyev did not hesitate to suggest that its weight had been measured incorrectly. He also predicted the properties of the "missing" elements, and very shortly his predictions proved correct with the discovery of the elements gallium, scandium, and germanium (Appendix 1).

The weight of an atom of an element is contained almost entirely in its **nucleus,** which contains protons (atomic weight = 1, electrical charge = 1^+) and neutrons (atomic weight = 1, electrical charge = 0). An element's **atomic number** is the number of protons in its nucleus, and this number is unique to that element. The weight of an atom—its **atomic mass**—is the sum of its nuclear protons and neutrons. For example, $^4_2$He denotes the element helium, which has 2 protons (denoted by the subscript) and 2 neutrons, for an atomic mass of 4 (superscript). Electrical neutrality of the atom is provided by balancing the positive proton charges by an equal number of negatively charged electrons orbiting in shells around the nucleus (◆ Figure 2.3). **Ions** are atoms that are positively or negatively charged due to a loss or gain of electrons (e^-) in the outer electron shell. Thus, sodium (Na) may lose an electron in its outer shell to become sodium ion (Na^+, a *cation*), and chlorine (Cl) may gain an electron to become chloride ion (Cl^-, an *anion*). *Valence* refers to ionic charge, and sodium and chlorine are said to have valences of 1^+ and 1^-, respectively. Elemental sodium is an unstable metallic solid, and chlorine is a poisonous gas. When ionized, they may combine in an orderly fashion to form the mineral halite (NaCl), common table salt, a substance necessary for human existence (◆ Figure 2.4).

Isotopes are forms (or species) of an element that have different atomic masses. The element uranium, for instance, always has 92 protons in its nucleus, but varying numbers of neutrons define its isotopes. For example, Uranium-238 (^{238}U) is the common naturally occurring isotope of uranium. It weighs 238 atomic mass units and contains 92 protons and 146 (238 *minus* 92) neutrons. Uranium-235 is the rare isotope (0.7% of all uranium) that has 143 neutrons. Similarly, ^{12}C is the common isotope of carbon, but ^{13}C and ^{14}C also exist. A modern periodic table of the elements that shows their atomic number and mass appears in Appendix 1.

Minerals

Earth's crust is composed of rocks, which are made up of one or more minerals. Although most people seldom think about minerals that do not have nutritional importance or great beauty and value such as gold and silver, the mineral kingdom encompasses a broad spectrum of chemical compositions. **Minerals** are defined as *naturally occurring, inorganic, crystalline* substances, each with a narrow range of *chemical compositions* and characteristic *physical properties.* Thus, neither artificial gems such as zirconia nor organic deposits such as coal and oil are minerals by definition. The crystal form of a mineral reflects an orderly atomic structure, which in turn determines the crystal shape. Solids that have random or noncrystalline atomic structures—glass and opal, for example—are described as **amorphous.** Minerals composed of a single element, such as copper and carbon (as in graphite and diamonds), are known as *native elements.* Most minerals, however, are composed of combinations of two or more elements. Although more than 3,000 minerals have been named and described, only about 20 make up the bulk of Earth's crustal rocks. The chemistry of minerals is the basis of their classification, and the most common minerals are primarily composed of the elements oxygen (O), silicon (Si), aluminum (Al), and iron (Fe). This is not surprising, because oxygen and silicon compose 75 percent of crustal rocks by weight. A memory aid for these elements in order is "OSAF."

Geologists classify minerals into groups that share similar negatively charged ions (anions) or ion groups (radicals).

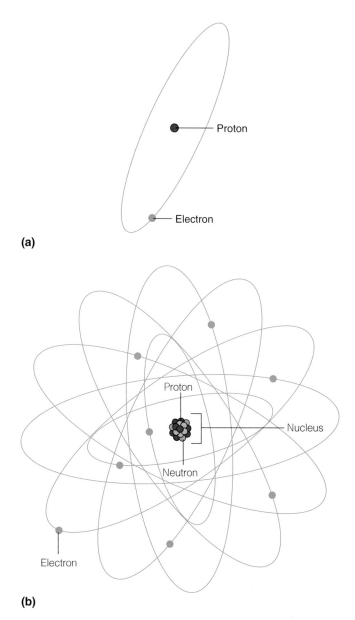

(a)

(b)

◆ **FIGURE 2.3** Structures of (a) a hydrogen atom, in which an electron orbits a single proton, and (b) an oxygen atom, in which 8 electrons orbit a dense nucleus containing 8 protons and 8 neutrons.

◆ **FIGURE 2.4** Two models of the atomic structure of the mineral halite (NaCl), common table salt. (a) A packing model that shows the location and relative sizes of the sodium and chloride ions. (b) A ball-and-stick model that shows the mineral's cubic crystal structure.

(a)

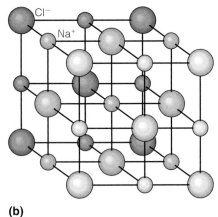

(b)

Oxygen (O^{-2}) may combine with iron to form hematite (Fe_2O_3), a member of the *oxide group* of minerals. The *sulfide minerals* typically are combinations of a metal with sulfur. Examples include galena (lead sulfide, PbS), chalcopyrite (copper-iron sulfide, $CuFeS_2$), and pyrite (iron sulfide, FeS_2), the "fool's gold" of inexperienced prospectors. *Carbonate minerals* contain the negatively charged $(CO_3)^{-2}$ ion. Calcite ($CaCO_3$), the principal mineral of limestone and marble, is an example. ✳ Table 2.1 summarizes some of the mineral groups most important to geologists.

The most common and important minerals are the *silicates,* which are composed of combinations of oxygen and silicon with or without metallic elements. The basic building block of a silicate mineral is the silica tetrahedron (◆ Figure 2.5a). It consists of one silicon atom surrounded by four oxygen atoms at the corners of a four-faced tetrahedron. The manner in which the tetrahedra are packed or arranged in the mineral structure is the basis for classifying silicates. The tetrahedra may be arranged in layers or sheets, as in the clay minerals and mica; in long chains, as in the amphibole and pyroxene groups; and in three-dimensional networks, as in quartz and feldspar (◆ Figure 2.5b and ■ Case Study 2.1 on page 39).

Rock-Forming Silicates

Most rocks are aggregates of minerals, and feldspar is the most abundant of the silicate minerals in Earth's crust (◆ Figure 2.6). Feldspar is actually a mineral *group* that ranges in chemical composition from potassium-rich orthoclase found in granite (◆ Figure 2.7) to calcium-rich plagioclase found in basalt and gabbro. The ferromagnesian silicates are rich in iron and magnesium in addition to silicon and oxygen. Most of them are dark colored, either black, brown, or green (◆ Figure 2.8). Important among these are hornblende (amphibole), augite (pyroxene), biotite mica, and olivine, which is believed to be the most abundant mineral just below the outer crust of the planet (✳ Table 2.2).

Mineral Identification

Serious students of mineralogy are able to identify several hundred minerals without destructive testing. They are able to do this because minerals have distinctive physical properties, most of which are easily determined and associated with particular mineral species (Appendix 2). With practice, one can build up a mental catalog of minerals, just like building a vocabulary in a foreign language. The most useful physical properties are hardness, cleavage, crystal form, and to lesser degrees, color (which is variable) and luster. Mineralogists use the **Mohs hardness scale,** developed by Friedrich Mohs in 1812 (✳ Table 2.3). Mohs assigned a hardness value (H) of 10 to diamond and of 1 to talc, a very soft mineral. Diamond scratches everything; quartz ($H = 7$) and feldspar ($H = 6$) can scratch glass ($H = 5\frac{1}{2}$–6), and calcite ($H = 3$) and your fingernail can scratch gypsum ($H = 2$).

✳TABLE 2.1	Some Important Mineral Groups*		
Mineral Group	Negatively Charged Ion or Ion Group	Examples	Composition
Carbonate	$(CO_3)^{-2}$	Calcite	$CaCO_3$
		Dolomite	$CaMg(CO_3)_2$
Halide	CL^{-1}, F^{-1}	Halite	NaCl
Hydroxide	$(OH)^{-1}$	Limonite	$FeO(OH) \cdot H_2O$
Native element	—	Gold	Au
		Diamond	C
Oxide	O^{-2}	Hematite	Fe_2O_3
Silicate	$(SiO_4)^{-4}$	Quartz	SiO_2
		Olivine	$(Mg,Fe)_2SiO_4$
Sulfate	$(SO_4)^{-2}$	Gypsum	$CaSO_4 \cdot 2H_2O$
Sulfide	S^{-2}	Galena	PbS

*A table of the elements and their symbols appears in Appendix 1.

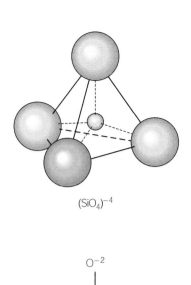

$(SiO_4)^{-4}$

O^{-2}

$O^{-2} — Si^{4+} — O^{-2}$

O^{-2}

		Formula of negatively charged ion group	Example
Isolated tetrahedra	▲	$(SiO_4)^{-4}$	Olivine
Continuous chains of tetrahedra		$(SiO_3)^{-2}$	Pyroxene group (augite)
		$(Si_4O_{11})^{-6}$	Amphibole group (hornblende)
Continuous sheets		$(Si_4O_{10})^{-4}$	Mica(muscovite)
Three-dimensional networks	Too complex to be shown by a simple two-dimensional drawing	$(SiO_2)^0$ $(Si_3AlO_8)^{-1}$ $(Si_2Al_2O_8)^{-2}$	Quartz Orthoclase feldspar Plagioclase feldspar

(a)   (b)

◆ **ThomsonNOW™ ACTIVE FIGURE 2.5** (a) Model of the silica tetrahedron, showing the unsatisfied negative charge at each oxygen that allows it to form (b) chains, sheets, and networks.

(a)

(b)

(c)

(d)

◆ **FIGURE 2.6** Some common rock-forming silicate minerals: (a) feldspar, (b) quartz, (c) muscovite, and (d) hornblende. (a) USGS; (b)–(d) Paul Silverman/Fundamental Photographs

◆ **FIGURE 2.7** This granite is an aggregate of the minerals quartz, biotite, and feldspar. Top left, Michael Dalton/Fundamental Photographs; top right and bottom left, Sue Monroe; bottom right, Paul Silverman/Fundamental Photographs

Quartz (mineral)

Granite (rock)

Biotite (mineral)

Feldspar (mineral)

Cleavage refers to the characteristic way particular minerals split along definite planes as determined by their crystal structure. Mica has perfect cleavage in one direction; this is called *basal* cleavage, because it is parallel to the basal plane of the crystal structure. Feldspars split in two directions; halite, which has *cubic* structure, in three directions; and so on, as shown in ◆ Figure 2.9. Minerals that have perfect cleavage can be split readily by a tap with a rock hammer or even peeled apart, as in the case of mica. Some minerals do not cleave but have distinctive **fracture** patterns that help one to identify them. The common crystal forms, shown in ◆ Figure 2.10, can be useful in identifying a particular mineral.

*TABLE 2.2　Some Common Rock-Forming Minerals

Mineral	Abundance in Crust, %	Rock in Which Found
Plagioclase*	39	Igneous rocks mostly
Quartz	12	Detrital sedimentary rocks, granites
Orthoclase**	12	Granites, detrital sedimentary rocks
Pyroxenes	11	Dark-colored igneous rocks
Micas	5	All rock types as accessory minerals
Amphiboles	5	Granites and other igneous rocks
Clay minerals	5	Shales, slates, decomposed granites
Olivine	3	Iron-rich igneous rocks, basalt
Others	11	Rock salt, gypsum, limestone, etc.

*A series of six minerals within the plagioclase group from albite ($NaAlSi_3O_8$) to anorthite ($CaAl_2Si_2O_8$).
**Feldspar group of minerals.

(a)

(b)

(c)

(d)

◆ **FIGURE 2.8** Some common ferromagnesian silicates: (a) olivine; (b) augite, a pyroxene-group mineral; (c) hornblende, an amphibole-group mineral; and (d) biotite mica. Courtesy Sue Monroe

*TABLE 2.3	Mohs Hardness Scale	
Hardness	Mineral	Common Example
1	Talc	Pencil lead 1–2
2	Gypsum	
		Fingernail 2½
3	Calcite	Copper penny 3
		Brass
4	Fluorite	Iron
5	Apatite	Tooth enamel
		Knife blade
		Glass 5½–6
6	Orthoclase	
		Steel file 6½
7	Quartz	
8	Topaz	
9	Corundum	Sapphire, ruby
10	Diamond	Synthetic diamond

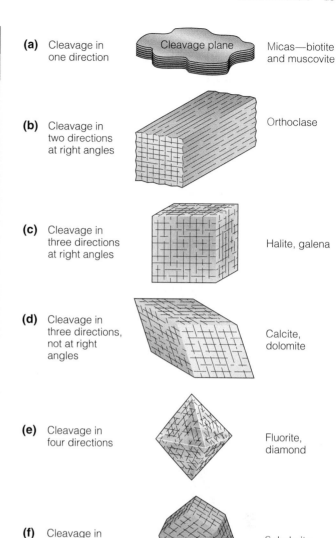

(a) Cleavage in one direction — Micas—biotite and muscovite

(b) Cleavage in two directions at right angles — Orthoclase

(c) Cleavage in three directions at right angles — Halite, galena

(d) Cleavage in three directions, not at right angles — Calcite, dolomite

(e) Cleavage in four directions — Fluorite, diamond

(f) Cleavage in six directions — Sphalerite

Color tends to vary within a given mineral species, so it is not a reliable identifying property. **Luster**—how a mineral reflects light—is useful, however. We recognize metallic and nonmetallic lusters, the latter being divided into types such as glassy, oily, greasy, and earthy. (■ Case Study 2.2 on page 40 discusses some gem minerals.)

Rocks

Rocks are defined as consolidated or poorly consolidated aggregates of one or more minerals, glass, or solidified organic matter (such as coal) that cover a significant part of Earth's crust. There are three classes of rocks, based upon their origin: igneous, sedimentary, and metamorphic. **Igneous** (Latin *ignis,* "fire") rock is crystallized from molten or partly molten material. **Sedimentary rocks** include both *lithified* (turned to stone) fragments of preexisting rock and rocks that were

◆ **FIGURE 2.9** Types of cleavage and typical minerals in which they occur.

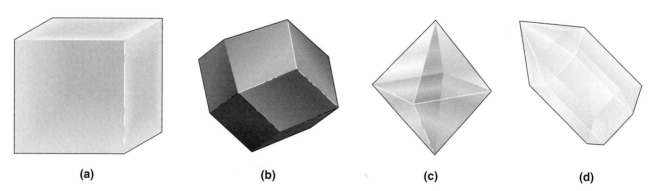

| (a) | (b) | (c) | (d) |

◆ **FIGURE 2.10** Mineral crystal shapes: (a) cube (halite), (b) 12-sided dodecahedron (garnet), (c) 8-sided octahedron (diamond, fluorite), and (d) 6-sided hexagonal prism (quartz).

formed from chemical or biological action. **Metamorphic rocks** are those that have been changed, essentially in the solid state, by heat, fluids, or pressure within the earth.

The **rock cycle** is one of many natural cycles on Earth. The illustration of it in ◆ Figure 2.11 shows the interactions of energy, earth materials, and geologic processes that form and destroy rocks and minerals. The rock cycle is essentially a closed system; "what goes around comes around," so to speak. In a simple cycle there might be a sequence of formation, destruction, and alteration of rocks by earth processes. For example, an igneous rock may be eroded to form sediment that subsequently becomes a sedimentary rock, which may then be metamorphosed by heat and pressure to become a metamorphic rock, and then melted to become an igneous rock.

Throughout this book we emphasize those rocks that, because of their composition or structure, are involved in geologic events that endanger human life or well-being or that are important as resources.

Igneous Rocks

Igneous rocks are classified according to their texture and their mineral composition. A rock's texture is a function of the size and shape of its mineral grains, and for igneous rocks this is determined by how fast or slowly a melted mass cools. If **magma**—molten rock within the earth—cools slowly, large crystals develop, and a rock with coarse-grained, **phaneritic texture** such as granite is formed (see Figure 2.7). The resulting large rock mass formed within the planet is

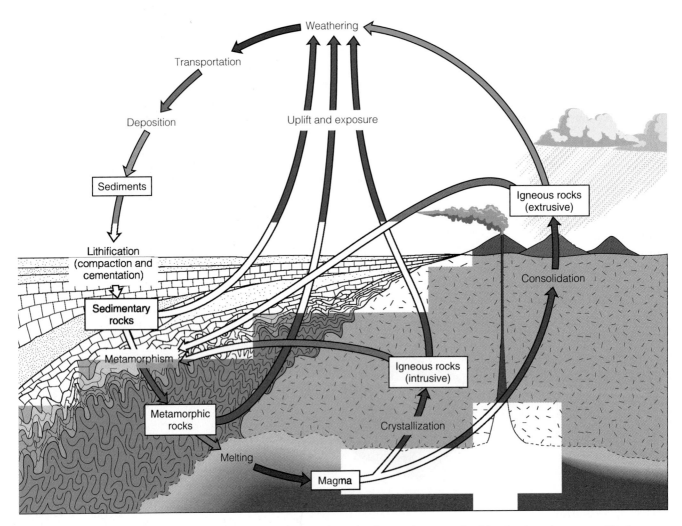

◆ **FIGURE 2.11** The rock cycle. The three rock types are interrelated by internal and external processes involving the atmosphere, ocean, biosphere, crust, and upper mantle.

known as a **batholith.** Greater than 100 square kilometers (39 mi^2) in area by definition, batholiths are mostly granitic in composition and show evidence of having invaded and pushed aside the *country rock* into which they intruded. Also, many batholiths have formed in the cores of mountain ranges during mountain-building episodes. Batholiths are a type of igneous mass referred to as *plutons,* and rocks of batholiths are described as **plutonic** (after Pluto, the Greek god of the underworld), because they were formed at great depth. The Sierra Nevada of California is an example of an uplifted and eroded mountain range with an exposed core composed of many plutons (◆ Figure 2.12).

Most igneous rocks—whether on Earth, the Moon, or Mars—are composed of silicate-mineral-containing silicon, oxygen, and aluminum. Silicon combined with oxygen is the compound *silica,* SiO_2. The percentage of silica in an igneous rock is a measure of how "distilled," or fractionated, its original magma was. The higher the percentage of silica in an igneous rock, the more steps of fractionation it has gone through. Minerals that are rich in magnesium and iron and low in silica (minerals such as pyroxene, amphibole, and olivine) will crystallize and settle out of the magma first. The resulting rocks, relatively rich in magnesium and iron and poor in silica, are thus designated **mafic** (*ma-* for magnesium, *-fic* for iron). The remaining magma has less magnesium and iron and a greater percentage of silica. When the next batch of minerals settles out, perhaps with quartz crystals, rocks of *intermediate* composition are formed. During the fractionation process, the magma becomes richer and richer in silica and more impoverished in magnesium and iron. This late-stage magma is largely silica, alumina, and other elements that combine at lower temperatures. The resulting rocks are rich in feldspar and silica, and are thus described as **felsic** (*fel-* for feldspar, *-sic* for silica). "Primitive" magmas (<50% SiO_2) produce mafic gabbro and its volcanic equivalent, basalt, the rock common to Hawaii volcanoes. More "evolved" magmas (>50% SiO_2) produce rocks of intermediate composition, such as diorite and its volcanic equivalent, andesite. Highly evolved magmas produce felsic rocks such as granite and its volcanic equivalent, rhyolite. Mafic rocks are black or dark colored, and felsic rocks are whitish and pinkish. Intermediate igneous rocks vary in color between these extremes according to their percentage of silica.

Lava is molten material at Earth's surface produced by volcanic activity. Lava cools rapidly, resulting in restricted crystal growth and a fine-grained, or **aphanitic,** texture. An example of a rock with aphanitic texture is rhyolite, which has about the same composition as granite but a much finer texture. The grain size of an igneous rock can tell us whether it is an **intrusive** (cooled within Earth) or an **extrusive** (cooled at the surface of Earth) rock. The classification by texture and composition of igneous rocks is shown in ◆ Figure 2.13. Note that for each composition there are pairs of rocks that are distinguished by their texture. Granite and rhyolite, diorite and andesite, and gabbro and basalt are the most common pairs found in nature. The end member shown in Figure 2.13, peridotite, is rarely found because it originates deep within Earth. Three important and relatively common glassy (composed of amorphous or finely crystalline SiO_2) volcanic rocks are obsidian, which looks like black glass; pumice, which has the composition of glass but is not really glassy-looking; and tuff, consolidated volcanic ash or cinders (◆ Figure 2.14). Tuff has a **pyroclastic** (literally "fire-broken") texture, resulting from fragmentation during violent volcanic eruptions.

Sedimentary Rocks

Sediment is particulate matter derived from the physical or chemical weathering of materials of Earth's crust and by certain organic processes. It may be transported and redeposited by streams, glaciers, wind, or waves. Sedimentary rock is sediment that has become **lithified**—turned to stone—by pressure from deep burial, by cementation, or by both of these processes. **Clastic sedimentary rocks** are those that are composed of *clasts,* fragments of preexisting rocks and minerals. Clastic sedimentary rocks are classified according to their grain size. Thus sand-size sediment lithifies to sandstone, clay to shale, and gravel to conglomerate (◆ Figures 2.15 and 2.16 a, b, and c). Other sediments result from chemical and biological activity. **Chemical sedimentary rocks,** which may be clastic or nonclastic, include chemically precipitated limestone, rock salt, and gypsum. **Biogenic sedimentary rocks** are produced directly by biological activity, such as coal (lithified plant debris), some limestone and chalk ($CaCO_3$, shell material), and chert (siliceous shells) (◆ Figure 2.16 d and e). ✻ Table 2.4 presents the classification of sedimentary rocks.

◆ **FIGURE 2.12** The Sierra Nevada batholith and Mount Whitney, looking west from Owens Valley; east-central California.

B. Pipkin

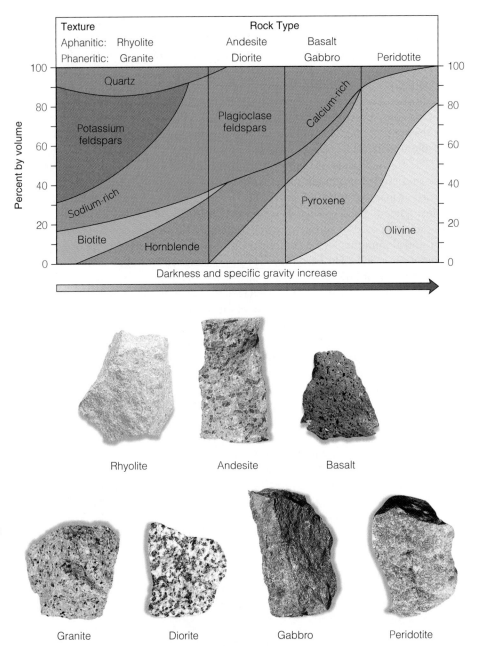

◆ **FIGURE 2.13** Classification of common igneous rocks by their mineralogy and texture. Relative proportions of mineral components are shown for each rock type. Fine-grained *aphanitic* texture results from rapid cooling of molten material. Coarse-grained *phaneritic* texture results from slow cooling. Rock photos courtesy Sue Monroe

A distinguishing characteristic of most sedimentary rock is bedding, or **stratification** into layers. Because shale is very thinly stratified, or *laminated,* it splits into thin sheets. Some sedimentary rocks, such as sandstone and limestone, may occur in beds that are several feet thick. Other structures in these rocks give hints as to how the rock formed. *Cross-bedding*—stratification that is inclined at an angle to the main stratification—indicates the influence of wind or water currents. Thick cross-beds and frosted quartz grains in sandstone indicate an ancient desert sand-dune environment (◆ Figure 2.17). Some shale and claystone show polygonal *mud cracks* on bedding planes, similar to those found on the surface of modern dry lakes; these indicate desiccation in a subaerial environment (◆ Figure 2.18).

CONSIDER   THIS

Forensic geologists are specialists who are sometimes called upon to help solve crimes. They can, for example, compare the mineralogy of soil on a suspect's shoes with the soil at the scene of the crime. They also use geologic clues to reconstruct events that happened millions of years ago. For instance, huge round scars (craters) on the surface of Earth can indicate ancient meteorite impacts. What are some of the "clues" in sedimentary rocks that tell us about the ancient environments in which they formed?

Ripple marks, low, parallel ridges in deposits of fine sand and silt, may be asymmetrical or symmetrical (◆ Figure 2.19). Asymmetrical ripples indicate a unidirectional current;

(a)

(b)

(c)

◆ **FIGURE 2.14** Extrusive igneous rocks: (a) glassy obsidian; (b) pumice, which is formed from gas-charged magmas; and (c) tuff. The lavas that form obsidian and pumice cool so rapidly that crystals do not grow to any size. The reference scale in each photo is 5 centimeters long (5 centimeters is about 2 inches).

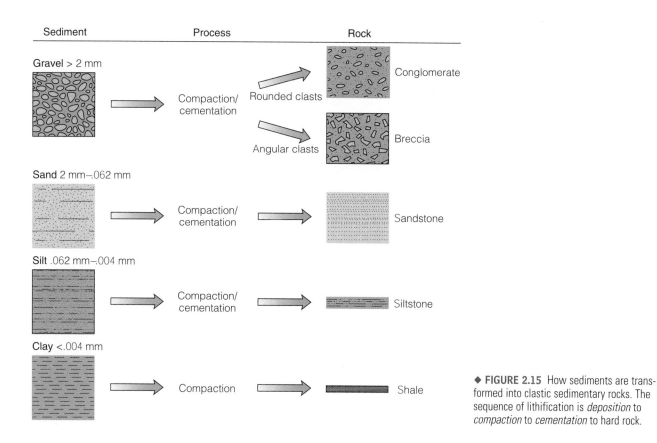

◆ **FIGURE 2.15** How sediments are transformed into clastic sedimentary rocks. The sequence of lithification is *deposition* to *compaction* to *cementation* to hard rock.

(a)

(b)

(c)

(d)

(e)

◆ **FIGURE 2.16** Common *clastic* sedimentary rocks: (a) shale, (b) sandstone, (c) conglomerate. *Biogenic* sedimentary rocks: (d) limestone composed entirely of shell materials (called *coquina*), (e) coal.

★TABLE 2.4   Classification of Sedimentary Rocks

Detrital Sedimentary Rocks (clastic texture)

Sediment	Description	Rock Name
Gravel (>2.0 mm)	Rounded rock fragments	Conglomerate
	Angular rock fragments	Breccia
Sand (0.062–2.0 mm)	Quartz predominant	Quartz sandstone
	>25% feldspars	Arkose
Silt (0.004–0.062 mm)	Quartz predominant, gritty feel	Siltstone
Clay, mud (<0.004 mm)	Laminated, splits into thin sheets	Shale
	Thick beds, blocky	Mudstone

Chemical Sedimentary Rocks

Texture	Composition	Rock Name
Clastic	Calcite ($CaCO_3$)	Limestone
	Dolomite [$CaMg(CO_3)_2$]	Dolostone
Crystalline	Halite (NaCl)	Rock salt
	Gypsum ($CaSO_4 \cdot 2H_2O$)	Rock gypsum

Biogenic Sedimentary Rocks

Texture	Composition	Rock Name
Clastic	Shell calcite, skeletons, broken shells	Limestone, coquina
	Microscopic shells ($CaCO_3$)	Chalk
Nonclastic (altered)	Microscopic shells (SiO_2), recrystallized silica	Chert
	Consolidated plant remains (largely carbon)	Coal

◆ **FIGURE 2.17** Wind-blown sandstone exhibiting large cross-beds; Zion National Park, Utah.

◆ **FIGURE 2.19** Ripple marks found in sedimentary rocks. (a) Asymmetrical ripple marks are common in streambeds and are also found on bedding planes in sedimentary rocks. (b) Symmetrical ripple marks are due to oscillating water motion; that is, wave action.

symmetrical ones, the back-and-forth motion produced by waves in shallow water. Only in sedimentary rock do we find abundant fossils, the remains or traces of life.

Metamorphic Rocks

Rocks that have been changed from preexisting rocks by heat, pressure, or chemical processes are classified as metamorphic rocks. The process of metamorphism results in new structures, textures, and minerals. **Foliation** (Latin *folium,* "leaf") is the flattening and layering of minerals by nonuniform stresses. Foliated metamorphic rocks are classified by the development of this structure. Slate, schist, and gneiss are foliated, for example, and they are identified by the thickness or crudeness of their foliation (◆ Figure 2.20). Metamorphic rocks may also form by **recrystallization.** This occurs when a rock is heated and strained by uniform stresses so that

◆ **FIGURE 2.18** Mud cracks in an old clay mine; Ione, California.

larger, more perfect grains result or new minerals form. In this manner a limestone may recrystallize to marble or a quartz sandstone to quartzite, one of the most resistant of all rocks (◆ Figure 2.21). ✳ Table 2.5 summarizes the characteristics of common metamorphic rocks.

Rock Defects

Some rocks have structures that geologists view as "defects"; that is, surfaces along which landslides or rockfalls may occur. Almost any planar structure, such as a bedding plane in sedimentary rock or a foliation plane in metamorphic rock, holds potential for rock slides or falls. The orientation of a plane in space, such as a stratification plane, a fault, or a joint, may be defined by its **dip** and **strike** (Appendix 3). **Joints** are rock fractures without displacement and they occur in all rock types. They are commonly found in parallel sets spaced several feet apart (◆ Figure 2.22). **Faults** are also fractures in crustal rocks, but they differ from joints in that some movement or displacement has occurred along the fault surface. Faults also are found in all rock types and are potential surfaces of "failure." We will examine the relationships of rock defects to geologic hazards when we discuss landslides, subsidence, and earthquakes.

CONSIDER THIS

Rock climbing is a popular sport in many parts of the world. A favorite spot in the U.S. West is Yosemite Valley, a picturesque area carved by glaciers into a uniform granite body known as the Cathedral Peak Granite (see Gallery Figure 3). Why do you suppose climbers would prefer to climb near-vertical cliffs of granite, as opposed to similar cliffs composed of schist, gneiss, or shale?

◆ **FIGURE 2.20** Metamorphic rocks: (a) coarsely foliated gneiss, (b) mica schist showing wavy or crinkly foliation, (c) finely foliated slate showing slaty cleavage.

Geologic Time

Interest in extremely long periods of time sets geology and astronomy apart from other sciences. Geologists think in terms of billions of years for the age of Earth and its oldest rocks—numbers that, like the national debt, are not easily comprehended. Nevertheless, the time scales of geologic activity are important for environmental geologists because they provide a way to measure human impacts on the natural world. For example, we would like to know the rate of natural soil formation from solid rock to determine whether topsoil erosion from agriculture is too great or not. Likewise, understanding how climate has changed over millions of years is vital to properly assess current global-

◆ **FIGURE 2.21** (a) Limestone recrystallizes to form white marble. (b) Quartzite, the hardest and most durable common rock, is metamorphosed sandstone. Rocks courtesy Sue Monroe

*TABLE 2.5	Common Metamorphic Rocks	
Rock	Parent Rock	Characteristics
Foliated or Layered		
Slate	Shale and mudstone	Splits into thin sheets
Schist	Fine-grained rocks, siltstone, shale, tuff	Mica minerals often crinkled
Gneiss	Coarse-grained rocks	Dark and light layers of aligned minerals
Nonfoliated or Recrystallized		
Marble	Limestone	Interlocking crystals
Quartzite	Sandstone	Interlocking, almost fused quartz grains

◆ **FIGURE 2.22** Joints in basalt flows near Chico, California.

warming trends. Clues to past environmental change are well-preserved in many different kinds of rocks.

Geologists evaluate the age of rocks and geologic events using two different approaches. **Relative-age dating** is the technique of determining *a sequence of geological events,* based upon the structural relations of rocks. **Absolute-age dating** provides the *actual ages* for rocks in years before the present. Relative age is determined by applying geologic laws based upon the structural relations of rocks. For instance, the Law of Superposition tells us that in a stack of undeformed sedimentary rocks, the stratum (layer) at the top is the youngest. The Law of Cross-cutting Relationships tells us

that a fault is younger than the youngest rocks it displaces or cuts. Similarly, we know that a pluton is younger than the rocks it intrudes (◆Figure 2.23).

Using these laws, geologists arranged a great thickness of sedimentary rocks and their contained fossils representing an immense span of geologic time. The geologic age of a particular sequence of rock was then determined by applying the Law of Fossil Succession, the observed chronologic sequence of life forms through geologic time. This allows fossiliferous rocks from two widely separated areas to be correlated by matching key fossils or groups of fossils found in the rocks of the two areas (Figure 2.23). Using such indicator

◆ **FIGURE 2.23** Geologic cross sections illustrating the Laws of Superposition, Cross-cutting Relationships (intrusion and faulting), and Fossil Succession. The limestone beds are correlative because they contain the same fossils. The numerals indicate relative ages, with 1 being the youngest.

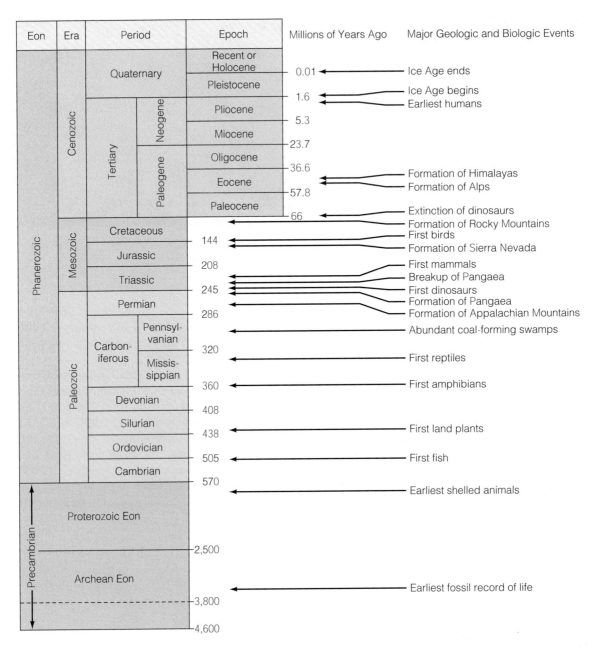

Eon	Era	Period		Epoch	Millions of Years Ago	Major Geologic and Biologic Events

◆ **FIGURE 2.24** Geologic time scale. Adapted from A. R. Palmer, Geology, 1983, 504.

fossils and radioactive dating methods, geologists have developed the geologic time scale to chronicle the documented events of Earth history (◆ Figure 2.24). Note that the scale is divided into units of time during which rocks were deposited, life evolved, and significant geologic events such as mountain building occurred. Eons are the longest time intervals, followed, respectively, by eras, periods, and epochs. The Phanerozoic ("revealed life") Eon began 570 million years ago with the Cambrian Period, the rocks of which contain the first extensive fossils of organisms with hard skeletons. Because of the significance of the Cambrian Period, the informal term *Precambrian* is widely used to denote the time before it, which extends back to the formation of Earth 4.6 billion years ago. Note that the Precambrian is divided into the Archean and Proterozoic Eons, with the Archean Eon extending back to the formation of the oldest known in-place rocks, about 3.9 billion years ago. Precambrian time accounts for 88 percent of geologic time, and the Phanerozoic for a mere 12 percent. The eras of geologic time correspond to the relative complexity of life forms: Paleozoic (oldest life), Mesozoic (middle life), and Cenozoic (most recent life). Environmental geologists are most interested in the events of the past few million years, a mere heartbeat in the history of Earth.

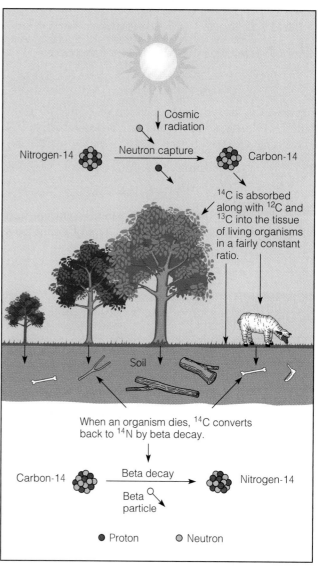

◆ FIGURE 2.25 (a) Alpha emission, whereby a heavy nucleus spontaneously emits a helium atom and is reduced 4 atomic mass units and 2 atomic numbers. (b) Emission of a nuclear electron (ß⁻ particle), which changes a neutron to a proton and thereby forms a new element without a change of mass.

Absolute age-dating requires some kind of natural clock. The ticks of the clock may be the annual growth rings of trees or established rates of disintegration of radioactive elements to form other elements. At the turn of the twentieth century, American chemist and physicist Bertram Borden Boltwood (1870–1927) discovered that the ratio of lead to uranium in uranium-bearing rocks increases as the rocks' ages increase. He developed a process for determining the age of ancient geologic events that is unaffected by heat or pressure—**radiometric dating.** The "ticks" of the radioactive clocks are radioactive decay processes—spontaneous disintegrations of the nuclei of heavier elements such as uranium and thorium to lead. A radioactive element may decay to another element, or to an isotope of the same element. This decay occurs at a precise rate that can be determined experimentally. The most common emissions are alpha particles ($^4_2\alpha$), which are helium atoms, and beta particles (ß⁻), which are nuclear electrons. New *radiogenic* "daughter" elements or isotopes result from this **alpha decay** and **beta decay** (◆Figure 2.25).

For example, of the three isotopes of carbon, ^{12}C, ^{13}C, and ^{14}C, only ^{14}C is radioactive, and this radioactivity can be used to date events between a few hundred and a few tens of thousands of years ago. Carbon-14 is formed continually in the upper atmosphere by neutron bombardment of nitrogen, and it exists in a fixed ratio to the common isotope, ^{12}C. All plants and animals contain radioactive ^{14}C in equilibrium with the atmospheric abundance until they die, at which time ^{14}C begins to decrease in abundance and, along with it, the object's radioactivity. Thus, by measuring the radioactivity of an ancient parchment, log, or piece of charcoal and comparing the measurement with the activity of a modern standard, the age of archaeological materials and geological events can be determined (◆Figure 2.26).

◆ FIGURE 2.26 Carbon-14 is formed from nitrogen-14 by neutron capture and subsequent proton emission. Carbon-14 decays back to nitrogen-14 by emission of a nuclear electron (ß⁻).

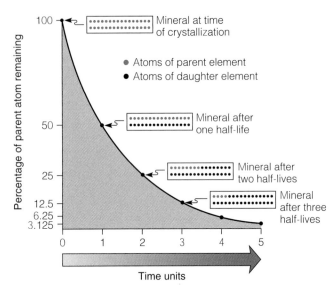

◆ **FIGURE 2.27** Decay of a radioactive parent element with time. Each time unit is one half-life. Note that after two half-lives one-fourth of the parent element remains, and that after three half-lives one-eighth remains.

Carbon-14 is formed by the collision of cosmic neutrons with ^{14}N in the atmosphere, and then it decays back to ^{14}N by emitting a nuclear electron (ß⁻).

$$^{14}_{7}N + \text{neutron} \longrightarrow {}^{14}_{6}C + \text{proton}$$

$$^{14}_{6}C \longrightarrow {}^{14}_{7}N + ß^{-}$$

Both carbon—the radioactive "parent" element—and nitrogen—the radiogenic "daughter"—have 14 atomic mass units. However, one of ^{14}C's neutrons is converted to a proton by the emission of a beta particle, and the carbon changes (or *transmutes*) to nitrogen. This process proceeds at a set rate that can be expressed as a **half-life,** the time required for half of a population of radioactive atoms to decay. For ^{14}C this is about 5,730 years.

Radioactive elements decay exponentially; that is, in two half-lives one-fourth of the original number of atoms remain, in three half-lives one-eighth remain, and so on (◆Figure 2.27). So few parent atoms remain after seven or eight half-lives (less than 1 percent) that experimental uncertainty creates limits for the various radiometric dating methods.

Whereas the practical age limit for dating carbon-bearing materials such as wood, paper, and cloth is about 40,000 to 50,000 years, ^{238}U disintegrates to ^{206}Pb and has a half-life of 4.5×10^9 years. Uranium-238 emits alpha particles (helium atoms). Since both alpha and beta disintegrations can be measured with a Geiger counter, we have a means of determining the half-lives of a geological or archaeological sample. ✶Table 2.6 shows radioactive parents, daughters, and half-lives commonly used in age-dating.

Age of Earth

Before the advent of radiometric dating, determining the age of Earth was a source of controversy between established religious interpretations and early scientists. Archbishop Ussher (1585–1656), the Archbishop of Armagh and a professor at Trinity College in Dublin, declared that Earth was

✶TABLE 2.6	Isotopes Used in Age-Dating			
Isotopes		Parent's Half-Life, Years	Effective Dating Range, Years	Material That Can Be Dated
Parent	*Daughter*			
Uranium-238	Lead-206	4.5 billion	10 million to 4.6 billion	Zircon Uraninite
Uranium-235	Lead-207	704 million		
Thorium-232	Lead-208	14 billion		
Rubidium-87	Strontium-87	48.8 billion	10 million to 4.6 billion	Muscovite Biotite Orthoclase Whole metamorphic or igneous rock
Potassium-40	Argon-40	1.3 billion	100,000 to 4.6 billion	Glauconite Hornblende Muscovite Whole volcanic rock Biotite
Carbon-14	Nitrogen-14	5,730 years	less than 100,000	Shell, bones, charcoal

formed in the year 4004 B.C. Ussher provided not only the year but also the day, October 23, and the time, 9:00 A.M. Ussher has many detractors, but Stephen J. Gould of Harvard University, though not proposing acceptance of Ussher's date, was not one of them. Gould pointed out that Ussher's work was good scholarship for its time, because other religious scholars had extrapolated from Greek and Hebrew scriptures that Earth was formed in 5500 B.C. and 3761 B.C., respectively. Ussher based his age determination on the verse in the Bible that says "one day is with the Lord as a thousand years" (2 Peter 3:8). Because the Bible also says that God created heaven and Earth in 6 days, Ussher arrived at 4004 years B.C.—the extra four years because he believed Christ's birth year was wrong by that amount of time. Ussher's age for Earth was accepted by many as "gospel" for almost 200 years.

By the late 1800s geologists believed that Earth was on the order of 100 million years old. They reached their estimates by dividing the total thickness of sedimentary rocks (tens of kilometers) by an assumed annual rate of deposition (mm/year). Evolutionists such as Charles Darwin thought that geologic time must be almost limitless in order that minute changes in organisms could eventually produce the present diversity of species. Both geologists and evolutionists were embarrassed when the British physicist William Thomson (later Lord Kelvin) demonstrated with elegant mathematics how Earth could be no older than 400 million years, and maybe as young as 20 million years. Thomson based this on the rate of cooling of an initially molten Earth and the assumption that the material composing Earth was incapable of creating new heat through time. He did not know about radioactivity, which adds heat to rocks in the crust and mantle.

Bertram Boltwood postulated that older uranium-bearing minerals should carry a higher proportion of lead than younger samples. He analyzed a number of specimens of known relative age, and the absolute ages he came up with ranged from 410 million to 2.2 billion years old. These ages put Lord Kelvin's dates based on cooling rates to rest and ushered in the new radiometric dating technique. By extrapolating backward to the time when no radiogenic lead had been produced on Earth, we arrive at an age of 4.6 billion years for Earth. This corresponds to the dates obtained from meteorites and lunar rocks, which are part of our solar system. The oldest known intact terrestrial rocks are found in the Acasta Gneiss of the Slave geological province of Canada's Northwest Territories. Analyses of lead to uranium ratios on the gneiss's zircon minerals indicate that the rocks are 3.96 billion years old. However, older detrital zircons on the order of 4.0–4.3 billion years old have been found in western Australia, indicating that some stable continental crust was present as early as 4.3 billion years ago (* Table 2.7). Suffice it to say that Earth is very old and that there has been abundant time to produce the features we see today (◆ Figure 2.28).

*TABLE 2.7	Earth's Oldest Known Materials	
Material	Location	Age, Billions of Years
Crust	Zircon minerals in rocks of western Australia	4.0–4.3
Rock	Zircon minerals in the Acasta Gneiss, N.W. Terr., Canada	3.96
Sedimentary rock	Isua Greenstone Belt, Greenland	3.7–3.75
Fossils	Algae and bacteria	3.5

Environmental geology deals mostly with the present and the recent past—the time interval known as the *Holocene Epoch* (10,000 years ago to the present) of the *Quaternary Period.* However, because the Great Ice Age advances of the Pleistocene Epoch of the Quaternary Period (which preceded our own Holocene Epoch) had such a tremendous impact on the landscape of today, we will investigate the probable causes of the "ice ages" in order to speculate a bit about what the future might bring. In addition, Pleistocene glacial deposits are valuable sources of underground water, and they have economic value as sources of building materials. We will see that ice ages have occurred several times throughout geologic history (see Chapter 11).

What is most impressive about geologic time is how short the period of human life on Earth has been. If we could compress the 4.6 billion years since Earth formed into one calendar year, *Homo sapiens* would appear about 30 minutes before midnight on December 31 (see Figure 2.30). The last ice-age glaciers would begin wasting away a bit more than 2 minutes before midnight, and written history would exist for only the last 30 seconds of the year. Perhaps we should keep this calendar in mind when we hear that the dinosaurs were an unsuccessful group of reptiles. After all, they endured 50 times longer than hominids have existed on the planet to date. At the present rate of population growth, there is some doubt that humankind as we know it will be able to survive anywhere near that long.

The Earth we see today is the product of earth processes acting on earth materials over the immensity of geologic time. The response of the materials to the processes has been the formation of mountain ranges, plateaus, and the multitude of other physical features found on the planet. Perhaps the greatest of these processes has been the formation and movement of platelike segments of Earth's surface, which influence the distribution of earthquakes and volcanic eruptions, global geography, mineral deposits, mountain ranges, and even climate. These *plate tectonic* processes are the subject of the next chapter.

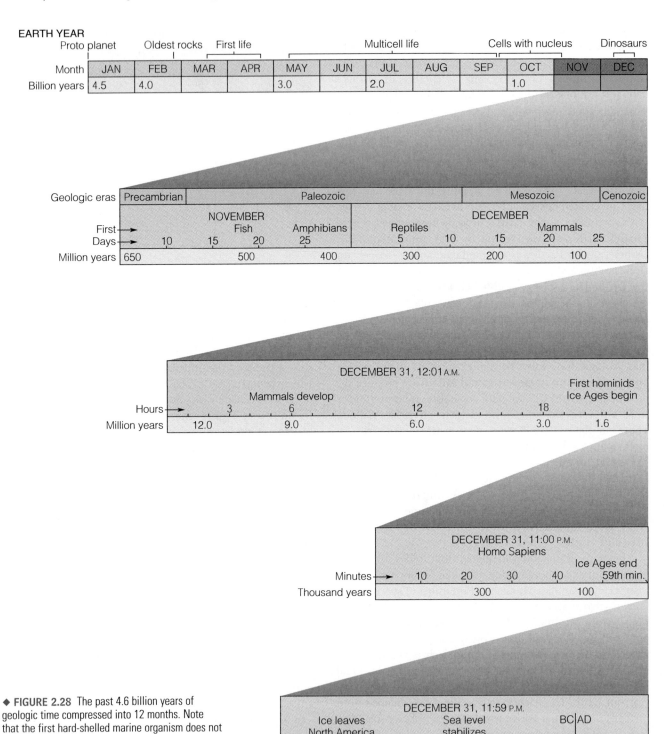

◆ **FIGURE 2.28** The past 4.6 billion years of geologic time compressed into 12 months. Note that the first hard-shelled marine organism does not appear until about November 1, and that humans as we know them have been around only since the last hour before the New Year.

CASE STUDY 2.1

Minerals, Cancer, and OSHA—Fact and Fiction

When an international health organization designated quartz as "probably" carcinogenic (cancer-causing) to humans, the U.S. Occupational Safety and Health Agency (OSHA) immediately went into action. It issued a mandate requiring products containing more than one-tenth of one percent (0.1%) of quartz or "free silica" (SiO_2) to display warning signs. Because quartz is chemically inert and because it is the most common mineral species, questions arose as to whether this requirement extended to sandpaper, beach sand, and unpaved roads that may produce clouds of fine-grained quartz dust. Questions—and more—arose when some Delaware truck drivers were "ticketed" for not displaying the required "quartz on board" signs during transport of crushed rock to construction sites. Such well-meaning OSHA actions have been perceived as ridiculous. They illustrate what happens when a government authority establishes health regulations without understanding the substances involved. In this case OSHA did not understand the where, how, and chemistry of the mineral—its mineralogy. Unless one has had a long-term craving to inhale beach sand or crushed rock, there are no health hazards in the examples cited. Nonetheless, because exposure to very large quantities of any substance, even table salt or vitamins, can be harmful to health, it is certain that long-term workplace exposure to dusts from some minerals can pose health problems.

The World Health Organization's Group 1 classification of "known" carcinogenic minerals includes asbestos minerals (there are six), erionite (a zeolite), and minerals containing arsenic, chromium, and nickel. Its Group 2 of "probable" carcinogenic minerals includes all radioactive minerals and minerals containing lead, beryllium, and silica. The classification is based upon suspected relationships between specific diseases and workplace exposure to the identified substances and on laboratory experiments with animals.

A major human health concern is the relationship between lung cancer and inhaling the fine fibers of asbestos minerals. The long, fibrous crystal forms of asbestos belonging to the amphibole group (see hornblende structure, Figure 2.7) are considered the most carcinogenic. Of these, blue asbestos, crocidolite (pronounced krō-sid'- əl-īt; ◆Figure 1), is thought to be most dangerous and is believed to cause mesothelioma, a relatively rare cancer of the lining of the heart and lungs. Although crocidolite constitutes only 5 percent of all industrial asbestos, its morbidity statistics are grim indeed. For example, a 1990 survey of 33 men who, in 1953, worked in a factory where crocidolite was utilized in manufacturing cigarette filters found that 19 of them had died of asbestos-related diseases.

Common white asbestos, chrysotile (pronounced kris'- ə-tīl; ◆Figure 2), is a sheet-structure mineral similar to mica. It appears under high magnification as long fibers, which are in reality rolled sheets, much like long rolls of gift-wrapping paper. Chrysotile constitutes 95 percent of all industrial asbestos and has never been demonstrated to cause cancer at the levels found in most schools and public

◆ **FIGURE 1** Deadly crocidolite, "blue asbestos," magnified about 100 times. The mineral appears in its characteristic blue and green colors when viewed through a petrographic microscope. It was used in only a small percentage of commercial products.

buildings. A study conducted in Thetford, Quebec, Canada evaluated persons who had been exposed to high concentrations of white asbestos in their workplace and found no deaths attributable to it. Many of the diagnosed chrysotile-related lung problems have been traced back to improper handling of the material and inadequate respiratory protection during asbestos removal procedures. Experimental studies at Virginia Tech have shown that respirable-sized 1-nannometer-diameter chrysotile fibers dissolve in about nine months under conditions

◆ **FIGURE 2** Chrysotile asbestos (×100) has many uses in homes, offices, and public buildings. Although it is the target of removal in thousands of structures, at low levels it poses no documented risk. Note the difference between chrysotile and crocidolite's crystal structures.

CONTINUED

expected in lung tissue. This very short lifetime is difficult to reconcile with the general observations that asbestos-related diseases appear in asbestos workers only after many years on the job.

Inhaling finely divided airborne asbestos fibers in large quantities is definitely a health hazard. Under the Toxic Substance Control Act of 1972, the EPA mandated in 1986 that *all* asbestos minerals be treated as identical health hazards, regardless of their mineralogy, and that they be removed. By the mid-1990s the cost of removal had amounted to hundreds of millions of dollars, and the total cumulative cost for remediation of rental and commercial buildings, litigation, and enforcement was estimated at $100 billion. The EPA requirements were sweeping. They applied to buildings containing the relatively benign white asbestos and to those where airborne concentrations were so low that they could not be measured. The fear of asbestos and the EPA regulations are based on the idea that there is no safe "threshold" concentration—that even one fiber can kill. No doctor or public health official would agree with this. A New York school district's administration was besieged by irate parents when it admitted that it could not *guarantee* that *all* asbestos had been removed from its buildings. The district had spent millions of dollars to remove it.

Industry and government can ill afford to squander capital and tax dollars on poorly conceived hazard-mitigation requirements based upon the "no threshold" theory of health risk; that is, that one molecule of pesticide or one asbestos fiber can cause health problems. Many government regulations regarding "toxic substances" address risks to humans that are no greater than those incurred by routinely drinking several cups of coffee each day or eating a peanut butter sandwich for lunch. The "no threshold" criterion forces "carcinogen" classification upon otherwise benign minerals and many other useful substances and needlessly increases public anxiety. (Remember when synthetic sweeteners and cellular telephones were labeled carcinogenic?) The costs of removal and liability protection in such cases are horrendous, and a fiscal crisis in the environmental field is acknowledged. Liability extends to building owners, real estate agents who sell the buildings, banks that lend money for property purchases, and purchasers of land upon which any material classified as hazardous is found.

A person's chances of being struck by a lightning bolt are about 35 per 1 million lifetimes, and the risk of a nonsmoker's dying from asbestos exposure is about 1 in 100,000—about a third of the chance of being struck by lightning. Incidentally, the risk of dying from cigarette-related diseases is about 1 in 5 for smokers. Certainly, some substances in the environment pose dangers, and the key to risk reduction and longevity is awareness. Just as a reasonable person would not play golf during a violent thunderstorm because of the risk of being struck by lightning on the course, one should not handle hazardous substances without wearing protective gear.

CASE STUDY 2.2

A Girl's Best Friend and Other Gems

Rarity and beauty are what make precious and semiprecious gems so desirable. Those shown in ◆ Figure 1 are but a sample of several hundred valued gem minerals and their varieties. The largest uncut diamond in the world, the Cullinan diamond (◆ Figure 1a), was recovered in 1905 from the Premier Mine at Kimberley, Transvaal, South Africa; the huge, colorless stone weighed 3,106 carats (1.3 pounds). The smooth face of the Cullinan replica shown in the photograph replicates the stone's natural cleavage surface, which indicates that it was not the entire stone. Unfortunately, the remainder of the Cullinan lies undiscovered in a deep volcanic pipe—which is where all diamonds originate. The Transvaal government bought the diamond for $1.6 million and gave it uncut to King Edward VII of England. After months of study, an Amsterdam diamond cutter's decisive blow yielded nine large stones and about 100 smaller ones, all of them flawless. All are now in the British crown jewels collection.

Diamonds are the high-pressure form of carbon and are the hardest natural substance known. Curiously, graphite, the high-temperature, low-pressure form of carbon, is among the softest minerals known.

Diamonds are found mostly in Africa, Australia, Russia, India, and South America (◆ Table 1). Near Yellowknife, Northwest Territories in Canada, the Ekati diamond mine opened in the late 1990s with great expectations. Diamond finds in the United States are shown on the map of ◆ Figure 2. Most are solitary finds, and their sources are unknown. At Murfreesboro, Arkansas, however, thousands of diamonds have been recovered from an eroded diamond "pipe," one weighing 40 carats. For the price of admission, one can dig for diamonds here in the "blue ground" of the eroded pipe. One lucky hunter uncovered a 15-carat stone.

Precious opal (Sanskrit *upâlā*, "precious stone"; ◆ Figure 1b) occurs in shallow surface diggings, and because it lacks crystalline form, it

(a)

(b)

◆ FIGURE 1 (a) Exact replica of the Cullinan diamond with the two largest stones cut from it, the Great Star of Africa (530.2 carats) and the Second Star of Africa (317 carats), which now reside in the British crown jewels collection. (b) Uncut precious opal. (c) Uncut emerald.

(c)

★TABLE 1	Major World Diamond Producers, 1997*	
Country		**Value, $ millions**
Botswana		$1,461
Russia		1,210
Angola		1,035
South Africa		971
Congo		715
Namibia		410
Australia		288

*Just seven countries account for 90% of all rough-diamond production.
Source: Larry Gordon, *Los Angeles Times*, November 4, 1998.

◆ FIGURE 2 Reported diamond finds in glacial drift in the Great Lakes region. Numerals indicate the number of diamonds found at the location; single finds have been reported at the other locations. After C.B. Gunn, *Gems and Gemology* 12, nos. 10 and 11 (1968), pp. 297–303, 333–334, © Gemological Inst. of America

actually is not a mineral. It is amorphous hydrated silica and gets its "fire" from an orderly arrangement of silica spheres interspersed with water molecules. Black and fire opals are the most desirable, and each stone is priced individually.

Emerald, the most valuable mineral carat-for-carat, is the precious variety of the silicate mineral beryl (◆ Figure 1c). It is found in coarse-grained granites called *pegmatites* (see Chapter 13) and in mica schist.

Quartz, plain old SiO_2, one of the most common minerals, has a host of semiprecious varieties such as purple amethyst, banded agate, yellow citrine, and smoky and rose quartz (◆ Figure 3). Searching for polishing-quality quartz varieties is the passion of many "rock hounds," and good crystal specimens also are cherished.

CONTINUED

(a)

(b)

(c)

(d)

(e)

◆ **FIGURE 3** Some varieties of quartz: (a) colorless crystals, (b) smokey quartz, (c) amethyst, (d) agate, and (e) rose quartz. (a) Smithsonian Institute; (b)–(e) Sue Monroe

CASE STUDY 2.3

Minerals, Cats, and the Litter Belt

Many of Lovell, Wyoming's 2,100 inhabitants once depended upon the oil industry for their livelihood. The people there mine bentonite, which is used in oil drilling. Mixed with water, bentonite forms a "mud" that is circulated through the drill pipe and back to the ground surface outside the pipe. It forms a filter cake on the walls of the hole that prevents entry of water and loss of the drilling fluid into porous formations. It also cools the drill bit as the drill churns through hard rock and carries the drilled rock debris up to the surface. Oil prices dropped in the late 1980s, and Lovell all but dried up (Chapter 14).

Bentonite is formed by geochemical alteration of volcanic ash to form clay minerals, the most important of which is *smectite*. One of smectite's unusual properties is that it can absorb water equivalent to many times its original volume. The clay may swell as it absorbs water, forming a gooey mess, or it may crumble into fluffy pellets, depending on the amount of water and the initial size of the clay aggregates. Land areas underlain by ben-

tonite may absorb so much water in the rainy season that they become impassable. Also, bentonitic soils can swell and cause severe damage to structures founded in it or on it (see Chapter 6). It has many uses. Native Americans once used it to remove oil and dirt from buffalo hides. It is used today in the landscaping of golf greens, to filter and clarify wine, to line landfills and ponds to prevent water loss, and in the manufacture of crayons.

Lovell was a potential ghost town without oil drilling. Bentonite to the rescue! It began when kitty litter replaced the sand box in 1948. The new product utilized a variety of clay-type minerals in the litter mix to absorb moisture. An enterprising chemist recognized the potential of bentonite, with its great moisture-absorbing properties, as cat litter. He reasoned that, with the proper grain size, the bentonite would clump when the cat did his duty, so that the soiled clumps could easily be removed from the litter pan. He was right, and the rest, as they say, is history (◆ Figure 1).

Today, almost all cat litter contains bentonite, and the Lovell mine is back in full-swing operation. The plant employs 60 people, and new houses are being built in the community to accommodate them. Bentonites in Wyoming are the result of volcanic eruptions in Cretaceous time, when dinosaurs roamed the land. The swath of mineable bentonites from Lovell to Casper has been dubbed the "Litter Belt" in Wyoming.

◆ **FIGURE 1** © 1994 Margaret Miller/ The National Audubon Society Collection/Photo Researchers

A Rock Collection

Specific rocks have had historical, aesthetic, and practical significance to humans; Plymouth Rock, the Rock of Gibraltar, the biblical Rock of Ages, and the Rosetta Stone are examples. Various geologic agents of erosion have shaped the rocks of the Grand Canyon, Bryce Canyon, Yosemite, and other national parks into areas that we admire for their great beauty. Early humans lived in rock caves and threw rocks to defend themselves against their enemies and to kill animals for food. Over time humans came to build crude rock shelters, and then rock fences, and eventually beautiful castles and abbeys. Today rock and rock products are important mineral resources, used mostly as building materials. The beauty and usefulness of rocks are celebrated in these photographs.

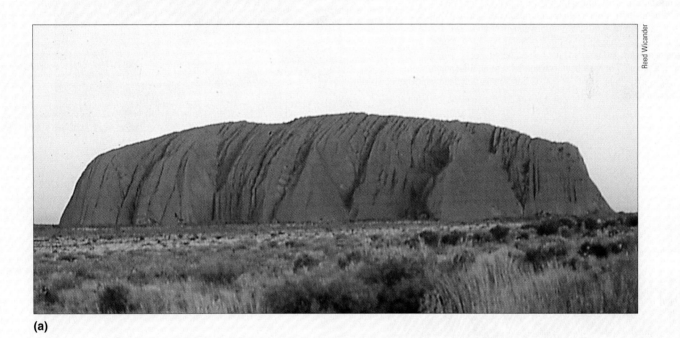

Reed Wicander

(a)

◆ FIGURE 1 Ayers Rock, the world's largest sand-stone monolith, is one of Australia's leading tourist attractions. An erosional remnant of a previous high-land, it rises abruptly above the surrounding flat land. In geological terminology it is called an *inselberg* (German "island mountain") because of its resemblance to an island rising from the sea. Aborigines (native Australians) call Ayers Rock *Uluru*. In 1958 Ayers Rock and the rocks of the Olgas nearby were incorporated into Uluru National Park. (a) Ayers Rock rises 348 meters (1,141 ft) above the surrounding plain, and is scaled by 80 percent of the visitors to the park. (b) The Olgas, a circular grouping of more than 30 red domes, is a subdued but still spectacular sandstone inselberg in Uluru National Park. Its highest point, Mt. Olga, rises 460 meters (1,500 ft) above the plain. The Olgas' Aboriginal name is *katajuta*, "many heads." Ayers Rock is in the background.

Reed Wicander

(b)

41

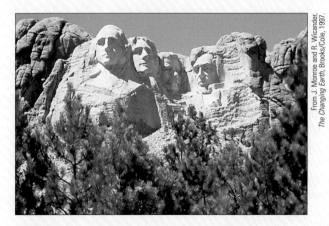

From J. Monroe and R. Wicander, *The Changing Earth*, Brooks/Cole, 1997.

◆ **FIGURE 2** Sixty-foot-high representations of the heads of four presidents were carved into Mount Rushmore's Harney Peak Granite in southwestern South Dakota between 1927 and 1941. The great work was possible because the Precambrian granite is relatively homogeneous (uniform) and not riddled with defects. Why would such a project not have been considered if Mount Rushmore were composed of slate, shale, or schist? Can you identify the presidents honored here?

Theodore Roosevelt Collection, Harvard Coll. Library

◆ **FIGURE 3** President Theodore Roosevelt (*left*) and naturalist John Muir at Yosemite Valley in 1903. The rock on which they were photographed is Cathedral Peak Granite, one of the many granite intrusions that make up the Sierra Nevada batholith. Note the rounded exfoliation domes in the background (see Chapter 6).

B. Pipkin

◆ **FIGURE 4** A skillfully assembled sandstone wall in Yorkshire, England. Yorkshire is the largest county (shire) in England, and literally thousands of kilometers of these walls are found there. This commonly occurring sandstone breaks readily into platy and blocky pieces, which makes it perfect for wall building.

Summary

Solar System

Description

Formed 5 billion years ago from an interstellar cloud (nebula).

Probable Cause

The nebula collapsed as a result of a gravitational attraction. The nebula started to spin and condense. The inner part of the cloud became the hot protosun and it was surrounded by a cooler, disc-shaped cloud, the solar nebula, which formed the large outer, Jovian planets. Rocky material closest to the sun formed the inner, terrestrial planets. Mars rocks are similar to Earth rocks.

Earth System

The Earth System has five interconnecting subsystems, or reservoirs, sometimes called "spheres." They are the solid Earth (includes lithosphere and soil), the atmosphere, the hydrosphere, the biosphere, and the extraterrestrial. Most are closed systems, such as the rock cycle and the hydrologic cycle, but energy is the exception. Continual interaction and recycling by these reservoirs is vital to the dynamic earth system.

Earth Materials

Crust

Outermost rocky layer of Earth composed of rocks that are aggregates of minerals.

Minerals

Naturally occurring inorganic substances with a definite set of physical properties and a narrow range of chemical compositions.

Classification By

Chemistry of anions (negative ions or radicals), such as oxides, sulfides, carbonates, etc. Silicates are the most common and important mineral group and are composed of silica tetrahedra $(SiO_4)^{-4}$ units that are joined to form chains, sheets, and networks.

Identification

Physical properties such as hardness, cleavage, crystal structure, fracture pattern, and luster.

Rocks

Consolidated or poorly consolidated aggregates of one or more minerals or organic matter.

Classes

Igneous—rock formed by crystallization of molten or partially molten material.

Sedimentary—layered rock resulting from consolidation and lithification of sediment.

Metamorphic—preexisting rock that has been changed by heat, pressure, or chemically active fluids.

Classification by

Texture and composition.

Structures

Many planar rock structures may be viewed as defects along which landslides, rockfalls, or other potentially hazardous events may occur. Stratification in sedimentary rocks and foliation in metamorphic rocks are common planar features. Faults and joints occur in all classes of rock.

Rock Cycle

A sequence of events by which rocks are formed, altered, destroyed, and reformed as a result of internal and external earth processes.

Geologic Time

Relative Time

The sequential order of geologic events established by using basic geologic principles or laws.

Geologic Time Scale

The division of geologic history into eons, eras, periods, and epochs. The earliest 88 percent of geologic time is known informally as Precambrian time. *Precambrian* rocks are generally not fossiliferous. Rocks of the Cambrian Period and younger contain good fossil records of shelled and skeletonized organisms. Environmental geology is concerned mainly with geologic events of the present epoch, the Holocene, and the one that preceded it, the Pleistocene.

Absolute Age

Absolute dating methods use some natural "clock." For long periods of time, such clocks are known rates of radioactive decay. A parent radioactive isotope decays to a daughter isotope at a rate that can be determined experimentally. This established rate, expressed as a half-life, enables us to determine the age of a sample of material.

Age of Earth

Comparing present U/Pb ratios with those in iron meteorites, we can extrapolate backward and obtain an Earth age of 4.6 billion years.

Rocks and Crust

The oldest known in-place rocks are 3.96 billion years old. Dating of minerals derived from older crust yields an age of 4.0–4.3 billion years for stable continental crust.

Key Terms

absolute-age dating	aphanitic texture	atomic number	biogenic sedimentary	chemical sedimentary
alpha decay	atom	batholith	rocks	rocks
amorphous	atomic mass	beta decay		clastic

clastic sedimentary rocks	foliation	lava	nucleus	rocks
cleavage	fracture	lithified	phaneritic texture	sedimentary rock
dip	half-life	luster	plutonic	stratification
element	igneous rocks	mafic	pyroclastic	strike
extrusive	intrusive	magma	radiometric dating	
fault	ion	metamorphic rocks	recrystallization	
felsic	isotope	mineral	relative-age dating	
	joint	Mohs hardness scale	rock cycle	

Study Questions

1. What physical and chemical factors are the bases of the rock-classification system? What are the three classes of rocks, and how does each form? Identify one characteristic of each class that usually makes it readily distinguishable from the others.

2. How and where do batholiths form? What type of rock most commonly forms in batholiths?

3. What are some of the planar surfaces in rocks that may be weak and thus lead to various types of slope failure?

4. How may structures in sedimentary rocks be used to reconstruct past environments?

5. How may absolute-age-dating techniques be used to the betterment of human existence?

6. Earth is 4.6 billion years old, and humans have been on Earth for only a few hundred thousand years. What changes of a global nature have humans invoked on Earth's natural systems (water, air, ice, solid Earth, and biology) in this short length of time? Which impacts are reversible, and which ones cannot be reversed or mitigated?

7. What is the most common mineral species? Name several rocks in which it is a prominent constituent.

8. What is cleavage? How can it serve as an aid in identifying minerals?

9. The most common intrusive igneous rock is composed mostly of (1) the most common mineral and (2) a mineral of the most common mineral group. Name the rock and its constituent minerals.

10. What mineral is found in both limestone and marble?

For Further Information

Books and Periodicals

Albritton, C. C. 1984. Geologic time. *Journal of geological education* 32, no. 1: 29–47.

Bowring, S. A., I. S. Williams, and W. Compston. 1989. 3.96 Ga gneisses from the Slave province, Northwest Territories, Canada. *Geology* 17: 971–975.

Brown, V. M. and J. A. Harrell. 1991. Megascopic classification of rocks. *Journal of geological education* 39: 379.

Dietrich, R. V. and Brian Skinner. 1979. *Rocks and rock minerals.* New York: John Wiley & Sons.

Eicher, D. L. 1976. *Geologic time,* 2nd ed. Englewood Cliffs, N.J.: Prentice-Hall, Inc.

Gunter, Mickey Eugene. 1994. Asbestos as a metaphor for teaching risk perception. *Journal of geological education* 42: 17.

Harvey, Carolyn, and Mark Rollinson. 1987. *Asbestos in the schools.* New York: Praeger.

Hurley, Patrick. 1959. *How old is the earth?* New York: Anchor Books.

Libby, W. F. 1955. *Radiocarbon dating.* Chicago: University of Chicago Press.

Mackenzie, Fred T. G. and Judith A. Mackenzie. 1995. *Our changing planet: An introduction to Earth system science and global environmental change.* Englewood Cliffs, N.J.: Prentice-Hall, Inc.

National Research Council, National Academy of Sciences. 1993. *Solid-earth sciences and society.* Washington, D.C.: National Research Council Commission on Geosciences, Environment, and Resources, National Academy of Sciences Press.

Newcott, William R. 1998. Return to Mars. *National geographic* 194, no. 2: 2–29.

Nuhfer, E. B., R. J. Proctor, and Paul H. Moser. 1993. *The citizen's guide to geologic hazards.* Arvada, Colo.: American Institute of Professional Geologists.

Parker-Pope, T. 1997. Cat litter breathes new life into region of bentonite mines. *The Wall Street Journal,* April 1.

Skinner, H. Catherine W. and Malcom Ross. 1994. Geology and health. *Geotimes* (Washington, D.C.: American Geological Institute), January: 11–12.

———. 1994. Minerals and cancer. *Geotimes,* January: 13–15.

Snow, T. P. 1993. *Essentials of the dynamic universe.* St. Paul, Minn.: West Publishing Company.

Monroe, James, Reed Wicander, and Richard Hazlett. 2006. *Physical geology: exploring the Earth.* Belmont, California: Brooks/Cole.

ThomsonNOW

Assess your understanding of this chapter's topics with additional comprehensive interactivities at http://www.thomson.com/login, which also has up-to-date web links, additional readings, and exercises.

Plate Tectonics

The prominent lineation down the center of this satellite photo is the Dead Sea rift zone, an active tectonic plate margin (◆ Figure 1). It is the Holy Land of biblical times and an area of political and religious conflict. Included in the view are the lands of Jordan, Israel, Syria, and part of Saudi Arabia and the Jordan River, the Mediterranean Sea, the Gulf of Aqaba, and the Dead Sea. The Dead Sea's shoreline is the lowest point on Earth's surface, averaging 396 meters (1,300 ft) below sea level. This valley was part of the sea 65 million years ago, and its desiccation may be the source of salt deposits in the region. The Dead Sea is fed by the Jordan River, but its level has dropped 19 meters (63 ft) in the past hundred years due to development along the river.

A well-known Old Testament story tells us that the Lord appointed Joshua to lead the Israelites to Canaan, the land of milk and honey. That "Promised Land" was in the vicinity of present-day Jericho. Jericho is at least 8,000 years old, the oldest almost continuously occupied city yet discovered by archaeologists. Karnak, Giza, and the tomb of Tutankamen are all young in comparison. The scriptures also tell us (in Joshua 6) that Joshua's orders were to march his army around the walled city for six days, blowing seven ram's-horn trumpets. On the seventh day, as the trumpets were blown, the walls of the city would fall flat, and the city could then be destroyed.

Jericho (see map) is in a rift valley formed by lateral slip on faults between the African plate to the west and the Arabian plate to the east (◆ Figure 2). Although both plates are moving northward, the African plate is moving more slowly, so the Arabian plate's *relative* motion is to the north, and the African plate's is to the south (◆ Figure 3). Motion of this type on faults results in a "pull-apart" basin, or **graben,** as shown in the figure.

◆ **FIGURE 1** Dead Sea rift zone.

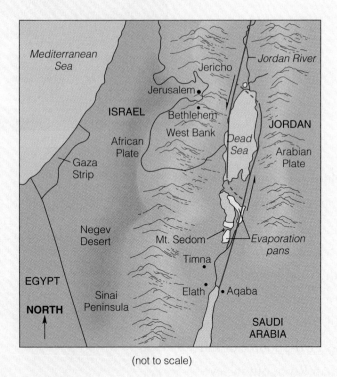

(not to scale)

◆ **FIGURE 2** The Dead Sea, Jordan River, and biblical villages and lands surrounding the sea.

(a)   **(b)**

◆ **FIGURE 3** (a) The Dead Sea transform fault, a special variety of strike-slip fault, separates two northward-moving plates, the slower-moving African plate (left) and the faster-moving Arabian plate. (b) Overlapping faults between the West Bank and Jordan outline a pull-apart basin in which the Dead Sea resides. D indicates displacement on the fault.

This explains how the floor of the valley came to be 400 meters (1,300 ft) below sea level (◆ Figure 4).

The ruins of Jericho included warehouses that contained grain. It was not the Israeli *modus operandi* to attack and destroy after a grain harvest. They usually attacked just before grain was harvested so that a siege period would be effective and they could later harvest the grain for themselves.

Similar plate boundaries at other places in the world have produced destructive earthquakes. Examples include California and Turkey. An alternative explanation for the Israelites' success at Jericho, and perhaps a more plausible one, is that the walls were felled by an earthquake caused by the Dead Sea faults so that the earth shook and the mud-brick "walls came tumbling down."

(a)   **(b)**

◆ **FIGURE 4** (a) The Dead Sea viewed from the western shore in Israel. This is the lowest dry land in the world. (b) The Gulf of Aqaba from Aqaba, Jordan—an example of a seaway, or arm of the ocean that floods a young rift valley. Someday the gulf of Aqaba may grow so wide that one can no longer see all the way across it at this location.

Continental Drift

From the time that the first complete maps of the Atlantic Ocean were published in the seventeenth century, thoughtful minds (including Francis Bacon) were struck by the similarity of the coastlines of Africa and South America. Various explanations for this included a popular one that the Atlantic is a gigantic river bed cut by Noah's flood. The banks of rivers, after all, tend to be parallel to one another. By 1910, however, enough scientific evidence had collected to begin pondering this similarity more seriously. Alfred Wegener (1880–1930), a German meteorologist, presented a paper to the Frankfurt Geological Society in which he expressed his opinion that Africa and South America, together with other continents, had once been joined together in a single gigantic landmass—a supercontinent— that somehow split apart. The fragments then separated thousands of kilometers from one another over a period of about 100 million years to produce the world map we see today. He called this hypothesis *die Verschiebung der Kontinente,* meaning "continental displacement," which English-speaking scientists translated to **continental drift,** the name that stuck. Wegener had no well-grounded explanation for how continental drift took place. He suggested speculatively that the spin of the Earth might have something to do with it. In any event, he thought that as the Americas drifted westward *(Westwanderung)* from the Old World, their edges crumpled into the mountains of the Andes and Rockies. This deformation resembles that seen in a rug slid against a wall. Likewise, as Australia drifted apart from southern Africa the Great Dividing Range grew along the Australian east coast.

Wegener and many Southern Hemisphere geologists including Victor Linz cited as field evidence for continental drift the distribution of late Paleozoic (Permian Period) glacial deposits and plant fossils known collectively as the **Gondwana Succession** (named after the Gond tribe of central India, whose region contains many of these fossils). These distinctive ancient land plants (◆Figure 3.1a) and their associated glacial deposits (◆Figure 3.2) are found only in South America, Africa, India, Australia, and Antarctica, which comprised the southern part of the original supercontinent. Wegener named this giant ancient landmass **Pangaea** from the Greek word meaning "All Earth" (◆Figure 3.3).

One famous fossil associated with the break-up of Pangaea is the freshwater reptile *Mesosaurus,* which inhabited Permian rivers, lakes, and swamplands in what are now Brazil and South Africa (Figure 3.1b). It is inconceivable that these freshwater creatures swam or island-hopped across the salty Atlantic Ocean to an identical freshwater habitat on the opposite side. It seems much more reasonable that *Mesosaurus* inhabited a single large homeland that geographically broke apart.

The evidence isn't restricted to fossils and glacial deposits alone. Belts of mineral deposits, and groups of similar rocks of the same age—even whole pre-Mesozoic mountain ranges—can be fit back together hand-in-glove by reassembling the continents as Wegener imagined.

Had most of the world's geologists and academic institutions been located in the Southern Hemisphere, Wegener and his advocates might have been taken far more seriously. But in the Northern Hemisphere evidence for continental drift wasn't so clear-cut because the shorelines of continents there did not fit together as well. Enormously thick ice-age glaciers had pressed the land down in northern latitudes, causing the ocean to flood continental margins in a highly irregular way (just glance at a map of western Europe). This made it difficult to discern the critical transoceanic linkages in fossils and other features that had

(a)   **(b)**

◆ **FIGURE 3.1** (a) Fossil leaves of the Gondwana Succession plant *Glossopteris,* from the Upper Permian Dunedoo Formation, Australia; (b) *Mesosaurus,* a freshwater reptile that inhabited Gondwana ecosystems.

(a)

(b)

Glaciated area
Arrows indicate the
direction of glacial
movement based on
striations preserved
in bedrock.

◆ **FIGURE 3.2** (a) The directions of glacial grooves preserved in bedrock on continents as they are now positioned show the direction of glacier movement during Permian (Gondwana Succession) time. For a large glacier or a number of glaciers to produce the directions of the observed grooves would otherwise require a source area in the Indian and South Atlantic Oceans. (b) With Gondwana continents reunited and an ice sheet over a south pole in present-day South Africa, the directions of glacier motion are resolved. (c) Glacial grooves at Hallet's Cove, Australia. Formed in Permian time, these grooves are more than 200 million years old. The width of the area shown in the photo is approximately 2 meters.

(c)

reportedly been seen in the warmer latitudes south of the equator. Since geologists did not travel as widely to do research then as they do now, the development of knowledge was sluggish by today's standards. To make matters worse, Wegener was not even a certified geologist. The courageous German spent the last years of his life defending his hypothesis in scientific papers and five editions of his classic book *The Origin of Continents and Oceans*. He disappeared in 1930 on an expedition to Greenland, where, it is said, his ideas were born decades earlier when he saw a giant iceberg float away from a calving glacier.

Wegener Vindicated

For various cultural reasons, resistance to Wegener's hypothesis was much greater in America than it was in Europe. Despite this discouragement, Professor Arthur Holmes, a British geologist and possibly the finest geology teacher of his day, developed an explanation for continental drift in 1926–1927 that ultimately proved to be spectacularly correct. Holmes suggested that the continents don't drift by plowing through sea-floor crust, like ships moving through sea ice. Rather, the continents move apart as new

Late Carboniferous Period (285–300 million years ago)

◆ ThomsonNOW™ ACTIVE FIGURE 3.3 The Earth of 285–300 million years ago according to Alfred Wegener. The supercontinent Pangaea began to break up about 100 million years ago, and the individual continents, roughly outlined as we know them today, have since then "drifted" to their present positions. The stippled areas represent widespread shallow seas over the continents in which sediments and fossils accumulated.

ocean floor grows *in between* them. The Atlantic and Indian oceans began as weak seams fracturing Pangaea. These ocean basins grew wider due to the eruption of basaltic lava along the crests of **mid-ocean ridges,** the belt of broad volcanic highlands that bisect the sea floor worldwide like the seams on a giant baseball. He further speculated that very old oceanic crust must be destroyed by sinking back into the deep earth through **marine trenches,** the steep-walled abyssal valleys fringing some ocean floors. Internal convection, a churning of hot rock within the Earth, could account for this activity. The evidence to test Holmes' bold explanation lay on the sea floor, a region largely out of reach in the 1920s, and not likely to get any closer without strong international collaboration and new technology.

As often happens in history, military conflict led to new inventions with unforeseen applications. The ship-borne magnetometer proved valuable in the detection of mines and Axis submarines threatening sea lanes during World War II. For the first time, too, a detailed map of the ocean floor could be made by means of echo sounding—a way of measuring the depth of the ocean by sending sound pulses to the bottom and retrieving the echoes on return. These techniques allowed oceanographers to map the seabed as never before, both bathymetrically and magnetically. The Cold War that followed provided many opportunities to apply this new technology cooperatively as Americans and Western Europeans sought military advantage and favor with Third World countries through prestigious scientific research.

The study of lava flows using the magnetometer in the 1950s led to several important breakthroughs. Each involved **magnetic polarity,** a property created by the

alignment of tiny iron-bearing mineral grains within Earth's magnetic field as molten lava cools into solid rock. The minerals act like natural compass needles, recording the direction toward the north magnetic pole existing at the time that they harden into place. They are "fossil magnetic field indicators." Because the Earth as a whole acts like a giant bar magnet, with a north (positive) magnetic pole presently situated in Northern Canada and a south (negative) pole near Antarctica, any change in the past orientation of the planetary magnetic field will be recorded in the polarity of ancient rocks formed just before and after a field change.

Geophysicists correctly assumed that the positions of Earth's magnetic poles almost continuously drift within just a few degrees latitude of the planet's geographic (rotational) poles. But researchers discovered that the magnetic polarity of different equivalent-aged ancient rocks on opposite sides of the Atlantic gave *different locations* for each of the magnetic poles. In other words, there appeared to be *multiple* north poles and south magnetic poles, each paired to a separate continent, and each with its own history of wandering through many latitudes across the face of the globe (◆Figure 3.4). Try as people might, this simply did not make any sense—there can only be two magnetic poles at any given time for a planetary magnetic field. However, if the Atlantic was made smaller and the continents rotated back closer to one another at specific increments of time, then the multiple-wandering-pole problem disappeared. This was indirect evidence of continental drift—but very compelling indeed.

Stimulated by the magnetic findings, U.S. geologist Harry Hess revived and advanced Holmes' speculations in 1960, to suggest a mechanism for continental drift that he called **sea-floor spreading**—the growth of new oceanic crust along the crests of mid-ocean ridges. He also supported the notion that oceanic crust must be destroyed as it grows old, cold, and heavy, nosediving back into the planet through marine trenches. Perhaps wary of Wegener's professional fate, Hess referred to this model as "geopoetry," but there was growing evidence that he was correct.

In addition to the magnetic data, seismology delivered some clues. In 1927, Japanese seismologist Kiyoo Wadati discovered that a zone of frequently occurring earthquakes, including some very destructive and powerful tremors, slants under Japan from the trench along the archipelago's eastern coast. Hugo Benioff later mapped similar zones worldwide, which are now called **Benioff–Wadati zones.** They mark the paths of sinking oceanic material extending hundreds of kilometers inside Earth mostly around the edge of the Pacific Basin (which is growing smaller as the Atlantic and Indian oceans grow wider). Fragments of broken slabs may actually settle several thousand kilometers, all the way to Earth's core. Geologists now call this process **subduction,** meaning "under-moving" (◆Figure 3.5). Further evidence for the correctness of the

POLAR WANDERING VERSUS...   CONTINENTAL DRIFT

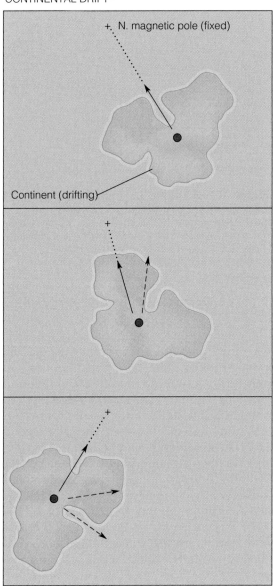

◆ **FIGURE 3.4** Two interpretations from the 1950s of magnetic polarities found in ancient rocks. The column to the left presumes that the continents remained fixed as the magnetic poles drifted to account for the variation seen in rock magnetization over time. The column to the right presumes just the opposite—that the continents drift through a magnetic field with fixed poles. Both models lead to the same present-day magnetic pattern for any given continent.

Holmes model comes from a simple consideration of the age of the sea floor. Whereas we've discovered continental rocks as old as 4 billion years, the oldest intact sea floor has an age of less than 200 million years. Where did all of the older material go, if it wasn't swallowed back up by the planet?

Researchers were close to verifying continental drift, but they still needed more evidence. They found it again as they continued studying patterns of natural rock magnetism. Geophysicists discovered that every few hundred

thousand to few million years something truly spectacular happens; Earth's magnetic poles swap positions entirely—in other words, the entire magnetic field suddenly flips over, and the poles become *reversed*. As a reversal approaches, the strength of the field simply weakens to the point of temporarily disappearing. When the field returns, each pole reappears in the opposite hemisphere from its former position. We regard the present time as having a "normal" magnetic field simply because of our place in time, with the field position "reversed" in other epochs

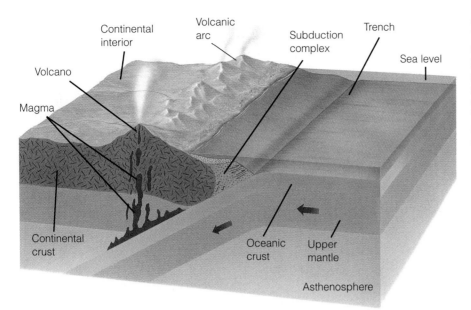

◆ ThomsonNOW™ ACTIVE FIGURE 3.5
The process of subduction is the sinking of the sea floor and a thick layer of underlying rock back into the planet. This process can generate huge earthquakes, and can create magma to feed a chain of volcanoes near the edge of the overthrusting landmass. Whereas sea-floor spreading at mid-ocean ridges create oceanic crust, subduction destroys it. From B. Murphy and D. Nance, *Earth Science Today,* 2nd ed., Brooks/Cole.

(◆Figure 3.6). (One can only speculate about what happens during a reversal to birds and marine creatures that depend upon the magnetic field to assist their migrations.)

In 1963, British researcher Fred Vine and Drummond Matthews and Canadian Lawrence Morley proved that rocks that formed when Earth's magnetic field was the same as today's yield a strong magnetic signal—or **positive anomaly**—whereas those that formed when the field was the opposite of today's field yield a weak signal—a **negative anomaly.** Vine, Matthews, and Morley reasoned that a striped anomaly pattern of sea-floor magnetization would develop if sea-floor spreading really happened. The pattern should be geometrically symmetrical about the mid-ocean ridges, assuming that sea-floor spreading rates are the same on both sides of a ridge crest. Oceanographers leapt to the challenge, and in 1966 confirmed the presence of this pattern in the northern Atlantic (◆Figure 3.7). Because over 170 reversals are known to have occurred during the past 76 million years, the striped magnetic record of sea-floor spreading is strikingly detailed, and geologists the world over gasped in unison.

All at once, the human race had its first holistic understanding of the physical world. Coupled with the first pictures of Earth from space, scientists began to look at our planet in terms of a *single system of integrated processes,* rather than an assortment of independent phenomena. This had important consequences politically as well as scientifically, including a surge in popular environmental interest. It is no coincidence that the first Earth Day took place in 1970.

The story of scientific breakthroughs leading to this revolution differs notably from that of Darwinian biology or Newtonian physics. Scientists from many diverse backgrounds independently provided vital clues to complete the picture. No one person can claim overwhelming credit for revolutionizing our understanding of the Earth.

ThomsonNOW™
Click **Geology Interactive** to work through an activity on plate boundaries through Plate Tectonics.

Plate Tectonics

In 1926, Vening Meinesz, a Dutch surveyor, introduced the term **plate** to describe broad regions of structurally distinctive crust, referring specifically to the Caribbean plate in a study that he had done for the U.S. Navy. In the late 1960s, Canadian geophysicist J. Tuzo Wilson revived Meinesz's work and helped popularize the term **plate tectonics** to give people a quick way of describing our new view of the physical world. "Tectonics" derives from the Greek word *tektonikos,* meaning "builder." The term "plate" refers to a rigid fragment of Earth's outermost skin. Plate tectonics radicalized notions about the forces responsible for shaping Earth's myriad landforms. Prior to the 1960s, most geologists thought primarily in terms of vertical force to account for the construction of mountain and valleys and other topographic features. But plate tectonics shows that vertical motions in Earth's crust are mostly a product of far greater *horizontal* movements (◆Figure 3.8). One reason the new theory challenged many older geologists was that their thinking had to be turned literally 90°.

There are seven major plates making up the surface of the Earth, and numerous smaller ones ranging in width from

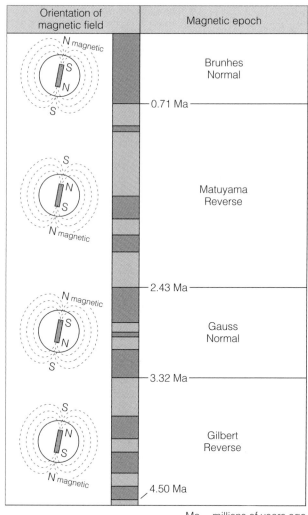

Orientation of magnetic field		Magnetic epoch
N magnetic / S		Brunhes Normal
	— 0.71 Ma —	
S / N magnetic		Matuyama Reverse
	— 2.43 Ma —	
N magnetic / S		Gauss Normal
	— 3.32 Ma —	
S / N magnetic		Gilbert Reverse
	— 4.50 Ma —	

Ma = millions of years ago

Normal

Reverse

◆ **FIGURE 3.6** Earth's magnetic field is much like the field that would be generated by a bar magnet inclined at 11° from Earth's rotational axis. Reversals of the field have occurred periodically, leaving "fossil" magnetism in rocks that can be dated. Each epoch is named after an important student of earth magnetism.

several hundred kilometers to only a few tens of kilometers (◆Figure 3.9). The plates interact with one another along their margins. As you will learn, all of human civilization and its environmental conditions are vitally linked to what happens along these margins. Essentially, three types of plate interactions take place (◆Figure 3.10):

- At **divergent boundaries** there is *tension;* stresses from Earth's interior act to move plates apart along these boundaries. Divergence within the continental crust creates features such as the East African Rift Valley,

(a)

(b)

↑ = Normal magnetic polarity

↓ = Reversed magnetic polarity

←→ = Direction of plate movement

mya = Millions of years ago

◆ **ThomsonNOW™ ACTIVE FIGURE 3.7** (a) Symmetric pattern of magnetic variation across part of the Mid-Atlantic Ridge southwest of Iceland. Colors indicate sea-floor rocks with matching polarity. (b) The origin of the magnetic anomaly pattern across mid-ocean ridges. Lava erupting along the crest of the ridge records Earth's prevailing magnetic polarity as it cools and solidifies. Sea-floor spreading then carries the rock away from the ridge in both directions as new lava erupts on the ridge axis.

while in the oceans, sea-floor spreading along mid-ocean ridges takes place. *Seaways* represent an intermediate stage of development between continental and

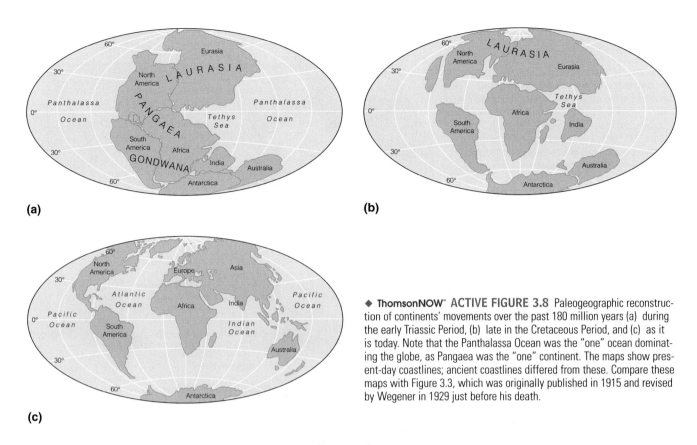

(a)

(b)

(c)

◆ **ThomsonNOW™ ACTIVE FIGURE 3.8** Paleogeographic reconstruction of continents' movements over the past 180 million years (a) during the early Triassic Period, (b) late in the Cretaceous Period, and (c) as it is today. Note that the Panthalassa Ocean was the "one" ocean dominating the globe, as Pangaea was the "one" continent. The maps show present-day coastlines; ancient coastlines differed from these. Compare these maps with Figure 3.3, which was originally published in 1915 and revised by Wegener in 1929 just before his death.

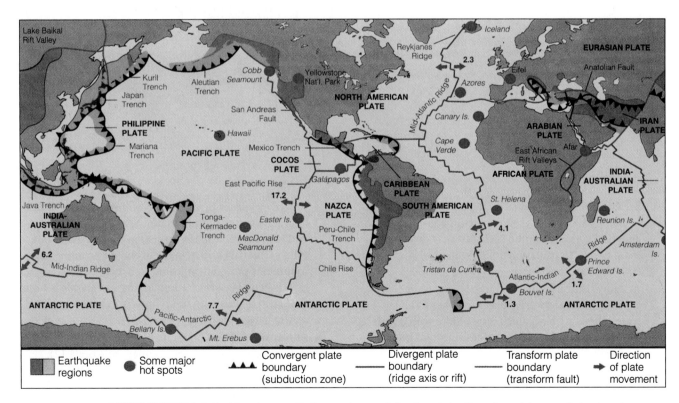

◆ **ThomsonNOW™ ACTIVE FIGURE 3.9** Earth's major tectonic plates and types of plate boundaries. Regardless of the type of plate boundary, each one is delineated by earthquake epicenters (not shown). The arrows indicate the present direction of plate motion; the numbers, the rate of spreading in centimeters per year. The rate of spreading is determined by dividing the distance to a magnetic anomaly (or rock) of known age in kilometers ($\times\ 10^5$ = cm) by the age of that anomaly in years (= cm/y).

◆ **FIGURE 3.10** (a) Divergent, convergent, and transform plate boundaries. Each type of boundary is characterized by a particular type of plate motion and stress. (b) Stresses found at plate boundaries: (1) *Compression.* Two forces acting in opposite directions in the same plane results in shortening of crust by folding and faulting. (2) *Tension.* Extension, or pulling the crust apart, causes faulting. (Rifting is shown.) (3) *Shear.* Two forces acting in opposite directions on different planes causes faulting and displacement between those planes.

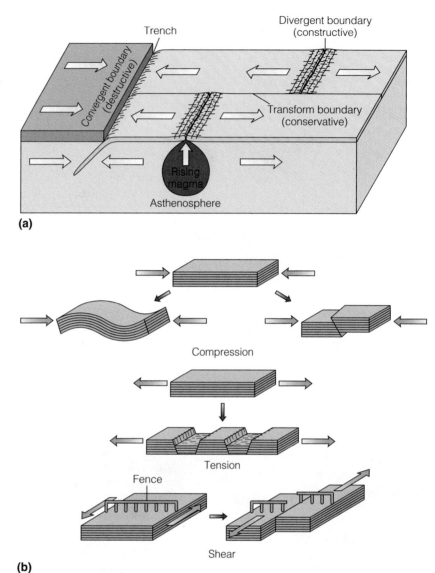

oceanic divergent boundaries (Figure 4 in the chapter opener and ◆Figure 3.11). Frequent small earthquakes and mild volcanic eruptions characterize divergent margins. Divergent boundaries are also called *spreading centers.*

■ At **convergent boundaries** there is *compression;* stresses converge to drive plates together. Where a plate capped with oceanic crust collides with a plate made up of continental material, as around much of the Pacific Rim, subduction takes place (Figure 3.5). This greatly disturbs the underlying mantle. The world's deadliest earthquakes and very explosive volcanic eruptions result from subduction. Volcanic mountain ranges such as the Andes mark the tectonic disturbance at the edge of the overriding plate along this convergent boundary.

■ Where *two* plates made up of continental material collide, a great range of mountains rises. The Himalaya and the Alps mountains formed in this way. Very powerful earthquakes often occur as the intracontinental mountains grow, but volcanic activity is essentially nonexistent, because the underlying hot mantle is little disturbed by this kind of ("Himalayan-style") convergence.

■ At **transform boundaries** *shear* forces cause plates to slide horizontally past one another (◆Figure 3.12). Long, linear faults mark transform boundaries in many places. Outstanding examples include the Alpine fault in New Zealand and the San Andreas fault in California. The strong earthquakes along both faults ease the world's biggest plate, the Pacific plate, past two other giant plates, the India–Australian and North

(a)

(b)

(c)

◆ **FIGURE 3.11** (a) Two large rift valleys are forming in East Africa as continental crust stretches along a divergent plate margin. The large lake between the rifts is Lake Victoria. The Red Sea and the Gulf of Aden exemplify more advanced ("seaway") stages of rifting and ocean development. (b) Looking down the Great Rift Valley of East Africa with Lake Magadi, Kenya, in the foreground. Because of high evaporation rates and lack of exterior drainage Lake Magadi is a soda lake rich in sodium carbonate, a salt that whitens mud flats on the lake's shore. (c) Satellite photo of the Sinai Peninsula, looking north. The Red Sea is at the bottom, the Gulf of Suez on the left, and the Gulf of Aqaba on the right. Very likely, the Red Sea resembles the South Atlantic Ocean of 270 million years ago. (a) From R. Wicander and J. Monroe, *Essentials of Geology*, 2nd ed., Brooks/Cole, 1999.

American plates. Whereas destructive earthquakes are a strong risk from these faults, virtually no volcanic activity takes places along transform boundaries.

Plate boundaries may also be described by what happens to the crust at that plate margin. Where plates diverge, new ocean crust is created, and we have a *constructive* plate boundary. Where an oceanic plate sinks and disappears at a subduction zone, the plate boundary is described as *destructive*. Finally, at transform boundaries crust is neither created nor destroyed, and we have a *conservative* boundary. Because these designations describe how the margin is modified, they also serve as a memory aid for what processes take place there (◆Figure 3.13).

CONSIDER   THIS

It is said that all knowledge of the natural world is potentially beneficial to humanity, even knowledge about past conditions that have subsequently changed. How might our knowledge of past and present plate positions and subsequent motions be applied to benefit the human race?

ThomsonNOW™

Click **Geology Interactive** to work through an activity on
- Plate boundaries and locations through Plate Tectonics
- Distribution of Volcanism
- Earthquakes and Tsunamis
- Seismic Risk

Richard Hazlett

◆ **FIGURE 3.12** Geology students standing next to a fresh rupture of the Motagua fault, the transform boundary between the North American and Caribbean plates in Guatemala. The land on which the students are standing is shifting to the left through time relative to the land in the foreground.

How Fast Do the Plates Move?

The rate at which the sea floor is spreading away from a mid-ocean ridge may be calculated by measuring the distance from the ridge to lava of known age that presumably erupted from that ridge. The magnetization of the volcanic rock can help verify its age and origin. Simply divide the distance traveled from the ridge by the age of the rock. That gives you the drift rate of the rock.

Plates typically move on the order of centimeters per year (about the same rate as human fingernail growth). For

example, Honolulu, Hawaii, now lies about 6 meters (20 ft) farther west-northwest than it did a hundred years ago. The East Pacific Rise is spreading at the fastest rate, up to 18 centimeters (7 in) per year, whereas the northern Mid-Atlantic Ridge is slowest, at about 2 centimeters (3/4 in) per year (see Figure 3.9). It may be that ocean basins fringed with subduction zones, like the Pacific, tend to have faster spreading centers within them, as the sinking plates around the edges strongly tug at the centers of the basins. Techniques using very-long-baseline radio interferometry (VLBI), satellite laser ranging (SLR), and the global positioning system (GPS) are now providing direct measurements that confirm the longer-term magnetic measurements. As use of these techniques expands, it will be possible to monitor surface deformation directly. This will contribute to our understanding of strain buildup that leads to earthquakes, volcanic eruptions, and plate movements.

CONSIDER THIS

How close is your home town or school to a plate boundary? What kind of plate boundary is it? Are there any geologic hazards associated with it about which you should be concerned?

What's Causing All This Restlessness?

Wegener had difficulty defending his hypothesis because he was haunted by the questions of why and how continental

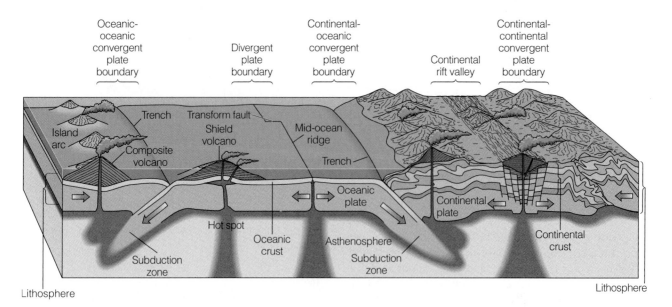

◆ **ThomsonNOW™ ACTIVE FIGURE 3.13** The plate tectonic model. Divergent and convergent boundaries and their relationships to sea-floor and continental volcanoes are shown. Transform faults on the sea floor are transform boundaries linking different segments of mid-ocean ridge. Rift-valley formation as a result of divergence under the continent is also shown.

drift takes place. In contrast, plate tectonicists have had abundant geophysical evidence to explain the plate motions that we observe. Important clues lie in Earth's deep interior. Seismologists have constructed an overview of the deep Earth based upon the way that earthquake shock waves travel through it. When waves hit a boundary between different layers, they reflect or refract back to the surface in mathematically predictable ways. The speed and type of seismic waves depend upon several factors, including the density of a rock layer and whether or not it is partly or wholly molten.

When Earth first formed, the densest material accumulated at the center of the planet, forming a metallic iron–nickel-rich **core.** Around this ball a thick shell of magnesium-silicate matter developed that we call the **mantle.** This is by far the thickest layer making up the planet (◆Figure 3.14). A thin "skin" of relatively lightweight aluminum and alkali (sodium and potassium)-rich silicate rocks, termed the **crust,** formed atop the mantle. The crust

is still evolving through processes of igneous activity, weathering, sedimentation, and metamorphism. There are two basic kinds of crust—*oceanic* and *continental.* Oceanic crust consists largely of basaltic rocks resulting from sea-floor spreading, and is typically 5–10 kilometers (3–6 mi) thick. The continental crust, made up largely of silica-rich igneous and sedimentary rocks (like granite and sandstone) and related metamorphic rocks ranges from 20–90 kilometers (12–56 mi) thick, with the greatest thicknesses found beneath mountain ranges. Oceanic rocks are typically darker and somewhat heavier (3.0 gm.cm^3) than continental rocks (2.7 gm.cm^3), because of a higher content of magnesium and iron. This difference in relative density helps explain why oceanic crust subducts during plate convergence. Because continental crust is thicker as well as lighter weight, it also stands topographically higher, mostly rising above the sea.

In addition to the compositional layers above, seismologists have also discovered other kinds of boundaries inside Earth. Within the upper mantle, typically between 100 and 350 kilometers (60–210 mi) down, is a seismic zone known as the **asthenosphere** (Greek, "weak sphere"). In the upper part of the asthenosphere is a zone of low seismic wave speeds, indicating that the mantle here is close to its melting point and may actually contain melted portions. It is a zone of mobility that detaches the overlying rigid outer shell of the planet from the hotter, more plastic interior. The rigid outer shell is called the **lithosphere** (Greek, "rocky sphere"), and it consists not only of the crust but also of **mantle lid,** a narrow layer of rigid upper mantle rock (◆Figure 3.15). Tectonic plates are actually fragments of lithosphere floating atop the mushy asthenosphere.

The asthenosphere owes its existence to the release of heat from Earth's interior. Most of this heat originates from

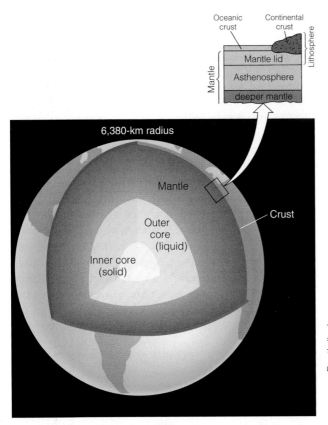

◆ **ThomsonNOW** ACTIVE FIGURE 3.14 Earth's internal structure. The lower part of the figure shows the layers that are defined by contrasts in density, as deduced from observations of seismic waves. The upper part of the figure illustrates the relative thickness of the crust in continental areas as compared with the sea floor. The lithosphere is comprised of the rigid tectonic plates moving on a plastic asthenosphere.

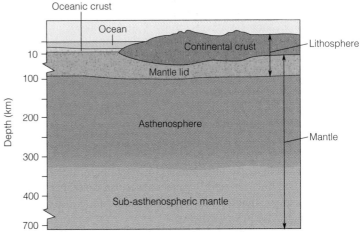

◆ FIGURE 3.15 Earth's outer layers are divided into *crust* and *mantle* based on rock type, and into *lithosphere* and *asthenosphere* based on rigidity.

◆ **FIGURE 3.16** Convection (a) in a pot of soup or rolled oats on a stove; (b) in the mantle, involving "whole mantle" overturn; and (c) an alternate model of mantle convection involving multiple layers, which is probably closer to reality than (b).

the slow decay of radioactive elements, such as uranium, lying in the core and lower mantle (Chapter 2). The pressure in the lower mantle is so great that the rock there remains solid, despite temperatures in the range of 3500–4000°C—hot enough to melt steel at Earth's surface. In the upper mantle, however, pressure is reduced just enough that the hot rock can become partly molten, even though its temperature is a cooler 1500°C at that depth.

The most efficient way for Earth's heat to escape is through the slow convective churning of mantle rock, much like the churning in a pot of rolled oats cooking on a stove (◆Figure 3.16). Hot rock wells up from the depths of the mantle, becomes partially molten and weakens in the asthenosphere, loses heat to the overlying lithosphere, and being denser because it is now cooler, sinks back down into the depths. The heat imparted to the lithosphere causes magma to form, contributes to earthquakes and volcanic eruptions, and slowly leaks from the ground into the air. (The percentage of this "Earth heat" is trivial in most places, however, compared to the warmth of ordinary sunlight).

What drives plate motion is still being debated, but it is most certainly a combination of gravity acting on the lithosphere (subduction) and thermal convection currents in the asthenosphere that drag the overlying plates along with them as though on a conveyor belt.

ThomsonNOW™
Click **Geology Interactive** to work through an activity on Earth's layers

The Dance of the Continents

The process of subduction means that the rocks of the ocean basins have been recycled back into the mantle many times. Therefore, no rocks or sediments older than the current cycle of sea-floor spreading would be expected. In fact, if we multiply the average spreading rate by the length of the mid-ocean ridge system, we find that new oceanic crust is forming at a rate of 2.8 square kilometers (1.1 mi²) per year. Because our oceans cover an area of 310 million square kilometers (120 million mi²), their beds could have formed in as little as 110 million years, and over the past two billion years, as many as 20 global ocean floors may have been created and destroyed. Land geology also records at least two and as many as five complete openings and closings of all the ocean basins.

The *Wilson cycle* is an evolutionary sequence for oceans named for its developer, J. Tuzo Wilson. He identified five stages in the tectonic birth and death of oceans (◆Figure 3.17):

Evolutionary stage	Example
Embryonic (Fig. 3.17 a–c)	Rift valleys of East Africa
Youthful (Fig. 3.17d)	Gulf of California, Gulf of Aqaba, Red Sea
Mature (Fig. 3.17e–f)	Atlantic Ocean (growing larger)
Declining (Fig. 3.17g)	Pacific Ocean (becoming smaller)
Terminal (Fig. 3.17 h–i)	Mediterranean Sea (closing, almost extinct)

◆ **FIGURE 3.17** The Wilson cycle.

Andean-type continental margin

Subduction begins as oceanic lithosphere breaks along continental margin

(g)

Supercontinent restored

Himalayan-type mountain range

(Mantle heat trapped once again)

(h)　　　　　　　　　　　　**(i)**

◆ **FIGURE 3.17** (Continued)

One explanation for the cyclical nature of supercontinent formation is that there is an ongoing tug-of-war between the forces of gravity and heat flow in the upper mantle. A supercontinent like Pangaea acts like a giant lid to trap heat trying to escape Earth's interior. (It is generally much easier for heat to escape through oceanic lithosphere than through thicker continental lithosphere.) As the trapped heat accumulates, the supercontinent wells up into a volcanically active *thermotectonic arch,* weakens, and rifts apart, creating a new divergent boundary. The sundered continental fragments drift away as a vigorous new Atlantic-type ocean grows, eventually becoming thousands of kilometers wide. The rifted continental margins fringing the ocean initially stand high as coastal mountain ranges, but as the lithosphere cools these ranges subside, and broad coastal plains replace them, an example being the Eastern Seaboard of the United States. These coastlines are termed **passive margins,** in contrast to active continental margins such as the west coast of South America, where vigorous mountain building and volcanism are taking place. An ocean can only grow so large, however, before the sea floor grows too old and heavy for the mantle to support it. Heavy loads of sediment dumping onto an aged sea floor from nearby passive margins help initiate subduction; and once subduction begins the ocean starts to close up. Subduction ultimately draws the sundered continental fragments back together to form a new supercontinent transected by a huge

mountain range marking the line of collision. Traces of unsubducted oceanic crust typically suture the range axis, and the cycle starts all over again. Europe and Africa are examples of former pieces of Pangaea in the process of rejoining as the Mediterranean Basin disappears between them, thanks to subduction beneath Italy and Greece. Elsewhere, Pangaea's fragments continue to drift apart.

The formation of a supercontinent (and associated mountain building) occurs about every 400–500 million years in Earth history. Geologists have discovered only scraps of evidence for the supercontinent preceding Pangaea, a landmass of about a billion years age that researchers have dubbed *Rodinia.* At that time, Antarctica, Australia, North America, and Europe were joined together. The Pacific Ocean did not yet exist.

CONSIDER　THIS

A stockbroker might speculate on what the market will do the next day, a business person might try to forecast six-month trends, but only an earth scientist will speculate on what the face of our planet will look like a million years from now. Here's your chance! What will be the fate of (1) the Mediterranean Sea, (2) the Atlantic and Pacific Ocean basins, and (3) the west coast of the United States exclusive of Alaska if the present plate motion continues for the next 20 million years? Hazard a guess.

Plate Tectonics and the Rock Cycle

The theory of plate tectonics also provides an excellent model for explaining the rock cycle, described in Chapter 2. Igneous rocks form from cooling magma bodies at divergent and convergent plate boundaries. Uplift at convergent boundaries exposes this rock to the harsh surface agents of weathering and erosion, which yields up the loose sediment needed to make sedimentary rocks. Further plate convergence metamorphoses the sedimentary rock, which under intense conditions of heat and pressure causes it to partially melt. This renews the material transfer of the rock cycle.

One tectonic consequence of the rock cycle is that a submerged continental shelf of soft muds and sands in one era can become a towering granitic mountain range in the next, with a net addition of new, hard crust to a continent. As a result, the total land area of the continents has enlarged over the past few billion years, with new growth concentrated along convergent plate boundaries. Earth is gradually becoming more of a land planet and less of a water world, although the growth in continents may be compensated by an overall deepening trend in the seas as well.

Hot Spots

Within some ocean basins there are chains of aligned volcanic islands that become progressively older in one direction. The Hawaiian Islands, Line Islands, and Tuamotus are such chains in the Pacific Ocean. Although the Galápagos Islands off the coast of Ecuador—made famous by the writings of Charles Darwin—are only roughly aligned, they are of similar origin. These lines-of-islands are not associated with plate boundaries, but have formed over areas of unusually hot rock, or **hot spots,** fixed in the asthenosphere. Many (though not all) geologists believe that hot spots are fed by plumes of material welling up from the deep mantle. These rising intraplate plumes penetrate the general convective circulation that drives plate motion and are independent of spreading centers. As a tectonic plate moves over a hot spot, the plate carries with it the volcanoes that form there, with new volcanoes growing in place of the older ones that are carried away (◆Figure 3.18). For example, Maui and Hawaii, the islands closest to the Hawaiian hot spot, are the only ones with active volcanism today. A line drawn from the Island of Hawaii to Kure Atoll, the oldest of the chain, would represent an arrow marking the direction and rate of movement of the Pacific plate in this region. The track of the Hawaiian Islands forms a "lazy L" with the Emperor Seamount chain, a line of submerged volcanoes that extends northward from Midway, tracing a different direction of plate movement prior to 40 million years ago. Of greater environmental concern because of population densities are hot spots that occur beneath the continents. Yellowstone National Park,

for example, is situated above a midplate hot spot fed by a mantle plume at least 500 km deep with a potential for destructive volcanic activity. About a third of the more than 120 identified hot spots that have been active within the last ten million years penetrate continental areas (see Figure 3.9).

ThomsonNOW
Click **Geology Interactive** to work through an activity on the distribution of volcanism.

Plate Tectonics and the Environment

Plate tectonic movements have shaped and changed past natural environments throughout the world. Some tectonically forced environmental changes have impacted the entire world, while others have focused only upon particular regions. An excellent example comes from research done by the Deep Sea Drilling Project of the U.S. National Science Foundation. During a series of cruises in the Mediterranean Sea, the researchers discovered thick salt deposits beneath the sea floor, indicating that about ten million years ago (Miocene time) the sea was isolated from the Atlantic Ocean and that the sea totally evaporated (◆Figure 3.19). Access of Atlantic Ocean water to the Mediterranean through the Strait of Gibraltar was cut off by uplift as the African plate moved northward, and also by a global lowering of sea level at the time. Further drilling yielded sediments indicating that the floors of the two Mediterranean basins once resembled the great dry lakes of present-day deserts in the western United States. Occasionally they were occupied by water when the connection with the Atlantic was periodically reestablished. About five million years ago the Strait of Gibraltar reopened, and the Atlantic Ocean flowed into the Mediterranean Sea as a waterfall or cascade of great magnitude (◆Figure 3.19b). This inflow filled the Mediterranean in a few thousand years. The sediments on top of the five-million-year-old salt-flat deposits contain fossils of marine organisms, indicating rapid filling with normal seawater, and no abnormal salinity, which would have occurred if the filling were slow.

Plate Tectonics and the Human Environment

Plate tectonic activity not only shapes the natural world, but also explains the global geography that has strongly influenced human history and the present distribution of the world's population. The origins of many natural resources are tied to plate movements. For example, valuable mineral deposits such as zinc and copper ore form around sea-floor hot springs and volcanic vents at divergent boundaries.

◆ **ThomsonNOW**˙ **ACTIVE FIGURE 3.18**
(a) Cross section of six islands formed and
forming over the Hawaiian "hot spot." The
Hawaiian Islands are sequentially older in a
northwest direction. The new volcano Loihi is
forming underwater off the southeast end of
the Hawaiian chain. (b) Kinked hotspot trajectories in the Pacific. The kink in each island chain
occurred about 40 million years ago due to a
change in the Pacific plate's direction of
motion. (b) B. Murphy and D. Nance, *Earth Science
Today*, 2nd ed., Brooks/Cole.

(a)

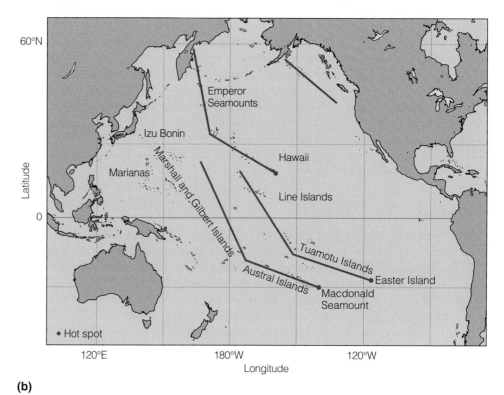

(b)

Upheaval of ancient oceanic lava flows rich in copper formed the Island of Cyprus in the eastern Mediterranean, which was a vital source of metal during the Bronze Age. One of the oldest known smelter sites in the world, at Timna in southern Israel (Figure 2, p. 48), extracted copper from the Dead Sea rift valley over 5,000 years ago. Metal from this site helped make Egypt a powerful kingdom during the time of Moses.

Along convergent boundaries, volcanoes erupt billowing clouds of volcanic ash, which fertilizes surrounding lands for agriculture. Largely because of the rich farms, about one out of every ten people in the world lives in a convergent plate setting today. On the Island of Java, which is notorious for its volcanic activity, there are as many as three harvests a year. On neighboring Borneo, however, a harvest may be possible only once every one or two years, because that island lies out-

side of the nearby volcanic zone. Gold, silver, tin, and mercury deposits form along convergent boundaries, too, helping support wild mining booms. The conquistadores braved treacherous conditions in Central and South America to overwhelm indigenous cultures in the quest for tectonic treasures. The unique character of modern Latin America begins essentially with its geology.

Passive margins have been even more vital to human affairs. Mature passive margins allow large rivers to form large floodplains and deltas as they flow to the sea, providing the most fertile environments for agriculture. Except for occasional bad weather and flooding, people living along passive margins have little to fear from natural disasters, and generally have plenty to eat—to begin with at least. (Unfortunately, coastal floodplains are also prone to become

◆ **FIGURE 3.19** Desiccation of the eastern and western Mediterranean basins about ten million years ago (Miocene time), when its connection with the Atlantic Ocean through the Strait of Gibraltar was blocked. (a) Total evaporation took as little as 1,000 years, during which salt was deposited and dry lakes or salt lakes existed in the basins. Some spillover from the Red Sea occurred in the eastern Mediterranean. (b) Two-kilometer-thick deposits of sediments and evaporites (especially gypsum and halite) beneath the floors of these basins indicate that the cycle of filling, evaporation, and refilling was repeated many times (2 km ≈ 6,500 ft or 1¼ mi).

the most crowded places in the world). The list of early civilizations below shows the influence of passive margins at the dawn of human history.

Civilization	Size of origin	Tectonic setting
Greco–Minoan	Small coastal floodplains	Convergent boundary
Roman	Near a small floodplain	Convergent boundary
Aztecs and Incas	Mountain valleys, lakeshore	Convergent boundary
Chinese	Initially fertile highlands and long, broad floodplains	Passive margin near convergent boundary
Sumerian	Long, broad floodplain	Passive margin near convergent boundary
Egyptian	Long, narrow floodplain	Passive margin
Harappan (Pakistan)	Long, broad floodplain	Passive margin

Mature passive margins have become even more important in recent times, because they also provide ideal locations for petroleum and natural gas reservoirs, upon which the modern world economy and political stability depend. Geologists use plate tectonic concepts in exploring for oil and gas, focusing especially on the sedimentary rocks of passive margins. Our technical civilization, standing on the two mutually dependent legs of metals and fuel, could never have developed without the phenomenon of plate tectonics.

CASE STUDY 3.1

Exotic Terranes—A Continental Mosaic

Because continental plates divide, collide, and slip along faults, it is not surprising that bits and pieces of continental crust existing within the oceans ultimately collide with continents at subduction zones and become stuck there. Because of their low density, they stand high above oceanic crust (due to isostatic equilibrium), and these microplates or microcontinents become plastered, *accreted,* to larger continental plates when they collide with them. The accreted plates are known as **terranes,** defined as fault-bounded blocks of rock with histories quite different from those of adjacent rocks or terranes.* In size they may be several thousand square kilometers or just a few tens of square kilometers, and they may become part of a continent composed of many terranes. Oceanic crust and the sediment resting on it may be scraped up onto the continents. Terranes may consist of almost any type of rock, but each one is fault-bounded, has a paleomagnetic signature indicating a distant origin, and has little geology in common with adjacent terranes or with the continental **craton**—the continent's stable core.

The terrane concept developed in Alaska when geologic mapping for land-use planning revealed that the usually predictable pattern of rocks and structures was not valid for any distance. In fact, the rocks the geologists found a few kilometers away were almost always of a "wrong" composition and age. Further studies revealed that Alaska is a collection of microplates (terranes)—tectonic flotsam and jetsam, if you wish—that have mashed together over the past 160 million years and that are still arriving from the south (◆ Figure 1). One block, the Wrangellia terrane, was an island during Triassic time and it has a paleomagnetic signature of rocks that formed 16° from the equator. It is not known whether Wrangellia formed north or south of the equator, because it is not known whether the magnetic field at the time was normal or reversed. In either case, the terrane traveled a long distance to become part of present-day Alaska (◆ Figure 2). It now appears that about 25 percent of the western edge of North America, from Alaska to Baja California, formed in this way; that is, by bits and pieces being grafted onto the core of the continent and thus enlarging it. In the distant future, part of California may become an exotic terrane of Alaska.

If you've deduced that terrane accretion onto the continents (also known as *docking*) is a characteristic of active continental margins, you are right (◆ Figure 3). The east coast of North America is a rifted (pulled-apart), or *passive,* margin. Material is added to it by river sediment forming flat-lying sedimentary rocks that become part of the continent. Such rocks are not subject to the mountain-building forces of active margins and they accumulate in thick, undisturbed sequences.

Terrane, as noted, is a geological term describing the area or surface over which a particular rock or group of rocks is prevalent. *Terrain* is a geographical term referring to the topography or physical features of a tract of land.

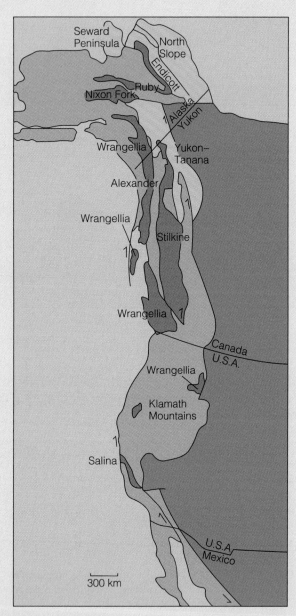

◆ **FIGURE 1** Accreted terranes of the west coast of the United States and Canada. The Salina, Wrangellia, Alexander, Stikine, Klamath Mountains, Ruby, and Nixon Fork blocks (dark brown) were probably once parts of other continents and have been displaced long distances. The terranes shown as light-green areas are probably displaced parts of North America, the stable North American craton (darker green). The lighter-brown areas represent rocks that have not traveled great distances from their places of origin.

◆ **FIGURE 2** An analysis of Wrangellia terrane trajectories for the period 180 Ma to 100 Ma, assuming initial position in the Northern Hemisphere. In this interpretation both Vancouver Island and the Alaskan terranes (see Figure 1) rode with the oceanic plate until they collided (docked) at their present positions on the North American continent about 100 million years ago. The data points (the dots) represent paleomagnetic evidence at the respective locations.

◆ **FIGURE 3** Formation of exotic terranes by a small continental mass and a submarine volcano being scraped off from the subducting plate and onto the continental mass. Many portions of the west coasts of the United States and Canada have grown in this manner.

Visions of How the Earth Works

The evolution of modern plate-tectonic theory started with Alfred Wegener's 1912 hypothesis of Continental Drift. Almost fifty years later the idea of sea-floor spreading was proposed. Although scientists were skeptical at first, this far-reaching concept led to the unifying theory of plate tectonics.

Bildarchiv Preussischer Kulturbesitz

◆ **FIGURE 1** Alfred Wegener formulated his hypothesis that continents move about on the face of the earth while sitting out a long Arctic winter in Greenland. His ideas were considered so outrageous that more than fifty years passed before scientists realized he was on the right track.

Rodney Supple

◆ **FIGURE 2** Evidence of colliding and sliding tectonic plates. Collision of the Indian and Asian plates produced the great Himalaya Mountains. The rocks of Nepal's Dhaulāgiri I (8,172 m, 26,810 ft), one of the highest peaks in the world, were uplifted and contorted by the continent–continent collision. The steep-sided south wall is 15,000 feet high. This view shows folded strata in the mountain's lower slope.

(a)

(b)

(c)

◆ **FIGURE 3** (a) "Black smokers" of mid-oceanic ridge. Hot brine loaded with minerals leached from basalt emanates from vents on ridges and builds tall "chimneys." (b) Giant tube worms thrive around the "smokers" and live on bacteria in the Galapagos Rift (see Chapter 5). (c) Clams more than 25 centimeters (10 in) long inhabit the warm waters near the vents in the Galapagos Rift.

Summary

Continental Drift

Description

Alfred Wegener's theory that during the Permian Period there was a single supercontinent, Pangaea, which split apart during Jurassic time into individual continents that have since migrated to their present positions.

Cause

The theory provided no explanation for a driving force.

Evidence

1. Similar glacial deposits and plant fossils in Permian rocks (the Gondwana Succession) in Africa, South America, India, Australia, and Antarctica.
2. Similarities between fossils, ages of rocks, and geologic provinces on opposite sides of the Atlantic Ocean.
3. The jigsaw fit of the continents if the Atlantic and Indian Oceans were closed.

Sea-Floor Spreading

Description

Theory proposed by Harry Hess that new oceanic crust is created at mid-ocean ridges and moves laterally across the ocean basins to trenches, where it sinks and returns to the mantle.

Cause

Convection cells in the mantle generated by thermal and density differences carry the rigid overlying crust (lithosphere) away from the ridges until the crust cools and descends toward the mantle at oceanic trenches.

Evidence

1. Distribution of deep-focus earthquakes at trenches.
2. Lack of ancient sediments on the sea floor.
3. Increasing age of sea-floor sediments away from mid-ocean ridges.

Plate Tectonics

Description

Theory that unifies and incorporates the earlier theories of continental drift and sea-floor spreading. According to it, the lithosphere is composed of seven large plates and a number of smaller ones that move about on the surface of the earth. Plates interact in only three ways: they *collide* at convergent boundaries marked by trenches or mountain ranges; they *move apart,* forming new sea floor, at divergent boundaries marked by mid-ocean ridges; or they *slip by one another* along transform boundaries.

Cause

Convection currents in the asthenosphere (the plastic layer of the upper mantle) carry the plates as passive passengers from divergent boundaries to convergent and conservative boundaries. Gravity pulls plates down into the mantle at convergent boundaries.

Evidence

1. Land geology, ocean drilling, and geophysical data support past openings and closings of the ocean basins (Wilson cycle).
2. Magnetic anomaly patterns ("stripes") on both sides of mid-ocean ridges.
3. Chains of oceanic volcanoes and seamounts that systematically increase in age with distance from the present locations of active volcanism (hot spots) indicate that plates are moving over fixed plumes of lava coming from deep in the mantle.
4. The geological and geophysical evidence for continental drift and sea-floor spreading also support plate tectonics.

Explains

1. The thick salt deposits beneath the Mediterranean Sea and its desiccation 10 million years ago.
2. The existence of narrow seas and gulfs such as the Gulf of California and the Red Sea as spreading centers.
3. The location and geology of the Himalaya Mountains.
4. The location of violent earthquakes and volcanoes at convergent margins.

Key Terms

anomaly	crust	mantle	plate tectonics
asthenosphere	divergent boundary	mantle lid	sea-floor spreading
Benioff–Wadati zone	Gondwana Succession	marine trench	subduction
continental drift	graben	mid-ocean ridge	terrane
convergent boundary	hot spot (plume)	Pangaea	transform boundary
core	lithosphere	passive margin	Wilson cycle
craton	magnetic polarity	plate	

Study Questions

1. What geologic and geographic evidence did Alfred Wegener cite for continental drift?

2. How do we know that Earth's interior is layered?

3. Why does convection occur? Give some examples of convection from everyday life.

4. What are the major spheres, or shells, of the earth's interior based upon composition? What is meant by the term *lithosphere*? Describe the lithosphere and tell how it is separated from the deep mantle.

5. What is a tectonic "plate"? Give an example (exact geographic location) of each type of plate boundary. How fast do plates move?

6. What geophysical observations and measurements support the model of sea-floor spreading and plate tectonics?

7. How can the change in direction of a line of oceanic islands—such as that between the Hawaiian Islands chain and the Emperor Seamount chain—be explained?

8. Draw a cross section of a typical convergent plate boundary (a subduction zone) and label the following: trench, volcanic areas, Benioff-Wadati zone, lithosphere, asthenosphere.

9. How might the distribution of the Permian Gondwana Succession be explained without invoking plate tectonics (ancient landmass, land bridges, etc.)? Might an alternative explanation be more reasonable than drifting continents and plate tectonics?

10. How have the narrow bodies of the Red Sea and the Gulf of California formed? Study a map, seeking an obvious relationship between the Red Sea and the Dead Sea.

For Further Information

Books and Periodicals

Ballard, Robert. 1983. *Exploring our living planet.* Washington, D.C.: National Geographic Society.

Bonatti, Enrico. 1994. The earth's mantle below the oceans. *Scientific American,* March: 44–51.

Cox, Allan. 1986. *Plate tectonics: How it works.* Palo Alto, Calif.: Blackwell Scientific.

Dalziel, Ian W. D. 1995. Earth before Pangaea. *Scientific American,* January: 58.

Debiche, M. G., Allan Cox, and D. Engebretson. 1987. *The motion of allochthonous terranes across the north Pacific basin.* Geological Society of America Special Paper 207, 49 pp.

Hallam, A. 1973. *A revolution in the earth sciences.* Oxford, U.K.: Oxford University Press.

Hsu, Ken. 1983. *The Mediterranean was a desert.* Princeton, N.J.: Princeton University Press.

Kearey, P., and F. J. Vine. 1996. *Global tectonics,* 2d ed. Palo Alto, Calif.: Blackwell Scientific.

Larson, Robert. 1995. The mid-Cretaceous superplume episode. *Scientific American,* January: 82–86.

Moores, E. M., ed. 1990. Shaping the earth: tectonics of continents and oceans. *Scientific American readings.* New York: W. H. Freeman.

Murphy, J. Brendan, and R. Damian Nance. 1992. Mountain belts and the supercontinent cycle. *Scientific American,* April: 84–91.

Nance, R. Damian, T. R. Worsley, and J. B. Moody. 1988. The supercontinent cycle. *Scientific American* 259: 172–79.

Orestes, N., 1999, *The Rejection of Continental Drift.* Oxford University Press.

Schneider, David. 1997. Hot spotting. *Scientific American,* April: 22–23.

Sullivan, Walter. 1974. *Continents in motion: The new earth debate.* New York: McGraw-Hill.

Tarling, D., and Maureen Tarling. 1970. *Continental drift: A study of the earth's moving surface.* New York: Anchor Books.

Uyeda, Seiya. 1977. *The new view of the earth.* New York: W. H. Freeman.

Wegener, Alfred. 1929, 1966 translation. *The origin of continents and oceans.* New York: Dover Publications.

Wilson, J. Tuzo. 1972. Continents adrift. *Scientific American readings.* San Francisco: W. H. Freeman.

ThomsonNOW

Assess your understanding of this chapter's topics with additional comprehensive interactivities at http://www.thomson.com/login, which also has up-to-date web links, additional readings, and exercises.

Earthquakes and Human Activities

ASSOCIATED PRESS, AUGUST 25, 1999 "TURKEY'S PRIME MINISTER has promised stricter building rules to prevent the shoddy construction blamed for the thousands of deaths from last week's massive earthquake. Eight days after the powerful 7.4-magnitude temblor reduced much of western Turkey to rubble, an estimated 200,000 survivors remained camped out in parks and on vacant lots."

The cause of the earthquake was a sudden rupture along northern Turkey's Anatolia fault. The severe ground motion that was generated collapsed hundreds of buildings, many of which had been built below earthquake-resistant standards. Interestingly, the Anatolia fault and California's infamous San Andreas fault have some striking geographic similarities; see ◆ Figure 1. Let's hope that is where the likeness ends.

◆ **FIGURE 1** The North Anatolian fault in Turkey and the San Andreas fault in California. The faults have the same sense of motion, are about the same age and length, and are capable of similar-magnitude earthquakes. The earthquake sequences shown on the North Anatolian fault represent events that occurred, one after the other from east to west, along the fault.

After experiencing an earthquake in Concepción, Chile, in 1835, Charles Darwin noted that "A bad earthquake at once destroys the oldest associations; the world, the very emblem of all that is solid, had moved beneath our feet like crust over a fluid." Darwin's reflections are vivid, and many of us have felt the same way when experiencing strong earthquake motion. What Darwin did not know was the cause of earthquakes and the resulting ground motion.

The Nature of Earthquakes

Earthquakes are the result of abrupt movements on **faults**—fractures in Earth's lithosphere. The types of faults and the Earth forces that cause them are shown in ◆ Figure 4.1. The

(a) Normal fault

(b)

(c) Reverse fault

(d)

(e) Right-lateral strike-slip fault

(f)

◆ **FIGURE 4.1** (a) Normal fault geometry and (b) examples in a road cut on I-40 near Kingman, Arizona. The normal fault at the right is in relatively soft sedimentary rocks. Fault at the left is also a normal fault with a small displacement of white sandstone between it and a small fault that shows reverse displacement. (c) Reverse fault geometry and (d) low-angle reverse fault displacing sandstone strata at Wasatch Plateau near Salina, Utah. (e) Right-lateral strike-slip fault geometry and (f) a plowed field displaced by a strike-slip fault in the Imperial Valley, California, in 1979.

(a) Original position

(b) Deformation

(c) Rupture and release of energy

(d) Rocks rebound to original undeformed shape

(e)

◆ **FIGURE 4.2** (a–d) The cycle of elastic-strain buildup and release for a right-lateral strike-slip fault according to Reid's elastic rebound theory of earthquakes. At the instant of rupture, (c), energy is released in the form of earthquake waves that radiate out in all directions. (e) Right-lateral offset of a fence by 2.5 meters (8 ft) by displacement on the San Andreas fault in 1906; Marin County, California.

movements occur as Earth's crustal plates slip past, under, and away from one another. Because the **stress** (force per unit area) that produces **strain** (deformation) can be transmitted long distances in rocks, active faults do not necessarily occur exactly on a plate boundary, but they generally occur in the vicinity of one. The mechanism by which stressed rocks store up strain energy along a fault to produce an earthquake was explained by Harold F. Reid after the great San Francisco earthquake of 1906. Reid proposed a mechanism to explain the shaking, which resulted from movement on the San Andreas fault, known as the **elastic rebound theory** (◆Figure 4.2). According to this theory, when sufficient strain energy has accumulated in rocks, they may rupture rapidly—just as a rubber band breaks when it is stretched too far—and the stored strain energy is released as vibrations that radiate outward in all directions (◆Figure 4.3).

Most earthquakes are generated by movements on faults within the crust and upper mantle that do not produce ruptures at the ground surface. We can thus recognize a point within the Earth where the fault rupture starts, the **focus,** and the **epicenter,** the point on the earth surface directly above the focus (Figure 4.3). Elastic waves—vibrations—move out spherically in all directions from the focus and strike the surface. Damaging earthquake foci are generally within a few kilometers of Earth's surface. Deep-focus earthquakes, on the other hand, those whose foci are 300–700 kilometers (190–440 mi) below the surface, do little or no damage. Earthquake foci are not known below 700 kilometers. This indicates that the mantle at that depth behaves *plastically* due

to high temperatures and confining pressures, deforming continuously as ductile substances do, rather than storing up strain energy.

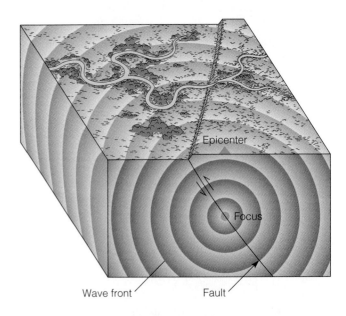

◆ **ThomsonNOW** **ACTIVE FIGURE 4.3** The focus of an earthquake is the point in the earth where fault rupture begins, and the epicenter is directly above the focus at the ground surface. Seismic-wave energy moves out in all directions from the focus. From *Essentials of Geology,* 2nd ed., by R. Wicander and J. Monroe, p. 228, Brooks/Cole, 1999

P-wave propagation →

Dilation   Compression   Dilation   Compression   Unstressed condition

(a)

S-wave propagation →

Vertical plane

(b)

Surface-wave propagation →

(c)

◆ **ThomsonNOW** **ACTIVE FIGURE** 4.4 Ground motion during passage of earthquake waves. (a) P-waves compress and expand the earth. (b) S-waves move in all directions perpendicular to the wave advance, but only the horizontal motion is shown in this diagram. (c) Surface waves create surface undulations that result from a combination of the retrograde elliptical motions of Rayleigh waves (shown) and Love waves, which move from side to side at right angles to the direction of wave propagation.

The vibration produced by an earthquake is complex, but it can be described as three distinctly different types of waves (◆Figure 4.4). Primary waves, **P-waves,** and secondary waves, **S-waves,** are generated at the focus and travel through the interior of Earth; thus, they are known as **body waves.** They are designated P- and S-waves because they are the first (*primary*) and second (*secondary*) waves to arrive from distant earthquakes. As these body waves strike the planet's surface, they generate surface waves that are analogous to water ripples on a pond.

P-waves (◆Figure 4.4a) are **longitudinal waves;** the solids, liquids, and gases through which they travel are alternately compressed and expanded in the same direction the waves move. Their velocity depends upon the resistance to change in volume (in compressibility) and shape of the material through which they travel. P-waves

travel about 300 meters (1,000 ft) per second in air, 300–1,000 meters (1,000–3,000 ft) per second in soil, and faster than 5 kilometers (3 mi) per second in solid rock at the surface. P-wave velocity increases with depth, because the materials composing the mantle and core become less compressible with depth. This increase causes the waves' travel paths to be bowed downward as they move through the Earth. P-waves speed through the Earth with a velocity of about 10 kilometers (6 mi) per second. At the ground surface they have very small amplitudes (motion) and cause little property damage. Although they are physically identical to sound waves, they vibrate at frequencies below what the human ear can detect. The earthquake noise that has been reported could be P-waves of a slightly higher frequency or some other, related vibrations whose frequencies are in the audible range.

◆ **FIGURE 4.5** Seismometer (*left*) and seismogram (*right*) used to demonstrate method of detecting and recording earthquakes. The record on the seismogram is not an earthquake, but represents the seismometer's detection of vibrations from students' footsteps amplified about 2,000 times.

S-waves (◆Figure 4.4b) are **transverse (shear) waves;** they produce ground motion perpendicular to their direction of travel. This causes the rocks through which they travel to be twisted and sheared. These waves have the shape produced when one end of a garden hose or a loosely hanging rope is given a vigorous flip. They can travel only through material that resists shearing—that is, material that resists two forces acting in opposite directions in different planes. Thus, S-waves travel only through solids, because liquids and gases have no shear strength (try piling water in a mound). S-wave ground motion may be largely in the horizontal plane and can result in considerable property damage. S-wave velocity is approximately 5.2 kilometers (3.2 mi) per second from distant earthquakes; hence, they arrive after the P-waves.

Unexpended P- and S-wave energy bouncing off Earth's surface generates the complex surface waves (◆Figure 4.4c). These waves produce a rolling motion at the ground surface. In fact, slight motion sickness is a common response to surface waves of long duration. The waves are the result of a complex interaction of several wave types, the most important of which are *Love waves,* which exhibit horizontal motion normal to the direction of travel, and *Rayleigh waves,* which exhibit retrograde (opposite to the direction of travel) elliptical motion in a plane perpendicular to the ground surface. Surface waves have amplitudes that are greatest in near-surface unconsolidated layers and are the most destructive of the earthquake waves.

Locating the Epicenter

A **seismograph** is an instrument designed specifically to detect, measure, and record vibrations in the Earth's crust (◆Figure 4.5). It is relatively simple in concept (◆Figure 4.6), but some very sophisticated electronic systems have been

developed. Seismic data are recorded onto a **seismogram** (◆Figure 4.7). Because seismographs are extremely sensitive to vibrations of any kind, they are installed in quiet areas such as abandoned oil and water wells, cemeteries, and parks.

When an earthquake occurs, the distance to its epicenter can be approximated by computing the difference in P- and S-wave arrival times at various seismograph stations.

◆ **FIGURE 4.6** The first earthquake detector, invented about A.D. 130 by Chinese scholar Chang Heng. Balls held in the dragons' mouths were aligned with a pendulum inside the vase. When an earthquake occurred the pendulum swung and pushed balls into the mouths of the frogs aligned with the pendulum's swing. If the frogs facing north and south contained balls, for example, Chang Heng could say that the earthquake epicenter was north or south of the instrument.

◆ **FIGURE 4.7** Seismogram of the main shock of the Northridge earthquake, January 17, 1994. The time in minutes and seconds after 4:00 A.M. appears at the bottom. Distance from the epicenter and direction and ground acceleration at the recording site are also indicated. (Acceleration is explained in the next section.)

Although the method actually used by seismologists today is more accurate and determines the depth and location of the quake's focus and its epicenter, what is described here serves to show how seismic-wave arrival times can be used to determine the distance to an epicenter. Because it is known that the two kinds of waves are generated simultaneously at the earthquake focus and that P-waves travel faster than S-waves, it is possible to calculate where the waves started.

Imagine that two trains leave a station at the same time, one traveling at 60 kilometers per hour and the other at 30 km/h, and that the second train passes your house one hour after the first train goes by. If you know their speeds, you can readily calculate your distance from the train station

of origin as 60 kilometers. The relationship between distance to an epicenter and arrival times of P- and S-waves is illustrated in ◆Figure 4.8. The epicenter will lie somewhere on a circle whose center is the seismograph and whose radius is the distance from the seismograph to the epicenter. The problem is then to determine where on the circumference of the circle the epicenter is. To learn this, more data are needed: specifically, the distances to the epicenter from two other seismograph stations. Then the intersection of the circles drawn around each of the three stations—a method of map location called *triangulation*—specifies the epicenter of the earthquake (◆Figure 4.9).

> **CONSIDER THIS**
>
> You are shopping for a house in earthquake country. How could an isoseismal map of an earthquake whose epicenter was near a house you think you would like to buy be useful? What patterns would you look for when examining the isoseismal map?

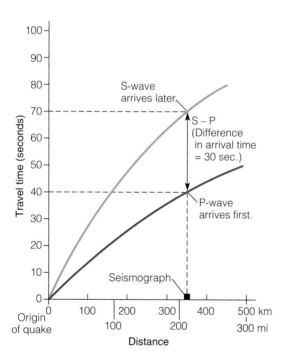

◆ **FIGURE 4.8** Generalized graph of distance versus travel time for P- and S-waves. Note that the P-wave has traveled farther from the origin of the earthquake than the S-wave at any given elapsed time. The curvature of both wave paths is due to increases in velocity with depth (distance from epicenter).

Earthquake Measurement

Intensity Scales

The reactions of people (geologists included) to an earthquake typically range from mild curiosity to outright panic. However, a sampling of the reactions of people who have been subjected to an earthquake can be put to good use. Numerical values can be assigned to the individuals' perceptions of earthquake shaking and local damage, which can then be contoured upon a map. One **intensity scale** developed for measuring these perceptions is the 1931 **modified Mercalli scale *(MM)*.** The scale's values range from *MM* = I (denoting not felt at all) to *MM* = XII (denoting widespread destruction), and they are keyed to specific U.S. architectural and building specifications. (See Appendix 4.) People's perceptions and responses are compiled from returned questionnaires, and then lines of earthquake intensity, called **isoseismals,** are plotted on maps. Isoseismals enclose areas of equal earthquake damage and can indicate

◆ **ThomsonNOW** **ACTIVE FIGURE 4.9** An earthquake epicenter can be closely approximated by triangulation from three seismic stations.

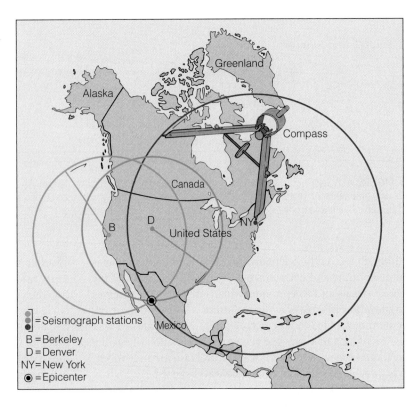

areas of weak rock or soil as well as areas of substandard building construction (◆Figure 4.10a). Such maps have proved useful to planners and building officials in revising building codes and safe construction standards.

Recently a new method of plotting shaking intensities has evolved that is faster and that compares favorably with the questionnaire method. It is the Community Internet Intensity Maps (CIIM), an example of which is shown in Figure 4.10b. The CIIM takes advantage of the Internet, and the time to generate intensity maps drops from months to minutes. The responses, which can take place within 3 minutes of the event, are summarized by computer, and an intensity number is assigned to each ZIP code area. This method is particularly useful in areas with sparse seismograph coverage. Although perhaps not as colorful as the map generated by the traditional *MM* intensities obtained by using postal questionnaires, the CIIM values agree well and have actually proved more reliable in areas of low shaking. However, neither method allows comparison of earthquakes with widely spaced epicenters because of local differences in construction practices and local geology.

Richter Magnitude Scale—The Best-Known Scale

The best-known measure of earthquake strength is the **Richter magnitude scale,** which was introduced in 1935 by Charles Richter and Beno Gutenberg at the California Institute of Technology. It is a scale of the energy released by an earthquake and thus, in contrast to the intensity scale,

may be used to compare earthquakes in widely separated geographic areas. The Richter value is calculated by measuring the maximum amplitude of the ground motion as shown on the seismogram using a specified seismic wave, usually the surface wave. Next, the seismologist "corrects" the measured amplitude (in microns) to what a "standard" seismograph would record at the station. After an additional correction for distance from the epicenter, the Richter **magnitude** is the common logarithm of that ground motion in microns. For example, a magnitude-4 earthquake is specified as having a corrected ground motion of 10,000 microns ($\log_{10}$ of 10,000 = 4) and thus can be compared to any other earthquake for which the same corrections have been made. It should be noted that because the scale is logarithmic, each whole number represents a ground shaking (at the seismograph site) 10 times greater than the next-lower number. Thus a magnitude-7 produces 10 times greater shaking than a magnitude-6, 100 times that of a magnitude-5, and 1,000 times that of a magnitude-4. Total energy released, on the other hand, varies logarithmically as some exponent of 30. Compared to the energy released by a magnitude-5 earthquake, a $M = 6$ releases 30 times (30^1) more energy; a $M = 7$ releases 900 times (30^2) more; and a $M = 8$ releases 27,000 (30^3) times more energy (◆Figure 4.11a).

The Richter scale is open-ended; that is, theoretically it has no upper limit. However, rocks in nature do have a limited ability to store strain energy without rupturing, and no earthquake has been observed with a Richter magnitude greater than 8.9—yet.

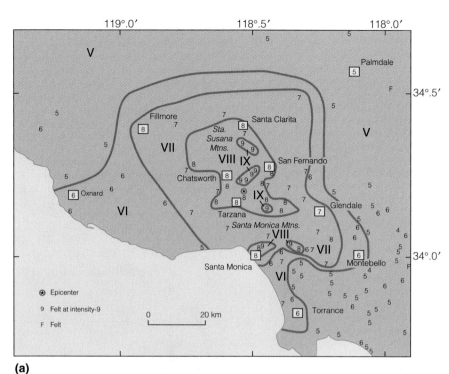

(a)

◆ **FIGURE 4.10** (a) Isoseismal map of the near-field (close to the epicenter) modified Mercalli scale intensities of the 1994 Northridge, California, earthquake. Intensity-IX values are assigned where there are spectacular partial collapses of modern buildings, destroyed wood-frame buildings, and collapses of elevated freeways (see Appendix 4). (b) Community Internet Intensity Map (CIIM) for the same earthquake. The main difference in appearance is due to the fact that the intensities were not contoured but assigned to ZIP code areas of the respondents. (a) SCEC data (b) USGS

(b)

Moment magnitude is derived from seismic moment, M_0 (in dyne centimeters), which is proportional to the average displacement (slip) on the fault *times* the rupture area on the fault surface *times* the rigidity of the faulted rock. The amount of seismic energy (in ergs) released from the ruptured fault surface is linearly related to seismic moment by a simple factor, whereas Richter magnitude is logarithmically related to energy. Because of the linear relationship of seismic moment to energy released, the equivalent energy released by other natural and human-caused phenomena can be conveniently compared to earthquakes' moment magnitudes on a graph (◆Figure 4.11b).

Moment magnitudes (M_w) are derived from seismic moments (M_0) by the formula: $M_w = (\frac{2}{3} \log M_0 - 10.7)$. This table compares the two most commonly used scales for selected significant earthquakes:

Earthquake	Richter Magnitude	Moment Magnitude
Chile, 1960	8.3	9.5
Alaska, 1964	8.4	9.2
New Madrid, 1812	8.7 (est.)	8.1 (est.)
Mexico City, 1985	8.1	8.1
San Francisco, 1906	8.3 (est.)	7.7
Loma Prieta, 1989	7.1	7.0
San Fernando, 1971	6.4	6.7
Northridge, 1994	6.4	6.7
Kobe, Japan, 1995	7.2 JMA*	6.9

*The Richter scale is not used in Japan. The official earthquake scale there is the scale developed by the Japanese Meteorological Agency (JMA).

Moment Magnitude—The Most Widely Used Scale

Seismologists have abandoned Richter magnitudes in favor of **moment magnitudes** (M_w or M) for describing earthquakes. The reason is that Richter magnitudes do not accurately portray the energy released by large earthquakes on faults with great rupture lengths. The seismic waves used to determine the Richter magnitude come from only a small part of the fault rupture and, hence, cannot provide an accurate measure of the total seismic energy released by a very large event.

◆ **FIGURE 4.11** Earthquake magnitude and energy. (a) Richter magnitudes of nine selected earthquakes, 1906–1994. (b) Equivalent moment magnitudes of energetic human-caused events (*squares*), natural events (*triangles*), and large earthquakes (*circles*). The erg is a unit of energy, or work, in the metric (cgs) system. To lift a one-pound weight one foot requires 1.4 x 10^7 ergs.

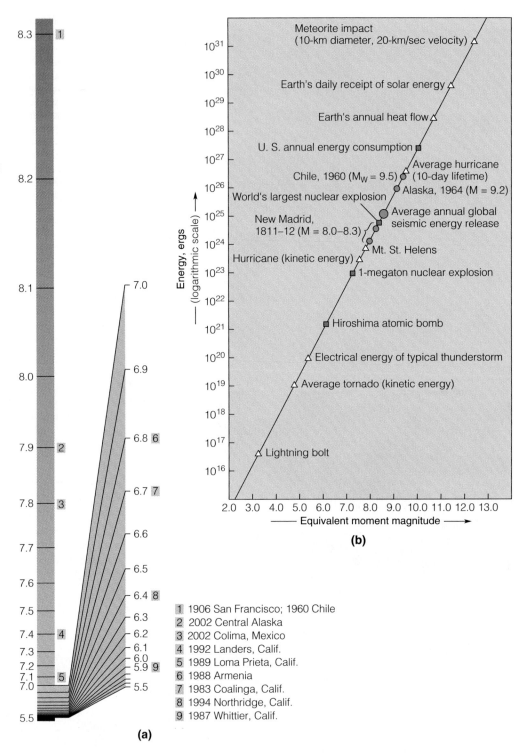

1　1906 San Francisco; 1960 Chile
2　2002 Central Alaska
3　2002 Colima, Mexico
4　1992 Landers, Calif.
5　1989 Loma Prieta, Calif.
6　1988 Armenia
7　1983 Coalinga, Calif.
8　1994 Northridge, Calif.
9　1987 Whittier, Calif.

(a)

Confusion arises because some of the earthquake magnitudes are reported as Richter magnitude (M_L, teleseismic body wave magnitude (m_b), duration magnitude (m_d), surface wave magnitude (M_s), or moment magnitude (M_w or M). This is simplified somewhat because most newspapers and the Internet report earthquakes as either Richter or moment magnitude.

At the close of the twentieth century the Chilean earthquake of 1960 ($M_w = 9.5$) still held the record for the greatest seismic moment and energy release ever measured; that is, it had the longest fault rupture and the greatest displacement. The Alaskan earthquake of 1964 had the highest Richter magnitude of the 1900s and theoretically more severe ground motion than the event in Chile. (See ■ Case Study 4.2 on page 103.)

"Then the Lord rained upon Sodom and Gomorrha brimstone and fire. . . . And he overthrew those cities, and all the plain about . . ." (Genesis 19: 24–25). Sodom and Gomorrha are believed to have been located near the modern industrial city of Sedom in Israel at the south end of the Dead Sea. Could some geological event have caused the destruction of these towns? If so, what events might have been possible?

ThomsonNOW

Click **Geology Interactive** to work through an activity on Earthquakes and Space and Time through Earthquakes and Tsunamis.

Fault Creep, the "Nonearthquake"

Some faults move almost continuously, or in short spurts, and do not produce detectable earthquakes. This type of movement, called **fault creep,** is well known but poorly understood. The Hayward fault, which is part of the San Andreas fault system, is an example of a creeping fault. It is just east of the San Andreas fault and runs through the cities of Hayward and Berkeley, California. (See the map in Figure 4.33.) Creep along this fault causes displacements of millimeters per year, and is one way that this plate boundary accommodates motion between the Pacific and North American plates. An alternative "accommodation" of plate motion on the San Andreas system is the storage of the strain energy and periodic release as a large displacement on a fault that generates a damaging earthquake. The obvious benefit of a creeping fault does not come without a price, as the residents of Hollister, California, can testify. The "creeping" Calaveras fault runs through their town and, as in Hayward, it gradually displaces curbs, sidewalks, and even residences.

A good strategy in areas subject to fault creep is to map the surface trace of the fault so that it can be avoided in future construction. The University of California–Berkeley Memorial Stadium was built on the Hayward fault before the hazard of fault creep was recognized. The fault creep caused damage to the drainage system that requires periodic maintenance. It is ironic that creep damage occurs at an institution that installed the first seismometer in the United States.

Forensic Use of Seismic Records

Seismic records can be used, in conjunction with other methods, to distinguish between earthquakes and nuclear explosions. The basis for the seismic method is that nuclear explosions are more concentrated in space and time and therefore excite more short-period seismic waves. This method requires extensive analysis of seismograms and is one of the tools that will be used to measure compliance by signers of the Comprehensive Test Ban Treaty. The following are select

anomalous seismic events from 1995 to 2003, some of which were believed to be nuclear explosions. Note that the August 12, 2000 event marks the tragic explosion and sinking of the Russian submarine *Kursk,* and the February 1, 2003 event marks the *Columbia* space shuttle disintegration. Although not on this list of special studies compiled by Lynn Sykes of Lamont–Doherty Earth Observatory of Columbia University, the collapse of the Twin Towers on September 11, 2001 was also recorded on seismographs at Lamont–Doherty.

Location	Date	Type of Event
Novaya Zemlya	January 13, 1996	earthquake
Kola Peninsula	September 19, 1996	chemical explosion
Germany	September 11, 1996	mine collapse
East Kazakhstan	August 03, 1997	chemical explosion
India	May 13, 1998	alleged nuclear explosions
Novaya Zemlya	September 23, 1999	alleged nuclear explosion
Kursk, Barents	August 12, 2000	chemical explosion
Novaya Zemlya	February 23, 2002	earthquake
U.S. space shuttle Columbia	February 01, 2003	explosion 100 seconds long

Seismic Design Considerations
Ground Shaking

Ground movements, particularly rapid horizontal displacements, are most damaging during an earthquake. Shear and surface waves are the culprits, and the potential for them must be evaluated when establishing design specifications. The design objective for earthquake-resistant buildings is relatively straightforward: structures should be designed to withstand the maximum potential horizontal ground acceleration expected in the particular region. Engineers call this acceleration *base shear,* and it is usually expressed as a percentage of the *acceleration of gravity* (*g*). On Earth, *g* is the acceleration of a falling object in a vacuum (9.8 m/sec^2, or 32 ft/sec^2). In your car it is equivalent to accelerating from a dead stop through 100 meters in 4.5 seconds. An acceleration of 1 *g* downward produces weightlessness, and a fraction of 1 *g* in the horizontal direction can cause buildings to separate from their foundations or to collapse completely. An analogy is to imagine rapidly pulling a carpet on which a person is standing; most assuredly the person will topple.

The effect of high horizontal acceleration on poorly constructed buildings is twofold. Flexible-frame structures may be deformed from cube-shaped to rhomb-shaped, or they may be knocked off their foundations (◆Figure 4.12). More rigid multistory buildings may suffer "story shift" if floors and

◆ **FIGURE 4.12** (a) Strong horizontal motion may deform a house from a cube to a rhomboid or knock it from its foundation completely. (b) A Coalinga, California, frame house that was deformed by the magnitude-6.3 earthquake in 1983. (c) A cripple-wall consists of short vertical members that connect the floor of the house to the foundation. Cripple-walls are common in older construction. (d) A Watsonville, California, house that was knocked off its cripple-wall base during the Loma Prieta earthquake of 1989. Without exception, cripple-walls bent or folded over to the north relative to their foundations.

◆ **FIGURE 4.13** Total vertical collapse as a result of "story shift"; Mexico City, 1985. Such structural failures are not survivable.

walls are not adequately tied together (◆Figure 4.13). The result is a shifting of floor levels and the collapse of one floor upon another like a stack of pancakes. Such structural failures are not survivable by inhabitants, and they clearly illustrate the adage that "earthquakes don't kill people; buildings do."

Damage due to shearing forces can be mitigated by bolting frame houses to their foundations and by *shear walls*. An example of a shear wall is plywood sheeting nailed in place over a wood frame, which makes the structure highly resistant to deformation. Wall framing, usually two-by-fours, should be nailed very securely to a wooden sill that is bolted to the foundation. Diagonal bracing and blocking also provide shear resistance (◆Figure 4.14). L-shaped structures may suffer damage where they join, as each wing of the structure vibrates independently. Such damage can be minimized by designing *seismic joints* between the building wings or between adjacent buildings of different heights. These joints are filled with a compressible substance that will accommodate movement between the structures.

Wave period is the time interval between arrivals of successive wave crests, or of equivalent points of waves, and it is expressed as T in seconds. It is an important consideration when assessing a structure's potential for seismic damage, because if a building's natural period of vibration is equal to that of seismic waves, a condition of resonance exists. **Resonance** occurs when a building sways in step with an oscillatory seismic wave. As a structure sways back and forth under resonant conditions, it gets a push in its direction of sway with the passage of each seismic wave. This causes the sway to increase, just as pushing a child's swing at the proper moments makes it go higher with each push. Resonance also may cause a wine glass to shatter when an operatic soprano sings just the right note or frequency.

Low-rise buildings have short natural wave periods (0.05–0.1 seconds), and high-rise buildings have long natural periods (1–2 seconds). Therefore, high-frequency (short-period) waves affect single-family dwellings and low-rise buildings, and long-period (low-frequency) waves affect tall structures. Close to an earthquake epicenter, high-frequency waves dominate, and thus more extensive home and low-rise damage can be expected. With distance from the epicenter, the short-period wave energy is absorbed or dissipated, resulting in the domination of longer-period waves.

CONSIDER THIS

Over time, tectonic stresses strain the rocks along a fault and increase the chance of sudden rupture and a potentially damaging earthquake. For this reason, it is generally believed that a region that has had many small earthquakes (magnitude <4.0) has a low probability for a large earthquake. Question: For a magnitude-7.0 earthquake with a 50-year recurrence interval, how many magnitude-4.0 earthquakes would be required to "balance the energy books"? How many small earthquakes a day is this? Is this belief realistic in a seismically active region based upon your calculations?

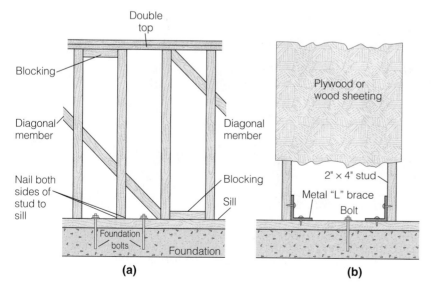

(a)   **(b)**

◆ **FIGURE 4.14** Methods of reinforcing structures against base shear. (a) Diagonal cross-members and blocks resist horizontal earthquake motion (shear). (b) Plywood sheeting forms a competent shear wall, and metal "L" braces and bolts tie the structure to the foundation.

◆ **FIGURE 4.15** Pictured is the site of the earthquake-induced rockslide at Red Mountain. The Madison River is just off the picture in the foreground. The rockslide was triggered by an earthquake and took place in schist with foliation planes inclined parallel to the mountain slope (see Chapter 7).

Landslides

Thousands of landslides are triggered by earthquakes in mountainous or hilly terrain; there were an estimated 17,000 during the Northridge earthquake alone (see ■ Case Study 4.1 on page 103). The 1989 Loma Prieta earthquake caused landsliding in the Santa Cruz Mountains and adjacent parts of the California Coast Ranges. Such areas are slide prone under the best of conditions, and even a small earthquake will trigger many slope failures. In the greater San Francisco Bay area there was an estimated $10 million damage to homes, utilities, and transportation systems because of landslides and surficial ground failures resulting from the Loma Prieta earthquake.

One of the worst earthquake-triggered tragedies in the United States occurred in August 1959, a short distance from Yellowstone Park. A landslide, in reality a massive rockslide (see Chapter 7), originated on Red Mountain above the Madison River in Montana. The rockslide was triggered by a moderate earthquake that caused the metamorphic rock (schist) composing the mountain to slide down its foliation planes, which were inclined parallel to the hill slopes (◆Figure 4.15). However, the rockslide occurred above a popular campground, and 26 people were killed by the falling rock. The slide generated a terrific shock wave of air that lifted cars, trees, and campers off the ground. In addition, the Madison River was dammed by the slide and a lake formed, later named "Quake Lake."

Ground or Foundation Failure

Liquefaction is the sudden loss of strength of water-saturated, sandy soils resulting from shaking during an earthquake. Sometimes called **spontaneous liquefaction,** it can cause large ground cracks to open, lending support to the ancient myth that the earth opens up to swallow people and animals during earthquakes. Shaking can cause saturated sands to consolidate and thus to occupy a smaller volume. If the water is slow in draining from the consolidated material, the overlying soil comes to be supported only by pore water, which has no resistance to shearing. This may cause buildings to settle, earth dams to fail, and sand below the surface to blow out through openings at the ground surface (◆Figure 4.16a). Liquefaction at shallow depth may result in extensive lateral movement or spreading of the ground, leaving great cracks and openings.

Ground areas most susceptible to liquefaction are those that are underlain at shallow depth—usually less than 30 feet—by layers of water-saturated fine sand. With subsurface geologic data obtained from water wells and foundation borings, liquefaction-susceptibility maps have been prepared for many seismically active areas in the United States.

Similar failures occur in certain clays that lose their strength when they are shaken or remolded. Such clays are called *quick clays* and are natural aggregations of fine-grained clays and water. They have the peculiar property of turning

(a)

(b)

◆ **FIGURE 4.16** (a) These apartment buildings tilted as a result of soil liquefaction in Niigata, Japan, in 1964. Many residents of the building in the center exited by walking down the side of the structure. (b) "House of cards" collapse of quick clay structure in Turnagain Heights, Anchorage, Alaska, in 1964. Total destruction occurred within the slide area, which is now called Earthquake Park.

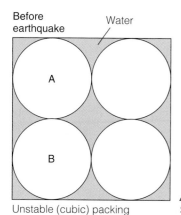

Before earthquake

Water

A

B

Unstable (cubic) packing

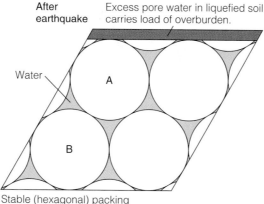

After earthquake

Excess pore water in liquefied soil carries load of overburden.

Water

A

B

Stable (hexagonal) packing

◆ **FIGURE 4.17** Liquefaction (lateral spreading) due to repacking of spheres (idealized grains of sand) during an earthquake. The earthquake's shaking causes the solids to become packed more efficiently and thus to occupy less volume. A part of the overburden load is supported by water, which has no resistance to lateral motion.

from a solid (actually a gel-like state) to a liquid when they are agitated by an earthquake, an explosion, or even vibrations from pile driving. They occur in deposits of glacial-marine or glacial-lake origin and are therefore found mostly in northern latitudes, particularly in Scandinavia, Canada, and the New England states. Failure of quick clays underlying Anchorage, Alaska, produced extensive lateral spreading throughout the city in the 1964 earthquake (◆Figure 4.16b).

The physics of failure in spontaneous liquefaction and in quick clays is similar. When the earth materials are water-saturated and the earth shakes, the loosely packed sand consolidates or the clay collapses like a house of cards. The pore-water pressure pushing the grains apart becomes greater than the grain-to-grain friction, and the material becomes "quick" or "liquifies" (◆ Figure 4.17). The potential for such geologic conditions is not easily recognized. In many cases it can be determined only by information gained from bore holes drilled deeper than 30 meters (100 ft). Because of this expense, many site investigations do not include deep drilling, and the condition can be unsuspected until an earthquake occurs.

Ground Rupture and Changes in Ground Level

Structures that straddle an active fault may be destroyed by actual ground shifting and the formation of a fault scarp (◆Figure 4.18). By excavating trenches across fault zones, geologists can usually locate past rupture surfaces that may reactivate. In 1970 the California legislature enacted the Alquist–Priolo Special Study Zones Act, which was renamed the *Earthquake Fault Zones Act* in 1995. It mandates that all known active faults in the state be accurately mapped and zoned for seismic safety. The act provides funds for state and private geologists to locate the youngest fault ruptures within a zone and requires city and county governments to limit land use adjacent to identified faults within their jurisdictions. Ironically, the faults responsible for the 1992 Landers earthquake ($M_w = 7.3$) were designated as Earthquake Fault Zones just prior to the June 28 event.

Changes in ground level as a result of faulting may have an impact, particularly in coastal areas that are uplifted or down-dropped. For instance, during the 1964 Alaskan event, parts of the Gulf of Alaska thrust upward 11 meters (36 ft), exposing vast tracts of former tidelands on island and mainland coasts.

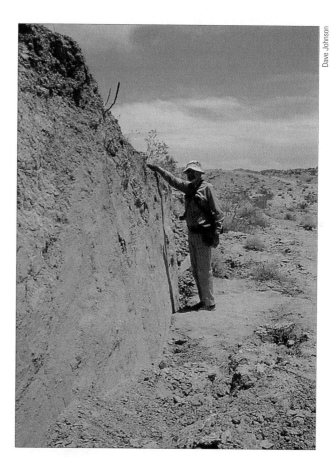

Dave Johnson

◆ **FIGURE 4.18** The 1992 Landers earthquake ($M_w = 7.3$) in the Colorado Desert of southern California was felt from Phoenix, Arizona, to Reno, Nevada. Right-lateral offset of 4.27 meters (14 ft) on the Johnson Valley fault created a 2-meter (6.5-ft) vertical scarp due to lateral offset of a ridge. The geologist is 185 cm tall.

Fires

Fires caused by ruptured gas mains or fallen electric power lines can add considerably to the damage caused by an earthquake. In fact, most damage attributed to the San Francisco earthquake of 1906 and much of that in Kobe, Japan, in 1995 was due to the uncontrolled fires that followed the earthquakes. The Kobe quake hit at breakfast time. In neighborhoods crowded with wooden structures, fires erupted when natural-gas lines broke and falling debris tipped over kerosene stoves. Broken water mains made fire-fighting efforts futile. One of the principal "do's" for citizens immediately after a quake is to shut off the gas supply to homes and other buildings in order to prevent gas leaks into the structure. This in itself will save many lives (see Figure 4.41).

Tsunamis

The most myth-ridden hazard associated with earthquakes (and submarine volcanic eruptions and landslides) is tsunami (pronounced "soo-nah-mee"), or seismic sea waves. **Tsunami** is a Japanese word meaning "great wave in harbor" and it is appropriate because these waves are impulsively generated and most commonly wreak death and destruction inside bays and harbors. They have nothing to do with the tides, even though the term "tidal wave" is commonly used in the English-speaking world. The Japanese written record of tsunamis goes back 200 years and their power is dramatically displayed in the well-known print by Hokusai (◆Figure 4.19). Tsunamis, their causes, and effects are treated in detail in Chapter 10.

ThomsonNOW
Click **Geology Interactive** to work through an activity on Tsunamis.

Five Earthquakes That Make a Point

Each year in the world, on average, there are at least two earthquakes of magnitude 8.0 or greater and 20 earthquakes in the magnitude 7.0 to 7.9 range. Release of seismic energy in the form of earthquakes has occurred throughout geologic time, and recorded history contains many references to strong earthquakes. More than 3,000 years of seismicity are documented in China, and Strabo's *Geography* mentions an earthquake in 373 B.C. in Greece. Thus, humans have probably always been subject to earthquakes (◆Table 4.1).

This section describes five earthquakes that occurred between 1994 and 2005. All five had very strong magnitudes but had quite different results because of differences in local foundation conditions, building standards, population density, and societal factors. The following is a synopsis of these events.

■ A magnitude-7.7 earthquake struck Gujarat, India at 8:46 A.M. on January 26, 2001. It was 60 times more powerful than the Northridge, California, earthquake of 1994 but the death toll was 400 times greater.

■ A magnitude-7.9 earthquake struck central Alaska on November 3, 2002. It was on the Denali fault and was one of the largest strike-slip ruptures in Alaska of the past two centuries. One minor injury was reported and the dollar loss was minimal.

■ A magnitude-7.8 earthquake struck the state of Colima, Mexico, on January 22, 2003. The destruction was widespread, but the death toll was only 29. The victims were mostly in dwellings that were poorly built and collapsed. Modern high-rise buildings faired well.

◆ **FIGURE 4.19** "The Breaking Wave off Kanagawa," wood-block color print by Katsushika Hokusai (1760–1849) from the series "Thirty-six Views of Mount Fuji," 1826–33. Metropolitan Museum of Art, H. O. Havemeyer Collection (JP 1847)

★TABLE 4.1   Selected Significant* World Earthquakes, in Chronological Order

Location	Year	Richter Magnitude**	Impact
San Francisco	1906	8.3	700 killed, $7 million damage, fire
Messina (Sicily)	1908	7.5	160,000 killed
Tokyo, Japan	1923	8.3	140,000+ killed, fire
Assam, India	1950	8.4	30,000 killed
Chile	1960	M_w 9.5	5,700 killed, 58,000 homes destroyed, tsunami
Alaska	1964	M_w 9.2	131 killed, tsunami
T'ang-shan, China	1976	7.9	330,000 killed
Mexico City	1985	8.1	10,000+ reported killed
Armenia	1988	6.8	55,000 killed
Loma Prieta (California)	1989	M_w 6.9	67 killed, $8 billion damage
Northridge, California	1994	M_w 6.7	60 killed, $25 billion damage
Kobe, Japan	1995	M_w 6.9	5,378 killed, $100 billion damage
Izmit (Kocaeli), Turkey	1999	M_w 7.4	15,370 killed, $10–$20 billion damage
Chi-Chi, Taiwan	1999	M_w 7.6	2,300+ killed
Gujarat, India	2001	M_w 7.7	Reported 20,000+
Alaska	2002	M_w 7.9	Little impact, no casualties
Colima, Mexico	2003	M_w 7.8	Widespread destruction, 27 fatalities
Bam, Iran	2003	M_w 6.5	30,000 believed killed, 30,00 injured
Simeulue, Sumatra	2004	M_w 9.3	230,000 killed, tsunami
Kashmir, Pakistan	2005	M_w 7.6	73,000 killed

*A "significant" earthquake is defined as one that registers a moment magnitude (M_w) of at least 6.5 or a lesser one that causes considerable damage or loss of life. The world averages 60 significant earthquakes per year.
**Estimated prior to 1935. M_w = Moment magnitude.
Sources: U.S. Geological Survey: *Earthquakes and Volcanoes;* California Division of Mines and Geology; *Academic American Encyclopedia* (1990, Grolier Electronic Publishing Company).

- A magnitude-9.3 earthquake struck the Andaman Islands and Sumatra on 26 December 2004. Despite the great shaking loss of life was due almost entirely to a tsunami.
- A magnitude-6.7 struck the San Fernando Valley at the community of Northridge on January 17, 1994. It is recognized as the second most costly natural disaster in U.S. history, second only to Hurricane Andrew (see Chapter 10).

Gujarat, India, 2001

A headline in a well-known American newspaper stated "Bad quake, worse buildings." This just about sums up the impact of this strong event in the state of Gujarat (◆Figure 4.20). It was a reverse-fault earthquake and the closest plate boundary lies many hundreds of kilometers away. It was felt 2000 km away and over an area 16 times that of the M_w = 7.8 San Francisco earthquake of 1906. Field investigation in Gujarat revealed no ground rupture, which is unusual for an earthquake of this magnitude. Liquefaction was widespread because of the high water table and thickness of unconsolidated sediment in the region. The quake occurred in an old rift system, which is a

well-known seismic zone that is very similar to parts of the central United States. One doesn't have to be a seismologist to know that an earthquake of this magnitude has real potential to cause devastation. Here, the lack of strict building codes governing construction methods, some of which date back to the British Colonial period, exacerbated the destruction that led to the loss of more than 20,000 lives. Here also, one can become an architect or building contractor without any special education or license. The damage covered an area over 500 km wide from the large city of Ahmedabad in the east to the Arabian Sea in the west. Severe damage was reported within an area 50 km by 70 km in which most high-rises (anything more than 3 stories) and low-rise cobble-stone structures collapsed.

What is surprising to geologists is that this earthquake occurred in an area of relative flat topography without the usual tectonic landforms suggestive of faulting and seismic activity. Strong earthquakes in India usually occur as the Indian plate moves northward against the Himalayas. However, a similar event occurred in 1819 in the Rann of Katchchh, also in the state of Gujarat, just to the southeast of the 2002 earthquake epicenter. This suggests a greater rate of tectonic (earthquake) activity than is indicated by the land forms there.

(a)

(b)

◆ **FIGURE 4.20** (a) The regional geography and plate tectonic setting of the Gujarat (Bhuj) earthquake. The epicenter is shown by the yellow dot. Bhuj lies 400–500 km from a plate boundary and a greater distance from the Himalayan range. Also shown are buried rift basins that are seismically active and very similar to those of the central United States (see page 94 on New Madrid). (b) Collapsed houses in the town of Ratnal, in the epicentral region of the Bhuj earthquake.

Geologists from the United States are particularly interested in this event because it may serve as an analog for mid-continent earthquakes and the New Madrid, Missouri, seismic zone (Figure 4.30). Major earthquakes are rare in intraplate regions like New Madrid and Gujarat, far from plate edges and the usual seismicity associated with the world's tectonic-plate boundaries. As pointed out, there is little evidence at the ground surface left by these earthquakes. Thus, each intraplate earthquake is an opportunity to study and better understand the hazards posed by these events.

Alaska, 2002

On November 3 a magnitude-7.9 earthquake occurred some 90 miles south of Fairbanks along the Denali fault (◆Figure 4.21). Denali is the native Tanana word for "high one," and the Denali fault is the best-known and studied active fault in the state. This earthquake was among the strongest ever recorded in the United States. It shut down the Alaska pipeline, and caused lakes to ripple in Iowa and water to slosh out of swimming pools as far south as Louisiana. The earthquake was shallow and its energy went directly to the surface to produce the distant effects. One resident of Porcupine Creek is quoted as saying "A charging brown bear I can handle. This (the earthquake) scared the heck out of me." Alaska has a history of strong earthquakes, demonstrated in 1964 when the Denali fault ruptured and left 159

dead and many communities in ruins, mostly due to tsunami. This most recent event is a reminder that the fault has a great potential for damage.

Colima, Mexico, 2003

On January 22 a magnitude-7.8 earthquake struck near the village of Tecoman in the state of Colima (◆Figure 4.22). Twenty-seven people lost their lives in Colima and two more in the adjoining state of Jalisco. In this shallow-focus quake, the epicenter occurred near the junction of three tectonic plates: North American plate to the northeast, the Cocos plate to the south, and the Rivera plate to the northwest. Both the smaller plates are being subducted beneath the North American plate, producing significant seismic activity in the region. Twenty of the fatalities occurred in the collapse of adobe-brick houses. Over 150 houses were reported destroyed in the city of 200,000 that dates back to sixteenth-century Spanish colonial times. Mexican structural engineers are very aware of the seismic hazards that exist in this part of the country and are quite good at designing buildings to be earthquake-resistant. As a result, no damage occurred to modern high-rise buildings from this powerful earthquake. However, it was felt strongly and caused some to panic in Mexico City, where an earthquake in 1985 with its epicenter in the same region took over 10,000 lives. Two 20-story buildings in the capital swayed so much that they actually collided, but did little damage.

(a)

(b)

◆ **FIGURE 4.21** (a) The magnitude-7.9 Denali fault earthquake of November 3, 2002, resulted from predominantly right-lateral offset along portions of the Denali and Totschunda fault systems in Alaska. Total length of the surface rupture was about 320 kilometers (200 mi). The western 49 km of the rupture shows mainly low-angle thrust offset as much as 1.5 m, with the northwest side up. Shown here are the epicenters of the November 3 event (red) and the magnitude-6.7 foreshock of October 23, 2002 (blue), as well as two previously recorded large shallow earthquakes (yellow) in the vicinity of the fault. (b) Aerial view of the Trans-Alaska Pipeline System (TAPS) line near the Denali fault, looking west. This is where the pipeline is supported by rails on which it can move freely in the event of fault offset. Here the line has slid toward the west end of the rails. Alyeska Pipeline Service Company reported no breaks to the line and therefore no loss of oil. Out of view to the left (south) is the 2.5 m (ft) right-lateral offset of the highway where it crosses the fault. Photo courtesy of Rod Combellick, Division of Geological and Geophysical Surveys, State of Alaska

Sumatra, 2004

The third deadliest and second most powerful earthquake in recorded history struck the northwest coast of Sumatra around breakfast time on December 26, 2004. In a mere six to eight minutes, the edge of the Indo-Pacific plate boundary flexed and lifted the coral-rimmed coasts of offshore islands closest to the 600-km-long fault rupture as much as 90 centimeters (35 in), while the shoreline of the main island of Sumatra sank below sea level, inundating important farmlands, roads, and built-up areas (◆Figure 4.23). An enormous tsunami radiated outward from the focal area and battered coasts as far away as eastern Africa, Sri Lanka, Myanmar, and Thailand. Because there was no early warning system in place to alert people of the approaching waves, nearly a quarter of a million people drowned. In one instance the sea waves derailed and washed away a crowded passenger train that happened to be traveling in the wrong place at the wrong time.

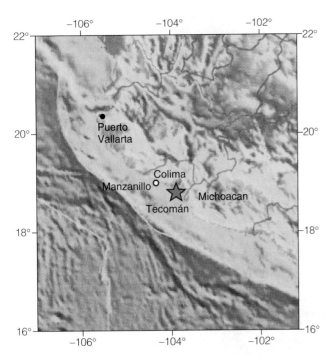

◆ **FIGURE 4.22** Magnitude-7.8 earthquake near Tecomán, Colima, Mexico, on January 22, 2003. USGS

For geologists, the Great Sumatran earthquake was geophysically interesting because it set the whole Earth ringing like a giant bell struck with a hammer. Every location on the planet—including the remote poles and the flat plains of Kansas, rose and fell at least a centimeter in slow, gentle

oscillations with periods ranging from every 20.5 to 54 minutes, too slow for people to notice without instrumental assistance. This wiggling continued with diminishing strength over a period of months. The quake was also strong enough to trigger aftershocks as far away as Alaska. Only a few months later, in March 2005, another great earthquake with a magnitude of 8.5–8.7—the biggest aftershock of all—struck the same area of Sumatra. Although it did not generate a large tsunami, 1300 people lost their lives, mostly on a single island.

Northridge, California, 1994

The largest earthquake in Los Angeles's short history occurred at 4:30 A.M. Monday, January 17, 1994, on a hidden fault below the San Fernando Valley. The $M_w = 6.7$ earthquake started at a depth of 18 kilometers (11 mi) and propagated upward in a matter of seconds to a depth of 5–8 kilometers (3–5 mi, ◆Figure 4.24). There were thousands of aftershocks, and their clustered pattern indicated the causative fault to be a reverse fault with a shallow dip of 35° to the south (Case Study 4.2 and Appendix 3). Such a low-angle reverse fault is called a *thrust fault*, and, because the thrust did not rupture the ground surface, it is described as

◆ **FIGURE 4.23** Porites coral heads on the west coast of Simeulue that were uplifted about 90 centimeters (35 in) by the December 26, 2004, earthquake.

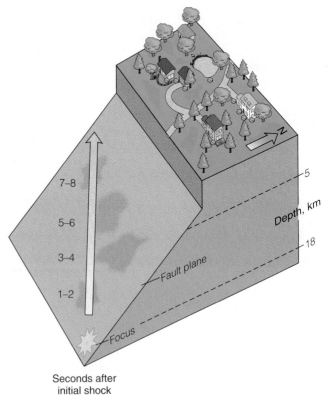

◆ **FIGURE 4.24** In the 1994 Northridge earthquake, the fault rupture progressed up the fault plane from the focus at the lower right of the figure to the upper left in 8 seconds. Rather than rupturing smoothly, like a zipper opening, it moved in jerks along the fault plane, as shown by the pink patches. Total displacement was about 4 meters (12 ft).

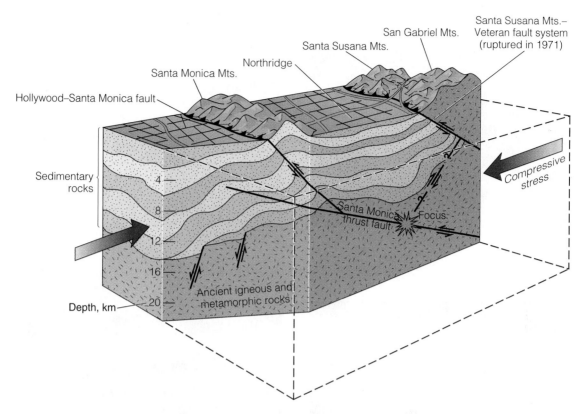

◆ **FIGURE 4.25** Interpretation of the fault system in the San Fernando Valley and surrounding area of Southern California. Compressive stresses built up over a long period, causing the subsurface blind thrust fault to rupture. The ensuing Northridge earthquake impacted the entire valley, and extended from the Santa Susana Mountains on the north to the city of Santa Monica on the south. USGS DATA

"blind" (◆Figure 4.25). Blind thrusts were first recognized after the 1987 Whittier earthquake 40 kilometers (25 mi) southwest of Northridge, but they were not fully appreciated until after the Northridge event.

Blind thrust faults were a newly identified seismic hazard, and there is evidence that a belt of them underlies the northern Los Angeles basin. They are especially dangerous because they cannot be detected by traditional techniques such as trenching and field mapping (thus they do not fall within the Earthquake Fault Zones Act as it is written) and yet, as we know now, they can generate significant earthquakes. Just as the residents of earthquake country were beginning to feel confident that geologists knew the location and behavior of most active faults, blind thrusts made their presence known.

Field inspection of the epicentral region was a depressing experience. Thirteen thousand buildings were found to be severely damaged; 21,000 dwelling units had to be ordered evacuated; 240 mobile homes had been destroyed by fire; 11 major freeway overpasses were damaged at 8 locations (■ Case Study 4.3 on page 104). The reason for the extensive damage was the high horizontal and vertical accelerations generated by the earthquake. Accelerations of more than 0.30 g are considered dangerous, and the vertical acceleration of 1.8 g measured by an instrument bolted to bedrock in nearby Tarzana probably set a world record. The high ground acceleration explains

why many people were literally thrown out of their beds and objects as heavy as television sets were projected several meters from their stands. Although the damage was not as visually spectacular as that at Mexico City in 1985, it was heartbreaking to many residents—brick chimneys, both reinforced with steel bars and unreinforced, came down; houses moved off their foundations; concrete-block walls crumbled; gaps broke open in plaster walls; the number of shattered storefront windows was beyond counting (◆Figure 4.26). The horizontal ground motion was directional; that is, it was strongest in the north–south direction. With few exceptions, block walls oriented east–west tipped over or fell apart, whereas those oriented north–south remained standing. Many two- and three-story apartment buildings built over open first-floor garages collapsed onto the residents' cars. The lack of shear resistance of these open parking areas led to failure of the vertical supports, and everything above came down.

California State University at Northridge sustained almost "textbook" earthquake damage. In its library is "Leviathan II," recognized as one of the most advanced automated book-withdrawal systems in the country. On this day it recorded a record withdrawal of about 500,000 books—all of them onto the floor of the library. Bottled chemicals fell off their storage shelves (a major concern at any university) and caused a large fire in the Chemistry

(a)

(b)

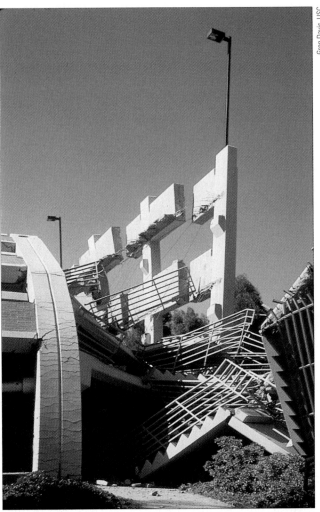

(c)

◆ **FIGURE 4.26** (a) Two wings of an apartment building that collapsed toward one another. (b) A staircase that leads to nowhere. In reality, it was the second-floor breezeway that collapsed onto the ground floor. (c) Part of the collapsed parking structure of Fashion Center, Northridge. Such collapses instigated new design criteria for open structures. Note the outside staircase that separated from the main structure.

Building. In addition, one wall of a large open parking structure collapsed inward to produce the stunning art deco architecture seen in ◆Figure 4.26c.

What We Can Learn

These five earthquakes reinforce the adage that "earthquakes don't kill people, falling buildings and tsunamis kill people." The magnitudes were in the range where destruction is certain if construction methods are not adequate. In Gujarat high-rise structures and stone dwellings alike collapsed due to inadequate design leading to a high death toll. In Alaska, where the population density is about one person per square mile, the strong temblor took no lives and really did minimal damage. On the other hand, the example in Mexico illustrates that even when high population areas are struck by a powerful earthquake, recognition of the importance of seis-

mic design criteria can reduce the loss of life as can an internationally organized tsunami early-warning alert network. The Northridge earthquake was an unusual case. There the combination of a blind thrust fault and very high ground accelerations, both vertical and horizontal, combined to cause the extensive damage in Southern California.

It should be noted that other factors beside construction, population density, and kind of fault movement can cause damage. Site effects are extremely important. During the 1989 Loma Prieta (San Francisco) earthquake the ground shaking around the bay area varied considerably. There was liquefaction and widespread destruction in the Marina District, where the two-level Interstate 880 was built on bay muds. Near Oakland it shook violently and failed (◆Figure 4.27) causing fatalities, whereas structures in San Francisco built on bedrock suffered much less or no damage. The seismograms shown in ◆Figure 4.28 illustrate this point (also see Case Study 4.3).

◆ **FIGURE 4.27** The I-880 freeway failed because it was built on bay muds that reacted to seismic waves like a bowl of gelatin. Pictured is the Cypress Street viaduct with the upper deck collapsed upon the lower one. There was loss of life here.

◆ **FIGURE 4.28** Seismograms for a magnitude-4.1 aftershock as recorded on (a) firm bedrock, (b) alluvium (stream-deposited sediment), and (c) areas of fill and bay muds. This is where the most damage occurred in the San Francisco earthquakes of 1906 and 1989. Data from EOS—American Geophysical Union

Site effects were noted almost 200 years ago when an observer of the New Madrid sequence (next topic) noted "The convulsion was greater along the Mississippi, as well as along the Ohio, than in the uplands. The strata in both valleys are loose. The more tenacious layers of clay and loam spread over the adjoining hills . . . suffered but little derangement" (see Drake, 1815, in For Further Information).

Does Earthquake Country Include Idaho, Missouri, and New York?

Even though the vast majority of the world's earthquakes occur at plate boundaries, areas hundreds and even thousands of kilometers away are not free of seismic activity. In the United States the five most seismically active states between 1980 and 1991 were

| | Earthquakes 1980–1991 | |
State	Number Recorded	Largest, M_w
Alaska	10,253	9.2
California	6,732	7.2
Washington	615	5.5
Idaho	536	7.3
Nevada	398	5.6

Although Alaska and California continue to lead the United States in the number of shakers, the earthquakes that have been felt over the largest area occurred in Missouri in 1811 and 1812, and significant seismic hazards are recognized in 39 states. No state is earthquake proof, as the seismic-risk map of the United States shows (◆Figure 4.29). It appears

that U.S. residents who want to be seismically safe should move to Texas, Florida, or Alabama.

Why do such strong earthquakes occur *intraplate*—that is, far from a plate boundary (⁎ Table 4.2)? Intraplate earthquakes have several characteristics in common (see also the Gujarat earthquake, this chapter):

1. The faults causing them are deeply buried and have not broken the ground surface.

2. Because the rocks of the continental interior are stronger than those at plate boundaries, which are laced with faults, they transmit seismic waves better, causing ground motion over a huge area. In the United States this is usually many states (◆see Figure 4.29).

3. They do not appear to be random events.

The Charleston, South Carolina, earthquake of 1886 was larger than the 1989 San Francisco shaker. It killed scores of people, ruined the city, and slowed the South's recovery from the Civil War. The New Madrid (pronounced "mad´rid") earthquakes of 1811 and 1812 caused extensive topographic changes, locally reversed the course of the Mississippi River, and may have been felt over a larger area than any other earthquake in recorded history. Ground motion was felt as far away as Washington, D.C., where it caused church bells to ring and scaffoldings on the Capitol to collapse.

Recent studies suggest that intraplate earthquakes are concentrated in areas where normally stable crust has been stretched and faulted. Such zones form where continents have been split apart *(rifted)*, forming two continents, as occurs at divergent plate boundaries (see Chapter 3). When North America was separated from Africa at the Mid-Atlantic Ridge

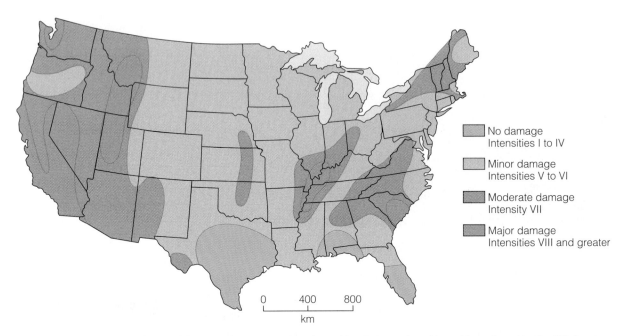

◆ **FIGURE 4.29** Seismic-risk map of the 48 contiguous states based upon historical records and intensities collected by the U.S. Coast and Geodetic Survey. The Coast and Geodetic Survey gathers intensity data from questionnaires after earthquakes. From M. L. Blair and W. W. Spangle, USGS prof. paper 941-B, 1979

Legend:
- No damage Intensities I to IV
- Minor damage Intensities V to VI
- Moderate damage Intensity VII
- Major damage Intensities VIII and greater

Scale: 0   400   800 km

about 180–200 million years ago, the continental crust being rifted at the ridge was thinned, stretched, and faulted. The North American continent was transported westward with the plate, and the weakened part of the crust along its eastern edge was hidden by a thick cover of younger sedimentary rocks. Buried rifted crust under the Eastern seaboard states forms the intraplate earthquake zone from the Carolinas to Canada.

The Midwest earthquake zone through Arkansas, Missouri, and Illinois is believed to be where an ancient (pre-Pangaea) divergent boundary started to form but "failed" for some reason, leaving behind a significant buried fault zone. Known as the *Reelfoot Rift*, the buried block of crust is down-dropped between faults (the hachured lines on the map of

◆Figure 4.31). The rift is 60 kilometers wide and 300 kilometers long (roughly 40 mi × 190 mi) and formed at least 500 million years ago. The linear trend of earthquakes from Marked Tree, Arkansas, northeastward to Caruthersville, Missouri, reveals upwarped sedimentary rocks along the rift axis. Detailed analysis of the geology across the Reelfoot fault scarp by trenching revealed evidence of three large earthquakes within the past 2,000 years, which yields a recurrence-interval estimate of 600–900 years for the fault, but the recurring earthquakes are not necessarily of the same magnitude as the 1811–1812 events. In fact, scientists estimate that a magnitude-6–7 earthquake will occur in the New Madrid seismic zone between 2000 and 2050 with a 90 percent probability.

⋆TABLE 4.2 Selected North American Intraplate Earthquakes			
Location	Year	Moment Magnitude⋆	Impact
New Madrid, Missouri	1811	8.2	Reelfoot Lake formed in NW Tennessee.
New Madrid	1812	8.3	Elevation changes caused Mississippi River to reverse its course locally.
New Madrid	1812	8.1	
Charleston, South Carolina	1886	7.6	Felt from New York to Chicago; 60 killed.
Charleston, Missouri	1895	6.8	Damage in 6 states (see Figure 4.28).
Grand Banks, Newfoundland	1929	7.4	Submarine landslides broke trans-Atlantic cable, disrupting communications.

⋆Moment magnitude is used in reconstructing the strength of "preinstrument" earthquakes, because we know something of fault length, rupture length, and area felt.

(a)

(b)

◆ **FIGURE 4.30** Mid-continent earthquakes. (a) Comparison of the effects of two earthquakes of similar magnitude. The 1895 Charleston, Missouri, earthquake impacted a relatively huge area in the central United States, whereas the 1994 Northridge earthquake's effects were limited to Southern California. Red indicates areas of minor-to-major damage to buildings and their contents. Yellow indicates areas where shaking was felt but there was little or no damage to objects, such as dishes. Data from USGS. (b) Damage from the 1886 earthquake along East Bay Street in Charleston, South Carolina.

Nobody knows how many people died in the 1811–1812 earthquakes. An amateur observer in Louisville, Kentucky, recorded almost 2,000 shocks with a homemade pendulum. Liquefaction was widespread along the Mississippi River, and the town of New Madrid, Missouri, was completely destroyed when it settled from 8 meters (25 ft) above sea level to only 4 meters (12 ft). Subsidence caused some swamps to drain and others to become lakes; an example is Reelfoot Lake in northwest Tennessee, which today is more than 50 feet deep. The New Madrid seismic zone is a major geologic hazard in the United States, and efforts are being made to reduce the impact of a future large earthquake there.

Iben Browning, a scientist with a Ph.D. in physiology but who is best known for his work on climate, predicted there would be a repeat of the 1811 New Madrid earthquake on December 3, 1990. His prediction was based upon alignment of the planets and consequent gravitational pull, which he believed would be sufficient to trigger an earthquake on that date. Although the prediction was discounted by scientists, it created considerable anxiety in Arkansas, Tennessee, Alabama, and Missouri. Months before "the day," earthquake insurance sales boomed, moving companies were booked up, and bottled-water sales rose dramatically—as did sales of quake-related souvenirs. One church sold "Eternity Preparedness Kits," and "Survival Revivals" were held. On the day of the scientifically discredited prediction nothing earthshaking occurred.

Many earthquakes with epicenters in weakened intraplate continental crust have shaken parts of the Midwest, eastern Canada, New England, New York, and the East Coast of the United States. New York does not have a major fault, but it has many faults. In the 1980s an earthquake in Westchester County ($M = 4.0$) toppled chimneys and caused enough panic for the state to implement new seismic codes that added 2–5

percent to building costs. In April 2002 the state experienced a magnitude-5.1 shaker that centered 15 miles southwest of Plattsburgh near the Canadian border. It rattled dwellings from Maine to Maryland and left cracks in foundations and chimneys. There were no injuries. The point here is that a relatively small intraplate earthquake can be felt over a huge area. By the mid 1990s New York and Massachusetts were the only Northeastern states that had earthquake building codes.

The Pacific Northwest

In years past, earthquake hazards were considered minor in Oregon and Washington. During the 1980s, however, research changed the perception, revealing geologic evidence that "major" (≥7.0 but <8.0) or "great" (≥8.0 but <9.0) subduction-zone earthquakes have occurred in the past and that they can occur in the future. The Cascadia subduction zone (◆Figure 4.32), extending 1,200 kilometers (740 mi) from northern California to Vancouver Island in Canada, has destructive earthquake potential. Geological evidence, consisting of carbon-dated tsunami deposits and drowned red-cedar forests, suggests that great earthquakes strike the Pacific Northwest roughly every 500 years, the last one in A.D. 1700, approximately 300 years ago. Minor earthquakes occur daily, however, and the cities of Portland, Seattle, and Vancouver, British Columbia, are in earthquake country (◆Figure 4.33). The states now are working to minimize damage should the "big one" occur on the subduction zone or on the Seattle fault, which runs through downtown Seattle.

The year 2000 marked the tricentennial of the last great (equal to or greater than $M = 8.0$) earthquake generated along the Cascadia Subduction Zone. To commemorate this, almost 100 earth scientists and public officials gathered at

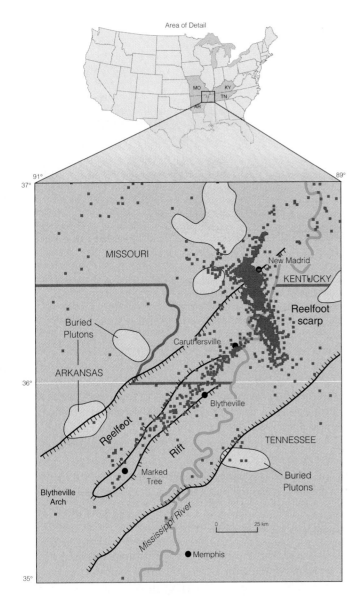

◆ **FIGURE 4.31** The New Madrid seismic zone covers parts of four states and consists of an ancient, fault-bounded depression (rift) buried below 1.5 kilometers (almost a mile) of sedimentary rocks. An area of major seismic hazard, it is studied intensively. USGS DATA

■ Deep earthquakes (>65 km or 40 mi deep)* occur when the oceanic plate descends beneath the continental plate. The largest deep earthquakes in recent times were in 1949 (*M* = 7.1) and in 1965 (*M* = 6.5).

● Shallow earthquakes (<17 km or 10 mi deep)* are caused by faults in the North American continent. Magnitude 7+ earthquakes have occurred along the Seattle fault in 1872, 1918, and 1946.

— Subduction earthquakes are huge quakes that occur when the subduction boundary ruptures. The most recent Cascadia Subduction Zone earthquake was 1700 and it sent a tsunami as far as Japan.

*Shallow and deep do not refer to focus of quake; rather, depth is subjective and is related to damage caused by faults in the Seattle area.

◆ **FIGURE 4.32** Faults and epicenters in the Seattle, Washington and Vancouver, British Columbia area. USGS

■ The recurrence interval for an event equivalent to the 1700 earthquake is 500–600 years.

Twenty years ago scientists were debating whether great earthquakes occurred at subduction zones. Now there are few doubters, and the 2000 meeting spent a great deal of time and effort in discussing methods of mitigating loss of life and damage. It is ironic that the conference hotel lies within the inundation zone of the 1700 tsunami.

Prediction

A guy ought to be careful about making predictions. Particularly about the future.
Yogi Berra, baseball player

Earthquake prediction has the great potential for saving lives and reducing property damage. A good prediction gives the location, time, and magnitude of a future earthquake with acceptable accuracy. Prediction was the hottest area of geophysical and geological research from the 1970s to the early 1990s, based upon the belief that measurable phenomena occurring before large and small earthquakes called **precursors** could be identified. Researchers studied earthquakes and seismograms where presumed precursors were seen. Such things as changes in the ratio of P-wave and S-wave velocities,

Seaside, Oregon, to assess the seismic hazard posed by the Cascadia Subduction Zone. Besides ways to mitigate great loss of life, selected major points of agreement were:

■ Most of the 1100 km of the subduction zone ruptured on January 26, 1700. A correlative tsunami struck Japan and the characteristics of the wave suggest a M_w of 9.0.

■ Cascadia earthquakes generate tsunami, the most recent of which was about 10 meters high based on studies of the inundation zone.

■ Strong ground shaking from a M_w −9.0 earthquake will last three minutes or more and will be damaging as far inland as Vancouver, Portland, and Seattle.

◆ **FIGURE 4.33** Seismic-hazard map of downtown Portland, Oregon. The hazard zones are based upon liquefaction potential, landslide potential, and the probable degree of ground shaking. Red denotes greatest hazard; pale yellow, the lowest hazard. Oregon Dept. of Geology and Mineral Industries

ground tilt, water-well levels, and emission of noble gases in ground water were measured and piles of data were accumulated. Unfortunately, the hope of finding precursors that would lead to reliable predictions seems to have evaporated. In fact, the U.S. Geological Survey is on record as saying that the prospect of earthquake prediction is very dismal. In short, earthquakes cannot be predicted because the mechanics of earthquake generation are, with the present state of our knowledge, too complicated to predict.

Forecasts

We are familiar with weather forecasts and are aware that accuracy declines as the time span of the prediction becomes longer. We can usually rely on one-week forecasts, but a year ahead would be asking too much. The same can be said of

earthquakes, only in reverse. There is an old saying in geology that "the longer it has been since the last earthquake, the sooner we can expect the next one."

A new approach is to evaluate the probability of a large earthquake occurring on an active fault during a given time period. This falls under the heading of long-term forecasting. An example of this is the U.S. Geological Survey and other scientists' conclusion that there is a 70 percent probability of at least one magnitude-6.7 or greater earthquake striking the San Francisco Bay region between 2000 and 2030. Such an event would be capable of causing widespread damage (◆Figure 4.34). Such forecasts are made on the basis of measured plate tectonic motion and slip on faults. The inexorable movement of the Pacific plate past the North American plate loads strain on the San Andreas network. Periodically this strain is released on one of the faults in the system and an earthquake occurs.

Statistical Approach

By compiling statistical evidence pertaining to past earthquakes in a region, we acquire basic data for calculating the statistical probability for future events of given magnitudes. These calculations may be done on a worldwide scale or on a local scale, such as the example in ◆Figure 4.35. Analysis of the graph indicates that for the particular area in Southern California, the statistical **recurrence interval**—that is, the length of time that can be expected between events of a given magnitude—is 1,000 years for a magnitude-8 earthquake (0.1/100 years), about 100 years for a magnitude-7 earthquake (1/100 years), and about 10 years for a magnitude-6 earthquake (almost 10/100 years). The probability of a magnitude-7 occurring in any one year is thus 1 percent, and of a magnitude-6, 10 percent. On an annual basis worldwide, we can expect at least two magnitude-8 earthquakes, 20 magnitude-7 earthquakes, and no less than 100 earthquakes of magnitude 6. Thus for seismically active regions, historical seismicity data can be used to calculate the *probability* of damaging earthquakes. Although these numbers are not really of predictive value as we defined it, they can be used by planners for making zoning recommendations, by architects and engineers for designing earthquake-resistant structures, and by others for formulating other life- and property-saving measures.

CONSIDER THIS

Humans have caused earthquakes by injecting fluids, such as oil-field waters and chemical warfare wastes, into deep wells. How does this open the possibility of controlling earthquake activity, and what might be a major deterrent to the effort?

Geological Methods

Research suggests that active faults and segments of long, active faults tend to have recurring earthquakes of characteristic magnitude, rupture length, and displacement. For

◆ **FIGURE 4.34** Probabilities that one or more magnitude-6.7 or greater earthquakes will strike on specific faults in the San Francisco Bay region between 2000 and 2030. The San Andreas, Rogers Creek, and Hayward faults have the highest probabilities. Total probability for the region is computed as 70% (± 10%). These probabilities were developed by scientists with the U.S. Geological Survey, part of the U.S. Department of the Interior, and thus constitute official long-term *forecasts*. The message is that all communities in the Bay region should keep preparing for earthquakes.

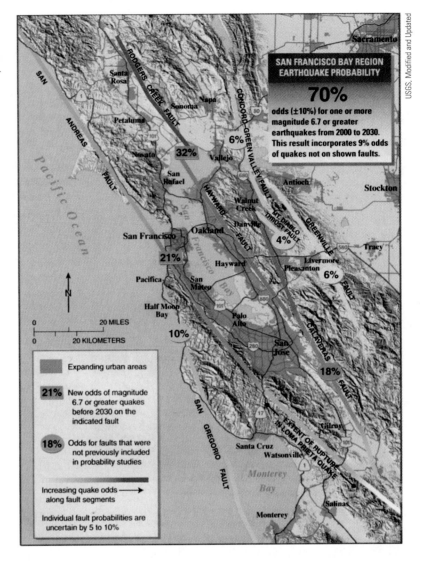

example, six earthquakes have occurred along the San Andreas fault at Parkfield since 1857 (◆Figure 4.36). They had Richter magnitudes of around 5.6, rupture lengths of 13–19 kilometers (8–12 mi), and displacements averaging 0.5 meter. These earthquakes have recurred about every 22 years since the earliest recorded earthquake. A 95 percent probability of an earthquake was predicted for this segment between 1988 and 1993, the first prediction in the United States to be endorsed by scientists and subsequently issued by the federal government. The prediction was a failure.

Geophysical and seismological precursors, as noted previously, have not proved to be reliable predictors of earthquakes. Seismic gaps, however, can indicate stretches of future fault activity. Seismic gaps are stretches along known active fault zones within which no significant earthquakes have been recorded. It is not always clear whether these fault sections are "locked" and thus building up strain energy, or if motion (creep) is taking place there that is relieving strain. Such gaps existed and were "filled" so to speak during the Mexico City

(1985), Loma Prieta (1989; Figure 4.36), and Izmit (1999) earthquakes. Seismic gaps serve as alerts or warnings of possible future events and can be used as forecasting tools.

Since recorded history in North America is short, geologists need other means of collecting frequency data of large prehistoric earthquakes. One method is to dig trenches into marsh or river sediments that have been disrupted by faulting in an effort to decipher a region's **paleoseismicity,** its rock record of past earthquake events. Kerry Sieh of the California Institute of Technology has done this across the San Andreas in Southern California (◆Figure 4.37). Sieh found an intriguing history of seismicity recorded in disrupted marsh deposits at Pallett Creek and liquefaction effects extending from the seventh century to a great earthquake in 1857. Ten large events, extending from A.D. 650 to 1857, were dated using [14]C. The average recurrence interval for these ancient earthquakes is 132 years, but they are clustered in four groups. Within each cluster, the recurrence interval is less than 100 years, and the intervals between the clusters are two to three centuries in length.

◆ **FIGURE 4.35** A graphing of 463 earthquakes of magnitude 4 or greater in a small area near a nuclear reactor in Southern California over a period of 44 years. Statistically, the graph shows that 600 magnitude-4 earthquakes can be expected in 100 years, or 6 per year on average. The probability of a magnitude-8 earthquake in 100 years is 0.1, which would be 1 in 1,000 years. Such plots can be constructed for a region or for the world. The graphs are all similar in shape; only the numbers differ.

The last big one, also the last one of a cluster, was in 1857. Thus it appears that this section of the San Andreas may remain dormant until late in the twenty-first century or beyond.

Earlier in this chapter we quoted a geologist saying about earthquake prediction that "the longer it's been since the last earthquake, the sooner we expect the next one." Unfortunately, this is about the status of our present predictive ability. We remain uncertain that a quake will follow well-defined precursory phenomena, such as wave velocity changes or anomalous animal behavior (see ■ Case Study 4.4 on page 106). It seems that no one phenomenon is a predictor, and many changes will have to be monitored over a long period of time before our knowledge of fault behavior is refined enough for reliable prediction.

ThomsonNOW™

Click **Geology Interactive** to work through an activity on Seismic Risk USA through Earthquakes and Tsunamis.

Mitigation

Reducing earthquake risks is an admirable goal of scientists and lawmakers. Building codes provide the first line of defense against earthquake damage and help ensure the public safety. It has been shown that strict building codes in seismic regions, such as the Pacific Rim, reduce damage and loss of life. Laws passed after the 1933 (Long Beach) and 1971 (Sylmar) California earthquakes have proven the effectiveness of strict earthquake-resistant design. A good example is the magnitude-6.2 Morgan Hill (California) earthquake that

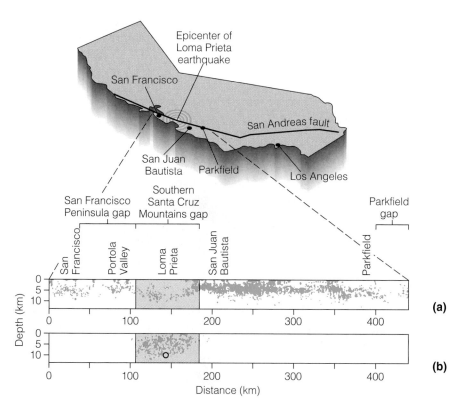

◆ **FIGURE 4.36** (a) Historic seismic activity of about 450 kilometers (275 mi) of the San Andreas fault south of San Francisco before the 1989 Loma Prieta earthquake. The southern Santa Cruz Mountains seismic gap, where Loma Prieta is located, is highlighted. Other seismic gaps apparent in this historical record at the time were one between San Francisco and the Portola Valley and one southeast of Parkfield. (b) Seismicity record of the Southern Santa Cruz Mountains portion of the fault after the 1989 earthquake. The former seismic gap had been "filled" by the earthquake (*open circle*) and its aftershocks.

Kerry E. Sieh, Seismological Laboratory, California Institute of Technology

◆ **FIGURE 4.37** Disrupted marsh and lake deposits along the San Andreas fault at Pallett Creek near Palmdale, California. Sediments range in age from about A.D. 200 at the lower left to A.D. 1910 at the ground surface. Several large earthquakes are represented here by broken layers and buried fault scarps.

shook West Valley College 20 miles from the epicenter. Seismic instruments on the gymnasium showed that the roof was so flexible that in a strong seismic event it could collapse (◆Figure 4.38). Flexible roofs were permitted by the code at that time and many gyms and industrial buildings were built that way. As a result of the experience at West Valley College the Uniform Building Code was revised—this is the code used by hundreds if not thousands of municipalities across the country. The revision requires that the roofs be constructed to be less flexible and thus able to withstand nearby or strong distant earthquakes. Most large cities in strong earthquake zones have their own building codes, patterned after the Uniform Building Code, that require construction to modern seismic standards. For instance, ground response due to differing soil types is now more appreciated as contributing to quake damage. ◆Figure 4.39 shows how the code has evolved from 1955 as we obtained more information. For example, soft clays react more violently with earthquake waves than do, say, granites, and this difference in response is now taken into consideration.

The primary consideration in earthquake design is to incorporate resistance to horizontal ground acceleration, or "base shear." Strong horizontal motion tends to topple poorly built structures and to deform more flexible ones. In California, high-rise structures are built to withstand about 40 percent of the acceleration of gravity in the horizontal direction (0.4 g), and single-family dwellings are built to withstand about 15 percent (0.15 g). *Base isolation* is now a popular design option. The structure, low- or high-rise, is placed upon Teflon plates, rubber blocks, seismic-energy dissipators that are similar to auto shock absorbers, or even springs, which allows the ground to move but minimizes building vibration and sway.

The ultimate earthquake resistance for large buildings is provided by "base isolation." The century-old Salt Lake City and County Building (◆Figure 4.40), scheduled at the time

◆ **FIGURE 4.38** Seismic records (upper right) obtained during the 1984 Morgan Hill, California, earthquake led to an improvement in the Uniform Building Code (a set of standards used in many states). The center of the gym roof shook sideways three to four times as much as the edges. The code has since been revised to reduce the flexibility of such large-span roof systems and thereby improve their seismic resistance. USGS

West Valley College
Gymnasium
in Saratoga, California

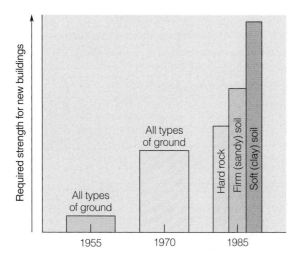

◆ **FIGURE 4.39** Earthquake requirements in building codes have increased over time as scientists and engineers have obtained new information. Note that recent codes specify separate criteria for different ground types. USGS data

◆ **FIGURE 4.40** Salt Lake City and County Building, Utah. Constructed in 1890, largely of brick, it is now seismically retrofitted to meet the modern building code.

for demolition, was cut from its foundation and retrofitted with 440 rubber base isolators. These permit the structure to move as a single unit during an earthquake while the ground shakes in all directions (◆Figure 4.41). About seventy-five percent of Utah's population live near the Wasatch Range and the fault responsible for the uplift. The retrofit of older public buildings is an example of the awareness of earthquake hazards by government officials and the public. In this case it saved an architectural treasure for future generations.

Survival Tips

Knowing what to do before, during, and after an earthquake is of utmost importance to you and your family.

Before an Earthquake:

◆ Figure 4.42 provides the Federal Emergency Management Agency's (FEMA) suggestions for minimizing the possibility of damage, fire, and injuries in the home.

During an Earthquake:

- Remain calm and consider the consequences of your actions.
- If you are indoors, stay indoors and get under a desk, bed, or a strong doorway.

◆ **FIGURE 4.41** Basement of the Salt Lake City and County Building. The building has been seismically retrofitted by cutting the massive structure from its foundation pillars (one shown on the far left, another in the center of the photograph), and lifting the building onto 440 large rubber isolators (one left of center, another at the extreme right of the photograph).

- If you are outside, stay away from buildings, walls, power poles, and other objects that could fall. If driving, stop your car in an open area.
- Do not use elevators, and if you are in a crowded area, do not rush for a door.

After an Earthquake:

- Turn off the gas at the meter.

- Use portable radios for information.
- Check water supplies, remembering that there is water in water heaters, melted ice, and toilet tanks. Do not drink waterbed or pool water.
- Check your home for damage.
- Do not drive.

1　Nail plywood to ceiling joists to protect occupants from falling chimney bricks.

2　Anchor hanging lamps with closed hooks or relocate.

3　Secure top-heavy furniture to wall studs with metal braces.

4　Keep all breakables in low or secure cabinets.

5　Know the locations of main electrical and gas switches for emergency shutoff.

6　Stabilize water heater with metal straps to wall studs.

7　Use flexible connectors where gas lines meet appliances, if local codes permit.

8　Keep fire extinguisher in accessible place.

9　Keep emergency supplies on hand, including drinking water, canned or dried foods, first-aid kit, flashlight, and portable radio with extra batteries.

10　Place secure latches on cupboards to prevent doors from swinging open.

11　Keep heavy, unstable objects away from exit routes, and anchor wheels.

12　Replace heavy hangings over beds with lightweight alternatives.

(a)

Shut-off valve positions

On　　Off

(b)

◆ **FIGURE 4.42** (a) How to minimize earthquake damage in the home in advance. (b) Keep a small crescent wrench at the gas meter. Turn off the gas by turning the valve end 90°. FEMA

CASE STUDY 4.1

Earthquakes, Landslides, and Disease

Dynamically induced landslides are not particularly newsworthy, even though the 1994 Northridge earthquake caused 17,000 of them. However, the soil dislodged during sliding caused an outbreak of *coccidioidomycosis* (CM), commonly known as "valley fever." Endemic to the Southwest, the disease causes persistent flu-like symptoms and in extreme cases can be fatal. The victims breathe in airborne *Coccidioides immitis* spores that are released from the soil during sliding. From January 24 to March 15, 166

people were diagnosed with valley fever symptoms in Ventura County, up from only 53 cases in all of 1993. Most of the cases were reported from the Simi Valley, an area in which only 14 percent of the county's population resides (◆ Figure 1).

Large clouds of dust hung over the Santa Susana Mountains for several days after the earthquake, promoted by the lack of winter rains preceding the quake. During this period, pressure-gradient winds known locally as "Santa Ana" winds of 10–15 knots (11–17 mph)

blew into the Simi Valley, carrying in spore-laden dust from the Santa Susana Mountains to the northeast. Researchers believe that the more "coherent" metamorphic rocks of the San Gabriel Mountains northeast of the San Fernando Valley probably account for the lack of cases reported in the epicentral region. This is the first report of an earthquake-associated outbreak of valley fever, even though many earthquakes have occurred in CM endemic areas.

◆ FIGURE 1 Histogram of the almost-epidemic outbreak of coccidioidomycosis (valley fever) in Ventura County in early 1994 following the Northridge earthquake.

CASE STUDY 4.2

Predictable "Future Shocks"

A large earthquake is normally followed by thousands of smaller-magnitude earthquakes known as aftershocks (◆ Figure 1). If the main shock is small—say in the magnitude-4.0–5.0 range—aftershocks are small and nonintimidating. Following Northridge-size and bigger earthquakes, however, the strongest aftershocks (*M* = 5.0–6.0 at Northridge) can cause

buildings damaged by the main earthquake to collapse and, even worse, can greatly increase anxiety in the already damaged psyche of the local citizenry. Aftershocks are caused by small adjustments (slips) on the causative fault or on other faults close to the causative one. For example, try this: push the eraser on the end of a lead pencil across

a desktop. You'll find that it does not slide smoothly; it moves in jerky jumps and starts. This is called "stick–slip" and it is what happens along faults that are adjusting after a big earthquake.

Los Angeles experienced 2,500 aftershocks in the week following the Northridge earthquake. Three strong ones, magnitude

CONTINUED

5 or greater, occurred the first day. The largest ($M = 5.6$) occurred eleven hours after the main shock, causing concern among rescuers digging for victims beneath the rubble and the already traumatized citizens. Aftershocks follow statistically predictable patterns, as exemplified by the Northridge sequence. On the first day there were 188 aftershocks of magnitude 3 or greater, and on the second day only 56 were recorded (◆Figure 2). By fitting an equation to the distribution of aftershocks during the first few weeks, seismologists were able to estimate the number of shocks to be expected in the future. Statistically, there was a 25 percent chance of another magnitude-5 or greater aftershock occurring within the following year, but it did not happen.

◆ **FIGURE 1** Seismogram of early aftershocks following the Northridge earthquake, one of them a magnitude-5.6. Southern California Earthquake Center (SCEC)

◆ **FIGURE 2** Daily record of aftershocks of magnitude 3.0 to 5.9 during the three weeks following the main shock at Northridge. Note the sharp drop in aftershock frequency in the first four days. Redrawn from F. Harp and R. Jibson, USGS

CASE STUDY 4.3

Rx for Failed Freeways

Extensive damage to freeway bridges and overpasses typically accompanies earthquakes in large urban areas. Such damage has occurred in Alaska, California, and Japan. Overpass damage commonly is due to failure of the shorter columns, which lack the flexi-bility of longer ones. During an earthquake the tall columns supporting a bridge or overpass system bend and sway with the horizontal forces of the quake. Because the parts of the overpass system are tied together, the stresses are transferred through the structure to the short columns, which are designed to bend only a few centimeters (◆Figure 1). Failure causes the short columns to bulge just above ground level, which breaks and pops off the exterior concrete, exposing the warped, "birdcaged" steel in the interior. In addition,

◆ FIGURE 1 The difference in flexibility of long and short columns results in failure of the short ones.

In a quake, long columns survive because they sway.

Short columns, unable to bend, absorb horizontal energy produced by longer columns and blow out.

high vertical accelerations can cause some columns to actually punch holes through the platform deck. With excessive horizontal motion some deck spans may slip off their column caps at one end and fall to the ground like tipped dominoes.

The California Department of Transportation in 1971 decided to retrofit 122 overpasses to alleviate these problems. One aspect of the retrofitting was jacketing the short columns with steel or a composite substance and filling the space between the jacket and the original column with concrete (◆ Figure 2a). This allows the columns to bend 12.5 centimeters (5 in), instead of 2.5 centimeters (1 in), without shattering. Another solution is to increase columns' horizontal strength by wrapping heavy steel rods around their vertical support bars, particularly on short columns. This allows the columns to bend but prevents "birdcaging" or perma-

nent bending (◆ Figure 2b). To prevent the decks from slipping off their supports and dropping to the ground, steel straps or cables are installed at the joints (◆ Figure 2c). Of the 122 overpasses that CalTrans retrofitted, not one collapsed in the 1994 Northridge earthquake. Ten of the eleven that collapsed were slated for future retrofitting.

Roadway

Jacket

Column

Concrete backfill

Soil

(a)

B. Pipkin

(b)

Straps keep joints from coming apart.

(c)

◆ FIGURE 2 Earthquake-resistant design for bridges and overpasses. (a) Short columns are retrofitted with steel or composite jackets that allow them to bend five times as much. (b) Old method of constructing highway support columns. The vertical steel supports have bent and "birdcaged." (c) Steel straps are used to hold deck sections together, preventing them from falling off their support columns. (a), (c) After *The Los Angeles Times*

Depressed Tigers, Restless Turtles, and Earthquakes!

Anomalous animal behavior preceding earthquakes is well documented. Domesticated animals such as barnyard fowl, horses, cats, and dogs have been known to behave so peculiarly before big events that they attracted the notice of people not knowledgeable in what is normal or abnormal animal behavior (◆Figure 1). Remember that although anomalous animal behavior precedes many earthquakes, it does not appear to precede every earthquake, and abnormal animal behavior is not always followed by an earthquake. Other natural phenomena, such as atmospheric disturbances, also can cause animals to behave strangely. Here are some reported incidents of unusual animal behavior noted before earthquakes:

- Tientsin Zoo, China, 1969: 2 hours before the magnitude-7.4 earthquake the tiger appeared depressed, pandas screamed, turtles were restless, and the yak would not eat.
- Haicheng, China, 1975: 1½ months before the magnitude-7.3 earthquake, snakes came out of hibernation; 1–2 days before, pigs would not eat and they climbed walls; 20 minutes before, turtles jumped out of the water and cried.
- Tokyo, Japan, 1855: 1 day before the magnitude-6.9 earthquake wild cats cried, and rats disappeared.
- Concepción, Chile, 1835: 1 hour and 40 minutes before the earthquake, flocks of sea birds flew inland, and dogs left the city.

- San Francisco, 1906: dogs barked all night before the magnitude-8.3 earthquake.
- Friuli, Italy, 1976: 2–3 hours before the magnitude-6.7 earthquake, cats left their houses and the village, mice and rats left their hiding places, and fowl refused to roost.

B. Pipkin

◆ **FIGURE 1** Anomalous animal behavior. An earthquake may be in the offing if your dog dons a hard hat.

Earthquakes Are Hard on Cars

The sight of cars buried beneath a pile of bricks and rubble after an earthquake seems to be standard fare for the press. We captured a few of these scenes just by coming upon them and hope you feel, as we do, that there is a light side to most bad natural disasters. The other photos were just too unusual or amusing to pass up.

B. Pipkin

◆ **FIGURE 1** This luxury car seems to be pursuing the garage in which it is normally kept. The house and garage slid down the hillside, but the car was parked with its rear wheels on the driveway, which was on stable ground. Nobody was hurt; Northridge, 1994

◆ **FIGURE 2** A row of cars in need of body-and-fender work because their owners were asleep in the apartment building at the time of the earthquake; Northridge, 1994

Frederick Larson, *SAN FRANCISCO CHRONICLE*

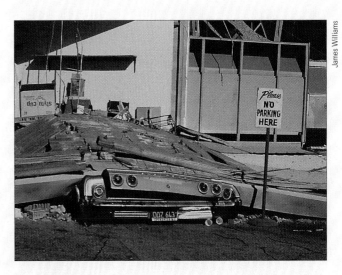

James Williams

◆ **FIGURE 3** Earthquakes have no respect for "No Parking" signs; Boys Market Sylmar, California, 1971

◆ **FIGURE 4** One hundred yard . . . dash? The September 21, 1999 earthquake (M_w = 7.8) in Taiwan was caused by movement on the Chelungpu fault. This running track at Kuang Fu High School was built across the fault that here had a vertical offset of 2.5 meters (8.1 ft). It is obvious that no 100-meter-dash records will be broken here.

Yi-Ben Tsai, National Central Univ., Taiwan

◆ **FIGURE 5** The Hector Mine earthquake of October 16, 1999 was a real bomb! The magnitude-7.0 event occurred in California's remote Mojave Desert. The fault scarp, shown here, forms a gash across the desert for 40 kilometers (25 mi), but the earthquake did little damage. This area happens to be a U.S. Marine Corps bombing range, as you can see, which made geologists' field work interesting.

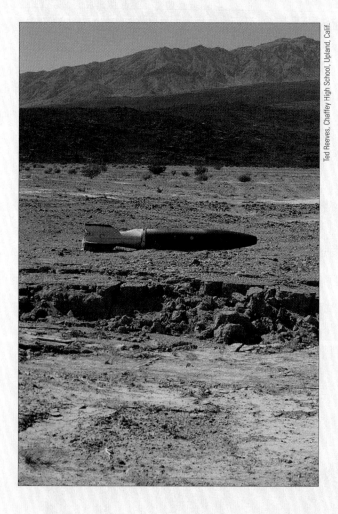

Ted Reeves, Chaffey High High School, Upland, Calif.

Summary

Earthquakes

Cause

Movements on fractures in the crust known as *faults* that result in three types of wave motion: P- and S-waves, which are generated at the focus of the earthquake and travel through the Earth, and surface waves.

Distribution

Most (but not all) large earthquakes occur near plate boundaries, such as the San Andreas fault, and represent the release of stored elastic strain energy as plates slip past, over, or under each other. Intraplate earthquakes can occur at locations far from plate boundaries where deep crust has been faulted, probably at "failed" continental margins.

Measurement Scales

Some of the scales used to measure earthquakes are the modified Mercalli intensity scale (based on damage), the Richter magnitude scale (based on energy released as measured by maximum wave amplitude on a seismograph), and the moment magnitude (based on the total seismic energy released as measured by the rigidity of the faulted rock, the area of rupture on the fault plane, and displacement).

Earthquake-Related Hazards and Mitigation

Ground Shaking

Damaging motion caused by shear and surface waves.

Ways to reduce effects—seismic zoning; building codes; construction techniques such as shear walls, seismic joints, and bolting frames to foundations.

Landslides

Hundreds of landslides may be triggered by an earthquake in a slide-prone area.

Ways to reduce effects—proper zoning in high-risk areas.

Ground Failure (Spontaneous Liquefaction)

Horizontal (lateral) movements caused by loss of strength of water-saturated sandy soils during shaking and by liquefaction of quick clays.

Ways to reduce effects—building codes that require deep-drilling to locate liquefiable soils or layers.

Ground Rupture/Changes in Ground Level

Fault rupture and uplift or subsidence of land as a result of fault displacement.

Ways to reduce effects—geologic mapping to locate fault zones, trenching across fault zones, implementation of effective seismic zonation like the Earthquake Fault Zones Act in California.

Fire

In some large earthquakes fire has been the biggest source of damage.

Ways to reduce effects—public education on what to do after a quake, such as shutting off gas and other utilities.

Tsunamis

Multidirectional sea waves generated by disruption of the underlying sea floor (see Chapter 10).

Earthquake Prediction

It is not feasible at this time to predict within useful limits the time, magnitude, and location of an earthquake. However, seismologists continue to search for clues to accurate prediction, which is what scientists do and what, we might add, science is.

Upside/downside—no proven large earthquakes predicted. Inaccuracies in short-term prediction have made the public wary.

Earthquake Forecasts

Based on plate movement and known fault movement there is a 70 percent chance there will be a magnitude-6.7 earthquake in the San Francisco Bay area between 2000 and 2030. This kind of forecast is the research thrust today and forecasts will vary for each seismic region.

Upside/downside—good for planning purposes but not for short-term warnings.

Statistical Methods

Tell us that worldwide there will be two $M = 8.0+$ and at least 20 $M = 7.0+$ earthquakes each year. Statistics can be applied for a smaller area in earthquake country.

Upside/downside—good for planning purposes but not for short-term warnings.

Geological Methods

Active faults are studied to determine the characteristic earthquake magnitudes and recurrence intervals of particular fault segments; sediments exposed in trenches may disclose historic large fault displacements (earthquakes) and, if they contain datable C-14 material, their recurrence intervals.

Upside/downside—useful for long-range forecasting along fault segments and for identifying seismic gaps; not useful for short-term warnings.

Key Terms

base isolation	epicenter	focus (pl. *foci*)	isoseismal
body wave	fault	forecasts	liquefaction
elastic rebound theory	fault creep	intensity scale	longitudinal wave

magnitude	P-wave	seismograph	transverse (shear) wave
modified Mercalli scale (*MM*)	recurrence interval	spontaneous liquefaction	tsunami (pl. *tsunamis*)
moment magnitude (M_w or M)	resonance	strain	wave period (*T*)
paleoseismicity	Richter magnitude scale	stress	
precursor	seismogram	S-wave	

Study Questions

1. What is "elastic rebound," and how does it relate to earth-quake motion?

2. Distinguish among earthquake intensity, Richter magnitude, and moment magnitude. Which magnitude scale is most favored by seismologists today? Why?

3. Why should one be more concerned about the likelihood of an earthquake in Alaska than of one in Texas?

4. In light of plate tectonic theory, explain why devastating shallow-focus earthquakes occur in some areas and only moderate shallow-focus activity takes place in other areas.

5. What should people who live in earthquake country do before, during, and after an earthquake (the minimum)?

6. Describe the motion of the three types of earthquake waves discussed in the chapter and their effects on structures.

7. Why do wood-frame structures suffer less damage than unreinforced brick buildings in an earthquake?

For Further Information

Books and Periodicals

Atwater, Bryan, and others. 1999. *Surviving a tsunami: Lessons from Chile, Hawaii, and Japan.* U.S. Geological Survey circular 1187, 19 pp.

Bolt, Bruce. 1998. *Earthquakes, newly revised and expanded.* New York: W. H. Freeman.

Brocher, Thomas M., 2000, Urban seismic experiments investigate Seattle fault and basis, *EOS, Transactions of the American Geophysical Union,* vol. 81, no. 46, November 14.

Celebi, M., P. Spudich, Robert Page, and Peter Stauffer. 1995. *Saving lives through better design standards.* U.S. fact sheet 176–95.*

Drake, D. 1815. *Natural and statistical view, or picture of Cincinnati and the Miami County, illustrated by maps.* Cincinnati, Ohio: Looker and Wallace.

Ellis, Michael, Joan Gomberg, and E. Schweig. 2001. Indian earthquake may serve as an analog for New Madrid earthquakes, *EOS, Transactions of the American Geophysical Union,* vol. 82, no. 32, August 7.

Field, Edward H. 2000. Accounting for site effects in probabilistic seismic hazard analysis of Southern California. *Bulletin of the Seismological Society of America,* vol. 90, no. 6b, December.

Gomberg, Joan, and Eugene Schweig. 2002. *East meets Midwest: An earthquake in India helps hazard assessment in the central United States.* U.S. Geological Survey fact sheet 007-02.

González, Frank I. 1999. Tsunami. *Scientific American,* May: 56–65.

Gore, Rick. 1995. Living with California's faults. *National geographic,* April:2–34.

Hickman, Steve, and John Langbein. 2000. *The Parkfield experiment—Capturing what happens in an earthquake,* U.S. Geological Survey fact sheet 049-02.

Iacopi, Robert. 1971. *Earthquake country.* Menlo Park, Calif.: Lane Books.

Knopoff, L. 1996. Earthquake prediction: The scientific challenge. In *Earthquake prediction: Proceedings of the National Academy of Sciences,* pp. 3719–3720.

Kockelman, William J. 1984. *Reducing losses from earthquakes through personal preparedness.* U.S. Geological Survey open file report 84-765.

Koper, Keith D., and others. 2001. Forensic seismology and the sinking of the *Kursk, EOS,* Transactions of the American Geophysical Union, vol. 82, no. 4, January 23.

Kovachs, Robert. 1995. Earth's fury: An introduction to natural hazards and disasters. Englewood Cliffs, N.J.: Prentice-Hall.

Michael, Andrew J., and others. 1995. *Major quake likely to strike between 2000 and 2030.* U.S. Geological Survey fact sheet 151–99.

Mori, James J. 1994. Overview: The Northridge earthquake: Damage to an urban environment. *Earthquakes and volcanoes* 25, no. 1 (special issue).

Renwald, Marie, Tammy Baldwin, and Terry C. Wallace. 2003. Seismic analysis of the space shuttle *Columbia* disaster (abstract). Geodaze Geoscience Symposium, University of Arizona, Tucson, p. 75.

Richter, C. 1958. *Elementary seismology.* New York: W. H. Freeman.

Wuethrich, Bernice. 1995. Cascadia countdown. *Earth: The science of our planet,* October: 24–31.

Yeats, Robert S. 1998. *Living with earthquakes in the Pacific Northwest.* Corvallis, Oreg.: Oregon State University Press.

*Fact sheets are one- or two-page condensations of a geological problem and are free of charge. Some are found on the Web at http://quake.usgs.gov. Hard copies may be obtained from the U.S. Geological Survey, Mail Stop 977, 345 Middlefield Road, Menlo Park, CA 94025.

ThomsonNOW

Assess your understanding of this chapter's topics with additional comprehensive interactivities at http://www.thomson.com/login, which also has up-to-date web links, additional readings, and exercises.

Volcanoes

"Ashes, Ashes, All Fall Down"

One night in 1982 a British Airways Boeing 747 on a routine flight from Kuala Lumpur, Malaysia, to Australia cruised at an altitude of 12,000 meters (37,000 ft). Just before midnight, sleeping passengers were awakened by a pungent odor. Through the windows, they saw the huge plane's wings lit by an eerie blue glow. Suddenly engine number 4 flamed out, followed almost immediately by the other three. The plane glided silently for an agonizing 13 minutes. At 4,500 meters (14,500 ft), engine number 4 was restarted, then numbers 2, 1, and 3. Nonetheless, an emergency was declared, and the plane landed in Jakarta, Indonesia, with only three engines operating.

This near-death experience gained the attention of the world's airline passengers and pilots. Before this, such a failure seemed virtually impossible in modern aircraft, which have backup systems for almost every contingency. Flying air-gulping jet engines through clouds of volcanic ash, however, is not one of them.

In December 1989, a KLM Boeing 747 encountered airborne ash from Redoubt Volcano at about 8,500 meters (28,000 ft) during a descent to land at Anchorage, Alaska (◆ Figure 1). All four engines flamed out, and the large aircraft suddenly became a glider. After a 4,100-meter fall (13,300 ft, more than 2 mi), the engines were restarted, and the plane went on to make what was described as an "uneventful" landing. All four engines required replacement, as did the windshield and the leading edges of the wings, flaps, and vertical stabilizer, which had all been "sandblasted." One may wonder what it takes to make a landing "eventful." The plane's interior was filled with ash, and the seats and avionic equipment had to be removed and cleaned. It cost $80 million to return the aircraft to service.

Joyce M. Warren and USGS

◆ FIGURE 1

(a)

(b)

◆ **FIGURE 2** More than 10,000 passengers and millions of dollars in cargo are flown daily on these North Pacific and Far East air routes. (a) The routings (red lines) pass over or near more than 100 active volcanoes (red triangles) on this subduction-zone complex. (b) Air traffic to the Far East and Asia was disrupted in September 1994 when Mount Kliuchevskoi (4,750 m, 15,580 ft) on the Kamchatka Peninsula erupted, spewing ash into high-altitude airlanes. This photo was taken by astronauts on board the Endeavor.

Ash clouds are difficult to distinguish from rain clouds, both visually and with radar. The ash cloud from Mount Pinatubo's 1991 eruption traveled westward more than 5,000 miles in three days from the Philippines to the east coast of Africa. Twenty aircraft were damaged by the cloud, most of them while flying more than 1,000 kilometers (600 mi) from the eruption.

North Pacific air routes are some of the busiest in the world. Since 1980, flying through ash clouds on those routes has caused damage to at least 15 aircraft (including the KLM flight), and worldwide there have been more than 100 inadvertent ash-cloud entries. The Alaskan Peninsula and the Aleutian Islands have 40 historically active volcanoes, and the Kamchatka Peninsula has even more (◆ Figure 2). In 1992 Mount Spurr Volcano on the Alaskan Peninsula disrupted air traffic several times in the United States and Canada (◆ Figure 3).

Historically, there are an average of 5 eruptions per year along the 2,400-nautical-mile great circle from Alaska to northern Japan. On average, volcanic ash is present 4 days

(a)

(b)

◆ **FIGURE 3** Mount Spurr Volcano, a potential hazard to aviation. (a) Scientists from the Alaskan Volcano Observatory and the University of Alaska install seismometers at Mount Spurr to detect magma activity below the volcano. (b) The ash cloud from Mount Spurr's 1992 eruption traveled across Canada and the United States on prevailing westerly winds.

each year above 9,300 meters (30,000 ft), where passenger jets fly. A massive effort in place to accurately forecast eruptions—the best way to address this potential hazard—involves the Alaskan Volcano Observatory (AVO), the U.S. Geological Survey (U.S.G.S.), University of Alaska, Federal Aviation Administration (FAA), National Oceanic and Atmospheric Administration (NOAA) Weather Service, Michigan Technological University, and the Russian Institute

of Volcanic Geology and Geochemistry in Petropavlovsk-Kamchatskii. Forecasting data are collected by monitoring seismic activity in the volcanic arc, reviewing satellite imagery to detect ash plumes, and making overflights of the 40 active volcanoes to measure gas emissions, which precede many eruptions—all to help make "flying the friendly skies" of the North Pacific and Far East safe for the traveler. (For more information see http://www.avo.alaska.edu/)

Although people commonly regard volcanoes and volcanic activity as environmentally harmful and life-threatening, volcanoes are not all bad. Many of them, such as Japan's Mount Fujiyama, are esthetically beautiful, some offer outstanding skiing and hiking opportunities, as do Oregon's Mount Hood and California's Mammoth Mountain; and volcanic soils, such as those on the Island of Hawaii, are highly productive. The eruption of Italy's Mount Vesuvius in A.D. 79 illustrated why volcanoes present a problem to humans (■ Case Study 5.1, page 135). An active volcano may be dormant for hundreds or even thousands of years, and human settlement may occur nearer and nearer to the volcanic cone during that time. Like a hibernating bear, the sleeping giant may suddenly awaken and vent an explosive eruption that wreaks havoc upon the surroundings, as did Mount St. Helens in 1980. Today, however, we can forecast an eruption with a good deal of accuracy, as explained later in the chapter. Knowing that a potential volcanic hazard exists allows policy makers and emergency managers to plan for various eruption and evacuation scenarios, thus reducing casualties when an eruption does occur.

Who Should Worry

Most geologic activity that is dangerous to humans occurs along plate boundaries. This is where we find earthquakes and active volcanoes. Explosive volcanic activity, which presents the greatest challenge to life and property, occurs mostly at convergent plate boundaries. Inspection of the Pacific Ocean basin shows that it is surrounded by trenches, which form at convergent plate boundaries. Associated with these subduction zones is the so-called Ring of Fire, the location of two thirds of the world's active violent volcanoes. A recent catalog of the 1,350 volcanoes that have erupted within the last 10,000 years (*Holocene time* to the geologist) shows 900 of them around the Pacific Rim. The largest number are found in New Zealand, Japan, Alaska, Mexico, Central America, and Chile (◆ Figure 5.1). Mount Erebus in Antarctica is the southernmost active volcano in

this belt. Some of the most famous active volcanoes are found in the Mediterranean, including Vesuvius, Etna, and Stromboli. Stromboli has been called the "lighthouse of the Mediterranean" because of the nearly continuous activity in its crater since the time of Greek colonization more than 2,000 years ago.

The most frequently active volcanoes tend to produce mild eruptions of fluid lava and occur along divergent plate boundaries at mid-ocean ridges. Hot-spot volcanism may be explosive or mild and may occur on continents or in ocean basins (see also Chapter 3).

There are twice as many dry land volcanoes north of the equator as there are south of it. This is particularly interesting to meteorologists, because large amounts of volcanic ash in the stratosphere result in a net heat loss for Earth, which affects climate. Any concentration of active volcanoes at a particular latitude must be considered as a potential agent of change in global climate. Although most climatic variability is related to causes other than volcanism, historical examples of volcanic eruptions affecting weather are those of Tambora (Indonesia, 1815), El Chichón (Mexico, 1982), and most recently, Mount Pinatubo (the Philippines, 1991). Because two thirds of the world's active volcanoes and land area are north of the equator, the Northern Hemisphere is more vulnerable to climatic impact by volcanic eruptions than is the southern half of the world.

Mapping of the potential volcanic risk in the United States, such as ◆ Figure 5.2, reveals that there is virtually no threat of volcanic outbursts east of New Mexico. This is understandable in light of plate tectonics. The odd-shaped projections from the high-risk area on the map are due to the estimated transport of ash on the prevailing winds. The northeast–southwest trending high-risk zone through Idaho and into the corner of Wyoming is the trace of the southwestward drift of North America over a stationary mantle hot spot. A zone of volcanic vents, ash deposits, and lava flows mark the drift path, with Yellowstone being the currently active center over the hot-spot plume.

The Cascadia subduction zone is responsible for the many potentially or recently active volcanoes in Washington (6),

Spreading ridges   Convergent plate margins   Volcanoes

◆ **FIGURE 5.1** Distribution of Earth's active volcanoes at plate boundaries and hot spots. Note the prominent "Ring of Fire" around the Pacific Ocean, which contains 900 (66 percent) of the world's potentially active volcanoes. The remaining 450 are in the Mediterranean belt (subduction zones) and at mid-ocean-ridge spreading centers (divergent boundaries). A few important volcanic centers are related to hot spots, such as those in the Hawaiian and Galápagos Islands. After R. I. Tilling, C. Heliker, and T. L. Wright, *Eruptions of Hawaiian Volcanoes: Past, Present, and Future* (USGS, 1987)

◆ **FIGURE 5.2** Map of potential volcanic hazards in the 48 contiguous states. The red areas are subject to lava flows, lateral blasts, ash falls, and mudflows. The severity of risk decreases from red (greatest), to green, to blue (least). After Hays, USGS prof. paper 1240-B, 1981

◆ **FIGURE 5.3** Active volcanoes and volcano clusters in the continental United States. The volcanoes of the Cascades are geologically related to the Cascadia subduction zone.

- Volcanoes that have short-term eruption periodicities (100–200 years or less) or that have erupted in the past 200–300 years, or both.

- Volcanoes that appear to have eruption periodicities of 1,000 years or greater and that last erupted 1,000 years or more ago.

- Volcanic centers that are greater than 10,000 years old, but beneath which exist large, shallow bodies of magma that are capable of producing exceedingly destructive eruptions. The Snake River plain is the track of the Yellowstone hot spot.

Oregon (21), and California (16; see ◆ Figure 5.3). The zone of active volcanoes extends 1,100 kilometers (700 mi) from Mount Lassen in California northward into British Columbia. Alaska ranks as the second-most active volcanic region in the world, and Hawaii is not far behind. Thus the study of volcanoes is important to citizens of the United States.

ThomsonNOW
Click **Geology Interactive** to work through activities on Distribution of Volcanism, Volcano Watch, and Seismic Case Study, Alaska, 1964, USA through Volcanism.

The Nature of the Problem

How a volcano erupts determines its impact on humankind. A cataclysmic eruption, such as that of Mount St. Helens in 1980, has serious results. Simple outpourings of lava such as at

Kilauea in Hawaii, on the other hand, can be good for tourism and business. Unfortunately, there is no scale for describing the "bigness" of volcanic eruptions as there is for earthquakes. ◆ Figure 5.4 shows some of the criteria commonly used to describe an eruption's "explosivity." **Volcanic Explosivity Index (VEI)** values range from 0 to 8 according to the volume of material ejected, the height to which the material rises, and the duration of the eruption. Its "Classification" scale associates the particular eruption with a well-known volcano that exhibited the same kind of activity. The "Description" scale employs adjectives such as those used in newspaper headlines to describe the eruption. The 1980 eruption of Mount St. Helens, for example, could be indexed as a *4* and appropriately described as an *explosive-to-cataclysmic* eruption.

In many (though not all cases) a volcano's potential explosivity has been found to increase with time since the start of its previous eruption (◆Figure 5.5). This fact allows a region's risk of volcanic eruptions to be assessed when the

◆ **FIGURE 5.4** Graphic representation of the Volcanic Explosivity Index (VEI). As an example, a VEI 5 would be a very large eruption, described as *cataclysmic, Vulcanian* in its type of eruption, and have an ash plume up to 25 kilometers (15 mi) high. There have been 19 historic VEI-5 eruptions. After T. Simpkin and L. Siebert, *Volcanoes of the World,* 2nd ed. (Tucson, Ariz.: Geoscience Press, 1994)

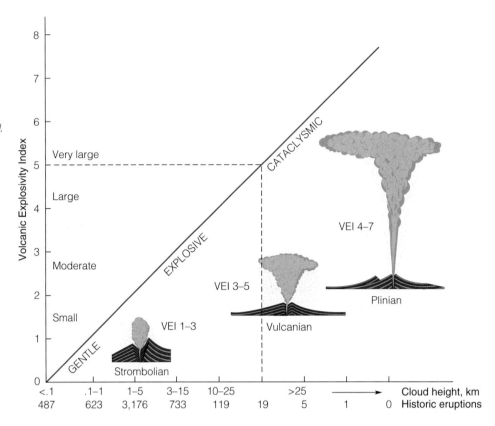

◆ **FIGURE 5.5** The longer the time interval since an eruption, the greater is the next eruption's potential explosivity. These data for 4,320 historic eruptions relate known intervals between eruptions to the Volcanic Explosivity Index (Figure 5.4). Also shown is the percentage of eruptions in each VEI that have caused fatalities. Data from T. Simpkin and others, *Volcanoes of the World* (Dowden, Hutchinson, and Ross)

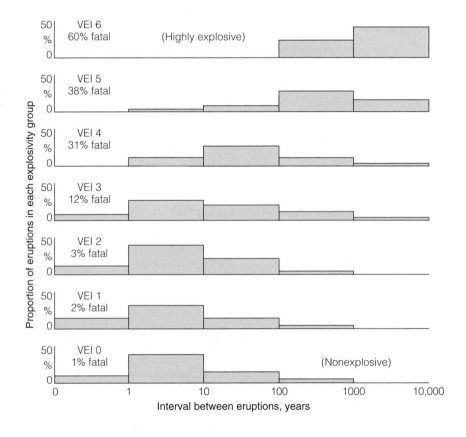

date of the volcano's last eruption is known. Some cataclysmic eruptions, such as the one that took place at Yellowstone hot spot 600,000 years ago, are considered a minor threat because of their rarity. Thus, both magnitude and frequency must be considered in evaluating volcanic hazards.

A magma's *viscosity*—its resistance to flow—is another determinant of a volcano's explosivity, and viscosity is a function of lava's temperature and composition. Viscosity varies inversely with temperature for most fluids, including magma: the higher the temperature, the less viscous; the lower the temperature, the more viscous, other factors being equal. A magma's composition, most importantly its silica (SiO_2) content, also influences its viscosity. The silicon-oxygen bond is very strong; considerable heat energy is required to break it. The fluidity of siliceous (high-silica) magmas depends on the continual breaking and remaking of this bond. Thus, the higher the SiO_2 content, the more viscous is the lava—again, other factors being equal.

Viscous magmas with a high gas content can build up such high gas pressures as to be explosive, whereas gases escape readily from fluid lavas and hence are much less dangerous. This fact gives us another method of categorizing large volcanoes and their activity: the nature of the magmas they tap. Magmas form at depths of 10 to 250 kilometers (6–150 mi), where temperatures are sufficiently high to melt rocks completely or partially. At mid-ocean ridges and hot spots, volcanoes draw from magmas in the upper mantle that contain abundant iron and magnesium and a relatively low amount of silica (50 percent or less). These are **mafic** magmas (*ma-* for magnesium and *-f-* for the Latin word for iron, *ferrum,* plus *-ic*), which yield fluid (low-viscosity) lavas that retain little gas and hence do not erupt violently. Volcanoes that are adjacent to subduction zones, on the other hand, tap magmas that derive from oceanic crust and sediment, upper-mantle material, and melted continental rocks. These are **felsic** magmas (*fel-* for feldspar and *-s-* for silica, plus *-ic*), which yield thick, pasty lavas with SiO_2 contents up to 70 percent. Even though hot lavas have lower viscosities and flow more readily than do cool ones, just as with honey and various other common fluids, the major determinant of magma fluidity is silica content.

High-silica, high-viscosity magmas retain gases, which leads to violent, explosive-type eruptions. The geologically important boundary between mild oceanic eruptions and the more explosive continental ones of the Pacific basin is called the **andesite line** (after the intermediate rock andesite from the Andes Mountains). The line is generally drawn southward from Alaska to east of New Zealand by way of Japan, and along the west coasts of North and South America. The andesite line is also a petrologic boundary between mostly mafic magmas, which yield basalt, and felsic magmas, which yield andesite or some other high-silica rock like rhyolite. Thus, explosive volcanoes are always found on the continental side of the andesite line, and gentle volcanoes are found within the Pacific Ocean basin.

Types of Eruptions and Volcanic Cones

The type of volcanic eruption determines the shape of the structure or cone that is built, and by appearance alone, one can get an idea of a volcano's hazard potential (◆Figure 5.6).

Effusive Eruptions
Shield Volcanoes
Shield volcanoes are built by gentle outpourings of low-silica fluid lavas from a central vent or conduit. The lavas cool to form basalt, the most common volcanic rock. A shield volcano's profile is gently convex upward like that of a shield laid on the ground. Mostly oceanic in origin, shield volcanoes are found in Iceland (where the *shield* name was first applied), the Galápagos Islands, and the Hawaiian Islands (◆Figure 5.7). They are built up from the sea floor, layer upon layer, to elevations thousands of meters above sea level. Mauna Loa ("long mountain") and Mauna Kea ("white mountain") volcanoes on the Island of Hawaii are shield volcanoes that project 4.5 kilometers (2.8 mi) above sea level, and their bases are in water about 5 kilometers (3 mi) deep. With a total height of 9.5 kilometers (31,000 ft), these are the

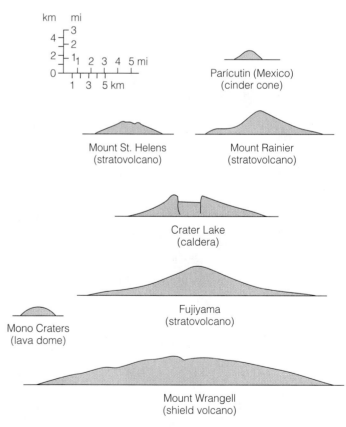

◆ **FIGURE 5.6** Comparative profiles and relative sizes of some Pacific rim volcanoes and the Mono Craters in the western interior of the United States.

◆ **FIGURE 5.7** Shield volcano Fernandina in the Galápagos Islands. This active volcano is related to the Galápagos "hot spot." Its convex profile is similar to those of the volcanoes of Hawaii.

highest mountains on earth, exceeding Mount Everest by about 650 meters (2,150 ft). (If one counts the fact that these volcanoes have also caused the sea floor to sink beneath them as they've grown, then each is more than 15,000 meters or 50,000 feet high!)

The Island of Hawaii (the "big" island to locals) is composed of five separate volcanoes that have built the island over the past 700,000 years (◆ Figure 5.8). Kilauea (Hawaiian, "much spreading") is the most easterly of the group and is the most active. This is exactly what one would predict as sea floor moves over the fixed Hawaiian hot spot.

A new volcano, Loihi ("the long one"), is growing on the flanks of Kilauea 28 kilometers southeast, providing further evidence of the northwest motion of the Pacific plate over a hot spot. The summit of Loihi is about 1,000 meters below sea level, and it rises 3,500 meters from the Pacific floor (◆ Figure 5.9). In 1996 it gave rise to the largest swarm of earthquakes ever recorded near any Hawaiian volcano— more than 4300 earthquakes in a month. Loihi is believed to be fed by the same 50-km-wide hot spot that is the source of Mauna Loa and Kilauea volcanic activity. Loihi will probably pop its head above water in about 50,000 years and become a tourist attraction.

It is not uncommon for a shield volcano to erupt from a *fissure* (crack or "rift"), on its flanks, rather than from a central vent. This is typical of Kilauea's east rift zone, where the countryside has been flooded under a sea of lava. Pu'u O'o ("hill of the o'o bird") is a large crater built upon a vent in the east fissure zone. Pu'u O'o's crater has reached impressive proportions as a result of scores of eruptions since 1983. During Pu'u O'o's eruptions, Kilauea's summit deflates slightly, rising again or reinflating between eruptive episodes. This indicates that the rift zone and Kilauea's vent plumbing are connected with the main magma reservoir beneath the

◆ **FIGURE 5.8** The Island of Hawaii. (a) Satellite photograph with north at the top. Mauna Kea and Mauna Loa are clearly visible. (b) The volcanoes that form the island have grown over 700,000 years in this order: Kohala (indicated by K), Mauna Kea (MK), Hualalai (H), Mauna Loa (ML), Kilauea (KI), and Loihi (L; submarine). Solid stars denote vigorous growth; open stars, waning growth; open circles, little activity. The island to the northwest is Maui. Its Haleakala Volcano is shown. Modified from Moore and Clague, 1992. Volcano World Web site. http://volcano.und.nodak.edu/

(a)   **(b)**

(a)

(b)

◆ **FIGURE 5.9** Locations of earthquakes near submarine Loihi Volcano, 1971–1972 and 1975. Similar earthquake swarms occurred in 1984–1985, providing further evidence that Loihi is an active volcano. USGS

summit. Lava flows associated with Pu'u O'o caused significant damage in the Royal Gardens subdivision near Kalapana about 8 kilometers (5 mi) from the vent. Flows destroyed at least 75 homes and covered 10 kilometers (6 mi) of residential streets (◆Figure 5.10). In addition, lava has built out hundreds of meters into the sea, adding over 200 hectares (500 acres) of new land to the island.

Spectacular lava fountains 400 meters (1,300 ft) high have occurred with fissure eruptions at Pu'u O'o (◆Figure 5.11). Some of the more fluid droplets set into glassy, tear-shaped blobs or tiny threads, known, respectively, as "Pele's tears" and "Pele's hair," named after the Hawaiian goddess of volcanoes (◆Figure 5.12). Birds have been known to make nests from some of the more pliable threads of volcanic glass.

Continental Flood Basalts

The landscapes of some areas of the world are dominated by thick, flat-lying basalt flows that form immense plateaus: the Columbia River plain in Washington, Oregon, and Idaho, and the Deccan plateau in northwestern India to name two

(c)

◆ **FIGURE 5.10** (a) A lava flow ignores a stop sign in the Royal Gardens subdivision below the east rift zone. (b) Lava advances through the Kalapana community, leveling everything in its path. (c) Firefighters arrest the speed of an advancing flow by dousing its front to create a resistant crust. This gives homeowners time to finish evacuating belongings.

J. B. Stokes, USGS

◆ **FIGURE 5.11** Lava fountaining at Pu'u O'o, Kilauea Volcano east rift zone, Island of Hawaii.

(◆ Figure 5.13). In scale they cover many times the area of the large volcanoes. When deeply eroded, these "flood basalts" form stairstep topography consisting of flat "treads" (soft rock) and vertical "risers" (hard rock). This geomorphic expression led early geologists to call the rocks collectively *traps*, the Swedish word for "staircase." When you hear or read terms like "the Deccan Traps" or "the Siberian Traps," this is the reason.

(a)

Pele, Goddess of Hawaii's Volcanoes, by artist Herb Kawainui Kane

B. Pipkin

(b)

◆ **FIGURE 5.12** (a) Artist's rendition of the revered Hawaiian fire goddess Pele. Her traditional home is at the summit of Kilauea Volcano. (b) "Pele's hair," thin filaments of glassy lava that have been carried by wind.

(a)

B. Pipkin

(b)

◆ **FIGURE 5.13** (a) Fissure eruptions forming a lava plain. (b) Antoja caves, Buddhist shrines excavated into the basalts of the Deccan lava plateau, India.

The Deccan Traps are 1–2 kilometers (3,000–6,000 ft) thick and cover a half-million square kilometers. What is the explanation for these great outpourings of lava? The process is believed to start as a giant plume of hot rock (see Chapter 3) originating at the mantle–core boundary that is several hundred kilometers in diameter. When the superplume rises to the base of the lithosphere it is 200°–300° C hotter than the surrounding mantle, and the rock at the base of the lithosphere rapidly melts. Over a period of just a few million years a basalt plateau grows on the surface above. Some plateaus can be matched across continents—the Parana of Brazil and the Etendeka of Namibia, for instance—giving more credence to Wegener's original ideas on drifting continents.

The Deccan Traps have been linked by some to the extinction of the dinosaurs 65 million years ago (end of the Cretaceous Period). They argue that the sulfurous fumes from the massive basaltic eruptions could have severely altered climates and poisoned ecosystems worldwide. Others cite even more compelling evidence that a meteorite impact in Central America at about the same time caused the die-off. The balance of fossil evidence favors the meteorite theory. However, the two events could be linked. Some geophysicists suggest that a large meteorite impact on one side of the earth might trigger an upwelling or superplume on the opposite side, causing vast outpourings of lava there. India and Central America, are (perhaps not coincidentally) positioned opposite one another on the globe.

Explosive Eruptions
Stratovolcanoes

A combination of effusive and explosive volcanic activity builds **stratovolcanoes,** sometimes referred to as *composite cones,* because they are composed of layers of both pyroclastic material and lava. Typically thousands of feet high and 10–20 kilometers (6–12 mi), across at the base, they have a concave upward profile and a central vent. They are stratified, thus the name *strato*volcano, consisting of alternating layers of ash, cinders, and lava.

The upper, steep slopes are formed mostly of pyroclastic volcanic ejecta, and the less steep, lower slopes are composed of alternating layers of lava and pyroclastics. These cones are some of the most beautiful tourist attractions in the world. Noteworthy examples are Mount Vesuvius in Italy, Mount Fujiyama in Japan, Mount Hood in Oregon, Mount Rainier in Washington, and Volcán San Cristobal in Nicaragua (◆Figure 5.14). They occur on the landward side of subduction zones, where melting of descending oceanic crust and mantle forms magma. The magmas rise because, as they melt, they expand, becoming more buoyant than the surrounding lithosphere. As the magma penetrates the continental rocks, partial melting occurs, and the magma becomes enriched in potassium and silica. This mixing and partial melting changes the volcanism from ultramafic basalt to explosive andesitic and high-silica rhyolitic volcanism. As the

(a)

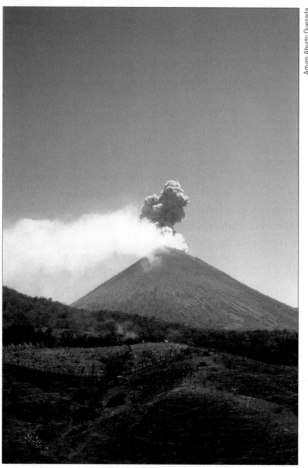
(b)

◆ **FIGURE 5.14** Three examples of stratovolcanoes. (a) Mt. Shasta, California, with Shastina, a parasitic stratocone on Shasta's northwest flank. Shasta, mantled in snow and ice, is deeply eroded, since the volcano's eruption frequency is waning. Shastina grew after the end of the last ice age, and preserves a youthful conical shape. (b) Volcán San Cristóbal, Nicaragua, shown here erupting in 1976. The dark cauliflower-shaped cloud is volcanic ash. The white cloud is volcanic gas and steam.

◆ **FIGURE 5.15** Crater Lake is a caldera, resulting from the explosion–collapse of a huge stratovolcano known as Mount Mazama, about 6,900 years ago.

magma rises it becomes gas-charged, and the high-silica lavas, rhyolites, dacites, and the like, are very viscous and thus do not flow easily. They may congeal in the volcano's central conduit (vent), which can cause gas pressures to build to explosive proportions. For this reason, stratovolcanoes present the most immediate threat to humans. Some eruptions have been so great that large cones have simply disappeared in the explosion. Crater Lake in Oregon represents the stump of the former Mount Mazama, a very large stratovolcano; it was probably the size of Mount Rainier. About 6,900 years ago, 70 cubic kilometers (17 mi³) of Mount Mazama disappeared, due in part to explosive activity, but mostly due to the collapse of the remaining cone into the deflated magma chamber beneath it. The "crater" of Crater Lake is a **caldera,** defined as a volcanic crater that is many times larger than the vent that feeds it (◆ Figure 5.15). Calderas may form by explosive disintegration of the top of a volcano, by collapse into the magma chamber, or by both mechanisms (see Case Study 5.1). Yellowstone National Park includes several huge calderas, as does Long Valley in the eastern Sierra Nevada, both of them lying above shallow bodies of magma that are capable of producing destructive eruptions. The Yellowstone calderas cover an area of 40 by 65 kilometers (25 by 40 miles).

Lava Domes

Lava domes are formed when bulbous masses of lava pile up around the vent because the lava is too thick and viscous to flow any significant distance from its source. Sometimes called *volcanic domes,* they usually grow by expansion from within. As the outer surface cools, the brittle crust breaks and tumbles down the sides, as at the Mono Craters on the east-ern Sierra Nevada of California (◆ Figure 5.16). Relatively small domes may form in the crater of a larger composite cone, such as the one that formed in the crater of Mount St. Helens after the 1980 eruption (◆ Figure 5.17). The source vents of large domes may be substantially plugged, which offers the potential for explosive eruptions, particularly where the lavas have access to underground water or seawater. Mount Pelée on Martinique in the West Indies and Mount Lassen and Mammoth Mountain in California are all dormant lava domes. They extrude lavas such as rhyolite with silica (SiO_2) contents of 65–75 percent, and they also extrude glassy rocks that cool quickly, such as obsidian and pumice.

◆ **FIGURE 5.16** Lava domes; Mono Craters, east-central California. The Sierra Nevada range is in the background.

Types of Eruptions and Volcanic Cones 121

(a)

(b)

◆ **FIGURE 5.17** (a) Steaming lava dome in the crater of Mount St. Helens, October 1981. (b) Oblique map of the same lava dome, October 8, 1981. Tao Rho Alpha

Cinder Cones

Cinder cones are the smallest and most numerous of volcanic cones (◆Figure 5.18). They are built of pyroclastic material of all sizes—from blocks and bombs to the finest ash (✳ Table 5.1). Pyroclastic material of all shapes and sizes is collectively known as **tephra**. *Bombs* are blobs of still-molten lava that assume an aerodynamically induced spindle shape and solidify before striking the ground (◆Figure 5.19). They can be found in great numbers around certain cinder cones, and collectors have impoverished many landscapes of their specimens. Cinder cone activity is local, within a few kilometers of the source vent, and is usually short-lived. The only new volcano to form in historic time in North America erupted in a farm field in 1943 near the village of Parícutin in the state of Michoacán, Mexico (Figure 5.18). Eruptions caused by frothing gases hurled blobs of lava into the air that

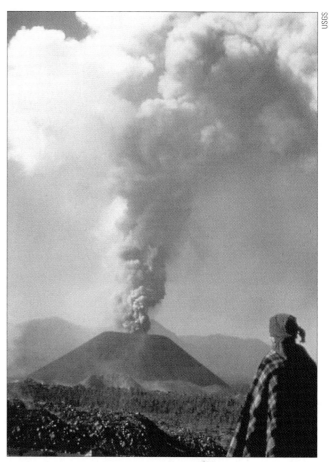

◆ **FIGURE 5.18** Parícutin Volcano, Michoacán, Mexico, in 1943. The only totally new volcano in North American history, it began as a fuming crack in a farmer's field. In a short time it was 400 meters (1,312 ft) high, and lava from it covered two nearby villages, leaving only a church steeple protruding through the lava. Volcanic activity decreased rapidly, and the volcano was inactive by 1952.

became cinders and then fell back around the vent, eventually building a cone nearly 400 meters (1,300 ft) high. An observatory was established on a nearby hill, and the volcano's every burp and belch was recorded for nine years. After the initial cone-building stage had passed, basaltic lava flowed from the base of the cone, inundating the nearby

✳TABLE 5.1	Classification of Pyroclastic Ejecta (Tephra)	
Name	Size	Condition When Ejected
Blocks	>32 mm	Cold, solid
Bombs	>32 mm	Hot, plastic
Lapilli (cinders)	4–32 mm	Molten or solid
Ash	¼–4 mm	Molten or solid
Dust	<¼ mm	Molten or solid

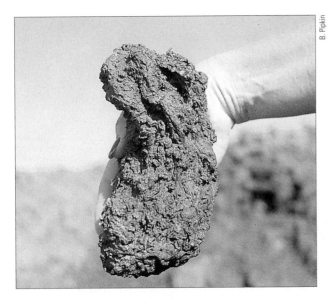

◆ **FIGURE 5.19** A volcanic bomb; Galápagos Islands, Ecuador. Note the spindle shape that the bomb acquired as it was flung through the air.

pueblo of San Juan and burying about 160 square kilometers (100 mi²) of agricultural land. Fortunately, no lives were lost. Cinder cones are generally thought to be one-shot events; that is, once the eruption sequence ends, it is rarely reactivated. Nonetheless, exceptions are known, and one usually finds many cinder cones clustered together.

ThomsonNOW
Click **Geology Interactive** to work through activities on Magma Chemistry and Explosivity and Volcanic landforms through Volcanism.

Benefits of Volcanic Action

Most of the atmosphere and hydrosphere that we know on Earth today has come from the interior of the earth via volcanic activity. Earth's primitive atmosphere was probably composed of hydrogen and helium, the two most abundant gases found in the universe. Because the young planet was still very hot, these gases most likely escaped to outer space. A second atmosphere came into being, sweated out from Earth's interior by volcanic eruptions and fumeroles (steam vents, see Figure 2 in the Gallery on page 144). Working on the principle that "the present is the key to the past," we assume that volcanic action spewed out the same gases then as it does today: water vapor (80%), carbon dioxide (10%), and the remainder mostly nitrogen and some rare gases. The predominantly water and carbon-dioxide atmosphere was continually modified by volcanic **outgassing** until sufficient water was supplied to form clouds, from which rain fell to form the oceans. (There is some evidence that cometary impacts also supplied large amounts of water to the early Earth.) From this start, plants evolved two to three billion years ago, and they consumed much of the carbon in the atmospheric CO_2. As the proportion of CO_2 decreased, the atmosphere became richer in oxygen and nitrogen. So we can credit volcanoes for our oceans and atmosphere. In fact, volcanic outgassing remains a vital player in maintaining Earth's habitability, even at present.

Volcanic activity also provides products that we utilize in many ways. The final polish your teeth receive when you get them cleaned is an example. Dental pumice is refined and flavored volcanic pumice with a hardness just slightly less than tooth enamel. "Lava" brand hand soap, a rough, abrasive bar soap, contains the same powdered rock. Light-weight bricks, cinder blocks, and many road-foundation and decorative stone products originated deep within the earth. Where volcanic cinders are mined for road base, they may also be mixed with oil to form asphalt pavement. The reddish pavement of state highways in Nevada and Arizona contains basalt cinders that are rich in oxidized iron, which gives it the red color. Pieces of rock pumice are sold in drugstores, supermarkets, and hardware stores for use as a mild abrasive for removing skin calluses and unsightly mineral deposits from sinks and toilets. Powdered, it is used in abrasive cleaners and in furniture finishing.

Glassy volcanic rock, such as obsidian, is easy to chip and form. Hence, Native Americans and stone-age people in many parts of the world used it to make tools and arrowheads. Today obsidian and many similar volcanic rocks are the raw material of "rock hounds" and artisans for producing polished pieces and decorative art.

Volcanoes provide opportunities for recreational activities, ranging from mountain climbing and skiing to more passive activities such as photography and birdwatching. Of course, skiing on an active volcano poses some measure of risk, as skiers at Mount Ruapehu in New Zealand found out in 1995 (see ■ Case Study 5.1 on page 137).

CONSIDER THIS

Although a few areas on the Island of Hawaii are regarded as relatively free from geologic hazards, you might not want to live in one of those "safe" places. Select an area on the island that appeals to you (for its view, beach access, culture, or some other amenity) and determine what geologic hazards you could encounter there.

Geothermal Energy

By far the most important and beneficial volcanic product is also the most hazardous; it is heat. The same heat energy that causes eruptions also drives geysers and hot springs and, when controlled, it can be converted to other uses. Not surprisingly, the prospects for geothermal energy are best at or near plate boundaries, where active volcanoes and high heat flow are found. The Pacific Rim (Ring of Fire), Iceland on the Mid-Atlantic Ridge, and the Mediterranean belt offer the most promise. Energy from earth heat is discussed at length in Chapter 14.

Volcanic Hazards

Sicily's Mount Etna (from the Greek *aitho,* "I burn") exhibits almost continuous activity in its crater. In 1992 eruptions and lava flows were threatening several villages. Empedocles (circa 490–430 B.C.), Greek philosopher and statesman, is perhaps most notable for throwing himself into the crater of Mount Etna to convince his followers of his divinity. His dramatic suicide inspired Matthew Arnold's epic poem "Empedocles on Etna," which bears no resemblance to the little rhyme attributed to Bertrand Russell:

> Empedocles that ardent soul—
> Fell into Etna and was roasted whole!

Volcanoes comprise the third most dangerous natural hazard globally in terms of loss of life, after coastal flooding (hurricanes and typhoons) and earthquakes. Following the Mount St. Helens eruption of 1980, U.S. civil defense agencies published suggestions for what to do when a nearby volcano erupts. The Federal Emergency Management Agency's suggestions appear later in the chapter. For now, however, let us examine the various types of hazards associated with eruptions, several of which might occur during a single eruptive phase (◆Figure 5.20).

Lava Flows

Most hazards, natural and human-made, decrease in severity with distance from the point of origin. This is true of earthquakes generally, tornadoes, and falls of volcanic ash, for example. Lava flows may be the exception to this, because they generally burn or bury everything in their path, even to their farthest limit. Holocene lava flows in Queensland, Australia, traveled 100 kilometers (62 mi) from their vents down riverbeds with very low gradients. Knowledge of the paths that flows might take from given vents makes it possible to delineate low- and high-risk volcanic-hazard areas. Basaltic lavas, such as those from Mount Etna in 1992, may emerge from a vent or fissure at temperatures in excess of 1,100° C and flow rapidly downslope like a river because of their low viscosity. As a flow cools, its viscosity increases, and then it may only "chug" along slowly. In either case, the

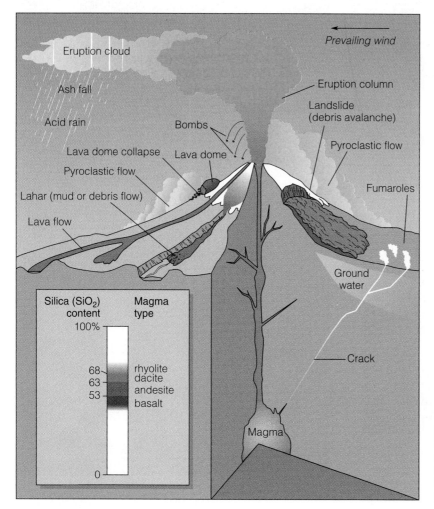

◆ **FIGURE 5.20** Volcanic hazards typical of those found in the western United States and Alaska. Some hazards, such as lahars and landslides, can occur even when a volcano is not erupting. Table 5.1 provides descriptions of pyroclastic ejecta portrayed here. USGS image, fact sheet 002-97, "What Are Volcano Hazards?"

end product is a layer of rock of varying thickness that covers everything in its path.

Two kinds of basalt flows are recognized. **Pahoehoe** ("pa-ho´-e-ho´e") forms when a skin develops on a flow and buckles up as the flow moves, making a smooth or ropy-looking surface (◆ Figure 5.21a). Other basalt flows develop upper and lower surfaces that are rough and blocky. This rough, angular lava is called **aa** ("ah´-ah") and it is characterized by a very slow advance in which the top, cold rubble rolls over the front of the flow, moving much like the track of a Caterpillar tractor (◆ Figure 5.21b).

A volcanic eruption cannot be prevented, but in some cases, it is possible to divert or chill a flow so as to keep it from encroaching onto croplands or structures. Flows have been diverted in Hawaii and Italy by constructing earthen dikes. Icelandic fire fighters have successfully chilled flow fronts by spraying them with large volumes of seawater from fire hoses. In the 1930s and 1940s the U.S. Army Air Corps tried, unsuccessfully, to divert lava flows by bombing them.

(a)

(b)

◆ **FIGURE 5.21** (a) Smooth, ropy pahoehoe lava; Galápagos Islands, Ecuador. (b) Rough, blocky aa flow in Hawaii. Human approach is possible because the flow moves very slowly.

Ash Falls

Roman naturalist and historian Gaius Plinius (Pliny the Elder, born A.D. 23) died during the eruption of Vesuvius in A.D. 79 from complications brought on by inhaling noxious fumes and by overexertion. He is revered as geology's first martyr, having been quoted by his nephew as saying, "Fortune favors the brave." Bravery was to be his undoing, however, as corpulent Pliny died in an area of heavy fallout from the eruption. Fortunately, however, Pliny had enjoyed life: he is credited with coining the phrase *In vino veritas* ("In wine there is truth"). Before he died, he witnessed a great vertical plume of ash with a mushroom- or anvil-shaped head rising from Vesuvius's summit. This roiling, high-speed column of steam, gas, and fragmented laval is called a **Plinian column** in commemoration of Pliny the Elder. Plinian columns typically penetrate the stratosphere as high as 15–25 kilometers (approximately 10–15 mi), and inject huge amounts of climate-cooling, sunset-altering dust and sulfur dioxide into the upper atmosphere. Plinian columns formed at the onset of the Mount St. Helens eruption in 1980 and at Mount Pinatubo (◆ Figure 5.22) in 1992. Acidic gases from

◆ **FIGURE 5.22** Ascending Plinian ash cloud over Mount Pinatubo.

◆ **FIGURE 5.23** A pyroclastic flow (*nuée ardente*) hurling down the slope of Augustine Volcano in Alaska, April 1986.

Pyroclastic Flows

Pyroclastic flows are turbulent mixtures of hot gases and pyroclastic material that travel across the landscape with great velocity. They are generated quickly and with such force that obstructions in their path may be blown down or carried away (◆Figure 5.23). The term **nuée ardente,** French for "glowing cloud," is commonly applied to this kind of eruption because of the intense heat in the cloud's interior. A nuée ardente caused most of the fatalities at Mount St. Helens and devastated an area in excess of 160 square kilometers (◆Figure 5.24).

One of the most infamous of all historic eruptions is that of Mount Pelée on the Island of Martinique in the West Indies on May 8, 1902. It caused the deaths of approximately 30,000 people in Saint-Pierre at the foot of the volcano and initiated the study of nuée ardentes and the unique volcanic deposits it forms. Pelée rumbled for some time before its main eruption. Because of this precursor activity, the population of Saint-Pierre swelled from 19,700 to at least 30,000 as refugees fled there from outlying villages. Local officials encouraged people to stay to participate in an upcoming election, claiming that Mount Pelée posed no more of a

(a)

(b)

◆ **FIGURE 5.24** Mount St. Helens. (a) A blast erupted from the volcano on Sunday morning, May 18, 1980, and culminated with a powerful pyroclastic flow. (b) The force of the pyroclastic flow was evidenced by the downed trees stripped of their bark in the "blow-down" area. This is the area where most of the fatalities occurred.

the 1912 Katmai, Alaska Plinian eruption—the largest eruption in the past century—ate clothes hanging on the line in Seattle, Washington, two thousand miles downwind! As a Plinian cloud spreads, its ash and pumice fall out, with the larger, heavier particles of pumice falling closest to the vent. An **ashfall** from the A.D. 19 eruption fell across Pompeii as people fled. Many carried mattresses and pillows on their heads as protection against the marble- and golf-ball-sized debris dropping from the sky. Farther downwind, the finer dust-like ash falls out. Some particles are so small that they cannot be seen, but certainly can be tasted. During the Mount St. Helens eruption, westerly winds carried ash eastward, causing difficulties in Yakima and Spokane, where several inches of ash were deposited. At Butte, Montana, about 750 kilometers (465 mi) east, the fine ash and dust in the atmosphere forced the closure of the airport. People in Yakima wore masks to filter out the choking dust. Bankers politely requested that all patrons remove their masks before entering their banks because of potential identification problems.

threat to St. Pierre than Vesuvius does to Naples(!). The concentration of sulfurous gases in the air became so great that citizens were forced to cover their faces with wet cloths. On the fateful day there was a tremendous explosion and a lateral blast from Pelée that boiled and rolled down the slopes of the mountain at a velocity estimated at 100 to 150 kilometers per hour (60–90 mph). The searing cloud engulfed the town in seconds and burned or suffocated all its inhabitants except for two survivors, one of them a condemned prisoner who had been in a dungeon and later went on circus tours to recount his horrible ordeal.

Such eruptions are common in the Lesser Antilles and similar subduction-related island arcs around the world (see ■ Case Study 5.2 on page 140).

The old Roman city of Pompeii was buried under six meters (20 ft) of volcanic ash over a period of several days when Mount Vesuvius erupted in A.D. 79 (◆ Figure 5.25). Uncovering the city and preserving its treasures marked

(a)

(c)

(b)

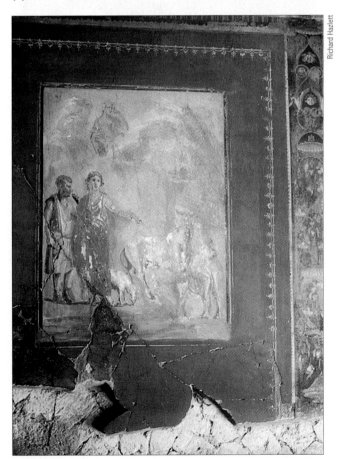

(d)

◆ **FIGURE 5.25** (a) The excavated wall of Terzigno quarry at the southeast base of Vesuvius. Find the dark bed in the lower center of the wall with the rippled upper contact. The ripples are furrows from an ancient Roman farm now buried under almost 8 meters (25 ft) of younger volcanic deposits. (b) Plaster casts of a person and a dog whose body molds were preserved in the A.D. 79 ash covering Pompeii. More than 2,000 body molds have been discovered. (c) A fully excavated Pompeii avenue. The wood bracing is to strengthen ancient walls weakened by modern earthquakes. (d) A fresco preserved on the wall of a Pompeiian home. The red color ("Pompeii Red") of these frescoes may not be original, but baked in by the heat of the eruption in A.D. 79.

the beginning of modern systematic archeology. Less well known, but more dramatic, was the eruption's impact on Pompeii's neighboring city Herculaneum, settled by the Greeks and named after Hercules. Herculaneum was overcome in a matter of minutes by a pyroclastic flow that buried the city to a depth of 20 meters (65 ft). The pyroclastic deposits are extremely hard, and a modern city, Ercolano, is now situated on the old city's grave. For this reason, only the equivalent of eight city blocks there have been excavated. Until the 1980s it was thought that Herculaneum's residents had escaped, because only 30 bodies had been recovered there, compared to 3,000 at Pompeii. Excavations since then along the former waterfront have uncovered hundreds of skeletons huddled together in cavelike openings in buildings used to store fishing boats. Apparently, the victims were overcome by the hot flows after running to the beach seeking refuge. More of this sad attempt of humans to escape the overwhelming forces of a volcanic eruption will be revealed in the continuing archeological excavations at Herculaneum.

Suffocating pyroclastic flows are a major volcanic hazard and have occurred in historic times in Alaska, Washington, and California. Prehistoric but geologically young pyroclastic-flow deposits of truly enormous size are found in all the Western states. They are known as ash flow or **welded tuffs**, because in certain layers the minerals and glass composing them were fused together by intense heat.

Lahars

Water from heavy precipitation, melting snow, a lake, or a river may mobilize debris on the flanks of a volcano and cause it to move a great distance downslope as a thick mush of rock, ash, and cinders. **Lahar** is the Indonesian word for such a fast-moving volcanic debris flow. A lahar accompanied the eruption of Mount St. Helens and filled the north fork of the Toutle River, a pristine mountain valley and stream before the eruption (◆Figure 5.26). Lahars are basically identical to nonvolcanic debris flows except for their volcanic source (see Chapter 7). Lahar-generating volcanoes may show little activity when such flows occur, and there may be little warning.

Another example of a destructive lahar is the one caused by the mild eruption of Colombia's Nevado del Ruiz, 5,432 meters (17,800 ft) high, in November 1985. Although, as one observer put it, the volcano simply "ran a fever and cleared its throat," a lahar generated by melting snow and ice cover covered the town of Armero 50 kilometers (30 mi) to the east in just a few minutes. A wall of mud 40 meters high (130 ft) careened down the narrow canyon of the Lagunilla River and overwhelmed the city at the canyon's mouth, leaving more than twenty thousand victims entombed in mud. Because the disaster struck at 11 o'clock at night, many of the victims were sleeping and unable to run to higher ground.

◆ **FIGURE 5.26** Lahar-filled north fork of the Toutle River at Mount St. Helens, formerly a pristine V-shaped stream valley. This photograph was taken in July 1980, well after the main eruption on May 18, and the lahar was still steaming.

The potential for destructive debris flows is predictable. The map of the Mount Rainier area in ◆ Figure 5.27 specifies the various identified potential volcanic hazards from this stratovolcano. Because Mount Rainier is covered with ice and has some areas of escaping steam and hot water, it is considered capable of generating lahars that could reach the suburbs of Seattle and Tacoma. Even a small eruption would subject the area at its base to inundation. Similar maps have been developed for most of the active volcanoes near urban areas along the west coast of the United States.

Tsunamis

Destructive tsunamis associated with volcanic activity are rare and they occur mainly in the western Pacific Ocean and around Indonesia. Of the 405 tsunamis recorded since 1900, 12 were caused by submarine volcanic eruptions, and only two of those resulted in significant damage. The most famous tsunami of all time, however, was caused by Krakatoa's eruption in 1883. Krakatoa Volcano lies in the Sunda Strait between the islands of Java and Sumatra. In 1883 an eruption destroyed the volcano and formed a 7-kilometer-wide (4 mi) caldera. The islands of Krakatoa, Verlaten, and Lang are remnants of this volcano. The eruption was so enormous (VEI = 6) that its explosion was heard 3,000 miles away, and it spewed a dust cloud 80 kilometers (50 mi) into the atmosphere. About 30 minutes after the climactic phase of the eruption began, a huge tsunami swept the west coasts of Java and Sumatra, rising to a height of 35 meters (115 ft) above sea level and killing an estimated 36,000 people. The wave traveled across the Pacific, still a meter high when it reached South America, and was noticed as far away as the English Channel. Since 1927 small eruptions in the caldera have been frequent, and a new volcanic island has appeared, Anak Krakatoa ("Son of Krakatoa";

◆ **FIGURE 5.27** Volcanic hazard map of Mount Rainier area in Washington. USGS data

◆Figure 5.28). It is characterized by explosive eruptions, with turbulent ash clouds rising 1,200 meters (4,000 ft) above the crater.

Weather and Climate

Benjamin Franklin is regarded as the first person to recognize the connection between cold weather and volcanic erup-

tions while he was serving as U.S. ambassador to France in 1783–84. Laki Fissure in Iceland erupted in June 1783, putting sufficient ash into the atmosphere that the following winter was extremely cold in Europe. The summer of 1783 was bleak in Iceland, resulting in famine and the loss of a fifth of its population and more than half its sheep, cattle, and horses. The eruption of Tambora Volcano in Indonesia in April 1815 hurled so much fine ash into the upper atmosphere that the

◆ **FIGURE 5.28** Anak Krakatoa, "Son of Krakatoa," in Indonesia. Krakatoa's 1883 eruption caused one of the largest tsunami in history and left a huge caldera. This "son" volcano formed in the caldera. It had nine episodes of explosive activity between 1963 and 2000. This view (1993) shows a rising ash cloud and dark-colored ash falling into the sea.

⋆TABLE 5.2	Dust Veil Indexes of Selected Volcanoes	
Volcano		DVI
Tambora, Indonesia, 1815		1,500
Krakatoa, Indonesia, 1883		1,000
Mount Pelée, Martinique, 1902		500
Mount St. Helens, Washington, 1980		1

Source: Lamb, H. H. Volcanic Dust in the Atmosphere (Phil. Trans. Royal Society of London, Ser. A, 266, 425–533).

following year became known as the "year without a summer." This led to a famine that killed no less than 80,000 humans, produced the coldest three years in British history, and brought snow to New England in July. Crop failures caused the price of flour to double in Great Britain during the two crop years of cold weather.

The reason for these drastic climate changes is that the tiny particles blown into the upper atmosphere by a volcano are very effective in reducing incoming solar radiation. The average length of time volcanic dust particles (0.0001–0.005 mm) remain in the upper atmosphere, the *residence time*, has been found to be 1 to 2 years. Sulfur dioxide gas emitted by volcanic action produces white coatings on the particles, which makes them superreflectors of solar energy. This loading of the upper atmosphere with volcanic dust reduces the amount of incoming radiation relative to outgoing radiation, resulting in a net heat loss for Earth. An attempt has been made to quantify these so-called dust veils into a Dust Veil Index (DVI) that can be used to relate a specific eruption to its impact on climate. Indexes for selected volcanoes are shown in ⋆ Table 5.2. As apparent in the table, Tambora and Krakatoa have had potentially the most significant effects on climate in recent history, whereas Mount St. Helens, with a DVI of 1, had little effect. Dust veils are obviously sporadic and transient, and many volcanoes would have to erupt in concert to produce significant long-term effects on climate.

CONSIDER THIS

Skiers flock to Washington, Oregon, and California's many popular ski resorts on dormant volcanoes but are seldom given instructions about what to do if one of them erupts. What evacuation instructions should skiers on the slopes of a volcano that "warms up" to the point that the snowpack begins to melt rapidly have? (This has occurred in New Zealand and is not at all improbable in the western United States.)

Gases

Denver, Mexico City, and Los Angeles have their smog; the Island of Hawaii, the "big island," has its *vog*—short for "*volcanic gas.*" Since 1986 Kilaeua Volcano near the island's southeast coast has been working almost nonstop producing lava

and, as a by-product, 1,000 tons of sulfur dioxide (SO_2) per day. This sulfurous gas quickly combines with water to form sulfuric acid, which is hazardous to health and corrosive to metallic components of structures and machinery. There are reports of the nails and hinges of houses being eaten away to such an extent that the structures have almost collapsed and of damage to plants and crops by the acidic gases. During most of the year trade winds blow the vog toward the west side of the island, where it swirls behind massive Mauna Loa and gets trapped over the island's main tourist area, the city of Kailua Kona and the Kona coast (◆ Figure 5.29). Health officials and citizens are concerned, and there is much debate about vog as a health hazard. However, the volcano itself will close the debate when this activity cycle ends.

Tree-killing emissions of CO_2 were discovered in 1990 at Mammoth Mountain, California. These emissions continue to this day and pose a serious hazard to campers and hikers (■ Case Study 5.3 on page 141). The intimate association of lethal carbon dioxide gas and volcanism yielded tragic results in 1986. A cloud of carbon dioxide gas emitted from a crater lake in Cameroon, West Africa, killed more than 1,700 people (see ■ Case Study 5.4 on page 143).

Selected historic volcanic eruptions and prehistoric eruptions indicated by thick, widespread tephra deposits of Holocene age are listed in ⋆ Table 5.3. Although other significant eruptions are known, those in the table were chosen to illustrate the volcanic hazards and impacts discussed in this chapter.

ThomsonNOW

Click **Geology Interactive** to work through an activity on Magma Chemistry and Explosivity through Volcanism.

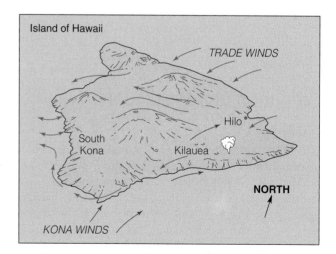

◆ **FIGURE 5.29** During trade-wind conditions the almost continuous stream of vog produced by Kilauea (white plume in figure) is blown to the west side of the Island of Hawaii. Traces have been found on Johnston Island 1,600 kilometers (1,000 mi) to the southwest. Onshore (daytime) and offshore (nighttime) winds, indicated by double-headed arrows, trap vog on the island's popular Kona Coast. When the light Kona winds blow (red arrows) the vog is concentrated on the east side of the island. Modified from USGS fact sheet 169-97, 1997

⋆TABLE 5.3   Selected Notable Worldwide Volcanic Eruptions⋆

Year	Volcano Name and Location	VEI	Comments
4895 B.C.±	Crater Lake, Oregon	7	Posteruption collapse formed caldera
1390 B.C.±	Santorini (Thera), Greece	6	Late Minoan civilization devastated
79	Vesuvius, Italy	5	Pompeii and Herculaneum buried; at least 3,000 killed
186	Taupo, New Zealand	7	16,000 km^2 devastated; largest eruption in last 5,000 years
1631	Vesuvius, Italy	4	Modern Vesuvius eruptive cycle begins
1783	Laki, Iceland	4	Largest historic lava flows; 9,350 killed
1792	Unzen, Japan	2	Debris avalanche and tsunamis killed 14,500
1815	Tambora, Indonesia	7	Most explosive eruption in history; 92,000 killed; weather changed
1883	Krakatoa, Indonesia	6	Caldera collapse; 36,000 killed, mostly by tsunamis
1902	Mount Pelée, Martinique, West Indies	4	Saint-Pierre destroyed; 30,000–40,000 killed; spine extruded from lava dome
1912	Katmai, Alaska	6	Perhaps largest 20th-century eruption; 33 km^3 of tephra ejected
1914–17	Lassen Peak, California	3	California's last historic eruption
1943	Parícutin, Mexico	3	New cone formed; event observed and documented from first eruption
1959	Kilauea, Hawaii	2	Lava lake formed that is still cooling
1963	Agung, Bali	4	1,100 killed; climatic effects
1968	Fernandina, Galápagos	4	Caldera floor drops 350 meters
1980	Mount St. Helens, Washington	4–5	Ash flow, 600 km^2 devastated
1982	El Chichón, Mexico	4	Ash flows kill 1,877; climatic effects
1991	Mount Pinatubo, Philippines	5–6⋆⋆	Probably the second largest eruption of the 20th century; huge volume of SO$_2$ emitted
1991	Unzen, Japan	4⋆⋆	Pyroclastic flows killed 41 people including 3 volcanologists; lava dome
1991–1993	Etna, Italy	1–2⋆⋆	Longest continuous activity (473 days) in 300 years ended; 300 million m^3 lava extruded
1983–	Kilauea, Hawaii	1–2⋆⋆	Longest continuing eruption, with more than 50 eruption events
1995–	Montserrat, West Indies	1–2⋆⋆	Pyroclastic flows and ash falls that have devastated this idyllic island

⋆Historic lava or tephra volume ≥2 km^3, Holocene >100 km^3, fatalities ≥1,500.
⋆⋆Author's estimate.
Source: Data adapted from Smithsonian Institution, Global Volcanism Program.

Mitigation and Prediction
Diversion

As mentioned earlier in the chapter, various tactics have been used in attempts to prevent lava flows from overwhelming the land. At various times, people have dammed them, diverted them, and even bombed them. Diversion barriers, high earth and rock embankments piled up by bulldozers, have been constructed on Mauna Loa to protect the city of Hilo, and also to divert potential flows away from the National Oceanographic and Atmospheric Administration (NOAA) observatory at Mauna Loa. Practically, diversion can be considered only if the topography allows the diverted lava to flow onto unimproved lands whose owners do not object to it. Flows have been slowed and even stopped by spraying them with seawater at Heimaey Island, Iceland (◆Figure 5.30). This was done in 1973 at the fishing village of Vestmannaeyjar. Both damming and diversion were used in Sicily in 1992 when eruptions of Mount Etna generated extensive lava flows.

Volcano Hazard Zones and Risk

The purpose of a hazard-zone map of any type is to give accurate information on the frequency and severity of the particular hazard. In the 1950s, the area below Kilauea's east rift zone on the Island of Hawaii was developed. The volcano had been dormant for 17 years and it had not erupted on the lower east rift zone since 1840. Kilauea became active in 1952, however, and by 1996 there had been 13 separate rift-zone eruptions, the last of which has been almost continuous since 1983 (◆Figure 5.31). In 1990 lava-flow hazard maps were prepared for the island, delineating zones ranging from low risk (9) for Kohala at the north end of the

USGS

◆ **FIGURE 5.30** Lava flows on Heimaey Island off the south coast of Iceland were successfully chilled by spraying them with seawater in 1973.

island to high risk (1 and 2) within and below the east rift zone (◆ Figure 5.32). The Royal Gardens residential subdivision, a development project of the 1950s, has been almost totally buried under lava (see Figure 5.10), and soon after the hazard-zone maps were published, the town of Kalapana was covered by aa flows. Had the developers known that 90 percent of the land surface of Kilauea had

been covered by lava since the arrival of the first Hawaiians 1,500 years earlier, they may have reconsidered building there. May have, that is!

Eruption Forecasting

A handful of volcano observatories exist in particular regions around the world to study volcanoes and forecast their eruptions. The oldest is the Vesuvius Volcano Observatory, established by the King of Naples in 1845. Researchers at the Hawaiian Volcano Observatory on the rim of Kilauea Caldera, established in 1912, developed many of the ground-based technologies used in forecasting eruptions (◆ Figure 5.33). More recently scientists at the Alaska Volcano Observatory working with laboratories in Kamchatka, Japan, and the U.S. Pacific Northwest have applied satellites very effectively to study eruptions across thousands of kilometers of little inhabited territory.

Prediction is the ability to identify when and where something will happen. Although volcano scientists have gotten very close to actually predicting some eruptions within a few days of their occurrence, it is more accurate to say that they are *forecasters*—that is, that they state in general terms the *probabilities* of eruptions taking place. Like hurricane forecasters, they do this by looking for certain precursory warning signs. The ability to forecast depends upon how well a volcano is monitored with instruments, and to a certain extent by how well its history of eruptions

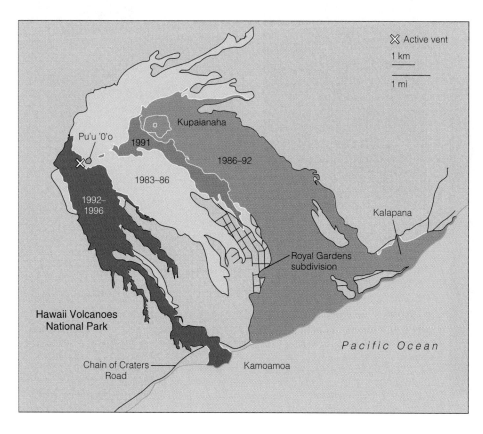

◆ **FIGURE 5.31** Lava flows on Kilauea Volcano's east rift zone. By late 1992 more than 83 square kilometers (33 mi²) had been covered by the 1983 to 1992 eruptive sequence shown here, and activity continued into the twenty-first century. USGS data

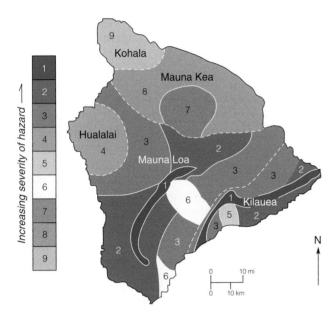

◆ **FIGURE 5.32** Lava-flow hazard zones for the Island of Hawaii. The zones range from low risk (9) to high risk (1). Volcano boundaries are denoted by dashed lines. USGS data

is known. Almost every volcano shows its own unique "personality" or eruptive behavior. Some show patterns of behavior that can be very useful in forecasting. Others are more chaotic, exhibiting great changes in their eruptive styles over time.

Scientists at the Hawaiian Volcano Observatory closely monitor the behavior of Kilauea and Mauna Loa, two among the world's most active volcanoes. Each shield contains a magma reservoir several kilometers below the surface that gradually fills with molten rock from weeks to years before an eruption. The whole mountain swells up just as if air were being blown into a balloon. The uplift causes the slopes of the mountain to steepen very gradually, a change that can be precisely measured using a *tilt-meter* (◆Figure 5.34). Gradually increasing earthquake activity typically accompanies the tilting. The locations of earthquake epicenters and foci indicate where the outburst is likely to occur. In the final hours leading up to an eruption, the reservoir suddenly deflates as molten rock works its way toward the surface. Simultaneously a continuous

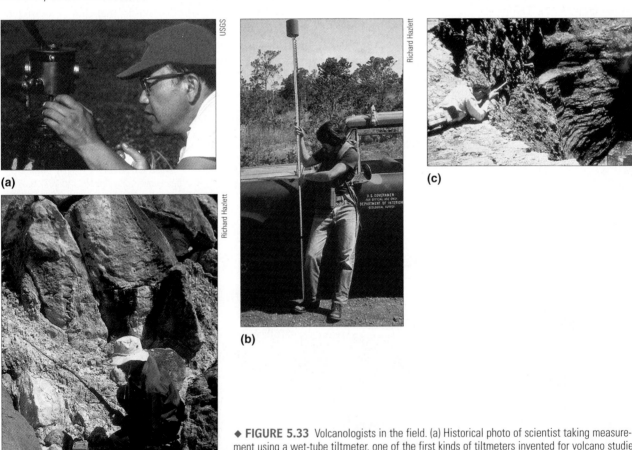

◆ **FIGURE 5.33** Volcanologists in the field. (a) Historical photo of scientist taking measurement using a wet-tube tiltmeter, one of the first kinds of tiltmeters invented for volcano studies. As the slope of a volcano changes, so too does the water level in three precisely spaced metal water pots connected by hoses that are set on that slope. (b) Hawaiian geologist Gary Puniwai with a proton-precession magnetometer, used to detect shallow magma intrusions. (c) U.S.G.S. researcher Donald Peterson measures the depth to a lava pool in a vent on the Kilauea east rift zone using a range-finder. (d) A student researcher collects fumarole gas samples using a gas chromatograph in the crater of Casita Volcano, Nicaragua.

shuddering of the ground, called *volcanic tremor,* takes place. The scientists alert civil defense authorities that an eruption may be imminent: Take no chances; it is time to evacuate!

Eruptions do not always follow these warnings. Magma may simply intrude at a shallow depth without breaching the surface. Nor do the warnings provide any clue as to the magnitude and duration of an eruption, should one occur. But it is better to be safe than sorry, and thousands of lives have been saved by successful eruption forecasting.

Other tools have also proved useful in studying volcanic activity. The ascent of magma into shallow reservoirs usually causes a change in Earth's gravity field, which can be measured using *gravimeters.* Change in the makeup of gases, especially in concentrations of chlorine relative to sulfur issuing from fumaroles, often accompanies the ascent of fresh magma. Tell-tale swellings may be detected using *satellite interferometry*—a method of comparing images from space at different times to detect even slight changes in the shape of a volcano. Interferometry is an excellent way to study

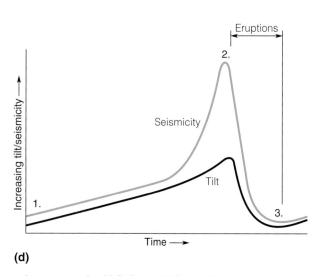

◆ **FIGURE 5.34** Three stages are apparent in Hawaiian volcanoes' typical eruption sequence. (a–c) Inflation and deflation of the cone are accompanied by (d) measurable changes in slope and seismicity. Eruptions occur after peak inflation and continue until magma is exhausted. USGS data

volcanoes that cannot be easily equipped with tiltmeters and seismometers. *Global Positioning System* (GPS) receivers are also placed to help measure landform changes.

Volcano scientists must also be skillful at dealing with the press and government officials, a craft that can only be learned on the job. Scientists must be careful to convey information accurately so that they do not cause panic or unnecessary and costly evacuations. At the same time, they must judge the precise moment when it is mandatory to urge people to leave their homes. These are not easy calls to make—and throughout a period of crisis the experts and authorities wrestle with life-threatening probabilities.

The ability to save lives from volcanic activity also depends upon the level of public education. Volcano scientists working through the United Nations and other organizations are eager to broadcast information about warning signs, potential hazards, and what people can do to protect themselves during an eruption. There are many troublesome misconceptions that people have about volcanoes.

One source of confusion is the terms "active," "dormant," and "extinct." Many people think of active volcanoes as ones that are *presently* in a state of eruption. Scientifically, however, an active volcano is one that has erupted frequently in historic time, and will almost certainly continue to do so in the future whether or not it is presently erupting. (Just what "frequently" means is a subjective term, however. Also, notice that the length of "history" differs from one region to another around the world.) An active volcano has to be regarded as threatening, whether it is actually erupting or not.

As a rule of thumb, a dormant volcano is one that shows signs of having erupted within the past few hundred or few thousand years, but which has not erupted in living memory. Many dormant volcanoes have only slightly weathered lava flows, appear not to be greatly eroded, and have little vegetation relative to the surrounding area. However, some dormant volcanoes are so heavily vegetated and eroded that people don't even know that they exist without a careful geologic study! Because a volcano is dormant does not mean that it is safe to live near. We simply don't know if or when it will erupt again. Moreover, if an eruption does occur it is likely to be dangerously explosive, due to the cap of old hardened rock that plugs the throat of the volcano. Examples of dormant volcanoes that have returned to life catastrophically include El Chinchon (Mexico), Mount Lamington (New Guinea), Mount Pinatubo, Vesuvius, and Mount St. Helens. Geologists do not know exactly how many dormant volcanoes there are in the world at present.

An extinct volcano is typically deeply eroded because it has not erupted in thousands if not millions of years. Cinder cones, however, are examples of extinct volcanoes that may have fresh, young appearances, because they tend to erupt only once in their lives. As you might guess, there are many more extinct volcanoes than dormant and active ones in the world today.

CONSIDER THIS

Volcanic activity is perhaps the most spectacular of all geologic hazards, and the destructive potential of many volcanoes is immense. Fortunately, hazards associated with volcanoes are not spread equally around Earth's surface. What areas in the United States are most likely to be affected by future volcanic eruptions, and how have they been identified?

What to Do When an Eruption Occurs

Based upon the experience of people at Mount St. Helens, the Federal Emergency Management Agency (FEMA) made the following suggestions to ease the trauma of a volcanic eruption.

At Home

- Stay calm and get children and pets indoors.
- If outside, keep eyes closed or use a mask and seek shelter.
- If indoors, stay there until heavy ash has settled.
- Close doors and windows, and place damp towels at door thresholds and other draft openings.
- Do not run exhaust fans or use clothes dryers.
- Remove ash accumulations from low-pitched roofs and gutters.

In Your Car

- Drive slowly because of limited visibility.
- Change oil and air filters every 50–100 miles (80–160 km) in heavy dust, or every 500–1,000 miles (800–1,600 km) in light dust (visibility up to 200 feet, or 60 meters).
- Use both windshield washer and wipers.
- Volcanic ash is abrasive and can ruin engines and paint.

Pets

- Keep pets indoors.
- Brush or vacuum them if they are covered with ash.
- Do not let them get wet, and do not try to bathe them.

ThomsonNOW
Click **Geology Interactive** to work through an activity on Seismic Risk USA through Earthquakes and Tsunamis.

CASE STUDY 5.1

New Zealand's Blast in the Past, a Skifield, and Fluidization

The two islands of New Zealand are clearly distinguishable geologically. Whereas North Island exhibits explosive volcanism and some of the most spectacular volcanic landforms in the world, South Island lacks volcanism and is more alpine in nature. North Island's volcanic zone includes Lake Taupo, the site of a cataclysmic volcanic eruption in A.D. 186 that was arguably the largest eruption on Earth in 5,000 years (◆Figure 1). A volcanic source, now beneath Lake Taupo, vented a column of hot gas, ash, and pumice more than 50 kilometers (30 mi) high, which spread downwind, forming light-yellow ash-fall deposits more than 5 meters (8 ft) thick in some places. At 100 kilometers (60 mi) distant the deposits are 25 centimeters (10 in) thick. Toward the end of the eruption sequence the hot column became so heavy that it collapsed and flowed outward in all directions as a dense mixture of expanding gases and volcanic fragments called a pyroclastic flow. Flow velocity is estimated to have been 600 kilometers per hour (375 mph), and the material traveled more than 80 kilometers (50 mi) from its source, overwhelming all the topography and vegetation in its path. Fortunately, the native New Zealanders, the Maori, had not yet settled the island when the eruption occurred. When they did come to the island about A.D. 1000, they regarded the Tongariro–Taupo area as sacred. They believed that their gods and demons had brought volcanic fire with them from Hawaiki, the Maori's ancestral homeland.

The aftermath of this eruption was a huge collapse basin or caldera, which is now filled with water and known as Lake Taupo. The area is still hot, and north of the lake are the Rotorua thermal springs and geysers, which attract many tourists, and the Wairaki geothermal energy complex (see Chapter 14).

How can a pyroclastic material move at such a phenomenal speed and travel such a great distance, seemingly defying friction and gravity? Some pyroclastic flows are **fluidized,** a process by which solids are transported that is well known in chemical engineering. A "fluidized bed" is a body of fine-grained solids through which a stream of high-pressure gas flows so that the grains separate and move as fluid. Many chemical engineering professors demonstrate this by forcing air through a powder on the bottom of a see-through box. As the air pressure is increased, the powder begins to quiver; then particles start dancing around, and eventually the whole mass is in motion. When the professor has it just right, he or she places a plastic duck (professor's choice) into the container, and it literally floats on the air–solid mixture. If "ducky" is pushed down, it immediately pops up, proving that it is floating on a denser medium. Part of the weight of the solids is taken by the air, reducing the interparticle friction to such a degree that the particles will not stand in a heap. The particles are not *entrained* (carried away bodily) like snowflakes in a blizzard; rather, the mass behaves as a fluid substance would. The point of this is that a well-understood process demonstrates how pyroclastic flows can fluidize and travel far from their source, destroying everything in their path.

At the south end of the Taupo Volcanic Zone is a cluster of stratovolcanoes in the Tongariro National Park. Two of the volcanoes are active and are popular playgrounds for New Zealanders, primarily for skiing and tramping (hiking). Mount Ruapehu, with a summit elevation of 2,797 meters (9,100 ft), is the highest point on North Island and has a lake in its summit crater. It is also the location of the Whakapapa Skifield, a very popular, well-equipped ski area. The terrane at Whakapapa (Maori, pronounced "whack-a-papa") is bare ragged lava and requires a lot of snow to be skiable (◆Figure 2). Throughout the skifield (or lava field, depending on the time of year) signs alert skiers and trampers to stay on high ground and out of the canyons should Ruapehu erupt, which it did in 1969, 1971, 1982, and sensationally in 1995. The eruptions are *phreatic;* that is, superheated water at the bottom of the lake flashes to steam and overflows the crater. The lake's surface-water temperature, which ranges from 20°C to 60°C (68°–140° F), is monitored as a potential eruption predictor. When the water heats up, some kind of activity can be expected. A lahar warning system at Whakapapa is based on detection of earthquake swarms, which precede phreatic and magmatic eruptions. Tongariro (Maori *tonga-,* "south wind," and *-riro,* "carried away") National Park is another case of humans putting nature to good use.

CONTINUED

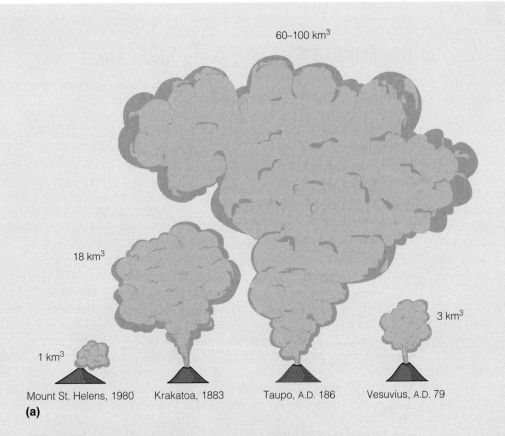

60–100 km³

18 km³

3 km³

1 km³

Mount St. Helens, 1980   Krakatoa, 1883   Taupo, A.D. 186   Vesuvius, A.D. 79

(a)

(b)

◆ **FIGURE 1** (a) The relative sizes of four large eruptions of the past 2,000 years based on estimated volumes of ejected tephra. (b) The very large Taupo eruption left a huge caldera that is now Lake Taupo. The cones in the foreground and in the distance suggest the lake's volcanic origin. (c) Tectonic setting of the Taupo Volcanic Zone, North Island, New Zealand. (a), (c), Karen Williams, *Volcanoes of the Southwind: A Field Guide to the Volcanoes and Landscape of Tangariro National Park* (Tongariro National History Society)

(c)

(a)

◆ **FIGURE 2** (a) Whakapapa Skifield is on volcanic Mount Ruapehu, the highest point on New Zealand's North Island and the site of a beautiful summit crater lake. Signs on the slopes warn skiers to stay out of canyons and low spots should a phreatic eruption create a dangerous lahar. (b) On September 25, 1995 a combination of hot magma and cold water produced a violent steam eruption that hurled boulders over the upper slopes of the Whakapapa Skifield. The eruption did little damage, but projectiles as big as cars were thrown over the rim. The Maori name for Ruapehu means "exploding pit."

(b)

CASE STUDY 5.2

Montserrat, Paradise Lost

The Soufrière Hills Volcano on Montserrat, a tidy little island and British crown colony in the eastern Caribbean Sea, began a series of eruptions in 1995 that continued episodically into 2000. The eruptions began with a dome of andesitic lava in the central crater that periodically collapsed, generating pyroclastic flows (◆Figure 1). Ash falls followed the flows and smothered most of Plymouth, the resort capital, and St. Patricks, a resort town. The world followed the eruptions on television and on the Internet, particularly the evacuation of half of Montserrat's 12,000 inhabitants away from the shadow of the smoldering peak. Volcanic hazard zones were established in September 1997 by the British Geological Survey's Montserrat Volcano Observatory (◆Figure 2). To add to Montserrat's problems, it was also subjected to the extreme hurricane season of 1999.

◆ **FIGURE 1** Pyroclastic flow moving down the slope of Soufrière Hills Volcano on the island of Montserrat, British West Indies. Seen here is one of many life-endangering flows that occurred during July 1997 and that threatened the city of Plymouth.

◆ **FIGURE 2** Map of Montserrat Island showing Soufrière Hills Volcano and the volcanic hazard zones. *Exclusion Zone:* no admittance except for scientific monitoring and national security matters. *Central Zone:* residents only on a heightened state of alert; all residents to have a rapid means of exit 24 hours a day and to wear hard hats and dust masks when outside. *Northern Zone:* significantly lower risk; suitable for residential and commercial occupation. Montserrat Volcano Observatory Web site map, Jan. 1998, British Geological Survey

CASE STUDY 5.3

Carbon Dioxide, Earthquakes, and the Los Angeles Water Supply

The Eastern Sierra Nevada is a mecca for tourists who want beautiful mountains and outstanding recreation. Much of the area's appeal results from volcanic action. About 760,000 years ago a huge eruption blew out 617 cubic kilometers (150 mi³) of magma that spread ash over nine states and as far to the east as present-day Nebraska (◆ Figure 1). The earth surface above the magma chamber sank 2 kilometers, forming the huge, oval caldera (16 km × 33 km) that is now called *Long Valley*. The eruption was 2,000 times the size of the 1980 Mount St. Helens eruption and it left hard welded tuff all over today's east-central California. Mammoth Mountain and Mono Craters, a linear chain of glassy domes (see Figure 5.16), formed within the last 400,000 years, and the people of Long Valley are living with the caldera's continuing restlessness.

The restlessness is manifest in hot springs, carbon dioxide emissions, and swarms of earthquakes, the most intense of which began in 1980 after two decades of quiescence. There were four strong, magnitude-6 earthquakes, three of them occurring on the same day. These quakes prompted studies by the U.S. Geological Survey that found uplift of 60 centimeters (about 2 ft) in the caldera center. Uplift, earthquake swarms, and gas emissions leave little doubt that magma is rising and getting closer to the ground surface. Late in 1997, just after the volcano movie *Dante's Peak* was released, the real volcano here acted up with more than 8,000 earthquakes larger than magnitude 1.2, and a couple of rattlers approached magnitude 5.0. More than 1,000 earthquakes occurred one day, and many scientists believe the volcano was waving a red flag signaling "danger."

Much of the water for the City of Los Angeles comes from Sierra Nevada snowmelt and travels from Mammoth Lakes to the city via open aqueduct. Should the volcano erupt, it would jeopardize or totally cut off this invaluable resource. Furthermore, the area's main highway access is aligned in the direction of the prevailing wind from the mountains. For this reason, an "escape road" was built in the opposite direction, toward the north, to provide an alternate route for the area's residents and visitors.

Mammoth Mountain, a large rhyolitic volcano, is still hot. Tree-killing emissions of CO_2 were discovered at the base of the mountain in 1990. This indicated magma activity at shallow depth (◆ Figure 2). By 1995 about 30 hectares (75 acres) of pine and fir trees had suffocated, and CO_2 concentrations of up to 90 percent of total gas were found in the trees' soil and root systems. Where CO_2 concentrations exceeded 30 percent, most of the trees were dead. One large campground had to be closed because park rangers found high levels of CO_2 in restrooms and cabins after campers exhibited symptoms of asphyxia (◆ Figure 3). It appears that carbon dioxide degasses from the magma and migrates into a deep gas reservoir. When earthquake swarms cause fractures to develop in the reservoir rock, the gas finds its way to the surface. It is estimated that between 200 and 1,000 tons of carbon dioxide flows into the soil and atmosphere per day. The good news is that gas emissions have been declining, which may indicate that the magma has exhausted its gas supply.

◆ **FIGURE 1** Mammoth Mountain and the Mono–Inyo Craters volcanic chain (red). The cataclysmic eruption 760,000 years ago that formed Long Valley ejected hot, glowing pyroclastic flows that cooled to form the Bishop Tuff (yellow). The inset map shows the distribution of Bishop Tuff and ash. USGS data

CONTINUED

(a)   (b)

◆ **FIGURE 2** The Horseshoe Lake tree-kill area, Mammoth Lakes, California. (a) Aerial view looking north toward Mammoth Mountain. Inyo–Mono Craters and Mono Lake are seen in the right background. The light-colored area (foreground) at the base of the Mammoth Mountain and on the shore of Horseshoe Lake is the tree-kill area. (b) Close-up of trees killed by leaking volcanogenic carbon dioxide gas.

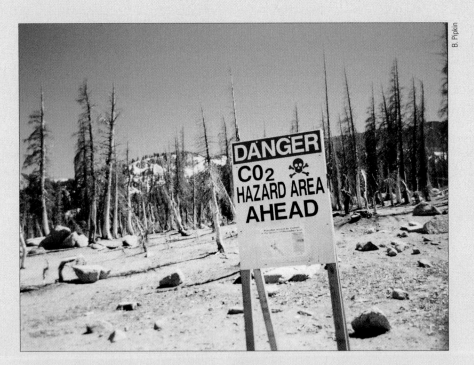

◆ **FIGURE 3** Looking south through the Horseshoe Lake tree-kill area on the south side of Mammoth Mountain. The trees have died from high levels of CO_2 in the root zone.

◆ **FIGURE 4** A small geyser of scalding water erupts in a formerly popular bathing pool at Hot Creek, not far from Mammoth Mountain. Activity picked up here in the spring of 2006.

CASE STUDY 5.4

Volcanic CO$_2$ and Fountaining Lakes

Lake Nyos is contained within a volcanic crater, one of 40 such craters that are roughly aligned southwest to northeast in Cameroon, West Africa. Specifically, the lake is in a **maar,** a low-relief crater produced by explosive interaction of magma with underground water. Such a high-pressure steam explosion, called a **phreatic eruption,** does not produce much new magmatic material, which is why the resulting crater is relatively shallow. Lake Nyos and several nearby crater lakes and springs are known to be highly charged with

carbon dioxide, CO$_2$, just as is a bottle of soda water.

On the evening of August 21, 1986, almost noiselessly and without warning, the lake erupted, discharging 80 million cubic meters (100 million yd^3) of CO$_2$ dissolved in its waters into the atmosphere. So much gas escaped from the lake that its level dropped 1 meter. Because carbon dioxide weighs about one and a half times as much as air, the suffocating gas descended downslope, following stream valleys and drainages for 16 kilometers

(10 mi). The CO$_2$ cloud was 50 meters (160 ft) thick and it killed all animal life in its path, including 1,200 residents of Nyos village and 500 persons in nearby communities. The entire event took less than an hour (◆ Figure 1).

What happened the evening of the tragedy that caused the gas in the lake to explode catastrophically? Was it a small volcanic disturbance, or did some other physical phenomenon upset the lake? It is known that lakes periodically *overturn;* that is, their surface water sinks to the bottom and is replaced

CONTINUED

by bottom water rising to the surface. This usually occurs in temperate climates in the fall, because as the surface water cools, it becomes denser than the bottom water and displaces it. Overturn usually requires a trigger, such as strong winds, a landslide, or a drastic change in atmospheric pressure. The best hypothesis appears to be that winds associated with the rainy season blew the lake's surface water to one side of the crater. This reduced the hydrostatic (confining) pressure on the bottom waters, which allowed the highly charged gas to come out of solution and form bubbles. The formation of bubbles

further reduced the density of the water, and the gas in solution frothed and rose with dramatic speed. That this sequence of events indeed happened is supported by stripped vegetation along the lake shore. The leaves and other parts of plants were most likely removed by a surge of water associated with the explosion—just as a fountain of foam is associated with popping the top of a warm can of soda.

Bantu folklore is filled with stories of exploding lakes and "rains" of dead fish. According to legend, there have been at least three earlier episodes of catastrophic lake

explosions. Dead fish found floating on the water surface during minor degassing events are believed by the local people to be gifts from their ancestors who live in the lake.

Since 1986 the gas content of the lake has increased by additions from subterranean springs and magmatic sources. Engineering studies indicate that Lake Nyos and other dangerous crater lakes in the region could be defused by installing pipes in them to bring charged water from the lake bottom to the surface as fountains. Once started, the fountains would be driven entirely by the lifting force of the released gas.

(a)

(b)

◆ **FIGURE 1** (a) Deadly carbon dioxide belched from the bottom of volcanic Lake Nyos, which stood muddy and full of debris for several days. The gas settled into the valleys below, tragically suffocating 1,700 people. (b) Cattle suffocated by carbon dioxide at Lake Nyos.

Volcanic Wonders

Volcanism creates landscapes that are attractive to humans. One of the most eye-catching volcanic features is *columnar jointing*, which forms as cooling volcanic rock contracts around many equally spaced centers, causing the lava to split into polygonal columns. Six-sided columns are most common, but four-, five-, seven-, and eight-sided columns also occur. An excellent example is seen at the Devil's Tower, Wyoming, a shallow intrusion (◆Figure 1).

◆ **FIGURE 1** Devil's Tower National Monument in northeastern Wyoming is an exposed volcanic neck with spectacular columnar jointing. Also known as "Grizzly Bear Lodge" and "Mato Tepee," it rises 865 feet above the surrounding landscape.

◆ **FIGURE 2** Nature's foot-warmer; Sarangson fumarole field, Minhasa, Celebes (Sulawesi). Fumarole temperatures range from 30° to 90° C.

143

◆ **FIGURE 3** Call the automobile club!

◆ **FIGURE 5** A mud volcano formed by volcanic gases escaping through fine-grained clay deposits; Imperial Valley, California.

The columns form perpendicular to the main cooling surfaces of the flows, which is why they are sometimes curved. The 264-meter-tall (865 ft) Devil's Tower, called "Grizzly Bear Lodge" and "Mato Tepee" by early Native Americans, is surrounded by colorful Cheyenne and Lakota Sioux legends. According to one legend, a number of children were being chased by a grizzly bear. The Great Spirit saw their plight and raised the ground they were on. The bear scratched deep grooves into the rocks in his attempts to reach the frightened children. Imagine the tribal elders passing on this legend to wide-eyed children. It is a much more memorable explanation for the origin of the columns than the scientific one.

Fumaroles represent the dying stages of volcanism. They emit heat, steam, and sulfurous gases and build brightly colored surface mounds. They also have other uses (◆Figure 2). The other gallery photos speak for themselves.

◆ **FIGURE 4** A DC-10 pointed skyward due to Mount Pinatubo ash on its tail; Cubi Point Naval Air Station, Philippines.

◆ **FIGURE 6** Surrealistic lava tree molds form when fluid lava surrounds a tree trunk and cools, leaving a cylinder of solidified rock; east rift zone, Kilauea Volcano, Hawaii.

Summary

Volcanoes

Defined
A vent or series of vents that issue lava and pyroclastic material.

Distribution
Adjacent to convergent plate boundaries around the Pacific Ocean (the Ring of Fire); in a west–east belt from the Mediterranean region to Asia; along the mid-ocean ridges; and in the interior of tectonic plates above hot spots in the mantle. In the U.S., a 1,100-kilometer (680-mi) belt extends northward from northern California through Oregon and Washington.

Measurement
The Volcanic Explosivity Index assigns values of 0 to 8 to eruptions of varying size.

Explosivity
Depends upon the lava's viscosity and gas content. Viscosity, a function of temperature and composition, determines the type of eruption: felsic (high-SiO_2) lavas are viscous and potentially explosive; mafic (low in SiO_2, high in magnesium and iron) lavas are more fluid and less explosive.

Types of Volcanoes and Volcanic Landforms

Shield (Hawaiian or "Effusive" Type)
Gentle outpourings of lava produce a convex-upward edifice resembling a shield.

Continental Flood Basalts
Lava erupts from long cracks, building up broad lava plateaus such as those found in the Columbia River Plateau (Oregon–Washington–Idaho), Iceland, and India. They are fed by mantle plumes.

Stratovolcanoes (Explosive Type)
Characterized by concave-upward cone thousands of meters high. Vesuvius (Italy), Fujiyama (Japan), and Mount Hood (Oregon) are examples. Crater Lake (Oregon) is the stump of a stratovolcano that exploded and collapsed inward, leaving a wide crater known as a *caldera*.

Lava Domes
Bulbous masses of high-silica, glassy lavas, such as found at Mono Craters (California). Domes may form in the crater of a composite cone after an eruption, such as at Mount St. Helens (Washington).

Cinder Cones
The smallest and most numerous of volcanic cones, composed almost entirely of tephra.

Benefits of Volcanic Activity

Atmosphere and Hydrosphere
Outgassed from Earth's interior.

Building Materials
Cinder blocks, road-base materials, pumice, light-weight concrete, decorative stone.

Geothermal Energy
Cooling magma at depth heats water that can be converted to steam to drive electrical generators.

Hazards

Lava Flows
Destroy or burn everything in their path, can travel a distance of 100 kilometers or more.

Ash Falls
Heavy falls of volcanic ash from Mount Vesuvius buried Pompeii in A.D. 79. There were heavy ash falls from Mount Pinatubo, the Philippines, in 1991. Vertical plumes of ash may rise many kilometers from a vent, which are then carried by the wind and blanket the terrain. Such plumes rising from a vent are known as *Plinian eruptions*.

Pyroclastic Flows
Pyroclastic flows are hot, fluid masses of steam and pyroclastic material that travel down the flanks of volcanoes at high speeds, blowing down or suffocating everything in their path. Such flows have killed thousands of people.

Lahars
Catastrophic mud flows down the flanks of a volcano. They cause the most volcanic fatalities, more than pyroclastic flows.

Tsunamis
Submarine volcanic eruptions (such as that of Krakatoa in 1883) create enormous sea waves that may travel thousands of miles and still do damage along a shoreline.

Weather
Sulfur dioxide coatings on ash and dust particles increase their reflectivity and cause cooling of weather, such as occurred after the eruption of Mount Pinatubo, 1991–1993. The effects of ash and dust in the stratosphere are short term—a few years.

Gases
Corrosive gases emitted from a volcano can be injurious to health, structures, and crops. Such gases are called *vog* (*v*olcanic *g*as) on the island of Hawaii. Carbon dioxide emitted from the bottom of volcanic Lake Nyos in Cameroon formed a cloud that sank to the ground and suffocated 1,700 people in 1986. Tree kills due to CO_2 have occurred at Mammoth Mountain, California.

Mitigation and Prediction

Diversion and Chilling

Flows have been diverted in Hawaii and elsewhere and have been chilled with seawater in Iceland.

Prediction

Prediction in Hawaii, based upon seismic activity (earthquake swarms and harmonic tremors) and the tilt of the cone as magma works its way upward, has become quite accurate. Similar phenomena were observed at Mount St. Helens and Mount Pinatubo.

Key Terms

aa	fluidization	nuée ardente	shield volcano
andesite line	lahar	outgassing	stratovolcano
ash fall	lava dome	pahoehoe	tephra
caldera	lava plateau	phreatic eruption	Volcanic Explosivity
cinder cone	maar	Plinian column	Index (VEI)
felsic	mafic	pyroclastic flow	welded tuff

Study Questions

1. What are the four kinds of volcanic cones, and what type of eruption can be expected from each kind? What are flood basalts, and how have they shaped the earth's landscape?

2. How would you expect the eruption of a volcano that taps mafic magma to differ from the eruption of one that taps felsic magma? What kind of rocks will result from each eruption?

3. Explain the distribution of the world's 1,350 active volcanoes in terms of plate tectonic theory.

4. List the six geologic hazards connected with volcanic activity in decreasing order of their threat to human life and limb.

5. Where in the United States are the most dangerous volcanic hazards encountered? Which geologic hazard related to volcanic activity presents the greatest danger to humans, and how can this hazard be mitigated, or at least minimized?

6. Why can eruptions on the Island of Hawaii be predicted more accurately than volcanic eruptions at subduction zones?

7. How may calderas be formed? What geologic evidence is found at Crater Lake, Oregon, that indicates it was formed by a special set of circumstances?

8. In what ways are volcanic activity and its products useful to humankind?

9. Name five volcanic areas of great scenic wonder and the geologic feature found there; for example, Crater Lake, caldera.

10. How do volcanic eruptions affect climate and weather? What impact does this have on populations, particularly Third World peoples?

11. In what ways do gases, including water vapor, emitted by a volcano impact the nearby area and people living there?

12. Define or sketch these volcanic features: aa, pahoehoe, lahar, Dust Veil Index, lapilli, tephra, welded tuff.

For Further Information

Books and Periodicals

Decker, Robert, and Barbara Decker. 1981 and 1997. *Volcanoes.* New York: W. H. Freeman.

Duennebier, F. K. (contact person) and the Loihi Science Team. 1997. Researchers rapidly respond to submarine activity at Loihi Volcano, Hawaii. EOS 78, no. 22 (3 June).

Evans, W. C., L. D. White, M. L. Tuttle, G. W. Kling, G. Tanyileke, and R. L. Michel. 1994. Six years of change at Lake Nyos, Cameroon, yield clues to the past and cautions for the future. *Geochemistry* 28: 139–162.

Fierstein, Judy, and others. 1997. *Can another great volcanic eruption happen in Alaska?* U.S. Geological Survey fact sheet 039-97.

Francis, Peter. 1993. *Volcanoes.* New York: Oxford University Press.

Hazlett, Richard W. 1987. *Kilauea volcano: Geological field guide.* Hilo, Hawaii: Hawaiian Natural History Association.

Hill, David, and others. 1996. *Living with a restless caldera, Long Valley, California.* U.S. Geological Survey fact sheet 108-96.

_____. 1997. *Future eruptions in California's Long Valley area: What's likely.* U.S. Geological Survey fact sheet 073-97.

Kling, George W., and others. 1987. The 1986 Lake Nyos gas disaster in Cameroon, West Africa. *Science* 236: 169–174.

McDonald, G. A., A. T. Abbott, and F. L. Peterson. 1983. *Volcanoes in the sea: The geology of Hawaii,* 2d ed. Honolulu: University of Hawaii Press.

McGee, Kenneth A., and others. 1997. *Impacts of volcanic gases on climate, the environment, and people.* U.S. Geological Survey open file report 97-262.

McPhee, John. 1989. *The control of nature.* New York: Farrar, Straus, and Giroux.

Myers, Bobbie, and others. 1997. *What are volcano hazards?* U.S. Geological Survey fact sheet 002-97.

Neal, Christina A., and others. 1997. *Volcanic ash: Danger to aircraft in the North Pacific.* U.S. Geological Survey fact sheet 039-97.

Schuster, Robert L., and J. P. Lockwood. 1991. Geologic hazards at Lake Nyos, Cameroon, West Africa. *Association of Engineering Geologists News,* April.

Sigvaldason, G. E. 1989. International conference on Lake Nyos disaster, Yaounde, Cameroon, 16–20 March 1987: Conclusions and recommendations. *Journal of volcanology and geothermal research* 39: 97–109.

Simkin, Tom, and others. 1981. *Volcanoes of the world,* Stroudsberg, Penn.: Hutchinson Ross Publishing Co.

Smith, A. L., and M. J. Roobol. 1991. *Mt. Peleé, Martinique: An active island-arc volcano.* Geological Society of America memoir 175.

Sorey, Mike, Bill Evans, Mack Kennedy, John Rogie, and Andrea Cook. 1999. Magmatic gas emissions from Mammoth Mountain. *California geology,* September/October.

Stager, Curt. 1987. Killer lake. *National geographic,* September: 404–420.

Sutton, Jeff, and others. 1997. *Volcanic air pollution: A hazard in Hawaii.* U.S. Geological Survey fact sheet 169-97.

Tilling, Robert I. 1984. *Monitoring active volcanoes.* Denver, Colo.: U.S. Geological Survey.

Williams, A. R. 1997. Montserrat: Under the volcano. *National geographic,* July.

Wright, Thomas L., and T. C. Pierson. 1992. *Living with volcanoes.* U.S. Geological Survey circular 1073. U.S. Geological Survey, Box 25425, Federal Center, Denver, CO 80225.

ThomsonNOW™

Assess your understanding of this chapter's topics with additional comprehensive interactivities at http://www.thomson.com/login, which also has up-to-date web links, additional readings, and exercises.

CHAPTER 6

Soils, Weathering, and Erosion

CHAPTER

A few inches between humanity and starvation . . .

Anonymous

The Wind Blew and the Soil Flew

THE GREAT DEPRESSION OF THE 1930s WAS exacerbated by a protracted drought in the Great Plains of Oklahoma, Colorado, Texas, New Mexico, and Kansas. This part of the Great Plains was totally dependent upon rainfall for crop production and, because the government had guaranteed wheat prices, farmers tilled thousands of acres. A longstanding agricultural practice was to plow the fields after the fall harvest, crop stubble and all, and let the land lie fallow all winter. This was good practice as long as it didn't rain too much—or too little. If too much rain falls, the soil is subject to extreme sheet and rill erosion by water, and if there is drought and the soil dries out, the result is the same: extreme soil erosion, only by wind.

There was drought, and the wind did blow in the southern Great Plains in the mid-1930s. Huge quantities of topsoil were simply blown away (◆Figure 1). Fine particles were lifted 5 kilometers (16,000 ft) in the air and carried eastward as far as Washington, D.C., and beyond. Five states that were the source of this airborne dust became known as the "Dust Bowl."

UPI/Bettmann/CORBIS

◆ **FIGURE 1** A dust storm hits a southwestern Great Plains village in October 1937. Storms like this one destroyed crops and buried pasturelands. Minutes after this photograph was taken the village was completely engulfed in choking dust.

Farming was impossible, and farm families, burdened by debt for equipment, seed, and supplies, left their farms to become migrant workers. Many traveled to California and became derisively known as "Okies" (◆Figure 2). These unfortunate victims of severe soil erosion were the subject of John Steinbeck's touching novel *The Grapes of Wrath*. Even today, wind erosion exceeds water erosion in many parts of the Dust Bowl states.

CORBIS

◆ **FIGURE 2** Dust Bowl America. In 1938 Dorothea Lange, who worked for the Farm Security Administration, took this historic photograph of a homeless migrant family of seven on a highway in Pittsburgh County, Oklahoma. By 1939, half of the families in Oklahoma were on relief.

Soil, the thin mixture of weathered rock and organic material below our feet, is Earth's most fundamental resource. We live on it, and through it, we produce much of our food. Soil supports forest growth, which gives us essential products including paper and wood. Soil material, organisms within the soil, and vegetation constitute an ecological system critical to life on this planet. It is through soil that the four ingredients needed for plant growth are recycled: water, air, organic matter, and dissolved minerals (◆Figure 6.1).

The multiple uses of **soil** are reflected in the many definitions and classification schemes that have been developed for soils. To the engineer, a soil is the loose material at Earth's surface; that is, material that can be moved about without first being dynamited and upon which structures can be built. The geologist and the soil scientist see soil as a mixture of weathered rock, mineral grains and organic material that is capable of supporting plant life. A farmer, on the other hand, is mostly interested in what crops a soil can grow and whether the soil is rich or depleted with respect to organic material and minerals.

The carrying capacity of our planet, the number of people Earth can sustain—depends on the availability and productivity of soil. This is why understanding how soil is formed and how it can be best cared for are so important. Soil erosion removes this precious resource and for all practical purposes, once productive topsoil is removed, it is lost to human use forever. Soil pollution can render areas harmful to enter or unable to grow edible food products. The goal of this chapter is to give you an appreciation of how important soil is to our environment by giving you the information you need to understand how soil is formed, how it can be impacted by human actions, and how we as a society can better care for this invaluable resource.

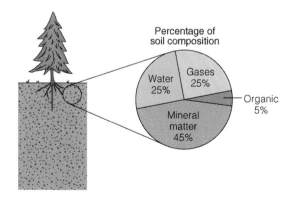

◆ **FIGURE 6.1** Composition of a typical soil. The organic component includes humus (decomposed plant and animal material), partially decomposed plant and animal matter, and bacteria. Mineral matter is what is left of the rock that weathered to form the parent material for the soil.

Weathering

Because soil is made up in large part of weathered rock, we start by approaching the question, how does rock weather and erode to produce parent materials on which soils develop?

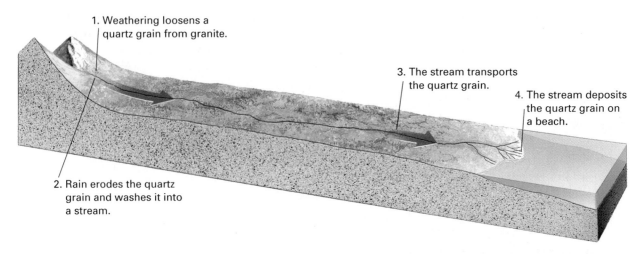

1. Weathering loosens a quartz grain from granite.

3. The stream transports the quartz grain.

4. The stream deposits the quartz grain on a beach.

2. Rain erodes the quartz grain and washes it into a stream.

◆ **FIGURE 6.2** Weathering is catalyzed by water and atmospheric gasses, which work together to loosen the quartz grains in the host rock, granite. The loosened grains are then transported, in this example by a stream, to a beach, which may be at a lake or at the ocean.

Weathering is a destructive process by which rocks and minerals are broken down by exposure to atmospheric agents. Specifically, **weathering** is the physical disintegration and chemical decomposition of earth materials at or near Earth's surface. **Erosion,** on the other hand, is the *removal and transportation* of weathered or unweathered materials by wind, running water, waves, glaciers, groundwater, and gravity (◆Figure 6.2).

Physical Weathering

Physical weathering makes little rocks out of big rocks by many processes. Rocks are wedged apart along planes of weakness by thermal expansion and contraction and by the activities of organisms. **Frost wedging** occurs when water freezes in joints or other rock openings and expands. This expansion, which amounts to almost a ten percent increase in volume, can exert tremendous pressures in irregular openings and joints, but only if the joint is somehow sealed or the ice constrained. As one would suspect, this process operates only in temperate or cold regions that have seasonal or daily freeze-and-thaw cycles. Water is not the only material to solidify in rocks and catalyze physical weathering. **Salt-crystal growth** (◆Figure 6.3a) can exert tremendous pressure and is known to pry loose individual minerals in a rock, even granites. It is particularly effective in porous, granular rock such as sandstone and occurs mainly in arid regions. Abrasion of rock by wind-driven sandblasting leaves tell-tale hints (the smoothing and streamlining of abraded surfaces) and is termed **ventification** (◆Figure 6.3b). Ventification is a common phenomenon in deserts where there is little vegetation to hold soil and sand in place.

Fire is a dramatic way to physically weather rock (◆Figure 6.3c). It's long been known that intense forest fires can shatter the surface of rocks, but only recently have people observed similar physical weathering when dry shrubs and thick grasses burn in deserts and semiarid areas. How is it that range fires passing in mere minutes can damage tough rocks like granite? Rocks are very poor conductors of heat, therefore when the fire passes by, the surface of the rock may heat to hundreds of degrees centigrade in a matter of just a few minutes, expanding the rock. Meanwhile, several centimeters below the surface, the rock remains cool. This differential expansion sets up huge stresses that can shatter even the toughest rock. Some people have speculated that diurnal cycles of heating and cooling in the desert could cause similar physical weathering, yet experiments to test this hypothesis have never yielded conclusive results.

Biota are important agents of physical weathering and help prepare rock for its conversion to soil and sediment. Roots of even the smallest plants can act as wedges in rock in any climate (◆Figure 6.3d). The most dramatic example of root wedging is probably the damage to paving and structures caused by tree roots. Animals also contribute significantly to weathering and soil formation by aerating the ground and mixing loose material. Insects, worms, and burrowing mammals, such as ground squirrels and gophers, move and mix soil material and carry organic litter below. Some tropical ants' nests are tunnels hundreds of meters long, for example, and common earthworms can thoroughly mix soils to depths of 1.3 meters (4.25 ft). Earthworms are found in all soils where there is enough moisture and organic matter to sustain them, and it is estimated that they eat and pass their own weight in food and soil minerals each day, which amounts to about ten tons per acre per year on average. An Australian earthworm is known that grows to a length of 3.3 meters (11 ft) and is a real earth mover! Charles Darwin was the first person to calculate just how much soil earthworms process.

◆ **FIGURE 6.3** (a) Crystallizing salt can help pry rock apart. This granite in the desert of Namibia is spalling in onion-skin-like layers as salt crystallizes in small cracks and splits the rock apart. A pen is used for scale. (b) Wind-driven sand can effectively erode rock. In the hyperarid Namibian desert of southern Africa, the hard granite has been physically weathered (polished and shaped) by sandblasting, otherwise known as ventifaction. (c) Range fire is a powerful means by which to physically weather rock. A range fire spreads rapidly through dry sage and grass in Owens Valley, California. Granitic rocks heated by these fires lose centimeter-thick sheets from their surfaces due to rapid heating and thermal expansion. (d) Tree roots and their trunk wedge openings in granite; Yosemite Valley, California.

Chemical Weathering

Chemical reactions alter rock and mineral debris at Earth's surface. These reactions are complex and involve many steps, but the fundamental processes are reactions between earth materials and atmospheric constituents such as water, oxygen, and carbon dioxide. The products of chemical weathering are new minerals and dissolved elements and compounds.

The most important chemical weathering reactions are *solution,* the dissolving of minerals; *oxidation,* the "rusting" of minerals; *hydration,* the combining of minerals with water; and *hydrolysis,* the complex reaction that forms clay minerals and the economically important aluminum oxides. ✳ Table 6.1 shows the formulas for the typical chemical-weathering reactions that are explained in the following discussion.

*TABLE 6.1 Examples of Chemical-Weathering Reactions	
Reaction	Example
Solution	
Step 1: A natural acid forms.	$CO_2 + H_2O \rightarrow H_2CO_3$ carbon dioxide water carbonic acid
Step 2. Acid dissolves limestone, forming calcium ions and bicarbonate ions in solution.	$CaCO_3 + H_2CO_3 \rightarrow Ca^{++} + 2(HCO_3)^-$ limestone carbonic acid calcium ions bicarbonate ions
Oxidation and Hydration Oxygen and water combine with iron, producing hydrated iron oxide ("rust").	$4Fe^{++} + 3O_2 + 6H_2O \rightarrow 2(Fe_2O_3 \cdot 3H_2O)$ iron minerals oxygen water limonite (rust)
Hydrolysis Orthoclase feldspar combines with acid and water, forming clay minerals and potassium ions.	$2KAlSi_3O_8 + 2H^+ + 9H_2O \rightarrow$ orthoclase feldspar acid ions water $Al_2Si_2O_5(OH)_4 + 2K^+ + 4H_4SiO_4$ clay minerals potassium ions soluble silica

Solution

Carbon dioxide released from decaying organic matter and from the atmosphere combines with water to form carbonic acid. This natural weak acid attacks solid limestone, dissolving it and yielding a watery solution of calcium and bicarbonate ions. Solution in limestone terrain creates caverns, such as the Mammoth Caves in Kentucky and Carlsbad Caverns in New Mexico. (Chapter 7 explains this.) Acid rain, which forms when sulfur dioxide or nitrogen oxides combine with water droplets in the atmosphere to form sulfuric and nitric acids, takes its toll on rock monuments (◆Figure 6.4).

Oxidation and Hydration

Oxidation produces iron-oxide minerals (hematite and limonite) in well-aerated soils, usually in the presence of water. It is the rusting commonly seen on metal objects that are left outdoors. Pyroxene, amphibole, magnetite, pyrite, and olivine are most susceptible to oxidation because they have high iron contents. It is the oxidation of these and other iron-rich minerals that provides the bright red and yellow colors seen in many of the rocks of the Grand Canyon and the Colorado Plateau.

◆ **FIGURE 6.4** Compare the weathering of granite obelisks, both believed to have been shaped 3,500 years ago (1500 B.C.). (a) Obelisk amid the ruins of Karnak near Luxor, Egypt but since exposed to radically different environments. The hieroglyphs are sharp, and the polished surface is still visible. (b) The red-granite obelisk known as "Cleopatra's Needle" that stands in New York's Central Park was a gift from the government of Egypt in the late 19th century. New York City's humidity and acidic pollution have caused chemical weathering of the incised hieroglyphs that had endured several thousand years in Egypt's arid climate.

(a)

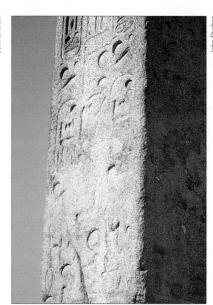

(b)

John Shelton

Hydrolysis

The most complex weathering reaction, hydrolysis, is responsible for the formation of clays, the most important minerals in soil. A typical hydrolytic reaction occurs when orthoclase feldspar, a common mineral in granites and some sedimentary rocks, reacts with slightly acidic carbonated water to form clay minerals, potassium ions, and silica in solution. The ions released from silicate minerals in the weathering process are salts of sodium, potassium, calcium, iron, and magnesium, which become important soil nutrients. Clay minerals are important in soils, because their extremely small grain size—less than 2 microns (0.002 mm)—gives them a large surface area per unit weight. Soil clays can adsorb significant amounts of water on their surfaces, where it stays within reach of plant roots. Also, because the clay surfaces have a slight negative electrical charge, they attract positively charged ions, such as those of potassium and magnesium, making these important nutrients available to plants. Other soil components being equal, the amounts of clay and humus in a soil determine its suitability for sustained agriculture. Sandy soils, for example, have much less water-holding capacity, less humus, and fewer available nutrients than do clayey soils. But overly clay-rich soils drain poorly and are hard to work.

The Rate of Weathering

The rate of chemical weathering is controlled by the surface environment, grain size (surface area), and climate. The stability of the individual minerals in the parent material is determined by the pressure and temperature conditions under which they formed. Quartz is the last mineral to crystallize from a silicate magma, and the temperature at which it does so is lower than the temperatures at which olivine, pyroxene, and the feldspars crystallize. For this reason, quartz has greater chemical stability under the physical conditions at Earth's surface. The relative resistances to chemical weathering of minerals in igneous rocks thus reflect the opposite order of their crystallization sequence in a magma. Most stable to least stable, the sequence is quartz (most stable; crystallizes at lowest temp.), orthoclase feldspar, amphibole, pyroxene, and olivine (least stable; crystallizes at highest temp.).

Micas and plagioclase feldspars form over a range of temperatures and thus vary in weathering stability. Note that ferromagnesian (iron and magnesium) minerals—olivine, pyroxene, and amphibole—are least stable and most subject to chemical weathering. Igneous rocks, such as basalt and gabbro, are made up of iron-rich minerals, and weather readily in humid climates.

A monolithic mass of rock is less susceptible to weathering than an equal mass of jointed and fractured rock. This is because the monolith has less surface area on which weathering processes can act. A hypothetical cubic meter of solid rock would have a surface area of 6 square meters. If we were

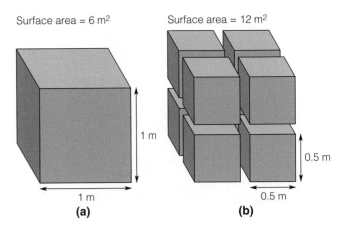

Surface area = 6 m²   Surface area = 12 m²

1 m   1 m   0.5 m   0.5 m

(a)   (b)

◆ **FIGURE 6.5** Surface area increases with decreasing particle size. A cube that is 1 meter on each side has a surface area of 6 m². If the cube is cut in half through each face, 8 cubes result that have a total surface area of 12 m².

to cut each face in half, however, we would have 8 cubes with a total surface area of 12 square meters (◆Figure 6.5). Thus smaller fragments have more area upon which chemical and physical weathering can act. For example, whereas soils have developed on volcanic ash in the West Indies after only 30 years, some nearly 200-year-old solid basalt flows in Hawaii have yet to grow a radish. This reflects differences in particle size and surface area.

The effect of climate has already been discussed. It is important to remember that chemical weathering dominates in humid areas, and physical weathering is most active in arid or dry alpine regions. (Figure 6.4 may help you remember this.) However, humans have accelerated chemical weathering by polluting the atmosphere with acid-forming compounds. Limestone monuments in English cemeteries require 250–500 years to weather to a depth of 2.5 centimeters and thus obliterate inscriptions. Buildings in northern England are known to weather more quickly on the side that receives sulfur-laden winds from nearby industrial areas. A sixteenth-century monastery in Mexico that was built of volcanic tuff has been ravaged by physical and chemical weathering to the extent that some of the carved statues on its exterior are barely recognizable (◆Figure 6.6a). A rock wall protecting Chicago's Lakeshore Drive was built of Indiana limestone. Chemical weathering by water overtopping the wall has dissolved clearly visible pits in a pattern known as "honeycomb" weathering (◆Figure 6.6b). You can see examples of weathering in your own community by visiting a cemetery. Compare the legibility of the inscriptions on monuments of various ages and materials. Some rock types hold up better than others, and younger inscriptions are easier to read than those that have been exposed to the elements for a century or two.

In the past 20 years geologists, teaming up with high-energy particle physicists, have come up with a new way to measure rates of erosion, the result of physical and chemical

◆ **FIGURE 6.6** (a) A 16th-century monastery in Mexico shows the ravages of weathering, mostly from wind and wind-driven rain. The rock is volcanic tuff. (b) A Lake Michigan seawall built of Indiana limestone is chemically weathered by waves overtopping the structure. Solution of the limestone has caused "honeycomb" weathering.

weathering of rock (◆ Figure 6.7). Measuring erosion is not a simple task, because in most cases what you are trying to measure, rock, is long gone. The trick to this method is the ability to count very rare atoms of several elements including beryllium, chlorine, and helium. Earth is constantly being bombarded by radiation (mostly neutrons) that originates outside the solar system. Most of this radiation passes through the rocks that make up our planet, but occasionally there is a direct hit and something like the nucleus of an oxygen atoms gets slammed so hard, it breaks apart. One of the pieces left is likely to be a Be atom with 4 protons and 6 neutrons giving it a mass of 10 atomic mass units—otherwise known as ^{10}Be. These rare creations are known as *cosmogenic isotopes*, because they are isotopes made (genesis) by cosmic radiation (cosmo).

Using expensive and exotic tools the number of ^{10}Be atoms can be counted. Because the neutrons that make ^{10}Be penetrate only a meter or two into rock, the number of ^{10}Be atoms reveals how quickly the rock is eroding. Lots of ^{10}Be, slow erosion. Not much ^{10}Be, fast erosion. Using this technique, researchers have shown that parts of Australia and Antarctica are exceptionally stable, eroding only a few tens of centimeters over a million years. In contrast, parts of the active mountain ranges, such as the Himalaya lose a kilometer or more of rock over the same length of time.

Geologic Features of Weathering

Spheroidal weathering is a combination of chemical and physical weathering in which concentric shells of decayed

◆ **FIGURE 6.7** (a) At Lawrence Livermore Laboratory, best known for designing nuclear weapons, is a machine of exquisite sensitivity, an atom sorter and counter known as an accelerator mass spectrometer. (b) In the highlands of Namibia two geologists collect samples of eroding rock to analyze on the same accelerator seen in 6.7a. The data showed this is a very stable outcropping of rock; it's eroding only about 3 meters every million years.

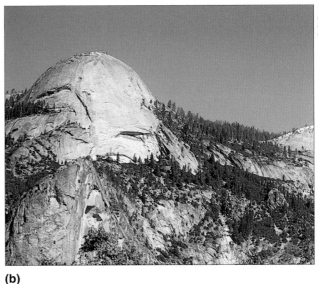

◆ **FIGURE 6.8** (a) Spheroidal weathering in jointed granite; Alabama Hills, California. Mount Whitney and the Sierra Nevada are in the background. (b) Sheet jointing has produced these two spectacular domes in granite. North Dome and Basket Dome; Yosemite Valley, California.

rock are separated from a block bounded by joints or other fractures (◆Figure 6.8a). It occurs when a rectangular block is weathered from three sides at the corners and from two sides along its edges, while the block's plane faces are weathered uniformly. It is also called "onionskin" weathering, because the layers of an onion provide a good analogy. **Exfoliation domes** (Latin *folium,* "leaf," and *ex-,* "off") are the most spectacular examples of physical weathering. These domes result from the unloading of rocks that had been deeply buried. As erosion removes the overlying rock, it reduces pressure on the underlying rocks, which in turn begin to expand. As the rocks expand, they crack and fracture along **sheet joints** parallel to the erosion surface. Slabs of rock then begin to slip, slide, or spall (break) off the host rock, revealing a large, rounded domelike feature. Sheeting along joints occurs most commonly in plutonic rocks like granite and in massive sandstone. Half Dome in Yosemite National Park, California and Stone Mountain in Georgia are granite exfoliation domes (◆Figure 6.8b).

Soils
Soil Genesis

Soils form by the weathering of **regolith,** the fragmental rock material at Earth's surface. By studying soils, we can make inferences about their parent materials and the climate in which they formed and can determine their approximate age. Five environmental factors determine the development of soils: (1) climate, (2) organic activity, (3) relief of the land, (4) parent material, and (5) the length of time that soil-forming

processes have been acting. These factors can be entered into the "CLORPT equation," a memory aid for these five factors: Soil = $f(Cl, O, R, P, T)$ where f is read "a function of" and Cl, O, R, P, and T represent climate, organic activity, relief, parent material, and time, respectively. The rate at which a soil develops is a function of climate and parent material, because the weathering of rock that started on the outcrop continues when fragments of rock become the parent material for soils.

Soil Profile

As we have noted, loose rock and mineral fragments at the surface of the Earth are referred to as *regolith*. Regolith may consist of sediment that has been transported and deposited by rivers or wind, for example, or it may be rock that has decomposed in place. Where weathering has been sufficient, a surface layer that can support plant life—soil—has developed. Climate is the most important factor in soil development; the influence of the parent material is most apparent in young soils such as decomposed granite, which contains quartz and feldspar grains, some of them having been altered to clay minerals.

A developed **soil profile** has several recognizable **soil horizons,** layers roughly parallel with the ground surface that are products of soil-forming processes (◆Figure 6.9). The uppermost soil horizon, the "A horizon," is the *zone of leaching.* Here, mineral matter is most strongly dissolved by downward-percolating water. It may be capped by a zone of organic matter (*humus*) of variable thickness called the "O horizon," which provides CO_2 and organic compounds that make the percolating water slightly acidic. As the dissolved

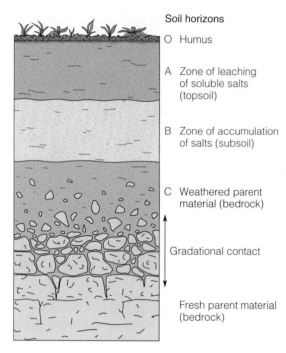

Soil horizons

O Humus

A Zone of leaching
   of soluble salts
   (topsoil)

B Zone of accumulation
   of salts (subsoil)

C Weathered parent
   material (bedrock)

Gradational contact

Fresh parent material
(bedrock)

◆ **FIGURE 6.9** An idealized soil profile. Heavily irrigated soils and very young ones exhibit variations of this profile.

chemicals move downward, some of them are redeposited as new minerals and compounds in the "B horizon," called the *zone of accumulation.* This horizon is usually lighter in color and harder than the A horizon. Below this is the "C horizon," the weathered transition zone that grades downward into fresh parent material.

CONSIDER **THIS**

Tennis is a sport that is played throughout the world on a variety of court surfaces. For example, the five most prestigious professional tennis tournaments are played on grass (in England), clay (in France and Italy), and concrete (in the United States and Australia). Why do you suppose clay-surface courts are more common in the eastern United States, and in tropical and humid countries, than in the south-western United States, where concrete is the preferred surface?

The thickness and development of the soil profile are profoundly influenced by climate and time. In desert regions of the American southwest, the A horizon may be thin or nonexistent, and the B horizon may be firmly cemented by white, crusty calcium carbonate known as **caliche.** Caliche forms when downward-percolating water evaporates and deposits calcium carbonate that has been leached from above. Also, if the water table is close to the ground surface, upward-moving waters may evaporate into the layers, leaving deposits of caliche. Some of these deposits are so thick and hard that unusual measures are required to till or excavate through them (◆Figure 6.10).

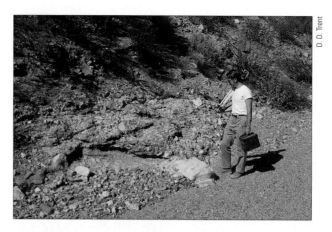

◆ **FIGURE 6.10** Caliche exposed in an arroyo near Tucson, Arizona.

Residual Soils

Residual soils have developed in place on the underlying bedrock. For example, in humid-temperate climates, rock decomposes into saprolite. If the parent rock were granite, the saprolite would contain quartz, weathered feldspar, and clay minerals formed from the weathering of feldspar. Saprolite can be mistaken easily for its parent rock except that one can often stick a shovel right into it and the density of saprolite can be tens of percent less than the density of the rock from which it was derived. Engineers and geologists call slightly weathered granite *decomposed granite,* or simply *d.g.* It is an excellent foundation material for structures and roads. On the other hand, heavy clay soils develop from the *in situ* weathering of shale bedrock. The expansive nature of some of these clays makes them troublesome. (This is discussed in the next section of this chapter.) Residual soils take tens to hundreds of thousands of years to develop, and they are always subject to erosion and removal by one of many geologic processes.

Transported Soils

Some soils have formed on transported regolith. These transported soils are designated by the geologic agent that is responsible for their transportation and deposition: *alluvial* soils by rivers, *eolian* soils by the wind, *glacial* soils, *volcanic* soils, and so on. ◆ Figure 6.11 illustrates a soil that developed on volcanic ash overlying an older basalt on which little or no soil had developed. Known as the *Pahala ash,* soil developed on this parent material supports such exotic and valuable crops as macadamia nuts, sugar cane, and papaya on the Island of Hawaii.

CONSIDER **THIS**

Decomposed granite (referred to as *d.g.* in the building trades) is the preferred sandy-soil material for making durable, attractive garden pathways, trails, and even driveways. What is the mineralogy of this immature soil, and what mineral makes it cohesive and firm when it is rolled?

B. Pipkin

◆ **FIGURE 6.11** Volcanic ash (horizontal layers) overlying weathered basalt; Pahala, Hawaii. This volcanic soil supports rich crops of sugar cane, pineapple, and macadamia nuts.

As Pleistocene glaciers expanded and moved over northern North America, they scraped off Canada's soils and regolith and redeposited them in a band across the United States from Montana to New Jersey. Soils formed on these widespread deposits—collectively known as *glacial drift*—are extremely variable; they may be thin or thick, bouldery or fine grained, fertile or relatively barren. Some areas of drift are so bouldery that they are impossible to farm. This is one of the reasons that pastures for grazing dairy cattle, rather than cultivated grain crops, are today the agricultural mainstay of such states as Wisconsin and New Hampshire (see Gallery ◆ Figure 2).

Loess (approximately "luss," to rhyme with cuss) is wind-blown silt composed of very small grains of feldspar, quartz, calcite, and mica. Covering about 20 percent of the United States and about 10 percent of Earth's land area (◆ Figure 6.12), loess is arguably Earth's most fertile parent material. The sources of loess are glacial deposits and deserts. Strong winds blowing off the Ice Age glaciers that covered most of Canada and the northern United States

swept up nearby meltwater deposits and redeposited them far away as loess in valleys and on ridge tops. In the United States, loess has produced especially rich agricultural lands in the Palouse region of eastern Oregon and Washington, and in the central Great Plains, sometimes called the "breadbasket" of the United States. The fertility of the Ukraine, formerly part of the Soviet Union but now a republic, is due to a favorable climate and its loessal soils. So highly regarded was this soil, that Adolph Hitler had large quantities of it moved to Germany during World War II. Loess derives its fertility from its loamy texture, which allows roots to penetrate easily and retains water well. In addition, many of the minerals in loess are small and not yet weathered. When they do weather in the soil, they release nutrients that plants can use.

The largest loess deposits are in China, where they cover 800,000 square kilometers (310,000 mi^2) and are as thick as several hundred meters. These deposits were derived from the Gobi and Takla Makan deserts to the north and west. On windy days airborne silt from these deserts is noticeable in Beijing, hundreds of miles away. Similarly, the loess in Africa's eastern Sudan was carried there by winds from the Sahara Desert. Even more impressive is the wind transport of dust from Asia to Hawaii, where small grains of windblown quartz can be found.

Loess has several noteworthy physical properties. It is tan to almost yellow in color and rather loosely packed (low density), which makes it easily excavated and eroded by running water. Loess has cohesive strength and thus is capable of standing in vertical slopes without falling (◆ Figure 6.13). These unusual properties served the Union and the Confederacy well in Mississippi during the Civil War. Both sides excavated tunnels, trenches, revetments, and other earthworks in the loess soil prior to the siege and battle at Vicksburg, which ultimately was won by Ulysses S. Grant's Union forces. In northern China's Shansi Province in the 1500s, elaborate caves scraped out of loess provided refuge for more than a million people. Unfortunately for the cave residents, loess is subject to collapse under dynamic stresses such as those of an earthquake, and an estimated 800,000 people were buried in their homes during the earthquake of 1556. The load of loess carried by the Huang Ho River as it flows through this area gave the river its other name, the *Yellow River*—which empties into the *Yellow Sea*.

Soil Color and Texture

Color is a good indicator of a soil's *humus* (organic material) and iron content. As the proportion of humus increases, soil color darkens from brown to nearly black. Oxides of iron impart a reddish or yellowish color found mostly in semitropical and tropical areas. Bright red soils occur where there is aeration and good drainage, whereas yellow hydrated-iron compounds form where there is poor drainage. In arid climates, white B horizons and white-coated soil fragments indicate

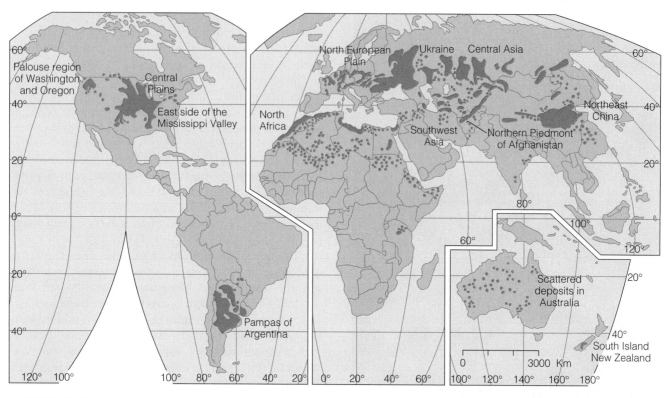

◆ **FIGURE 6.12** Loess-covered regions of the world. Note that the largest areas are in China, central and western Asia, and North America.

calcium carbonate or other salts including gypsum (Calcium sulfate) and halite (sodium chloride). Because both gypsum and halite are water soluble, their presence in soils indicates very low amounts of rainfall. Such soils are found in the driest deserts of the world, for example the southern Negev in Israel.

A soil's texture—size of the individual grains (particles) composing it—is a major determinant of its utility. A sample of any particular soil, excluding any gravel or boulders in it, consists of three basic grain sizes: sand, silt, and clay. The grain-size range used by the U.S. Department of Agriculture for each texture category is shown in ◆Figure 6.14a. Based upon the percentages of sand, silt, and clay in a soil sample, the soil can be classified as loam, sandy loam, and so forth (◆Figure 6.14b).

◆ **FIGURE 6.13** Villagers in Askole, Pakistan, have dug caves in these vertical loess cliffs.

(a)

(b)

◆ **FIGURE 6.14** (a) Grain-size scale adopted by the U.S. Department of Agriculture and used by most soil scientists. (b) Soil texture classification triangle. Each side of the triangle is a scale for the percentage content of one of the three textural grades—sand, silt, or clay. A hypothetical soil sample has been found to be 60% silt, 20% sand, and 20% clay. Using this triangle, thick black lines are followed inward from the respective percentages to learn the textural class of the soil, "silt loam." USDA data

The texture of a soil has practical significance, as it determines the soil's properties—its looseness, workability, drainage, and so on. For example, coarse-textured soils are easily worked, readily penetrated by plant roots, and easily eroded. Cemeteries in glaciated regions are almost always dug in sand and gravel. Fine-textured (clayey) soils tend to be heavy, harder to work, and sticky when wet. Water retention and infiltration are also functions of soil texture. Loose, sandy soils tend to allow water to pass through them readily, but they have low water retention capacity. The opposite is true of fine-textured soils; they have large water-retention capacity but low infiltration rates. This condition leads to poor drainage and excessive water runoff. Loamy soils are generally considered most favorable for agriculture because they provide a balance between the coarse- and fine-textured soils, as shown in Figure 6.14b.

Soil Classification

Pedologists (Greek *pedon,* "soil," and *logos,* "knowledge of ") have long known that soils that form in tropical regions are different from those that form in arid or cold climates. They also know that soils change over time as iron-rich materials oxidize (rust) and grow redder, organic matter accumulates, and clays that form by weathering are transported into the soil by gravity and water, a process called **illuviation**. Where rainfall is heavy, soils are deep, acidic, and dominated by chemical weathering. Soluble salts and minerals are leached (removed) from the soil, iron and aluminum compounds accumulate in the B horizon, and the soil supports abundant plant life. In arid regions, on the other hand, soils are usually alkaline and thinner, coarse-textured or rocky, and dominated

by physical weathering. Because of low precipitation in arid regions salts are not leached from soils, and when soil moisture evaporates, it leaves additional salts behind (■Case Study 6.1 on page 172). These salts may form crusts and lenses of caliche ($CaCO_3$ and other salts), most commonly in the B horizon.

These understandings led to the development of a system of soil orders that are used to classify soils. In this system, soils are classified by their physical characteristics, soils that have been modified by human activities are classified along with natural soils, and most importantly, soil names convey information about their physical characteristics. There are eleven soil orders (see ◆ Figure 6.15a and b) that can be arranged to follow patterns of age and climate. This type of ordering shows just how useful this soil classification scheme can be to geologists working in the field who want to understand environments and landscape history (◆ Figure 6.16). An example might be locating a site for a septic system for waste disposal. Such systems require well-aerated soils that are not saturated by water. After meeting with the landowner, the first thing to do is go to the library and consult the county soil survey. If the land is dominated by spodsols (◆ Figure 6.17), the soils are probably well drained. But if there are histosols, they are wetland soils. The next step is to start digging pits. If there are, mottled, Cg horizons, it is a histosol, and not a good place to site a septic system because the ground will be saturated at least part of the year. In actuality, soil orders are the highest level of classification. Below them are suborders, families, and series. The number of soil entries increases astronomically at the lower levels (illustrated by the fact that 14,000 soil series are recognized in the U.S.).

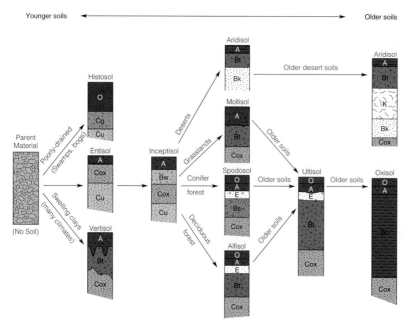

O horizon: Surface horizon dominated by organic material, dark
A horizon: Surface horizon or beneath O horizon, dominated by mineral material but with enough organic material to be dark
E horizon: Subsurface horizon, leached gray by acids from conifer needles
Bw horizon: Subsurface horizon, young and slightly reddened by iron oxide
Bs horizon: Subsurface horizon, reddened where organic matter, aluminum and iron accumulate
Bk horizon: Subsurface, lightened by the accumulation of calcium carbonate
Bt horizon: Subsurface horizon that is reddened by iron and where clay has accumulated
Bo horizon: Subsurface horizon, deeply weathered and very red with iron, found in very old, tropical soils (laterite)
Cox horizon: Subsurface horizon of oxidized parent material, red from iron
K horizon: Subsurface horizon similar to Bk but so enriched in calcium carbonate that it is white
Cg horizon: Subsurface horizon that has patchy colors of grey and green because it is usually saturated with water
Cu horizon: unweathered parent material

(a)

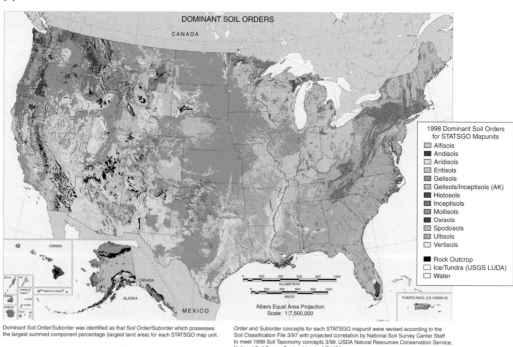

Dominant Soil Order/Suborder was identified as that Soil Order/Suborder which possesses the largest summed component percentage (largest land area) for each STATSGO map unit.

Order and Suborder concepts for each STATSGO mapunit were revised according to the Soil Classification File 3/97 with projected correlation by National Soil Survey Center Staff to meet 1998 Soil Taxonomy concepts 3/98. USDA Natural Resources Conservation Service, National Soil Survey Center, Lincoln, NE USA.

(b)

◆ **FIGURE 6.15** (a) The classification of eleven soil orders is an organized way to understand where different types of soils form and how soils change as they age. Source: Birkeland, Soils and Geomorphology, figure 2.7 (b) Wonder where to find your favorite soil order? Check the map! If you are in the United States, can you figure out what soil order likely underlies where you are sitting right now, reading this book? Source: http://soils.ag.uidaho.edu/soilorders/

◆ **FIGURE 6.16** Here is an Oxisol, a deep red soil that has formed as the result of extended weathering in a tropical climate. This is Madagascar. You are looking at the Bo horizon; the A and O horizons have been eroded. This type of soil is also known as a laterite.

◆ **FIGURE 6.17** A classic spodsol. With a light grey, leached E horizon and the red B horizon below. At the top is the dark A horizon and decayed vegetation (the O horizon). This soil is formed on parent material of sandy, glacial outwash in Michigan, most likely under the acid needles of conifers.

Soil Problems

Soil Erosion

Although soil is continually being formed, it is for practical purposes a nonrenewable resource, because hundreds or even thousands of years may be necessary for soil to develop. Ample soil is essential for providing food for Earth's burgeoning population, but throughout the world it is rapidly disappearing. Although the United States has one of the world's most advanced soil conservation programs, soil erosion remains a problem after 60 years of conservation efforts and expenditures of billions of dollars, even though rates of erosion have been reduced. Erosion removed an estimated two billion tons of topsoil from U.S. farmlands in 1992—down from slightly more than three billion tons a decade earlier. With the average annual soil loss estimated as 10–12 tons per hectare (4–4.8 tons/acre) and an assumed annual soil-formation rate of 2–4 tons per hectare (0.8–1.6 tons/acre), three to five times as much soil is being lost as is being formed in the United States. Not only does soil erosion destroy fertility, but tons of soil settle in lakes and clog waterways and drainages with sediment, pesticides, and nutrients each year. Losses of only 2–3 centimeters (1 in) of topsoil represent about 200 tons per hectare. Such erosion cuts crop yields and over time renders land less productive.

On a global basis, an area the size of China and India combined has suffered *irreparable degradation* from agricultural activities and overgrazing—mostly in Asia, Africa, and Central and South America (◆Figure 6.18). Lightly damaged areas can still be farmed using the modern conservation techniques explained later in this chapter, but "fixing" serious erosion problems is beyond the resources of most Third World farmers and their governments.

Erosion Processes

The agents of soil erosion are wind and running water. Heavy rainfall and melting snow create running water, which removes soil by sheet, rill, and gully erosion. **Sheet erosion** is the removal of soil particles in thin layers more or less evenly

◆ **FIGURE 6.18** World soil degradation, 1945–1991. The areas degraded are given both in percentage of the arable area (pie-shaped areas in orange) and in hectares (a hectare is 10,000 square meters = 2.47 acres). Table 6.3 (on page 163) summarizes the various causes of soil degradation in the world.

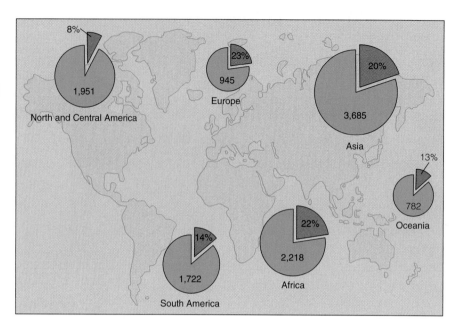

from an area of gently sloping, bare land. It goes almost unnoticed and can easily be stopped by planting a cover crop. The roughness provided by the vegetation as well as the effective cohesion provided by roots keeps soil in place.

Rill erosion, on the other hand, is quite visible as discrete streamlets carved into the soil (◆Figure 6.19a). If these rills become deeper than about 25–35 centimeters (10–14 in), they cannot be removed by plowing, and gullies form. Estimated annual U.S. cropland soil loss from sheet and rill erosion is shown by state in ◆Figure 6.20a. Tennessee headed the list in 1980, followed by Hawaii, Missouri, Mississippi, and Iowa, as shown in ⁕ **Table 6.2.** Gullies are created by the widening, deepening, and headward erosion of rills by water

both running over the surface and moving through pores in the soil and parent material. **Gullying** is a problem because it removes large areas of land from production or even transit (◆Figure 6.19b). The U.S. Army worries about gullies on its training grounds because entire tanks have fallen into gullies during night maneuvers.

Wind erodes soils when tilled land lies fallow and dries out without vegetation and root systems to hold it together. The dry soil breaks apart, and wind removes the lighter particles. If the wind is strong, a dust storm may occur, as it did in the 1930s, creating the Dust Bowl (described at the beginning of the chapter). Much of the reason for the Dust Bowl was the widespread conversion of marginal grasslands, which

(a)

◆ **FIGURE 6.19** (a) Rill erosion in cultivated soil. The rill will probably be plowed under. (b) Gullies have eaten away at the landscape, dramatically limiting the availability of tilled land near Lumpkin, Georgia (width of area in photo about .25 km).

(b)

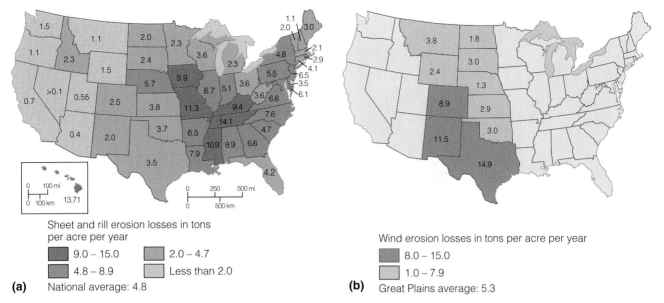

◆ **FIGURE 6.20** Estimated annual rates of cropland soil loss in the United States, 1980. (a) Sheet and rill erosion losses. (b) Wind erosion losses in the Great Plains. (Light green represents <1 ton/acre per year.)

★TABLE 6.2	Significant U.S. Soil Erosion by State, 1980	
Rank	State	Tons/(acre × year)
	Sheet and Rill Erosion	
1	Tennessee	14.1
2	Hawaii	13.7
3	Missouri	11.3
4	Mississippi	10.9
5	Iowa	9.9
	Wind Erosion	
1	Texas	14.9
2	New Mexico	11.5
3	Colorado	8.9
4	Montana	3.8
5	Oklahoma	3.0
	Total Soil Erosion, Water and Wind*	
1	Texas	18.4
2	Tennessee	14.1
3	Hawaii	13.7
4	New Mexico	13.5
5	Colorado	11.4

*The U.S. average annual rate of total soil erosion is estimated at 4.0–4.8 tons/acre (10–12 tons/hectare).

Source: *Environmental Trends* (Washington, D.C.: Council on Environmental Quality, 1981), cited in Sandra Batie, *Soil Erosion: A Crisis in America's Cropland?* (Washington, D.C.: The Conservation Foundation, 1983).

receive only 25–30 centimeters (10–12 in) of rainfall per year, to cropland. Unfortunately, this is still occurring in some places in the United States and in the rest of the world. ◆ Figure 6.20b presents estimates of the amount of soil lost each year to wind erosion in the Great Plains states. When the 50 states' estimated wind and water erosion losses are combined (see Table 6.2), the state with the greatest annual loss is Texas, followed by Tennessee, Hawaii, and New Mexico, respectively. ★ Table 6.3 summarizes the recognized causes of accelerated soil erosion worldwide and assesses their relative impact.

In addition to the soil erosion caused by overgrazing, deforestation, and bad agricultural practices, recreational and military pursuits (see ■**case study** 6.2) cause soil erosion, particularly those that involve off-road vehicles (ORVs). A 1974 study indicated that recreational pressure on semiarid lands of southern California by ORVs was

★TABLE 6.3	Causes of World Soil Erosion and Deterioration
Cause	Estimated % of Total
Overgrazing	35
Deforestation	30
Bad agricultural practices	28
Other causes, natural and human	7

Source: World Resources Institute, United Nations Environment and Development Program, *World Resources: A Guide to the Global Environment* (New York: Oxford University Press, 1992).

◆ **FIGURE 6.21** Hill-climbing motorcyclists have devastated this slope in Jawbone Canyon in the Mojave Desert, California. The bikers have compacted the soil surface, causing reductions in vegetation and soil permeability. The reduced soil moisture content has seriously harmed the local plant and animal ecology. Desert rains have eroded the tire tracks, transforming them into gullies, which increases water runoff and sediment yield (erosion).

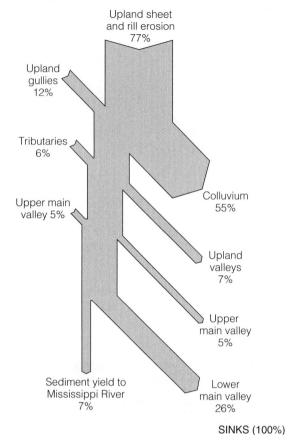

SOURCES (100%)

Upland sheet and rill erosion 77%

Upland gullies 12%

Tributaries 6%

Upper main valley 5%

Colluvium 55%

Upland valleys 7%

Upper main valley 5%

Sediment yield to Mississippi River 7%

Lower main valley 26%

SINKS (100%)

◆ **FIGURE 6.22** "Trimblegram" for Coon Creek a stream that is a tributary of the Mississippi River in Wisconsin. The diagram shows sources of eroded soil and sinks where the eroded soil has gone between 1938 and 1975. Most of the eroded soil ends up as colluvium, the poorly sorted mass of material at the base of hillslopes. Source: Trimble, 1983, American Journal of Science

"almost completely uncontrolled" and that those desert areas had experienced greater degradation than had any other arid region in the United States (◆ Figure 6.21). In the two decades since that study, much has been accomplished in controlling off-road traffic in California and other states, but ORVs continue to exert severe impacts upon areas established for their use.

Although significant soil erosion has gone on for millennia, starting with the beginning of intensive agriculture in the Middle East, it has not always been clear where the eroded soil goes and how far and fast it travels. More recent work, particularly that of Stan Trimble, a geographer, suggests that most eroded soil does not go far at all. Trimble tracked soil eroded from slopes in the Midwest and found that only a small percentage of it has made the journey all the way to the Mississippi River. Most of the eroded soil is sitting at the bottom of hillslopes or on valley bottoms (◆ Figure 6.22). This is also the case in the eastern states. In Pennsylvania, Dorothy Merritts and Bob Walter found that small mill dams, built by colonial settlers to power the mills that were the backbone of their economy, have trapped much of the soil eroded from the then clear-cut slopes. Today these dams are an environmental disaster waiting to happen. They are failing or being removed, and all that sediment, eroded more than 200 years ago but in storage ever since, is headed downstream to the Chesapeake Bay, one of the most important estuaries in the country, and a place where millions of dollars are being spent to improve water quality and fisheries.

The Impact of Cropland Loss on Humans

The main concern when addressing soil loss—whether the loss is due to erosion or the conversion of cropland to nonagricultural uses—is that soils are biological and chemical factories that produce food. Increasingly, the U.S. population is moving into urban areas, and to accommodate them, cities are expanding outward onto agricultural land. About 20 percent of the United States was under cultivation in 1992 (◆ Figure 6.23), and each year more of that land is urbanized or converted to forestland, particularly in the northeastern and southeastern states. This trend is also seen in India and other nations with high growth rates. Between 1950 and 1998 the amount of grain-growing land per person worldwide declined. World cropland decreases had not been regarded as a major problem until the late 1900s, because increases in productivity had been great. Increases in productivity leveled off in 1990, however, and it is doubtful that future increases will keep pace with increasing population and decreasing cropland soils.

It is also important to consider that much of the increase in agricultural productivity has been leveraged off of the use of fossil fuels to power large-scale industrial agriculture in developed nations. This cheap energy also allows for the

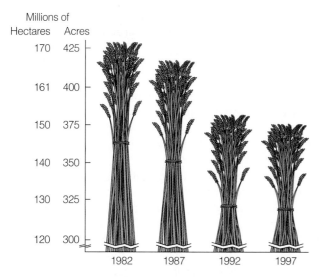

Millions of
Hectares   Acres

◆ **FIGURE 6.23** Total U.S. cropland, 1982 to 1997. Reductions were due to urbanization, conversion to other uses, and soil erosion. American Geological Institute

◆ **FIGURE 6.24** Terracing steep hillsides is an ancient soil conservation practice; China.

shipment of food products long distances so that in the dead of winter people in Maine or Wisconsin can eat tropical fruits from Hawaii or lettuce from southern California. If energy prices continue to increase and fossil fuels supplies tighten, one needs to ask: is there still enough fertile and available land nearby to support the food needs of the local population? The answer in many intensively developed areas may well be no.

Mitigation of Soil Erosion

Thomas Jefferson was among the first people in the United States to comment publicly on the seriousness of soil erosion. He called for such soil conservation measures as crop rotation, contour plowing, and planting grasses to provide soil cover during the fallow season. These practices are now common in industrialized nations but, unfortunately, only minimally employed in developing countries. Proper choices of where to plant, what to plant, and how to plant are primary components of soil conservation. The major erosion mitigation practices are described here.

- *Terracing*—creating flat areas, terraces, on sloping ground—is one of the oldest and most efficient means of saving soil and water (◆Figure 6.24).
- *Strip-cropping*, by which close-growing plants are alternated with widely spaced ones, efficiently traps soil that is washed from bare areas and also supplies some wind protection. An example of this is alternating strips of corn and alfalfa.
- *Crop rotation* is the yearly alternation of soil-depleting crops with soil-enriching crops. Rotating corn and wheat with clover in Missouri, for example, has been found to reduce soil runoff from 19.7 tons/acre for corn

to 2.7 tons/acre, a huge loss reduction. Groundcovers such as grasses, clover, and alfalfa tend to be soil-conserving, whereas row crops like corn and soybeans can leave soil vulnerable to runoff losses. Retaining crop residues, such as the stubble of corn or wheat, on the soil surface after harvest has been found to reduce erosion and to increase water retention by more than half.

- *Conservation-tillage* practices minimize plowing in the fall and encourage the contour plowing of furrows perpendicular to the field's slope so that they will catch runoff, increasing water infiltration.
- *No-till* and *minimum-till* practices also conserve soil. With no-till farming, seeds are planted into the soil through the previous crop's residue, and weeds are controlled solely with chemicals. Specialized no-till equipment is required. No-till has been especially successful in soybean farming. In 1993 U.S. farmers left 30 percent of their crop debris on 37 million cultivated hectares (92 million acres), nearly a third of all cultivated land in the United States. Ten percent of the U.S. planted acreage was not plowed at all. No-till agriculture is most beneficial during times of drought, when plowed fields dry out and topsoil is more vulnerable to wind erosion. No-till practices saved much of the agricultural soil that would have otherwise been eroded by floodwaters of the Great Flood of 1993 in the Mississippi River valley.

Wind-caused soil losses can also be reduced by planting windbreaks of trees and shrubs near fields and by planting

Edward B. Nuhfer and AIPG

◆ **FIGURE 6.25** This well-built concrete-block wall in Colorado was uplifted and tilted by stresses exerted by the underlying expansive soil.

row crops perpendicular to the prevailing wind direction. Wind losses are almost zero with cover crops such as grasses and clover.

Expansive Soils

Certain clay minerals have a layered structure that allows water molecules to be absorbed between the layers, which causes the soil to expand. (This process differs from the *adsorption* of water to the surface of nonexpansive soil clays.) Soils that are rich in these minerals are said to be **expansive soils** and fall in the **soil order,** *vertisol.* Although this reaction is reversible, as the clays contract when they dry, soil expansion

can exert extraordinary uplift pressures on foundations and concrete slabs, with resulting structural and cosmetic damage (◆ Figure 6.25). Damage caused by expansive soils costs about $6 billion per year in the United States, mostly in the Rocky Mountain states, the Southwest, and Texas and the Gulf Coast states (◆ Figure 6.26). The swelling potential of a soil can be identified by several standard tests, usually performed in a soils engineering laboratory. A standard test is to compact a soil in a cylindrical container, soak it with water, and measure how much it swells against a certain load. Clays that expand more than 6 percent are considered highly expansive; those that expand 10 percent are considered critical. Treatments for expansive soils include (1) removing them, (2) mixing them with nonexpansive material or with chemicals that change the way the clay reacts with water, (3) keeping the soil moisture constant, and (4) using reinforced foundations that are designed to withstand soil volume changes. Identification and mitigation of damage from expansive soils is now standard practice for U.S. soil engineers.

> **CONSIDER THIS**
>
> Expansive soil is the soil problem most likely to be encountered in maintaining a home. Assuming that you, as a homeowner, found that your newly purchased dream house is built on expansive soil, what could you do to minimize its impact on your home?

Permafrost

The term **permafrost,** a contraction of *permanent* and *frost,* was coined by Siemon Muller of the U.S. Geological Survey in 1943 to denote soil or other surficial deposits in which temperatures below freezing are maintained for several years. More than 20 percent of Earth's land surface is underlain by permafrost, and it is not surprising that most of our

◆ **FIGURE 6.26** Distribution of expansive soils (shown in brown) in the United States.

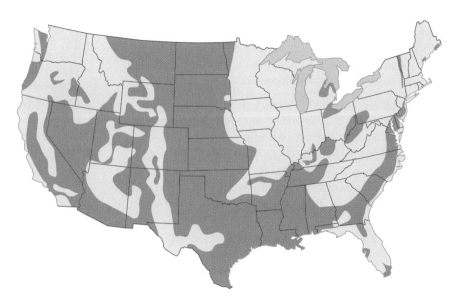

knowledge about frozen ground has been derived from construction problems encountered in Siberia, Alaska, and Canada. Permafrost becomes a problem for people when we change the surface environment by our activities in ways that thaw the near-surface soil ice. Such melting results in soil flows, landslides, subsidence, and related phenomena. Permafrost forms where the depth of freezing in the winter exceeds the depth of thawing in the summer. If cold ground temperatures continue for many years, the frozen layer thickens until the penetration of surface cold is balanced by the flow of heat from Earth's interior. This equilibrium between cold and heat determines the thickness of the permafrost layer. Thicknesses of as much as 1,500 meters and 600 meters (almost 5,000 and 2,000 ft) have been reported in Siberia and Alaska, respectively. Such thick layers are very old; they must have formed over hundreds of thousands to perhaps millions of years as Earth cooled during repeated Pleistocene glaciations.

The top of the permanently frozen layer is called the **permafrost table** (◆Figure 6.27). Above this is the **active layer,** which is subject to seasonal freezing and thawing and is always unstable during summer. When winter freezing does not penetrate entirely to the permafrost table, water may be trapped between the frozen active layer and the permafrost table. These unfrozen layers and lenses, called *talik* (a Russian word), are of environmental concern, because the unfrozen groundwater in the talik may be under pressure. Occasionally, pressurized talik water moves toward the surface and freezes, forming a dome-shaped mound 30–50 meters (100–160 ft) high called a *pingo*. The presence of ice-rich permafrost becomes evident when insulating vegetation, usually tundra, is stripped away for a road, runway, or building. Thawing of the underlying soil ice results in subsidence, soil flows, and other gravity-induced mass movements (◆Figure 6.28). Even the casual crossing of tundra on foot or

◆ **FIGURE 6.28** Utility poles extruded from permafrost ground; Alaska. One solution has been to support the poles with tripods placed on the ground surface.

in a jeep can upset the thermal balance and cause thawing. Once melting starts, it is impossible to control, and a permanent scar is left on the landscape (◆Figure 6.29).

Structures that are built directly on or into permafrost settle as the frozen layers thaw (◆Figure 6.30). Both active and passive construction practices are used to control the problem. Whereas active methods involve complete removal or thawing of the frozen ground before construction, passive methods build in such manners that the existing thermal regime is not disturbed. For example,

- a house can be built with an open space beneath the floor so that the ground can remain frozen (◆Figure 6.31a),
- a building can be constructed on foundation piers whose temperature is held constant by heat dissipaters or coolant (◆Figure 6.31b), and

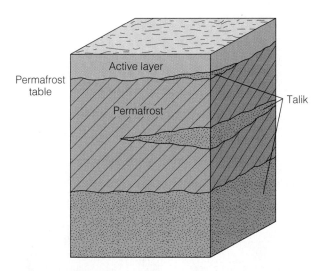

◆ **FIGURE 6.27** Permafrost zones. Talik, unfrozen layers and "lenses," may occur in the active layer and in the permanently frozen layer. USGS

◆ **FIGURE 6.29** Scars made by vehicles on tundra soil remain for many years; Alaska.

◆ **FIGURE 6.30** Differential melting of permafrost caused this cabin to subside at one end. Note that part of the foundation of the cabin is open to the atmosphere, which prevented the permafrost from melting.

Larry Hinzman, Univ. of Alaska

■ roads are constructed on top of packed coarse-gravel fill to allow cold air to penetrate beneath the roadway surface and keep the ground frozen.

The most ambitious construction project on permafrost terrain to date is the 800-mile oil pipeline from Prudhoe Bay on Alaska's North Slope to Valdez on the Gulf of Alaska. About half the route is across frozen ground, and because oil is hot when it is pumped from depth and also during transport, it was decided that the pipe should be above ground so as to avoid the thawing of permafrost soil (◆Figure 6.32).

The four-foot-diameter pipeline also crosses several active faults, three major mountain ranges, and a large river. The pipeline's above-ground location allows for some fault displacement and for easier maintenance if it should be damaged by faulting. Placing the pipeline above ground accommodates the longstanding migratory paths of herding animals such as caribou and elk.

Permafrost is likely to be one of the most troublesome victims of global climate change. All climate models and much recent observational data (such as the dramatic thinning of

(a)

©Bryan & Cherry Alexander Photography/Alamy

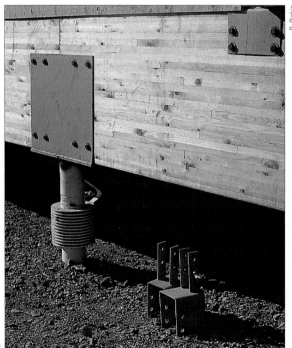

B. Pipkin

(b)

◆ **FIGURE 6.31** Two methods of mitigating permafrost damage: (a) Apartments raised on pilings in Anadyr Chukotka, Siberia. (b) Heat-dissipating foundation piers on a modern structure; Kotzebue, Alaska

(a)

(b)

◆ **FIGURE 6.32** The 800-mile Alaskan oil pipeline was constructed to accommodate permafrost and wildlife. (a) The meandering pattern allows for expansion and contraction of the pipe and for potential ground movement along the Denali fault, which it crosses (see Ch. 4). The pipeline supports feature heat-dissipating radiators. (b) Caribou are able to pass beneath the elevated pipeline.

arctic sea ice) indicate that the warming of Earth as CO_2 levels continue to rise will not be a uniform affair. Climate change is predicted to have some of its most extreme impacts in the polar regions with warming several times greater than at midlatitudes. The effects will be dramatic, with areas of permafrost that have existed since the end of the last ice age disappearing. Once permafrost is gone, traditional building techniques can be employed, but the real problems will come during the decades-long transition when once-solid frozen ground melts, and structures, roads, and other engineering works that depend on that solid, frozen base are damaged and destroyed.

Settlement

Settlement occurs when a structure is placed upon a soil, rock, or other material that lacks sufficient strength to support it. Settlement is an engineering problem, not a geological one. It is treated here, however, because settlement and specific soil types are inextricably associated. All structures settle, but if settlement is uniform—say, two or three centimeters over the entire foundation—there is usually no problem. When differential settlement occurs, however, cracks appear or the structure tilts.

The Leaning Tower of Pisa in Italy is probably the best-known, most-loved example of poor foundation design. It may have scientific importance as well, as Galileo is said to have conducted gravity experiments at the 56-meter (183 ft) structure. Begun in 1174, the tower started to tilt when the third of its eight stories was completed, sinking into a two-meter-thick layer of soft clay just below the ground surface. At

first, the tower leaned north, but after the initial settlement and throughout the rest of its history it has leaned south. To compensate for the lean, the engineer in charge had the fourth through eighth stories made taller on the leaning side. The added weight caused the structure to sink even further. At its maximum lean, it tilted toward the south about 5.2 meters (17 ft) from the vertical, about 5.5 degrees, which gives one an ominous feeling when standing on the south side of the tower (◆ Figure 6.33).

In 1989 a similarly constructed leaning bell tower at the cathedral in Pavia, Italy collapsed, causing officials to close the tower at Pisa to visitors. In 1990, the Italian government established a special commission of structural engineers, soils engineers, and restoration experts to determine new ways to save the monument at Pisa. The commission's goal was to reverse the tilt 10–20 centimeters (4–8 in), which they believed would add 100 years to the lifetime of the 800-year-old structure. After considering many plans, it was decided to remove soft sediment from the north side of the tower, causing it to reverse its lean to the south. The method of soil extraction was proposed by a commission member and professor of soil mechanics, John Burland of London's Imperial College. This method was simple in concept but difficult to implement. It was done with drills 200 mm (about 8 in) in diameter, which remove cores of soil about 15–20 liters (4.8–5.2 gal) in volume. The weak sediment under the north side foundation quickly filled the void left by the drill and the tower started to straighten; that is, tilt back toward the north. The concept was simple compared with installing stabilizing cables or constructing enlarged and stronger foundations. After being shut down for eleven years, the tower was

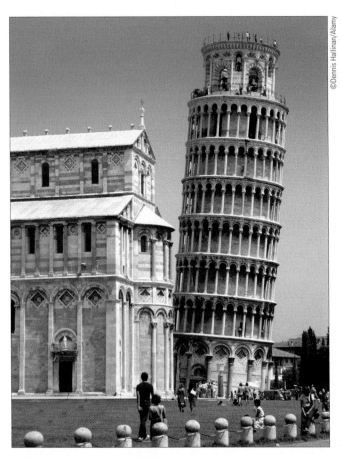

◆ **FIGURE 6.33** Inadequate foundation investigation and design; Pisa, Italy.

canopies of jungle vegetation. But if the trees are cut and the land used for agriculture, the soils can bake in the sun. They become brick-hard when they dry out and of little use (◆ Figure 6.34). Indeed, the famous Buddhist temple complex at Angkor Wat in Cambodia is partly constructed of laterite bricks that have endured since the thirteenth century. Deforestation of areas underlain by laterites is an invitation to this hardening, as U.S. forces discovered in Vietnam when they attempted to grade roads and runways on lands that had been defoliated for military reasons. Deforested laterites make for swampy conditions during the rainy season, because they lack permeability; there is little infiltration of the water. This can raise havoc with wheeled vehicles and restrict mobility in such regions.

Desert soils can also be quite fragile as many military forces have discovered. The dry desert conditions limit plant growth, and what organic matter is produced is rapidly oxidized leaving soils with only a minimal A horizon. Often a delicate biologic crust of algae, bacteria, and lichen forms on desert soils along with a pavement of stones that allows the soils to resist erosion by both wind and water. When this crust or armoring is disturbed, the soils can erode rapidly. It can take decades for the crust to become reestablished. After

reopened, still leaning, but 40 cm (16 in) and 0.5 degrees less. It is estimated that the realignment will add 300 years to the life of the tower. The project cost $30 million, but that is dwarfed by the enthusiasm of the four million visitors who come to the tower each year.

It should be noted that tilting towers are not exceptional in Italy. Few of the 170 campaniles (bell towers) still standing in Venice are vertical, for example, and many other towers throughout Italy and Europe tilt. These graceful towers are certainly testimony to past architects' ability and talent, but also to their failure to understand that a structure can be truly vertical only if local geology permits.

Other Soil Problems

There are a number of other problems that can affect soils. Usually these problems arise when people take actions that impact either the chemical or physical properties of soil; many such problems are region-specific.

In the tropics, where weathering conditions are extreme due to high rates of rainfall and warm temperatures, soils are very susceptible to damage. These oxisols or laterites are bright red and clay rich. They are typically covered by dense

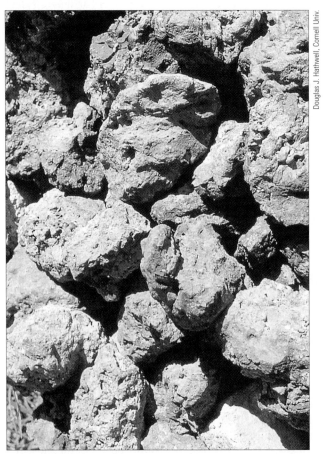

◆ **FIGURE 6.34** Dried and hardened laterite; Brazil. This soil is so hard that soil scientists call it "ironstone."

disturbance, dust is the biggest issue, and clouds of it can be raised by traffic and wind once the soil's protective armor has been removed. This dust can choke the engines of vehicles operating in the desert, clogging their air filters and bringing them quickly to a halt. It fills the lungs of people living and working nearby. At best, it leads to the "concrete boogers" that plug the nose of every scientist who has ever worked in the desert. At worst, it leads to poisoning when the dust is laden with toxic metals such as selenium.

Have you ever hiked on a trail through the woods that became a stream after an afternoon thunderstorm passed? If so, you have seen the effect of soil compaction firsthand. In the woods there is no flowing water; it's all being absorbed by the soil. Moving people and vehicles across soils changes soil structure by collapsing the pores that allow water and air to pass between grains. Some of these pores are microscopic, not visible with the naked eye. Others are large enough to put your hand in, perhaps the abandoned burrow of a gopher or the cavity left when an old root rotted away. When these pores are crushed, there is nowhere for the water to go except to run off the surface. The pounding of hiking boots is one way to compact soil. The tires of automobiles are an even better way (◆Figure 6.35). Park on a lawn a few times. The ability of the soil to soak up rainwater might go down by a factor of two. Park in the same place until the grass is dead and the soil packed tight and what was once a lawn now behaves like asphalt. Repeat this process across a city, and storm sewers that used to be able to handle all the runoff in a good rainstorm no longer can because so much more water is spilling into the streets every time it rains. However, with a pick axe, some compost, some fencing, and handful of grass seed, the problem can be fixed. Soil, once aerated and protected from future compaction will regain its ability to absorb water.

CONSIDER THIS

It is jokingly said that the twelfth-century architect of the Leaning Tower of Pisa saved money by not having a foundation investigation. Had engineers and geologists with today's knowledge and tools existed at that time, what routine tests would they have performed on borehole soil samples that would show settlement was inevitable? What recommendations might they have made to the client?

(a)

(b)

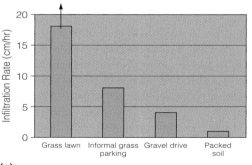

(c)

◆ **FIGURE 6.35** Soil compaction is a significant urban and suburban problem caused in large part by large objects that we drive. (a) Cars parked on what used to be lawn near college student apartments in Burlington, Vermont. (b) University of Vermont undergraduate research students measure how little water infiltrates on a part of campus where hundreds of people walk over the soil every day. Here, they are simulating a rainstorm and measuring runoff. (c) The results of many such infiltration tests shows how well lawns soak up rainfall and how packed soil has almost no ability to infiltrate rainfall.

Salinization and Waterlogging

Irrigation is an amazing thing, allowing the desert to bloom and many hungry mouths to be fed. But irrigation can adversely impact soils. When irrigated, some soils get so salty that plants can't grow. This salinization is the oldest soil problem known to humans, dating back at least to the fourth century B.C. At that time a highly civilized culture was dependent upon irrigation agriculture in the southern Tigris–Euphrates Valley of Iraq, the "Cradle of Civilization." By the second century B.C. the soils there were so saline that the area had to be abandoned. Soils in parts of California, Pakistan, the Ukraine, Australia, and Egypt are now suffering the same fate.

Salinization can be human induced by intensive irrigation, which raises underground water levels very close to the soil. Capillary action then causes the underground water, containing dissolved salts, to rise in the soil, just as water is drawn into a paper towel or sugar cube. The soil moisture is then subject to surface evaporation, leaving behind salts that render the soil less productive and eventually barren (see ◆ Figure 1). The productivity of 15 percent of all U.S. cropland is totally dependent upon irrigation, and 30 percent of U.S. crops are produced on this land.

For millennia, annual flooding of the Nile River added new layers of silt to the already rich soil and removed the salts by dissolving them and flushing them downstream. After completion of the Aswan Dam in 1970, however, the yearly flooding and flushing action stopped, and salts have now accumulated in the soils of the floodplain. Salinization is particularly evident in the arid Imperial Valley of California. Soils of the Colorado Desert, or any desert for that matter, can be made productive if enough water is applied to them. Because deserts have low rainfall, irrigation water must be imported, usually from a nearby river. The All-American Canal brings relatively high salinity water from the Colorado River to the Imperial Valley, where it is used to irrigate all manner of crops, from cotton to lettuce. In places, the water table has risen to such a degree that the cropland lies barren, its surface cov-

ered by white crusts of salt. The Imperial Valley's Salton Sea is one of the largest saltwater lakes in the United States, and it grows saltier and larger every year by the addition of saline irrigation water. This internally drained basin has no outlet, so all the salt that comes in, stays in, unless of course it dries and blows away. The return of degraded irrigation water in canals to the Colorado River in southern Arizona has required that a desalinization facility be established near Yuma to make the water acceptable for agricultural use in Mexico.

Soil salinization can be reversed by lowering the water table by pumping and then applying heavy irrigation to flush the salts out of the soil. Salinization can also be mitigated, or at least delayed, by installing perforated plastic drainpipes in the soil to intercept excess irrigation water and carry it off-site. Neither remedy is an easy or inexpensive solution to this age-old problem.

◆ **FIGURE 1** Accumulation of salts at the soil surface due to evaporation of irrigation and groundwater; Imperial Valley, California.

General Patton's soils decades later

Most people know General George S. Patton (◆ Figure 1) as a legendary military commander who used his tank corps to defeat the Germans in North Africa during World War II; however, few know that he was a great compactor of soil.

In preparation for the North Africa campaign, Patton ordered the building of a dozen training camps in desert southwest, camps with names like Iron Mountain. There, tens of thousands of recruits, most of whom had never seen the desert, came to live and train

for months. Imagine the shock coming from the woods of Minnesota or the bayous of Louisiana to the Mojave Desert where the biggest plant was a sage brush bush, and there wasn't anything green for miles. The camps were spartan places with rows of tents and roads bulldozed onto the gently sloping expanse of the desert. The soldiers, who we can only assume were more than a bit home-sick at times, did what they could to make the place home, building stone walls and intricate stone designs around their tents. Indeed, only the roads and little stone walls remain today. When the war was won, the camps were abandoned and never reoccupied. For 60 years they have been a ticking experiment in how quickly desert soils recover from the pounding of soldiers' boots and tons of force that tank treads impose on the landscape.

In the late 1990s, geologists from the University of Vermont and Duke University reoccupied one of Patton's camps in order to see how the desert soils had recovered over the more than 50 years since Patton and his men had packed up and gone home. They used all sorts of tools to understand how the landscape and soils behaved, including high precision surveys (◆ Figure 2), low-tech soil pits, and measurements of ^{10}Be (see the explanation earlier in the chapter). One of them set out lines of small painted pebbles, 1600 in all, to track how pebbles moved over several years (◆ Figure 3).

The impacts of Patton's men more than half a century ago are very much affecting the area today: soil compaction in deserts is a long-lasting insult. The soil beneath the aban-doned roads is still compacted, and water flows along these roads during rainstorms rather than through natural drainage ways. Some of the pebbles moved in the several years that they were tracked. The pebbles in channels moved the farthest and fastest as they were swept away by moving water (it rained several times during the three-year experiment). Even the pebbles away from channels moved a bit, probably by the action of gophers or other clumsy animals. The rock berms that the soldiers made to outline the walkways might seem insignificant, but they were a major influence on which way the water moved.

So, what can be done? At present, nothing because this camp is a protected area, but this 50-year experiment suggests some sim-ple ways in which the impact of future camps on desert soils might be minimized. When a camp is abandoned, plow up the roads and disturb the soils to reduce compaction. This will accelerate erosion initially but allow the system to more quickly reestablish natural drainage patterns in the long run. All of this should make us all wonder about the impact people have had and are having on the expan-sive deserts of the Middle East where so much of our petroleum exploration and mili-tary activity goes on these days.

◆ **FIGURE 1** General George S. Patton, tank commander and desert soil compactor.

◆ **FIGURE 2** A survey rod equipped with a prism reflects laser light allowing precise measurement of distance. In the background a specially designed GPS unit is used to measure locations to within a centimeter or two. Hundreds of locations will be measured in a day and the data will be used to map the walkways and channels that carry water over this desert surface.

◆ **FIGURE 3** University of Vermont geologists lay out lines of numbered and painted pebbles at General Patton's Iron Mountain camp in the Mojave Desert. Several years of suurveying will show how fast these pebbles move.

CASE STUDY 6.3

Rx for Contaminated Soils

For millennia soil has been a convenient place to dump waste nobody wanted as the waste would seem to disappear, and soil was plentiful. Indeed, the use of soil for disposal has been a gold mine for archeologists who routinely sort through century-old privies to find the remains of long-vanished civilizations. But today, the stakes are higher as we manufacture and process many chemicals far more hazardous than what went into colonial outhouses—heavy metals, toxic pesticides, oil wastes. We rely on groundwater for drinking, and much of what is in the soil eventually finds its way into the groundwater. Sadly, it took us a while to realize how bad the problem was so we've been playing catch up as a society for several decades now. Although spills of hazardous materials frequently contaminate soils, the Environmental Protection Agency (EPA) did not include a soil component in their system for ranking Superfund cleanup sites until 1990. Fortunately, soil contamination is reversible, and soils can be "cleaned," *remediated,* by a variety of methods. A large soil remediation industry has sprung up in response to EPA and state environmental protection requirements.

Various soil remediation techniques are used, depending upon the thickness of the soil to be cleaned and the chemical nature of the contaminant. *Dilution,* mixing contaminated soil with clean soil, is one technique. It works, but it is expensive and it contaminates an even larger volume of soil. The old saying "the solution to pollution is dilution" is not really a solution.

Bioremediation, a natural process, uses microorganisms to degrade and transform organic contaminants. Bacteria and fungi flourish naturally in soils where oil, sewage sludge, or food-production waste has been discarded. Biodegradation can be stimulated by increasing the amount of air in the soil through cultivation, vapor-extraction pumping (see below), or stockpiling the soil and forcing air into it. Adding easily decomposed organic matter such as hay, compost, or cattle manure also speeds up degradation of organic contaminants. Bioremediation is relatively inexpensive, even if some contaminated soils simply require turning (disking or plowing) to speed up oxidation.

A successful bioremediation project at Mobil Oil Company's natural-gas refinery at Liberal, Kansas, is shown in ◆ Figure 1. The soil contained up to 26,000 parts per million (2.6%) of hydrocarbons—an oily mess. To help degrade these oils, the contaminated soil was spread in a layer less than 20 centimeters (8 in) thick and then a nutrient and microbial amendment, cow manure, was applied. The soil was periodically stirred to promote biological

activity and was subsequently reclaimed and planted (◆ Figure 1b).

Vapor extraction is used for removing volatile (easily evaporated) organic compounds such as cleaning solvents from soils. Air is drawn through the soil by means of dry wells connected to vacuum pumps. The air passing through the soil evaporates the compounds and exhausts them either to the atmosphere or to charcoal filters where they are trapped and later treated. This technique is especially desirable for cleaning soils beneath buildings or roads, because no excavation is required except for the drilling of shallow wells. The downside is that it may take months or even years to remove most of the contamination.

Phytoremediation, the use of plants to remove contaminants, is used mainly for extracting salts. This has been used in the Netherlands where periodic seawater flooding contaminates soils with salt. Plant scientists are also developing *hyperaccumulator* plants that clear soils of heavy metals such as cobalt, nickel, and zinc by concentrating these metals in the plant tissues. The cost of phytoremediation materials, equipment, and labor is relatively low, but up to a decade can be required to remediate soil to the point that it can be used again. Of course, the metal- and salt-laden plants need to be disposed of correctly, too.

(a)

(b)

◆ **FIGURE 1** A successful bioremediation project. (a) Oil-contaminated soil (2.6% hydrocarbons) at a Kansas refinery is removed for bioremediation by a bulldozer. Note the patchy distribution of the oil contamination. The soil is spread in a layer about 20 centimeters (8 in) thick. Nutrient amendment (cow manure) is added to stimulate biological degradation of the hydrocarbons. (b) Remediated soil (<.01% hydrocarbons) is spread and planted with grass. Note the clods of manure and the white chunks of caliche in the redistributed soil. The structure in the background is a grain silo in which wheat is stored.

Soils as an Album of History

History is written on our landscapes and in our soils, and you can learn an amazing amount once you know the language and some of the vocabulary. These two images tell a story of settlement and agriculture. ◆Figure 1 shows just how much information about what life used to be like and how humans and their actions have impacted the landscape can be gleaned from a soil pit. ◆Figure 2 works the other way and is all about clues—clues that a landscape gives you about what lies beneath in the soils. Here, stone walls tell of rocky glacial soils and the toils of long-dead farmers to clear their fields.

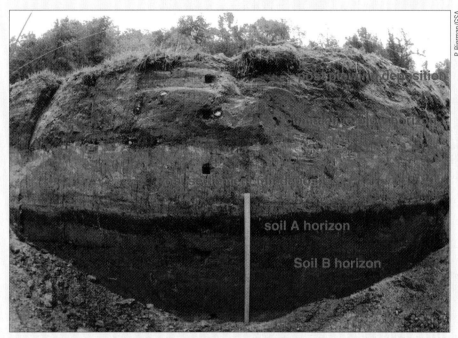

P. Bierman/GSA

◆ **FIGURE 1** A fish-eye view of a soil that has lots of stories to tell. The bottom two layers are forest soil, an inceptisol with a well-developed A and Bw horizon. The A horizon is a meter below today's surface. The material burying the soil came pouring off the slope above when settlers first cleared this site in Huntington, Vermont 200+ years ago. There is a sharp line between the dark and light grey material that marks the bottom of the plow zone; it's a really distinctive way to know that soils have been plowed and planted. The thickness of the plow zone is more than twice the depth to which plows can reach. Which means that every time it rained and the slope eroded, it had to be plowed again. Source: Bierman, P., Lini, A., Davis, P. T., Southon, J., Baldwin, L., Church, A., and Zehfuss, P., 1997, Post-glacial ponds and alluvial fans: recorders of Holocene landscape history: GSA Today, v. 7, p. 1-8. Reprinted with permission of Paul Bierman and GSA Today.

Robert Thayer/Projections

◆ **FIGURE 2** Remnants of a stone wall in an area that was once cleared for agriculture; Attleboro, Massachusetts. Rocky glacial soils are difficult to farm because freezing and thawing cycles continually lift boulders into the soil root zone. This produces a new "crop" of rocks each spring in some areas. Stone walls are seen in fields and forests throughout the northeastern United States.

Summary

Soil

Defined

Many definitions depending upon use (engineering, agriculture, geology, etc.). For our purposes, however, soil is defined as weathered rock and mineral grains that can support plant life.

Environmental Factors of Soil Formation

Climate, organic activity, relief (topography), parent material, and time. Soils form from the weathering of regolith.

Weathering

Physical and chemical breakdown of bedrock and regolith. They are linked processes.

1. *Physical weathering* is caused by temperature differences and disruption by plants and animals.
2. *Chemical weathering* processes include solution, oxidation, hydration, and hydrolysis. Chemical weathering is important in the formation of clays, the most important mineral group in soils. Clays are important because they hold moisture and exchange nutrients with plants.

Rate of Weathering

Depends upon the rock or regolith's mineral composition and surface area as well as climate. Smaller particles weather faster than large masses, and iron-rich minerals weather faster than quartz or feldspar.

Features and Landforms

Spheroidal weathering and exfoliation domes are common features.

Soil Profile

Defined

Distinguishable layers, or horizons, in mature soils composed of the organic-rich O horizon on the top, the dark A horizon or zone of leaching (where minerals are dissolved), and a lower B horizon known as the zone of accumulation, where salts and clays accumulate. Below this is the C horizon of weathered parent material. The thickness of the horizons and the development rate of soil are profoundly influenced by climate.

Residual Soil

Developed in place on underlying bedrock and also known as saprolite. Oxisols, or laterites, are the brick-red soil of humid (subtropical and tropical) regions that represents intensive weathering of parent rock.

Transported Soil

Developed on regolith transported and deposited by wind (eolian), glaciers, rivers, or volcanic action. Loess, for example, is an eolian soil associated with ice-age continental glaciation. It is highly productive and is found throughout the central U.S. "breadbasket."

Soil Classification

A classification of soils into 11 orders by their physical characteristics that often reflect soil age and climate.

Soil Problems

Erosion

A major problem, because soil determines Earth's carrying capacity. Globally, irreparable soil degradation has impacted an area the size of China and India combined. U.S. soil losses vary greatly with location.

Processes

Sheet erosion by running water (thin layer is removed) can become rill erosion (defined streamlets are carved in the soil), which leads to gullying (the most destructive). Sheet and rill erosion can be halted, but once gullying starts, it is extremely difficult and costly to mitigate. Wind erodes soil on marginal lands that were once cultivated and then dried out. Without plant root systems to hold the soil, wind erosion can lead to "dust bowl" conditions. Off-road vehicles also seriously degrade soils.

Mitigation

Good agricultural practices include terracing, no-till and minimum tillage, strip cropping, and crop rotation. Wind losses can be minimized by planting windbreaks, strip crops, and cover crops such as clover.

Other Soil Problems

Expansive Soils

Certain clay minerals absorb water and expand, exerting high uplift pressures that can crack or even destroy structures. Mitigated by removal of soil, mixing, or keeping the moisture content constant.

Permafrost

Permanently frozen ground underlies (soil or rock) more than 20 percent of Earth's surface. Structures built directly on soil permafrost will settle, so mitigation involves building with an open space below the structure or thermal isolation so as not to disturb the thermal regime in the soil and melt the permafrost. Climate change will likely cause issues in permafrost regions.

Settlement

Occurs when the applied load is greater than the bearing strength of the soil; e.g., Leaning Tower of Pisa. An engineering problem that can be mitigated by proper design or by strengthening of the underlying soil.

Miscellaneous Soil Problems

Salinization and waterlogging (high water table), hardening of laterites due to deforestation and desiccation, compaction, and dust generation.

Contamination

Brines, petroleum products, crude oil, and chemicals of all sorts may contaminate soils. Common methods of cleansing the soil are bioremediation (bacteria), phytoremediation (plants), and vapor extraction (oxidation).

Key Terms

active layer
bioremediation
caliche
erosion
exfoliation dome
expansive soils
frost wedging
gullying (erosion)

illuviation
laterite
loess
pedologist
permafrost
permafrost table
phytoremediation
regolith

residual soil
rill erosion
sheet erosion
sheet joint
soil
soil horizon
soil profile
soil order

spheroidal weathering
trace elements
tundra soils
vapor extraction
weathering

Study Questions

1. Sketch a soil profile and describe each soil horizon.
2. Distinguish chemical weathering, physical weathering, and erosion.
3. What kinds of soils would you expect to develop on basalt in Hawaii, New Jersey, and Arizona? Explain the differences in terms of the CLORPT equation.
4. What is permafrost, and where is it found?
5. What soil problem does permafrost cause structures, and what techniques are used to prevent damage?
6. What is expansive soil, and what problems and challenges does it pose to soils engineers? What can be done to prevent distress due to this condition?
7. Soil erosion and degradation are two of humankind's oldest problems. How has human-induced soil loss come about?
8. What agricultural practices have led to salinization and water-logging of soils?
9. An inscribed rock obelisk dating from 1500 B.C. was resurrected from the ruins at Karnak, Egypt. Its inscriptions were crystal clear when it was brought to New York's Central Park as a gift of the Egyptian government in 1880, but today they are totally illegible. Explain the reason for this.
10. Laterites or oxisols present special problems when they are deforested. Why?
11. Compare the rates of soil erosion and soil formation in the United States.

For Further Information

Books and Periodicals

Batie, Sandra S. 1983. *Soil erosion: A crisis in America's croplands?* Washington, D.C.: The Conservation Foundation.
Brady, Nyle C. 1990. *The nature and properties of soils.* New York: Macmillan Publishing Co.
Brevik, Eric. 2002. Problems and suggestions related to soil classification as presented in introduction to physical geology textbooks, *Journal of Geoscience Education,* vol. 50, no. 5, November.
Brown, K.W. 1994. New horizons in soil remediation. *Geotimes* (American Geological Institute), September.
Brown, Lester. 1999. *State of the world.* New York: W.W. Norton & Co.
Ferrians, O. J. and others. 1969. *Permafrost and related engineering problems* U.S. Geological Survey professional paper 678.
Heiniger, Paolo. 1995. The Leaning Tower of Pisa. *Scientific American* 273, no. 6: 62–67.
Loynachan, Thomas E., Kirk W. Brown, Terence H. Cooper, and Murray Milford. 1999. *Sustaining our soils and society.* Alexandria, Virginia: American Geological Institute.
Singer, M. J. and D. N. Munns. 2002. *Soils: an introduction,* 5th ed. Upper Saddle River, New Jersey: Prentice Hall.
Winkler, Erhard M. 1998. The complexity of urban stone decay. *Geotimes* (American Geological Institute), September.

ThomsonNOW

Assess your understanding of this chapter's topics with additional comprehensive interactivities at http://www.thomson.com/login, which also has up-to-date web links, additional readings, and exercises.

Mass Wasting and Subsidence

A Bad Slice on the Golf Course

Golf's explosion in popularity in the late 1990s led to many new golf courses. Some are in resort communities, but others are in urban and suburban areas, like the beautiful Ocean Trails Golf Course south of Los Angeles on the Palos Verdes Peninsula, now known as the Trump National Golf Club (◆ Figure 1). Geologists know the peninsula well for its many landslides, due in part because it is uplifted 370 meters (1,300 ft) above sea level and in part to the sea, which is constantly battering the cliffs' base with waves. It's easy to see in 30- to 50-meter cliffs where the layers are exposed that the stratified sedimentary rock underlying the course inclines gently to the sea. Just as a slice of bread slides down a breadboard when tilted, some weak layers have slid toward the sea in the past, carrying houses and roads with them. Ocean Trails Golf Course was almost ready for its early summer 1999 opening when, without warning, a fissure opened parallel to the cliff, and 300 meters of the 18th fairway slid into the ocean. Local resident Tony Baker and his dog were temporarily stranded

◆ **FIGURE 1** Ocean Trails golf course, Palos Verdes Peninsula, California, shortly after the "slice" occurred, disrupting grand opening plans.

178

on a precarious 215-meter-(700 ft)-long island between fissures. "I heard crumbling earth and started seeing dust rising," Baker said later. "The trail started cracking up. I was doing a little running around, jumping over big cracks . . . I just found a place and hunkered down. I wasn't sure if I was going to make it back."

After three years of wrangling, the developers and lenders reached an impasse, and the landslide stabilization work stopped. The beautiful golf course, now only 15 holes long, was blemished by the scar of the landslide and stabilization work. Enter Donald Trump, the New York entrepreneur, real estate magnate, and enthusiastic golfer. He bought the troubled project (at a bargain price) in 2002 and vowed to finish the project by the summer of 2003 (not quite fulfilled). On January 20, 2006 the Trump National Golf Club officially opened with all 18 holes, and the buttress fill designed to stabilize the "slice" on the course is buried under the last two holes.

Mass wasting is the general term that denotes any downslope movement of soil and rock under the direct influence of gravity. Mass-wasting processes include landslides, rapidly moving debris flows, slow-moving soil creep, and rockfalls of all kinds. Annual damage from landsliding alone in the United States is estimated at between one and two billion dollars and is widespread, affecting much of the country (◆ Figure 7.1). If we include other ground failures, such as subsidence, expansive soils, and construction-induced slides and flows, total losses are on average many times greater than the annual combined losses from earthquakes, volcanic eruptions, floods, hurricanes, and tornadoes—unless of course it happens to be the year that hurricane Katrina strikes.

Mass wasting and subsidence are global environmental problems. Earthquake-triggered landslides in Kansu Province in China killed an estimated 200,000 people in 1920, and debris flows left 600 dead and destroyed 100,000 homes near Kobe, Japan in 1938. The largest loss of life from a single landslide in U.S. history, 129 fatalities, occurred at Mameyes, Puerto Rico in 1985. Landslides and debris flows are terrifying environmental phenomena that test our very certainty that Earth will always be stable below our feet.

The goal of this chapter is to reveal the variety of ways in which mass movements and subsidence can occur and place people and their property in harm's way. We will consider the relevant physical processes and means by which different types of Earth-movement hazards can be effectively mitigated or avoided.

Classifying Mass Movements

The classification of mass movements used in this book is similar to the one widely used by engineering geologists and soil engineers (◆ Figure 7.2). The bases of the classification are

- the type of material involved, such as rock or soil;
- how the material moves, such as by sliding, flowing, or falling;
- how fast the material moves, its velocity.

For instance, soil creep occurs at imperceptibly slow rates; debris flows are water saturated and move swiftly; and slides are coherent masses of rock or soil that move along one or more discrete failure surfaces, or **slide planes.** Failure occurs when the force that is pulling the slope downward (gravity) exceeds the strength of the earth materials that compose the slope. Because the force of gravity acting on a given slope is constant, either the earth materials' resistance to sliding must decrease, or the gradient of the slope must increase in order for sliding to occur. The presence of water is key, as it has the potential to diminish the resisting force that makes slopes stable. The strong shaking of a major earthquake can momentarily change the balances of forces on a just-stable landslide block and send it screaming down slope.

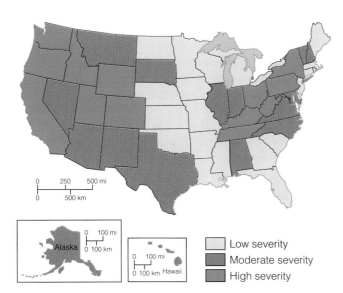

◆ **FIGURE 7.1** Severity of landsliding in the United States. Note that the most serious problems are found in the Appalachian Mountains, the Rocky Mountains, and the coastal mountain ranges of the Pacific Rim.
From J. P. Krohn and J. E. Slosson, "Landslide Potential in the U.S.," *California Geology* 29, no. 10 (1976)

◆ **FIGURE 7.2** Classification of landslides by mechanism, material, and velocity.

MECHANISM		MATERIAL			VELOCITY
		Rock	Fine-grained Soil	Coarse-grained Soil	
SLIDE		Slump	Earth slump	Debris slump	Slow
		Block glide	Earth slide	Debris slide	Rapid
FLOW		Rock avalanche	Mudflow, avalanche	Debris flow, avalanche	Very Rapid
		Creep	Creep	Creep	Extremely slow
FALL		Rockfall	Earthfall	Debrisfall	Extremely rapid

Flows
Types of Flows

Creep is the slow (a few millimeters per year) downslope movement of soil and rock on steep slopes. It involves any number of specific and different processes that are all typically lumped together in this one term. Physical creep involves deforming or changing the shape of the slope materials. Some deformation of weak materials, such as soft clay, may be driven completely by gravity. For other materials, freezing and thawing or alternate wetting and drying of a hill slope, which causes upward expansion of the ground surface perpendicular to the face of the slope, causes creep. As the slope dries out or thaws, the soil surface drops vertically, resulting in a net downslope movement of the soil (◆ Figure 7.3a). Biota of all sorts contribute to soil creep, and burrowing animals can move soil onto steep slopes. More of that soil ends up moving downslope than upslope; the net result is downslope transport. Trees are an important catalyst for soil creep. Every time one blows over and its root wad tips up (◆ Figure 7.3b), soil is moved, usually downslope.

How do we know soil creep is active? Bent trees, leaning fence posts and telephone poles, and bending of rock layers downslope are all evidence of soil creep (◆ Figure 7.3c). Homes built with conventional foundations 45–60 centimeters (18–24 in) deep may develop cracks due to soil creep. This is seldom catastrophic; typically it is a cosmetic and maintenance problem. The influence of soil creep can be overcome by placing foundations through the creeping soil into bedrock.

Debris flows are dense, one-phase, fluid mixtures of rock, sand, mud, and water. The one-phase part is important. Add too much water and the sediment settles out. Don't put

enough water in the recipe and the debris flow won't flow. Debris flows are often generated quickly during heavy rainfall or snowmelt where there is an abundant supply of loose soil and rock. They often begin as landslides, which mobilize and break up as they move downslope. Moving with the consistency of wet concrete, debris flows are very destructive, with velocities up to many meters per second. Because of their high viscosity and high density, commonly 1.5–2.0 times the density of water, debris flows are capable of transporting large boulders, automobiles, and even houses in their mass (◆ Figure 7.4).

Areas most subject to debris flows are characterized by sparse vegetation and intense seasonal rainfall, or are in regions that are subject to drenching rains (see ■ Case Study 7.1 on page 201). Debris flows are relatively common in steep, alpine, and desert environments worldwide. Debris flows associated with volcanic eruptions (lahars) are potential hazards in all volcanic zones of the world. They pose a particular danger in populated areas near volcanoes and are the most significant threat to life of all the mass movement hazards (see Chapter 5).

Causes, Behavior, and Prediction of Debris Flows

The recipe for debris flows is pretty short. Take a steep slope, provide plenty of loose material including some clay and silt, add just enough water to get everything wet but not too wet, mix well, and let the mixture loose down a stream channel or steep canyon. But something needs to start the flow and get things mixed up. Often that something is a small landslide or sediment collapsing off a steep bank. Once initiated, debris flows usually follow tracks or stream channels, often bulking

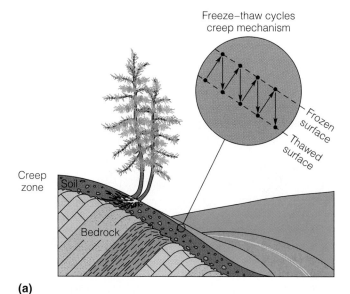

Freeze–thaw cycles
creep mechanism

Frozen
surface

Thawed
surface

Creep
zone

Soil

Bedrock

(a)

(b)

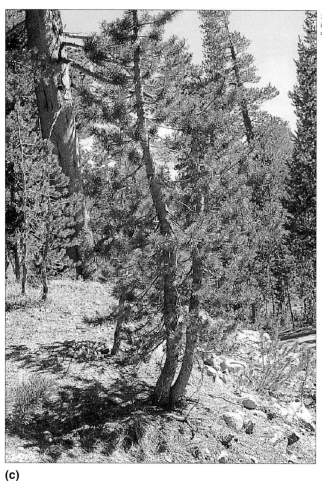

(c)

◆ **FIGURE 7.3** (a) Diagram of soil creep. (b) Soil creep on an Oregon scale. Here, in the Drift Creek Wilderness area, geomorphologist Tom Dunne (1.8 m) shows just how large tip ups and root wads can be. This is an old growth forest and when a tree falls on the 25 degree slopes, soil moves. (c) Soil creep, east slope of the Sierra Nevada, California.

up as they move by incorporating rocks and water from the stream. Small flows may end at the bottom of their track on a debris fan (◆ Figure 7.5)

Depending on the slope and its composition (the amount of water and the type of sediment), debris flows can just creep along or they can thunder down canyons at speeds in excess of 50 kilometers per hour (30 mi/hr). Several flows may merge and travel many miles from their source area. Because debris flows have a finite yield strength (unlike water, which will flow on any slope), at some combination of low slope and critical thickness (or thinness if you like), they will cease to flow and just sit there, slowly drying up and solidifying.

Although predicting the timing and location of specific debris flows isn't possible, the conditions that lead to debris-flow initiation are well known. Researchers have collected the field data required to create what are called intensity/duration envelope diagrams (◆ Figure 7.6). Simply put, these are

graphs that show the combination of how long it needs to rain and at what rainfall intensity before debris flows will begin. Reading the graphs, it's clear that really heavy rain need fall for only short periods of time to trigger flows, whereas moderate rain needs to fall for much longer before slopes will give way. Antecedence, or the amount of rain that's fallen over the past week or two, is also important. As you might suspect, saturated or nearly saturated soils are more likely to fail than those that have plenty of dry pore space available to soak up the rainfall.

Intensity/duration data have been compiled for flows and slides in the San Francisco Bay area of northern California (see Figure 7.6). These curves show that for a rainfall intensity of 0.5 inch per hour, the threshold time for the onset of debris flows is 8 hours in Marin County and 14 hours in Contra Costa County. The differing rainfall thresholds in these relatively close areas are due to the variability of geologic materials and topography. The lower curve of Figure 7.6

(b)

◆ **FIGURE 7.4** (a) Two debris flows in 1.5 hours hit and moved the farmhouse and destroyed several other buildings. The farm structures were on an alluvial fan without a well-defined main channel. The flow occurred in Madison County, Virginia, which shows that debris flows are not limited to the southwestern United States. (b) These are old boulders on a debris flow fan in Madison County. The boulder in the background is the size of a small house; a debris flow dropped these two where they sit today. The soils that partially bury them suggest repeated debris flows have covered this fan over the past tens of thousands of years.

(a)

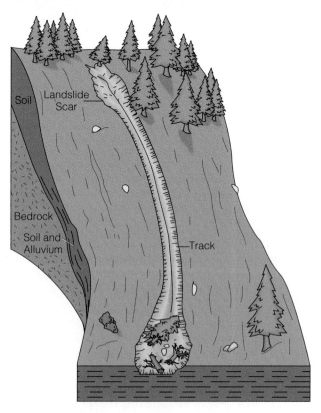

◆ **FIGURE 7.5** Debris flow track and zone of deposition. A debris flow may travel thousands of feet beyond the base of the slope.

shows that less-intense rainfall will produce debris flows in semiarid and arid areas of California. This is because these dry areas have little vegetation with root systems that retain soils and, therefore, have abundant loose surface debris. Although these curves are regional, they serve to alert residents in critical areas once the threshold conditions for flows have been attained.

Not all debris-flow seasons are created equal. Heavy rains (◆ Figure 7.7) associated with El Niño events (the change in Pacific Ocean water temperature distribution) have resulted in exceptional landslide and debris-flow activity, particularly along the west coasts of North and South America. The major El Niño of 1982–1983 was marked by widespread landsliding (slumps, slides, and flows) in various parts of the western hemisphere. The 1997–1998 El Niño, possibly the largest of the twentieth century, also had exceptional flows and slides. Hard hit was the San Francisco Bay area, where some of the 85,000 landslides shown on the thematic maps of the region were reactivated. This is an excellent example of interaction between the atmosphere, hydrosphere, and solid-earth systems.

Mountain slopes burned by range and forest fires during the dry season are very susceptible to debris flows during the wet season. John McPhee, in *Control of Nature*, does a marvelous job of describing the fire/storm/flow continuum in

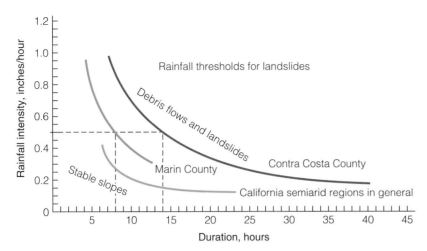

◆ **FIGURE 7.6** Rainfall thresholds for debris flows and landslides for two central California counties and California semiarid regions in general. For example, a rainfall intensity of 0.5 inch/hour for 8 hours is sufficient to initiate flows in Marin County. The same intensity for 14 hours is the threshold for Contra Costa County. *California Geology* data from CDMG

the hills overlooking the Los Angeles basin as well as the societal response (or lack thereof). High in those very steep hills, wildfires (◆ Figure 7.8 a) scorch the scrubby chaparral vegetation, releasing waxy chemicals that essentially waterproof the ground. When the winter rains come, the soils are impermeable, and with the vegetation burned off, they quickly lose all strength, letting loose debris flows that sweep through canyons, not caring one bit whether people or their homes and vehicles are in the way (◆ Figure 7.8 b). This cycle repeats itself over and over again. In October 2003 extreme forest fires burned in Southern California. In December of that year, when the rains came, 13 people lost their lives in a campground at the mouth of one of the burned canyons in the San Gabriel Mountains.

Debris flows are not limited to just the arid and semiarid Southwest and West; they occur anywhere slopes are steep, water is available, and loose sediment is ready to move. In

(a)

◆ **FIGURE 7.7** Rainfall was plainly in excess of normal in the San Francisco Bay area during El Niño years 1982–1983 and 1997–1998. These heavy rainfalls translated directly into a greater frequency of landslides and debris flows as saturated and nearly saturated soils failed and came roaring down slopes.

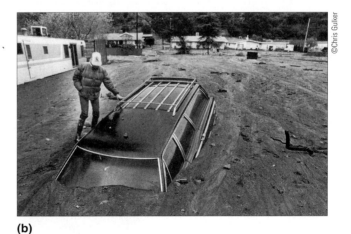

(b)

◆ **FIGURE 7.8** Fire, flood, and flow. (a) Wildfires rage in the forest and chapparal above Los Angeles. Once scorched and the vegetation removed, the land is primed to generate debris flows. (b) The results of a debris flow that came down La Tuna canyon in 1984.

Madison County, Virginia in 1995 an intense, long-lasting thunderstorm dumped more than 10 inches of rain on the steep slopes of the Blue Ridge Mountains, triggering landslides that set off numerous debris flows, which roared down steep stream channels, carrying boulders the size of houses (Figure 7.4) and devastating the area. Livestock were killed and buildings, bridges, roads, and crops were damaged. There was one loss of life directly attributable to the debris flows. It's estimated that such damaging debris flows may occur every three years somewhere in the Blue Ridge and southern Appalachian Mountains. Often they are triggered by the intense rains of tropical storms and hurricanes as the warm, moist air is lifted over the steep mountains.

Not all debris flows and avalanches are triggered by intense rainfall. On May 30, 1983 a debris flow was generated on Slide Mountain, Nevada that killed one person, injured many more, and destroyed a number of homes and vehicles, all in less than 15 minutes. How did this happen without any rainfall? About 720,000 cubic meters of weathered granite gave way from the mountain's steep flank and slid into Upper Price Lake. This mass displaced the water in the lake, causing it to overflow into a lower lake, which in turn overflowed into Ophir Creek gorge as a water flood. Picking up sediment as it went, it became a debris flow that emerged from the gorge, spread out, destroyed homes, and covered a major highway.

Landslides That Move as a Unit

The term **landslide** encompasses all moderately rapid mass movements that have well-defined boundaries and that move downward and outward from a natural or artificial slope. Landslides can range widely in size from a small planar failure no bigger than a car, to the largest landslide on record, the sector failure of Mt. St. Helens, during which the entire north side of the mountain slid away. Landslides occur in all 50 states and are an economically significant factor in more than 25 of them (see Figure 7.1). Areas with the highest slopes are at highest risk, because gravity is the force that drives landslides. For example, more than two million landslide scars dot the steep slopes of the Appalachian Mountains between New England and Alabama. Almost ten percent of the land area of Colorado is landslide terrain; and landslides and debris flows in Utah caused $300 million worth of damage in 1983–84. In southern California, eight wet years between 1950 and 1993 averaged $500 million in landslide damage. Slope stability problems have such impact that a national landslide-loss-reduction program was implemented by the U.S. Geological Survey in the mid-1980s. A high priority of the program is to identify and map landslide-prone lands.

Types

Two kinds of coherent slide masses are recognized, distinguished by the shape of the slide surface. They are **slumps,** or **rotational slides,** which move on curved, concave-upward slide surfaces and are self-stabilizing; and **block glides,** or **translational slides,** which move on inclined slide planes (see Figure 7.2). A block glide moves as a unit until it meets an obstacle, the slope of the slide plane changes, or the block disintegrates into a debris flow.

Slumps

Slumps are the most common kind of landslide and range in size from small features a few meters wide to huge failures that can damage structures and transportation systems. They are spoon shaped, having a slide surface that is curved concave-upward and exhibiting a backward rotation (◆ Figure 7.9). The rotation part is key to the definition. If you cleaned away the landslide and looked just at the failure plane, it would be curving and bowl shaped. Slumps occur in geologic material that is fairly homogeneous, such as soil or badly weathered or fractured bedrock or clay, and the slide surface cuts across geologic boundaries. Slumps move about a center of rotation; that is, as the toe of the slide rotates upward, its mass eventually counterbalances the downward force, causing the slide to stop (◆ Figure 7.9b). Slumping

◆ **FIGURE 7.9** A rotational landslide. (a) Oblique stylized view showing ideal spoon shape and crown and toe of landslide. (b) Oblique view of rotational landslide (slump) showing toe with earth flow and potential headward growth of landslide.

(a)

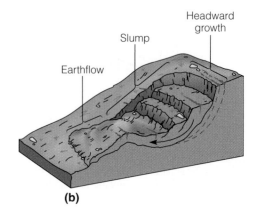

(b)

produces repeated uniform depressions and flat areas on otherwise sloping ground surfaces. Slumps grow headward (upslope) and are encouraged by undercutting at the toe. This is because as one slump mass forms, it removes support from the slope above it. Thus, a stair step surface is common in landslide terrain. Slump-type landslides are the scourge of highway builders, and repairing or removing them costs millions of dollars every year.

Block Glides

Block glides are coherent masses of rock or soil that move along relatively planar sliding surfaces (failure planes), which may be sedimentary bedding planes, metamorphic foliation planes, faults, or fracture surfaces. Block glides are translational landslides—imagine the landslide block moving down a plane, just like sliding your cell phone down the cover of your notebook. For a block glide to occur, it is necessary that the failure plane be inclined *less steeply* than the inclination of the natural or manufactured hill slope. Slopes may be stable with respect to block glides until they are steepened by excavating for building subdivisions or roads, thus leading to landsliding (◆ Figure 7.10).

A classic block glide of about ten acres is seen along a sea cliff undercut by wave action at Point Fermin in San Pedro, California. Movement was first detected there in January 1929, and by 1930 the landslide had moved two meters seaward. It has been intermittently active ever since (◆ Figure 7.11). The rock of the slide mass is coarse sandstone (not the type of earth material usually involved in block glides), but a thin layer of **bentonite** dipping 15 degrees seaward forms the slide plane. Bentonite was volcanic ash that has chemically weathered to clay minerals, which become very weak and slippery when wet (see Case Study 2.3). Bentonite is very commonly involved in slope failures; addition of water is all that is needed to initiate a landslide where the slope of the bentonite layer is as little as 5 degrees.

Some of these translational slides, an alias by which fast-moving block glides are also known, are large and move with devastating speed and tragic results. In 1985, tropical storm Isabel dumped a near-record 24-hour rainfall that averaged almost 470 millimeters (18.5 in) on a mountainous region near the city of Ponce on the south coast of Puerto Rico. Rainfall intensities peaked in the early morning hours of October 7, reaching 70 millimeters (2.8 in) per hour in some places.

◆ **FIGURE 7.10** Cutting a natural slope for homesites can lead to potential landslides on bedding or foliation planes. (a) After cutting a natural slope for a building pad the manufactured slope exposes potential slide planes. (b) A slide plane (smooth surface) and moving mass of shale after toe was cut; Santa Monica Mountains, California. (c) Striations gouged in clay on the slide plane by the sliding mass above it as shown in (b).

◆ **FIGURE 7.11** The Point Fermin landslide at San Pedro, California is a rock block glide that has moved intermittently since 1929. Damaged homes have been removed from the slide area in the foreground. The slide plane emerges just in front of the houses in the background, which are on relatively stable ground.

At 3:30 that Monday morning, much of the Mameyes residential district was destroyed by a fast-moving rock block glide initiated during the most intense period of rainfall. This resulted in the worst loss of life from a landslide in U.S. history—129 deaths. The landslide was in a sandstone with stratification that parallels the natural slope of the slide mass, a condition called a *dip slope.* It moved at least 50 meters (165 ft), probably on a clay layer in the sandstone, before breaking up into the large blocks. The scarp at the top of the slide was 10 meters high (32 ft), and the maximum thickness observed at the toe of the landslide was 15 meters (49 ft).

A similar landslide occurred in the Alps of northeastern Italy in 1963 at Vaiont Dam, the highest thin-arch dam in the world at the time (275 m; 900 ft). The geology at the reservoir consists of a sedimentary-rock structure that is bowed downward into a concave-upward **syncline** with its axis parallel to the Vaiont River canyon. Limestones containing clay layers dip toward the river and reservoir from both sides of the canyon due to this structure (◆ Figure 7.12).

Slope movements and slippage along clayey bedding planes above the reservoir had been observed before the dam was constructed. This condition gave engineers and geologists sufficient concern that they placed survey monuments on the slope above the dam for monitoring such movement. Heavy rains fell for two weeks before the disaster, and slope movements as large as 80 centimeters (31 in) per day were recorded as slow-moving block glides began.

Then, on the night of October 9, without warning, the speed of the glides dramatically accelerated, and a huge mass of limestone slid into the reservoir so fast it generated a wave 100 meters (330 ft) high. The wave burst over the top of the dam and flowed into the Piave River valley, destroying villages in its path and leaving 2,500 people dead. The landslide velocity into the reservoir was so speedy and the slide block

so large that the slide mass almost emptied the lake. The dam did not fail and it is still standing today—a monument to excellent engineering but poor site selection.

Slump (rotation) and block glides (translation) are the most common types of landslides, but there are also **complex landslides,** combinations of the two types. These landslides have elements of both rotational and translational failure, and there are many examples, most of them large landslides such as the Slumgullion landslide in Colorado (■ Case Study 7.2 on page 202).

Falls

Rockfalls are the simplest type of mass movement. They occur when a mass of rock detaches from a cliff and literally falls to the bottom. They usually occur very rapidly and are among the most common of mass-wasting processes. Signs alerting motorists to watch for falling rocks are a common sight. Chunks of rock of all sizes simply fall from vertical or very steep cliffs, having separated from the main mass along joints, faults, foliation planes, and other rock defects. The rocks are loosened by root growth, frost wedging, and heavy precipitation. A pile of rock debris may build up at the base of a cliff, forming a slope called **talus** (◆ Figure 7.13). Two huge rockfalls in Yosemite Valley in 1996 killed one visitor and injured 14 others. The force of the shock-wave from the rockfall toppled nearby trees and stripped bark from more distant ones. Rockfalls may well increase as a side effect of global warming. Here's how. As the Earth warms, alpine glaciers are retreating ever more rapidly (most alpine glaciers have been in retreat since the Little Ice Age began waning several hundred years ago). As these glaciers melt away, they leave steep bedrock walls in the canyons they used to occupy. Without the buttressing of ice, these walls are often unstable.

(a)

(b)

◆ **FIGURE 7.12** The 1963 Vaiont Dam landslide. (a) Map of the slide mass that hurtled into the reservoir and the area that was impacted by the giant wave and flooding. Longarone and several other villages along the Piave River below the dam were devastated. (b) Cross-section through the Vaiont River valley showing a syncline with the sedimentary layers dipping toward the valley axis. The principal slide plane and resultant slide mass are indicated. The cross-section line is shown in (a).

In summer 2006 the famous Eiger face in the Swiss Alps, a victim of glacial retreat, collapsed, dumping 20 million cubic feet of rock on the glacier below, equal to about half the volume of the Empire State Building (◆ Figure 7.14).

CONSIDER THIS

You must choose between two hillside homesites. One site is underlain by bedded sandstone, the other by homogeneous granite. Which site would you choose, and why?

Lateral Spreading

In just the right geologic conditions, nearly flat ground can give way and collapse into a morass of sliding blocks. In what are termed lateral spreads, coherent blocks move horizontally, overlying a liquefied layer of sediment at depth. Such spreads involve elements of translation, rotation, and flow. Typically triggered by earthquakes, lateral spreading results from the spontaneous liquefaction of water-saturated sand layers or the collapse of **sensitive clays**—also known as **quick clays**—which lose all strength when they are shaken

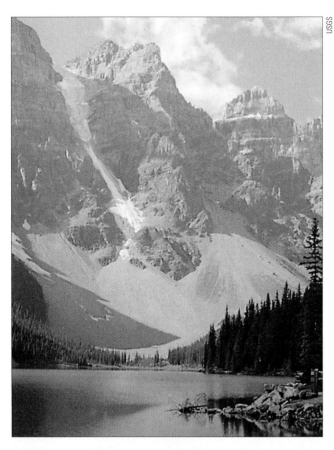

◆ **FIGURE 7.13** Talus slopes caused by frost wedging and other physical weathering processes; Banff National Park in the Canadian Rocky Mountains.

(see Chapter 4). Much of the damage in the Marina district of San Francisco in the 1989 earthquake was due to lateral spreading caused by liquefaction of debris piled there after the 1906 earthquake (and then built upon). The most dramatic damage in Anchorage, Alaska during the massive 1964 quake was due to quick-clay-induced lateral spreads in the Turnagain Heights residential neighborhood and the downtown area. The spreading was so extensive that two houses that had been more than 200 meters (more than 2 football fields) apart collided within the slide mass. The Turnagain Heights area is now a tourist attraction known as "Earthquake Park" (◆ Figure 7.15). Such quick clays are usually marine in origin and can also be found in Norway and eastern Canada.

The Mechanics of Slides: a Matter of Balance

Let's briefly examine the physics of landslides, because by understanding how landslides work, you will be better able to understand how they can be predicted and controlled. Landslides occur when the balance of forces shifts (◆ Figure 7.16). Really, there are only two forces to consider. There is the **driving force,** pulling the landslide block downslope. That force is Earth's gravity filtered through the steepness of the slope. Opposing the driving force is the **resisting force:** the strength of whatever material makes up the landslide. So there we have it, a face off between gravity and the strength of earth materials. If the slide material is strong and the driving force is weak (say the slope is gentle), nothing happens, the potential landslide is stable, and it will remain so until something changes the balance. If the slide mass is just stronger than the driving force, then the landslide is primed to fail. If things keep changing, just as the driving force exceeds the resisting force, the landslide occurs. It's all about balance.

Now, let's understand more about what goes into this balance. First, consider the driving force. As mentioned above,

◆ **FIGURE 7.14** With climate warming, melting glaciers have left crumbling rock faces unsupported. Soon after the glacial ice melts, the rock gives way. Here, hikers watch Eiger Mountain, where hundreds of tons of rock are expected to fall, above Grindelwald, Switzerland, in July 2006.

◆ **FIGURE 7.15** Turnagain Heights as it appeared after the "quick clay" lateral spread that was triggered by the 1964 Alaskan earthquake.

gravity is the big player. The gravity force is directed downward, toward the center of Earth. Indeed, it's what keeps your feet planted solidly on the ground (◆see Figure 7.16a). Now imagine a block-glide-type of landslide on a 15 degree slope (◆see Figure 7.16b). We can take that gravity force and partition it into two separate forces: one is oriented downslope, trying to get the block to slide and the other is pushing onto the slope; this one is called the **normal** force, and

it's helping to anchor the slide block. Now, let's crank up the slope to 45 degrees (◆see Figure 7.16c). The partitioning of forces have now changed. More of the gravity force is oriented downslope and less into the slope. Imagine what the partitioning must look like on a 70 degree slope. The message is that the steeper the slope, the more the gravity force is directed downslope, and it is more likely the landslide will fail.

(a)

Normal force

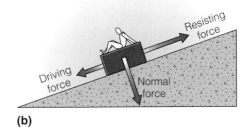

(b)

Resisting force

Driving force

Normal force

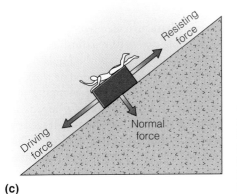

(c)

Resisting force

Driving force

Normal force

◆ **FIGURE 7.16** Landslide physics is all about balance. (a) In the middle of the Great Plains, all of the gravity force is directed straight down and there are no landslides. (b) Long arrows mean big forces. Small arrows mean little forces. As slopes steepen, some of the gravity force is directed downslope and makes up the driving force. Some of the gravity force is directed into the slope as the normal force. (c) Here's a slide about to happen on a steep slope. Look carefully at the length of the arrows compared to 7.16b. What happens to the driving, normal, and resisting forces? How do you know this slope is about to fail?

The resisting force is all about the physical character of the rock or soil that makes up the landslide. It has two components; both are familiar through life experiences. The first component is cohesion or the tendency of the material to hold together. Consider clay. It has **cohesion** and can hold a vertical face; you can mold and shape it. Now, consider sand, a common **granular** material with no cohesion. It has what is termed **frictional strength,** the result of frictional interaction between grains. The harder you push the grains together, the stronger sand becomes. So, as the slope gets steeper and the normal force holding sand grains together decreases, you soon reach a critical point. For sand, that critical point where the friction between grains is no longer able to resist the downslope pull is about 35 degrees, which is termed its angle of repose. Try as you might, you'll never be able to stack dry sand any steeper than 35 degrees nor can nature. Just get out your protractor and measure the slope of any nearby sand dune.

Most materials that make up landslides have both cohesion and frictional strength. Even granular materials, such as sand and gravel, have small amounts of cohesive strength in nature where networks of tree roots provide effective cohesion, binding the grains together. The strongest earth materials have both frictional and cohesive strength. Rocks are stronger than soils because they have very high cohesive strengths. For sedimentary rocks, cohesion is provided by the cements holding grains together. For igneous and metamorphic rocks, interlocking mineral grains cause the high cohesion values.

Geologists and engineers have come up with many different ways to quantify this balance of forces, most of which involve physical measurements and mathematical models. All of this experimentation and computation can be reduced to one number, referred to as the **factor of safety**, which is a ratio between the resisting and driving forces. When the two forces are equal, the factor of safety equals 1.0, and the slide is teetering on the brink of failure. When resisting forces are greater than driving forces, the factor of safety is greater than 1.0 and all is well. The moment the resisting forces are less than driving forces, the factor of safety is less than 1.0 and the landslide starts. Most modern building codes require that manufactured or natural slopes have a factor of safety of 1.5 or greater to provide a margin of error in the measurements and calculations.

Several times in this chapter we have mentioned that water has a great influence on slope stability and that in wet years, landslides are very common. Why is this? Let's go back to the force balance and your personal experience in swimming pools and at the beach. When rainfall saturates a landslide block with water, some of the weight of the grains is buoyed up by that water just like when you are swimming and feel lighter. This buoyancy is caused by the pressure of groundwater in the soil and rock pores; it's referred to as pore pressure, and it partially offsets the gravity force hold-ing the slide on the slope. Because the water pressure supports a portion of the block's weight, it reduces the normal force, thus reducing the frictional strength of the material and the all-important resisting force. Sometimes this reduction in strength can be just enough to tip the balance, drop the factor of safety below 1, and trigger the slide. The greatest effect of heavy rains, rising groundwater tables, and increasing pore pressure is on landslides that are made up of low cohesion material such as sand and gravel or weathered rock.

To trigger a landslide, something must change the factor of safety so that it falls below one and driving forces exceed resisting forces. A short-term change in this balance is most often driven by water. Water usually saturates slopes as the result of heavy rain but occasionally human errors like leaky swimming pools and sprinkler systems are the cause. Other human triggers of landlslides include cutting away their toes (which is equivalent to steepening the slope) or the addition of weight at the top of a slope, such as by building a house, which increases the driving force. Over the longer term, minerals in rock and soil will weather, weakening the material, especially if the weathering products are clay. This is the underlying factor in many basalt landslides such as those which plague parts of the Oregon Coast Range.

Reducing Losses from Mass Wasting

Landslide Hazard Zonation

The first step in reducing losses due to mass-wasting over the long term is to make a careful inventory or map of known landslide areas. Ancient landslides have a distinct topography characterized by hummocky (bumpy) terrain with knobs and closed depressions formed by backward-rotated slump blocks. On topographic maps, slide terrain can be evidenced by curved, closely spaced, amphitheater-shaped contour lines indicating scarps at the heads of landslides. In the field, one may see scarps, trees, or structures that are tilted uphill; unexpected anomalous flat areas; and water-loving vegetation such as cattails where water issues at the toe of a landslide.

With an adequate database provided by maps and field observations, it is possible to define landslide hazard zones. Maps can be generated that show the *landslide risk* in an area, and then these areas can be avoided or work can be done to stabilize them (◆Figure 7.17). Mapping programs do not prevent slides, but they offer a means for minimizing the impact on humans. The human tragedy of landslides in urban areas is that they cause the loss of land as well as of homes. ✳ Table 7.1 summarizes mitigating measures that can slow or stop landsliding and other mass-wasting processes.

Explanation

Stable

Generally stable

Moderately unstable

Single isolated small landslide deposits

Subject to liquefaction

Moderately stable

Unstable

◆ **FIGURE 7.17** Map of the relative slope stability of parts of Contra Costa County and adjacent counties near San Francisco, CA, derived by combining a slope map, a landslide-deposit map, and a map of susceptible geologic units. The area shown here is 15 kilometers (9 mi) wide. USGS

Building Codes and Regulations

Building codes dictate which site investigations must be performed by geologists and engineers and the way structures must be built. Chapter 70 of the *Uniform Building Code,* which deals with slopes and alteration of the landscape, has been widely adopted by cities and counties in the United States. It specifies compaction and surface-drainage requirements and the relationships between such planar elements as bedding, foliation, faults, and slope orientation. Code requirements for manufactured slopes in Los Angeles resemble the specifications found in codes elsewhere (◆Figure 7.18). The maximum slope angle allowed by code in landslide-prone country is 2:1; that is, 2 feet horizontally for each foot vertically (27°). The rationale for the 2:1 slope standard is that granular earth materials (such as sand and gravel) have a natural angle of repose of about 34 degrees; 2:1 slopes allow for a factor of safety.

Losses have been cut dramatically by enforcement of grading codes, and they will continue to decrease as codes become more restrictive in hillside areas. For instance, before grading codes were established in Los Angeles in 1952, 1,040 building sites were damaged or lost by slope failures out of each 10,000 constructed—a loss rate of 10.4 percent. With a new code in effect between 1952 and 1962 that required minimal geologic and soil-engineering investigation, losses were reduced to 1.3 percent for new construction. In 1963 the city enacted a revised code requiring extensive geological and soils investigations. Losses were reduced to 0.15 percent of new construction in the following six years, which included 1969, the largest rain year in recent history.

✶TABLE 7.1 Summary of Mass-Wasting Processes and Their Mitigation		
Landslides		
Cause	Effect	Mitigation
Excess water	Decreased strength	Horizontal drains, surface sealing
Added weight at top	Increased driving force	Buttress fill, retaining walls, decrease slope angle
Undercut toe of slope	Decrease resistance	Retaining walls, buttress fill
"Daylighted" bedding	Exposure of unsupported bedding planes in cut or natural slope	Buttress fill, retaining walls, decrease slope angle bolt
Other Mass-Wasting Processes		
Process	Mitigation	
Rockfall	Rock bolts and wire mesh on the slope, concrete or wooden cribbing at bottom of the slope, cover with "shotcrete"	
Debris flow	Diversion walls or fences and catch basins	
Soil creep	Deep foundations	
Lateral spreading	Dewater, buttress, retain (difficult to mitigate), abandon	

◆ **FIGURE 7.18** Part of a typical grading ordinance (code) that shows the limitation of cut-slope steepness, the required benches on slopes for collecting rainfall and reducing slope-face erosion, and an approved method of constructing a fill slope with bedrock benches for increased stability.

Control and Stabilization

The basic principles behind all methods of preventing or correcting landslides relate to strengthening the earth materials (increasing the resisting forces) and reducing the stresses within the system (decreasing the driving forces). For a given slide mass, this requires halting or reversing the factors that promote instability, which will probably be accomplished by one or more of the following: draining water from the slide area, excavating and redistributing the slide mass, and installing retaining devices. Debris flows require special devices that divert the path of the flow away from structures and property.

Water Drainage and Control

Water is the major culprit in land instability, and surface water must be prevented from infiltrating the potential slide mass. Water within the slide mass can be removed by drilling horizontal drains, called *hydrauger* (water bore) holes, and lining them with perforated plastic pipe. This is commonly done on hillside terrain where underground water presents a problem. In some areas, the land surface of a building site above a sus-

pect slope is sealed with compacted fill to help keep surface water from percolating underground. Also, plastic sheeting is widely used to cover cracks and prevent water infiltration and erosion of the slide mass (◆Figure 7.19a). The efficacy of drainage control and planting is shown in ◆Figure 7.19b.

Excavation and Redistribution

Recontouring is one method of stabilizing a slide mass. Material is removed from the top of the landslide and placed at the toe. Compacted-earth structures called *buttress fills* are often designed to retain large active landslides and known inactive ones believed to be vulnerable. They are constructed by removing the toe of a slide and replacing it, layer by layer, with compacted soil. Such fills can "buttress" huge slide masses, thus reclaiming otherwise unusable land. The finished product is required to have concrete terraces (for intercepting rainwater and preventing erosion) and downdrains for conveying the intercepted water off the site (◆Figure 7.20). Buttressing unstable land has aesthetic and economic advantages, in that the resulting slope can be landscaped and built upon. The cost of the additional work needed to stabilize

(a)

(b)

◆ **FIGURE 7.19** Excess water is the culprit in initiating many landslides. (a) Plastic sheeting placed over the head scarp of a landslide. This is, perhaps, closing the barn door after the horse has bolted but is common practice in landslide-prone areas. (b) Surface-water erosion prevention measures on a graded slope; San Clemente, California. Whereas slope planting and terracing have kept the middle slope in good condition, the slope on the left has gullied badly and will need maintenance in the future.

(a)

(b)

◆ **FIGURE 7.20** (a) Buttress fill with horizontal drains for removing water and surface drains for preventing erosion. The fill acts as a retaining wall to hold up unstable slopes such as those that result from excavation. (b) A slope with benches and surface drains built according to accepted standards.

unstable land is usually offset by a relatively low purchase price, which can make it economically "buildable." Of course, the ultimate mitigating measure is total removal of the slide mass and reshaping of the land to buildable contours.

Retaining Devices

Many slopes are oversteepened by cutting back at the toe, usually for the purpose of obtaining more flat building area. The vertical cut can be supported by constructing steel-reinforced concrete-block retaining walls with drain (weep)

holes for alleviating water-pressure buildup behind the structure (◆Figure 7.21). Retaining devices are constructed of a variety of materials, including rock, timber, metal, and wiremesh fencing. An interesting if not particularly attractive means of stabilizing weak slopes is the application of a cement cover. This material is known as shotcrete and is sprayed onto rock slopes where it hardens into a skin.

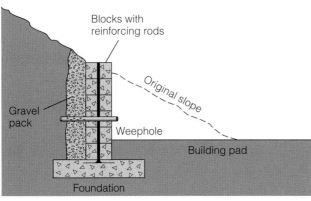

(a)

◆ **FIGURE 7.21** (a) Typical retaining wall with drain (weep) holes to prevent water retention and the buildup of hydrostatic pressure behind the wall. The wall is constructed of concrete blocks with steel reinforcing rods and concrete in their hollow centers. (b) A steel cage is about to be placed in an 80-foot hole, which will then be filled with concrete. Thirty-nine of these "caissons" were installed and tied together with a horizontal beam to retain ten homes at the top of a landslide.

(b)

(a)

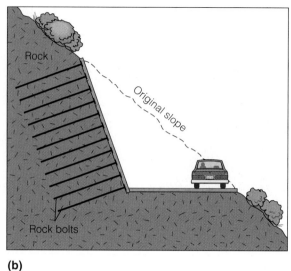

(b)

◆ **FIGURE 7.22** (a) Typical rock bolt installation in a tunnel or mine opening. (b) Rock bolts support jointed rocks above a highway.

Steep or vertical rock slopes that are jointed or fractured are often strengthened by inserting long rock bolts into holes drilled perpendicular to planes of weakness. This binds the planes of weakness together and prevents slippage. Rock bolts are used extensively to support tunnel and mine openings. They add considerably to the safety of these operations by preventing sudden rock "popouts." They are also installed on steep roadcuts to prevent rockfalls onto highways (◆ Figure 7.22). Retaining devices also are effective for mitigating rock and debris falls.

Mitigating Debris Flows

Mitigating debris flows presents a different challenge than landslides, because flows can originate some distance away from the site of interest. How can one avoid debris-flow hazards? The most obvious answer is to live away from steep slopes, and if you choose to live in a mountainous area, stay away from canyon bottoms and the mouths of canyons that act as conduits for debris flows. Home sites by streams seem attractive until that stream is filled with a raging mixture of rock and mud. This is particularly true in areas of high mean annual rainfall, areas that are subject to sudden cloudbursts, and areas that have been burned, such as in the tragic October 1993 firestorms in southern California. As long as people continue to build houses in the "barrels" of canyons, as is done in the foothills of southern California, debris flows will continue to take their toll.

Debris-flow insurance is expensive, but the cost can be less if *deflecting walls* are designed into the house plans (◆ Figure 7.23a). These walls have proven to be effective in protecting dwellings, but they could have adverse consequences if they divert debris onto neighbors' structures, in which case neither an architect nor a geologist would be as helpful as a lawyer. Los Angeles has taken a larger-scale approach to debris-flow mitigation. It has built a series of large catch basins designed to trap debris flows before they can harm property (◆ Figure 7.23b). These basins are situated in the upper reaches of deep canyons that drain the mountains and, until they fill, are effective means of capturing flows. Of course the basins need to be cleaned out with great frequency and the material dumped somewhere else. Some have argued that the debris basins, similar to flood-control levees, provide a false sense of security for those living beneath them and encourage development in what are actually very hazardous places to live. John McPhee's book (see listing at end of chapter) has wonderful descriptions of these basins, including stories of how they do and don't work.

CONSIDER THIS

In many parts of the world, large numbers of people live on or close to potentially unstable hillslopes. How do grading codes help to reduce the risk of landslides? Do you think they are effective if they are enforced?

(a)

(b)

◆ **FIGURE 7.23** (a) The outlet of a debris-flow diversion structure; San Fernando Valley, California. See Figures 7.4 and 7.8 to view what damage the lack of a debris-flow diversion structure can produce.
(b) One way to deal with debris flows is to try and capture them before they can harm people and property. Los Angeles tries to do this with a series of debris basins. Sometimes this approach works well, but other times the flows are so large that they overtop the basins and cover the houses below. Can you find the result of just such an overtopping in this figure?

Snow Avalanches

The mechanics of snow avalanches are similar to those of landsliding, the differences being in the material and the velocity. Although snow avalanches have been around as long as there have been mountains and snow, the relatively recent emergence of the recreational skiing industry as big business and the growing interest in backcountry over-snow travel has made avalanche awareness and control all the more critical. Unfortunately, it's too late for Hannibal. His crossing of the Alps in 218 B.C. was plagued by avalanches. Purportedly 18,000 of his troops and who knows how many of his elephants were killed by avalanches. It's also too late for others. During World War I, 6,000 troops were buried in one day by avalanches in the Dolomite Mountains of northern Italy. During this war, armies intentionally triggered avalanches with the hope of burying their opponents. Avalanches in high mountain regions have wiped out villages, disturbed railroad track alignments, blocked roads, and otherwise made life difficult for millennia. Even eastern North America is affected. In many years on Mount Washington, above tree line, a skier or climber dies in Tuckerman's Ravine when an avalanche buries him or her alive.

Snow stability is determined by exactly the same factors that determine the stability of landslides—the driving and resisting forces. In the case of snow, strength changes can happen in just a few hours as snow warms and weakens or wet snow freezes into a strong, solid mass. Many avalanches are caused by an addition of new snow (an increase in driving force). Indeed, the most hazardous time to be in the mountains is when it's snowing hard and the wind is blowing strongly. During such high avalanche-hazard conditions, snow is rapidly loaded onto slopes and avalanches may occur constantly. Avalanches have one resisting force that landslides don't—**terrain anchors**. Trees are probably the most effective terrain anchor, but large rocks can help too. These roughness elements on the landscape hold snow and minimize avalanche hazard by providing an additional resisting force.

Most avalanches run on weak layers in the snow pack. One such weak layer is an ice crust to which the snow above is not well bonded. **Ice crusts** can form from freezing rainstorms or when bright sun melts the snow, which then refreezes. Other weak layers are **surface hoar,** the delicate crystals of ice that form on top of the snow during cold, moist nights and depth hoar. **Depth hoar** forms when the ground beneath the snow pack is moist and warm, and the air above the snow pack is very cold. Water vapor moving upward forms a layer of very large and weak crystals, which can fail catastrophically. Depth hoar is common at high altitude, in thin snowpacks, and on north-facing slopes in places like the Rockies and Wasatch Range. In these situations, the gradient in temperature and moisture is extreme between the ground and the air.

There are several different kinds of avalanches. A **slab avalanche** is a coherent mass of snow and ice that hurtles down a slope (◆Figure 7.24a) —much like a magazine sliding off a tilted coffee table. This type of avalanche is most frequent on slopes between 35 and 40 degrees, just about black-diamond territory (◆Figure 7.24b). Slab avalanches account for the majority of avalanche deaths because of their size and their tendency to solidify when they stop. **Climax avalanches** occur in spring when the snowpack melts and weakens. They often run over the ground snapping off trees and burying anything in their run-out zones with thick, wet heavy snow. **Powder-snow avalanches** are most common during storms. These "dry" avalanches are dangerous because they entrain a great amount of air and behave like a fluid. Furthermore, the strong shock wave that precedes them can uproot trees and flatten structures. Victims of dry avalanches tend to be buried in light snow close to the surface, which makes their chances of being rescued alive better than those of wet-avalanche victims.

CONSIDER   THIS

Why do you think slab avalanches are most common on moderate slopes of angles between 35 and 40 degrees? What happens to snow on steeper and less steep slopes that makes it less of a hazard?

Avalanches can be triggered by snow loading, rockfalls, skiers, loud noises, or explosives. Mimicking nature, avalanche control is usually achieved by triggering an avalanche with explosives or cannon fire when dangerous snow conditions exist in areas frequented by people, such as ski areas or roads. The explosions collapse the depth hoar, break loose slabs, or detach powder snow, causing a "controlled" avalanche. Various other means have been developed for mitigating the destructive might of avalanches. Where structures already exist, fences can be built to divert avalanches away. In some areas in the Alps, the uphill sides of chalets are shaped similar to a ship's prow so that they will divert avalanching snow (◆Figure 7.24 c). Railroads and highways can be protected by building snow sheds along stretches adjacent to steep slopes (◆Figure 7.24 d). On some slopes high in the

(a)

(b)

(c)

(d)

◆ **FIGURE 7.24** Avalanches can be devastating. (a) A slab avalanche scar. The headscarp from which the slab avalanche detached is clearly visible. (b) Percentage of avalanches versus slope angle in degrees. (c) What a great place to have your home, until the avalanches from the bare slope above come roaring down. Look carefully and you will see the rock prow that defends the up slope side of this home in the Swiss Alps above Davos. (d) In Davos itself more intensive avalanche control measures are used to keep the road open. Here is an avalanche shed designed to let the traffic go under and the snow go over. Source: B. Data from Knox Williams, Avalanche Formation and Release, *Rock Talk*, Colo. Geological Survey 3, no. 4, Oct. 2000.

Alps, miles of large concrete, metal, and wood barriers have been built to help anchor snow to the slopes.

The best personal defense against avalanche hazard is to stay away from steep open slopes, especially when conditions are hazardous. Avalanche forecasts and hotlines exist for most mountain areas near population centers. If you spend time in the backcountry or ski out of bounds, take an avalanche safety course, and learn how to read the snow. It could very well save your life.

Subsidence

Two million people live below the high-tide level in Tokyo. The canals of Venice overflow periodically and flood its beloved tourist attractions (■ Case Study 7.3 on page 204). The Houston suburb of Baytown subsided almost three meters in the 1900s, and 80 square kilometers (31 mi²) of this coastal region is permanently underwater. Earthen dikes prevent the sea from flooding the land in some places in California, and Mexico City's famous Palace of Fine Arts rests in a large depression in the middle of the city (✳ Table 7.2). These areas suffer from natural and human-induced **subsidence,** a sinking or downward settling of Earth's surface. Subsidence is not usually catastrophic, and loss of life due to it is rare, but land subsidence is currently observed in 45 states and is estimated to cost $125 million annually. In the United States the area of human-induced subsidence is estimated as at least 44,000 square kilometers (17,000 mi²), about the size of Maryland and New Jersey combined; but the actual area is probably even greater. Planners and decision makers need to be aware of the causes and impacts of subsidence in order to assess the risks and reduce material losses.

Human-Induced Subsidence

Human-induced subsidence occurs when humans extract underground water, engage in mining or oil and gas production, and when they cause loose sediments at the ground surface to consolidate or compress. The effects may be local or regional in scale. In the United States and Mexico alone, an area the size of Vermont has slowly subsided 30 centimeters (1 ft) due to withdrawal of underground water. Sinking of the land changes drainage paths, and it is particularly damaging to coastal areas and lands adjacent to rivers because it increases flood potential. Subsidence can also result from compaction of sediments rich in organic matter. Parts of the city of New Orleans, built upon cypress swamps of the delta of the Mississippi River and now isolated from the sediment-laden floods of that same river, are now below river level and sea level (see Chapter 9).

Annual losses from subsidence due to fluid withdrawal along the Texas Gulf Coast, for example, were estimated at $109 million between 1943 and 1973. Lowering of the water table in areas of cavernous limestone and gypsum has caused surface subsidence and collapse, costing many millions of dollars each year (see the Chapter 9 discussion of hydrologic hazards). Each year subsidence of the land surface into abandoned coal mines costs the United States $30 million. About a quarter of the seven million acres that have been mined for coal has subsided, and some of this area underlies cities.

Natural Subsidence

Natural subsidence is caused by earthquakes, volcanic activity, and the solution of limestone, dolomite, and gypsum. Earthquake-related subsidence occurs rapidly. It is best known in Alaska and California but also occurs in other states including Oregon and Washington. Displacement along large faults can raise or lower the land surface over a large area. For instance, subsidence of one meter over 180,000 square kilometers (70,000 mi²) took place during the Alaskan earthquake of 1964. Much of the subsidence was along the coast, and the subsided area is now flooded at high tide. In fact, the land actually tilted, and a large area of the Gulf of Alaska was uplifted several meters.

Severe ground shaking that leads to liquefaction may also lower the ground surface. This happened along the valley of the Mississippi River during the New Madrid earthquakes of 1811 and 1812 and in the Marina district of San Francisco in 1989. A small-scale subsidence problem is the collapse of roofs of shallow lava tunnels and tubes in volcanic areas. Volcanic activity that empties magma chambers can

✳TABLE 7.2 Subsiding Cities, 1986			
World		United States	
City	Maximum Subsidence, cm*	City	Maximum Subsidence, cm
Mexico City	850	Long Beach	900
Tokyo	450	(San Joaquin Valley)	880
Osaka	300	San Jose	390
Shanghai	263	Houston	270
Niigata, Japan	250	Las Vegas	66
Bangkok	100	Denver	30
Taipei, Taiwan	190	New Orleans	22
London	30	Savannah	20

*Since measurement began
Source: R. Dolan and H. Grant Goodell, "Sinking Cities," *American Scientist* 74 (1986), no. 1.

cause collapse and subsidence over much larger areas when it forms calderas (see Chapter 5). Subsidence caused by tectonic (mountain-building) processes occurs so very slowly that it is not considered an environmental hazard.

A Classification of Subsidence

One method of classifying land subsidence is according to the depth at which the subsidence is initiated. *Deep subsidence* is initiated at considerable depth below the surface when water, oil, or gas is removed. *Shallow subsidence,* on the other hand, takes place nearer the ground surface when underground water or solid material is removed by natural processes or by humans. In addition, many poorly consolidated shallow deposits such as peat are subject to compaction by overburden pressures, groundwater withdrawal, and in some soils, simply by being saturated with water.

Settlement differs from subsidence. It occurs when an applied load—such as that of a structure—is greater than the bearing capacity of the soil onto which it is placed. Settlement is totally human induced and it is a soils- and foundation-engineering problem. The Leaning Tower of Pisa is a classic example of foundation settlement; its interesting construction history is discussed in Chapter 6.

Deep Subsidence

Removal of fluids—water, oil, or gas—confined in the pore spaces in rock or sediment causes deep subsidence. Porewater pressure—that is, the hydrostatic pressure of water in the pores between sediment grains—helps support the overlying material. As pressure is reduced by extraction, the weight of the overburden gradually transfers to mineral-and-rock-grain boundaries. If the sediment was originally deposited with an open structure, the grains will reorient into a closer-packed arrangement, thus occupying less space, and subsidence will ensue (◆Figure 7.25). Because clays are more compressible than sands, most compaction takes place in clay layers.

At least 22 oil fields in California have subsidence problems, as do many fields in Texas, Louisiana, and other oil-producing states. A near world record for subsidence is held by the Wilmington Oil Field in Long Beach, California, where the ground has dropped 9 meters (about 30 ft). This field is the largest producer in the state, with more than 2,000 wells tapping oil in an upward-arched geologic structure called an *anticline* (see Chapter 14). The arch of the Wilmington field's anticline gradually sagged as oil and water were removed, causing the land surface to sink below sea level. Dikes were constructed to prevent the ocean from flooding the adjacent Port of Los Angeles facilities and the naval shipyard at Terminal Island.

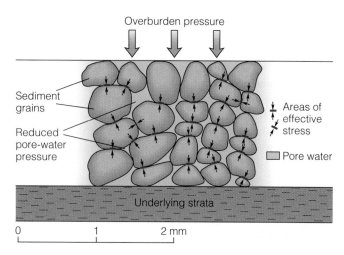

◆ **FIGURE 7.25** A reduction of pore pressure causes increased effective stress and rearrangement and compaction of sediment particles.

People who have their boats moored on Terminal Island must actually walk *up* to board them at sea level. When it rains it is necessary to pump water out of low spots upward to the sea, and oil-well casings and underground pipes have "risen" out of the ground as the land has sunk. To remedy the situation, in 1958 the city of Long Beach initiated a program of injecting water into the ground to replace the oil being withdrawn. Subsidence is no longer a problem, and the surface has even rebounded slightly in places.

Visible effects related to groundwater withdrawals are water-well damage, cracking of long structures such as canals, and development of tension cracks and fissures. In the Antelope Valley, California, home of Edwards Air Force Base, water levels beneath the dry lake have been lowered by more than 60 meters (200 ft). The dry lakebed at Edwards is the landing strip for the space shuttle and other high-performance aircraft. A ground fissure appeared in the lakebed that, initially only a few centimeters wide, became greatly enlarged by surface-water runoff and erosion. This halted operations on the lakebed until repairs could be made. Similar fissuring has occurred in Arizona, New Mexico, Texas, and Nevada. In Arizona, groundwater withdrawal in some places has caused subsidence of 5 meters (more than 15 ft) and the development of cracks and earth fissures, particularly along the edges of some basins (◆Figure 7.26). The subsidence has changed natural drainage patterns and caused highways to settle and crack. The magnitude of the subsidence due to groundwater withdrawal is similar to oil-field subsidence. In the San Joaquin Valley of California, for example, 8.9 meters (29 ft) of subsidence resulted from 50 years of water extraction for agricultural irrigation (◆Figure 7.27).

Mexico City sits in a fault valley that has accumulated nearly 2,000 meters (6,600 ft) of lake sediments, mostly of pyroclastic (volcanic) origin. In 1925 it was demonstrated that subsidence was occurring there due to the withdrawal of

■ **FIGURE 7.26** An old earth fissure at Queen Creek, Arizona, due to subsidence caused by groundwater removal that reopened in August 2005 from erosion resulting from heavy rain. This is a small segment of a fissure system that is over a mile long and locally up to 30 feet wide. The crack system is over 260 meters (50 ft) deep. One fissure system in Arizona is more than 11 kilometers (6.5 mi) long and over 100 meters (324 ft) deep.

water from these sediments. Total subsidence varies throughout the city, but almost 6 meters (20 ft) of subsidence had occurred by the 1970s in the northeast part of the city, mostly in the water-bearing top 50 meters (160 ft) of sediment. In 1951 an aqueduct was completed that brought water to the city and, as a result, a number of wells were closed. The effect on subsidence rates was dramatic, and by 1970 subsidence had decreased to less than 5 centimeters per year. The famous Our Lady of Guadalupe (the "brown Madonna") Cathedral tilts because its foundation is partly on lava flows and partly on the subsiding lake sediments.

◆ **FIGURE 7.27** Subsidence due to excessive groundwater withdrawal for agriculture in the San Joaquin Valley, California. The numbers on the pole indicate the ground level for the years indicated. The area is still subsiding, but at a much slower rate. You can see this declining rate of subsidence by examining how much the land level changed over different periods of time.

CONSIDER THIS

Subsidence of coastal cities such as Venice, Houston, and New Orleans is particularly dangerous because it threatens them with severe flooding. What can be done to prevent or slow such potential catastrophes?

Shallow Subsidence
Collapsing Soils

Subsidence that results from heavy application of irrigation water on certain loose, dry soils is called **hydrocompaction.** The in-place densities of such "collapsible" soils are low, usually less than 1.3 grams per cubic centimeter, about half the density of solid rock. Upon initial saturation with water, such as for crop irrigation or the construction of a water canal, the open fabric between the grains collapses and the soil com-

pacts. Subsidence of monumental proportions has occurred because of hydrocompaction. In the United States, it is most common in arid or semiarid regions of the West and Midwest where soils are dry and moisture seldom penetrates below the root zone. Known areas of hydrocompaction are the Heart Mountain and Riverton areas of Wyoming; Denver, Colorado; the Columbia Basin in Washington; southwest and central Utah; and the San Joaquin Valley of California.

Collapsing soils were a major problem for designers of the California Aqueduct in the San Joaquin Valley. In order to maintain a constant ground slope for the flow of water, it was necessary to identify those areas of loose soil that could not be avoided. Sediments were field-tested by saturating large plots and measuring subsidence at various levels beneath the surface. Subsidence was found to average 4.2 meters (close to 14 ft) over a period of 484 days, during which thousands of gallons of water had been applied to the

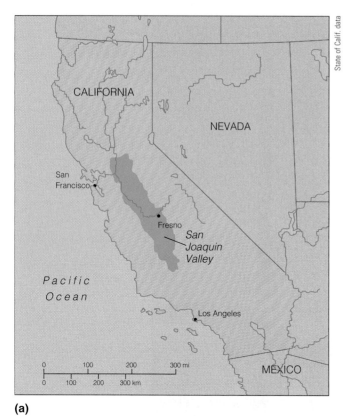

State of Calif. data

(a)

James L. Ruhle & Associates

(b)

◆ **FIGURE 7.28** (a) Location of the San Joaquin Valley. Collapsible soils occur almost entirely along the western border of the valley, whereas subsidence due to underground-water withdrawal is found throughout the valley. (b) Water-soaked test plot in the valley's collapsible soils. Total subsidence at this plot is on the order of 3 meters (10 ft).

test plots (◆Figure 7.28). On the basis of the field tests, 180 kilometers (112 mi) of the aqueduct alignment in the valley was "presubsided" by soaking the ground three to six months before construction. This assured that the gradient would be maintained after construction, and water would continue to flow where it was intended.

Mitigation

The best strategy for minimizing losses is to restrict human activities in areas that are most susceptible to subsidence and collapse. Unfortunately, most instances of land subsidence due to fluid withdrawals were not anticipated. But knowledge of the causes, mechanics, and treatment of deep subsidence has increased with each damaging occurrence, so that we can now implement measures for reducing the incidence and impact of these losses.

Some of the measures now taken to minimize subsidence are controlling regional water-table levels by monitoring and

limiting water extraction, replacing fluids by water injection, and importing surface water for domestic use in order to avoid drawing on underground supplies.

Underground-mining operators are now required to leave pillars to support mined-out coal beds, and mine openings are being backfilled with compacted mine waste to support the overburden. This latter procedure, however, may introduce chemicals that could contaminate underground water unless the backfill is first stripped of pollutants. Pennsylvania's Mine Subsidence Insurance Act of 1962 allows some property owners to buy subsidence insurance after inspection of their property. Another Pennsylvania bill allows homeowners to buy the bituminous coal beneath their property at a fair price and therefore exercise control over mining operations.

Collapsible soils along canals are now routinely precollapsed by soaking, thereby anticipating in advance any adjustments of the canal gradient. Relatively inexpensive geophysical techniques are available for locating shallow limestone caverns beneath potential building sites.

CASE STUDY 7.1

Dynamic Real Estate in Oregon

By volume, the Columbia River is the largest river flowing into the Pacific Ocean and the second-largest river in the United States. Its narrow gorge is a site of great scenic beauty, with towering basalt cliffs, beautiful river views, and boreal forests beyond description. No wonder people want to live there.

There is a problem, however. On a stretch of the gorge between the towns of Warrendale and Dodson, Oregon, massive debris flows have occurred every 50 to 100 years since the gorge formed 13,000 years ago. The record-setting 1996 snowfall of 4 meters (12 ft) and then 32 centimeters (13 in) of rain on the 2,000–4,000-foot cliffs above the towns changed the idyllic environment to an agonizing one. About 3:00 A.M. on February 6, 1996, Dodson resident Mark

Chandler went outside to call the family dog. He lived on Tumult Creek and could not help but notice when the creek's rampaging waters suddenly stopped. He stared unbelievingly at the creek and then heard an ominous rumbling in the distance, like "two Union Pacific trains colliding" on the nearby tracks. Realizing that something was amiss, he dashed back to the house with the dog, awakened his family, and got them all out immediately.

A giant landslide had dammed Tumult Creek and was mobilized by the water to form a debris flow. With boulders the size of minivans, the flow broke off 20-meter (65-ft) pine trees, filled houses with mud, and blocked I-84 and the railroad. When it was all over, geologists calculated that there was enough debris

to cover a football field with mud and boulders 215 meters (700 ft) thick (◆ Figures 1 and 2).

In all, seven landslides struck the gorge between the two towns. County officials quickly placed restrictions on building along this stretch of the gorge and designated the towns as "hazardous areas." This means residents will have to hire a geological consultant for any building whatsoever. Property values have plummeted, and some owners think the government should buy them out. Others want to rebuild, but with government help. The last major slide in the area had occurred in about 1920, and the lessons learned then apparently have been forgotten. Remarkably, no one was killed, only one person was injured, and a horse and a dog that were caught in the muck were rescued.

◆ **FIGURE 1** This home was submerged to its second floor in the Tumult Creek debris flow. The beautiful high cliffs of basalt in the background were the source area of the landslide/rockfall and ensuing debris flow.

◆ **FIGURE 2** The thickness and size of boulders in the flow are apparent in this photo. Again, note the precipitous basalt cliffs in the background.

CASE STUDY 7.2

Colorado's Slumgullion Landslide—A Moving Story 300 Years Old

The Rocky Mountain states, particularly Colorado, have some of the nation's highest levels of landslide hazard. Each year landslides in the Rockies take several lives and cause millions of dollars in damage to forests, roads, pipe and electrical-transmission lines, and buildings. What may be the largest active landslide in the United States is between Gunnison and Durango, Colorado, and bears the unusual name *Slumgullion*, a name that was probably bestowed upon it by early prospectors (◆Figure 1).

> **slumgullion** (slum-gul´yn), *n.* 1 *Slang.* a meat stew with vegetables, as potatoes and onion. 2. *Mining.* a muddy red residue in the sluice. (*Webster's New International Dictionary*)

Slumgullion, the stew, was a standard of mining camp cooks, and slumgullion, the red residue, was what miners usually found instead of gold in the sluice box.

The Slumgullion landslide originated 700 years ago when highly weathered and altered Tertiary volcanic rocks gave way on a ridge above the Lake Fork tributary of the Gunnison River. The slide site is a few kilometers upstream from Lake City, a historic mining town in the San Juan Mountains. The landslide dammed Lake Fork River, forming the largest natural lake in Colorado, Lake San Cristobal. The landslide is huge—6 kilometers (3.6 mi) long, 1 kilometer (0.6 mi) wide, and an average of 40 meters (132 ft) thick. As ◆Figure 2 shows, the Slumgullion is a landslide within a landslide; its 300-year-old active portion is flowing within the larger, 700-year-old mass. The total drop from head scarp to toe is about 762 meters (2,500 ft), and the slide moves at about 6 meters (20 ft) per year. The Slumgullion exhibits three distinct regions of deformation (◆Figure 3):

- The top of the slide is in tension (extension). Normal faulting dominates this region.
- The middle region flows as a rigid block, called *plug flow*. Nearly vertical strike-slip faults are found along the plug's lateral edges.
- The toe is a region of compression. It exhibits thrust (reverse) faults.

Within the active landslide, the terrain is jumbled, and trees are either highly tilted or dead.

The landslide poses several geologic hazards. If it overruns Colorado Highway 149, it will isolate recreational development upstream. Downstream flooding will result if the lake level rises and overtops the natural dam. For these reasons, the U.S. Geological Survey is conducting multidis-ciplinary studies of the area. In addition to 30 years' worth of observation data, the USGS is evaluating:

- precise measurements of the landslide's rate of movement using conventional survey techniques as well as Global Positioning System (GPS) technology.

◆ **FIGURE 1** The Slumgullion landslide in southwestern Colorado has a tremendous length and a sinewy path. The head scarp is more than 500 meters (1,600 ft) high. Landslide outlined in dashes.

Robert Schuster, USGS

◆ **FIGURE 2** Generalized contour map showing the 300-year-old active landslide within an inactive older slide mass. Lake San Cristobal formed when the landslide dammed the Lake Fork River. Redrawn from Lynn Highland, *Earthquakes and Volcanoes* 24, no. 3 (1993)

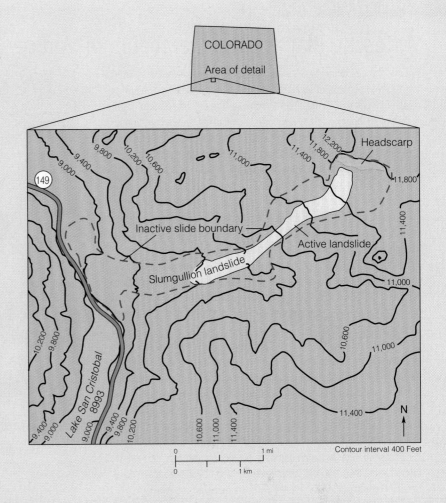

- old photographs of the area. These enable the researchers to estimate the slide's rate of headward growth. Because headward growth feeds rock debris to the head of the slide, it serves to stimulate movement and growth of the slide.

- Lake San Cristobal and its landslide dam. These will provide information that is applicable to other landslide dams in Colorado and the Rocky Mountains.

- three-dimensional models of the active and inactive portions of the slide based upon the accumulated data. Such models facilitate prediction of the slide's future behavior.

◆ **FIGURE 3** Flow regions within the landslide. Extension (pull apart) at the top of the landslide leads to slumping there. The coherent plug flow in the middle of the landslide moves with lateral slip at the sides of the plug. Thrusting takes place at the toe of the landslide as the coherent plug attempts to override the shattered but stable toe. Redrawn from Lynn Highland, USGS

CASE STUDY 7.3

A Rescue Plan for the Merchants of Venice

Called "the city where streets are paved with water," Venice has special interest because of its historical importance, priceless antiquities, and beauty, as well as its charming canals. The city has a major flooding problem, however. St. Mark's Square and other squares are flooded during periods of extremely high tides the locals call the *aqua alta* (Italian, "high water"). It is said that the first Venetians settled here in 421 A.D. "to escape the barbarian Goths" sweeping down from the north. Sitting on a low mud bank in a lagoon sheltered by barrier islands (see Chapter 10), the city has subsided about three meters (10 ft) relative to sea level since it was founded. The sinking is due in part to the existence of 20,000 water wells in the region (now water is brought in by aqueduct), settlement into the soft sediments on which it was built, and rising sea level. The traditional building practice was to drive wooden piles into the soft sediment to form level foundations on which to build structures and, of course, timbers rot and settle. According to records, one cathedral is founded on more than a million timbers.

During periods of *aqua alta*, the avenues and squares of Venice become flooded, and gondola traffic comes to a screeching halt (◆ Figure 1). The *aqua alta* occurs when an onshore flow of water (a storm surge) from the Adriatic Sea coincides with high tides. There were an average of 30 high waters per year between 1957 and 1967, and the number had increased to 40–60 floods annually by 1990 (◆ Figure 2). Dan Stanley of the Smithsonian Institution in Washington, D.C., likens Venice to a man standing in a swimming pool: His feet are embedded in lead, and the water level is rising. It's already to his nose. He'd better not make any waves.

The solution? Install 78 movable floodgates at the entrances to the 90-mile-perimeter lagoon that can temporarily cut the lagoon off from the sea. The cost? Four-and-a-half billion dollars. Estimated time of completion? 2011. The idea is to raise the floodgates like dams in anticipation of high water, and then to reopen them when the water level drops. There are environmental reasons as well as financial ones that make the project controversial. Assuming a sea level rise of 5 cen-

◆ **FIGURE 1** When the *aqua alta* floods St. Mark's Square in Venice, raised boardwalks are provided for pedestrians.

timeters over the next century (a conservative estimate), the gates would have to be raised 70 times a year, and that would interfere with boat traffic and tourism. According to British expert Edmund Penning-Rowsell, "The problem is that as sea level rises, they will have to be closed off so often that they will be quite ridiculous." Yet in the face of global warming and rising sea level, is there anything else to do? Should we abandon Venice?

◆ **FIGURE 2** Frequency of *aqua alta* flooding in Venice since 1910. The increase in frequency is due to subsidence, settlement, and rising sea level. Adapted from P. Gatto and L. Carbognin, "The Lagoon of Venice," *Hydrological Sciences Bulletin* 26, no. 4 (1981)

CASE STUDY 7.4

Water, Water Everywhere

New Orleans has the flattest, lowest, and youngest geology of all major U.S. cities. The city's "Alps," with a maximum elevation of about 5 meters (16 ft) above sea level, are natural levees built by the Mississippi River, and the city's average elevation is just 0.4 meters (1.3 ft). No surface deposits in the city are older than about 3,000 years. The city was established in 1717 on the natural levees along the river. The levees' sand and silt provided a dry, firm foundation for the original city, which is now called *Vieux Carré* (French "old square"), or the "French Quarter." Farther from the river, the land remained undeveloped because it was mainly water-saturated cypress swamp and marsh formed between distributaries of the Mississippi River's ancient delta. These areas are underlain by as much as 5 meters (16 ft) of peat and organic muck (◆ Figure 1).

When high-volume water pumps became available in the early 1900s (see Chapter 10 Case study), drainage canals were excavated into the wetlands to the north. Swamp water was pumped upward into

◆ **FIGURE 1** High-altitude false-color image of New Orleans, a city almost completely surrounded by water. The light spot in the lower center is the city. Note that the Mississippi River meanders through it, Lake Pontchartrain is to the north, and smaller Lake Borgne is to the northeast. Low, swampy delta lands appear brownish to the east and south. The land width in the photo is approximately 200 kilometers (125 mi).

Lake Pontchartrain, a cutoff bay of the Gulf of Mexico. About half the present city is drained wetlands lying well below sea and river level. The lowest parts of the city, about two meters below sea level, are also the poorest parts of the city and the parts most devastated by the flooding of hurricane Katrina.

Subsidence is a natural process on the Mississippi River delta due to the great volume and the sheer weight of the sediment laid down by the river. The sediment compacts, causing the land surface to subside. The region's natural subsidence rate is estimated to have been about 12 centimeters (4 in) per century for the past 4,400 years. This estimate is based upon carbon-14 dating of buried peat deposits and does not take into account any rise in sea level during the period. Urban development in the 1950s added to the subsidence. Compaction of peaty soils in reclaimed cypress swamps coincided with the construction of drainage canals and the planting of trees, both of which lowered the water table. Peat shrinks when it is dewatered, and also oxidation of organic matter and compaction contribute to subsidence. Most homes constructed on reclaimed swamp and marsh soils in the 1950s were built on raised-floor foundations. These homes are still standing, but they require periodic leveling. Unfortunately, homes built on concrete-slab foundations, a technique that had just been introduced, sank into the muck and became unlivable.

Other home foundations were constructed on cypress-log piles sunk to a depth of 10 meters or more (at least 30 ft). These houses have remained at their original level, but the ground around them has subsided. This *differential subsidence* requires that fill dirt be imported in order to make the sunken ground meet the house level. It is very common to see carports and garages that have been converted to extra rooms when subsidence has cut off driveway access to them (◆ Figure 2). One also sees many houses with an inordinate number of porch steps; the owners have added steps as the ground has sunk. In 1979, Jefferson and Orleans parishes (counties are called "parishes" in Louisiana) passed ordinances requiring 10- to 15-meter-deep wooden-pile foundations for all houses built upon former marsh- and swamp-land. This has been beneficial, but differential subsidence continues to damage New Orleans' sewer, water, and natural-gas lines as well as its streets and sidewalks. And it's this subsidence that will require ever-higher levees to protect New Orleans against storm surges and Mississippi River floods.

CONTINUED

B. Pipkin

◆ **FIGURE 2** Differential subsidence around this pile-supported house has left the carport high and dry. The carport was converted to a family room, and fill was imported to bring the yard surface up to the previous level.

When the Trees Come Down, So Do the Hills

Trees do so much for us. Their wood holds up our homes while their trunks and leaves store carbon that would otherwise warm our climate. They give us oxygen to breathe and shade under which to relax on a warm day. But trees do something you may not have given much thought to before. They hold up many of our hillslopes. Trees have a dense network of roots that serves to bind the soil together. In terms of resisting forces, these roots provide cohesion until the tree dies and the roots rot, or maybe the stumps are pulled so that sheep can graze on open slopes. On dry days and for soils with high natural cohesion, the loss of roots and their assistance in holding the soil together matters little. But let it rain—let it rain for a long time on sandy soils—and the hillside will fail in landslides, perhaps sending debris flows hurtling down steep slopes to the valley below.

If the trees are grown for wood products, then the slope will soon be replanted for the next rotation. The window is short between when the old roots rot and the new roots are numerous and big enough to hold up the slope—perhaps a decade or less (◆Figure 1). If no big storms hit in this window, everything's OK. But if the slope is kept clear and not replanted, then it's only a matter of time before the mass movements will start. We know this because the experiment has been

run over and over again. Not by scientists, but by the people who settled North America. First they cleared the mid-Atlantic states and the slopes failed, then New England, then the southeast, and finally the Pacific Northwest. Everywhere the loggers went, the slopes responded. The erosion is well documented in writings of the time (see the work of George Perkins Marsh, writing *Man and Nature* in the 1850s, who lamented the clearing of hillslope and the erosion that followed). More recently, scientists like Lee Benda, David Montgomery, and Beverley Wemple, geomorphologists who specialize in debris flows and erosion, have directly observed the effects of land clearance.

There is another data source, often overlooked, but available just about everywhere—historic images. Chances are, with a little detective work, you can find 100-year-old images of where you live today, and with those images, do your own research about forest clearance and landscape response. Let's look at what the historic images of Vermont can tell us about the results of that clear-cutting experiment our ancestors ran more than a century ago.

Study ◆Figure 2. It's an attractive image of a stream in one of the most picturesque towns in Vermont, a town best know for having the longest-running agricultural fair in the state. First, find the river

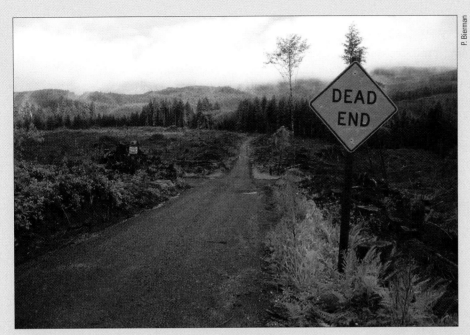

◆ **FIGURE 1** A logging road in southwestern Washington goes through a recently clear-cut stand of timber. In the distance are forests of different age, because each was replanted after it was cut.

terraces, they are the three flat surfaces. Then, see if you can find the alluvial fans. Here's a hint, find the horse. It's standing at the apex of one of the fans. Then, look above the horse and you'll see the eroding hillslope and the gully that is feeding the sandy sediment to the alluvial fan. Can you find a second fan? Can you find more erosion coming from the terrace below the alluvial fan? Geologists, graduate students, and faculty have dug up more than a dozen alluvial fans like the one in the photograph. Everyone of them was covered with at least a meter and sometimes four meters of sediment deposited after land clearance; today all the fans and the slopes above them are stable, covered in trees. But here in the photograph is the smoking gun: evidence that the cleared slopes eroded and fed sediment to the fans.

◆ **FIGURE 2** Here are the deforested slopes of Tunbridge, Vermont in the late 1800s. The sandy river terraces are being ripped apart by gullies and small landslides. All the sand is landing on the alluvial fans below.

Slip, Slide, and Fall

Undeniably, the results of mass-wasting processes can be tragic and devastating, as explained throughout this chapter. Sometimes the stories that go along with landslide images are every bit as interesting as the images themselves. Examine ◆Figure 1. It's a typical New England scene in the late 1800s: lots of clear cutting. Look in the distance and see a perfect landslide scar and then wonder, is the man sitting on an old growth stump that is all that's left of the first forest that was cleared at settlement, maybe 100 years earlier? Now try to figure out what is happening in ◆Figure 2. Can you match up the top of the telephone pole and its base? The pole now hangs from the wires it formerly

◆ **FIGURE 1** A man stares out at clearcut slopes sometime in the late 1800s. Can you find the shallow, translational landslide he's looking at? The slope failed because the trees were cut and the effective cohesion their roots provided was lost.

University of Vermont, Special Collections, Bailey-Howe Library

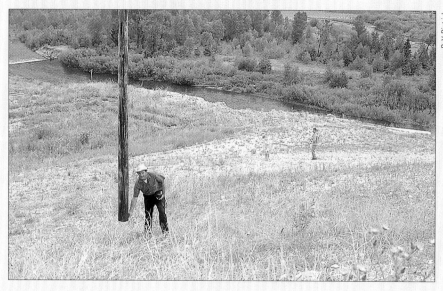

◆ **FIGURE 2** An active block glide in Montana. The person standing downslope is near the "stump" of the pole.

R. V. Dietrich

supported, and the base of the pole has moved some 70 feet downslope. This is all due to a landslide that occurred along Highway 89 and sent the base downslope while the wires (and most of the pole) stayed put. A beautifully developed landslide complex on the planet Mars shows that geologic processes also operate on this rocky planet (◆ Figure 3). The real question now is, what was the fluid that helped these mass movements move? Was it water? Was it CO_2? Perhaps only exploration of Mars will give us the answer.

◆ **FIGURE 3** A Martian landslide. Oblique view from the south toward the Olympus Mons landslide complex, Mars. The arcuate landslide crown scarp in the background is about 25 kilometers (15 mi) wide and 4 kilometers (2.4 mi) high. The landslide debris flowed as far as 65 kilometers (39 mi) from the scarp toward the observer. Mass wasting is widespread on this rocky planet.

NASA/JPL

Summary

Mass Wasting

Defined
Downslope movement of rock and soil under the direct influence of gravity. The term *landslide* includes falls, flows, and slides that have well-defined boundaries.

Classification by
1. Type of material—rock or earth.
2. Type of movement—flow, slide, or fall.
3. Moisture content.
4. Velocity.

Falls

Defined
Free fall of earth materials from a steep cliff or slope.

Types
1. Rockfall—involves hard bedrock of any size.
2. Debris fall—the collapse of weathered rock material and/or soil from a steep slope or cliff.

Flows

Defined
Mass movement of unconsolidated material in the plastic or semi-fluid state.

Types
1. Creep—slow downslope movement of rock and soil particles.
2. Debris flow—dense fluid mixture of rock, sand, mud, and water that is fast moving and destructive.

Causes
Heavy rainfall on steep slopes with loose soil and sparse vegetation.
Most common in arid, semiarid, and alpine climates and where dry-season forest fires expose bare soil.

Slides

Defined
Movement of rock or soil (landslide) as a unit on a discrete failure surface or slide plane.

Mechanics
Driving force (gravity) exceeds resisting forces (friction and cohesion).

Types
1. Rotational slide (slump) on a curved, concave-upward slide surface.
2. Translational slide (block glide) on an inclined plane surface.
3. Complex landslide, a combination of (1) and (2).
4. Lateral spreads of water-saturated ground (liquefaction of sand and quick clays).

Causes
1. Weakening of the slope material by saturation with water and weathering of rock or soil minerals.
2. Steepening of the slope by artificial or natural undercutting at toe.
3. Added weight at the top of the slope such as by a massive earth fill.
4. A change in effective gravity force such as that provided by the strong shaking of an earthquake.

Reduction of Losses(?)

Geologic Mapping
To identify active and ancient landslide areas and so avoid them.

Building Codes
To limit the steepness of manufactured slopes and specify minimum soil and fill conditions as well as surface-water drainage from the site.

Control and Stabilization

Insert Drainpipes
To drain subsurface water and lower pore water pressure.

Excavation
To redistribute soils and rock from the head of the potential slide to the toe. This decreases driving forces and increases resisting force.

Buttress Fills and Retaining Devices
To retain active slides and potentially unstable slopes by increasing resistance.

Rock Bolts
To stabilize slopes or jointed rocks.

Deflection Devices
To divert debris flows around existing structures.
Debris basins capture flow material, hopefully before it impacts buildings and people.

Snow Avalanches

Types

Slab avalanche is old snow and ice that moves as a coherent mass. Powder snow avalanche is composed of new snow that moves like a fluid at high velocities.

Causes

Weak boundary layer between unstable layer above and stable mass below.
Loading by new snow from wind or heavy storm

Mitigation

Controlled avalanching by shooting with light cannons, diversion structures, and snow sheds.

Subsidence

Defined

A sinking of Earth's surface caused by natural geologic processes or by human activity such as mining or the pumping of oil or water from underground.

Types

1. Deep subsidence caused by the removal of water, oil, or gas from depth.
2. Shallow subsidence of ground surface caused by underground mining or by hydrocompaction, the consolidation of rapidly deposited sediment by soaking with water.
3. Collapse of ground surface into shallow underground mines or into natural limestone caverns, forming sinkholes.

4. Settlement occurs when the load applied by a structure exceeds the bearing capacity of its geologic foundation.

Causes of Deep Subsidence

Removal of fluids confined in pore spaces at depth transfers the weight of the overburden to the grain boundaries, causing the grains to reorient into a closer-packed arrangement.

Causes of Shallow Subsidence and Collapse

The ground surface may collapse into shallow mines (usually coal). Sinkhole collapse is due to a lowering of the water table, which reduces the buoyant forces of underground water. Most sinkholes result from the collapse of soil and sediment cover into an underground limestone or dolomite cavern (see Chapter 9). Heavy irrigation causes some loose, low-density sediments and soils to consolidate (hydrocompaction). Compaction due to dewatering of peat and cypress-swamp (delta) clays and oxidation of the highly organic sediments causes subsidence.

Subsidence Problems

Ground cracking, deranged drainage, flooding of coastal areas, and damage to structures, pipelines, sewer systems, and canals. Whole buildings may disappear into sinkholes.

Mitigation

Underground water can be monitored and managed. Extracted crude oil can be replaced with other fluids. Mine operators are now required to leave pillars to support the mine roof, and rock spoil can be returned to the mine to provide support. Collapsible soils along canals can be precollapsed by soaking. Foundations on organic deltaic sediments should be on piles seated on firm geologic material. This protects structures from damage if the surrounding land subsides.

Key Terms

angle of repose	factor of safety	powder-snow avalanche	subsidence
bentonite	frictional strength	resisting force	surface hoar
block glide	granular material	rotational landslide	syncline
climax avalanche	hydrocompaction	quick clay	talus
complex landslide	ice crusts	sensitive clay	terrain anchors
cohesion	landslide	settlement	translational landslide
creep	lateral spreading	slab avalanche	
debris flow	mass wasting	slide plane	
driving force	normal force	slump	

Study Questions

1. What grading and land-use practices can reduce the likelihood of landslides?
2. How can vegetation, topography, and sediment characteristics aid in identifying old or inactive slumps, slides, and debris flows?
3. Name the processes that move earth materials downslope (gravity is the *cause,* not the *process*). On what factors does each depend?
4. Modern building codes require a factor of safety of 1.5 or greater in order to build on or at the top of a cut slope. What is the factor of safety, and why should it be 1.5?
5. What are some common, cost-effective methods of landslide control and prevention?
6. How did geologic structure factor into the disaster at Vaiont Dam?

7. What is the difference between settlement and subsidence? What can be done in advance to prevent settlement?

8. Distinguish between subsidence and collapse that are due to natural causes and due to human causes.

9. What can be done to slow or stop subsidence that is caused by withdrawal of water or petroleum?

10. What engineering problems make constructing canals and aqueducts in areas of hydrocompaction such an insidious geologic hazard?

11. What surface manifestations of subsidence due to groundwater withdrawal make it a serious problem, particularly in California and Arizona?

12. What hazard does subsidence present in coastal areas?

For Further Information

Books and Periodicals

California Department of Conservation. 1998. Hazards from mudslide, debris avalanches and debris flows in hillside and wildfire areas, California Div. of Mines and Geology, note 33, February.

Dolan, R. and H. Grant Goodell, 1986. Sinking cities. *American scientist* 74, no. 1: 38–47.

Fellows, Larry D. 1995. Land-subsidence and earth fissure information. *Arizona geology* 25, no. 2.

Fleming, R.W. and T. A. Taylor. 1980. *Estimating the costs of landslides in the United States.* U.S. Geological Survey circular 832.

Gori, Paula L., Carolyn Driedger, and Sharon L. Randall. 1999. *Learning to live with geologic and hydrologic hazards.* U.S. Geological Survey Water Resources Investigations Report 99-4182.

Highland, Lynn. 2000. *Landslide hazards.* U.S. Geological survey fact sheet FS-071-00, May.

Highland, Lynn M. 1993. Slumgullion: Colorado's natural landslide laboratory. *Earthquakes and volcanoes* 24, no. 5: 208.

Highland, Lynn, J. Godt, David Howell, and W. Z. Savage. 1998. *El Niño 1997–1998: Damaging landslides in the San Francisco Bay area.* U.S. Geological Survey fact sheet 089-98 (free).

Highland, Lynn, Ellen Stephenson, Sarah Christian, and William Brown III. 1997. *Debris flow hazards in the United States.* U.S. Geological survey fact sheet FS-176-97.

Holzer, T. L., Ed. 1984. Man-induced land subsidence. *Geological Society of America reviews in engineering geology* VI.

Krohn, J. P. and James Slosson. 1976. Landslide potential in the United States. *California geology*, October.

Larsen, Matthew C., Gerald F. Wieczorek, and others. 2001. *Natural hazards on alluvial fans: The Venezuela debris flow and flash flood disaster.* U.S. Geological Survey fact sheet FS 103-01, October.

McPhee, John. 1989. Los Angeles against the mountains. *The control of nature*, ch. 3. New York: Farrar, Straus & Giroux.

Monastersky, Richard. 1999. Against the tide: Venice's long war with rising water. *Science news* 156, no. 4 (24 July): 63.

National Academy of Sciences. 1978. *Landslides: Analysis and control.* Transportation Research Board special report 176. Washington, D.C.: National Academy Press.

Nilsen, Tor H. and others. 1979. *Relative slope stability and land-use planning in the San Francisco Bay region, California.* U.S. Geological Survey professional paper 944.Washington, D.C.: U.S. Government Printing Office.

Pearson, Eugene. 1995. *Environmental and engineering geology of central California: Salinian block to Sierra foothills.* National Association of Geology Teachers, Far Western Section, Fall Conference, University of the Pacific, Stockton, California.

Reid, Mark E., R. G. LaHusen, and William Ellis. 1999. *Real-time monitoring of active landslides.* U.S. Geological Survey fact sheet 091-99.

Saucier, Robert T. and Jesse O. Snowden. 1995. Engineering geology of the New Orleans area. *Geological Society of America annual meeting field trip guidebook,* nos. 6a and 6b.

Schultz, Arthur and Randall W. Jibson, Eds. 1989. *Landslide processes of the eastern United States and Puerto Rico.* Geological Society of America special paper 236, 102 pp.

State of California, Resources Agency. 1965. *Landslides and subsidence.* Geologic Hazards Conference, Los Angeles.

Tremper, Bruce. 1993. Life and death in snow country. *Earth: the science of our planet,* no. 2.

U.S. Geological Survey. 1982. *Goals and tasks of the landslide part of a ground-failure hazards reduction program.* U.S. Geological Survey circular 880.Washington, D.C.: U.S. Government Printing Office.

Varnes, D. J. and W. Z. Savage, Eds. *The Slumgullion earth flow: A large-scale natural laboratory.* U.S. Geological Survey bulletin 2130.

_____. 1995. *Debris-flow hazards in the San Francisco Bay region.* U.S. Geological Survey fact sheet 112-95 (free).

Varnes, David. 1984. *Landslide hazard zonation: a review of principles and practice.* Paris: UNESCO.

Wieczorek, G. F., B. A. Morgan, and R. H. Campbell. 2000. Debris flow hazards in the Blue Ridge of Central Virginia. *Environmental and engineering geoscience,* February.

Williams, Knox. 2000. Avalanche formation and release. *Rock talk.* Colorado Geological Survey publication no. 4, October.

Wilshire, Howard, Keith A. Howard, C. M. Wentworth, and Helen Gibbons. 1996. *Geologic processes at the land surface.* U.S. Geological Survey bulletin 2149.

ThomsonNOW

Assess your understanding of this chapter's topics with additional comprehensive interactivities at http://www.thomson.com/login, which also has up-to-date web links, additional readings, and exercises.

Fresh-Water Resources

CHAPTER 8

The High Plains Aquifer and Water Sharing

MARK TWAIN, A WRITER WHO COULD TWIST A PHRASE, is credited with saying "whiskey is for drinking, water is for fighting." There is much truth in the saying, as demonstrated in the conflict over water in the early settlement of the western United States. History may record that twenty-first century conflict in the Middle East was not over terrorists, territory, or even oil—but water. Most of the water in this region comes from three rivers: the Jordan, the Tigris-Euphrates, and the Nile. By 2025 the populations of water-scarce countries will be between 2.5 and 3.5 billion people, or about

Suddenly, from behind the rim of the moon, in long, slow-motion moments of immense majesty, there emerges a sparkling blue and white jewel, a light, delicate sky-blue sphere laced with slowly swirling veils of white, rising gradually like a small pearl in a thick

© L. Lefkowitz/Taxi/Getty

◆ **FIGURE 1** For decades, groundwater from the High Plains aquifer has irrigated our nation's "breadbasket." This irrigation system draws water from a well that taps the aquifer. The well's potential yield was estimated at 4,000 liters per minute (about 1,000 gallons per minute), 24 hours a day. But the real question remains: Is that rate sustainable over the long term when rates of water withdrawal outstrip rates of groundwater recharge?

sea of black mystery. It takes more than a moment to fully realize this is Earth . . . home. Edgar Mitchell, USA, Astronaut

viewing Earth from space (from http://www.solarviews.com/eng/earthsp.htm#quote)

half the world's population in 2003. Syria, Iraq, Israel, Jordan, and Egypt will be no exception to the population increase and they will need more water for their people. You can bet that water-sharing will be high on the agenda of any future peace talks between the leaders of these countries.

The same might be true, without the threat of military action, in the water wars over the High Plains aquifer. The High Plains aquifer contains as much water as Lake Huron and underlies 480,000 square kilometers (147,000 mi^2) of parts of Kansas, Colorado, New Mexico, Wyoming, South Dakota, Nebraska, Oklahoma, and Texas. Water distributed by the irrigation system in the photo is from a well drilled into the aquifer's water-bearing strata that can produce 4,000 liters per minute (about 1,000 gals/min) 24 hours a day. Indeed, 97 pecent of the water drawn from this aquifer is used for irrigation.

When the amount of water withdrawn from an aquifer exceeds the amount replenished to it by rainfall and rivers, an overdraft condition exists, a shortfall, and as with shortfalls of all kinds, it will have to be reckoned with later if not sooner. This overdraft condition is called groundwater *mining,* because the resource is being exploited without replenishment, and water levels in the strata have been dropping dramatically (see Figures 8.21 and 8.22). The latest data suggest water levels are continuing to fall. As of summer 2006 federal legislation that would authorize the U.S. Geological Survey to study the aquifer in its entirety remains stalled in congress. So senators worry the bill is the first step toward federalizing groundwater resources, which they think should be dealt with on a state-by-state basis. This chapter will show that ground and surface water have no respect for political boundaries.

When people go into space and are able to view Earth from afar, they cannot help but be struck by our planet's heavy cloud cover and its expanse of ocean, clear indications that Earth is truly "the water planet." Water is indeed what distinguishes our planet from other bodies in our solar system. Three quarters of Earth's surface is covered by water, and even the human body is 65 percent water. Water provides humans with means of transportation, and much human recreation is in water—and *on* it where it exists in solid form as ice and snow. Since water is not equally distributed on Earth's surface, we have droughts, famine, and catastrophic floods. The absence or abundance of water results in such marvelous and diverse features as deserts, rain forests, picturesque canyons, and glaciers. In this chapter, we investigate the reasons for this uneven distribution and its consequences. Water is involved in every process of human life; it is truly our most valuable resource.

The goals of this chapter are to show just how interconnected the hydrologic system truly is and how we as humans are dependent on clean, plentiful water for life. As the chapter progresses, we will demonstrate how closely connected ground and surface water systems are and just how fragile the balance can be that separates drought and plenty. We hope that you come away from reading this chapter with an understanding of how and why we need to protect our water resources.

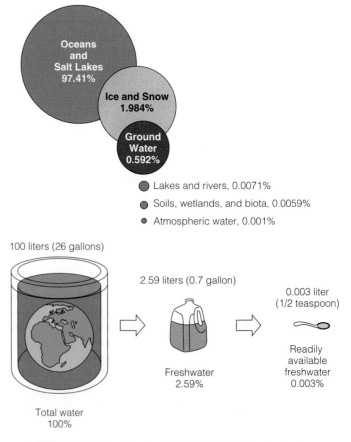

◆ **FIGURE 8.1** The planet's water budget. Only a tiny fraction by volume of the world's water supply is fresh water available for human use.

Water as a Resource

Water is the only common substance that occurs as a solid, a liquid, and a gas over the temperature range found at Earth's surface. Little more than 97 percent of Earth's water is in the oceans, and 2 percent is in ice caps and glaciers; about 0.6 percent is readily available to humans as underground or surface fresh water (◆ Figure 8.1). Fortunately, water is a renewable resource, which is illustrated by the **hydrologic cycle,** Earth's most important natural cycle (◆ Figure 8.2). Water that is evaporated from the ocean or land surface goes back into the atmosphere and forms clouds. Precipitation from these clouds that falls over land areas eventually flows in streams back to the sea, and the cycle is repeated. Remarkably, very little water is in the atmosphere at any one time, about 0.001 percent of the total. Because of this, we know that water must recycle continuously in order to supply the precipitation we measure. The average annual rainfall over the surface area of the 48 contiguous states is about 75 centimeters (30 in or 2.5 ft).

Evapotranspiration is the term for both the direct return of surface water to the atmosphere by evaporation and its indirect return through transpiration from the leaves of plants. It accounts for the return of about 55 centimeters (22 in) of the average annual precipitation. River runoff to the sea and infiltration into the ground account for the

remaining 20 centimeters, but runoff varies from 2.5 centimeters per year in the dry West to more than 50 centimeters per year in the East. Even though runoff varies greatly with location, the net water transport from land to sea must over time balance the net transport from sea to land. The sources and users of public water supplies are shown in ◆ Figure 8.3. The data do not include water used for agriculture or water that is self-supplied.

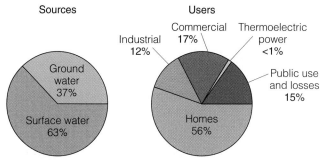

153,000 million liters (40,400 million gallons) per day

◆ **FIGURE 8.3** The sources and users of the U.S. public water supply in 1995. This does not include fresh water supplied for agricultural use or water that is self-supplied.

◆ **ACTIVE FIGURE 8.2** The hydrologic cycle. From *Essentials of Geology,* 2nd ed. by R. Wicander and J. Monroe, Brooks/Cole, 1999.

Fresh Water at Earth's Surface
Rivers

Rivers provide abundant water to cities, some far from the river's location. Usually rivers, as water suppliers, have to be dammed and the waters metered out downstream. Planners recognize several categories of river-water use:

- *Instream use*—all uses that occur in the channel itself, such as hydroelectric power generation and navigation.

- *Offstream use*—the diversion of water from a stream to a place of use outside it, such as to your home. The amount of water available for offstream use along any stretch of a river is the total flow *minus* the amount required for instream purposes and for maintaining water quality (◆Figure 8.4).

- *Consumptive use*—water that evaporates, transpires, or infiltrates and cannot be used again immediately. Forty-four percent of all water that is withdrawn is used consumptively, and agriculture accounts for about 90 percent of that.

- *Nonconsumptive use*—water that is returned to streams with or without treatment so that it can be used again downstream. Interestingly, domestic (household) water is used nonconsumptively: it is returned to the cycle through sewers and storm drains.

In many areas, particularly the western United States, consumption exceeds local water supplies. This necessitates importing water from other areas or mining groundwater. For example, about 75 percent of Southern California's water is imported from sources more than 200 miles away. Two aqueducts import water from west and east of the Sierra Nevada, and a third aqueduct brings water from the Colorado River. Irrigation utilizes about 40 percent of the total water withdrawn in the United States, and a startling 80 percent in California. It is not surprising then that California, with the largest population and a huge irrigation system, is the largest U.S. consumer of water, using almost as much as the two next-largest consumers, Texas and Illinois, combined (◆Figure 8.5).

Total world withdrawals of water for offstream purposes amount to about 2,400 cubic kilometers per year (1.7 trillion gal/day, *gpd*), of which 82 percent is for agricultural irrigation. This is expected to increase manyfold to 20,000 cubic kilometers (14.5 trillion gpd) by the year 2050, which is beyond the dependable flow of the world's rivers. Availability of water will limit population growth in the twenty-first century, either by statute in developed countries or by natural means, most likely drought and famine, in developing nations. Repetition of the terrible droughts experienced in Africa in the 1970s and 1980s, compounded by overtaxed water supplies, would be disastrous for those countries and their people.

Lakes

Lakes are bodies of water in landlocked basins that are formed by many different geologic processes. The geologic origin of the Great Lakes (except Lake Superior) is glacial, Crater Lake is volcanic, and the Great Salt Lake is a down-faulted basin, to name just a few. Lakes are not important quantitatively in the global water balance, providing less than 0.4 percent of all continental fresh water; however, they are of great local importance for agriculture, recreation, and as a source of water. It is significant that about 80 percent of all the water in lakes worldwide is held in fewer than 40 lakes.

Lakes are important as a source of fresh water, and salt lakes can be useful for transportation and mineral extraction. Whether a lake is fresh, salt, or even dry depends on the balance between precipitation (P) and runoff (R) into the lake, and evaporation (E) and outflow (O) from the lake. If a condition exists where $P + R = E + O$, the result is a fresh-water lake. If $P + R = E$ and there is no outflow, the result is a salt lake with a balance that is similar to the oceans. However, in the southwestern United States, the condition exists where $P + R < E + O$, producing in time a dry lake bed, also called a *playa*. Dry lake beds, especially the salt flats of the Great Salt Lake, have been used for automobile speed trials because they are among the most level surfaces above sea level. Rogers Dry Lake in California has the distinction of being used as the landing strip for the space shuttle and is the

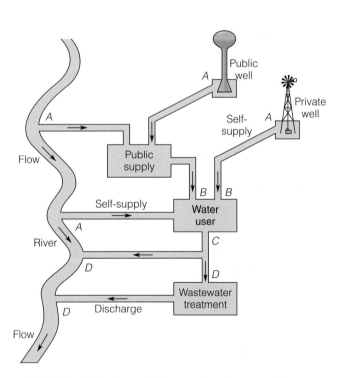

◆ **FIGURE 8.4** Water is supplied to users from streams and from public and private wells (A). Consumptive use (C) is the difference between the amount delivered to users (B) and the amount returned to the system (D). USGS data

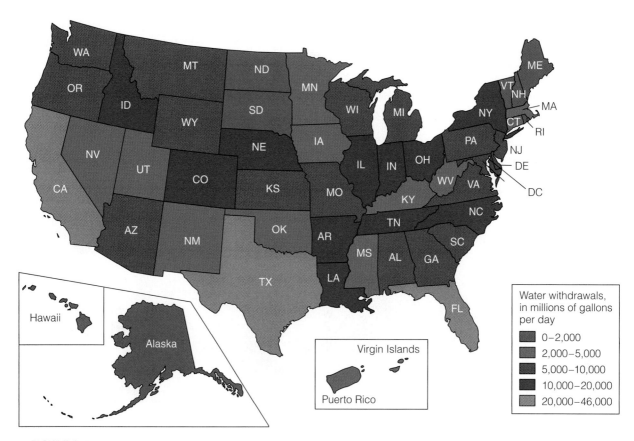

◆ **FIGURE 8.5** Total water withdrawals by state, 2000. USGS

home of Edwards Air Force Base. Playas are also known for a variety of salts and useful clays, products found in their sediments. Some lakes have their source of water cut off by humans, usually for agriculture, occasionally with catastrophic results (■ Case Study 8.1 on page 235).

Changing climate can dramatically alter the water balance in lakes. Consider this: If you had visited the southwestern United States 15,000 years ago there would have been lakes in the Mojave Desert. Those lakes would have been connected by rivers with rapids and waterfalls, places to swim and take a drink of fresh water. The glacial climate was cooler and cloudier, so evaporation was lower and precipitation may in some places have been higher. Even Death Valley, one of the hottest and driest places in the United States today, had a lake in it, Lake Manix. How do we know? Because the shorelines and lake-bottom sediments of this and other now-vanished lakes can easily be found. All of this should make you wonder what might be some of the unintended consequences of global climate change?

A process that keeps the bottom waters in lakes from becoming stagnant is **overturning.** This occurs in lakes in temperate and cool climates where surface waters are subject to near-freezing temperatures. The temperature of maximum density of fresh water is 4°C; that is, at this temperature it is heavier per unit volume than water that is warmer or colder. In the summer the lake is stratified and the warmer less dense

surface water is separated from the cooler, denser bottom waters by the *thermocline,* which acts as a floor for the surface water and a ceiling from the bottom waters. As it gets colder in the fall, the surface water lowers to 4°C and the thermocline weakens; that is, the temperature of the lake becomes about equal or *isothermal.* The surface water sinks and the bottom waters that are oxygen-deficient rise to replace them. As ◆ Figure 8.6 illustrates, the bottom waters stagnate during the winter but are refreshed again in the spring when the surface-water temperature rises to 4°C and sinks, and the bottom waters rise. The net result is oxygenation of the lake waters and recycling of nutrients, which are transported from the bottom to the surface. This makes for abundant plankton and good fishing.

Another factor in the well-being of lakes and their suitability as a source of water is how well "nourished" they are. Nourishment consists of inorganic compounds (nitrate, phosphate, and silica) that are carried into the lake by streams and produced by decaying organic matter at the bottom. *Oligotrophic* lakes are usually deep, with clear water, and low in nutrients, with a relatively low fish population (◆ Figure 8.7). They are a source of good drinking water and are usually visually appealing. Crater Lake is an example. A *eutrophic* lake is "well fed" with nutrients. Such lakes are often shallow, have plants, contain a population of so-called trash fish like carp, have a low oxygen content, and usually

◆ **FIGURE 8.6** Fall and spring overturn occurs in lakes in temperate and cold regions. Overturn is a mechanism whereby deep lake waters are reoxygenated and do not become stagnant.

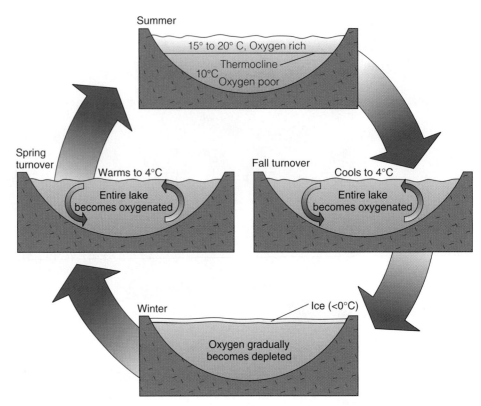

◆ **FIGURE 8.7** Over time, lakes go through a nutrient cycle that may be accelerated by waste products from humans living around the lake or by agricultural chemicals.

Low nutrient input, low plankton and fish population, clear water.

Good nutrient balance, good plant growth, plankton and fish population.

High nutrient input, many plants, low oxygen in bottom waters, low fish population, may have a surface mat of algae.

support a rich growth of algae or other plants at the surface (◆Figure 8.8). In between the two extremes are the *mesotrophic* lakes that have a well-balanced nutrient input and output. The result is a good fish population, a variety of shore and bottom plants, and an abundance of plankton (see Figure 8.7).

Fresh Water Underground

Some of the water in the hydrologic cycle infiltrates underground and becomes **groundwater,** one of our most valuable natural resources. In fact, most of Earth's liquid fresh water exists beneath the land surface; its geologic occurrence is the subject of many misconceptions. For example, it is commonly believed that groundwater occurs in large lakes or pools beneath the land. The truth is that almost all groundwater is in small pore spaces and fractures in rocks. Another misconception is that deposits of groundwater can be found by people with special skills or powers, people referred to as *water witches* or *dowsers.* They locate underground water using two wires bent into L shapes, forked branches, or other forked devices called *divining rods.* A dowser locates an underground "tube" or lake of water by walking over the ground, holding the divining rod in a prescribed manner until it jerks downward, pointing to the location of groundwater, a mineral deposit, or a lost set of keys (◆Figure 8.9).

Some dowsers claim they can locate good places to drill water wells using only a map of the land. The divining rod is

◆ **FIGURE 8.8** A eutrophic lake in western New York State. It is covered with a growth of slimy algae and bacteria and is not suitable for swimming, fishing, or as a water supply. Many eutrophic lakes are the result of seepage from cesspools and other human-waste facilities around their perimeter. Eutrophication caused by human activities is known as "cultural eutrophication."

passed over the map until it jerks downward where presumably a well should be located (X marks the spot). Water dowsers are found throughout the world, particularly in rural areas, and many of them will guarantee finding water. This is one difference between dowsers and groundwater geologists, or **hydrogeologists.** Hydrogeologists will not make this guarantee. However, some people will swear that experienced dowsers can find water reliably. Could it be that after years of work in the field, dowsers get to know an area and use subtle landscape clues to find places where water is likely to be found?

Groundwater Supply

Groundwater provides 40 percent of public water supplies and 30 to 40 percent of all water used exclusive of power generation in the United States. It is by far the cheapest and most efficient source of municipal water, because obtaining it does not require the construction of expensive aqueducts and reservoirs. Furthermore, groundwater usually requires far less cleaning and purification than surface water. Thirty-four of the largest 100 cities in the United States depend entirely upon local groundwater supplies; Miami Beach, San Antonio, Memphis, Honolulu, and Tucson are just a few. Groundwater provides 80 percent of the water for rural domestic and livestock use, and it is the only source of water in many agricultural areas. It is not surprising that some of the largest agricultural states, such as Texas, Nebraska, Idaho, and California, are the largest consumers of groundwater, accounting for almost half of all the groundwater produced. Groundwater is important even to communities that import water from distant areas, because in almost every case, local groundwater provides a significant low-cost percentage of their water supply.

Although it is not generally known, groundwater maintains streamflows during periods when there is no rain. This process, by which water from the surrounding landscape finds its way into streams, maintains what is known as baseflow. Baseflow is critical for maintaining the ecological integrity of streams as it keeps water flowing long after rains have ceased. In arid climates where there are permeable water-saturated rocks beneath the surface, groundwater seeping into stream channels may be the only source of water for rivers. The fabled oases of the Sahara and Arabian deserts occur where underground water is close to the surface or where it intersects the ground surface, forming a spring or watering hole.

© Bettmann/CORBIS

◆ **FIGURE 8.9** Early dowsers looking for water. After Abbé de Villemont, *Traité de la Physique Occulte* (undated engraving).

Location and Distribution

Between the land surface and the depth at which we find groundwater is the *zone of aeration,* a zone where voids in soil and rock contain only air and water films. This is also known as the unsaturated zone. The contact between this zone and the *zone of saturation* below it is the **water table** (◆ Figure 8.10). Above the water table is a narrow moist zone, the *capillary fringe.* In the saturated zone, free (unattached) water fills the openings between grains of clastic sedimentary rock, the fractures or cracks in hard rocks, and the solution channels in limestones and dolomites (◆ Figure 8.11).

Water-saturated geologic formations whose porosity and permeability are sufficient to yield significant quantities of water to springs and wells are known as **aquifers.** A rock's **porosity** (root word *pore*) is a function of the volume of openings, or void spaces, in it and is expressed as a percentage of the total volume of the rock being considered. Without such voids, a rock cannot contain water or any other fluid. **Permeability** is the ease with which fluids can flow through an aquifer; it is thus a measure of the connections between pore spaces.

Hydraulic conductivity is the term hydrologists prefer, but *permeability* will suffice for our purposes, as it has a long history of use and is easy to remember (see ■ Case Study 8.2). **Aquicludes** are rocks or sediments such as shale and clay that lack significant permeability and hence transmit little water. In some places aquicludes occur as *lenses* that trap water and prevent it from percolating down to the water table. Such a condition creates a **perched water table** (see Figure 8.10).

Aquifers are important because they transmit water from *recharge areas*—areas where water is added to the zone of saturation—to springs or wells. In addition, they store vast quantities of drinkable water. In terms of the hydrologic cycle, we can view aquifers both as transmission pipes and as storage tanks for groundwater. The Nubian Sandstone in the Sahara Desert, for instance, is estimated to contain 600,000 cubic kilometers (130,000 mi³) of water, which is just now being tapped. It is the world's largest known aquifer and is a resource of great potential for North Africa. However, it, like the High Plains

◆ **FIGURE 8.11** A rock's porosity is dependent upon the size, shape, and arrangement of the material composing the rock. Whereas (a) a well-sorted sedimentary rock has high porosity, (b) a poorly sorted one has low porosity. (c) In soluble rocks such as limestones, porosity can be increased by solution, whereas (d) crystalline metamorphic and igneous rocks are porous only if they are fractured.

aquifer, contains much fossil water so that extracting large amounts is indeed unsustainable mining. Started in 1984, the Great Man-Made River Project, a brainchild of Libya's leader, Muammar Al Qadhafi, now carries 6.5 million cubic meters of water each day from desert wells to the cities and agricultural fields of this arid nation (◆ Figure 8.12).

Static Water Table

Unconfined aquifers are formations that are exposed to atmospheric pressure changes and that can provide water to wells by draining adjacent saturated rock or soil

◆ **FIGURE 8.10** Schematic cross section of groundwater zones showing a static water table with a capillary fringe. A perched water table exists where a body of clay or shale acts as a barrier (otherwise known as an aquiclude) to further infiltration.

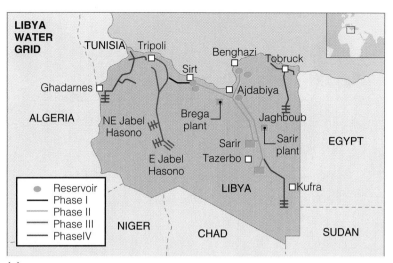

(a)

◆ **FIGURE 8.12** Libya's leader, Muammar Al Qadhafi, has overseen an ambitious plan to water his nation with fossil water from the Nubian Sandstone aquifer. (a) Map of Libya and the system that brings ancient water (recharged during cooler, moister glacial times) to the cities of today. (b) A billboard showing Qadhafi and the water system. (c) One of the 4-meter-wide pipes that carries the water.

(b)   **(c)**

(◆ Figure 8.13a). As the water is pumped, a **cone of depression** forms around the well, creating a gradient that causes water to flow toward the well (◆ Figure 8.13b). A low-permeability aquifer will produce a steep cone of depression and substantial lowering of the water table in the well. The opposite is true for an aquifer in highly permeable rock or soil. This lowering, or the difference between the water-table level and the water level in the pumping well, is known as **drawdown.** Stated differently, low permeability produces a large drawdown for a given yield and increases the possibility of a well "running dry." As pointed out, a pumping well in permeable materials creates a small drawdown and a gentle gradient in the cone of depression. Some closely spaced wells, however, have overlapping "cones," and excessive pumping in one well lowers the water level in an adjacent one (◆ Figure 8.14). Many lawsuits have arisen for just this reason. Water law is discussed briefly in ■ Case Study 8.3.

A good domestic (single-family) well should yield at least 11 liters (2.6 gal) per minute, which is equivalent to about 16,000 liters (3,700 gal) per day, although some families use as little as 4 liters per minute (1,350 gal/day). Many people get by with domestic wells that yield considerably less water than this. The reason is simple. If the well casing is long, large amounts of water can be stored in the well itself. For a six inch well, which is typical for a residence, each foot of casing stores

about 1.5 gallons of water. So a deep well of 200 feet gives people a several-hundred-gallon buffer, good enough for that very long shower but not enough to fill the family swimming pool.

The water table rises and falls with consumption and the season of the year. Generally, the water table is lower in late summer and higher during the winter or the wet season. Trees use lots of groundwater, extracting it with their roots. When deciduous trees lose their leaves in the fall and cease evapotranspiring, water tables rise. Thus water wells must be drilled deep enough to accommodate seasonal and longer-term climatic fluctuations of the water table (◆ Figure 8.15). If a well "goes dry" during the annual dry season, it definitely needs to be deepened.

Streams that are located above the local water table are called **losing streams,** because they contribute to the underground water supply (◆ Figure 8.16a). Beneath such streams there may be a mound of water above the local groundwater table known as a *recharge mound.* Losing streams are most commonly found in the desert where water tables are often far below the ground surface and stream water more often than not originates from runoff in high mountains towering above the desert floor. A stream that intersects the water table and is fed by both surface water and groundwater is known as a **gaining stream** (◆ Figure 8.16b). These streams are most common in humid regions where precipitation is regular and

(a)

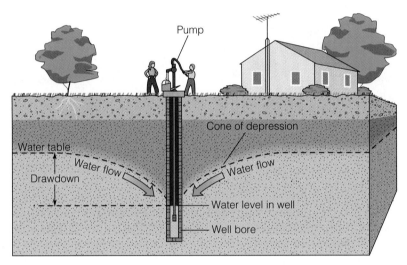

◆ **FIGURE 8.13** (a) A horizontal (static) water table. The water table will remain static until pumping begins. (b) When pumping begins, the water table is drawn down an amount determined by the pumping rate and the aquifer's permeability. The development of a cone of depression creates a hydraulic gradient, which causes water to flow toward the well and enables continuous water production. The amount of water the well yields per unit of time pumped depends upon the aquifer's hydrologic properties.

(b)

◆ **FIGURE 8.14** Cones of depression overlap in an area of closely spaced wells. Note the contributions to groundwater from septic tanks.

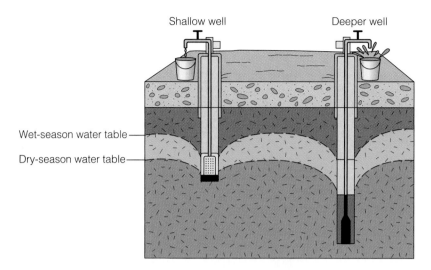

Shallow well   Deeper well

Wet-season water table

Dry-season water table

◆ **FIGURE 8.15** The effect of seasonal water-table fluctuations on producing wells. A shallow well may go dry in the summertime.

abundant, keeping groundwater tables near the surface. A stream may be both a gaining and a losing stream, depending upon the time of year and variations in the elevation of the water table. The gaining of water by streams is what makes up baseflow.

Where water tables are high, they may intersect the ground surface and produce a spring. Springs also are subject to water-table fluctuations. They may "turn on and off" depending upon rainfall and the season of the year. ◆ Figure 8.17 illustrates the hydrology of three kinds of springs.

(a)

(b)

◆ **FIGURE 8.16** Hydraulic gradient (*v/h*) in (a) a losing stream that contributes water to the water table, and (b) a gaining stream that gains water from the water table.

CONSIDER THIS

As explained in Case Study 8.3, the legal issues surrounding the withdrawal and use of groundwater are complex, and several legal doctrines apply to them. From a philosophical viewpoint, which of the four doctrines seems fairest for multiple users of an aquifer? Please explain your choice.

Pressurized Underground Water

Pressurized groundwater systems cause water to rise above aquifer levels and sometimes even to flow out onto the ground. Pressurized systems occur where water-saturated permeable layers are enclosed between aquicludes, and for this reason they are called **confined aquifers** (◆ Figure 8.18). A confined aquifer acts as a water conduit, very similar to a garden hose that is filled with water and situated so that one end is lower than the other. In both cases a water-pressure difference known as a *hydraulic head* is created. Water gushes from the low end until there is no longer a pressure difference. At that point the water level stabilizes, becoming *static*.

Wells that penetrate confined aquifers are called *artesian wells*, after the province of Artois, France, where they were first described. Water in some artesian wells is under enough pressure that it flows out onto the ground. In other cases, water simply rises up the well casing above the top of the aquifer. Artesian systems are distinguished by a water pressure gradient called the **artesian-pressure** or **piezometric surface** (◆ Figure 8.19). This "surface" is the level to which water will rise in a well at a given point along the aquifer. It is important to note that the slope of the water table of an unconfined aquifer is also a pressure surface. Underground water moves from areas of high hydraulic head to areas of low hydraulic head (pressure).

Contour maps of the pressure surface can be very useful, because they indicate the direction of groundwater flow and the slope of the hydraulic gradient (◆ Figure 8.20). If an

(a)

(b)

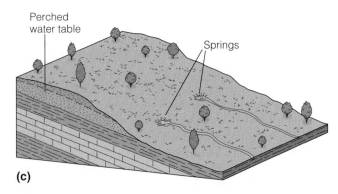

(c)

◆ **FIGURE 8.17** Geology and hydrology of three kinds of springs. (a) Springs form where a high water table in cavernous limestone intersects the ground surface. (b) Artesian springs. A fault barrier can cause pressurized water in a confined aquifer to rise as springs along irregularities in the fault. (c) Springs form where a perched water table intersects the ground surface. Such springs are intermittent, because the small volume of perched water is quickly depleted.

(a)

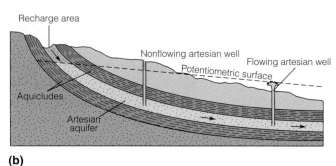

(b)

◆ **ACTIVE FIGURE 8.18** Water under pressure. (a) The hydraulic head in a hose lowers as water flows out the low end. Eventually a static condition prevails. (b) A confined aquifer, commonly called an *artesian* aquifer. The artesian-pressure surface is the level to which water will rise in wells at specific points above the aquifer. Why is one well flowing while the other is not?

aquifer's hydraulic conductivity can be estimated or measured, the rate and volume of groundwater flow can be determined using Darcy's Law (see ■Case Study 8.2 on page 237).

Artesian wells differ from water-table wells in that the latter depend upon pumping or topographic differences to create the hydraulic gradient that causes the water to flow. Because the energy required to raise water to the surface is the greatest expense in tapping underground water, artesian systems are much desired and exploited (see ■Case Study 8.4 on page 239). Not all artesian wells flow to the ground

surface, because the pressure surface lowers as water is extracted; water may rise naturally only part way up the well bore. Nevertheless, a natural rise of water any distance reduces the cost of its extraction.

Many bottled-water and beverage producers attempt to convince us that deep-well or artesian water is purer than other kinds of water. *Artesian* refers only to an aquifer's hydrogeology and has no water-quality connotation except that recharge zones for artesian wells are often in high-elevation, mountainous zones, which are less densely settled than valleys and less likely to be impacted by industrial waste dumping and polluting agricultural practices. Because artesian aquifers are under pressure where they are tapped as water supplies, water leaks out of them rather than in, protecting water quality. Do not be misled by advertisements attributing greater purity to artesian or deep-well water. Such waters may or may not have low levels of dissolved contaminants.

Groundwater Storage and Management

In order to manage underground water supplies in a groundwater basin intelligently, the hydrologist or planner must have two measurements: the quantity of water stored in the

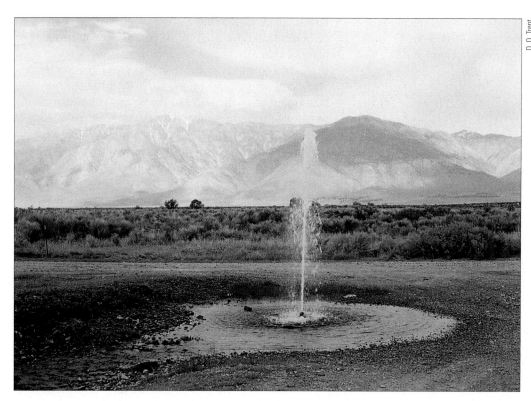

◆ **FIGURE 8.19** An artesian well in the Owens Valley, near Bishop, California in the shadow of the White Mountains. Note that artesian pressure raises the water above the ground and that the well flow is not regulated in any manner. Given what you see in the image, where do you think the water that is issuing from the well recharges?

basin, and the **sustained yield** to the amount of water the aquifers in the basin can yield on a day-to-day basis over a long period of time.

A groundwater basin consists of an aquifer or a number of aquifers that have well-defined geological boundaries and *recharge areas*—places where water seeps into the aquifer (see Figure 8.18b). To determine the amount of usable water in the basin, we rely on the concept of specific yield of water-bearing materials. **Specific yield** is the ratio of the volume of water an aquifer will give up by gravity flow to the total volume of material, expressed as a percentage. For example, a saturated clay with a porosity of 40 percent may have a specific yield of 3 percent; that is, only 3 percent of the clay's

volume will be able to drain into a well. The remaining water in the pore spaces (37 percent) is held by the clay-mineral surfaces and between clay layers against the pull of gravity. This "held" water is its *specific retention*. Similarly, sand with a porosity of 35 percent might have a specific yield of 23 percent and a specific retention of 12 percent. Note that the sum of specific yield and specific retention equals the porosity of the aquifer material.

Thus the total water-storage capacity of an aquifer may be calculated by multiplying the specific yield by the volume of the aquifer determined from water-well data. The process is a bit more complicated for artesian aquifers, but it follows the same procedure after accounting for the compaction of

(a)

(b)

(c)

152.31 LOCATION OF WELL AND
○   ALTITUDE OF WATER TABLE
         ABOVE SEA LEVEL, IN FEET

—*140*— WATER-TABLE CONTOUR—
         Shows altitude of water table.
         Contour interval 10 feet.
         Datum is sea level

         GROUND-WATER
         FLOW LINE

◆ **FIGURE 8.20** Using known altitudes of the water table at individual wells (A), contour maps of the water-table surface can be drawn (B), and directions of groundwater flow along the water table can be determined (C) because flow is perpendicular to the contours. Elevations are in feet above a datum, usually sea level, as English units are used almost exclusively on pressure-surface contour maps in the United States. USGS circular 1139 the aquifer and expansion of the water when the pressure is reduced. The amount of water available to us in a groundwater basin can be determined fairly accurately if the basic data are available from numerous wells.

As noted, sustained yield is the amount of water that can be withdrawn on a long-term basis without depleting the resource. Sustained yield is more difficult to assess than aquifer storage capacity, because it is affected by precipitation, runoff, and recharge. One of the real challenges facing groundwater resource managers today is how to deal with the effect of climate change on rates of rainfall, evaporation, and thus aquifer recharge. Nevertheless, sustained yield must be at least estimated for intelligent management of the resource.

Groundwater Mining

As explained in the chapter opening, when the amount of water withdrawn from an aquifer exceeds the aquifer's sustained yield, an overdraft condition called *groundwater mining* exists (◆Figure 8.21). The Ogallala Sandstone makes up about 80 percent of what is collectively known as the High Plains aquifer. The Ogallala's average thickness is 60 meters (about 200 ft), but thicknesses as great as 425 meters (1,400 ft) have been measured. In general, water levels in this important aquifer are dropping. In Texas, overdrafts have exceeded 65 percent, and overdrafts of 95 percent are known in a few places. In the latter case, 20 times more water was extracted from the aquifer each year than was recharged during that year. This magnitude of overdraft is a serious problem because much of the water in the aquifer infiltrated during wetter glacial climates more than 10,000 years ago. Much of the water pumped from the aquifer is fossil water.

The High Plains aquifer was not massively tapped until the 1950s, and by 1980 the water-saturated zone had decreased an average of 3 meters, and as much as 30 meters under some parts of Texas and Nebraska (◆Figure 8.22). Government subsidies have encouraged growing water-gulping corn, rather than less-water-intensive wheat, sorghum, and cotton.

In the early 1980s the rate of water-table decline decreased because of heavy rain and snow, better water management, and new technologies. New *LEPA* (low-energy, precision-application) irrigation nozzles use less water and less energy and decrease evaporation by as much as 98 percent from the amounts lost with spray-type irrigation. Furthermore, treated wastewater is now being recycled on fields, and rainfall has been induced by cloud seeding in attempts to recharge the aquifer in Kansas.

A 1982 Department of Commerce study found that 6 million hectares (15 million acres) were being irrigated with water drawn from 150,000 wells in the Ogallala and other High Plains aquifers. By the year 2020, according to the study report, about a fourth of the aquifer's water will have been mined at the present rate of withdrawal. A 1995 estimate of the total overdraft of the Ogallala is that it equals one year's flow of the Colorado River. The Ogallala aquifer is certainly the life-blood of High Plains agriculture, and most users of its water are aware that mining the resource must be discontinued. Strict management that includes conservative usage, monitoring, and utilization of new technologies is required for an attempt at balancing its recharge and withdrawals (◆Figure 8.23). As a postscript to the Ogallala story, the aquifer's name is derived from that of the Ogallala Tribe of the Sioux Nation. Led by Chiefs Red Cloud and Crazy Horse, the tribe fought to retain tribal lands in the late 1800s.

Groundwater mining causes shallow wells to go dry, increases the cost of lifting water to the surface as water levels drop, and may eventually cause ground subsidence (see Chapter 7). Currently groundwater pumping is twice the volume of natural recharge in Arizona's Tucson groundwater basin, and it has been necessary to import water from the Central Arizona Project to end the overdraft. One inadvertent but very useful product (for hydrologists) of nuclear testing in the 1950s and early 1960s was radioactive tritium. This rare isotope of hydrogen has two neutrons and one proton (most hydrogen has no neutrons). It has a short half-life of little more than a decade and so rapidly, over several decades, disappears from the aquifer. Tritium has been used as a tracer of groundwater recharge, because water older than the mid-1950s and modern water both contain very little

◆ **FIGURE 8.21** The effect of groundwater mining on the water table. The drop from the initial level to the present level is the *overdraft,* the amount of water that has been mined.

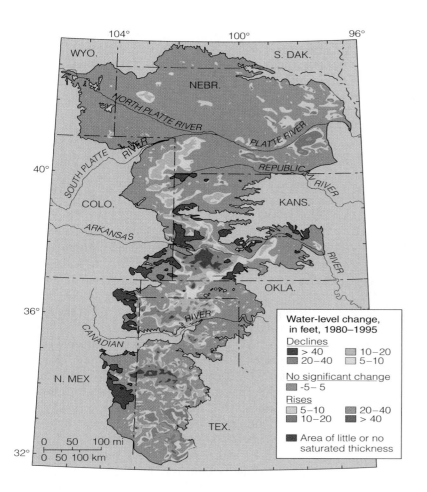

◆ **FIGURE 8.22** Water-level change in the High Plains aquifer, 1980–1995. USGS

tritium. This type of testing was done in the Tucson basin on alluvial fans of the adjacent Catalina and Rincon Mountains. The study indicates that both old and young water exist in the basin and that recharge rates are quite variable.

The Santa Clara Valley of central California is a classic case of regional overdraft. Water levels there declined 46 meters (150 ft) between 1912 and 1959, and downtown San Jose dropped 2.76 meters (9 ft). As a final example, overpumping in Alabama dropped the pressure surface in one aquifer 62 meters (200 ft); it is now below sea level more than 80 miles inland from the sea. The solution to such a problem is *artificial recharge,* or "water spreading," which is accomplished by importing or diverting surface water and ponding it where it can percolate into the aquifer. Such a program was initiated in the Santa Clara Valley in 1959, which, in combination with decreased pumping, has restored the water table to 1912 levels. Raising the water table does not bring the land back to its original level, however, because pore spaces are irreversibly lost as subsidence occurs.

Groundwater–Saltwater Interaction

Aquifers in coastal areas may discharge fresh water into the ocean, creating bodies of diluted seawater. If the water table is lowered by pumping to or near sea-level elevation, however,

saltwater invades the freshwater body, causing the water to become saline *(brackish)* and thus undrinkable. The direction of flow between the two water masses is determined by their density differences. Seawater is 2.5 percent (1/40th) denser than fresh water. This means that a 102.5-foot-high column of fresh water will exactly balance a 100-foot-high column of seawater (◆Figure 8.24a). Fresh water floats on seawater under the Hawaiian Islands, the Outer Banks of North Carolina, Long Island, and many other coastal areas (■ Case Study 8.3 on page 238).

This relationship is known as the *Ghyben–Herzberg lens*—named for the two scientists who independently discovered it and for the lenslike shape of the freshwater body (◆Figure 8.24b) that floats on the denser saltwater. In theory, the mass of fresh water extends to a depth below sea level that is 40 times the water-table elevation above sea level. If the water table is 2.5 feet above sea level, the freshwater lens would extend to a depth of 100 feet below sea level. Any reduction of water-table elevation would cause the saltwater to migrate upward into the freshwater lens until a new balance is established. If the water table drops below the level necessary for maintaining a balance with denser seawater, wells will begin to produce brackish water and eventually saltwater. Thus it is important to maintain high water-table levels in coastal zones so that the resource is not damaged by

◆ **FIGURE 8.23** Should the High Plains aquifer be treated as a bath-tub or an egg carton? The egg carton analogy assumes that a user is not subject to water depletion by the action of neighboring irrigators because of the local nature of the cone of depression. The bathtub analogy assumes that the aquifer acts as a common pool and the water level responds as if water were being drawn from a lake or bathtub. The actual situation lies somewhere between these two analogies.
USGS circular 1186, p. 47

saltwater encroachment. This level maintenance is accomplished by good management combined, when necessary, with artificial recharge using local or imported water (water spreading), or with the injection of imported water into the aquifer through existing wells.

Groundwater–Surface Water Interaction and Usage Trends

As has been emphasized thus far, surface water and groundwater are not separate entities. Nearly all surface-water features—lakes, streams, rivers, artificial lakes, and wetlands—interact with water underground. Some surface-water bodies gain water and acquire a different chemistry from groundwater, and other surface waters contribute to underground water and may even pollute it. Thus, it is important in water planning to have a clear understanding of the linkages between groundwater and surface water and of the geology that controls both.

The greatest volume of fresh water is used for irrigation, and the greatest total volume of water, both fresh and saline, is used for power generation. However, 98 percent of the water used for power generation is returned to streams or other reservoirs; only 2 percent is consumed. How water is used affects the reuse potential of returns flows. For example, irrigation water may be too salty or contaminated by pesticides and insecticides to have any reuse potential unless it is purified naturally or artificially. On the other hand, water used in power generation has great reuse potential because the principal change is usually an increase in its temperature and location (or head) as it is released downstream.

Since 1950 national water-use statistics have been compiled every five years (see W. B. Solley, For Further Information section). There was a steady increase in per-person water

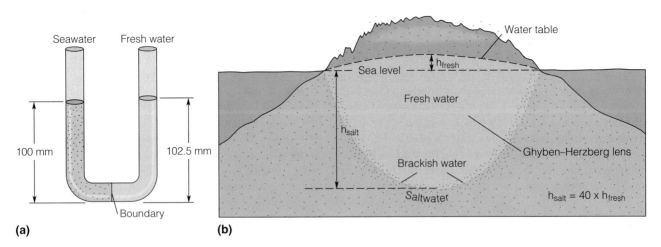

◆ **FIGURE 8.24** (a) Illustration of the density contrast between fresh water and seawater. Because seawater is 2.5% denser than fresh water, 102.5 millimeters of fresh water are required to balance 100 millimeters of salt water. (b) Hypothetical island and Ghyben–Herzberg lens of fresh water floating on seawater. The freshwater lens extends to a depth 40 times the height of the water table above sea level. Not to scale.

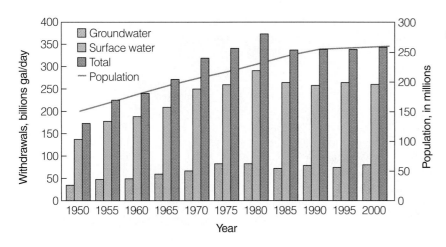

◆ **FIGURE 8.25** Trends in fresh ground- and surface-water withdrawals and population, 1950–2000. USGS

usage from 1950 to 1980, the all-time high. Between 1990 and 2000, there was greater than a 10 percent decrease in water use per person (in 2000 the average was 1430 gallons a day per person), but the U.S. population grew by 33 million people (◆Figure 8.25), so total withdraws were steady at 408 billion gallons per day. It was estimated that the United States was saving 144 billion liters (38 billion gal) per day in 1995, enough to fill Lake Erie in a decade. Some of the reasons cited for this decrease were the development and use of more efficient irrigation methods, conservation programs, increased water recycling, and a downturn in farm economies.

Geologic Work by Underground Water

Solution (a chemical reaction discussed in Chapter 6) of limestone and gypsum by underground water leads to the formation of caves, caverns, disappearing streams, and high yielding and extensive groundwater sources such as the Edwards aquifer (■ Case Study 8.4 on page 239). Land area exhibiting these features is called **karst terrane** (German *Karst*, for the Kars limestone plateau of northwest Yugoslavia; ◆Figure 8.26). Urbanization on karst terrane typically results in problems such as contamination of underground water and collapse of cavern roofs to form sinkholes.

The first sign of impending disaster in Winter Park, Florida occurred one evening when Rosa Mae Owens heard a "swish" in her backyard and saw, to her amazement, that a large sycamore tree had simply disappeared. The hole into which it had fallen gradually enlarged, and by noon the next day her home had also fallen into the breach. Six Porsches in a nearby storage yard suffered the same fate, as did a city swimming pool and two residential streets. Deciding to work with nature, the City of Winter Park stabilized and sealed the sinkhole, and converted it to a beautiful urban lake (◆Figure 8.27). Few people who read of this notorious sinkhole in May 1981 realized the extent of the sinkhole problem in the southeastern United States.

Sinkholes are most commonly found in carbonate terranes (limestone, dolomite, and marble), but they are also known to occur in rock salt and gypsum. They form when carbonic acid (H_2CO_3) dissolves carbonate rock, forming a near-surface cavern. Continued solution leads to collapse of the cavern's roof and the formation of a sinkhole. About 20 percent of the United States and 40 percent of the country east of the Mississippi River is underlain by limestone or dolomite. The states most impacted by surface collapse are Alabama, Florida, Georgia, Tennessee, Missouri, and Pennsylvania.

Tens of thousands of sinkholes exist in the United States, and the formation of new ones can be accelerated by human activities. For example, excessive water withdrawal that lowers groundwater levels reduces or removes the buoyant support of shallow caverns' roofs. In fact, the correlation

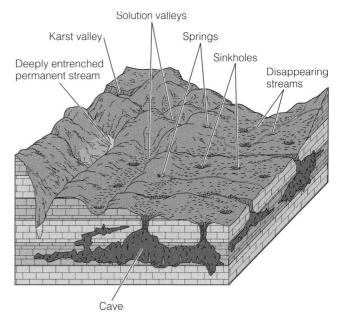

◆ **FIGURE 8.26** Surface and subsurface features as well as discontinuous surface drainage are indicative of karst topography.

◆ **FIGURE 8.27** Sinkhole in Winter Park, Florida. (a) Air view that shows its almost perfect symmetry. (b) Plugged and landscaped, the sinkhole area is now an urban park.

(a)

(b)

between water-table lowering and sinkhole formation is so strong that "sinkhole seasons" are designated in the Southeast. These seasons are declared whenever ground-water levels drop naturally because of decreased rainfall and in the summer, when the demand for water is heavy. Vibrations from construction activity or explosive blasting also can trigger sinkhole collapse. Other mechanisms that have been proposed for sinkhole formation are fluctuating water tables (alternate wetting and drying of cover material reduces its strength) and high water tables (which erode the roofs of underground openings).

Although the development of natural sinkholes is not predictable, it is possible to assess a site's potential for collapse resulting from human activities. This requires extensive geologic and hydrogeologic investigation prior to site development. Under the best of geologic conditions, good geophysical and subsurface (drilling) data can tell us *where* collapse is most likely to occur, but they cannot tell us exactly *when* a collapse may occur. Armed with this information, planners and civil engineers can implement zoning and building restrictions that will minimize the hazards to the public.

CONSIDER THIS

You could become a millionaire if you developed a relatively inexpensive method of locating caverns that may collapse and form sinkholes. Got any ideas? If not, what types of more sophisticated (and expensive) methods might be employed to locate caverns?

Water Quality
Dissolved Substances

Varying concentrations of all the stable elements known on Earth are dissolved in natural waters. Some of these elements and compounds, such as arsenic, are poisonous. Others are required for sustaining life and health; common table salt is one, and it occurs in almost all natural waters. Some are nuisance pollutants that either make the water taste bad or appear unattractive. ⋆ Table 8.1 lists some common water-problem symptoms and suggestions for correcting them.

Years ago the U.S. Public Health Service established **potable** (drinkable) **water** standards for public water supplies based on purity, which is defined as allowable concentrations

★TABLE 8.1 Common Water Quality Problems		
Problem	Probable Cause	Correction
Mineral scale buildup	water hardness	water softener or hardness inhibitor (such as Calgon)
Rusty or black stains	iron and/or manganese	aeration/filtration; chlorination; remove source of Fe/Mn
Red-brown slime	iron bacteria	chlorination filtration unit; remove source of slime
Rotten-egg smell or taste	hydrogen sulfide and/or sulfate-reducing bacteria; low oxygen content	aeration; chlorination filtration unit; greensand filters
Salty taste	chloride—seawater or other saline water	reduce pumping to raise water table
Gastrointestinal diseases, typhoid fever, dysentery, and diarrhea	coliform bacteria and other pathogens from septic tanks or livestock yards	remove source of pollution; disinfect well; boil water; chlorinate; abandon well and relocate new well away from pollution source
Petroleum smell or film	fuel oil, diesel fuel, or lubricating oil	remove source of pollution

Source: D. Daly, "Groundwater Quality and Pollution" (Geological Survey of Ireland Circular 85–1, 1985), in J. E. Moore and others, *Ground Water: A Primer,* American Geological Institute, 1994.

of particular dissolved substances in natural waters. Today, the Environmental Protection Agency (EPA) is responsible for administering the *National Primary Drinking Water Regulations (NPDWRs)*. These are legally enforceable standards that apply to public water systems. In fact, if you get your water from such a centralized system, once every year, along with your water bill, you will get a pamphlet letting you know how well the water you drink meets these standards and what your water company is doing to help make the water even cleaner. These primary standards protect your health by limiting the levels of potentially harmful chemicals in your drinking water. These concentrations are expressed in weight per volume, which is milligrams per liter (mg/L) in the metric system. The standards can also be expressed in a weight-per-weight system. For example, in the English system, one pound of dissolved solid in 999,999 pounds of water would be one part per million (ppm). The standards allow only minuscule amounts of pollutants in public water supplies. For example, 1 ppm or 1 mg/L is equal to about 1 ounce of a dissolved solid in 7,500 gallons of water, or 0.0001 percent. The standard for "sweet" water—the preferable quality classification for domestic use—is less than 500 ppm of *total dissolved solids (tds),* and the standard for "fresh" water is less than 1,000 ppm of total dissolved solids.

The quality of groundwater can be impaired either by a high total amount of various dissolved salts or by a small amount of a specific toxic element. High salt content may be due to solution of minerals in local geological formations, seawater intrusion into coastal aquifers, or the introduction of industrial wastes into groundwater. (Organic contaminants, mainly animal wastes, solvents, and pesticides, also

degrade water. They are discussed in the next subsection.) Several types of standards have been set. The most important enforcement standard is the **maximum contaminant level** (MCL), which is the highest level of a contaminant that is allowed in drinking water. **Maximum Contaminant Level Goal** (MCLGs) are the level of a pollutant at and below which there is no known or expected risk to health. MCLs are set as close to MCLGs as is politically and scientifically feasible while considering the available treatment technology and taking cost into consideration. ★Table 8.2 lists EPA limits for some of the inorganic substances that occur in groundwater and impair its safety.

Water with high salt content, particularly bicarbonate and sulfate contents, can have a laxative effect on humans. Dissolved iron or manganese can give coffee or tea an odd color, impart a metallic taste, and stain laundry. Concentrations greater than 3 ppm of copper can give the skin a green tinge, a condition that is reversible, and lead is both poisonous and persistent.

A *persistent pollutant* is one that builds up (or bioaccumulates) in the human system because the body does not metabolize or excrete it. The Romans, for example, used lead plumbing pipes, and skeletal materials exhumed from old Roman cemeteries retain high lead concentrations. Lead concentrations in the water supply greater than about 0.1 ppm can build up over a period of years to debilitating concentrations in the human body. Arsenic is also persistent, and the standards for arsenic and lead are similar, less than 0.05 ppm, preferably absent. Nitrates in amounts greater than 10 ppm are known to inhibit the blood's ability to carry oxygen and to cause "blue baby syndrome" *(infantile methemoglobinemia)* during pregnancy. The element with the greatest

★TABLE 8.2 Health Effects of Significant Concentrations of Common Inorganic Environmental Pollutants

Inorganic Pollutant	Standard, mg/L	Health Effects
Arsenic	0.01	dermal and nervous-system toxicity effects, paralysis
Barium	2.0	gastrointestinal effects, laxative
Boron	1.0	no effect on humans; damaging to plants and trees, particularly citrus trees
Cadmium	0.005	kidney effects
Copper	1.3	gastrointestinal irritant, liver damage; toxic to many aquatic organisms
Chromium	0.1	liver/kidney effects
Fluoride	4.0	mottled tooth enamel
Lead	0.015	attacks nervous system and kidneys; highly toxic to infants and pregnant women
Mercury	0.002	central-nervous-system disorders, kidney disfunction
Nitrates	10.0	methemoglobinemia ("blue baby syndrome")
Selenium	0.05	gastrointestinal effects
Silver	0.1	skin discoloration (argyria)
Sodium	20–170	hypertension and cardiac difficulties
	70.0	renders irrigation water unusable

★TABLE 8.3 Water Hardness Scale*

Concentration of Calcium^{2+}, mg/L	Classification
0–60	soft
61–120	moderately hard
121–180	hard
>180	very hard

*Hardness is expressed here as milligrams of dissolved Ca^{2+} per liter. Dissolved calcium and magnesium in water combine with soap to form an insoluble precipitate that hampers water's cleansing action.

impact upon plants is boron, which is virtually fatal to citrus and other plants in concentrations as low as 1.0 ppm.

Dissolved calcium (Ca^{2+}) and magnesium (Mg^{2+}) ions cause water to be "hard." In hard water, soap does not lather easily, and dirt and soap combine to form scum. Hard water is most prevalent in areas underlain by limestone ($CaCO_3$) and dolomite ($CaMgCO_3$). A water softener simply exchanges sodium (Na^+) for calcium and magnesium ions in the water using a zeolite (a silicate ion exchanger) or mineral sieve. Water with more than 120 ppm of dissolved calcium and magnesium is considered hard (★Table 8.3). Because sodium is known to be bad for persons with heart problems (hypertension) and water softeners increase the sodium content of water, those people on low-sodium diets should not drink softened water.

The good news regarding dissolved ions is that fluoride ion (F^-) dissolved in water reduces tooth cavities when it is present in amounts of 1.0–1.5 ppm. The explanation for this is that tooth enamel and bone are composed of the mineral apatite, $Ca_5(PO_4)_3(F, Cl, OH)$, whose structure allows the free substitution of fluoride F^-, chloride Cl^-, or hydroxyl $(OH)^-$ ions in the mineral structure. In the presence of fluoride, the crystals of apatite in tooth enamel are larger and more perfect, which makes them resist decay. Too much fluoride in drinking water, however—concentrations greater than 4 ppm—can cause children's teeth to become mottled with dark spots. Indeed, it was this cosmetic blemish, among children of Colorado Springs, Colorado in particular, that led to the discovery of the beneficial effect of flouride ion and to the establishment of concentration standards for it.

The story is great. In 1908, Dr. McKay, a Colorado Springs dentist, described the malady he called, *Colorado Brown Stain*. It was a discoloration of the tooth enamel that we now know results from ingesting too much fluoride. Not only did nearly 90% of school kids in Colorado Springs have stained teeth, they had far fewer cavities than their peers in Boulder. It took decades and many different studies to prove that fluoride was an effective way to dramatically reduce tooth decay. Now much of the nation drinks fluoridated water and gets far fewer fillings. Dissolved fluoride is also believed to slow osteoporosis, a bone-degeneration process that accompanies aging.

Groundwater Pollutants

The term *water pollution* refers to the introduction of chemical, physical, or biological materials into a body of natural water that affects its future use. Pollution is more widespread than formerly thought, as revealed by studies by state and federal agencies and by complaints from users. It is a serious problem because thousands of years may be required to flush contaminated water from an aquifer and replace it with clean water. River water, in contrast, is exchanged in a matter of hours or days.

Residence time, the average length of time a substance remains (*resides*) in a system, is an important concept in water-pollution studies. We may view it as the time that passes before the water within an aquifer, lake, river, glacier, or ocean is totally replaced and continues on its way through the hydrologic cycle. Residence time can be calculated simply by dividing the volume of the water body (m³) by the flow rate into and out of it (m³/second), assuming everything is in balance. The average residence time of water in rivers has been found to be a few days; of water in large lakes, several decades; in shallow gravel aquifers, a few days; and in deeper, low-permeability aquifers, perhaps thousands or even hundreds of thousands of years. This knowledge allows us to estimate the approximate time a particular system will take to clean itself naturally and indicates those cases in which a pollutant must be removed from a water body artificially by human means because of a long residence time.

Although most pollution is due to careless disposal of waste at the land surface by humans, some is the result of the leaching of toxic materials in shallow excavations or mines. Groundwater pollution occurs in urban environments due to improper disposal of industrial waste and leakage from sewer systems, old fuel-storage tanks, wastewater settling ponds, and chemical-waste dumps (◆Figure 8.28a). In suburban and agricultural areas, septic-tank leakage, fecal matter in runoff and seepage from animal feedlots, and the use of inorganic fertilizers, such as nitrates and phosphates, and of weed- and pest-control chemicals all can serve to degrade both surface and subsurface water (◆Figure 8.28b).

Leaking gasoline-storage tanks have been recognized in the last few decades as an important cause of soil and groundwater pollution (◆Figure 8.28c). By federal law, all underground tanks now must be inspected for leakage, and if gasoline is found in the adjacent soil, the tanks must be removed and the soil cleaned. (Although the problem is not amusing, the technology created by the need for hydrocarbon cleanup has come to be lightly referred to as *yank-a-tank.*) If gasoline is found floating on groundwater, it must be removed. Both the gasoline and the decontaminated groundwater are then usable. Soils can be cleansed of hydrocarbons biologically with bacteria, a process known as **bioremediation,** or by aeration and oxidation of the hydrocarbon films (see Case Study 6.3 on page 174).

Table 8.4 lists some of the detrimental effects of selected organic pollutants. Water standards for common organic pollutants of water bodies are given in Table 8.5. The very low limits allowed for the pesticides lindane and endrin indicate their toxicities. Some of these toxic chemicals are also carcinogenic (cancer causing), which makes them doubly dangerous.

Density differences between groundwater and particular pollutants often govern the remedial measures that can be used; for example, gasoline and oil float on groundwater, whereas salt brines from industry or agriculture and some organic chemicals sink to lower levels. In some cases it is possible to skim a layer of gasoline from the top of the water table. Gasoline or fuel oil that is floating on the capillary fringe may yield vapors that can rise and be trapped

Groundwater is polluted by industrial and municipal wastes, leaking sewers, and lawn fertilizers, pesticides, and herbicides.

(a) Urban areas

Groundwater is polluted by septic tanks, animal feedlots, and crop fertilizers, pesticides, and herbicides.

(b) Rural areas

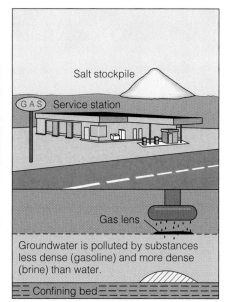

Groundwater is polluted by substances less dense (gasoline) and more dense (brine) than water.

(c) Density effects

◆ **FIGURE 8.28** (a) Urban-area and (b) rural-area pollution sources. (c) Some pollutants float and others sink due to differences in density between groundwater and the pollutants.

TABLE 8.4 Health Effects of Common Organic Pollutants		
Organic Substance	Human Health Effects	Environmental Effects
Dieldrin	convulsions, kidney damage	toxic to aquatic organisms
DDT	convulsions, kidney damage	reproductive failure in animals, eggshell thinning
PCBs	vomiting, abdominal pain, liver damage	eggshell thinning in birds, liver damage in mammals
Benzene	anemia, bone-marrow damage	toxic to some fish and aquatic invertebrates
Phenols	death at high doses	decreased phytoplankton productivity
Dioxin	acute skin rashes, systemic damage, mortality	lethal to aquatic birds and mammals

*Insecticides or compounds used in their manufacture.
Source: U.S. Public Health Service; Environmental Protection Agency.

beneath or in the walls of buildings. Since gasoline fumes contain BTX (*b*enzene, *t*oluene, and *x*ylene), they are carcinogenic. "Air-stripping" is currently the preferred method of removing volatile organic pollutants such as BTX compounds and trichloroethylene (TCE) and tetrachloroethylene (PCE) cleaning solvents from groundwater. (The origin of these substances is usually connected to refinery, industrial, or military activities.) The polluted water is brought to the ground surface, where the contained volatile pollutants (TCE or BTX) are gasified (air-stripped) and either vented to the atmosphere or captured on charcoal filters.

TABLE 8.5 Water Standards for Common Organic Pollutants	
Substance	Maximum Contaminant Level (EPA), mg/L
Cyanide	0.2
Lindane	0.0002
Endrin	0.002
2,4-D	0.07
Toluene	1.0

*Insecticides, fuel and animal-control compounds.
Source: Environmental Protection Agency.

Conservation and Alternative Sources

Many parts of the United States are experiencing drought conditions as this is being written. Excessive groundwater withdrawals have led to water mining in many areas, particularly the Southwest. Remedies to cure water-deficient conditions include desalinization of seawater, recycling wastewater, tugging huge Antarctic icebergs up the coast of South America to drier areas in the northern hemisphere, and 35-ton water bags floated down from the northwestern United States to southern California. But in the long run, as population increases, we will be required to conserve water. Voluntary water conservation has been quite successful, reducing consumption by as much as 15 percent, and even greater reductions have been achieved where rationing is mandatory. The advent of Energy Star appliances, such as water efficient dishwashers and front loading clothes washers, lets each of us contribute while often earning rebates from local utilities. Despite conservation, global water use is increasing everywhere. The world's 6 billion people are intercepting 54 percent of all fresh water from rivers, lakes, and aquifers. Humans will intercept 70 percent by 2025 as just the result of population growth. If total consumption rises at the current rate, humans could be using 90 percent of all available fresh water, leaving 10 percent for the rest of life on Earth. We should think "conservation."

CASE STUDY 8.1

Who Shrunk the Aral Sea?

The Aral Sea was once the fourth-largest lake in the world, and second only to the Caspian Sea in the former Soviet Union (◆ Figure 1). The level of the sea in 1960 was about 53 meters above sea level, and it contained a fish population that supported more than 60,000 persons in fishing and processing. In 2003 the level of the Aral was only 30 meters above sea level, and it ranked as the world's sixth-largest lake, having lost more than 74 percent of its surface area since 1960. The result of this shrinkage is that the fishing industry is no more (◆ Figure 2). Additionally, the salinity of the sea has increased from 10 g/l (about 1%) to over 100 g/l (10%) in some areas, making it inhospitable to most life. This story leaves a question that begs an answer: What caused this ecocatastrophe?

Agricultural demands of the former Soviet Union deprived this great salt lake of a water inflow sufficient to sustain itself. Two major rivers feed the lake: the Amu Darya (*darya, river*) flowing into the lake from the south, and the Syr Darya, which reaches the sea at its north. The Soviet leaders wanted exportable crops, and cotton, a great water gulper, was high on their list. Irrigated agriculture was expanded and the Kara Kum Canal was opened in 1956, which diverted water from the Amu Darya into the deserts of Turkmenistan. Millions of hectares of arid lands came under irrigation. By 1960 the level of the sea began to drop, and where in the past it received 59 km^3 of water annually, this amount fell to zero by the early 1980s. As the lake area receded, the salinity increased, and by 1977 the fish catch dropped to one-fourth its level before water diversion. By 1990 the area of the Aral was cut in half, and its water volume was but a mere one-third its historic amount. The lowering of the sea exposed 30,000 km^2 of salt- and chemical-filled lakebeds (◆ Figure 3). Blowing dust, particularly south of the lake, has resulted in air pollution producing a high incidence of throat cancer, eye and respiratory diseases, anemia, and infant mortality. In addition, the shoreline habitat was lost and delta wetlands desiccated. Animal populations shifted, because conditions favored animals better adapted to drought and high salinity. By any measure, the desiccation of the Aral Sea is an ecological disaster. The central Asian republics that surround the sea—Kazakhstan, Turkmenistan, Uzbekistan, and the little-known Karakalpak Republic (within Uzbekistan)—are the poorest of the former Soviet bloc and have no money to invest in rebuilding irrigation systems. In addition, Afghanistan and Iran, with small areas within the drainage basin, have little interest in the problem.

A sad Uzbek poem goes, "You cannot fill the Aral Sea with tears."

◆ **FIGURE 1** Location map of Aral Sea Redrawn from Philip Micklin, Western Mich. Univ.

CONTINUED

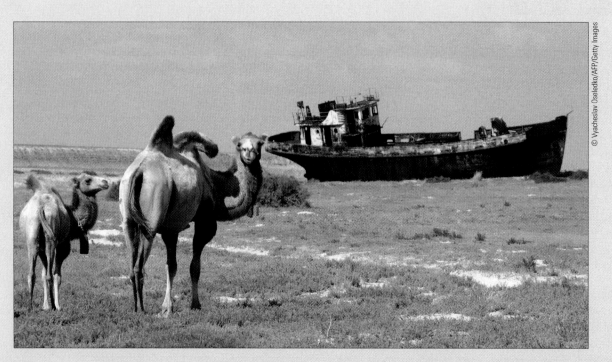

◆ **FIGURE 2** Fishing boat grounded with shrinkage of the Aral Sea. This spelled doom to a thriving fishing industry and to an important source of protein for the local inhabitants.

◆ **FIGURE 3** The shrinkage in area of the Aral Sea from 1960 to 2003, with its estimated reduction projected to 2010. By 2003, compared to 1960, the sea lost 74 percent of its area and 90 percent of its volume. Redrawn from Philip Micklin, Western Mich. Univ.

CASE STUDY 8.2

Fluid Flow in Porous Rocks

Porosity is the ratio of the volume of pore spaces in a rock or other solid to the material's total volume. Expressed as a percentage, it is

$$P = \frac{V_p}{V_t} \times 100$$

where P = porosity
V_p = pore volume
V_t = total volume

If an aquifer has a porosity of 23 percent, a cubic meter of the aquifer is composed of 0.77 cubic meters of solid material and 0.23 cubic meters of pore space, which may or may not be filled with water. Porosities of 20 to 40 percent are not uncommon in sand and gravel aquifers.

Permeability is a measure of how fast fluids can move through a porous medium and is thus expressed in a unit of velocity, such as meters per day. Knowing the permeability of an aquifer allows us to determine in advance how much water a well will produce and how far apart wells should be spaced. To determine permeability we use **Darcy's Law,** which states that the rate of flow (Q in cubic meters) is the product of hydraulic conductivity (K), the **hydraulic gradient,** or the slope of the water table (I in meters per meter), and the cross-sectional area (A in square meters). Thus,

$$Q = K \times A \times I$$

where "Q" is the rate of flow

Hydraulic conductivity, K, is a measure of the permeability of a rock or a sediment, its water-transmitting characteristics. It is defined as the quantity of water that will flow in a unit of time under a unit hydraulic gradient through a unit of area measured perpendicular to the flow direction. K is expressed in distance of flow with time, usually meters per day.

If we use a unit hydraulic gradient, then Darcy's Law reduces to:

$$Q = K \times A$$

Unit hydraulic gradient is the slope of 1-unit vertical to 1-unit horizontal ($I = 1/1 = 45°$), and it allows us to compare the water-transmitting ability of aquifers composed of materials with different hydraulic conductivities. Flow rates may be less than a millimeter per day for clays, and many meters per day for well-sorted sands and clean gravels. In general, groundwater moves at a snail's pace.

Pumice provides an interesting example. It is a porous but almost impermeable rock. It has porosities as high as 90 percent but few connected pore spaces. Pumice will float for a time because it has low density and its low permeability prevents immediate saturation. A cubic meter of pumice may weigh as little as 200 kilograms (440 lbs), a tenth of the weight of solid rock of the same composition.

◆ **FIGURE 1** The unit hydraulic gradient (I) and unit prism (1 m²) of a sandstone aquifer. When the hydraulic conductivity (K) is known, then the discharge (Q) in liters or cubic meters per day per square meter of aquifer can be calculated.

CASE STUDY 8.3

Groundwater Law

Ownership of groundwater is a property right and has traditionally been regulated as such by individual states. Each state applies one or more of four legal doctrines to groundwater rights, none of which considers the geological relationship between surface-water infiltration and groundwater flow. The doctrines are

- *Riparian doctrine* (Latin *ripa,* "river or bank") holds that landowners overlying well-defined underground "streams" have absolute right to that water. They may exercise that right whenever they wish without limitation.

- *Reasonable-use doctrine* restricts a landowner's right to groundwater to "reasonable use" on the land above that does not deprive neighboring landowners of their rights to "reasonable use." This doctrine results in a

more equal distribution of water when there is a shortage.

- *Prior-appropriation doctrine* holds that the earliest water users have the firmest rights; in other words, "first-come, first-served."

- *Correlative-rights doctrine* holds that landowners own shares to the water beneath their collective property that are proportional to their shares of the overlying land.

In the San Joaquin Valley of California, for example, surface-water rights are governed by the doctrine of prior appropriation (first-come, first-served), whereas groundwater rights are governed by the doctrine of correlative rights (proportional shares). In the late nineteenth century the Sierra Nevada to the east of the valley and the lower ranges to the

west maintained high water tables, and they both contributed water to the flow of the San Joaquin River (◆ Figure 1). By 1966, however, heavy groundwater withdrawals on the west side of the San Joaquin Valley had reversed the regional groundwater flow, so that the river was losing water underground, rather than gaining. The San Joaquin had become a losing stream. Imagine a courtroom scenario in which hundreds of people with first-come, first-served rights to *surface* water sue thousands of people holding proportional shares rights to *underground* water for causing their surface water to go underground.

As explained throughout this chapter, it is impossible to treat groundwater and surface water as separate entities. Surface water contributes to underground water supplies, and groundwater contributes to streamflow and springs.

◆ **FIGURE 1** Groundwater flow in the central San Joaquin Valley in (a) 1906 and (b) 1966. Note that the San Joaquin River was a gaining stream in 1906 and a losing stream in 1966. The change reflects intensive development and extraction of underground water.
AIPG, *Ground Water: Issues and Answers,* 1985

CASE STUDY 8.4

The Edwards Aquifer, a Texas Bonanza

The Edwards aquifer in south-central Texas is one of the most prolific aquifers in North America (◆Figure 1). It provides water for two million people, including the city of San Antonio. A well drilled for the city in 1991 is reportedly the world's greatest flowing well, yielding 95,000 liters per minute (25,000 gal/min). The aquifer is composed of limestone of Cretaceous age that is a *karstified* flow system; that is, it is honeycombed with solution cavities, caves, and caverns and feeds many springs. About 80 percent of the aquifer's recharge is from losing streams that flow over its exposed outcrops; the rest is from direct infiltration of precipitation. Where the aquifer dips down below the ground surface toward the south, it is under pressure, and water rises in well bores and sometimes to the ground surface (see Figure 8.19). At depth, the water quality and potability deteriorate to a zone marked on maps by the "bad-water line." The region served by the aquifer is one of the fastest growing areas in the United States, and water supply is critical to this growth. Recharge areas are environmentally sensitive to pollutants, and the resource is threatened by disregard for this potential problem (◆Figure 2). Threats are from human sewage, highway construction, agricultural chemicals, runoff from paved surfaces, and leaking underground storage tanks, to name a few. Government agencies at all levels are committed to protecting the aquifer. The federal government designated the aquifer a Sole Source Aquifer, which makes it eligible for funding for some protection projects. The state declared the Edwards aquifer the most susceptible to pollution in the state and established conservation districts for overseeing its protection.

Recharge zone

Extent of Edwards aquifer potable water

---- Bad water line

◆ **FIGURE 1** Area of south-central Texas's Edwards aquifer.

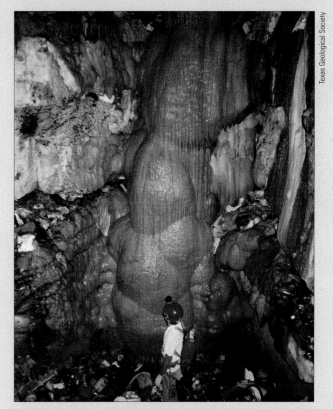

◆ **FIGURE 2** Midnight Cave in the Edwards aquifer before cleanup, 1993; southern Travis County near Austin, Texas. The trash is household garbage, oil filters, pesticide bottles, partially filled turpentine cans, and automobile parts. Trash had floated up to higher ledges of the cave during high-water aquifer conditions. Cleanup efforts involved conservation groups, government agencies, and cavers. An estimated 3,000 cubic feet of trash was removed from the cave.

CASE STUDY 8.5

Long Island, New York—Saltwater or Fresh Water for the Future?

By far, Long Island's most important source of fresh water is its aquifers, which are estimated to hold 10–20 trillion gallons of recoverable water (◆Figure 1). This water infiltrated underground over centuries and the excess was discharged naturally to the sea. Groundwater was exploited as the island was urbanized, causing the water table on the mainland side of the island to drop below sea level. By 1936 saltwater had invaded the freshwater aquifer. Pumping wells were converted to recharge wells using imported water, and by 1965 the water tables had recovered to acceptable elevations above sea level.

To the east in Queens County, pumping had increased and recharge had diminished due to the construction of sewers and the paving of streets. Treated wastewater was thus being carried to the sea, rather than infiltrating underground as it would with

cesspools and septic tanks. With lowered water tables, saltwater invaded the aquifers below Queens County, and the State of New York in 1970 asked the U.S. Geological Survey to conduct groundwater studies.

The basic challenge was to offset groundwater withdrawals of 1.7 million cubic meters per day with equal amounts of surface infiltration or injection. A line of injection wells was proposed for replacing the decreased natural recharge. These wells would inject treated sewage effluent or imported water and build a freshwater barrier against saltwater intrusion (◆Figure 2). Spreading highly treated sewage effluent and natural runoff into recharge basins could be carried out along with injection into the deeper aquifer. In both the injection-well and the spreading-basin alternatives, the treated sewage is purified to drinking-water standards so that it does not affect local shallow wells. Recharge,

like injection, builds a freshwater ridge that keeps saltwater at bay. An unusual but viable method is to allow controlled saltwater intrusion so that a true Ghyben–Herzberg lens of fresh water floating on saltwater develops. This method has the distinct advantage of salvaging much of the fresh water that otherwise would flow through aquifers into the ocean. In addition, this alternative would increase the yield of the aquifer by several hundred million cubic meters per day, although it would decrease the total volume of fresh water in the reservoir.

Each method of balancing outflow and inflow—injection wells, spreading basins, and controlled saltwater intrusion—has advantages and disadvantages. As is the case with many geological problems, applying a combination of methods yields the most fruitful and cost-effective solution. Kings and Queens Counties now rely entirely upon

◆ **FIGURE 1** Hydrologic relationship between fresh and salty underground water; Long Island, New York. Arrows indicate direction of water movement in the hydrologic cycle. After B. L. Foxworthy, USGS prof. paper 950, 1978

importation for their freshwater needs. Public water in Nassau and Suffolk Counties is entirely underground water, and only a very small amount of seawater intrusion occurs in the southwest corner of Nassau County.

Currently, there is a network of recharge basins that collect surface-water runoff and allow it to percolate underground into the shallow aquifer (◆Figure 3). The counties require developers to dedicate land for recharge basins within their housing or commercial projects. This method of recharge has proven effective in maintaining the balance between seawater and fresh water.

◆ **FIGURE 2** Method of balancing freshwater outflow and seawater inflow; Long Island, New York. The aquifer is recharged with highly treated wastewater (*T*) using injection wells. This method reverses saltwater intrusion and also improves the outlook for long-term water yield. After B. L. Foxworthy, USGS prof. paper 950, 1978

◆ **FIGURE 3** A recharge basin for capturing surface-water runoff; Nassau County, New York.

Groundwater Wonders

Karst terrane exists in many parts of the United States, but it is particularly prevalent in parts of Florida and Kentucky. Perhaps the most spectacular karst area in the world is along the Li River in the predominantly limestone region of Kwangsi in southern China near Canton (Guangzhou). Solution of limestone has reduced the landscape there but left enormous pinnacles of resistant limestone, called "tower karst," that present an almost extraterrestrial appearance (◆Figure 1). The towers and other karst features draw tourists from all over the world.

In many places, water containing dissolved calcium carbonate percolates downward through soil and rock into caverns, where evaporation and precipitation form needlelike **stalactites**—extending down from the ceiling—and the more irregular **stalagmites**—rising up from the floor (◆Figure 2). These freshwater limestone features in caves are called **dripstone,** because they build up drip by drip. Carlsbad Caverns in New Mexico and Mammoth Cave in Kentucky offer spectacular examples, but literally hundreds of other limestone caves also exhibit these features and are open to the public. **Speleology** is the study of caves, and spelunking, or "caving," is an exciting recreational pastime for many people. Cavers explore and map natural underground openings. Much of what we know about caves and caverns is attributable to these hobbyists' efforts and talents.

Mineralization by underground water is also responsible for transforming organic material into hard rocks. The replacement mineral is typically silica or calcium carbonate, and replacement may take place cell by cell as in the case of petrified wood (◆Figure 3).

◆ **FIGURE 1** The Stone Forest, 126 kilometers (80 mi) southeast of Kunming, People's Republic of China, is a high-relief karst landscape formed by the dissolution of carbonate rocks.

Reed Wicander

Scott Fee, Am. Speleological Society

◆ **FIGURE 2** Dripstone stalactites, stalagmites, and pillars in a limestone cavern.

Visuals Unlimited

◆ **FIGURE 3** Petrified wood from Arizona. Woody tissue is replaced cell by cell with mineral matter from groundwater.

Summary

The Hydrologic Cycle

Less than one percent of Earth's water is readily available to humans. It is accessible because of the hydrologic cycle: continuous evaporation from the oceans, precipitation on land, runoff back to the oceans, and storage of fresh water in lakes and underground.

Water Use

1. Consumptive use—water that cannot be immediately reused. Where consumptive use exceeds supplies, water must be imported.
2. Irrigation and thermoelectric power plants are the largest consumers. Irrigation water is usually highly degraded, whereas 98 percent of power-plant water is returned to the system, the only change being a higher temperature and elevation.
3. Worldwide about 82 percent of water use is for irrigation. Water availability will limit population growth in the twenty-first century, either by statute in developed countries or by drought and famine in developing nations. The world population projected for 2050 will require water beyond the reliable flow of the world's major rivers.

Lakes

Defined

Lakes are bodies of water in landlocked basins formed by many geologic processes.

   Budget—depends on precipitation plus inflow equaling outflow plus evaporation. If these do not balance in the long term, the result is an ephemeral or salt lake which when dry is known as a playa.

   Overturn—in temperate regions overturn, driven by changing lake temperature with season, keeps lake water oxygenated.

   Nutrients—oligotrophic lakes are relatively sterile and have a small nutrient input. Eutrophic lakes have a high nutrient input and can be choked with plant life. Mesotrophic lakes are in between and have a good balance between inflow and outflow of nutrients.

Rivers and Streams

Dams are built to impound fresh water, for power generation, flood control, and to improve navigation. In the U.S. dams are unpopular because of loss of land by inundation and the subsequent relocation of humans and wildlife.

Groundwater

Defined

Loosely defined as all water underground, as distinct from surface water; the water in the hydrologic cycle that infiltrates underground.

Zones

1. The *zone of aeration,* where the voids in rock or sediment are filled with air and water films.
2. The lower *zone of saturation,* where voids are filled with water.

Water Table

The contact between the zone of aeration and the zone of saturation.

Aquifers

Defined

Bodies of porous and permeable rock or sediment that are saturated with water.

1. *Porosity*—the volume of pore spaces in a geologic material, expressed as a percentage of the total volume.
2. *Permeability*—ease with which fluids flow through a geologic material.
3. *Aquiclude*—a geologic material of very low permeability and inhibits water flow.

Types

1. Unconfined—an aquifer in which the water table is exposed to atmosphere directly. A slope, or gradient, of the water surface is required to induce subsurface flow in a given direction. A well that taps the static water table creates a cone of depression, which provides the necessary gradient for water to flow to the well. Drawdown is the amount of lowering of the water table in a pumping well.
2. Artesian—an aquifer that is confined between aquicludes. The hydraulic head causes water to rise in a well when the aquifer is penetrated. The height to which water will rise at any point along the aquifer is known as the artesian pressure or piezometric surface.

Groundwater Management

Defined

Managing the amount of water contained in a groundwater basin so that it will produce water in the future.

1. *Sustained yield*—the amount of water an aquifer will yield on a day-to-day basis and which is compensated by recharge.
2. *Specific yield*—the amount of water a body of rock or sediment will yield by gravity drainage alone.
3. *Specific retention*—the amount of water held by a body of rock or sediment against the pull of gravity. Specific yield *plus* specific retention *equals* porosity.

Seawater Encroachment

The invasion of coastal aquifers by saltwater. Management requires maintaining high freshwater tables to balance the incursion of denser saltwater.

Groundwater–Surface Water Interaction

Surface water and groundwater cannot be treated as separate entities; what affects one impacts the other.

Surface Water Sources

Lakes, rivers, streams, and artificial reservoirs.

U.S. Use Trends

U.S. water use increased from 1950 until 1980. Between 1980 and 1995 it decreased 10 percent, even though population increased by 37 million people. Reasons include more economical application of irrigation water, public conservation programs, recycling, and a downturn in farm economies.

Solution by Groundwater

1. Solution of limestone and gypsum by underground water forms caves, caverns, disappearing streams, sink holes, and prolific groundwater aquifers. When terranes underlain by carbonate rocks exhibit these features, they are said to have *karst* topography.
2. Water and carbon dioxide from carbonic acid, a weak natural acid, which, over long periods of time, will dissolve carbonate rocks and gypsum.
3. Urbanization on karst terrane results in increased flooding, contamination of underground water, and collapse of the ground surface to form sinkholes.
4. Forty percent of the country east of the Mississippi is underlain by carbonate rocks. States most impacted by karst and sinkhole formation are Alabama, Florida, Georgia, Tennessee, Missouri, and Pennsylvania.

Water Quality

Defined

Purity or drinkability (potability) of water as established by the U.S. Public Health Service. Dissolved constituents are measured in milligrams per liter (volume) or parts per million (weight).

Standards

Less than 500 ppm total dissolved solids for "sweet" water, and limits on specific ions and molecules that impair the quality of water.

Pollution

Defined

Chemical, physical, or biological materials that impair the current and future use of water and that may be a health hazard.

Residence Time

The average length of time a given substance will stay in a system, such as water in a lake or aquifer. Whereas the residence time of human-generated smog in the atmosphere of large cities is on the order of ten days, pollutants may reside in some aquifers for thousands of years.

Common Pollutants

Hydrocarbons, carcinogenic BTX chemicals (benzene, toluene, and xylene), fertilizers, pesticides, livestock fecal matter, and gasoline.

Conservation and Alternative Sources

Conservation means include the use of treated wastewater for irrigation and recharging aquifers, water-saving irrigation devices, water-spreading during wet years, and voluntary water conservation. Desalinization and importation are the only viable alternative sources of water at present.

Key Terms

aquiclude
aquifer
artesian-pressure surface
bioremediation
cone of depression
confined aquifer
darcy's law
drawdown
dripstone

evapotranspiration
gaining stream
groundwater
hydraulic conductivity
hydraulic gradient
hydrogeologist
hydrologic cycle
karst terrane
losing stream

maximum contaminant level (MCL)
maximum contaminant level goal (MCLG)
overturn
perched water table
permeability
piezeometric surface
porosity

potable water
residence time
specific yield
speleology
stalactites
stalagmites
sustained yield
unconfined aquifer
water table

Study Questions

1. Sketch a hydrogeologic cross section that shows the groundwater zones and the static water table.

2. Sketch and define a confined aquifer. Explain the artesian-pressure surface and its importance in production of water from an artesian well.

3. How does topography affect the shape of the static water table?

4. How does one determine the amount of water a well that taps the static water table might produce on a long-term basis?

5. Explain the distinction between gaining and losing streams.

6. Explain the relationship between the amount of drawdown in a water well and the aquifer's permeability.

7. What states are the largest consumers of groundwater, and why is their usage so heavy?

8. What is meant by groundwater *mining*? Cite the case history of an aquifer where this has happened.

9. Many beverage manufacturers claim the water in their drinks is purer because it comes from artesian wells or springs. Comment on these claims.

10. What are the Public Health Service standards for total dissolved solids in drinking water?

11. Name three organic compounds sometimes found dissolved in groundwater that are hazardous to human health.

For Further Information

Books and Periodicals

Alley, William M., Thomas Reilly, and O. Lehn Franke. 1999. *Sustainability of ground-water resources.* U. S. Geological Survey circular 1186.

American Institute of Professional Geologists. 1985. *Ground water: issues and answers.* Arvada, Colo.: A.I.P.G.

Baldwin, H. L. and C. L. McGuinness. 1963. *A primer on ground water.* Washington, D.C.: U.S. Geological Survey.

Cohen, P., O. L. Franke, and B. L. Foxworthy. 1970. *Water for the future of Long Island, New York.* New York Division of Water Resources, Department of Environmental Conservation, in cooperation with the U.S. Geological Survey.

Dunne, T. and Leopold, L., 1978, *Water in environmental planning.* New York: Freeman, 818 p.

Galloway, Devin, David Jones, and S. E. Ingebritsen. 1999. *Land subsidence in the United States.* U.S. Geological Survey circular 1182.

Hauwerrt, Nico M. and Shawn Vickers. 1994. *Barton Springs/Edwards aquifer: hydrogeology and ground water quality.* Austin, Texas: Texas Water Development Board, Barton Springs/Edwards Conservation District.

Kidd, Mary A. 1996. *Nutrients in the nation's drinking water: Too much of a good thing?* U.S. Geological Survey circular 1136.

Moore, John E., A. Zaporozed, and James W. Mercer. 1994. *Ground water: a primer.* Environmental awareness series. Alexandria, Va.: American Geological Institute.

Sharp, John M., Jr. and Jay L. Banner. 1997. The Edwards aquifer: A resource in conflict. *G.S.A. Today* (Geological Society of America), August.

Solley, Wayne B., Robert R. Pierce, and Howard A. Perlman. 1998. *Estimated use of water in the United States in 1995.* U.S. Geological Survey circular 1200.

U.S. Geological Survey. 1999. *The quality of our nation's waters—nutrients and pesticides,* circular 1225.

Winter, Thomas C., Judson, Harvey O. Lehn Franke, and William M. Alley. 1998. *Ground water and surface water: A single resource.* U.S. Geological Survey circular 1139.

Zwingle, Erla. 1993. Ogallala aquifer: Well spring of the High Plains. *National geographic* 183, no. 3 (March).

ThomsonNOW

Assess your understanding of this chapter's topics with additional comprehensive interactivities at http://www.thomson.com/login, which also has up-to-date web links, additional readings, and exercises.

CHAPTER 9

Hydrologic Hazards at the Earth's Surface

The Blue Danube?

During the summer (August) of 2002, land along rivers in eastern Europe and western Russia was under water, as these areas experienced their worst flooding in a century (◆Figures 1 and 2). The flooding was driven by exceptionally heavy rains over large areas. The losses have been estimated in excess of $20 billion, which would place it on a par with the Northridge, California earthquake of 1994 in terms of dollar loss, but greater in terms of loss of life. There were 59 deaths in Northridge versus an estimated 105 for the 2002 flood—62 in Russia alone near the Black Sea coast. Global climate models suggest that such heavy precipitation events are likely to become more common in this area over the next 100 years if greenhouse gas emissions continue at present rates.

- Twelve countries were affected: Russia, Ukraine, Romania, Bulgaria, Croatia, the Czech Republic, Austria, Slovakia, Switzerland, France, Germany, and Italy.
- Along the Elbe River in Germany a dam broke, threatening a town of 16,500 people.

◆**FIGURE 1** The Danube River at Regensburg, Germany, during the great flood of August 2002. Note that the river walk behind the high-water (Hochwasser) sign is inundated.

(a)   (b)

◆ **FIGURE 2** Diners enjoy a Sunday lunch in a restaurant below the flood level of the Danube River in Regensburg, Germany. The water is kept at bay by the red inflatable flood-fence around the dining area.

- More than 400 houses were destroyed and at least 7,000 were damaged in Russia.

- About 220,000 residents living near the Vltava River (German Moldau) in the Czech Republic were displaced.

- More than 20,000 persons were evacuated in Dresden, Germany.

- A 30-meter-long steel bridge in Schwertberg, Germany was torn loose by the flooded Danube River.

Probably the worst flood impact, after the human loss, was the toll on the Prague Zoo. Zoos are a habitat that most humans don't think about during a flood. At the peak of the flood the lower half of the zoo was completely under water. A 12-year-old seal named Gaston made headlines by swimming 120 kilometers in the river before being recaptured in Dresden, Germany. An elephant and hippo were lost, but another hippo, which was believed to have died, was saved after the floodwaters began to recede. Ten big animals were lost, including an aging lion and a bear considered too old to evacuate. The big loss was Pong, a popular gorilla and one of five in the zoo, who is believed to have drowned in the evacuation effort. More than 1,000 animals were saved.

Water is life. Without it, Earth would be a dead planet, its surface pock-marked with craters like the moon. There would be no rivers, no mountain streams, no lakes, and no oceans. Forests, grasslands, and swamps wouldn't exist. Most days, water is a good thing. Moving water supports whole ecosystems and provides for recreational and economic activities. Rivers are tapped for drinking water and irrigate our fields, allowing crops to grow in the desert. But some days, some weeks, some places, water turns deadly. Floodwaters ravage riverside towns, storm surges rip homes from their foundations, flash floods carry people to their deaths, and tsunami waves sweep away entire families and communities. Water—and its agents, rivers, streams, and oceans—perform most of the work of erosion and deposition that shape and modify Earth's landscape.

Hydrologists are scientists who deal with water, its properties, circulation, and distribution on Earth and in the atmosphere. They can be engineers or geologists who make their living solving the very practical problems of water supply, river flooding, and water quality. In this chapter, we take the view of a practical hydrologist, examining the way in which water moves across the landscape. We focus here on hydrologic hazards, which means flooding. Why devote a whole chapter to flooding? That's easy: Flooding is the most globally pervasive, environmentally diverse, and continually destructive of all natural hazards. In order to understand flooding, you need to know a bit about where water comes from and where it goes. We'll start the chapter by examining the different types of floods and the forces that drive them. The focus will be on rivers and streams, because they carry most of the water moving over Earth's surface. Our goal is for you to understand not only why, where, and how often floods happen but how society can deal with water in all the wrong places.

Weather and Climate

Because most floods are driven one way or another by precipitation, it makes sense to start by understanding a little about weather and climate. Rain and snow occur when the atmosphere becomes saturated with water and that water condenses from a diffuse vapor to a localized droplet of liquid or an ice crystal. Then, gravity takes hold and down comes the rain, snow, hail, and sleet. If the precipitation falls as rain, it's ready to cause floods right then and there. If the precipitation is frozen, it may linger on the ground for days, weeks, months, years, or even millennia before melting and once again moving through the hydrologic cycle.

Precipitation is not equally spread over Earth's surface; rather, there are wet spots and dry spots predictably arranged around the world (◆Figure 9.1). In the tropics, such as Hawaii or Puerto Rico, moist air evaporated from warm ocean waters generates intense downpours. In contrast, downwind of cold ocean currents, such as in Peru and Namibia, hyperarid deserts are found where rain may fall only several times a decade. Mountains are almost always wetter than adjacent valleys. Air masses forced up and over high terrain cool, and the moisture in the air condenses, falling as rain or snow (◆Figure 9.2). This wringing out of moisture by lifting air over mountaintops is termed the *orographic* effect, and it is why many floods get their start up high. Downwind of mountainous terrain, the now-dry air descends. Many valley-bottom deserts of the western United States, such as the Mojave, are the result of mountains to their west having stolen the Pacific moisture before it could move inland.

Precipitation doesn't fall equally over time, either. Storms or low-pressure systems are disturbances in Earth's atmosphere that come and go day by day and with the seasons. For example, heavy thunderstorms are a summer phenomenon, the result of an atmosphere made unstable by strong solar heating. They affect mostly smaller drainage basins with torrential rains capable of generating flash floods. In contrast, extended winter rains commonly cause floods along the western coast of North America as Pacific storms come ashore. On the east coast, hurricanes can drop a foot of rain in the summer and fall while nor'easters batter the Atlantic coast with rain, wind, and sometimes very heavy snow mostly in the winter and spring. In the winter of 1888, much of New England got over 4 feet of snow in March from a nor'easter (◆Figure 9.3).

The most dramatic rainfall occurs when storms and topography interact. Let's have a look at southeastern Texas, perhaps not what you would think of as a flooding hotspot, but it is. Near Austin, the Balcones Escarpment rises up to 500 feet above the coastal plain. Moisture streaming north from the warm Gulf of Mexico on southerly and southeasterly winds is forced to rise up the escarpment and onto the Edwards Plateau, a rural farming area. Incredible rains can result, swelling normally dry riverbeds into raging torrents in a matter of minutes. During the 1954 flood, the Pecos River, often a dry stream, carried over a million cubic feet per second, the average discharge of the Mississippi River, yet its drainage is only one-third of one percent of the Mississippi (◆Figure 9.4). Some of the highest rainfall rates in the continental United States have been measured on the Balcones Escarpment as well as the greatest 18-hour rainfall total (36 in). There, in 1987, ten people died when their church bus was swept away by flash flooding. There are dramatic images of students being plucked from trees by helicopter rescue teams as floodwaters swirled around them.

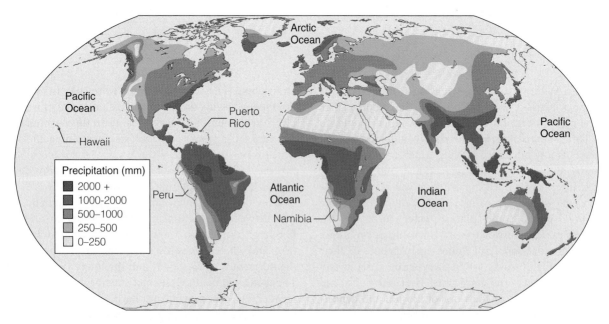

◆ **FIGURE 9.1** This map shows the global distribution of precipitation. Can you find areas near tropical oceans where it is very wet? Can you find areas downwind of major mountain ranges where it is very dry?

◆ **FIGURE 9.2** Air masses forced up and over mountain ranges cool, allowing the moisture in them to condense and rain out. After passing over the peaks, the air descends and warms, drying the landscape below. Can you predict which side of the mountain range will be cloudier and wetter? Source: USGS circular 1245, Large floods in the United States, p. 9, 2004

Vermont Historical Society

◆ **FIGURE 9.3** The blizzard of 1888, a classic nor'easter, took the east coast by surprise in mid-March. Temperatures plummeted from the 50s to a little above zero, and snow fell from Maryland to Maine. Here, in Brattleboro, Vermont, several feet of snow blanketed the city.

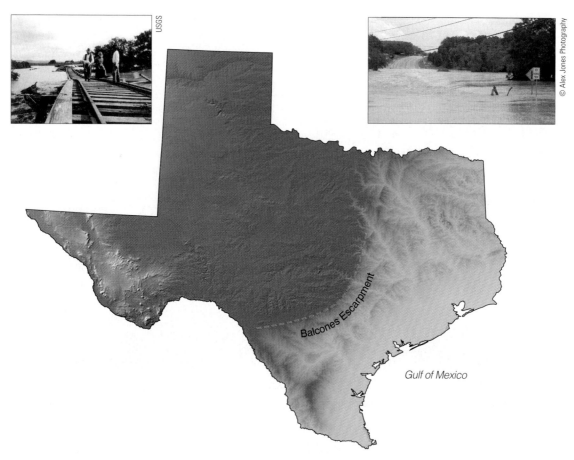

◆ **FIGURE 9.4** Texas is the place for floods. The digital elevation model shows the topography of Texas and the steep escarpment as it rises from the coastal plain ready to intercept storms and warm, moist air from the Gulf of Mexico. Inset (left) is an image of the damage caused by the July 13–18, 1900 flood on the Guadalupe River at Comfort. The river has flooded many times since, as shown by the modern image (right) taken on July 5, 2002.

Types of Floods

Floods are dramatic reminders of the power of natural forces. Hydrologic hazards result from a variety of solid Earth, surface, and atmospheric processes. Let's have a look at what causes floods (◆Figure 9.5). **Precipitation** in one form or another is the source of most flooding. Be it the 1962 Ash Wednesday nor'easter affecting 1,000 kilometers of coastline for several days, hurricane Katrina pounding New Orleans with torrential rains for hours, or a thunderstorm parked over Big Thompson Canyon in the Colorado Rockies, water falling from the sky faster than it can be absorbed by the ground or transported downstream sends rivers out of their banks. Warm winds and early spring rains on deep snow packs are particularly devastating as melting snow adds to the runoff. These rain-on-snow events have caused devastating floods all over the United States from southern Pennsylvania to the Cascades of Washington State. Ice-jam floods occur when

river ice breaks up, moves downstream, and wedges against obstacles in the channel. The short-lived ice dam quickly raises water levels upstream. Ice-jam floods are common anywhere rivers freeze over and often occur during rain-on-snow events (see Case Study 9.3 on page 266).

Water need not come from the sky during a storm to cause a flood; it might come from the ocean. When hurricanes or nor'easters make landfall, they push before them a wall of water driven by wind and accentuated by low atmospheric pressure near the storm. These surges of water can rapidly raise sea level by meters, inundating low-lying coastal areas in minutes. The effect of *storm surges* isn't just limited to the coast. Storm surges can move inland up coastal rivers. When they do, flood waters trying to move downstream are blocked, and flooding further intensifies.

Dams are supposed to control floods. Most of the time they do, but some devastating floods have been caused by the failure of dams both natural and constructed. Natural dams,

◆ **FIGURE 9.5** There are several ways to trigger devastating floods. (a) In late September of 1938, one of the strongest hurricanes to hit New England roared ashore, smashing into Long Island and racing north. The image shows massive flooding on the Merrimack River following hurricane passage. The hurricane was a fast mover, traveling 600 miles in 12 hours. (b) In mid-March 1936, the St. Patrick's Day flood struck Pennsylvania as rain melted the winter's snow. Shown here is a Harrisburg city bus nearly submerged. (c) The Big Thompson flood devastated the canyon on the east side of the Rocky Mountains in July 1976. Triggered by a slow-moving thunderstorm that dumped a foot of rain in just a few hours, the flood killed nearly 150 people, destroyed hundreds of homes, and resulted in tens of million of dollars in damages.

formed when landslides or glacial moraines block streams, can fail catastrophically. Failure of an earth-fill dam in Johnstown, Pennsylvania, in 1889 killed over 2,200 people as they were swept downstream by a wall of water 40 feet high. The stories are horrific. Riverside homes lifted from their foundations were carried downstream intact, and wedged up against a massive stone bridge in such a pile that no one could escape the fires that started when wood-fired cookstoves overturned. Victims were burned alive while their houses floated.

Earthquakes can do more than shake, rattle, and roll: they can cause floods in several ways. The Indian Ocean tsunami of 2004 generated rapid, but short-lived flooding, as massive tsunami waves washed ashore. But earthquakes can cause flooding in another way: by changing land level. In the Pacific Northwest, buried marsh soils and standing dead trees, their roots drowned by saltwater, are compelling evidence that giant quakes have yoyo-ed the land up and down over the past hundreds to thousands of years, intermittently flooding the coast. In Alaska, after the 1964 magnitude 9+ quake, land level fell far enough that villages were partially submerged, and there was no choice but to abandon them (◆ Figure 9.6).

Not all flooding is so obvious or rapid. Consider changing climate and its impact on sea level. At the peak of the last glaciation, 21,000 years ago, wooly mammoths roamed across North America and sea level was about 100 meters lower than today. As the climate warmed and the ice sheets melted, water flowed back into the ocean and sea level rose, rapidly at some times, more slowly at others, but rise it did. The camping sites of the first Americans along the Alaskan

(a)   **(b)**

◆ **FIGURE 9.6** Inundation is a devastating effect of floods. (a) In Portage, Alaska the land dropped several meters during the great 1964 earthquake, allowing seawater to flood much of the town. (b) After the floodwaters of Katrina receded, mold was a devastating problem in the warm, moist environment.

coast are now deep under water, and the Chesapeake Bay, once a river, is now drowned. Today, with climate warming and most glaciers retreating, the scientific consensus is that sea level will continue to rise, perhaps quite rapidly if melting of the Greenland or Antarctic ice sheets accelerates. It takes only a few meters of sea-level rise to inundate parts of many major and important world cities such as New York, Miami, Venice, London, Hong Kong, and New Orleans.

Impacts of Floods

Imagine a flood and its effects. You are probably thinking of rising, muddy water covering fields, homes, and cars. Indeed, the most common impact of floods is **inundation**, and because floods tend to carry large amounts of fine sediment, not only do things get wet, they get very muddy. The aftereffects of inundation can be more devastating than the flood itself. After the inundation of New Orleans, hundreds of thousands of automobiles were damaged because their engines and electrical systems had filled with floodwater. Many homes needed to be gutted or torn down, not because they were structurally unsound, but because their flood-soaked walls couldn't be dried and had mildewed so badly that inhabiting the buildings was impossible (see Figure 9.6).

Floods do more than get things wet. As flood waters move down river channels, they pick up sediment, both loose material from the channel bottom and solid material from the banks. At bridge abutments, this tendency of moving water to entrain material from the river bottom can lead to disaster as support is removed and the bridge eventually collapses

(◆Figure 9.7). In the past, not everyone realized that bank erosion and channel migration, processes most active during floods, are critical and normal aspects of river function. Human attempts to stabilize rivers using any variety of engineering solutions, with concrete and straightened channels at their core, have typically failed over time as these "solutions" ignore the dynamic nature of flowing water. Today the emphasis is on river-corridor management and river-channel restoration to accommodate the natural behavior of flowing water.

In the long term, rapidly moving water is a dynamic force, shaping Earth's surface. Large, rare floods can cause river channels to shift dramatically, abandoning their old course and establishing a new channel, sometimes with disastrous results. Some of the most spectacular features on our planet are deep canyons cut into rock. Research suggests that it takes massive and therefore rare events—the biggest floods—to generate enough power to rip rock away and carve canyons with moving water. In the Himalayas, raging rivers fed by the Asian monsoon can erode millimeters of rock per year. Surprisingly, the Potomac River, just outside of Washington, D.C. cut through hard rock at rates almost this fast during the last glaciation, cutting driven presumably by big floods (◆Figure 9.8).

River Systems

A stream's ability to erode (Latin *erodere*, "to gnaw away") the land and impact humans is related to the speed at which the flowing water moves (its velocity) and the amount of water moving through the stream (its discharge). With equal discharge—the same volume of water flowing past a point in a river channel in a given time period—a fast-flowing stream

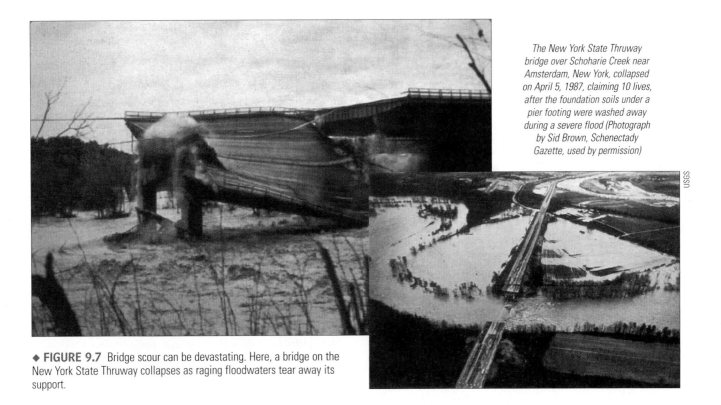

The New York State Thruway bridge over Schoharie Creek near Amsterdam, New York, collapsed on April 5, 1987, claiming 10 lives, after the foundation soils under a pier footing were washed away during a severe flood (Photograph by Sid Brown, Schenectady Gazette, used by permission)

◆ **FIGURE 9.7** Bridge scour can be devastating. Here, a bridge on the New York State Thruway collapses as raging floodwaters tear away its support.

erodes its banks more significantly than does a slow-moving one. In the United States velocity (V) is usually expressed in feet per second (ft/sec), and **discharge** (Q), the amount of water, in cubic feet per second (cfs). A cubic foot contains about 7.4 gallons of water. With increased velocity and discharge, there are increases in the stream's erosion potential and its sediment-carrying capacity (◆ Figure 9.9).

The longitudinal profile, or side view, of a stream channel has a slope known as its **gradient,** which can be expressed as the ratio of its vertical drop to the horizontal distance it travels (in meters per kilometer or feet per mile). A mountain stream may have a steep gradient of several tens of meters per kilometer and an irregular profile with rapids and waterfalls. As the same stream approaches the lowest level to which it can

(a)

(b)

◆ **FIGURE 9.8** Only big floods can erode rock. Here, at Great Falls on the Potomac River just 12 miles from the Capitol, most flows spill gracefully over the rocks. But when hurricanes or rain-on-snow events strike, the river becomes a raging torrent that can erode rock. (a) A calm November day with flow of several hundred cubic meters per second. (b) After hurricane Isabel in 2003, the river channel is filled as almost 5000 cubic meters per second pour over the falls.

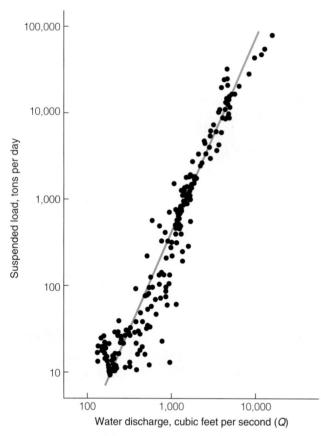

◆ FIGURE 9.9 The relationship between water discharge (Q) and the suspended load for a typical stream. The points represent separate measurements. A tenfold increase in water discharge results in almost a 100-fold increase in sediment load. Look carefully at the axes of this graph. Can you see that the units increase in multiples of 10 because these are logarithmic scales? Consider how variable these measurements are. For any one discharge, suspended sediment load can vary by a factor of more than 50!

erode, an elevation known as **base level,** its gradient may be almost zero, the water surface is nearly flat. Longitudinal profiles of graded streams are generally concave-upward from source to end. Gradients decrease in the lower reaches of a river (◆Figure 9.10), and this is where sedimentation often occurs as streams overflow their banks onto adjacent **floodplains.** Decreased water velocity on the floodplain results in the deposition of fine-grained silt and clay adjacent to the

main stream channel. This productive soil, commonly known as *bottomland,* is much desired in agriculture (Case Study 9.1).

Stream Features

In both humid and arid environments, streams lose the ability to transport sediment as they flow from confined channels in mountainous terrain onto wide open, flat valley floors. Here, where the slope changes, we find conspicuous depositional features known as **fans** (◆Figure 9.11). These landforms are in fact fan shaped and build up as the main stream branches, or splays, outward in a series of *distributaries,* each "seeking" the steepest gradient. Fans can provide beautiful, interesting views of surrounding terrain, but they also can be subject to flash floods and debris flows from intense seasonal storms in nearby mountains.

CONSIDER THIS

We generally associate high sediment loads with high river discharge, but there are other variables that determine the sediment transported by a river. With this in mind, would you expect the suspended sediment load per cubic meter of water to be greater in an area dominated by soft rocks, such as the sediments of the Dakota badlands, or hard rocks, such as the granites of the Sierra Nevada mountains? What role do you think vegetation might play in determining sediment load? Imagine the color of the water coursing down a stream draining a mountain catchment before and after clear cutting or a wildfire has removed all the vegetation, the roots of which once bound the soil together.

Deltas form where running water moves into standing water, causing sediment carried by the water to drop out. The Greek historian Herodotus (484–420 B.C.) applied the term to the somewhat triangular shape of the Nile delta in recognition of its resemblance to the Greek letter delta (D). Deltas are characterized by low stream gradients, swamps, lakes, and an ever-changing channel system. The "arcuate" (arc-shaped) delta of the Nile and the "bird's foot" delta of the Mississippi also are described by their appearance on maps (◆Figure 9.12). The tremendous sand output of the Nile has created the huge coastal dunes east of Alexandria that formed the background for the famous World War II battle at El Alamein (see the Chapter 12 opener). The Ganges-Brahmaputra delta of

◆ FIGURE 9.10 Cross sections, or longitudinal profiles, of the Arkansas River in Colorado and the Sacramento River in California. The vertical scale is exaggerated 275 times, meaning that these diagrams make the rivers look far steeper than they really are.

◆ **FIGURE 9.11** Here is a small fan in the Swiss Alps near the town of Durbodden. It's indicated by the black line. The fan was created when sediment from the steep mountains above was carried by streams and in debris flows to the valley bottom where the slope was less and thus, the sediment could move no more.

Bangladesh consists of tidal flats and many low-lying sand islands offshore (Figure 9.12c). Because deltas are at or near sea level, they are subject to flooding by tropical storms. Coastal flooding is the most deadly of natural disasters, even more deadly than earthquakes or river floods. This type of flooding was particularly disastrous in Bangladesh in 1970 when more than 500,000 people were drowned by a surge of water that moved onshore along with a tropical cyclone.

Streams and rivers with low gradients and floodplains form a number of features that both aggravate and alleviate flood damage. The courses of such rivers follow a series of S-shaped curves called **meanders,** after the ancient name of the winding Menderes River in Turkey. Straight rivers are the exception, rather than the rule, and it appears that running water of all kinds will meander—ocean currents, rivers on glaciers, and even trickles of water on glass. The key to these

◆ **FIGURE 9.12** River deltas. (a) Birdsfoot delta of the Mississippi River. The main channel and subordinate distributaries are separated by swamps and wetlands. (b) Arc-shaped delta of the Nile River is predominantly wetlands and rice-growing areas. The barrier islands are sand and they contribute to large coastal dunes to the west. (c) The Ganges–Brahmaputra delta of Bangladesh. The small islands rise above the tidal flats. Though subject to catastrophic floods, they are nonetheless densely populated.

regularly spaced curves is the river's ability to erode, transport, and deposit sediments. As a stream meanders, it erodes the outside curve of each meander and deposits sediment on each inside curve, producing a deposit known as a **point bar.** ◆ Figure 9.13 shows the velocity distribution around a stream meander, which explains the erosion-deposition pattern. Erosion occurs where water moves rapidly. Deposition occurs where water moves slowly. Meanders widen stream valleys by lateral cutting of valleyside slopes, causing landslides and eventually creating an alluvium-filled floodplain adjacent to the river. It is across this surface that the river meanders, sometimes becoming so tightly curved that it shortcuts a loop to form a **cutoff** and **oxbow lake** (◆ Figure 9.14). This is quite the hazard if your farm field happens to be on the other side of the cutoff.

River-bottom lands, with wide floodplains, meanders, cutoffs, and oxbow lakes, are prime places for flooding. Every time the river goes out of its banks and the raging flood waters slow, sand and silt are deposited adjacent to the channel (◆ Figure 9.15), helping to build **natural levees.** People, following nature's lead, raise or imitate these natural levees using all sorts of engineering approaches to hold back the floodwaters. **Artificial levees** keep floodwaters channelized so that the water level in the stream rises above the level of the adjacent floodplain, sometimes far above. This is a tenuous situation, because a breach in the levee causes immediate inundation of the floodplain. Even when the levees hold and protect one area

(a)   **(b)**

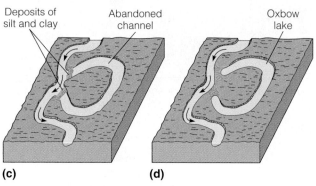

(c)   **(d)**

◆ **ThomsonNOW** FIGURE 9.14 (a–d) Over time, cutbanks erode, sometimes bringing meanders closer together (a and b). When the two meanders finally join (c), a cutoff forms, shortening the river channel but leaving an oxbow lake where the river used to flow (d).

(a)

(b)

◆ **ThomsonNOW** FIGURE 9.13 Erosion and deposition patterns on a meandering stream. (a) Erosion of the cutbank and deposition of a point bar on the gently sloping side of the meander. Longer arrows indicate faster flow. Shorter arrows indicate slower flow. (b) Rillito Creek rampaged through Tucson, Arizona, during the flood of 1983. Damage occurred when the cutbank of the meander migrated west (left) into vacant property immediately upstream from the townhouses (center left). This allowed erosion to occur behind a concrete bank that was protecting the townhouse property. Note the prominent point bar that developed (bottom center) as the meander migrated westward.

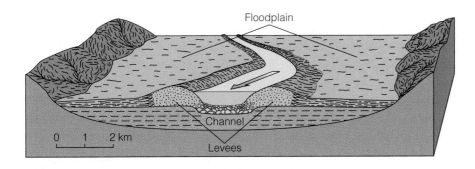

Floodplain

Channel

Levees

0   1   2 km

◆ **FIGURE 9.15** Relationship between natural levees and floodplain to a hypothetical stream. The coarsest sediment is deposited in the stream channel, where the stream's velocity is greatest, and finer silt and clay are deposited on levees and the floodplain as velocity diminishes during overflows.

from flooding, they speed the passage of floodwater, exacerbating flooding downstream, particularly in unleveed areas. What's the typical response? Build more levees.

During the 1993 floods in the Midwest, artificial levees saved some cities in the Mississippi River drainage basin, notably St. Louis, where the flood crested at 49.4 feet and the levee height is 52 feet. Quincy, Illinois, lacking artificial levees, was inundated; but the levees at Hannibal, Missouri, on the opposite side of the river held and spared the town. Some levees were intentionally breached in order to reduce flood-crest elevation downstream by allowing water to move onto the floodplain (where it belongs). More than 800 of the 1,400 levees in the nine-state disaster area were breached or overtopped. Most of these levees were simple dirt berms built by local communities, which explains why so many small towns were almost completely submerged by the floodwaters. However, more than 30 levees built by the U.S. Army Corps of Engineers also failed during this record flood event.

When There Is Too Much Water

Excess water, whether in rivers, lakes, or along a coast, leads to flooding. The basic hydrologic unit in fluvial (river) systems is the **drainage basin,** the land area that contributes water to a particular stream or stream system. Individual drainage basins are separated by **drainage divides.** A drainage basin may have only one stream, or it may encompass a large number of streams and all their tributaries.

Unless rainfall rates are exceptionally high or the ground has been compacted and there is little vegetation, most of the rain that falls within a particular drainage basin after a dry period infiltrates (seeps) into the uppermost layers of soil and rock; little water runs off the land. As the surface materials become saturated or if rainfall rates are extreme, some rainfall cannot infiltrate, and runoff begins. Runoff begins in saturated areas, flows into small tributary streams, and finally is consolidated into a well-defined channel of the main stream in the watershed. Whether or not a flood occurs is determined by several factors: the intensity of the rainfall, the amount of antecedent (prior) rainfall, the amount of snowmelt (if any), the topography, and the vegetation.

Upland floods occur in watershed areas of moderate or high topographic relief. They may occur with little or no warning, and they are generally of short duration, hence the name *flash floods.* Such floods result in extensive damage due to the velocity of the flowing water. Lowland, *riverine floods,* on the other hand, occur when broad floodplains adjacent to the stream channel are inundated. The typical damage is that things get wet or silt covered. The difference in these types of floods is due to watershed morphology (shape). Mountain streams occupy the bottoms of V-shaped valleys and cover most of the narrow valley floor; there is no adjacent floodplain. Heavy rainfall at higher elevations in the watershed can produce a wall of fast-moving water that descends through the canyon, destroying structures and endangering lives (see Figure 9.5c). Lowland streams, in contrast, have low gradients, adjacent wide floodplains, and meandering paths.

A **hydrograph** is a graph showing a water body's discharge, velocity, stage (height), or some other characteristic over time, and it is the basic tool of hydrologists (◆ Figure 9.16). The "synthetic" hydrographs in ◆ Figure 9.17 graphically illustrate the basic difference between upland (flash) floods of short duration and the longer-lasting lowland floods. The timing of flood crests on the main stream—whether they arrive from the tributaries simultaneously or in sequence—in large part determines the severity of lowland flooding. Floods are normal and, to a degree, predictable natural events. Generally, a stream will overflow its banks every year or two, gently inundating a portion of the adjacent floodplain. Over long periods of time, catastrophic high waters can be expected. Depending upon their severity, these events are referred to as fifty-, one-hundred-, or five-hundred-year floods, denoting the average period of time passing between events of similar magnitude. The more infrequent the event, the more widespread and catastrophic is the inundation (◆ Figure 9.18).

Floods from all causes are the number-one natural disaster in the world in terms of loss of life. Fifteen disastrous U.S. floods are listed in ⁎ Table 9.1. Although by no means a complete listing of severe floods, the table gives an idea of the distribution of riverine floods, flash floods, coastal floods, and dam-break floods in the United States. Coastal flooding due to hurricanes and typhoons is the greatest single killer. The record-holding river floods are due to dam failures. The

◆ **FIGURE 9.16** A synthetic hydrograph that relates precipitation and discharge to time. Note that peak discharge (+) occurs after the peak rainfall intensity (*). The drainage basin includes the main stream and all its tributaries.

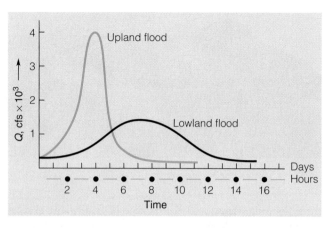

◆ **FIGURE 9.17** Synthetic hydrographs of an upland flash flood and lowland riverine flood.

legendary 1889 Johnstown flood killed over 2000 people, and the 1928 St. Francis Dam failure in southern California killed 450 people.

Flood Measurement

Flood studies begin with hydrographs for a particular storm on a river within a given drainage basin. These graphs are generated from data obtained at a stream-gauging station, where stage (the water elevation) is measured and related to discharge. Rapid runoff in a drainage basin is accompanied by high stream discharge and high water velocity. As discharge increases, the water rises to the *bank-full stage* and then spills onto the adjacent floodplain at *flood stage*. ◆Figure 9.19 shows such a condition. It is a hydrograph superimposed on the cross section of a stream valley. A *stage hydrograph* is most useful for flood-planning purposes, because it relates water height over time. One can see at a glance at what point the stream will overflow its banks and at what elevations flood waters will contact with specific structures. Note that both stage and discharge are shown in ◆Figure 9.20, which is for the Potomac River, just downstream

of where the photographs in Figure 9.8 were taken. This flood, triggered by the torrential rains of hurricane Isabel several days before, is the type of event that occurs on the Potomac once or twice every decade.

Flood Frequency

One of the most useful relationships that can be derived from long-term flood records is that of **flood frequency**, or **recurrence interval;** that is, how often on average a flood of a given magnitude can be expected in a particular location. With this kind of information, we are better equipped to design dams, bridge clearances over rivers, sizes of storm drains, and the like.

The information needed for determining recurrence intervals is a long-term record of annual *peak discharge* (the largest flow for each year) for the particular location on the river. The longer the period of record, the more reliable the statistics will be. The peak discharges are then ranked according to their relative magnitudes, with the highest discharge being ranked as 1, the second-largest as 2, and so forth. To serve as an example, selected annual peak discharges on the

◆ **FIGURE 9.18** The probable extent of flooding over long time intervals on a floodplain. The 1–2 year flood just goes over the stream bank onto the adjacent floodplain. The 100-year flood inundates the low terrace (Terrace 1), which formed when the river stood at a higher level. The 500-year event inundates an even higher terrace (Terrace 2) and all lower terraces and the floodplain.

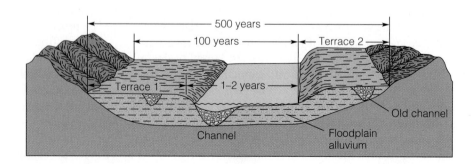

★TABLE 9.1   Selected U.S. Floods since May 1889

Type	Date	Location	Lives Lost	Estimated Damage $ millions
Regional flood	September 13, 1928	Lake Okeechobee, Florida	1,836	26
	March 1938	Southern California	79	25
	September 21, 1938	New England	600	306
	September–October 1983	Tucson, Arizona	<10	50–100
	Summer 1993	Upper Mississippi River drainage basin	50	12,000
	January–February 1996	Oregon, Washington, Idaho, Montana	1	89*
	October 1998	South-central Texas, San Antonio to Houston, Guadalupe River	29	400
Hurricane	September 8, 1900	Galveston, Texas	6,000	30
	August 17–18, 1969	Mississippi, Louisiana, and Alabama (Hurricane Camille)	256	1,421
	September 1999	North Carolina, Hurricane Floyd and post-hurricane rains	47	5,000+
Flash flood	July 1976	Big Thompson River, Colorado	139	30
Dam failure	May 1889	Johnstown, Pennsylvania	3,000	–
	March 12–13, 1928	California, St. Francis Dam	450	14
	February 1972	Buffalo Creek, West Virginia	125	10
	June 1976	Southeast Idaho, Teton Dam	11	1,000

Source: Various sources, including U.S. Geological Survey.

Rio Grande near Lobatos, Colorado, are listed in ＊ Table 9.2, with their ranks and recurrence intervals. A recurrence interval, T, is calculated as

$$T = (N + 1) \div M$$

where N is the number of years of record (76 years in our example), and M is the rank of the event.

The analysis predicts how often floods of a given size can be expected to occur in a watershed if the watershed and climate conditions have not changed. In this example, a flood the size of the 1906 flood ($M = 10$) would be expected to occur on average about once every 7.7 years [$(76 + 1) \div 10$]. If 100 years of records are available, the largest flood to occur during that period ($M = 1$) would have a recurrence interval

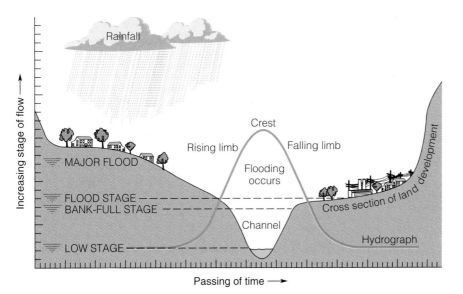

◆ **FIGURE 9.19** A stage hydrograph superimposed on a schematic stream valley illustrates the impact of increasing stage height on the flooded area.

◆ **FIGURE 9.20** Combined hydrograph showing both stage and discharge for the Potomac River at Little Falls after the passage of hurricane Isabel in fall, 2003. Note that the flood exceeds both the bankfull and flood stages. The blue line are data collected at the gauging station. The green dots are predicted stage values calculated by the advanced hydrologic prediction service based on rainfall information and gauge data from upstream. Such predictions are available for many North American rivers at: http://newweb.erh.noaa.gov/ahps2/

of about 100 years on average. This is the so-called 100-year flood. The 100-year flood can also be obtained by projecting rainfall or stream flow data beyond the period of record, although such extrapolation is extremely uncertain and may be misleading.

TABLE 9.2 Annual Peak Discharges on the Rio Grande River near Lobatos, Colorado, 1900–1975

Year	Discharge, m³/sec	Rank (M)	Recurrence Interval (T)
1900	133	23	3.35
1901	103	35	2.20
1902	16	69	1.12
1903	362	2	38.50
1904	22	66	1.17
1905	371	1	77.00
1906	234	10	7.70
1907	249	7	11.00
1908	61	45	1.71
1909	211	13	5.92
1974	22	64	1.20
1975	68	43	1.79

Source: U.S. Geological Survey.

How often can the "100-year flood" occur? The term is misleading, because it implies that a flood of the particular size can happen only once in 100 years. The 100-year flood is really a statistical statement of the probability that a flood of a given *rank* will occur in any one year; that is, $1/T$. For the 100-year flood, there is a 1 percent chance (1/100) of its occurring in any one year; and for the 50-year flood (1/50), a 2 percent chance. The U.S. Geological Survey suggests that a better term would be "the 1-in-100 *chance* flood." Viewed as a probability phenomenon, it is more understandable that we might get big floods in successive years or every few years. Keep in mind that the longer the rainfall or stream-flow record, the better and the more robust the statistical inference. Look at the stream-flow data collected between 1940 and 1996 on the Chehalis River in Washington State in ◆Figure 9.21. Note that the 1-in-100 chance flood calculated for data from 1940 to 1975 is lower than the same 1-in-100 chance flood based upon data for a period 21 years longer. This illustrates the importance of long-term data collection in assessing the magnitude of the 1-in-100 chance flood. There is, however, no meteorological or statistical prohibition against more than one 100-year flood occurring in a century, or even in one year, for that matter. Recurrence intervals are not exact timetables; they merely indicate the statistical probability of a given-size flood. However, even rough estimates of the scale of flood discharge that can be expected in a river system every 25, 50, or 100 years enables us to plan better against the flooding that is certain to occur eventually.

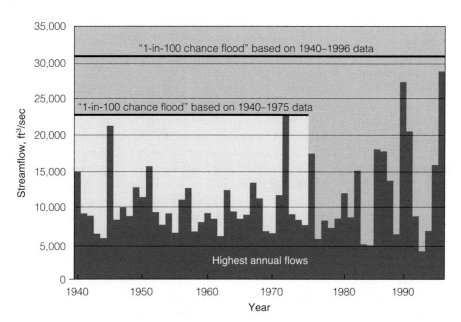

◆ **FIGURE 9.21** Annual maximum discharge data for the Chehalis River near Doty, Washington. Note the difference in the predicated value for the 100-year flood based upon a 35-year data-collection period and one of 56 years in length.

Once we have determined recurrence intervals from the historical record, it is possible to construct flood-frequency graphs like the ones in ◆ Figure 9.22. Such graphs allow us to estimate at a glance how often a flood-level or discharge of a particular magnitude should occur. For example, if we wish to build a warehouse with a useful life of 50 years on the floodplain of the Red River at Grand Forks, we see in the figure that the river reaches a reference elevation of about 49 feet every 50 years on average. We

would probably want to build the warehouse above that elevation because there is a significant chance of a flood within the 50-year window of interest (and our chances for insurance would be better too). However, urbanization, artificial levees, and other human-generated changes can alter the amount and timing of runoff and cause flood events to become more common. In urbanized areas, a 10-year flood can become the 2- or 3-year flood.

Land-use changes, engineering modifications of the river channel, and long-term climatic changes require that recurrence intervals, flood levels (stages), and floodplain management must be updated periodically. Indeed, changing climate and climate cycles influence flood frequency.

Mitigation
Options
Dams: The Solution or the Problem?

In the contiguous 48 states there are more than 75,000 dams more than two meters high, and nearly every major river is controlled by at least one dam. Dams provide such societal benefits as cheap electricity, flood control, recreation, and reduction of the fear of drought. However, the negative side is loss of habitats, loss of the natural cycles of flooding and sediment deposition, changes in aquatic and riverine biology, and destruction of important spawning grounds for migratory fish such as salmon. The days of big dam construction in the United States are over. Although more dams are being built in developing countries (see Case Study 9.4), only a few sites in the United States, Canada, and Europe are seriously being considered in the early twenty-first century.

◆ **FIGURE 9.22** Flood-frequency curve for the Red River at Grand Forks, North Dakota, using water elevation as the standard.

The water emerging from a dam has different physical properties than the water upstream. Sediment-free outflow water scours the riverbed below the dam; because the temperature is different, native fish are stressed and some die. Even with fish ladders, adults have trouble migrating upstream to spawn, and many fry cannot survive the trip back downstream. Different **riparian** communities arise in the downstream area as the frequency and magnitude of disturbance change (floods are now controlled). In addition, some dams fail, and dam-failure floods have caused loss of life (see Table 9.1).

For all these reasons, dams are being dismantled and some are being altered to make them more ecologically friendly. The Kennebec River in Maine now flows freely because the 162-year-old Edwards Dam in Augusta was breached in 1999. Other dams scheduled for breaching (to make way for spawning Pacific salmon) are the Elwha Dam in Washington State, which backs up water into Olympic National Park and ten hydroelectric dams on the Deerfield River in Vermont and Massachusetts (to allow passage by Atlantic salmon and other migratory species). This dismantling is occurring because of a 1996 federal law requires that environmental concerns be addressed before dams can be relicensed. Dam removal is by no means straightforward. Excessive sediment loads after removal must be considered as decades of trapped sediment are released. Some of these sediments can be rich in nutrients as well as toxic metals and organic compounds.

Artificial Levees: The Solution or the Problem?

Dams, retaining basins, floodwalls, and artificial levees are means of flood control, all of which attempt to keep floodwaters within the river channel or store water for slow release at a later time (◆ Figure 9.23). Ironically, these flood control structures may increase flood risk because flood-plain development occurs in response to speculation that flood control has been achieved. Population and property values adjacent to and below flood-control structures increase, placing people and their property at risk when the levees fail. For example, many artificial levees were built along the Mississippi River to protect farmland. The flood-plain was then urbanized, and the existing levees, though adequate to protect farmland, which can tolerate occasional flooding, were not adequate for protecting homesites.

An artificial levee is usually built upward upon a natural levee or riverbank so as to increase the amount of water the channel can accommodate and thus prevent the natural periodic flooding on adjacent land. When stream flow is high, the area's would-be floodwater flows downstream to areas that have lower natural levees or no levees, which then experience greater flooding than they would if the artificial levee had not been built upstream. Some of these downstream communities will build their own artificial levees to prevent flooding in the future. Artificial levees are thus self-perpetuating, and the Mississippi River today is largely contained within them. Even at nonflood river levels, the water surface is above adjacent floodplains, so the danger of flooding is ever present.

Riverside land adjacent to the old French Quarter of New Orleans is extremely valuable tourist property. Here, the natural levees were about 2.1 meters (7 ft) above sea level (*ASL*) in the 1700s, and natural flood stages probably never exceeded 3.0 meters ASL. However, confinement of the river upstream by artificial levees raised the flood level to 6.5 meters (21 ft) in modern times, and artificial levees were constructed. Due to the real estate's historic and economic value, it was felt that additional protection should be provided as a safety factor—it was decided to construct a **floodwall** just landward of the existing levee's crest. The floodwall has gates that close during flooding events (◆ Figure 9.24).

(a)

(b)

◆ **FIGURE 9.23** (a) Earthen levees are a popular engineering solution to flood protection, but they are massive structures such as this one protecting an industrial area northeast of New Orleans. (b) Some important features of earthen levees. Adapted from *Scientific American*, Feb. 2006, page 93.

The 13-kilometer-long (8-mi) wall looks innocent enough, but it is built of 2-foot-thick reinforced concrete resting on a continuous wall of wooden piles driven 7.6 meters (25 ft) into the ground. The "sheet" piles in turn rest upon concrete piles that extend down another 15 meters (almost 50 ft). The sheet piles prevent underseepage of water during floods. New Orleans's solution to the flooding problem served the city well for some time as it dodged this hurricane and that, but eventually hurricane Katrina and its storm surge breached many of the city's levies and flood walls, and as the *New York Times* reported for all to read, leaving nearly 80 percent of the land within the city limits underwater.

Insurance, Floodproofing, and Floodplain Management

The National Flood Insurance Act of 1968 provides federally subsidized insurance protection to property owners in flood-prone areas. The Federal Insurance Administration chose the 100-year-flood level as the **Regulatory Floodplain** on which to establish the limits of government management and set insurance rates. Maps have been developed that delineate regulatory floodplains in thousands of communities in the United States. The subsidized flood insurance is not available on new homes within the regulatory floodway (◆ Figure 9.25). Pre-1968 houses in the floodway were "grandfathered" (allowed to stay and to be insured under the government program), but they cannot be rebuilt at that site with flood-insurance money if they are more than 50 percent damaged by flooding.

Three methods of "flood-proofing" are (1) raising structures above the 100-year-flood level by artificial filling with soil, (2) building walls and levees to resist floodwaters, and (3) using water-resistant building materials. Good floodplain management limits the uses of floodplains in chronically flood-prone areas. Desert regions provide a particular challenge to flood hazard management. Here, the problem is less inundation and more the migration of channels during large flood events. In some cases, channels have moved laterally hundreds of feet without overflowing as banks were undercut by high flows. The National Academy of Sciences recently came up with a different flood hazard evaluation strategy more appropriate for arid regions; it explicitly considers the likelihood of channel movement during floods.

Development has literally poured onto floodplains in the United States. Annual flood damage (in constant dollars) almost tripled between 1950 and the mid-1990s to an average of $3 billion per year. As a result of the great flood of 1993 in the Midwest, the Senate Committee on Environment and Public Works stopped legislation that would have authorized dozens of new flood-control projects. The new belief is that flood policies must be changed, because traditional structural solutions—levees and dams—contribute to the problem.

Floods are natural and inevitable, as demonstrated in this chapter. A congressional report perhaps summed it up best in noting that "Floods are an act of God. Flood damages result from acts of men."

(a)

◆ **FIGURE 9.24** (a) The French Quarter as seen from atop the natural levee on the Mississippi River. Note that the levee slopes downward toward the French Quarter. The wall and gate are part of a floodwall built to hold back floodwaters should the river overtop the levee. (b) Here's what a flood wall looks like. The sheet piling helps stabilize the wall and keep water from seeping underneath. Adapted from *Scientific American*, Feb. 2006, p. 93.

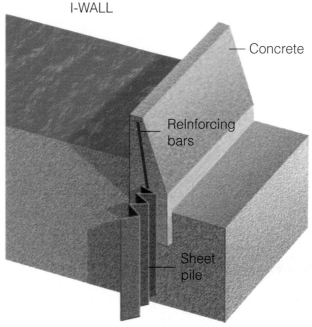

(b)

◆ **FIGURE 9.25** Fluvial flood-hazard areas as defined by the U.S. government. No building is allowed in the regulatory floodway, and only protected or raised structures are allowed to be built in the floodway fringe area.

Regulatory floodway—Kept open to carry flood water: no building or fill permitted.

Regulatory floodway fringe—Use permitted if protected by fill, flood-proofed, or otherwise protected.

Regulatory flood limit—based on technical study; outer limit of the floodway fringe.

Standard project flood (SPF) limit—Area subject to possible flooding by large floods.

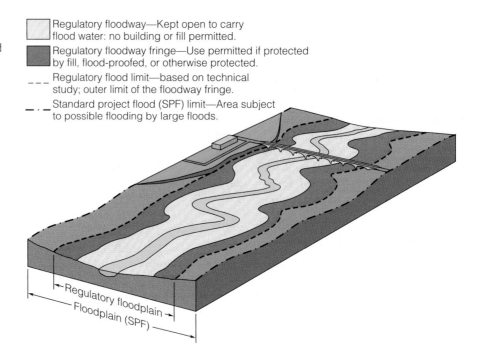

Regulatory floodplain →
Floodplain (SPF)

CASE STUDY 9.1

The Nile River—Three Cubits between Security and Disaster

Flooding is a natural part of the hydrologic cycle, and as farmers, hydrologists, and geologists know, it can be beneficial.

The annual flood on the Nile River, the longest river in the world (depending upon how one measures the Amazon), was a source of life for at least 5,000 years. Eighty percent of the water for these floods came from the faraway Ethiopian Highlands, and it replenished the soil moisture and deposited a layer of nutrient-rich silt on the floodplain (◆Figure 1). The Greek historian and naturalist Herodotus, in 457 B.C., recognized the importance of annual flooding when he spoke of Egypt as "the gift of the Nile." The priests of ancient Egypt used principles of

astronomy to calculate the time of the river's annual rise and fall. Records of the height of the flood crests go back to 1750 B.C. (some say to 3600 B.C.), as measured with stepped wells connected to the river and known as Nilometers (◆Figure 2). Water height was measured in

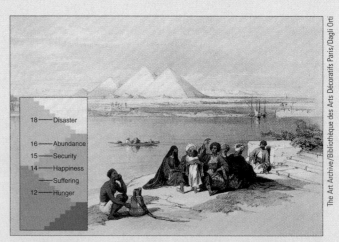

◆ **FIGURE 2** The Nile outside of Cairo as it flows past the pyramids. Inset is a schematic view of a Nilometer, a stepped well that allowed measurement of river stage or height. Water height was measured in cubits, a cubit being the distance between one's elbow and the tip of the middle finger (usually about 18 in). The environmental interpretations shown here were used during the time of Pliny the Elder (C.E. 23–79) of Mount Vesuvius fame. Source: *A Journey in Egypt*, R. Bianucci.

◆ **FIGURE 1** Farmers work in fields outside of Cairo, Egypt along a channel of the Nile River.

cubits, one cubit being the distance from one's elbow to the tip of the middle finger, approximately 0.5 meter.

The annual flooding cycle has changed since completion of the Aswan High Dam on the Upper Nile in southern Egypt in 1970. The dam's purposes were to increase the extent of arable land, generate electricity, improve navigation, and control the flooding on the Lower Nile. It is accomplishing all of those goals. Now that the flooding is controlled, however, crop maintenance depends upon irrigation. Severe environmental consequences have resulted, including depletion of the soil nutrients that are beneficial to farming (necessitating the use of artificial fertilizers) and the proliferation of parasite-bearing snails in irrigation ditches and canals. *Schistosomiasis* is a human disease found in communities where people bathe or work in irrigation canals containing snails serving as temporary hosts to parasitic flatworms (schistosomes).

These creatures, commonly called blood flukes, invade humans' skin when they step on the snails while wading in the canals. The flukes live in their human hosts' blood, where the females release large numbers of eggs daily, which cause extensive cell damage. Next to malaria, *schistosomiasis* is the most serious parasitic infection in humans. Its outbreak in Egypt is a result of controls on the river that prevent the generous floods that formerly flushed the snails from canals and ditches each year.

Another negative consequence is the loss of a huge shrimp fishery off the Nile delta; the dam traps the nutrients that encouraged the growth of plankton, upon which the shrimp larvae fed. Every dam has a finite useful lifetime that is determined by how fast the lake it impounds fills with sediment. Lake Nasser, behind the Aswan Dam, is rapidly filling with the (precious) sediment that formerly enriched the floodplain of the lower Nile and the waters off the delta.

CASE STUDY 9.2

New Orleans, The Flood Happens

New Orleans has always been a city about water and about risks. Built on the banks of the Mississippi River, scarcely above sea level and flanked by the expansive waters of Lake Poncitrain to the north, the city has faced flooding since the first building went up 300 years ago in what today is the French Quarter. Thanks to the invention and installation of a huge pumping network in the late 1800s (◆ Figure 1), the marshes were drained, the groundwater table lowered, and storm water removed, allowing the city to expand. It took an intricate system of levees and canals to move the water around, but one by one these were built, first of earth and then of steel and concrete. In the last half a century, the Army Corps of Engineers has managed this levee system, which allows much of New Orleans to exist even though it's below sea level.

Ironically, the combination of pumping and levees has caused the city to sink even further below sea level as dried, organic-rich soils decay and compact and the river's floods, which used to deposit sediment and raise the land, are funneled south, beyond the city's reach. Indeed, by walling in a city that now exists below sea level, engineers and politicians made it possible for people to live in a flood-hazard zone and created the potential for disaster. The levees and flood walls were designed to withstand flooding from a rapidly moving category 3 hurricane, a moderately severe storm.

Several times in the last few decades the levee system has been threatened, but each time the hurricanes changed course at the last minute, sparing New Orleans their full fury. In general, the levees have held and flooding of the city has not been catastrophic, until Katrina hit

◆ **FIGURE 1** Massive pumps keep New Orleans from filling with water. In 1913, Albert Baldwin Wood, an engineer with the New Orleans sewer and water board, designed a screw pump that could lift huge amounts of water—a million gallons every five minutes. Here are some of those pumps. Their invention made the draining and thus the growth of New Orleans possible.

CONTINUED

in August 2005. The storm hammered the city with wind and rain, but the real flooding came a day later, when the storm surge breached the flood-control system in numerous places allowing water from Lake Poncitrain to pour into the city. Nearly 80 percent of New Orleans was flooded (◆ Figure 2), 1300 died and nearly a million were homeless. This was flooding and destruction on a scale the United States had never seen.

An independent commission (**www.ce.berkeley.edu/~new_orleans**) examined why the levee and floodwall system failed. They determined that some sections were underdesigned and others poorly installed. The levees failed in several ways (◆ Figure 3). Some, those that were not built high enough, were overtopped by water. As this water poured over the levees, it eroded and undermined them, leading to failure. Other flood control features, built on soft soils, were simply pushed aside by the pressure of the water they were meant to contain as the soils beneath them gave way. Sometimes water moved under the levees in what are termed "piping failures" eroding material under the levee until it lost support and collapsed. These engineering failures can be remedied by improved design and construction techniques; however, the commission pointed out that what really needed to be fixed was the administrative system that allowed the design and construction of substandard flood control when millions of people's lives were at stake.

◆ **FIGURE 2** Map of flooding in New Orleans shows just how bad the situation was on September 3, five days after Katrina swept ashore. The map is based on combination aerial photography and laser elevation data. The color coding conveys water depth in the flooded areas. Clearly, most of the city is at least partially submerged.

◆ **FIGURE 3** Levees and floodwalls can fail in several different ways. (a) Water can pour over the top scouring away the base. (b) Weak soils beneath can fail allowing the levee to be pushed outward. (c) Water can move under the levee, called piping, a process by which the levee is demolished by erosion from below. Source: *Scientific American*, Feb 2006, page 93.

CASE STUDY 9.3

When Ice Melts and Moves

One moment, it's a pleasant early spring day by the river; the first robins appeared and it's warm enough to pull off your wool hat for the first time since December. The snow around your feet is soggy; it's a good thing you are wearing high rubber boots. It rained hard last night and the river should be rising, but you can't see it though the cover of punky, gray ice. Suddenly, there's a deafening crash, and the ice on the river breaks up before your eyes. Blocks of ice, half a meter thick and the length of small cars move downstream in a crazy jumble, grinding past one another, ripping trees from the river banks and jamming against the bridge piers just downstream. You watch in amazement as more and more ice stacks up against the bridge, ignorant of the water rising over your boot tops until it cascades down to your toes, bathing you and your wool socks in an extension of the icy-cold river. The rising water and your soaking feet are telling you that an ice-jam flood has started, and it's time to move to high ground—fast!

◆ **FIGURE 1** Ice jams have been damaging human constructs for as long as people have lived near frozen rivers. Here, as shown in this 1863 stereoview, an ice jam diverted the White River right down Main Street in Hartford, Vermont.

Ice-jam floods can happen anywhere that streams freeze in the winter; that means northern latitudes and high elevations. These floods occur when warm winds melt the snow pack, rain pummels icy slopes, and river ice weakens. Rising floodwaters can tear ice cover apart, rapidly adding immensely to the hazard. When ice jamming occurs, water levels rise fast as dams of ice block downstream flow and pond water. Unlike most river floods during which stage rises gradually and predictably, ice-jam floods are fast, devastating, and hard to predict. There's little warning. But it's not quite that grim. Many times, ice jams, and the floods they trigger, happen in the same place where natural or manmade obstacles force ice blocks to hang up (◆ Figure 1). Just imagine a bridge abutment or a tight meander bend. Can't you see the blocks of ice stacking one behind the next, the temporary pond behind them growing and spilling over the riverside road, filling the Jones' basement and bathing their new pickup truck in icy, muddy floodwater? What's the remedy? If you can be patient, time—to melt the ice. If people or their homes are in danger, dynamite and heavy equipment will do the trick, destroying the ice dam and letting the river flow free again (◆ Figure 2).

◆ **FIGURE 2** When ice jams cause flooding, big tools are used to remove them. Sometimes dynamite is the tool of choice; other times, like shown here along the Winooski River in Vermont, it's heavy machinery that opens the river once again to flow.

CASE STUDY 9.4

Dams—"In" or "Out"

Damming has long been a means for making river water more or less available to humans. The Three Gorges Dam on the Yangtze River in China is the most talked about modern example (◆Figure 1). Begun in 1993, it is 181 meters (594 ft) high and should be completed in 2009 at a cost in excess of $24 billion. Its main functions are power generation, flood control, and improved navigation. In 2003 the first electricity was generated and the first ship lock was operating. The dam has been criticized because of cost, resettlement of displaced persons, environmental impact, and adverse effects on local culture and history. In response, the protagonists say the electrical transmission will eventually pay for the dam, millions of people downstream will be better off, most of the important historical sites are being moved before they are inundated, shipping will become faster and cheaper, and hydroelectric power is cleaner than other large-scale energy sources such as coal.

In the United States the view on dams is somewhat different. More dams are coming out than going in. At least for now, the era of large dam building in the United States is over because many of the prime sites are already dammed and because of concern about environmental impacts, specifically changes in river dynamics, the loss of land by impounded water, and the resulting dislocation of wildlife and plants. There are 7,700 large dams in the country, and the total number of dams exceeds 75,000. Some existing dams serve a useful purpose—energy, flood control, recreation, and as a water source. Others are relics of a time when hydropower was a mainstay of industry.

Lloyd Olson

◆ **FIGURE 1** Three Gorges Dam Project (TGDP) under construction on the Yangtze River in summer of 2002.

CASE STUDY 9.5

A Very Wet Fall

New England is not the kind of place one imagines floods that take out a thousand bridges, destroy towns of 6,000 people, and remove miles of roadway; rather, people think of Vermont and New Hampshire as pastoral places where snow blankets the landscape in winter and gentle rains nurture the maple trees that provide syrup in the spring and flaming orange hillslopes every fall. Not so in the fall of 1927.

October 1927 was dreary and wet in New England. It rained and it rained. Many towns got twice their average rainfall. By early November the ground was sodden and the trees, having lost their leaves, weren't pumping water from the ground. Groundwater levels were on the rise. Then, on November 4, 1927, the rain began, driven by moist, tropical air from the south trying to override cold air from the north. As the warm air rose over the Green Mountains of Vermont, the moisture was squeezed out of the saturated atmosphere. Over the next

48 hours, mountainous parts of Vermont saw over 8 inches of rain fall from the sky; even the lowlands recorded 4 to 6 inches of rain. Since the ground was already soaked from the October rains much of this rain ran off into creeks and streams, driving river levels up. Riverside homes that had stood for 150 years were swept away, railroads were twisted into pretzels, and bridges were ripped from their piers and swept downstream (◆ Figures 1 and 2).

The flood is now the legend to which every other flood is compared. On the Winooski, the main river draining northern Vermont, the flood of '27 was the flood of record, the largest flood to affect the basin since western settlement. At the flood's peak, 113,000 cubic feet per second of water were flowing downstream, 2.5 times the second largest flood on record and almost 70 times the average flow. Simple calculations suggest that '27 was the 100-year flood, but this is misleading because

Fairbanks Museum and Planetarium, St. Johnsbury, VT

◆ **FIGURE 1** The 1927 flood picked up houses and dropped them in some pretty unusual places. This robust post and beam farm house survived the half-mile trip from its foundation to the railroad tracks intact. How do you think today's balloon framed homes might do in a similar situation?

Fletcher Free Library, Burlington, VT

◆ **FIGURE 2** Rampaging flood waters carried away over 1,000 bridges in the tiny state of Vermont, devastating the transportation network. This picture was taken just before the bridges washed away. A pontoon bridge linked the mills of Winooski (shown in the background) with the city of Burlington until a permanent bridge could be rebuilt the next year.

CONTINUED

it doesn't plot in line with other floods on the flood-frequency curve. This was an odd event, a perfect combination of widespread heavy rain on saturated ground. Miraculously, only 84 Vermonters (and 111 people in New England) died in the flood, but the region was forever changed. It took years to rebuild the lost bridges, and in many places rivers found new paths, leaving fields as islands separated from their farms.

So, just how rare was the 1927 flood? Lake mud answers that question. It wasn't that rare. Geologists from the University of Vermont ventured onto frozen lakes for several winters, bringing back cores of lake sediment that had been secreted away on lake bottoms for the last 14,000 years since the glaciers left (◆Figure 3). When they cut open those cores, they found lots of black, sticky, stinky mud. But every once

in a while, they would cut open a core to find a layer of bright gray sand carried into the lake when big storms struck the drainage basin (◆Figure 4). By dating these sand layers from lakes all over New England, the geologists, led by graduate student Anders Noren, determined that really big storms hit New England on average every few hundred years. What's even more interesting is that the frequency of these storms has changed over time and if the past is a clue to the future, the forecast for the next 600 years is an increase in big storms.

◆ FIGURE 3 Collecting 10,000 years worth of lake sediment is serious business easily accomplished off the winter ice. Here, one author (Bierman) and University of Vermont graduate student (Josh Galster), struggle to loosen a piece of coring equipment before the ice melts on this fine March day.

◆ FIGURE 4 Once the cores are cut open, storm layers clearly stand out from the black, organic-rich, and foul-smelling pond sediment. Here's a 10-cm-thick light-colored layer of sediment likely washed into Ritterbush Pond by a big storm about 6,800 years ago. At the top of the image are two very thin storm layers.

The Impermeable Flood

What do you think about when you imagine the cause of floods? Probably heavy rain, storm surges, and by now, ice jams. Do you think about people as a cause of floods? In urban and suburban areas, people and their developments dramatically change the way water moves over and into the ground. How can a new house, a nicely mowed two-acre lawn, and an SUV parked on the grass make any difference?

When a raindrop falls to Earth, it can take various paths (◆Figure 1). If the ground isn't already saturated with water and rain isn't falling too heavily, the raindrop will be absorbed and flow underground.

Sometimes groundwater will move just below the surface in pores large and small between soil grains or along natural pipes made as roots rot away. Sometimes groundwater will move deeply through the underlying rock or sediment. In forested areas all over the world, almost all rainwater follows these paths. However, if the ground is already saturated or if the raindrop falls on something impermeable, perhaps clay-rich soil or a hiking trail compacted by hundreds of footsteps or a paved parking lot, then the rainwater runs off, pouring off the slopes and into streams and rivers.

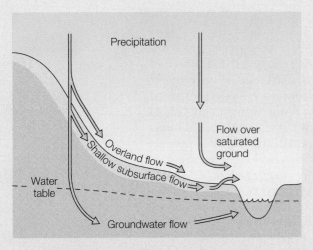

◆ **FIGURE 1** Water, falling from the sky as rain, can move various ways when it hits the ground. Development and other human impacts usually reduce the ability of the ground to absorb water, forcing more rainfall downslope as overland flow. Source: Adapted from Dunne and Leopold, *Water in Environmental Planning*, W.H. Freeman

So, what's development got to do with floods? As forests or grasslands are replaced by parking lots or 6,000-square-foot homes with shingle roofs, water that used to soak into the ground now pours into storm drains and enters rivers and streams rapidly. When forests covered the land, there were deep pits and high mounds where trees had tipped up and roughened the forest floor. These pits held rainwater, allowing it to slowly infiltrate. When the trees were cleared for the new development and its five-acre lots, the bulldozers smoothed the forest floor and uniform, tile-drained grass lawns took the place of rotting logs. Even in the city, the conversion of grassy lawns to parking areas can make a big difference (◆Figure 2). The response is dramatic. Water levels in streams and rivers rise rapidly and attain higher peaks as rain is more quickly and efficiently moved off the landscape. Floods may not last as long, but they can be more devastating. The slug of floodwater, moving at high velocity, tends to erode and deepen channels causing other unintended consequences.

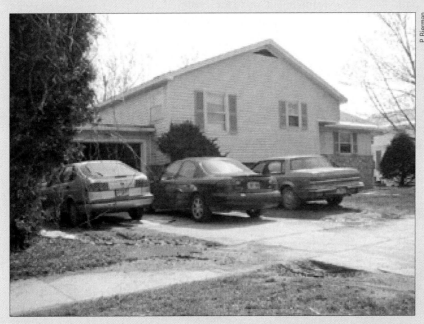

◆ **FIGURE 2** When cars park on lawns, the mud starts quickly. Here, several vehicles in Burlington, Vermont have repeatedly driven over the grass, killing it, compacting the soil beneath, and forming deep ruts. When it rains, that compacted soil can't infiltrate the water and muddy puddles result. The good news is, with fencing, rototilling to break up the compaction, and time, the soil will once again be able to absorb rainfall.

Going . . . Going . . . Gone! Dam Failure

Ask any geologists about dam failures and you'll likely hear at least one of three stories—pick your place, California, Idaho, or Pennsylvania. Each one has a devastating tale to tell. Johnstown, PA holds the record for lives lost. A private, earth-fill dam, holding back a lake used for recreation by the wealthy, failed during a very heavy storm. A wave of water swept through a series of towns, killing over 2,000 people and wrapping many of their homes around stone bridges (◆ Figure 1). Perhaps the most famous U.S. dam failure was that of the St. Francis Dam in southern California. That 1928 failure took 450 lives. The dam was part of an aqueduct system bringing water from the east slope of the Sierra Nevada to semiarid Los Angeles and its growing suburbs. The left abutment of the concrete dam was founded in sandstone, and the right abutment in mica schist (◆ Figure 2). The two rock formations were in contact along a 2-meter-wide shattered fault zone at the left abutment. The dam was completed in 1926, and more than two years were required to fill the reservoir with 38,000 acre feet (12.5 billion gallons) of water. On March 12, 1928, just one week after the reservoir had filled, the dam failed. Traditional theory has it that the dam failed along the fault zone in the left abutment because the rocks there contained gypsum. Water percolating through the fault zone dissolved the gypsum and eventually, full reservoir pressure blew out the weakened sandstone. Newer analysis, however, suggests that the right abutment was placed into an unrecognized landslide in the schist, and that the slide mass collapsed when the reservoir filled, leading to failure of the right abutment and the dam. Whatever the cause, the man who built the dam, William Mulholland, took the failure personally and died a short time later. He is said to be the four hundred fifty-first victim of the flood. The Teton Dam failed in Idaho, June, 1976. Fourteen people died when a wall of water swept downstream. The earthen dam failed as it was filled with water for the first time.

◆ **FIGURE 1** The Johnstown, Pennsylvania flood swept huge amounts of debris downstream when the dam failed. Trees and homes are piled high against a stone bridge. A crane is being used to remove the debris.

National Park Service

(a)

(b)

◆ **FIGURE 2** (a) The St. Francis Dam in San Francisquito Canyon, southern California, early March 1928. The right abutment is in Pelona schist; the left abutment is (center of photo) in the Sespe Formation, which is mainly sandstone. (b) All that remained of the dam on March 13, 1928. Security Pacific National Bank Historical Collection, Los Angeles County Library

◆ **FIGURE 3** The earth-filled Teton Dam fails. Water seeping through the dam weakened it so much that the entire dam failed catastrophically.

Summary

River Systems

Drainage Basin

The fundamental geographic unit or tract of land that contributes water to a stream or stream system. Drainage basins are separated by divides.

Discharge

The amount of water flowing in a stream channel depends upon the amount of runoff and subsurface flow from the land, which in turn depends upon rainfall or snowmelt, the degree of urbanization, and vegetation.

Erosion

The erosive power of a stream is a function of its velocity—the greater the velocity, the greater the erosion. Stream velocity is determined by discharge, channel shape, and gradient.

Base Level

The lowest level to which a stream or stream system can erode. This is usually sea level, but there are also temporary base levels such as lakes, dams, and waterfalls.

Graded Stream

A stream that has reached a balance of erosion, transporting capacity, and the amount of material supplied to it. This condition is represented by a concave-upward profile of equilibrium.

Stream Features

Alluvium

Sediment deposited by a stream, either in or outside the channel.

Alluvial Fan

A buildup of alluvial sediment at the foot of a mountain stream.

Delta

Forms where a sediment-laden stream flows into standing water. An example is the delta of the Nile River.

Floodplain

A low area adjacent to a stream that is subject to periodic flooding and sedimentation; the area covered by water during flood stage.

Meanders, Oxbow Lakes, and Cutoffs

Flowing water will assume a series of S-shaped curves known as meanders. The river may cut off the neck of a tight meander loop and form an oxbow lake.

Flooding and Flood Frequency

Floods

Upland floods come on suddenly and move rapidly through narrow valleys. Upland floods are often "flash" floods; the water rises and falls in a matter of a few hours. Lowland floods, on the other hand, inundate broad adjacent floodplains and may take many days, weeks, or even months to complete the flood cycle.

Hydrograph

A graph that plots measured water level (stage) or discharge over a period of time.

Recurrence Interval

The average length of time (T) between flood events of a given magnitude. Mathematically, $T = (N + 1) \div M$, where N is the number of years of record and M is the rank of the flood magnitude in comparison with other floods in the record. Recurrence interval calculations enable engineers and planners to anticipate how often floods of a given size may occur and to what elevation the water may rise.

Flood Probability

The chance that a flood of a particular magnitude will occur within a given year based on historical flood data for the particular location. Using the calculation for T established for the recurrence interval, probability is calculated as $1/T$. Thus a 100-year flood has a 1 percent chance of occurring in any one year. It is the 1-in-100 *chance* flood.

Mitigation

Structures

Dams, retaining basins, artificial levees, and raising structures on artificial fill are common means of flood protection. They also present problems.

Flood Insurance

The National Flood Insurance Act of 1968 provides insurance in flood-prone areas, provided certain building regulations and restrictions are met.

Urban Development

Hydrology

Urbanization causes floods to peak sooner during a storm, results in greater peak runoff and total runoff, and increases the probability of flooding. Floods, including coastal flooding during hurricanes, are the greatest natural hazards facing humankind.

Planning and Survival

Flooding is the most consistently damaging natural disaster in the United States. Never drive through flood waters.

Key Terms

alluvial fan	drainage basin	gradient	oxbow lake
alluvium	drainage divide	hydrograph	point bar
artificial levee	flood frequency	hydrology	precipitation
base level	floodplain	inundation	recurrence interval
delta	floodwall	meander	Regulatory Floodplain
discharge	graded stream	natural levee	riparian

Study Questions

1. How does stream erosion shape the landscape?

2. How can we prevent floods or at least minimize the property damage caused by flooding?

3. How is the velocity of a stream related to its erosive power?

4. What has been the impact of urbanization on flood frequency and peak discharge?

5. According to the local newspaper, your town on the Ohio River has just experienced a 50-year flood. What is the probability of a repeat of this event the following year?

6. How does the hydrograph record of an upland flash flood differ from that of a lowland riverine flood?

7. Where is flash flooding most frequent and what precautions should be observed in such areas?

8. What has the federal government done to alleviate people's suffering due to flooding? Do you believe this is a good thing? Support your answers with examples and rationales.

9. Consider a stream whose headwaters are 1,500 meters (4,900 ft) above sea level and that flows 300 kilometers (180 mi) to the ocean. What is the average gradient of the stream in m/km and in ft/mi?

10. What benefits do river dams impart to humans? What are some negative impacts of dams upon human beings and the environment?

For Further Information

Books and Periodicals

Carrier, Jim. 1991. The Colorado: A river drained dry. *National geographic*, June.

Collier, Michael and others. 1996. *Dams and rivers: a primer on the downstream effects of dams*. U.S. Geological Survey circular 1126.

Devine, Robert S. 1995. The trouble with dams. *Atlantic monthly*, August: 64–74.

Dinacola, Karen. 1996. The "100-year flood." U.S. Geological survey fact sheet FS-229-96.

EOS. 1996. *Controlled flood of Colorado River creates stream of data*. Transactions of the American Geophysical Union 77, no. 24 (June 11).

Federal Emergency Management Agency. Guidelines for determining flood hazards on alluvial fans.

Fischetti, Mark. 2001. Drowning New Orleans. *Scientific American*, October.

Gosnold, William and others. 2000. Floods and climate. *Geotimes*, May.

Holmes, Robert R., Jr. and Amit Kapadia. 1997. Floods in northern Illinois, July 1996. U.S. Geological Survey fact sheet FS-097-97.

Lucchitta, Ivo and Luna B. Leopold. 1999. *Floods and sandbars in the Grand Canyon. GSA today* 9, no. 4 (April).

McPhee, John. 1989. *The control of nature*. New York: Farrar, Straus & Giroux.

National geographic. 1993. Water: the power, promise and turmoil of North America's fresh water. Special edition, October.

Perry, Charles A. 2000. Significant floods in the United States during the 20th century. U.S. Geological Survey fact sheet FS-024-00, March.

Rogers, J. David. 1992. Reassessment of the St. Francis dam failure. In Pipkin, B.W. and Richard Proctor, Eds. *Engineering geology practice in southern California*. Belmont, Calif.: Star Publishing Co.

Saarinen, T. F., V. R. Baker, R. Durrenberger, and T. Maddock, Jr. 1984. *The Tucson, Arizona, flood of October 1983*. Washington D.C.: National Research Council, National Academy Press.

Teller, R.W. and M. J. Burr. 1998. Floods in north-central and eastern South Dakota, Spring 1997. U.S. Geological Survey fact sheet FS-021-98.

U.S. Geological Survey. 1993. Mississippi River flood of 1993. *U.S. Geological Survey yearbook:* 37–40.

ThomsonNOW

Assess your understanding of this chapter's topics with additional comprehensive interactivities at http://www.thomson.com/login, which also has up-to-date web links, additional readings, and exercises.

CHAPTER 10

Coastal Environments and Humans

"For the Earth, it was just a twinge. For a planet where landmasses are in constant motion across geological time, the event was no great moment. But for people—who make the calendar in days and months rather than eons—a monumental catastrophe had begun, not only the largest

Reefs in Peril

CORAL REEFS ARE UNIQUE AND ARE RIVALED by only a few other ecosystems. Charles Darwin may have been the first to recognize that they are the largest and most important ecosystems in the marine environment. Corals are animals, related to jellyfish, that secrete a hard skeleton of calcium carbonate (limestone). They grow only in warm water (above 20° C, which is approximately 70° F) within the zone of light. Corals require light because they live in symbiosis with the tiny marine algae *zooxanthellae*. These plants live within the coral polyp and give the calcareous skeleton its color (◆Figure 1).

Coral reefs help people in diverse ways. They form barriers to beach erosion, build atoll islands upon which people live, support fisheries, and attract tourism. Unfortunately, they are being destroyed worldwide at a phenomenal rate. Mining reefs for limestone, dumping mine tailings on reefs, fishing by use of explosives or cyanide, land reclamation, and polluted river runoff all take their toll. Seawater temperature increases due to global warming and El Niño events are causes of reefs' destruction. Reefs in Indonesia, North America, Hawaii, and the Great Barrier Reef of Australia are just a few at risk. At higher temperature, coral polyps expel *zoo-xanthellae*, lose their color, and eventually die if the warm water persists. The bleaching turns a beautiful underwater garden into a spiny waste-land (◆Figure 2). The newest threat to coral

◆ **FIGURE 1** Healthy coral reefs exhibit a variety of colors and diversity. A healthy reef off the Bahama Islands, with the staghorn coral, *Acropora palmata*, growing to the low-tide water level.

B. Pipkin

is acidification of near-surface ocean waters, caused by human-induced increases in atmospheric CO_2, the result of burning fossil fuels. The growing acidity of ocean waters as atmospheric CO_2 dissolves in the ocean makes it increasingly difficult for marine creatures to fix $CaCO_3$, which dissolves in acidic waters.

◆ **FIGURE 2** A bleached reef in the Bahamas that has lost most of its symbiotic algae. The limestone of the coral skeleton is clearly visible. If the environmental stress is not removed, the coral polyps will die. The coral here is elkhorn coral, Acropora cervicornis.

earthquake in 40 years but also the displacement of billions of tons of water, unleashing a series of mammoth waves: as tsunami."

Barry Bearak, *New York Times Magazine*, The Day the Sea Came, November, 2005, writing about the Indonesian Tsunami.

Many people want to live near a beach. Coastal areas in the United States and around the world experienced enormous population growth in the late twentieth century. Fifty percent of the U.S. population can now drive to a coastline in less than an hour. Yet, as events of 2004 and 2005 clearly show, the coast can be a dangerous place to be, with tsunamis and hurricanes damaging properties and taking hundreds of thousands of lives. There are more subtle and ongoing coastal hazards such as the slow erosion of sea cliffs and the retreat of barrier islands. Increasing global sea level ensures that these hazards will not only continue, but likely grow worse over the next century. Human actions sometimes contribute to the hazards. For example, wetlands are being filled, drained, and made into marinas, reducing their ability to dampen storm surges. Shoreline modifications continue to silt in harbors and erode beaches.

In order to understand and approach the environmental issues that are so important in the coastal zone, it is critical that we understand the relevant Earth processes. That's the goal of this chapter. Wind-driven waves that arise in the open ocean eventually strike shorelines, constantly altering beaches. Massive tsunami waves, generated by impulses including earthquakes and submarine landslides, can change thousands of kilometers of coastline in a matter of minutes. Hurricanes pound smaller stretches of coast for hours while nor'easters batter long stretches of eastern North America, sometimes for days at a time. Armed with the knowledge of how waves erode beaches and of the fate of eroded materials, we are all better equipped to understand and deal with coastal environmental issues.

Wind Waves

Waves in Deep Water and at the Shore

When wind blows over smooth water, surface ripples are created that enlarge with time to form local "chop" (short, steep waves) and, eventually, wind waves. The factors that determine the size of waves at sea and ultimately the size of the surf that strikes the shoreline are

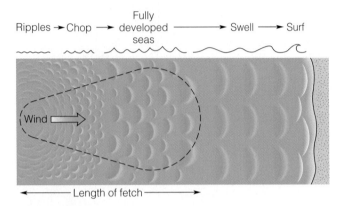

◆ **FIGURE 10.1** The evolution of wind-generated sea waves from a rippled water surface to fully developed seas (storm waves). Long waves with very regular spacing and height that outrun the storm area are called *swell*.

■ the wind velocity,

■ the length of time the wind blows over the water, and

■ the **fetch,** the distance along open water over which the wind blows (◆ Figure 10.1).

For a given fetch, wind velocity, and wind duration, wave dimensions will grow until they reach the maximum size for the existing storm conditions. This condition, known as a *fully developed sea*, represents the maximum energy that the waves can absorb for wind of a given velocity. For example, theoretical wave heights of 32 meters (100 ft) are possible for a 50-knot (93 km/h, 58 mph) wind blowing for 3 days over a fetch of 2,700 kilometers (1,600 mi). Wind waves will move out of the area of strong atmospheric disturbance as regularly spaced, long waves known as *swell* and eventually become huge breakers on a distant shoreline.

Important dimensions of wind waves are their length, height, and *period*—the length of time between the passage of equivalent points on the wave. These dimensions are measures of the amount of *energy* the waves contain, that is, their ability to do work (◆ Figure 10.2). Although waves with long wavelengths and long periods are the most powerful, both long and short waves are capable of eroding beaches.

The actual water motion in a wind-generated wave describes a circular path whose diameter at the sea surface is equal to the wave height. This circular motion diminishes with depth and becomes essentially zero at a depth equal to half the wavelength (*L*/2), the depth referred to as **wave base.** Wave base is the maximum depth to which waves can disturb or erode the sea floor. (This explains why divers and submersibles at depth are not tossed about during storms as surface ships are.) Although the waveform moves across the water surface with considerable velocity, there is no mass forward movement of water. Such waves are called **waves of oscillation.** Floating objects simply bob up and down with a slight back-and-forth motion as wave crests and troughs pass.

As waves approach a shoreline and move into shallow depths, the sea floor interferes with the oscillating water particles. This friction causes wave velocity to decrease. This in turn causes the wave to steepen; that is, the wavelength shortens and the wave height increases, a phenomenon easily seen by surf watchers. Eventually the wave becomes so steep that the crest outruns the base of the wave and jets forward as a "breaker." Breakers are **waves of translation,** because the water in them physically moves landward in the surf zone. Where the immediate offshore area is steep, we find the classic tube-shaped *plunging breakers* typical of Sunset Beach and Waimea Bay on the north shore of Oahu (◆ Figure 10.3). This is because the wave peaks rapidly on a steep sea floor. On a flat near-shore slope, on the other hand, waves lose

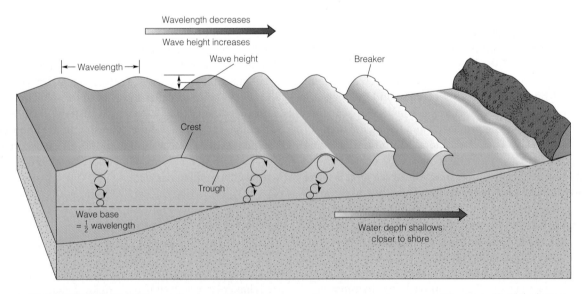

◆ **ACTIVE FIGURE 10.2** Wave motion is complex and changes as the wave approaches shore and begins to "feel" the bottom. Motion of water in a wave and the terminology of wave geometry. Note that the orbital water motion decreases with depth until it is essentially nil at a depth of one-half the wave length (*L*/2), a depth called *wave base*.

◆ **FIGURE 10.3** (a) Plunging (tubular) breakers form where there are steep offshore slopes. The front of the wave steepens until the top of the wave "jets" forward and down. This one is at Waimea Bay, Oahu, Hawaii, famous for large waves and surfing tournaments. (b) Spilling breakers form where there are gently sloping offshore areas, such as Waikiki Beach on Oahu, Hawaii. The forward face of the wave steepens and the crest spills down the front of the wave.

energy by friction, so they build up slowly, and the crest simply spills down the face of the wave. This latter type is called *spilling breakers.* They are typical of wide, flat near-shore bottoms such as that at Waikiki Beach on Oahu (see Figure 10.3). Regardless of the type of wave, *swash*—the water that rushes forward onto the foreshore slope of the beach—returns seaward as *backwash* to become part of the next breaker. A common misconception is the existence of a bottom current called *undertow* that pulls swimmers out to sea. The strong pull seaward one feels in the surf zone is simply backwash water returning to be recycled in the next breaker.

Wave Refraction

Where waves approach a shoreline at an angle, they are subject to **wave refraction,** or bending. Waves slow first at their

shallow-water ends while their deeper-water ends move shoreward at a higher velocity. Thus a fixed point on a wave crest follows a curved path to the shoreline (◆Figure 10.4).

Because waves seldom approach parallel to the shore, some water is discharged along the beach as a weak current within the surf zone called a **longshore current.** The greater the angle at which the wave approaches the shoreline, the greater the volume of water that is discharged into the longshore-current stream. This current is capable of moving swimmers as well as sand grains down the beach. Sand becomes suspended in the turbulent surf and swash zone and moves in a zigzag pattern down the beach's foreshore slope (see Figure 10.4). Beaches are dynamic: the sand grains present on the foreshore today will not be the same ones we see there tomorrow. Beach-sand transport parallel to the shore in the surf zone is known as **longshore drift,** and its

◆ **ACTIVE FIGURE 10.4** (a) Refraction, or bending, of wind waves and the generation of a longshore current parallel to the beach. The longshore current transports beach sand, resulting in a dynamic process called *longshore drift.* (b) Wave refraction along a relatively straight shoreline near Santa Barbara, California.

◆ **FIGURE 10.5** Wave refraction leads to concentration of energy on points and dissipation in embayments. The arrowed lines, called *orthogonals*, are constructed perpendicular to the wave crest and show the wave path. E_1, E_2, and so on represent equal parcels of wave energy and, therefore, equal ability to erode. Note that energy is focused toward the points and spread out in the bays. This is not abstract knowledge! Rather, erosion hazards are highest on the point and least in the embayments. Remember this when you go to buy a home by the coast.

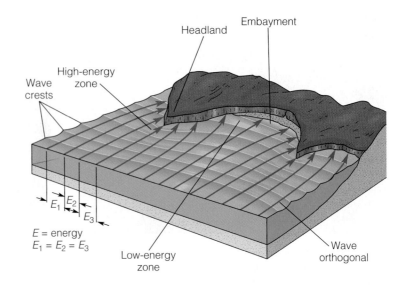

rate is usually expressed in thousands of cubic meters or cubic yards of sand per year.

Another consequence of wave refraction is the straightening of irregular shorelines. This occurs because the concentration of wave energy at points causes shoreline erosion, and the dissipation of wave energy in embayments allows sand deposition (◆Figure 10.5).

Longshore currents are likened to rivers on land, with the beach and the surf zone constituting the two banks. Just as damming a river causes sedimentation to occur upstream and erosion to occur downstream, so does building structures perpendicular to the beach. Such a structure slows or deflects longshore currents, causing sand accretion up-current from the structure and erosion down-current (◆Figure 10.6). **Groins** (French *groyne*, "snout") are constructed of sandbags, wood, stone, or concrete, ostensibly to trap sand and create a wider beach. For groins of equal length and design, the severity

of the erosion-deposition pattern is a function of the strength of the waves and the angle at which they strike the shoreline. Most groins are short and are intended to preserve or widen a beach in front of a private home or resort. Unfortunately, because this causes neighbors' beaches down-current from the groin to narrow, many of those neighbors build groins to preserve and widen *their* beaches, and so on. Like artificial levees on a river, groins tend to generate more groins, and we generally see fields of them along a given stretch of beach instead of just one (◆Figure 10.7).

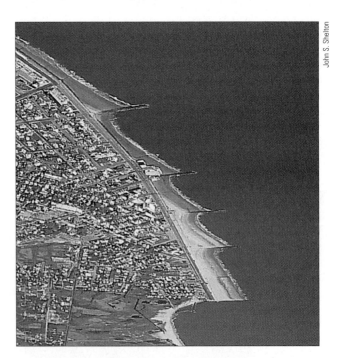

◆ **FIGURE 10.6** Accretion and erosion of beach sand at jetties constructed to improve an inlet to a navigable lagoon at Boca Raton, Florida. Can you use information in the image to determine which direction the longshore drift is moving the sand?

◆ **FIGURE 10.7** Groin field at Cape May, New Jersey. Note the breadknife, or sawtooth, appearance that has resulted from sand accretion and erosion above and below the groins. Can you use information in the image to determine which direction the longshore drift is moving the sand?

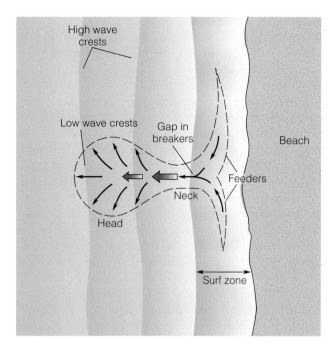

◆ **FIGURE 10.8** A rip current is characterized by relatively weak *feeder currents,* a narrow *neck* of strong currents, and a head outside the surf zone, where the rip dissipates.

Just as rivers overflow their banks, longshore currents may overflow through the surf zone, particularly during periods of big surf. Overflow (really *out*flow to the open ocean) occurs because the water level within the surf zone is higher than the water level outside the breakers, making for a hydraulic imbalance. The higher water inshore flows seaward to lower water offshore as a **rip current** through a narrow gap, or *neck,* in the breakers (◆Figure 10.8). Because the location of rip currents, erroneously called rip *tides,* is con-

trolled by bottom topography, they usually occur at the same places along a beach. Rip currents can become a problem to swimmers under big-surf conditions, when velocities in the neck may reach 4–5 knots. Awareness can save your life, so be alert to a gap in the breakers, white water beyond the surf zone, and objects floating seaward—all of which are evidence of a strong rip current flowing out to sea (◆Figure 10.9). Should you find yourself in a rip current, swim parallel to the beach until you are out of the narrow neck region of high velocity.

Impulsively Generated Waves
Tsunamis

Tsunamis, the tidal waves of the popular press, can be one of the most devastating environmental hazards, causing water levels to rise dramatically in just minutes, sweeping away people, buildings, and entire communities. Tsunami (pronounced "soo-nah-mee") is a Japanese word meaning harbor (tsun) and wave (ami) because harbors are where these waves "resonate" and are most observable. In Japanese, the singular and plural are the same, but we will follow the custom of English writers and add the "s" for the plural. After the devastating Indonesian tsunami of December 26, 2004, most people know the devastation these waves can cause—nearly a quarter million people died as water swept onto coasts all around the Indian ocean. Few natural phenomena can do so much harm so quickly.

Tsunamis are produced mostly by underwater earthquakes and less commonly by volcanic eruptions, submarine landslides, or meteorite impacts (⁎ Table 10.1). These impulses give rise to waves that move out from their source in all directions—analogous to those produced when you

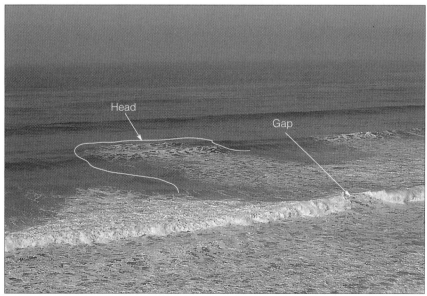

◆ **FIGURE 10.9** Small rip currents. Note the gap in the breakers and the white water seaward of the surf zone.

B. Pipkin

★TABLE 10.1	Causes of Tsunamis in the Pacific Ocean Region over the Last 2,000 Years			
Cause	Number of Events	Percentage of Events	Number of Deaths	Percentage of Deaths
Landslides	65	4.6	14,661	3.2
Earthquakes	1,171	82.3	390,929	84.5
Volcanic	65	4.6	51,643	11.2
Unknown (meteorite?)	121	8.5	5,364	1.2
Total	1,422	100	462,597	100

Source: National Geophysical Data Center and World Data Center A for Solid Earth Geophysics, 1998, and Intergovernmental Oceanographic Commission, 1999, in Bryant, 2001.

drop a rock into a pond. Tsunamis in deep water may have velocities exceeding 800 kilometers per hour (480 mph) and could easily keep pace with a Boeing 747. With wavelengths in excess of 160 kilometers (100 mi) and wave heights of only a meter or two in the open ocean, tsunamis have such gentle slopes that they go unnoticed at sea (◆Figure 10.10). As the leading waves move into shallow water, they slow to freeway speeds, and the waves behind begin to overtake them—a

(a) Earthquake! Sea floor drops, sea level falls with it.

(b) Water rushes into low spot.

H = 1 m
L = 160 km

Waves steepen and rise in shallow water

(c) Tsunami generated.

◆ **FIGURE 10.10** Formation of a tsunami when a portion of the sea floor is down-faulted and the water surface over the fault is lowered. Water rushes in to fill the low spot and creates an impulsively generated wave, then moves out in all directions with a very high velocity (hundreds of km/h).

process called *shoaling*. Thus, the energy contained in many waves is condensed into a smaller volume of water, and the waves increase in height and steepness. Eventually, the wave runs ashore as a huge breaking wave, as a wall of white, foamy water, or as a tide-like flood.

Fortunately, most underwater earthquakes do not generate tsunamis. In almost 100 years (1861–1948), only 124 major tsunamis were recorded despite there being more than 15,000 sea-floor earthquakes. The west coast of South America, a seismically active area, experienced 1,100 earthquakes in the same period and only 20 tsunamis. One of the reasons is that many tsunamis have such small amplitudes that they go unnoticed. In addition, earthquake-induced tsunamis require shallow-focus quakes with surface-wave magnitudes greater than 6.5. The Atlantic Ocean experiences only two percent of the tsunamis, whereas the Pacific Ocean experiences 80 percent of them. Why do you think the Pacific Ocean is so tsunami-rich (hint: consider what you know about plate tectonics)?

Earthquake-induced tsunamis may rise to heights of more than 30 meters. The time between crests of the incoming waves varies, and the first crest may not be the largest. The *trough* of the initial wave may arrive first; many lives have been lost by curious persons who wandered into tidal regions exposed as water withdrew, some in search of an easy seafood meal. In Lisbon, Portugal, on All Soul's Day in 1755, many people were in church when an earthquake struck. The worshipers ran outside to escape falling debris and fire, many of them joining a group seeking safety on the waterfront. There was a quiet withdrawal of water followed by a huge wave minutes later. Sixty thousand people died. The length of time of strong shaking has been estimated from historical accounts of how many *Ave Marias* and *Pater Nosters* the churchgoers recited during their fearful experience.

Water withdrawal before the first high wave also contributed to fatalities in the 1946 Hawaiian tsunami; many people walked offshore to collect exposed mollusks just before the first wave crest arrived. A good rule is to head for high ground at once should you witness a sudden recession of water along a beach or coastline or feel an earthquake near the shore.

Tsunamis are generated mostly by large-scale reverse faulting in subduction zones that ring the Pacific and Indian Ocean basins. Japanese studies have shown that strike-slip faulting seldom produces tsunamis. In the late twentieth century, earthquake-generated tsunamis around the Pacific Rim damaged Chile (1960), Alaska and the Pacific Northwest (1964), Nicaragua (1992), and New Guinea (1998). The Hawaiian Islands are very tsunami-prone due to multiple tsunami source areas. Between 1850 and 2000, the Islands averaged a damaging tsunami every two years (◆Figure 10.11). A tsunami's damage potential depends upon the earthquake mechanism, the distance the waves travel to the shoreline, the offshore topography, and configuration of the coastline. In 1998 a community on a low, coastal sandbar in Papua, New Guinea was obliterated by tsunami waves of up to 15 meters (50 ft) high that killed 2,200 people and left few survivors.

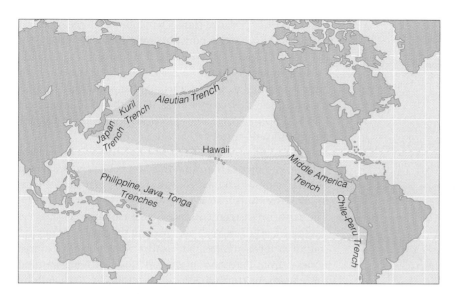

◆ **FIGURE 10.11** Tsunami sources and travel paths to the Hawaiian Islands, 1900–1983. USGS data

Experts were puzzled because the magnitude-7.1 earthquake was considered too small to generate such huge waves. This led to speculation (later confirmed by high-resolution sonar images) that the earthquake triggered a submarine landslide just offshore that caused the tsunami, which came ashore so soon after the quake that residents had no time to respond.

In 1992 twenty-six towns along 250 kilometers (150 mi) of Nicaragua's Pacific coast were struck by a 10-meter-high (33-ft) wave that killed 170 people and left 13,000 homeless. Normally, coastal inhabitants run for high ground when they feel rapid earthquake shaking. Only slight tremors were experienced in this case, however, and people did not suspect danger. Most of the earthquake energy was transmitted in much longer waves (long period, up to 200 seconds) that were not noticed or were ignored. This kind of quake, known as a "slow" earthquake, was first described by Hiroo Kanamori of the California Institute of Technology. Kanamori believes these quakes may be ten times as strong as the magnitude determined from short-period seismometer readings. Slow earthquakes of local origin are particularly dangerous in coastal areas, because they produce little precursory ground shaking that serves to warn people that a tsunami may be imminent. Up to ten percent of all tsunamis may be caused by this kind of earthquake.

The entire Pacific Rim is vulnerable to tsunami inundation. Geologic evidence indicates that within the past several thousand years many large earthquakes have generated destructive tsunamis on the shores of Washington, Oregon, and northern California. The risk becomes clearer when we recognize that 90 percent of the deaths in the Alaska earthquake of 1964 were tsunami related, and that the geology of the Cascadia subduction zone (off the coasts of Washington, Oregon and northern California) is very similar to the Alaska coast (◆ Figure 10.12)—long, linear, coast-parallel, subduction zone. Indeed, tsunamis have struck the Pacific Northwest quite recently. In 1964 tsunami waves originating

from the magnitude 9.2 Alaska subduction-zone quake destroyed much of Crescent City, California, killing at least 10. In April 1992 a magnitude-7.1 earthquake generated a small tsunami at Cape Mendocino, California. Estimates suggest a major Cascadia tsunami could cost the region billions of dollars and endanger more than half a million people who work, live, and play near the Pacific Northwest coast.

◆ **FIGURE 10.12** U.S. earthquake zones capable of generating tsunamis are the Alaska–Aleutian seismic zone and the Cascadia subduction zone. The five Pacific states are subject to tsunamis. The insert shows a tsunami detector that rests on the sea floor. It transmits acoustic signals to a surface buoy, which relays signals to a NOAA satellite and then to ground-based warning centers. From *EOS* 79, no. 2, June 2, 1998

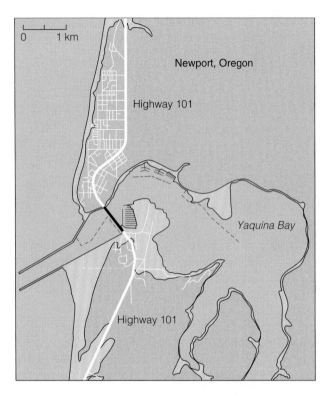

◆ **FIGURE 10.13** Potential tsunami inundation areas (green) at Newport, Oregon. From *EOS* 79, no. 2, June 2, 1998

The best defenses against tsunami risk are an educated public who knows how to respond, maps showing high-hazard areas so land-use decision can be made wisely (◆ Figure 10.13), and an early-warning system. Tsunami drills and standardized warning signs are now common in the Pacific states that are most likely to be impacted. Hazard maps have been or are being prepared, and the beginning of a warning system is in place. Useful (life-saving) warning times for the people who live and work in potential tsunami-inundation areas of the

Pacific Northwest range from a few minutes in the southern part of the Cascadia subduction zone to 20–40 minutes in the northern parts of the zone. The current Pacific-wide warning system is based on earthquake foci, and about an hour is required to issue a warning; that's too long because it's useful for only coastal areas more than 750 kilometers (465 mi) from the tsunami source, the approximate distance a tsunami could travel in that amount of time.

The goal now is to place real-time deep-ocean tsunami detectors on the sea floor that transmit data acoustically to a floating buoy, which relays the information to a satellite that, in turn, transmits it to a ground station (see Figure 10.12). The sensitive instruments can detect tsunamis as small as 3 centimeters (1.2 in) high and transmit the data to the ground station in three minutes. For nearby tsunami sources, three minutes from detection to an alert is a life-saving warning time. Seven instruments were in operation by 2004, and the plan is that 20 instruments will be installed and maintained in the Pacific Ocean by 2011. Lest you think that only the Pacific Northwest, Hawaii, and Alaska are at risk, tsunamis are purported to have struck Santa Barbara, California, in 1812 and Santa Monica, California, in 1930.

Tsunamis Initiated By Submarine Landslides

Recent research now includes landslides as a significant process in tsunami generation. This new awareness may save lives in population centers around both the Pacific and Atlantic margins that are currently under the false impression that tsunamis are not a hazard. San Francisco, Santa Barbara, Los Angeles, and San Diego are some of the cities that could be affected by tsunami-generating landslides on the steep, nearby continental slope. Known landslide-generated tsunamis resulted from sea-floor instability after the Alaskan earthquake in 1964, the Papua-New Guinea earthquake in 1998, and the Grand Banks earthquake in 1929 (◆ Figure 10.14). The latter quake (magnitude 7.2) is better known for the 12 transatlantic

◆ **FIGURE 10.14** Epicenter of Grand Banks earthquake and Burin Peninsula.

cables severed sequentially by the turbidity currents it triggered than for the tsunami waves (3 to as much as 27 m high) that struck the Burin Peninsula of Newfoundland about 2.5 hours after the seismic event. Several dozen people are reported to have perished in that event.

More than just the Grand Banks and Lisbon tsunamis (◆Figure 10.15a) have affected the Atlantic Ocean, and geological evidence indicates that some Atlantic tsunamis could be massive. Mapping of huge offshore landslide complexes on both sides of the Atlantic Ocean hints of what could happen. On the European shore, there is ample evidence that large underwater landslides have indeed triggered massive tsunami waves. About 8000 years ago, on the eastern edge of Norway, in a place called Storegga, a massive underwater landslide let loose (◆Figure 10.15b). The tsunami it generated ran up more than 25 meters in parts of the Shetland Islands off the coast of Scotland. On the other side of the Atlantic, off the coast of Virginia and North Carolina, there is evidence of a massive submarine landslide that occurred

some 18,000 years ago. This slide, which contained over 33 cubic miles of material, came off the edge of the continental shelf and must have generated a substantial tsunami. North of this ancient slide are tension cracks suggesting another slide may be imminent (◆Figure 10.15c).

Landslides Generated by Submarine Volcanic Action

The explosion of Krakatoa (Indonesia) on August 27, 1883 was one of the largest volcanic eruptions and subsequent tsunamis ever recorded. The volcano collapsed into its own magma chamber and, because it was an island in the Sunda Strait between Java and Sumatra, the ocean flowed in where the rock had once been. The eruption was disastrous, but the death toll of more than 37,000 from the tsunami was the worst effect. The tsunami had a maximum run up of 42 meters and traveled 5 kilometers inland over low-lying areas. The largest wave struck the town of Merak, because of the funnel

(a)

(b)

(c)

◆ **FIGURE 10.15** The Atlantic Ocean sees its share of tsunamis too. (a) The Lisbon tsunami of 1755 was triggered by a magnitude 9.0 earthquake that occurred 200 km off the Portuguese coast. (b) The Storegga submarine landslide (shown in yellow) let loose about 8000 years ago triggering waves that inundated coastlines of the British Isles. (c) In an article published in 2000, several geologists mapped large landslide scars and tension cracks on the continental slope of eastern North America. These features suggested to them that large tsunamis have been and will be generated just offshore. Source: (a) Univ. Cal. (b) David Smith; (c) Professor Neal Driscoll/Scripps Institution of Oceanography. Driscoll, Weissel, and Goff, *Geology*, May 2000, v. 28, no. 5, p. 407–410.

shape of its harbor. There the 15-meter wave increased to 40 meters due to concentration of energy, and coral blocks weighing over 600 tons were transported onshore. About 5,000 boats were destroyed and for months afterward bloated bodies washed ashore along with blankets of pumice.

Bolide Impacts

Bolides are bodies from space—comets or meteorites—that impact Earth. Most meteorites come from the asteroid belt between Jupiter and Mars and incinerate during their trip through the atmosphere before reaching Earth. Comets have a greater variety of orbits, some of which are extremely long, taking them away from Earth for hundreds to thousands of years. Bolides that penetrate the atmosphere and land in a body of water are capable of generating tsunamis. Hollywood has picked up on this particular tsunami-generating process and produced such fine movies as *Deep Impact* and *Armageddon*, both of which feature devastating and massive tsunamis created when bolides landed in the ocean. Indeed, there is good evidence in the geologic record of a major bolide impact and associated tsunami 65 million years ago: the Cretaceous–Tertiary boundary, a time of great extinction. Boulder beds are an indication of the great size of the wave, while the extinction of the dinosaurs and about 70 percent of all other creatures that lived at that time are testament to the devastation that the impact wrought. Recently, the crater, 180 kilometers in diameter, has been found in the northern Yucatan Peninsula, at a place called Chicxulub.

Shorelines

Where the sea and land meet, we find *shorelines,* some of which are shaped primarily by erosional geologic processes and others by depositional geological processes. Shorelines that are exposed to the open ocean and high-energy wave action are likely to be *erosional* and display such erosional features as sea cliffs or broad, wave-cut platforms. Shorelines that are protected from strong wave action, by offshore islands or by the way they trend relative to the direction of dominant wave attack, are characterized by *depositional* features such as sand beaches. Of course, not all sand beaches are stable, as we'll discover in the next few pages.

The shoreline is the distinct boundary between land and sea that changes with the tides, whereas the *coast* is the area that extends from the shoreline to the landward limit of features related to marine processes. Thus, a coast may extend inland some distance, encompassing estuaries and bays.

Beaches

In addition to their usefulness as recreational areas, beaches also serve to protect the land from the erosive power of the sea. They are where the energy of waves is dissipated. Beaches are composed of whatever sediment rivers and waves deliver to them. For example, in some places in Hawaii, black sand forms from weathered basalt and also from hot lava that disintegrates when it flows into the sea. In contrast, reef-fringed oceanic islands are characterized by beautiful white coral sand and shell beaches. Mainland beach materials are largely quartz and feldspar grains derived from the breakdown of granitic and sedimentary rocks. *Shingle* beaches are composed of gravels; they typically occur where the beach is exposed to high-energy surf. Amusing or not, tin cans from a local dump once formed a beach at Fort Bragg, California.

Beaches change shape with the season. As a rule, winter beaches are narrow or nonexistent, because high energy winter-storm waves erode sand from the upper part of the beach (the berm) and deposit it in offshore sandbars parallel to the beach (◆Figure 10.16). You may have found just such an offshore sandbar while wading in waist-deep water that abruptly shallowed as you walked onto the bar. Winter beaches are also more likely to be covered in gravel rather than sand as the sand is more easily moved offshore. With the onset of long, low-energy summer waves, the sand in the offshore bar gradually moves back onto the beach, and the beach berm widens. Thus, the natural annual beach cycle is from narrower and coarser in the winter to wider and sandier in the summer. On the East Coast, beach narrowing is related to

◆ **FIGURE 10.16** Winter and summer beach profiles and some beach terminology. From *Essentials of Geology,* 2nd ed., by R. Wicander and J. Monroe, p. 348, Brooks/Cole, 1999

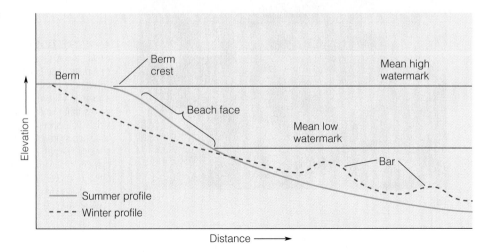

storm events that may occur at any time of the year but are more likely in the winter.

Barrier Islands

Barrier islands form the most extensive and tenuous beach system in the United States. They extend southward from Long Island and Coney Island, New York, to Atlantic City, continuing as the Outer Banks of North Carolina (see ■ Case Study 10.2 on page 302) and then down the coast of Florida to Daytona Beach, Cape Canaveral, Palm Beach, and Miami Beach. The barrier system begins again on the west coast of Florida and continues to the Padre Islands in Texas, interrupted only by the Mississippi River delta. These barrier beaches are transient fea-

tures; formed and reoriented by wave action, they are frequently overtopped by storm surges. Barrier beaches are separated from the mainland by shallow lagoons and marshland over which they migrate as large storms overwash the islands, transporting sand from their seaward sides to their landward sides.

Hog Island, Virginia, is a barrier island that was a popular hunting and fishing spot of the rich and famous in the late 1800s. Its town of Broadwater had 50 houses, a school, a cemetery, and a lighthouse. After a 1933 hurricane inundated the island, killing its pine forest, Broadwater was abandoned. Today Broadwater is underwater a half-kilometer offshore. Typical shoreward migration rates for an Atlantic-coast barrier island are 2 meters per year, but extraordinary displacements have been reported (see ■ Case Study 10.2). The rate of barrier-island migration is likely to increase as rates of sea-level rise increase in response to global warming and the resultant melting of glaciers and the thermal expansion of seawater. Although heavily developed in many parts of the United States, barrier islands are hazardous places to be in the face of any major coastal storm. They are routinely ravaged by hurricanes and nor'easters (◆Figure 10.17).

(a)

(b)

◆ **FIGURE 10.17** Barrier Islands are fragile places where disaster is waiting to strike. (a) This diagram shows the landward movement of barrier islands and the likely effects of storms on homes. (b) The day after hurricane Isabel (9/19/2003) on a barrier island near Manteo, North Carolina.

(a) **(b)**

◆ **FIGURE 10.18** Indiana Dunes National Lakeshore. (a) Glacially deposited sands were reworked by wave action and then by wind to form these impressive coastal dunes on the south shore of Lake Michigan. (b) Someone's beach home was buried when sand was blown to the lee side of the 25-meter-high (80-ft) coastal dunes. This is an example of dune migration (see Chapter 12).

Beach Accumulation and Erosion—The River of Sand

A beach is stable when the sand supplied to it by longshore currents replaces the amount of sand removed by waves. Where the amount of the supplied sand is greater than the available wave energy can remove—typically near the mouth of a river or rapidly eroding cliffs—the beach widens until wind action forms sand dunes. Significant areas of coastal dunes occur in Oregon, on the south shore of Lake Michigan in Indiana, near the Nile River in Egypt, and on the Bay of Biscay on France's west coast, to name but a few (◆Figure 10.18). The more usual

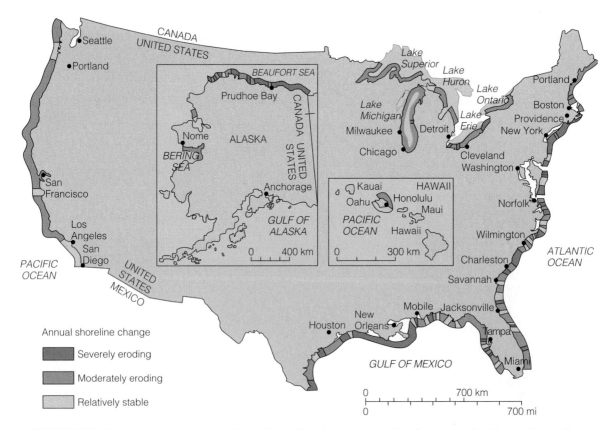

◆ **FIGURE 10.19** Present coastal erosion in the United States. Note that most of the shorelines are eroding. Uncolored coastal areas on the map represent shorelines for which data are not available. After R. Dolan and others, 1985, "Coastal Erosion and Accretion," *USGS National Atlas*

case is for wave action and longshore currents to move more sand than is supplied, and here we find eroding beaches or no beaches at all. All 30 of the U.S. coastal states have beach erosion problems of varying magnitudes resulting from both human activities and natural causes (◆Figure 10.19).

Inasmuch as sand comes to beaches by way of rivers, we should look to the land for causes of long-term beach erosion. Water-storage and flood-control dams trap sand that would normally be deposited on beaches. The need for upland flood protection is clear, but it can conflict with other needs, including the need for well-nourished beaches. Urban growth also increases the amount of paving, which seals sediment that might otherwise be eroded, find its way into local rivers, and ultimately to the beach and then the ocean. Significant natural causes of beach erosion are protracted drought and rising sea level over geologic time frames, for example, since the last glaciation peaked about 20,000 years ago (◆Figure 10.20). Little runoff occurs during drought conditions, and therefore, little sand is delivered to beaches. Rising sea level means that waves are likely to pound frequently at the bottom of sea cliffs, eroding them.

A rise in sea level could have catastrophic results. On a shorter time scale, it has been estimated that as Earth warms through the next century, sea level will rise 1 to 3 meters (up to 10 ft) due to thermal expansion and melting of glacial ice. On flat coastal plains where slopes are as gradual as 0.2–0.4 meters per kilometer, a sea-level rise of 2.5 centimeters (1 in) would cause the shoreline to retreat between 62 and 125 meters (200–400 ft). If the coast is subsiding, this shoreline migration landward would be magnified. On the other hand, tectonic uplift along parts of the Alaska and California coasts is faster than sea-level rise, which makes for a net shoreline retreat seaward. Careful tidal-gauge measurements at New York City, where the shoreline is tectonically stable, indicated a sea-level rise of 25 centimeters (almost 10 in) between 1900 and 1970. If that trend continues, plan to take a boat to the Statue of Liberty's big toe and to say goodbye to Long Island, Miami Beach, and much of Texas's Galveston County by the middle of the next century.

Erosion Examples

Long-term beach erosion is aggravated locally by poorly conceived engineering works, such as *breakwaters* built to create quiet water for safe yacht anchorage, and long **jetties** built to prevent sedimentation in harbor or river inlets. Such structures cut off the littoral flow, the movement of sand along beaches, causing accretion of sand in the immediate vicinity of the structure and erosion on their downcurrent side. Here are a few examples that show ways in which human interaction with coastal processes has not worked out so well.

CONSIDER THIS

After a few hours of frolicking in the surf, you find you have drifted along the shore to a spot where the waves aren't breaking. Suddenly, you find yourself being drawn seaward by an invisible hand, no matter how vigorously you swim toward the beach. What is happening? What should you do, and why?

Ocean City, Maryland, is at the south end of Fenwick Island, one of the chain of barrier islands extending down the U.S. east coast from New York to Florida. It is a major and highly developed destination beach resort for the millions of people who live in the Baltimore/Washington/Philadelphia corridor. Long jetties were constructed near Ocean City in the 1930s to maintain the inlet between Fenwick and Assateague Island to the south. As a result, the beach has been stabilized at Ocean City—the north jetty blocked the southward long shore transport of sand—and the Assateague

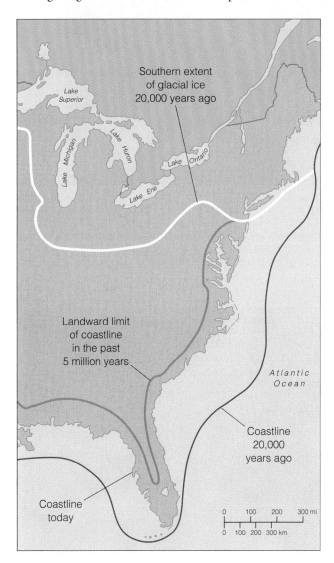

◆ **FIGURE 10.20** Position of the coastline in the eastern United States in late Pleistocene time (20,000 years ago), Miocene time (5 million years ago), and today. USGS data

(a)

Position of shoreline
▨ 1980
⬚ 1840

(b)

(c)

◆ **FIGURE 10.21** (a) Jetties built at Ocean City inlet in the 1930s cut off the supply of sand from the north. The north end of Assateague Island is now 500 meters shoreward of the south end of Fenwick Island. Source: J. S. Williams et. al., *Coasts in Crisis,* USGS circular 1075 (b) Using large pipes to pump sand from offshore onto the beach at Ocean City, Maryland. (c) Beach replenishment project at Ocean City, which is doing what it is designed to do, protect the buildings and give beachgoers more room to play.

Island beach has been displaced 500 meters (1,650 ft) shoreward due to sand starvation (◆Figure 10.21). Even though the Ocean City beach is relatively stable, the building of many large hotels and apartments mandates that the barrier island can migrate only at great expense. Indeed, it remains vulnerable despite all the building. A strong storm in March 1962 inundated all but the highest dune areas, causing $7.5 million worth of damage. Today the beach at Ocean City is routinely nourished by sand pumped from offshore. One can argue that this multimillion dollar investment in sand makes sense given the number of people who vacation there and the property that the beach protects.

In the 1920s Santa Barbara's civic leaders decided to mold their community into the "French Riviera" of California. In spite of unfavorable reports by the Corps of Engineers, city officials authorized construction of a long, L-shaped breakwater for a yacht anchorage in 1929 (◆Figure 10.22). The predominant drift direction here is southeasterly, and as the beach west of the breakwater grew wider, near-record erosion

◆ **FIGURE 10.22** The Santa Barbara, California, breakwater in 1988. Sand accumulation in the harbor is clearly visible, as is the dredge used to pump sand to the beaches downdrift.

★TABLE 10.2	Rates of Littoral Drift at Selected U.S. Locations	
Location	Drift Rate, yds³/yr	Direction
West Coast (all California)		
Newport Beach	300,000	south
Port Hueneme	290,000	south
Santa Barbara	250,000	south
Santa Monica	160,000	south
Anaheim Bay	90,000	south
East Coast		
Fire Island Inlet, N.Y.	350,000	west
Rockaway Beach, N.Y.	260,000	west
Sandy Hook, N.J.	250,000	north
Ocean City, N.J.	230,000	south
Palm Beach, Fla.	130,000	south
Great Lakes		
Waukegan, Ill.	43,000	south
Racine Co., Wis.	23,000	south

Sources: U.S. Army Corps of Engineers and other sources.

occurred on the beaches east of the structure. Eventually, the southeast-moving littoral drift traveled around the breakwater, forming a sandbar in the harbor entrance. The bar built up, diminishing the size of the harbor and creating a navigational hazard that remains to this day. When the Santa Barbara city fathers asked Will Rogers, the noted American humorist, what he thought of the harbor in the 1930s, he is alleged to have replied, "It would grow great corn if you could irrigate it." The drift rate here is about 250,000 cubic yards per year, which necessitates dredging sand from the harbor and pumping it to the beach about a mile downdrift. Summerland Beach, about 16 kilometers (10 mi) downdrift, retreated 75 meters (250 ft) in the decade following construction of the breakwater. ★ Table 10.2 compares this drift rate to that at other locations.

Communities along the shores of the Great Lakes have erosion problems also. Early in this century protective structures were built on the Lake Michigan shoreline. Many of these have now deteriorated, particularly during the record high lake-level of 1984 (582.9 feet above mean sea level). Lake levels began dropping around 1960, and there was little concern at the time about shoreline erosion. Since 1964 (record low of 576.6 feet above mean sea level), levels have been rising, and there is increasing public pressure to put more protective structures on the shoreline.

Sea Cliffs

Most people enjoy ocean views, particularly from atop a 100-foot-high sea cliff. Such cliffs are dynamic places, eroded both by wave action at the toe and by mass-wasting processes on the face and the top. An **active sea cliff** is one whose erosion is dominated by wave action. The result is a steep cliff face and little rock debris at the base. The erosion of an **inactive sea cliff** is dominated by running water and mass-wasting processes. Its slopes are much gentler, and angular debris accumulates at the toe. The nature of the debris at the foot of a sea cliff can aid in determining whether it is active or inactive. Wave erosion produces rounded cobbles, whereas mass wasting debris (talus) is angular. Long term, average rates of cliff erosion vary from a few centimeters to tens of centimeters per year, depending on the geology, climate, tectonic setting, and relative sea-level changes. Erosion can be gradual, grain-by-grain detachment, or can occur in large dramatic events such as rockfalls and landslides.

It is standard practice to consider 50 years as the lifetime of a house or other structure. Therefore, a structure should be set back from the top of a cliff at least 50 times the annual rate of cliff retreat. In all too many cases, the rates are not known or people choose to ignore them, with inevitable results (◆Figure 10.23). Orrin Pilkey of Duke University (see For Further Information) has developed a checklist for people to use when they are considering buying property on cliffs and bluffs. Pilkey's list includes such items as looking for evidence of failure at the toe of the cliff, determining rock hardness, and learning the history of cliff recession in the area from local land records and photographs.

Mitigation of Beach Erosion

Most coastal engineering works are built to protect the land from the sea. It is perhaps presumptuous to think we can build works that will shelter us from the rise of sea level or withstand enormous storm surges, but that does not keep some people from trying. Here are some examples of what has been done.

Rock revetments and concrete seawalls are built landward of the shoreline and parallel to the beach not to protect the beach but rather to protect the land and property behind them. Commonly, these "hard" structures reflect wave energy downward, removing sand and undermining the structure. There is a question among coastal engineers and geologists that goes something like "Do you want a revetment, or do you want a beach?" Because waves reflecting off hard shoreline structures remove the beach material in front of them, the best-designed rock revetments have sufficient permeability to absorb some of the wave energy. Another problem is that wave action erodes around the ends of revetments. When that happens, they must be extended to prevent damage to structures located there.

CONSIDER THIS

Several states have outlawed hard protective structures between beaches and the land. Why did they do this? Should other states, including those on the Great Lakes, enact similar legislation?

(b)

(a)

◆ **FIGURE 10.23** (a) Rapid sea-cliff retreat near Big Lagoon, Humboldt County, California. These cliffs near the Oregon border are composed of sandy and gravelly uplifted marine sediments. As shown by the photograph, they are subject to direct wave attack. (b) Drastic undercutting by wave action has left this house in San Diego County, California, in a precarious position. The near-vertical cliff and the rounded cobbles at the base indicate that this is an active sea cliff.

Groins are constructed to trap sand for the purpose of widening beaches. They trap sand on their upcurrent sides, thus depriving downcurrent beaches of sand. Once sand has built out to the end of a groin, it flows around the tip of it and begins filling in the eroded area downcurrent. Frequently another groin is built to widen *that* beach, and the cycle is repeated. The result is a beach with groins every few hundred feet and a shoreline with a scalloped or bread knife appearance (see Figure 10.7). The northern New Jersey shore and Miami Beach are textbook examples of multiple-groin shorelines. Permeable groins are often constructed today. They allow some sand to filter through them for nourishing downcurrent beaches. Jetties are similar to groins but longer and often installed in pairs on both sides of a harbor entrance or where a river flows into the sea. They have caused entire beaches and whole communities to disappear. The jetties at Ocean City, Maryland, have already been cited.

Breakwaters intended to create quiet water for yacht sanctuary can create unintended environmental problems. We have already seen the results of breakwater construction at Santa Barbara, California (see Figure 10.22). Venice Beach, California, a community with a reputation for the unusual, built a parallel breakwater. It was constructed so close to shore that the sand deposited in the wave "shadow" behind the breakwater has connected the breakwater to the land. This sand feature is called a **tombolo** (◆Figure 10.24).

At present, the designs of most long structures built perpendicular to the shoreline incorporate permanent *sand-bypassing works*. These features allow for the pumping of sand from the upcurrent side of the structure to nourish the beaches downcurrent. In addition, downcurrent beaches can

be artificially nourished by pumping in sand from offshore areas or by transporting it to them from land sources (Figure 10.21). Unfortunately, artificially nourished beaches are generally short-lived. One reason is that the imported sand is often finer than the native beach sand and is thus easily removed by the prevailing waves. The other reason is that artificial beaches usually have a steeper shore face and are therefore more subject to direct wave attack than are gently sloping, natural shorelines, which better dissipate wave energy offshore. Artificial beach nourishment is expensive, and it is most commonly done when large amounts of tourist dollars or infrastructure are at stake.

Although theory and models of shoreline behavior are improving, many shoreline-impact studies use scale models to evaluate various remediation schemes before they are

◆ **FIGURE 10.24** This breakwater at Venice, California, was built so close to the beach that sand deposited behind it has connected the breakwater to the beach, forming a tombolo.

◆ FIGURE 10.25 Scale model of King Harbor Marina, Redondo Beach, California. The model was built after the big storm of 1988 to aid in assessing potential damage from waves of varying height and source direction. Data from the model will be used to make future design improvements.

built. Physical modeling makes sense because beaches are complex systems with many feedbacks that might not be obvious at first glance or might be difficult to handle in a mathematical model. Such a model is an exact replica of the project but requires careful scaling of the materials and flows to compensate for differences in scale. The U.S. Army Corps of Engineers at its facility in Vicksburg, Mississippi has been at the forefront of such modeling efforts (◆Figure 10.25).

Hurricanes, Nor'easters, and Coastal Effects

Andrew, Mitch, Camille, Gilbert, Floyd, and *Katrina* are inno-cent sounding names, but onshore surges of water and intense rainfall produced by hurricanes (◆Figure 10.26) with such names are the greatest natural threat to humans. Hurricanes (called *typhoons* in the North Pacific Ocean and *cyclones* in the South Pacific and Indian Oceans) get their

(a)

(b)

◆ ACTIVE FIGURE 10.26 (a) Circulation patterns within a hurricane, showing inflow of air in the spiraling arms of the cyclonic system, rising air in the towering circular wall cloud, and outflow in the upper atmosphere. Subsidence of air in the storm's center produces the distinctive calm, cloud-less "eye" of the hurricane. (b) Satellite photograph of Hurricane Katrina as it comes ashore near New Orleans on August 29, 2005. Katrina's rotation and central eye are clearly visible.

energy from the equatorial oceans in the summer and early fall months when seawater is warmest, usually above 25°C (about 80°F). Hurricanes begin as tropical depressions when air that has been heated by the sun and ocean rises, creating reduced atmospheric pressure, clouds, and rain. As atmospheric pressure drops, the warm air moves toward the center of low pressure, what later may become the eye of the impending hurricane. When the moist rising air reaches higher elevations, the water vapor in it condenses and releases heat, causing the air to rise even faster and creating even lower atmospheric pressure and greater wind velocities. Wind blowing toward the center of low pressure is given a counterclockwise rotation by the Coriolis force in the northern hemisphere and a storm is born (see Figure 10.26).

How hurricanes cause damage

What began as a localized tropical disturbance, a few thunderstorms in the tropical Atlantic, can grow to be a monster storm, 800 kilometers (500 mi) across, with wind velocities far in excess of 120 kilometers per hour (74 mph), the lower velocity limit for hurricane designation. Hurricanes travel as coherent storms with forward velocities of 10 to 35 knots (12–40 mph). Their speed and course, and thus where and if they will strike land, are set by steering winds, which are controlled by the arrangement of large high and low pressure systems. In general, these steering winds guide hurricanes from their birth in the eastern Atlantic westward and then northward to their

graves over the cool North Atlantic or the continent of North America. However, hurricane tracks vary as widely as the arrangements of steering winds that guide them (◆Figure 10.27). Hurricanes are storms of the late summer and early fall because they need the energy contained in warm ocean water to grow strong (◆Figure 10.28).

CONSIDER   THIS

Although spring can be quite warm, there are rarely spring hurricanes. Why do you think that is the case?

What makes hurricanes so dangerous? Certainly the heavy rains they spawn cause massive flooding, but the worst actor in the hurricane story is wind. To understand the distribution of wind-induced damage from hurricanes, you must know something about where and how quickly hurricane winds blow. Let's start with the hurricane itself. The winds are wrapping counterclockwise around the eye as they do in all northern hemisphere storms (◆Figure 10.29). But this isn't the entire story, because the hurricane isn't standing still; it's moving along, being carried by the steering winds. Imagine yourself a television reporter. You are stationed to the east of New Orleans as hurricane Katrina comes ashore. The hurricane has winds of 120 mph, and it's moving toward you from the south at 12 mph. What wind speed do you feel

◆ **FIGURE 10.27** Hurricanes follow many different paths from their birth place in the tropical Atlantic to their demise, usually far to the west and north. Shown are tracks of all hurricanes from 1851 to 2006. NOAA/Ethan Gibney

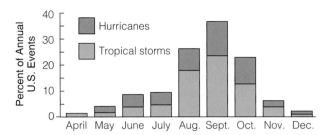

◆ **FIGURE 10.28** Hurricanes and tropical storms are most common in the late summer and early fall after the ocean has warmed in the strong summer sun. Source: From Zebrowsk, Perils of a restless planet, Fig 8.2, p 238, 1997 Cambridge Univ Press.

(◆Figure 10.30)? Since both the hurricane and steering winds are blowing in the same direction (from the south), you add them and feel winds of 132 mph. Now your colleague, working for the other network, happens to be stationed west of New Orleans. Here, the steering winds are blowing from the south, but the hurricane winds are blowing from the north. The result, your colleague feels only 113 mph winds (125 mph − 12 mph) winds. Still fierce, but 24 mph less than what you are feeling and showing your viewers. When a roof is about to fail, the 20 or 30 mph wind speed difference from one side of the hurricane to the other can make all the difference.

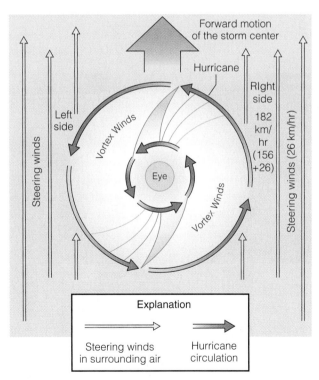

◆ **FIGURE 10.29** The hurricane is being steered by winds of 26 km/hr. The storm winds are 156 km/hr. On the right side of the storm, people on the ground feel 182 km/hr winds (156+26). What wind speed do people on the left side of the storm experience? Source: Modified from Nicholas Coch, 1994, Geologic Effects of Hurricanes, Geomorphology

◆ **FIGURE 10.30** Wind speed in hurricanes can be so high that it is difficult to stand unless of course you lean into the wind as this fellow is doing on August 25th, 2005 in south Florida where hurricane Katrina first made landfall.

Hurricane winds also drive **storm surges,** the mound of water pushed ahead of the hurricane that can cause sea level to rise many meters above the normal high-tide level (◆Figure 10.31). The storm surge is highest where the winds are moving most quickly (consider the scenario above). Katrina's storm surge that overtopped levees and flooded New Orleans came from the east of the city, where the right side of the hurricane and its strongest winds passed. The reduction in atmospheric pressure associated with a hurricane also causes sea level to rise—like fluid rising by suction in a soda straw. Average sea-level atmospheric pressure is 1,013 millibars (or 29.92 inches of mercury), and the rise in sea level is about 1 centimeter for every millibar of pressure drop. Hurricane Camille in 1969, the strongest storm to hit the U.S. mainland, had a near-record low barometric pressure of 905 millibars (26.61 inches of mercury). Hurricane surge and winds devastated the entire Gulf Coast from Florida to Texas.

◆ **FIGURE 10.31** Katrina's wind-driven storm surge was massive and severely damaged low-lying areas along the Gulf coast. Here the surge is coming over Highway 90 near Gulfport, Mississippi on August 29th, 2005.

◆ **FIGURE 10.32** The track a hurricane takes makes all the difference. Coast-parallel (CP) hurricanes do little damage to the east coast of North America because their strong winds and storm surge remain offshore. But when a hurricane hits the coast straight on (a coast-normal (CN) storm), the damage can be immense. Witness the storm surge in hurricane Katrina and the 1938 New England hurricane. Source: Image comes from Nicholas Coch, Geologic Effects of Hurricanes, Geomorphology, 1994

Hurricane tracks determine where and how severe the damage will be. Consider a hurricane approaching the coast (◆Figure 10.32). If the hurricane moves parallel to the coast, the strongest winds and the storm surge stay offshore. These are referred to as coast parallel or CP hurricane tracks. A hurricane that hits the coast at a right angle is a coast-normal or CN track. The full force of the storm surge is pushed ashore and the highest winds (remember where they are and why) slam into the coast. Katrina was a coast-normal storm both when it moved across Florida (going west) and when it moved over Louisiana (going north) and battered New Orleans (◆Figure 10.33). No wonder the damage was so immense.

Katrina was not the only coast normal storm to wreak havoc on the United States. Almost 70 years ago, long before weather satellites and hurricane chasers followed the every move of these storms, a late season hurricane of great fury snuck up on New England (◆Figure 10.34). The 1938 hurricane or New England hurricane (this was in the time before hurricanes were given proper names) slammed into Long Island with no warning. It was a fast-moving but devastating storm with steady winds of 121 mph and gusts reported to 186 mph. Wave heights of 50 feet were recorded in Gloucester, Massachusetts, and the storm surge rose 17 ft above normal high tide along the Rhode Island coast. Nearly 9,000 buildings and about 3,300 boats were destroyed; 63,000 people were left homeless. Even where there was little flooding, the winds on the right side of this

◆ **FIGURE 10.33** The track a hurricane takes makes all the difference. All three times hurricane Katrina hit land it was a coast normal storm pushing its highest winds and storm surge (to the right of the eyewall) ashore. Can you see from the graphs how wind speed and barometric pressure are related? What happens to both of these indications of storm strength after Katrina comes ashore? Source: These are NOAA data from the National Hurricane Center.

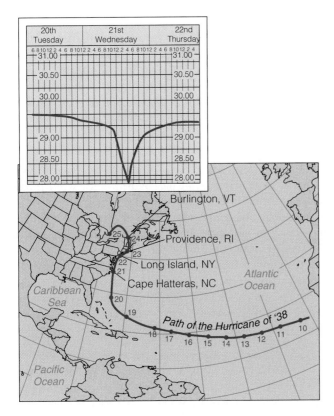

◆ **FIGURE 10.34** The 1938 hurricane roared into New England, slamming into Long Island and taking just about everyone by surprise. It was a fast-moving, coast-normal hurricane, which meant high wind speeds and a massive storm surge pounded communities to the right or east of the eye. Can you tell from the barometer trace how long the storm lingered over Long Island? Source: WGBH

fast moving storm caused terrible damage (◆ Figure 10.35), destroying 2 billion trees, many of which were in New Hampshire.

Hurricane examples

In 1969 Camille killed 130 people and three thousand homes simply disappeared. Yet real estate was resold, and new homes were built on the same sites where homes had been removed by the storm. Camille was rated as a category-5 hurricane, the highest category on the Saffir–Simpson Scale (⁎ Table 10.3). Indeed the number of intense hurricanes seems to be on the rise. A recent analysis published in *Science* magazine suggests that in the 1970s, there was a global average of fewer than a dozen category-4 and -5 hurricanes per year. Since 1990 that number has increased, averaging 18 per year globally. In 2005 three category-5 storms approached the United States; that's half the number of category-5 storms on record.

Some hurricanes veer eastward and follow a track up the U.S. East Coast, causing flooding and beach erosion from the Carolinas to Maine. In 1989 hurricane Hugo struck the coast just north of Charleston, South Carolina with sustained winds of more than 215 kilometers per hour and a storm surge of 6 meters (20 ft). Hurricane Floyd was the 1999 storm in North Carolina that wouldn't go away; it dropped 55 centimeters (20 in) of rain. Although not a strong hurricane, it created flooding of massive proportions in the eastern part of the state, aided by hurricane Dennis, which dropped 25 centimeters (10 in) of rain two weeks earlier. Thousands of square miles were underwater for weeks, and the flood area became a fetid swamp with the bodies of 10,000 hogs and 2.5 million chickens and turkeys.

CONSIDER THIS

"Why sweat a swamp?" is what some developers say about the fuss over preserving estuaries and marshlands. Is this attitude justified, or are these features valuable to the environment?

(a)

(b)

◆ **FIGURE 10.35** Damage from the 1938 New England hurricane differed depending on location. (a) Near the coast, huge waves and the storm surge ripped apart infrastructure and tossed homes around like toys as shown here in eastern Connecticut. (b) Further inland, wind was the primary agent of destruction. In Hartford, Vermont homes were damaged as massive trees were felled by the hurricane's wind.

★TABLE 10.3   Saffir–Simpson Hurricane Scale

Category	Wind Velocity		Damage	Examples
	km/h	mph		
1	119–153	74–95	minimal	Agnes, 1972
				Juan, 1985
2	154–178	96–110	moderate	David, 1979
				Bob, 1991
3	179–210	111–130	extensive	Betsy, 1965
				Frederic, 1979
4	211–250	131–155	extreme	Hugo, 1989
				Andrew, 1992
				Opal, 1995
5	>250	>155	catastrophic	Labor Day, 1935
				Camille, 1969

Source: Coastal Weather Research Center, University of South Alabama, Mobile.

In 1970 a tropical cyclone in East Pakistan (now Bangladesh) resulted in perhaps the deadliest coastal flooding of all times, with a death toll of more than 300,000 people. Dissatisfaction with the central government of Pakistan's response to the tragedy led to the formation of Bangladesh, a new country separated from Pakistan. Another tragedy in 1991 that killed 60,000 led to the formation of a tropical-cyclone forecasting center. Experts at the center recommended construction of raised concrete bunkers above storm-surge level for refuge. A fierce cyclone in 1998 left thousands homeless but killed only 200 people. One of the problems in less-developed countries is overpopulation, which forces people to settle on land that is subject to life-threatening natural hazards. Bangladesh is about the size of Wisconsin, with a population of 117 million, about half the population of the United States. Even in areas where people were warned of the 1991 storm, many were reluctant to leave their few possessions to looters.

Lest we think such tragedies are limited to less-developed countries, we should look to Galveston, Texas, in September 1900. A hurricane traveled across the Gulf of Mexico and struck the barrier island upon which Galveston is built. The hurricane struck with such force that it smashed 3,600 wooden structures and drowned over 6,000 people, the largest toll from a natural disaster in American history. Nellie Carey, who lived through the disaster, wrote in a letter: "Thousands of dead in the streets—the gulf and bay strewn with dead bodies . . . . Not a drop of water—food scarce. The dead are not identified at all—they throw them on drays and take them to barges, where they are loaded like

cord wood, and taken out to sea to be cast into the waves . . . ." The letter was reprinted in its entirety in a book published shortly after the disaster. Today, Galveston is one of the leading cities to deal with evacuation in case of a hurricane. Given the failure to promptly and completely evacuate low-lying areas of New Orleans in the face of hurricane Katrina, it's not clear we as a society have learned all we can from past disasters.

Hurricane Predictors

We know that hurricanes are part of the tropical weather pattern and that they will occur seasonally every year. Meteorologist William Gray at Colorado State University has developed an empirical prediction system that can foretell the severity of the upcoming hurricane season. His work is based on understanding the two most important ingredients needed to make strong hurricanes: warm sea-surface temperatures and an atmosphere with little shear so that hurricanes, once they start to form vertical circulations, are not ripped apart by the steering winds. Gray's model uses the following data:

- Tropospheric winds up to an altitude of 12,000 meters (40,000 ft). Strong winds in the troposphere work against hurricanes by shearing off the tops of their circulation.

- West African climate. Dry years in Africa promote high altitude winds from the west above the tropical Atlantic, increasing the shear between upper and lower levels of the atmosphere and diminishing the strength of hurricanes. During wet years, winds blow from the east at 12,000 meters, greatly reducing wind shear and thus promoting hurricane-strength storms.

- El Niño. The warming of the equatorial Pacific Ocean promotes westerly winds that blow into the Caribbean and Atlantic basins, where trade winds blow at lower levels from the east. This promotes wind shear that knocks down hurricane buildups. Between 1991 and 1994 repeated El Niños resulted in few hurricanes. In 1995 and 1999 El Niños gave way to a cooling of the equatorial Pacific Ocean (La Niña), and hurricane activity greatly increased.

- Atmospheric pressure. Low atmospheric pressure in the Atlantic Ocean and Caribbean Sea indicates areas of warm water, which fuel hurricanes, promote convergence of air masses, and stimulate vertical buildups of moisture-laden clouds.

Although Gray's model has a good record of predicting the intensity of any one hurricane season, it's up to seasoned forecasters to predict both the track and strength of any individual hurricane after it is born. The National Weather service is charged with this duty, and they have made great advances in the accuracy of their predictions over the past two decades. Forecasters are aided in their

(a)   (a)

◆ **FIGURE 10.36** Hurricane prediction capability is improving. (a) Satellite image of Hurricane Isabel before it made landfall. (b) The National Weather Service 5-day-forecast track for Hurricane Isabel, showing where the storm was likely to go and when. Such data form the basis for informed decisions about who to evacuate and when those evacuations should begin. Source: NOAA

work by several sources of data. First, they use sophisticated atmospheric models to predict the behavior of steering winds that help determine both the track of the hurricane and the degree of shearing that could tear the storm apart. Second, they use data collected real-time by hurricane—hunter planes that fly right through the beasts, collecting wind and pressure data. Third, they rely on over 100 years of hurricane history to understand how such storms behave along different parts of the Gulf and Atlantic coasts. The work of many forecasters at the National Hurricane Center in Miami is condensed into track and intensity prediction maps (◆ Figure 10.36). The improvement in hurricane forecasting accuracy is impressive. Today the accuracy of 5-day hurricane forecasts matches that of the 3-day forecasts only a decade ago.

Nor'easters

The east coast of North America is lucky enough to be affected by major coastal storms pretty much all year round. Although we and the media focus heavily on the hurricanes that threaten eastern North America in the summer and fall, during the winter, other powerful storms, termed nor'easters, threaten the Atlantic Coast. Their name comes from the direction that their winds most frequently blow on shore as the storms track north just off the east coast. These are winter and spring storms that differ not only in season but in many other ways from hurricanes. Nor'easters are cold storms, born in the western Atlantic. They are usually triggered by small low pressure systems moving from the west and then develop explosively along the east coast, often getting their start off Cape Hatteras. Nor'easters are huge and can be slow moving, lingering for days. Their strength and persistence create particular hazards

as they can bring record winter snows (see Figure 9.3) and dramatically alter coastlines as wave heights can build over days and relentlessly pound beaches and sea walls.

Perhaps the best known nor'easter is the Halloween storm of 1991, which pummeled New England with huge seas and is featured both in the book and movie, *The Perfect Storm*. The Halloween storm was massive and devastating, affecting much of the northeastern United States and Atlantic Canada (◆ Figure 10.37). It took the lives of fisherman at sea, (yes, George Clooney went down with the ship), and demolished many shorefront homes that had stood for a century or more. The Bush family compound in Kennebunkport, Maine suffered serious damage from the pounding surf.

◆ **FIGURE 10.37** Here's the Perfect Storm, the Halloween Storm, or the nor'easter of late October 1991 as it batters the northeastern United States and Atlantic Canada. The storm is so large it extends from Georgia to Labrador!

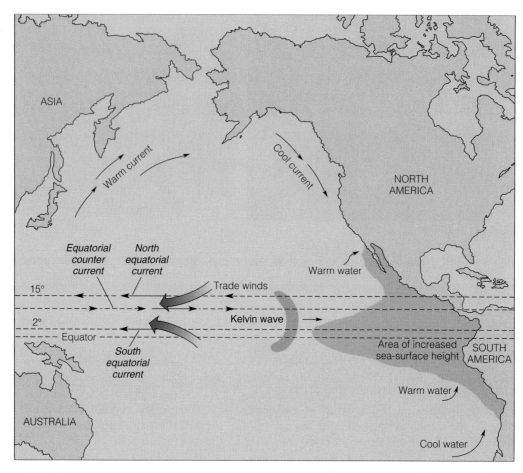

◆ **FIGURE 10.38** Oceanography, meteorology, and geography of an El Niño. At the onset, tradewinds maintain warm equatorial currents toward the east. As El Niño begins, the tradewinds weaken, and the equatorial countercurrent strengthens. This creates Kelvin waves, surges of warm water moving eastward. When a Kelvin wave reaches the Americas, it divides northward and southward, traveling along the west coasts.

El Niño and the Coastal Zone

El Niño is a perturbation, or disruption, of the normal coldwater conditions that exist along the west coasts of North and South America. During El Niño years high-pressure cells replace the normally low atmospheric pressure of the western Pacific Ocean. Because the pressure difference that drives the trade winds between the eastern Pacific and the western Pacific lessens, the trade winds stop, or may even reverse direction. A bulge of warm surface water (as much as a meter high) called a *Kelvin wave* surges eastward toward the coast of the Americas and displaces the cooler water there (◆Figure 10.38). First noticed by Peruvian fishermen around Christmas time in 1892, this invasion of warm water was dubbed the *Corriente del Niño* ("Current of the Christ Child"). Today, the atmospheric pressure reversal in the western Pacific region,

called the *southern oscillation,* is known to be the trigger for El Niño events. We now call this connection and the ensuing warm-water events the **El Niño–Southern Oscillation,** usually shortened to its easily articulated acronym, **ENSO.**

Significant El Niño events of 1972–1973 and 1976–1977 and the super El Niño of 1982–1983 established it as a global phenomenon. An almost continuous El Niño condition persisted from 1991 to 1994 (◆Figure 10.39), and then another super El Niño occurred in 1997–1998. During El Niño years, because of atmospheric convection shifts, there have been drought in Africa, Australia, and Indonesia; flooding in California, Ecuador, Peru, and Tahiti; and impressive storm waves and beach erosion along both the east and west coasts of the United States. More bad news was the unprecedented number of landslides and debris flows in California, Oregon,

◆ **FIGURE 10.39** The numbers on the left side of the graph are an ENSO index that incorporates these measured parameters: air temperature, atmospheric pressure, cloudiness, and wind speed and direction. El Niño events are shown in red (+); La Niña events, in blue (−). From *Meteorology Today*, 6th ed., by C. D. Ahrens, Brooks/Cole, 2000

and Washington during the 1997–1998 event. According to Jim O'Brien at the Center for Ocean–Atmosphere Prediction Studies (COAPS) at Florida State University, there is also good news. El Niño:

- decreases Atlantic hurricane activity;
- reduces forest fires in Arizona, Texas, and New Mexico;
- reduces tornadoes;
- produces better citrus and vegetable crops; and
- improves the fishing off California because of warm water.

Interestingly, Hawaiian hurricanes occur only during El Niño years. El Niño is a good example of Earth functioning as a system—the atmosphere, hydrosphere, and lithosphere interacting to create natural events. El Niño's "sister," La Niña, appears to be a media concoction. La Niña is a cold-water condition, which most experts call the normal condition for the west coast of the Americas. Even though it has been linked to drought and increased hurricane activity by the media, a direct scientific connection has yet to be demonstrated.

CASE STUDY 10.1

Distant Tsunamis—The Silent Threat

Ample warning had been given the residents of Hawaii as the Chilean tsunami raced across the Pacific Ocean at jetliner speeds. A warning had been issued about 6:45 P.M. on May 22, 1960 that large waves were expected to reach Hilo on the Island of Hawaii at about midnight. Coastal warning sirens had wailed at 8:30 P.M., and continued for half an hour.

At midnight a wave arrived, but it was only a few feet high. Hundreds of people had stayed home, and those who had left assumed the danger was over and returned home. Then, another wave appeared, and another. The highest wave struck at 1:04 A.M. (◆ Figure 1). Sixty-one people died, and another 282 suffered severe injuries. A restaurant memorialized the event with a waterline on its window (◆ Figure 2).

The city of Hilo, with its bay facing northeast toward the Aleutian trench, is a coastal section with high expected wave heights. This is due to its orientation and the bay's funnel shape, which concentrates tsunami energy. An engineering study in the aftermath of the 1960 tsunami resulted in some interesting recommendations for mitigating tsunami damage in that city. For example, parking meters in the run-up

◆ **FIGURE 1** Water-level measurements beneath the Wailuku River bridge during the first hours of the tsunami of May 23, 1960.

CONTINUED

area were bent flat in the direction of debris-laden wave travel (◆Figure 3), with the direction varying throughout the affected area. It was recommended that new structures be situated with their narrowest dimension aligned in the direction indicated by nearby bent parking

meters. Several waterfront structures had open fronts that allowed water to pass through them. Waterfront buildings are now designed with open space on ground level, so that damage from the impact of water and debris can be minimized.

◆ **FIGURE 2** A line painted on the window of a rebuilt restaurant commemorates the height to which the tsunami waters rose. Can you explain why the tsunami waves are not tidal waves as the notation on the window suggests?

◆ **FIGURE 3** Parking meters bent by the 1960 tsunami at Hilo, Hawaii. The meters resemble arrows aligned with the direction of wave runup.

CASE STUDY 10.2

A Moving Experience

Cape Hatteras Lighthouse, with its black-and-white, candy-cane paint job, is the tallest brick lighthouse in the world. Built in 1870 with state-of-the-art lenses, the 63-meter (208-ft) structure is so distinctive that it is on the National Register of Historic Places. Besides saving lives, the lighthouse has hosted millions of visitors. It is one of the most enduring landmarks in North Carolina and the nation. This part of the Outer Banks, designated the Cape Hatteras National Seashore by Congress, is a protected environment (◆Figure 1).

Fixed structures built on the shifting sands of barrier islands are inevitably at the mercy of beach erosion and, ultimately, direct wave action. This is because all U.S. barrier islands have been "migrating" shoreward due to the rise in sea level over the past few thousand years. When it was built in 1870, the lighthouse was 463 meters

(1,500 ft) from the ocean. By 1919 the sea had come to within 100 meters (310 ft) of its base and, by 1935, to within 30 meters (100 ft). When it comes to a battle of man against the sea, the sea eventually wins. Illustrating the futility of shore-protection efforts during times of rising sea level, the National Park Service and the Corps of Engineers spent millions of dollars attempting to save the beloved lighthouse—constructing groins to trap sand, replenishing beaches and artificially depositing a barrier-sand-dune system in front of the structure, installing offshore wave-energy dissipaters, and finally, constructing hard structures such as seawalls that reflect wave energy. By the 1980s the sea was lapping at the base of the lighthouse, and more extraordinary measures were required to save the structure. The National Park Service decided to move the lighthouse in 1990.

Moving structures of great weight has become easier with the development of modern hydraulic systems. The massive Cape Hatteras Lighthouse was moved by using horizontally mounted "pusher" jacks that pushed it along a track system in five-foot increments. The move took just 22 days, 19 of which were "pushing" days. A remarkable engineering feat, indeed (◆ Figure 2).

The powerful light that had been out for nine months was relit on Saturday, November 13, 1999 at ceremonies on the original lighthouse site in Buxton, North Carolina.

◆ **FIGURE 1** North Carolina's Outer Banks are a chain of islands composed of sand that form a barrier between lagoons and the ocean. Cape Hatteras, near the center of the photo, juts the farthest out into the Atlantic.

◆ **FIGURE 2** Ready . . .

Rolling . . .

Home safe

CASE STUDY 10.3

Katrina—How could it be so bad?

New Orleans and hurricanes are the stuff of textbooks and movies. Earlier editions of the book you are now reading and just about every other geology, geography, and natural hazards textbook and hurricane movie has for years presented New Orleans as the city waiting to flood. So why then, with increasingly accurate hurricane track and intensity forecasts (see Figure 10.36) and a scientific consensus that the city was a sitting duck, did more than 1,300 people die, and why were nearly a million more left homeless? The simple answer is that the levees failed, some before their design limits had been met (see Case Study 9.2). Once the levees breached (◆Figure 1), water from the storm surge poured in and inundated the low-lying areas of the city (◆Figure 2). The pumps were overwhelmed and the damage had been done. The more complex answer, stated so clearly by Michael Ignatieff in the *New York Times*, is

that the unstated societal contract between the American people and their government was broken—the federal and local governments were simply not there when tens of thousands of people were left to fend for themselves in squalid conditions under the roofs of the damaged convention center and Superdome (◆Figure 3).

Katrina will not be the last major hurricane to slam a North American city. Indeed, it may be one of many in the coming years. The year 2005 was the most active hurricane season on record in the Atlantic. There were more named storms than ever before, forcing the weather service to start over with the first letters of the Greek alphabet as they named late season storms. Why the uptick in storms? Perhaps it's because hurricane frequency is known to vary over decadal cycles; but perhaps it's due to warming of the sea surface. Because hurricanes are heat engines, driven

by warm ocean water, this is a plausible mechanism for increasing the energy available for storm formation and maintenance. Two recent studies now suggest that the total energy released by hurricanes, as well as the frequency of strong hurricanes, is increasing. (◆Figure 4). This is a frightening finding. As global warming raises sea level, storms last longer and their winds blow harder—a triple whammy.

What can be done in the face of rising sea-level and increasing storm frequency and energy release? Proposals for New Orleans include raising and strengthening the levee system, raising the land with fill before rebuilding, abandoning low-lying neighborhoods, and restoring the marshlands that help dissipate storm energy. Only time will tell if there is sufficient political will to act responsibly on the scientific data that already exist.

◆ **FIGURE 1** A week after hurricane Katrina, a helicopter drops a load of sandbags into a New Orleans levee breach.

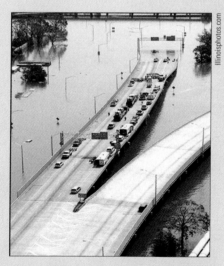

◆ **FIGURE 2** Search and rescue teams in the days after Katrina used interstate highway ramps as boat launches to rescue people from flooded parts of the city.

◆ **FIGURE 3** Residents of New Orleans who could not or would not evacuate lining up to enter the Superdome as a shelter of last resort from hurricane Katrina.

◆ **FIGURE 4** Two studies that came out in *Science* and *Nature* within weeks of hurricane Katrina striking New Orleans suggest that the potential for hurricane damage has been rising over the past 30 years. Could it be that global warming and the increase in sea surface temperatures it causes is the driving force behind changing hurricane dynamics? Time will tell. (a) The number of strong hurricanes (category 4 and 5) has been increasing globally since 1970. (b) Both sea surface temperature and total energy release from tropical storms in the Atlantic Ocean have been increasing in lockstep over the past 50 years. Storms are lasting longer and their winds are more intense. Does correlation mean causation in this case? Source: (a) Webster et al., *Science*, vol. 309, p., 1844; (b) Kerry Emanuel, *Nature*, vol. 436 (4), August 2005.

CASE STUDY 10.4

Tsunami—A Quarter Million Perish

Indonesia is no stranger to earthquakes, volcanic eruptions, and other spasms of our restless planet. Yet, within hours after the largest earthquake to strike Earth in 40 years (since the Alaskan and Chilean quakes of 1964) shook the region on December 26, 2004, the shoreline was unrecognizable and hundreds of thousands of people lay dead or dying. What happened that December day?

The magnitude 9.0 quake originated 10 kilometers below the surface, where the Indian and the Burma plates meet in a locked subduction zone. When over 1000 kilometers of the fault slipped, the seafloor rose 15 meters in places. Areas close to the quake had little warning as waves, moving at the speed of jet

planes, followed the quake within tens of minutes. One coastal city, Banda Ache, on the island of Sumatra, was hit especially hard and fast. Nearly a third of its residents were dead or missing as the result of numerous tsunami waves that surged through the city. The waves, and the debris they carried, smashed everything in their path. Field measurements show that the tsunami waves, when they came ashore, were astonishingly high; in some places run ups exceeded 30 meters. Homes, businesses, and people were simply swept away (◆ Figure 1).

The damage was not limited to area near the quake. As the waves spread across the Indian Ocean, so did the tragedy (◆ Figure 2).

In just a few hours, beach resorts in Thailand were demolished. Just after, the coast of Sri Lanka was assaulted by the waves and finally, hours later, the east coast of Africa, where sufficient warning prevented tragedy. The wave moved across the Indian Ocean for thousands of kilometers and could even be detected in the Atlantic Ocean.

What can be done to prevent this and similar tragedies from reoccurring (◆ Figure 3)? Simple measures such as public education about what to do when the Earth shakes can save lives. A coordinated, regionwide warning system that relays information (much like that already in place to warn of cyclone hazards) would likely save even more lives.

CONTINUED

Establishing a direct tsunami monitoring system in the Indian Ocean (much like the one in the Pacific Ocean, see Figure 10.12) is under discussion. In an eerie parallel to post-Katrina analyses, some in India have suggested replanting mangroves to diffuse tsunami energy. The coastal trees and the swamps they create moderate tsunami waves in the same way coastal wetlands tame storm surges. Some people are taking matters into their own hands. If you live in the region and own a Nokia cell phone, you can download a program that uses real-time USGS earthquake data to warn of potential tsunami hazards.

◆ **FIGURE 1** A week after the December 26, 2004 tsunami, flooding and damage to a village near the coast of Sumatra, Indonesia is on a scale so massive that it is hard to comprehend. Can you find the limit of inundation in this image that indicates how far the tsunami ran inland?

◆ **FIGURE 2** The Indonesian tsunami affected countries all around the ocean basin. Some of the waves traveled thousands of kilometers before crashing ashore. Source: USGS Soundwaves, Issue 68, Dec 2004/January 2005.

◆ **FIGURE 3** The Indonesian tsunami may be the most deadly we know of but it is not the first nor will it likely be the last tsunami to cause major losses of life and property. Source: Adapted from Spacedaily.com/Michael Paine. Data from *Tsunami: The Underrated Hazard*, Edward Bryant, Cambridge Univ. Press, 2001

GALLERY

Reminders of Nature's Force

The following photographs are good examples of the earth system at work—the interaction of solid earth, the atmosphere, and the oceans. ◆Figure 1 reminds us of the futility of human efforts to hold back the sea. Hurricane Camille also left her reminder of nature's forces (◆Figure 2). The State of New York has proved to be a slow learner as elevated stilt houses, formerly at sand level, have made their appearance because big surf of nor'easters and hurricanes moved the beach out from below. (◆Figure 3).

◆ **FIGURE 1** A revetment's half-ton to one-ton stone blocks were lifted and hurled through the walls and windows of a living space they were intended to protect; Hurricane Hugo, 1989.

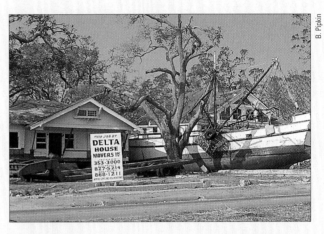

◆ **FIGURE 2** Delta House Movers appeared to have added boat-moving services after Hurricane Camille in 1969; Gulfport, Mississippi.

◆ **FIGURE 3** "Watch that first step!" would be a good warning to anyone exiting these stilt houses that once rested on the beach. Strong waves reduced the beach level almost four meters during one storm; Westhampton, New York.

307

Summary

Waves

Cause

Wind blowing over the water surface creates ripples, then stormy irregular seas, and finally regularly spaced swell that outruns the source area.

Factors of Size

Wave size depends upon wind velocity, the length of time wind blows over the water, and fetch. A fully developed sea has the highest waves attainable for the three variables.

Motion

Water parcels move in circular paths to a depth of half the wavelength, called *wave base*. This wind causes movement of the waveform known as *waves of oscillation*. Water physically moves shoreward when waves break in the surf zone. These breaking waves are called *waves of translation*.

Types of Breakers

Steep offshore slopes develop plunging breakers, and gentle slopes produce spilling breakers.

Wave Refraction

Waves generally approach the shore at some prevailing angle. This results in longshore currents that move sand along the beach. The transported sand is known as *longshore drift*. Groins act as dams to longshore drift, causing sand to be deposited upcurrent and eroded downcurrent. Wave refraction concentrates wave energy on points and dissipates it in bays, thus tending to straighten an irregular shoreline.

Impulsively Generated Waves

Also known as tsunamis (Japanese for harbor wave), they are mostly generated by seismic activity, but also are generated by submarine volcanic action, landslides, or bolide impacts. They have long wave lengths (hundreds of kilometers) and low amplitudes (about a meter) at sea, but transform to an impressive breaker or surge at the shoreline. Causes and death tolls over the last 2,000 years are given, as well as regions most susceptible to tsunamis. The 2004 Indonesian tsunami killed nearly a quarter million people.

Beaches

Defined

Narrow strips of shore that are washed by the waves or tides, usually covered by sand or pebbles.

Beach Erosion

Defined

Less sand is supplied by longshore drift than is removed by wave action.

Natural Causes

1. Drought
2. Rising sea level

Human Causes

1. Dams that impound sediment on rivers
2. Groins, jetties, and breakwaters that impound sediment
3. Hard structures such as seawalls and revetments
4. Human-induced climate warming and the resulting rise in sea level.

Mitigation

Design of groins, breakwaters, and jetties can incorporate features that allow sand to pass through or around them. Seawalls, revetments, and artificial nourishment are only temporary solutions. Model studies of existing structures and shorelines help us better understand the problem and thus to effect remedies.

Sea Cliffs

Defined

Cliffs formed and/or maintained by wave action.

Types

Active and inactive.

Erosion

Annual rates between a centimeter and tens of centimeters.

Mitigation

Structures' optimal (safest) setback from the edge of a cliff can be determined when the erosion rate is known.

Estuaries

Defined

Basins open to the sea in which fresh water mixes with seawater.

Types

1. Coastal-plain estuaries, drowned river valleys (Chesapeake Bay, site of an ancient bolide impact)
2. Fiords, drowned glacial valleys (Alaska)
3. Fault-block estuaries (south San Francisco Bay)
4. Bar-formed estuaries landward of barrier beaches (Laguna Madre, Texas)

Importance

Estuaries and their surrounding wetlands are areas of high biological productivity for marine life and waterfowl.

Human Impact

Used for dumping sewage, commercial fishing, transportation, and recreation. Structures are built on filled marshland.

Coastal Flooding

Hurricanes

Storms in the Atlantic Basin generated at sea and characterized by counterclockwise winds greater than 120 kilometers/hour (74 mph). They travel across the sea at velocities of 10–35 knots (12–40 mph).

Flood Danger

A storm surge is a "mound" of water pushed up by high winds and low atmospheric pressure. It may be many meters above normal high-tide levels. Storm surges on low-lying deltas such as the Ganges River delta in Bangladesh are the greatest natural hazard to human life.

Case Histories

Hurricanes Camille (1969), Hugo (1988), Floyd (1999), Isabel (2003) and Katrina (2005) are described.

El Niño (ENSO)

Associated with floods, landslides, and accelerated beach erosion. Also associated with decreased hurricane activity in the Atlantic, fewer tornadoes in the Midwest and fewer forest fires in the Southwest, and better fruit and vegetable crops. Hawaii experiences hurricanes only in ENSO years.

Hurricane Prediction

Utilizes models of steering winds and data on tropospheric winds, West African climate, El Niño, sea-surface temperature, and atmospheric pressure. Heat is the fuel that drives hurricanes.

Key Terms

active sea cliff	inactive sea cliff	spit	wave of translation
barrier island	jetty	storm surge	wave refraction
bolide	longshore drift	tombolo	
fetch	longshore current	wave base	
groin	rip current	wave of oscillation	

Study Questions

1. Why do submarines not experience severe storms at sea?
2. What shoreline structures impede littoral drift and cause beach erosion? How may these structures' impact be mitigated to minimize damage?
3. Where and when do hurricanes originate, and how do they obtain their energy? Distinguish a hurricane from a typhoon and a cyclone.
4. Name two types of breaker shapes and explain what causes one or the other to occur along a given shoreline.
5. How does the width of a beach vary naturally over the year? Where is the sand stored that is removed from the beach in winter and returned to the foreshore in summer?
6. What is a storm surge, and why is it such a danger in low-lying coastal communities?
7. How do long shore currents develop, and how do they impact beaches and *swimmers* in the surf zone?
8. How can hazardous currents in the surf zone be recognized?
9. Why do warm ocean temperatures stimulate hurricane development?

For Further Information

Books and Periodicals

American Geophysical Union. 2006. Hurricanes and the U.S. Gulf Coast: science and sustainable rebuilding. http://www.agu.org/report/hurricanes/

Bascom, Willard. 1964. *Waves and beaches*. Garden City, N.Y.: Doubleday.

Beardsley, Tim. 2000. Dissecting a hurricane. *Scientific American*, 282, no. 3, March.

Bearak, Barry. 2005. The day the sea came. *New York Times Magazine*, November 27.

Bryant, Edward. 2001. *Tsunami—the underrated hazard*. Cambridge, U.K.: Cambridge University Press.

Coch, N. K. 1994. *Geologic effects of hurricanes*. Geomorphology and natural hazards. M. Morisawa. Amsterdam, Elsevier: 37–64.

Dean, Cornelia. 1999. *Against the tide: the battle for America's beaches*. New York: Columbia University Press.

Field, M. E., Susan Cochran, and Kevin R. Evans. 2002. *U.S. coral reefs—imperiled national treasures*. U.S. Geological Survey fact sheet 025-02, 4 pp.

Gonzalez, Frank. 1999. Tsunami, *Scientific American,* May, p. 56–65.

Griggs, G. and L. Savoy, Eds. 1985. *Living with the California coast.* Durham, N.C.: Duke University Press.

Ignatieff, Michael. 2005. The broken contract. *The New York Times Magazine,* September 25, p. 15–17

Kaufman W. and Orrin Pilkey. 1979. *The beaches are moving.* Garden City, N.Y.: Anchor Press/Doubleday.

National Oceanographic and Atmospheric Administration (NOAA). 1996. *Hurricanes—a preparedness guide.* Washington D.C.: U.S. Government Printing Office.

Scientific American. The oceans. 1998. *Scientific American Quarterly.* Fall.

Sheets, Bob and Jack Williams. 2001. *Hurricane watch.* New York: Vintage Books.

Shinn, E. A. 1993. Geology and human activity in the Florida Keys. *Public issues in energy and marine geology* (U.S. Geological Survey), October.

Williams, J. S., K. Dodd, and Kathleen Gohn. 1990. *Coasts in crisis.* U.S. Geological Survey circular 1075.

Wolanski, Eric, Robert Richmond, Laurence McCook, and Hugh Swanson. 2003. Mud, marine snow and coral reefs. *American Scientist* 91, pp. 44–51, January.

ThomsonNOW™

Assess your understanding of this chapter's topics with additional comprehensive interactivities at http://www.thomson.com/login, which also has up-to-date web links, additional readings, and exercises.

Glaciation and Long-Term Climate Change

Perhaps the most visually obvious example of current climate change is the worldwide retreat of mountain glaciers. Some 80 percent of Kenya's Mount Kilimanjaro's has disappeared since about 1970, and of the 150 glaciers that graced Montana's Glacier National Park in 1910, fewer than 30 remain (◆ Figure 1). Changes in these mountain glaciers are significant because they

(a)

(b)

◆ **FIGURE 1** (a) Grinell Glacier, Glacier National Park, Montana, in 1911.(b) Grinell Glacier in 1998. In the 87 years since photo (a) was taken, about 120 glaciers within Glacier National Park have disappeared.

> The ice was here, the ice was there, The ice was all around; It cracked and growled and roared and howled, Like noises in a swound!
>
> —Samuel Taylor Coleridge, *The Rime of the Ancient Mariner* (1798)

are highly sensitive to temperature fluctuations. Their reaction time is much shorter than the vast ice sheets of Antractica and Greenland, and they provide significant information about twentieth-century global warming.

The discovery by two hikers in 1991 of the remains of a 5,200-year-old Neolithic "ice man" that had melted out of a glacier high in a mountain pass in northern Italy made eye-catching newspaper headlines (◆ Figure 2). The discovery proved to be a treasure trove of information for archeologists about the life of a Neolithic person who lived and died well before the time of ancient Greek civilization. A glacier typically melts only in its lower part, but because the "ice man" was found high up on an Italian glacier at 3,200 meters (10,500 ft), the discovery signified to glaciologists and climatologists that the ice was undergoing intensive melting throughout as a consequence of climate warming. Such shrinkage of glaciers is seen worldwide: in South America, the European Alps, Greenland's outlet glaciers, central Asia, tropical Africa, Irian Jaya, northwest America, California's Sierra Nevada, Svalbard, Scandinavia, Iceland, New Zealand, and Alaska.

◆ **FIGURE 2** The "ice man," the 5,200-year-old remains of a man discovered melting out of high-mountain ice by hikers in northern Itlay.

Less-obvious consequences of global warming are the decreased snowfalls in New England, 15 percent since 1953; Australia, 30 percent since 1960; rising ocean temperatures, up to 2° F since 1985; a global rise in sea level, as much as 7.8 inches during the twentieth century; and, beginning in the 1960s, the shifting of the ranges of plants, birds, and insects to higher latitudes and to higher altitudes in order to accommodate warming. No longer is it a question of whether global warming is happening. Instead, it is a question of what can we do about it.

Glaciers advance and retreat in response to cyclic changes in Earth's orbital elements and to global climate changes and consequently may provide evidence of past climates. In order to understand better global climate changes over time, and the effects of such changes on the landscape, we will first examine glaciers and glaciation. Important in understanding climates are the interrelationships of the atmospheric, oceanic, and biologic systems with plate tectonics and the orbital elements of the Earth-Sun-Moon system.

Glaciation

About 97 percent of Earth's water is in the oceans, and three-fourths of the remainder (2.25%) is in **glaciers.** A tenth of Earth's land area is covered by glaciers at present, the same amount that is cultivated globally. During the Pleistocene Epoch, which radiometric dating places as beginning 1.6 million years ago and lasting until about 10,000 years ago,

as much as 30 percent of Earth was covered by glaciers (◆ Figure 11.1). Today's glaciers store enormous amounts of fresh water, more than exists in all of the lakes, ponds, reservoirs, rivers, and streams of North America. Farmers in the Midwest grow corn and soybeans in soils of glacial origin, Bunker Hill in Boston is a glacial feature, and the numerous smooth, polished, and grooved bedrock outcroppings in New York City's Central Park were eroded by a glacier that flowed out of Canada. Glaciers in the Himalayas, Norway, Switzerland, Alaska, Washington State, Alberta, and British Columbia exert a vital effect on regional water supplies during dry seasons. They do this by supplying a natural base flow of meltwater to rivers that helps to balance the annual and seasonal variations in precipitation. Meltwater from glaciers serves as the principal source of domestic water in Switzerland. The Arapahoe Glacier is an important water source for Boulder, Colorado, so much so that Boulder residents take pride in telling visitors that their water comes from a melting glacier. (Actually, the glacier is only one part of a drainage basin of several tributaries that together supply the city's water.)

The steady water supply provided by melting glaciers during long periods of summer drought is widely used as a water resource for generating hydroelectric power in many temperate regions of the world. Utilization of glacial meltwater is highly developed in Norway and Switzerland, for example. Switzerland's hydropower stations, built mainly in the 1950s and 1960s, use water from melting snow and glacial ice. Dams store the meltwater in the summer, when electrical consumption is low in that country, and in winter,

(a)

(b)

◆ **FIGURE 11.1** Major centers of ice accumulation and the maximum extent of Pleistocene glaciation in (a) North America and (b) Europe.

when demand is highest, half of the country's electrical production is generated by water released from the reservoirs.

Origin and Distribution of Glaciers

Glaciers form on land where for a number of years more snow falls in the winter than melts in the summer. Such climatic conditions exist at high latitudes and at high altitudes. The pressure increases that occur as the thickness of the snowpack increases cause the familiar six-sided snowflakes to change into a coarse, granular snow called **firn** ("corn snow" to skiers). Continued accumulation increases the pressure and causes much of the trapped air to be expelled from the firn. Recrystallization into larger crystals occurs, and eventually the dense crystals of "blue" glacial ice form.

Once the ice attains a thickness of about 30 meters (100 ft), it begins to deform as a viscous fluid, flowing due to its own weight. It moves downslope if in mountains, or radially outward if on a relatively flat surface. This kind of behavior of an apparently solid material, described as *plastic flow*, takes place in the lower part of the glacier called the **zone of flowage** (◆Figure 11.2). The upper, surficial layer of ice behaves in a more familiar manner as a brittle solid, often breaking into a jagged chaotic surface of *crevasses*—ominous deep cracks—and *seracs*—towering prominences of unstable ice. It is the deformation by plastic flow that distinguishes glaciers from the perennial snow fields that persist at higher elevations in many mountain ranges. Glaciers are more than just masses of frozen water. Although they are largely ice, they also contain large quantities of meltwater and vast amounts of rock debris acquired from the underlying bedrock or mountains where they originated and across

which they have moved on their journey downslope. There are several types of glaciers; ⁕ Table 11.1. lists their classifications.

Glacier Budget

When the rate of glacial advance equals the rate of wasting, the front (terminus) of the glacier remains stationary, and the glacier is said to be in equilibrium. Glaciers **ablate,** or waste away, by melting or, if they terminate in the ocean, by

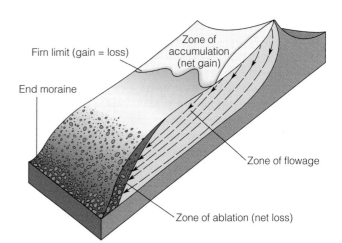

◆ **FIGURE 11.2** Typically, about two-thirds of a glacier lies at elevations above the firn limit in the zone of accumulation, where more snow falls in winter than melts in summer. Below the firn limit is the zone of ablation, where glacial ice and the entrained rock debris are exposed by melting in the summer. The ridge of rock debris formed at the edge of the melting ice is an end moraine.

★TABLE 11.1	Classification of Glaciers	
Type	Characteristic Location	Example
Valley (alpine)	mountain valleys	Vaughan Lewis Glacier, Alaska
Ice-field	extensive mountain glaciers that bury many adjoining valleys, leaving only the highest peaks and ridges rising above the ice	Juneau Ice Field, Alaska
Ice-cap	relatively smooth land surfaces in high latitudes or mountain summits where ice flows radially outward	Vatnajökull, Iceland
Piedmont	at the foot of mountain ranges where several valley glaciers emerge, flow laterally, and coalesce	Malaspina Glacier, Alaska
Continental (ice-sheet)	vast land areas	Greenland and Antarctica
Outlet	glacier tongue that originates from an ice sheet or mountain ice-field	Exit Glacier, Alaska

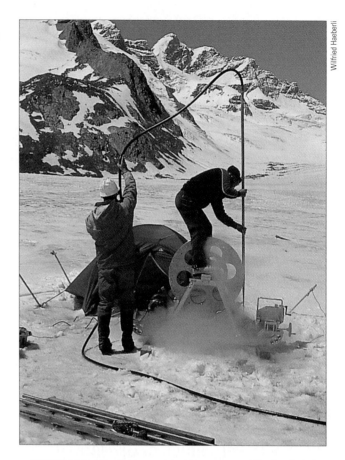

Wilfried Haeberli

◆ **FIGURE 11.3** Scientists use a jet of hot water to drill a borehole in a glacier. A stake will be placed in the hole that will enable scientists to measure the glacier's movement and summer ablation.

calving. **Calving** is the breaking off of a block of ice from the front of a glacier that produces an iceberg. It is important to realize that glacier ice always flows toward its terminal or lateral margins, irrespective of whether the glacier is advancing (when the net gain of snow and ice in the accumulation zone exceeds the net loss in the ablation zone), is in equilibrium (when the accumulation zone covers about two-thirds of the glacier's total length), or is retreating (when the net loss in the ablation zone exceeds the net gain in the accumulation zone). Glaciers move at varying speeds. Where the slopes are gentle, they may creep along at rates of a few centimeters to a few meters per day; where slopes are steep, they may move 8–10 meters (26–32 ft) a day (◆Figure 11.3). Some glaciers, under exceptional conditions, may episodically accelerate with speeds up to 100 meters (328 ft) a day, a condition known as *surging*.

Probably the best-documented and most dramatic retreat of a glacier is found at Glacier Bay National Park, Alaska. When George Vancouver arrived there in 1794, he found Icy Strait, at its entrance, choked with ice and Glacier Bay only a slight dent in the ice-cliffed shoreline. By 1879, when John Muir visited the area, the glacier, by then named

the "Grand Pacific," had retreated nearly 80 kilometers (50 mi) up the bay. The Grand Pacific Glacier had retreated another 24 kilometers (15 mi) by 1916, and today a 104-kilometer (65-mi)-long fjord occupies the area that just 200 years ago held a valley glacier that was as much as 1,220 meters (4,000 ft) thick (◆Figure 11.4).

CONSIDER THIS

If an Alaskan glacier's ice accumulates at an average rate of 50 centimeters a year and the glacier is 500 meters thick, how many years will be recorded in a complete core drilled to the base of the glacier?

Glacial Features

Glaciers carry all manner of rock debris that is deposited directly by melting ice as unsorted rock debris, or **glacial till.** **Moraines** are landforms composed of till and named for their site of deposition. **End moraines** (also called *terminal moraines*) are deposited at the ends of the melting glaciers. **Recessional moraines** are series of nested end moraines that record the stepwise retreat, or meltback, at the end of an ice age (◆Figure 11.5).

◆ **FIGURE 11.4** Map of Glacier Bay National Park, Alaska, showing the terminal positions of the retreating Grand Pacific and other glaciers from AD 1750 to the present. NPS data.

◆ **FIGURE 11.5** Recessional moraines; Coteau des Prairies, near Aberdeen, South Dakota.

After melting, continental and ice-cap glaciers leave a subdued, rounded topography with a definite "grain" that indicates the direction of glacial movement. They may also leave behind numerous **kettle lakes,** water-filled, bowl-shaped depressions without surface drainage (◆ Figure 11.6). For example, there are about a dozen kettle lakes in northern Indiana's Valparaiso moraine. These lakes are believed to have formed when large blocks of stagnant ice that were wholly or partly buried in the deposits left behind by retreating glaciers melted (◆ Figures 11.6 and 11.7). End moraines now form the hilly areas extending across the Dakotas, Minnesota, Wisconsin, northern Indiana, Ohio, and all the way to the eastern tip of Long Island, New York. Some Chicago suburbs have names that reflect their location on high areas of hilly moraines: Park Ridge, Palos Hills, and

◆ **FIGURE 11.6** Kettle lakes at Kewaskum, Wisconsin.

(a)

Labels: End moraine; Subglacial river; Ice block left by retreating glacier

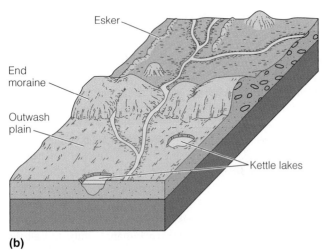

(b)

Labels: Esker; End moraine; Outwash plain; Kettle lakes

◆ **FIGURE 11.7** Formation of end moraines, kettle lakes, and eskers (a) during glaciation and (b) after glaciation.

Arlington Heights, for example. In addition, poor drainage or deranged drainage characterizes many areas that have undergone continental glaciation.

Following a period of glaciation, a fjord formed when the seaward end of a coastal U-shaped valley, eroded by a valley glacier, is drowned by an arm of the sea (◆Figure 11.8).

CONSIDER THIS

How can a "retreating" glacier still be flowing downhill during a time of global warming?

The Effects of Glaciation

Although the great ice sheets of the Pleistocene Epoch seem remote in time and modern glaciers seem remote in distance, both have impacts on modern society that are far from trivial.

◆ **FIGURE 11.8** A fjord, Gastineau Channel at Juneau, Alaska.

◆ **FIGURE 11.9** Rocky soil developed on glacial till; Adirondack Mountains, New York.

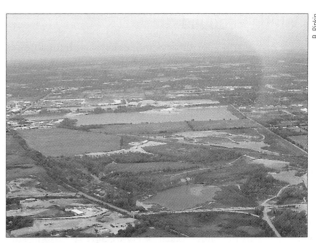

◆ **FIGURE 11.10** Part of a vast plain, underlain by Pleistocene glacial outwash near Elgin, Illinois. Outwash sediments, deposited along the margins of the melting continental ice sheets, are spread for thousands of square kilometers across the north-central United States. The ponds in the photograph are the excavations remaining from sand and gravel mining operations.

Distribution of Soils

Farming and forestry generally depend upon the distribution and quality of Pleistocene deposits. Some of the best agricultural soils in the world lie on sediments deposited in former glacial lakes and on glacio-eolian (loess) deposits (see Chapter 6). As Pleistocene glaciers expanded and moved over western Europe and North America, they scraped off soils from the underlying land and redeposited them as moraines of glacial till where the ice melted. Today some till-covered areas are excellent forestland and excellent-to-poor farmland (◆ Figure 11.9). Locally, in some locations such as south of Buffalo, New York, where the till is clay-rich, the clay may become unstable in places like road cuts along highways, and flow following significant wetting.

Groundwater Resources

Glacial outwash is sediment that was deposited by meltwater rivers originating at the melting edge of a glacier. The great Pleistocene ice sheet that extended out of Canada into the northern Mississippi River valley released copious amounts of sediment-laden meltwater, resulting in vast sheets of outwash sediments. Some of these glacial-outwash deposits serve as important groundwater aquifers in the end-moraine regions of the Midwest. Moraines associated with the outwash are poor aquifers due to the low porosity and permeability of the clays they contain. Thus geophysical exploration, test-drilling, and careful mapping are necessary in order to delineate the aquifers of porous and permeable sands within the buried stream channels. Glacial outwash can serve as an important source of sand and gravel (◆ Figure 11.10).

Sea-Level Changes

The transfer from the oceans to the continents of the millions of cubic miles of water that became the enormous Pleistocene continental ice sheets caused sea level to lower about 100 meters (330 ft). This exposed extensive areas of continental shelves. Consider that a drop of this amount today would increase the area of Florida real estate by more than 30 percent, would leave New Orleans high and dry, and would cause the Panama Canal to drain. Conversely, if all the polar ice were to melt, sea level would rise on the order of 40 meters (130 ft), and London, New York, Tokyo, and Los Angeles would be mostly underwater. As sea level dropped during the Ice Ages, the rivers in coastal regions began downcutting across the exposed continental shelves as they adjusted to the new conditions. When sea level rose to its present level, about 5,000 years ago, the mouths of the coastal rivers were drowned, forming what are now harbors and estuaries.

The formation of land bridges due to the lowering of sea level during the Ice Ages was of major importance in establishing the current biogeography of Earth. Among the land bridges at this time was the Bering bridge. It had existed during much of Cenozoic time and is especially significant because the two-way traffic across the bridge accounts for horses, mammoths, and other large mammals crossing between North America and Asia. About 20,000 to 30,000 years ago, during the lowered sea level of the last major Ice Age, humans used the bridge to cross from Asia into North America. Rising sea level beginning about 13,000 years ago drowned the bridge, and the 90-kilometer (54-mi) stretch of ocean between Alaska and Siberia now blocks temperate-climate organisms from migrating.

Isostatic Rebound

The Ice Age continental glaciers and ice caps, with thicknesses of two miles or more, were so massive that the crust beneath them was depressed by their weight. In the time since the ice retreated at the end of the last ice age, 8,000 to 11,000 years ago, the land regions exposed by the retreating ice sheets in Scandinavia, Canada, and Great Britain have risen due to the geologically rapid removal of the great load of ice. Uplift of the crust due to unweighting is caused by **isostatic rebound,** the slow transfer by flowage of mantle rock to accommodate uplift of the crust in one area that causes subsidence in another area. Evidence of isostatic rebound in deglaciated areas is seen in the raised beaches around Hudson Bay, the Baltic Sea, and the Great Lakes (◆ Figure 11.11). Careful surveying in Europe shows that as Scandinavia and Great Britain have been rising, a corresponding subsidence of Western Europe has occurred that is especially pronounced in the Netherlands. The uplift and subsidence in these regions remain active. Above the modern shorelines of the Gulf of Bothnia in Finland and Sweden are raised beaches that show a maximum uplift of 275 meters (900 ft). It is estimated that an additional 213 meters (700 ft) of rise will occur before equilibrium is reached. The rise is so rapid in some places in Scandinavia that docks used by ships are literally rising out of the sea. Uplift in Oslo Fjord, Norway is about 6 millimeters (¼ in) per year, which adds another 60 centimeters (2 ft) of elevation per century. Sea-level mooring rings the Vikings used for tying up their dragon boats a thousand years ago are now 6 meters (20 ft) above sea level. Not even the tallest Viking would be able to moor his boat to those rings today. Similar uplifting is recorded along the northern shores of Hudson Bay, where the average uplift is about a meter (3 ft) per century (◆ Figure 11.12).

Uplifting in the Great Lakes region is slow but continuing, and eventually it may cause problems for the residents of Chicago and elsewhere in Illinois. The rebound threatens to cause a drainage change that will force more of Lake Michigan to drain southward into the Mississippi River system.

The rapid unloading of the crust at Glacier Bay, Alaska, in the last 200 years has resulted in measurable rebound in the lower parts of the bay. Small islands are slowly emerging, and existing islands are rising at a rate of about four centimeters (1½ in) per year.

Human Transportation Routes

Beginning in 1980, the Columbia Glacier on Prince William Sound, Alaska began a catastrophic retreat by calving thousands of icebergs each year, some of them as large as houses. The glacier had been in equilibrium at much the same position for at least 200 years—it was first observed in the late eighteenth century—when it began to show evidence of retreat in the late 1970s. Fortunately, the moraine shoal at its terminus is sufficiently shallow to trap the larger icebergs and prevent them from drifting into Prince William Sound, where they would pose a major threat to the supertankers passing through these waters to and from the oil-loading terminal at Valdez. Because the terminus of the glacier has retreated some 15 kilometers (9 mi) since 1982, it appears that a new fjord is forming.

Juneau, Alaska is the only state capital in the United States without highway access, even though it is only about 160 miles (by air) west of the nearest highway in Canada. A highway connecting Juneau with Canada would be desirable, but it is not to be because the advancing Taku and Hole-in-Wall Glaciers threaten to close off the only

◆ **FIGURE 11.11** Isostatically raised beach ridges at Richmond Gulf, Hudson Bay, Quebec, Canada. The highest ridge in the photo lies about 300 meters (984 ft) above sea level and is about 8,000 years old.

C. Hillaire-Marcel

◆ **FIGURE 11.12** Locations of maximum postglacial (after glaciation) isostatic uplift in the Hudson Bay region and of land features resulting from the retreat of the late Pleistocene ice sheet about 10,000 years ago. Proglacial lakes (temporary, ice-marginal lakes) overflowed at different times through various spillways. One of the arrows east of the Finger Lakes represents the spillway pictured in Figure 11.17. The spillway draining Lake Agassiz in South Dakota is pictured in Figure 11.18. Windblown loess was deposited adjacent to major glacial meltwater systems. Waters from Lake Michigan drained southwestward into the Mississippi River at the time, which may occur again as isostatic uplift continues. After Dott and Batten, *Evolution on the Earth*, 3rd ed., p. 514, McGraw-Hill, 1981

possible route along the west shoreline of Taku Inlet (◆ Figure 11.13).

Whereas glaciers impede transportation in some areas, in other areas they have served to facilitate it. In wet boggy regions in the early days of New England, the crests of **eskers** provided good travel routes. Eskers are long, winding, steep-sided ridges of stratified sand and gravel deposited by subglacial or englacial streams that flowed in ice tunnels in or beneath a retreating glacier. Hence, especially in Maine, the eskers were called *horsebacks* (see Figure 11.7b and ◆ Figure 11.14).

Pleistocene Lakes

The cooler climates of the Pleistocene brought increased precipitation, less evaporation, and the runoff of glacial meltwater. Lakes dotted the basins of North America. Accumulations of water, mostly in valleys between the fault-block mountain ranges in the Great Basin, formed hundreds of lakes far from continental glaciers (◆ Figure 11.15). Today many of these valleys contain aquifers that were probably charged by waters of the Ice Age lakes. California had dozens of lakes, now mostly dried up; among them were Owens Lake, Lake Russell (the ancestor of Mono Lake), and China Lake. Lake Manley covered the floor of what is now Death Valley National Park, named after the Manly party that suffered great hardships there in 1849; and Rogers Dry Lake, near Lancaster, California, is the location of Edwards Air Force Base and a

landing site for the space shuttle. The Great Salt Lake in Utah is all that remains of the once-vast Pleistocene Lake Bonneville (◆ Figure 11.16). The Bonneville Salt Flats, an area that is ideal for setting automobile speed records, formed by evaporation of the ancient Pleistocene lake. Further east, the Great Lakes and the Finger Lakes of New York State are of glacial origin. In the Pleistocene Epoch, when drainage to the north from the Great Lakes and the Finger Lakes was blocked by ice, these lakes drained through various spillways at different times (Figure 11.12 and ◆ Figure 11.17). Major disruptions in drainage produced large temporary ice-marginal lakes, called **proglacial lakes,** which were dammed partly by moraines and partly by glacial ice.

Ice Age lake sediments are the basis of the rich soils of the northern United States and southern Canada. The rich wheat lands of North Dakota and Manitoba, for example, formed as sediments in Pleistocene Lake Agassiz (see Figure 11.12). Centered in present-day Manitoba, the lake was the largest known North American lake; its area of more than 518,000 square kilometers (200,000 mi²) was more than twice that of the five present-day Great Lakes combined. (It was named after Louis Agassiz, the nineteenth-century scientist who fostered the theory of the Ice Ages.) The lake formed when the great Canadian ice sheet blocked several rivers flowing northward toward Hudson Bay. For a time, a large spillway channel carried outflow southward from the lake, forming what is now the 200-foot-deep Browns Valley on the border between

◆ **FIGURE 11.13** Map recording the behavior of the retreating Norris Glacier and the advancing Taku Glacier, Alaska, from 1890 to 1990. The reason for the different behavior of the neighboring glaciers is that the Norris Glacier has a much smaller and lower-elevation accumulation zone than the Taku. Only two percent of the Norris's accumulation zone is above 1,370 meters (4,500 ft), whereas about 40 percent of the Taku's is above that elevation. Data from Foundation for Glacier and Environmental Research

◆ **FIGURE 11.14** Esker with a road on its crest; Malingarna area, southern Sweden.

Rolf A. Larsson

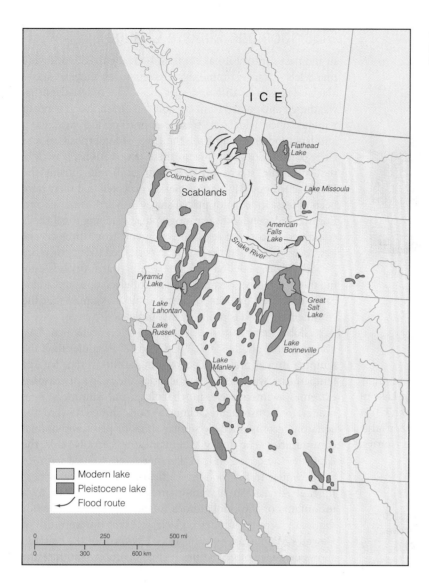

◆ **FIGURE 11.15** Pleistocene pluvial lakes in the western United States. After Weiss and Newman "The Channeled Scablands of Eastern Washington," USGS pamphlet, 1973

ICE

Flathead Lake

Columbia River

Scablands

Lake Missoula

American Falls Lake

Snake River

Pyramid Lake

Lake Lahontan

Great Salt Lake

Lake Russell

Lake Bonneville

Lake Manley

Modern lake
Pleistocene lake
Flood route

0   250   500 mi
0   300   600 km

◆ **FIGURE 11.16** Terraces on the flanks of the Wasatch Mountains that mark former shorelines of Pleistocene Lake Bonneville, at Brigham City, Utah. See Figure 11.15.

D. D. Trent

D. D. Trent

◆ **FIGURE 11.17** Typical subdued terrain resulting from continental glaciation at Lake George, New York. The lake is dammed by an end moraine. The break in the ridge on the right marks the channel of the ancient river that carried meltwater southward from the Pleistocene glacier. See Figure 11.12.

South Dakota and Minnesota (◆Figure 11.18). The many remnants of Lake Agassiz include Lake Winnipeg and Lake of the Woods. Northwest of this area are Great Bear Lake, Great Slave Lake, and Lake Athabaska, descendants of other large ice-marginal lakes in the present-day Northwest Territories, Alberta, and Saskatchewan.

CONSIDER THIS

If there had been no large-scale Pleistocene continental glaciation in North America, what differences might we find in today's midwestern states? (Hint: Carefully examine Figures 11.1a and 11.2.)

Glaciation and Climate Change

In the past century it has come to be recognized worldwide that Pleistocene—commonly referred to as the Ice Age—glacial deposits of different ages exist. The oldest deposits, weathered and gullied from erosion, have been found beneath younger ones, which are fresher appearing, less weathered, and less eroded. By applying the Laws of Superposition and Cross-cutting Relationships to these observations, it is clear that multiple stages of glaciation occurred during the Pleistocene Epoch. It is now generally accepted that there have been at least four major glacial stages in North America and Eurasia. Independently, oceanographers studying fossil shells contained in cores of sea-floor sediments from three oceans have determined that the oceans experienced twenty or more periods of deep cooling with intervening warm periods during the Pleistocene. Because evidence of glaciations on land is easily destroyed by later ice advances, it is assumed that the continental record is probably incomplete.

Global temperatures during the Pleistocene Ice Ages averaged only about 4° to 10° C (7° to 18° F) cooler than the temperatures at present. The lowering of the average Ice Age temperature was not as significant as the range of seasonal extremes; winters were much colder, but summers were moderate. Consequently, climate zones shifted toward the equator, accompanied by similar shifts of plant and animal communities. The Rocky Mountains, the Sierra Nevada, the Alps, the Caucasus, and the Pyrenees were topped with ice fields similar to the modern ice field in the mountains near Juneau, Alaska. Small mountain glaciers existed in high mountains of the midlatitudes much closer to the equator than any similar modern glaciers. Even the summit of Hawaii's Mauna Loa volcano, only 19° north of the equator, shows evidence of glaciation. It also was cooler south of the

◆ **FIGURE 11.18** Big Stone Lake now occupies part of Lake Agassiz's spillway channel. It is in Browns Valley on the boundary between western Minnesota and northeastern South Dakota. See Figure 11.12.

John S. Shelton

equator, but because the landmasses in the southern hemisphere's middle latitudes are small or narrow, extensive glaciation was limited to the South Island of New Zealand and the southernmost part of the Andes in South America. Antarctica and Greenland were ice covered much the same as they are today.

The recognized relationships between cyclic global climate change and multiple stages of glaciation lead to speculation about common underlying causes. In order to better understand global climate changes over time and why Earth experiences periodic ice ages, we next survey the factors that control climate.

Climate
Factors That Control Climate

Climate is the long-term average of day-to-day weather. Its definition also includes the annual extremes of weather elements within a specific region. Understanding climate requires recognizing that it is determined by the interactions of the geospheres that comprise the Earth System—the atmosphere, hydrosphere, biosphere, and lithosphere—coupled with the orbital elements of the Earth–Sun–Moon system (see Chapter 2). The **climate controls,** the relatively constant factors that dictate a region's climate, are

1. the intensity of the sun, which heats Earth and the atmosphere,
2. the distribution of land and water masses,
3. winds and atmospheric circulation,
4. circulation of the oceans, and
5. mountain barriers.

Some of these controls are treated in more detail in Chapter 12.

Heating of Earth and Its Atmosphere

Earth's surface and atmosphere is warmed by radiant energy from the Sun. Because part of the Sun's radiation is reflected back to space by clouds and the atmosphere, about 51 percent of the solar energy that could reach Earth actually does. This energy received from the sun is mainly visible light and near-infrared radiation, particular wavelengths of solar radiation that do not "see" the atmosphere through which they pass on their way to Earth, where they heat the ground and oceans. The intensity of the Sun's heat at a particular place on Earth's surface varies with the angle at which the Sun's rays hit Earth (◆Figure 11.19). This incoming solar radiation is sometimes referred to as *short-wave radiation.* Because all warm objects radiate heat, the warmed surface of Earth radiates energy back to the atmosphere, but at longer wavelengths known as *infrared,* or *long-wave, radiation.* The atmosphere is warmed by this long-wave radiation due mainly to the absorption and reradiation of heat by atmospheric CO_2, water vapor, and other trace gases. Consequently, the atmosphere acts as a blanket that absorbs most of the long-wave radiation and keeps Earth warm. This process, called the **greenhouse effect** by analogy to the solar-heating method that warms greenhouses, serves to keep Earth's surface temperature from dropping excessively during winter and night.

Winds and Atmospheric Circulation

Wind is movement of air from a region of high pressure to a region of low pressure due to unequal heating of Earth's surface. Because the Sun's rays strike Earth more directly at the equator than at other places, more radiation (heat) per unit area is received there (◆Figure 11.20). Solar heating at the equator warms the air, and it rises, creating a zone of low atmospheric pressure known as the **intertropical convergence zone (ITCZ),** and the **doldrums.**

In polar regions, the Sun's rays strike Earth at a low angle, resulting in less-intense heating per unit area. There the colder, drier, denser air creates a zone of high pressure known as the **polar high.** The cold, dry, polar air sinks and moves laterally into areas of lower pressure at lower latitudes. Upper-level airflow from the equatorial regions moves toward the poles. When it reaches approximately 30 degrees north and south of the equator, it sinks back to Earth's surface as dense, dry air to form high-pressure belts known as the **subtropical highs,** or the **horse latitudes.** Winds, then, are driven by differences in air pressure caused by unequal heating, but as they move they do not follow straight paths. Instead, they are deflected by the Coriolis effect.

The **Coriolis effect** is caused by the rotation of the earth. A simple analogy of the Coriolis effect is to consider two

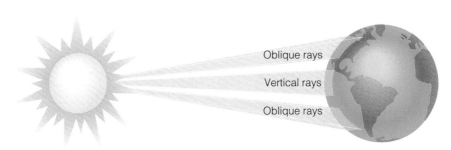

◆ **FIGURE 11.19** The intensity of the sun's heat depends upon the angle at which the sun's rays hit Earth. The intensity and heating is greatest where the rays hit vertically.

Oblique rays

Vertical rays

Oblique rays

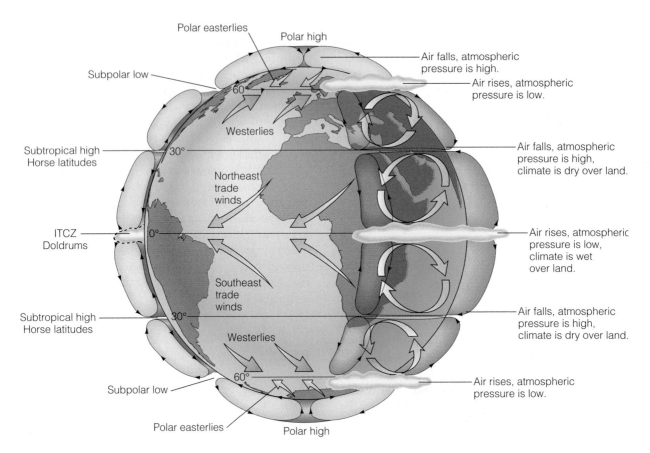

ThomsonNOW™ ACTIVE FIGURE 11.20 In the general scheme of global atmospheric circulation, heat transfer occurs in steps generating three cells between each pole and the equator. This results in persistent global air-circulation patterns that generate atmospheric pressure zones and surface wind belts. Descending air causes zones of high pressure (the polar highs and the subtropical highs), and rising air produces zones of low pressure (the ITCZ and the subpolar lows). From B. Murphy and D. Nance, *Earth Sciences Today*, p. 331, Brooks/Cole, 1999

people playing catch on a merry-go-round (◆ Figure 11.21). If the merry-go-round is stationary, the ball will follow a straight path. An apparent paradox occurs when the merry-go-round is turning, however. As seen by stationary observers not on the merry-go-round, the thrown ball still travels in a straight path, but to the people on the turning merry-go-round, the ball appears to follow a curved path. The reason for this paradox is that the merry-go-round and

its passengers are turning below the ball as it travels from one person to the other. To the people on the merry-go-round, the path of the ball appears to be deflected as though some force is acting on it. The curve will be to the right if the merry-go-round is turning counterclockwise, the same direction Earth rotates if observed from above the North Pole. The deflection of freely moving objects also occurs on Earth. Rifle bullets, ballistic missiles, ocean currents, and

FIGURE 11.21 The Coriolis effect in a game of catch. (a) The path of the ball is straight when the game is played on a stationary platform, and an observer perceives it as straight. (b) On a rotating platform the ball still follows a straight path, but to an observer on the platform, the path appears to be curved. This is the Coriolis effect.

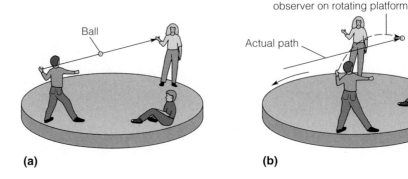

winds that travel long distances all appear to follow curved paths because of Earth's rotation. The path is deflected to the right in the northern hemisphere and to the left in the southern hemisphere.

The rising warm air in the equatorial belt expands and cools as it rises. Cooling reduces the air's ability to hold moisture, resulting in the formation of clouds and heavy precipitation. For this reason, the intertropical convergence zone (ITCZ) is one of the rainiest parts of the world. We generally do not find deserts there. Air also rises at latitudes of approximately 60° north and south, where cold polar surface air and mild-temperature surface air converge but tend not to mix. At this boundary, called the **polar front,** surface air rises, forming a zone of low pressure called the **subpolar low.** It is along the polar front that rising air causes storms to develop. In the subtropics, in contrast, cool, dry air sinks, forming high-pressure regions. As the air sinks, it is compressed, which causes its temperature to increase. This warming enables the air to absorb water and precludes the formation of clouds. Thus the climate belts of subtropical highs, from about 30° to 35° north and south of the equator, the so-called horse latitudes, experience warm, dry winds with generally clear skies and sunny days. It is here that we find most of the world's hot deserts. (Deserts are the topic of Chapter 12.)

CONSIDER THIS

The old expression "caught in the doldrums" is sometimes used to describe a person who lacks motivation and is listless. What is the relationship of this expression to the traditional term for the ITCZ?

Oceanic Circulation

Unequal heating of Earth's surface by the Sun moves the atmosphere, and the resulting winds drive the surface currents of the oceans. Each major ocean basin is distinguished by currents that rotate clockwise in the northern hemisphere and counterclockwise in the southern hemisphere in accordance with the Coriolis effect (◆ Figure 11.22). In both hemispheres, these currents carry heat from the equator toward the poles along the west sides of the ocean basins and, in turn, carry cooled water from polar latitudes back toward equatorial regions along the east sides of the ocean basins. This transfer of heat occurs in all oceans. For example, the California Current cools the west coast of North America, imparting mild summer temperatures to San Diego. In contrast, at the same latitude, the warm Gulf Stream on the east coast imparts hot, humid summers to Savannah, Georgia.

A major oceanic process affecting coasts in the "trade-wind" belts north and south of the ITCZ (see Figure 11.20)

ThomsonNOW™ ACTIVE FIGURE 11.22 Major wind-driven oceanic surface currents. Warm currents are shown in red; cool currents in blue. Currents rotate clockwise in the northern hemisphere and counterclockwise in the southern hemisphere.

is **upwelling.** Upwelling occurs when winds blowing from the land to the sea (*offshore winds*) sweep surface water away from the shore, creating a condition of hydraulic instability. The displaced nearshore water is replaced by nutrient-rich, cold waters from depths in excess of 200 meters (650 ft; Figure 12.8, page 356, illustrates this). During upwelling, coastal waters nearshore are colder than offshore water, which further moderates local weather. Conditions for coastal upwelling are most commonly found along the western sides of continents in the tradewind belts, as, for example, along the coasts of Peru and California. Upwelling brings dissolved phosphates and nitrates to the surface, which leads to the proliferation of marine plankton, which in turn promotes large fish populations and gives rise to commercial fisheries. However, if the tradewinds break down or weaken and upwelling ceases, major climatic upsets such as El Niño may occur, causing floods and severe storms in some areas (see Chapter 10).

ThomsonNOW™
Click **Geology Interactive** to work through an activity on World Currents and Dissect a Current through Waves, Tides, and Currents.

Causes of Climate Change
Variations in Earth's Orbit

Once scholars recognized that cyclic global climate changes were responsible for the multiple stages of glaciation, they began to seek answers to questions about underlying causes. An early answer was provided in the late nineteenth century by Scottish geologist John Croll. Serbian astronomer Milutan Milankovitch expanded upon Croll's work with elegant mathematics in 1941. Both of these scientists recognized that the cyclic pattern of the Pleistocene ice ages could result from periodic minor changes in Earth's rotation and revolution around the Sun, with the cold periods of ice advance occurring when three variations in Earth's rotational and orbital elements were synchronous. The three variations are

1. the **obliquity,** or tilt, of Earth's axis;
2. the **eccentricity,** or shape, of Earth's orbit; and
3. the **precession,** or wobble, of Earth's axis.

See ◆ Figure 11.23. Earth's *obliquity* relative to the sun has been found to vary between 21.8° and 24.5° over a 41,000-year cycle; Earth's present tilt is in the middle of this range. This slight change causes variations in the temperature range between summer and winter. When Earth is at the minimum tilt, sunlight hits the polar regions at a higher angle, and the global seasonal temperature variation decreases. Every 100,000 years, the orbit of Earth changes from nearly circular to more *eccentric*. Seasonal variation in temperature is greater when the orbit is more eccentric. Even at its maximum eccentricity, the annual variation in the total sunlight reaching Earth is

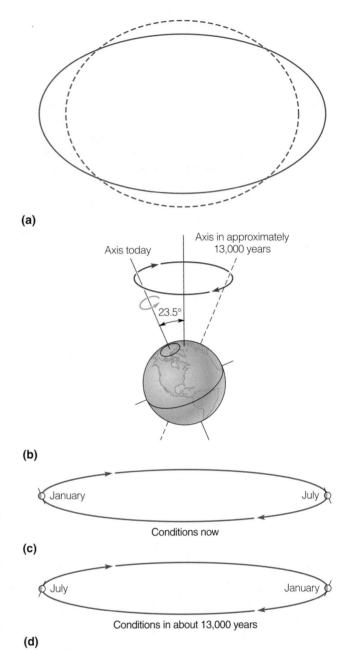

FIGURE 11.23 Geometry of variation in Earth's orbital eccentricity, axial precession, and axial obliquity. (a) The orbital eccentricity varies from nearly circular (dashed line) to elliptical (solid line) to nearly circular and back again over a period of 100,000 years. (b) Earth's axis slowly precesses, like a spinning top tracing out a cone in space, taking about 26,000 years for a complete cycle. (c) Conditions today. Earth is closest to the Sun in January while the northern hemisphere is experiencing winter. (d) Conditions in about 13,000 years. Earth will be closest to the Sun in July while the northern hemisphere is experiencing summer. www2.jpl.nasa.gov/basics/bsf2-1.html precession cycle = 26,000 yrs. (approx.)

less than one-tenth of a percent. Nevertheless, this seemingly trivial difference can cause Earth's temperature to rise or fall by a whopping 16° C (9° F). Earth's present eccentricity is not great, resulting in only a six percent difference in heat energy received between January and July. However, at its most eccentric orbit, the difference amounts to 20 to 30 percent. The axis of Earth, which now points to Polaris, the North Star, *precesses* like a spinning top when its axis is disturbed. This precession causes the axis to trace out a cone in space, taking 26,000 years to trace out a complete cone. Consequently, the northern and southern hemispheres "trade" their respective winter and summer seasons every 13,000 years.

Each of these periodic factors alone could cause the limited global cooling that might lead to a "little ice age." More important, however, is the interaction of the three cycles. When their cooling effects coincide, there is a sufficient change in the global heat budget to trigger glacial–interglacial episodes, though not enough to explain fully the 4° to 10° C cooling required for the major glacial cycles of the Pleistocene Epoch. In other words, the rotational and orbital factors adequately explain the timing of the glacial–interglacial cycles, but not the amount necessary to cause the *changes in global temperature.* There must be other factors.

Plate Tectonics and Variation in Atmospheric Carbon Dioxide

For glaciers to exist, the continents must be in the middle to higher latitudes, and high-standing mountains are "desirable." Plate tectonics can account for both the positioning of continents at "appropriate" latitudes and the uplifting of vast continental areas. Such repositioning of continents and higher elevations of land areas alters the circulation patterns of both the atmosphere and oceans, which leads to long-term climate change. In addition, the higher the continental land masses, the greater is the rock surface area exposed to chemical weathering by atmospheric gases. As the rocks weather, they combine with water and atmospheric carbon dioxide (CO_2), which reduces the amount of the gas in the atmosphere. Further, input of CO_2 from volcanic activity is reduced when, at the end of a tectonic cycle, the volcanic fires at oceanic ridges cool down and the ridges become less active. Because CO_2 is the major greenhouse gas, these reductions promote global cooling. (In the earlier phases of the cycle, the ridges are active, which increases the CO_2 input to the atmosphere, and sea level is high, which reduces weathering. These two factors reinforce each other to increase atmospheric CO_2.) The relationship of CO_2 concentrations in the atmosphere, oceans, and biosphere is enormously complicated, and several feedback mechanisms exist that are not understood. For example, diatoms, the microscopic oceanic plants that can be thought of as the "grass of the sea," may be part of a feedback loop in the biosphere that affects climate. Diatoms may step up productivity when there is excess atmospheric CO_2, thus drawing down the CO_2 content and cooling the climate.

Variations in Solar Radiation

Measurements by sophisticated instruments carried by satellites indicate that the output of solar radiation may vary considerably more than was once thought. Furthermore, it is known that the Sun's energy output changes slightly with sunspot activity. *Sunspots*—enormous magnetic storms on the Sun's surface that mark cooler regions surrounded by very bright areas radiating great bursts of energy—occur in cycles, with the maximum sunspot size and number occurring about every 11 years. During such times the sun produces about 0.1 percent more energy than it does at times of sunspot minimum. The 11-year cycle appears to collapse from time to time, as it did in the seventeenth century (at a time known as the *Maunder minimum*), when there were few if any sunspots. This "minimum" occurred during the coldest period of the Little Ice Age, when the average global temperature was about 0.5° C (1° F) lower than the long-term average.

Correlated with the 11-year sunspot cycle is a 22-year cycle, the time required for completion of the sun's *magnetic cycle*—and an interval that closely corresponds to the 20-year cycle of drought on the Great Plains. The Sun's general magnetic field increased 2.3 times between 1901 and 2000, and because the general magnetic field varies in time with the 11-year sunspot cycle, the varying magnetic field is also related to the Sun's brightness. Furthermore, the impact of the Sun's magnetic field on Earth appears to be related to cloudiness. (The field influences the amount of cosmic rays that enter Earth's atmosphere, which in turn may affect the formation of electrically charged particles, on which water condenses to form cloud droplets.)

Moreover, solar brightness also affects the stratospheric ozone layer. The 0.1 percent increase in solar energy produced during the 11-year maximum is ultraviolet radiation. Ultraviolet rays' wavelengths are absorbed by stratospheric ozone, the level of which also varies with the sunspot cycle. Because the time of maximum ozone content is also the time of maximum sunspot activity, additional ozone at such times absorbs the additional ultraviolet radiation.

If increased solar radiation were currently involved in global warming, it would be warming the upper and lower atmosphere as well as Earth's surface. This is not the case. The upper atmosphere is cooling, while the lower atmosphere and Earth's surface are warming. Eventually it may be found that fluctuations in solar radiation account for some long-term climate changes, but much more research is needed. Correlation is not necessarily causation.

Greenhouse Gases

Scientists have been measuring and recording the level of carbon dioxide in the atmosphere since 1880. Their measurements over the years show that the concentrations of CO_2 and other greenhouse gases, as well as average global temperatures, have risen steadily (◆Figure 11.24). This increase in

◆ **FIGURE 11.24** Atmospheric CO_2 and temperature changes since 1880. (a) Changes in the concentration of CO_2 obtained from ice cores (smooth curve) and measured annual oscillations at Mauna Loa, Hawaii. The sawtooth effect results from the seasonal changes in uptake and release of from northern forests (b) Average annual global surface-air temperature, plotted as a deviation from the average, denoted as zero (0). Nansen and Lebedeff, Global Trends of Surface-Air Temperatures, *Journal of Geophysical Research* 29, no. D11 fig. 15, p. 13370, (Nov. 20, 1987). Copyright 1987. Reproduced by permission of American Geophysical Union.

(a)

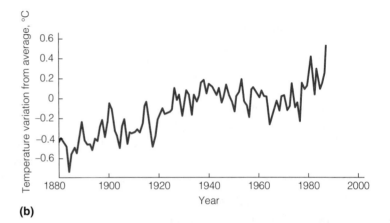

(b)

atmospheric CO_2 is unprecedented in human history, and it is believed to be largely due to humankind's dependence upon fossil fuels. Other "greenhouse gases" include:

- methane (CH_4), which is expelled as flatulence from the world's cattle population, from rice paddies, and of all things, from termites in tropical rainforests;

- nitrogen oxide (NO_x) from fertilizers and automobile exhausts; and

- **chlorofluorocarbons (CFCs),** largely from air conditioners and spray-can propellants.

- water vapor

These substances combine to increase global warming.

In addition to being a greenhouse gas, CFCs play another role in the atmosphere; they break down the upper-atmospheric (the stratospheric) ozone layer 10 to 48 kilometers (6–30 mi) above Earth's surface. Ozone, a form of oxygen, serves as a vital shield that protects Earth's organisms from harmful solar ultraviolet radiation. The chlorine in one molecule of CFC has the potential to destroy as many as 100,000 ozone molecules before it becomes inert. Any thinning of the ozone shield leads to global change.

Using data from satellites and airborne sensors, scientists discovered in the late 1970s and early 1980s that stratospheric ozone levels were decreasing at an alarming rate. By the spring of 1987, an "ozone hole" the size of the United

States and Mexico combined had developed over Antarctica. **Ozone hole** is a misleading term. It is a thinning out, not a complete elimination of ozone that is observed, although there was a complete disappearance of ozone, primarily in the 1990s, that posed a dangerous situation for people working in polar regions during the spring when they were exposed to the full impact of dangerous forms of space radiation, just as though they were working on the surface of another planet). The "hole" continued to enlarge, the thinning recognized over the North Pole and the midlatitudes as well. Ozone loss in the stratosphere causes warming on Earth's surface as well as dangerous cooling in the stratosphere.

A thinning of the atmospheric ozone layer threatens humans with increased risks of skin cancer and cataracts and of weakening the immune system. The increased ultraviolet radiation reaching Earth also threatens to damage crops and phytoplankton, the microscopic plants that are the basis of ocean food chains. Some medical authorities reported that a person's chance of developing skin cancer by the 1990s was about one in 75, up from one in 1,500 about 40 years earlier. Humans, of course, can protect themselves from ultraviolet radiation, but other animals cannot. For example, ultraviolet-radiation damage to DNA has been shown to account for severe losses of fertilized eggs in at least two species of Cascade Mountain frogs.

Also contributing to the depletion of the ozone layer is the burning of aviation fuel at altitudes above 9 kilometers (5.5 mi). Nitrogen oxides (NO_x) and water-vapor molecules released at altitudes between 9 and 13 kilometers (5.5 and 8 mi)—the usual cruising altitude for commercial jetliners—stay in the atmosphere about 100 times longer than those released near ground level. Although it seems contradictory, NO_x emissions can either increase or decrease ozone concentrations in the atmosphere. In the lower atmosphere, where we live, NO_x, together with hydrocarbons, forms ozone (a major component of smog) in the presence of ultraviolet light. In the upper atmosphere, however, NO_x breaks down ozone. CFC climate modeling, which does not take NO_x emissions from air traffic into account, has underestimated the amount of ozone depletion. According to researchers, the amount of ozone loss over the northern hemisphere is about twice that calculated using only CFC climate modeling. Regular (subsonic) air traffic is believed to be responsible for a 10 percent increase in the nitric acid concentration at 21 kilometers (13 mi) above sea level, which may be the most critical altitude for ozone holes. Clearly, the chemistry of the atmosphere is complex, and it is the subject of continuing scientific research.

In the 1990s a few radio-talk-show hosts and some government policymakers expressed doubts about the danger of CFCs and the depletion of the stratospheric ozone layer. They argued that chlorine from CFCs is trivial in comparison with the great quantities of chlorine released to the atmosphere from natural sources such as volcanic eruptions, which have been contributing chlorine to the atmosphere for many hundreds of millions of years. In spite of this, the ozone layer still exists, so, they argued, the concern about CFCs is overstated. Their argument was spurious, however, because natural chlorine is chemically reactive in the lower atmosphere and soluble in water; consequently, it gets rained out before it can reach the stratosphere. CFCs, in contrast, are absolutely inert and thus insoluble in the lower atmosphere. This allows them to rise through the lower atmosphere and into the stratosphere, where ultraviolet rays cause the release of chlorine. It was recognition of their chemical inactivity in the lower atmosphere—they react with *nothing*—that made them so appealing as coolants and propellants.

Despite commentary by radio-talk-show hosts and howls of protest from industry about the costs of prohibiting the use of CFCs, representatives of twenty countries signed a protocol, the Vienna Convention for the Protection of the Ozone Layer, in 1985. Had this agreement not been successful, by 2050 the middle latitudes of the northern hemisphere would have lost half their UV protection, while the middle altitudes in the southern hemisphere would have lost 70 percent. By 2001 recovery of the ozone layer was taking place and the Protocol had limited damage to about 10 percent of what it would have been otherwise. An especially cold winter at the pole will produce greater-than-normal ozone thinning in the spring, with severe thinning in 1996, 2003, and 2005.

This does not portend well, but in fact the rate in decline in stratospheric ozone at the lower latitudes over much of the rest of the world has slowed; it is still deteriorating, but at a reduced pace.

Key players supporting approval of the Protocol were Margaret Thatcher, then British prime minister, who had a college degree in chemistry and could appreciate the science that revealed the hazard (it pays to have a leader educated in science as well as schooled in law and politics) and President Ronald Reagan, a conservative Republican who overrode his free-market advisors and surprised the political pundits. Some think that his endorsement grew from his major skin cancer surgeries shortly before the Protocol meeting convened, but it may have been that Margaret Thatcher, whom he much admired, had bent his ear. The ozone Protocol has been strengthened twice, in 1990 and 1992, and oddly enough, the reduction of CFCs has resulted in a net savings to the companies involved and to the global economy; sometimes government regulation can be good for the economy. By 1997 satellites confirmed that the level of CFCs in the stratosphere had begun to drop, although current models indicate that it won't be until sometime in 2020 to 2035 before there is a net increase in stratospheric ozone and sometime after 2060 before the ozone levels return to normal.

Dust and Aerosols

Studies of glacial ice cores not only verify the Croll–Milankovitch theory of cyclic ice ages (Figure 11.23), but also reveal that the atmosphere was dusty during glacial stages. Winds apparently lifted fine dust from glacial deposits and arid regions, causing the skies to become hazy. This haziness would have scattered incoming solar radiation back into space, causing further cooling of Earth.

Volcanic activity has been suggested as a contributor to global cooling, both because of the dust ejected by eruptions and due to volcanic releases of sulfur dioxide (SO_2), which is converted to sulfate-aerosol droplets in the atmosphere. The sulfate aerosols, acting like tiny mirrors, cool the atmosphere by reflecting sunlight away from Earth. An illustration of the role played by volcanic eruptions in global climate is provided by the 1815 eruption of Tambora in Indonesia. After that event, with the spread of the eruption's aerosols and dust through the stratosphere, the amount of solar radiation reaching Earth was so reduced that the ensuing global cooling caused widespread crop failure. The starvation that followed caused the deaths of more than 90,000 people. Because the global cooling resulted in rain, late snows, and failed crops in Europe and in New England, 1816 became known as the "year without a summer."[1] Similar reductions in average global

---

[1] This cold summer made the *Old Farmer's Almanac* famous. When the printer was setting type for the 1816 issue, he found July's weather forecast to be incomplete. He decided to predict snow for the Fourth of July. Astoundingly, on that date, it *did* snow in New England, where a large proportion of Americans lived at the time, thereby establishing a solid reputation for that almanac's reliability.

temperatures due to stratospheric sulfate aerosols and dust following volcanic eruptions in modern times are recognized, such as those after the 1982 eruptions of El Chichón in Mexico and (for two years following) the 1991 eruption of Mount Pinatubo in the Philippines (see Chapter 5).

Scientists once thought that all sulfate aerosols made clouds more reflective, thus helping *cool* Earth. But that is true only of aerosols resulting from volcanic emissions, as they are blasted high into the stratosphere. In contrast, it is now recognized that sulfate aerosols released by coal-burning power plants and industry and by motor vehicles reside in the lower atmosphere, where they form droplets that make clouds dirtier and less reflective, thereby *increasing* global warming.

Change in Ocean Currents

Vagaries in ocean currents, too, seem to play a role in plunging Earth into glacial and interglacial climates. A giant, salty "conveyor-belt" current snakes through the world's oceans (◆ Figure 11.25). Originating in the North Atlantic by northward-flowing warm, salty (and thus dense) water because of evaporation, the belt is chilled as it moves northward, which further increases its density. It sinks into the depths flowing southward out of the Atlantic and into the other oceans, much of it rising in the Pacific, where it offsets the evaporation losses there. This conveyor is the main agent of oceanic heat transfer, with one part of it a deep, cold, salty (and thus dense) current (shown in green in Figure 11.25), and the other part of it a warm, less salty, surface current (shown in yellow). The northward-flowing surface water averages 8° C warmer than the cold, deep water flowing south.

When the conveyor is operating, the climate of the North Atlantic is mild, like that of today. It is vulnerable to abrupt disruptions and shutdowns, however, which can cause drastic shifts in global climate and force the North Atlantic into bitter, ice-age cold.

When excessively large volumes of cold fresh water from melting icebergs or runoff enter the North Atlantic, the conveyor shuts down and winter temperatures drop by five or more degrees.

Breaking the Ice: Evidence of Climate Change

Glacial ice provides evidence of cyclic changes in atmospheric chemistry, temperature, and amount of atmospheric dust that correlate with periods of cooling and warming during the Pleistocene Epoch. As snow accumulates and is packed down into ice, it carries information with it that gets locked into glaciers. The relative abundance of two slightly different oxygen atoms—the oxygen-18 to oxygen-16 isotope ratio, symbolized $^{18}O/^{16}O$—in ice molecules indicates what the temperature was when the snow fell from which the ice formed. During a glacial period, when seawater evaporates from a cold ocean and precipitates on land to form glaciers, water containing the lighter isotope, ^{16}O, is more readily evaporated than is water containing the heavier ^{18}O. Thus, the oceans come to contain more of the heavy isotope, and glaciers to contain more of the light isotope. Furthermore, each year's snowfall forms an easily recognized line in glacial ice. When core samples of glaciers are examined, these lines act like tree rings, allowing scientists to determine the years, and the $^{18}O/^{16}O$ ratios allow each year's temperature to be estimated. Together, these data allow a generalized overview and time scale of global climate change.

The bubbles of ancient atmosphere trapped in glacial ice obtained from 3,348-meter (10,981-ft)-deep cores drilled at the Vosstok Station in Antarctica, at the Greenland Ice Sheet Project 2 (GISP2), and the Greenland Ice-Core Project (GRIP), provided a 420,000-year record of variations in the atmosphere's temperature and composition. The Vostok

ThomsonNOW ACTIVE FIGURE 11.25 The giant "conveyor belt" current that snakes through the world's oceans. Two surface currents of major importance in determining the modern climates in Greenland, eastern North America, and western Europe are shown. The cold Labrador (*L*) and East Greenland (*EG*) currents (both shown in blue) cool the adjacent coasts. The Gulf Stream (*G*, red) transfers heat northward, influencing Arctic air currents and warming the coasts of Iceland, Greenland, and western Europe. This current was deflected southward toward North Africa during the coldest part of the last maximum glaciation. The importance of these currents, in combination with the atmospheric wind system, is illustrated by comparing the modern equitable temperature of northern Scandinavia, which is essentially unglaciated, with that of Greenland, which, at the same latitude, is covered by an enormous ice sheet. Data from W. S. Broecker, "Chaotic Climate," *Scientific American* 273, no. 5 (Nov. 1995).

record catalogs four full glacial-interglacial cycles, that is, the atmospheric conditions during four major interglacial periods and the preceding glacial periods. In 2004, a consortium of European scientists, the European Project for Ice Coring in Antarctica (EPICA), almost doubled the earlier Vostok climate record by pulling a new ice core from Dome C, about 300 miles from the Vostok station (◆Figure 11.26) The ice layers there go back 740,000 years and record eight glacial cycles (◆Figure 11.27). The study of this core illustrates that greenhouse gases play a significant role in the glacial-interglacial cycle and, on a human time scale, the ice reveals that since preindustrial times, the level of CO_2 has increased about 40 percent and that CH_4 has increased more than 100 percent. The interglacial period following the termination of one glacial stage was exceptionally long—28,000 years in contrast to the 12,000 years so far in the present interglacial stage. The similarities in the character of the earlier warm period and that of today suggests that without human intervention, a climate similar to what we now enjoy may extend well into the future.

Changes in Modern Glaciers

Modern glaciers provide relevant information because they respond to climate changes by either advancing or retreating. Their behavior serves as an indicator of climate change and also as a "filter," smoothing out the record of seasonal and annual variations in temperature and precipitation. Because of their small size and ice volume, mountain (alpine and ice cap) glaciers in the mid- and low latitudes are remarkably sensitive indicators of climate change: they respond quickly even to small perturbations in climatic elements. A worldwide survey of 160,000 mountain glaciers and ice caps reveals that the volume of the world's glacier ice is declining, and the rate of loss is increasing. For instance, in Glacier National Park in Montana's Northern Rocky Mountains, glacial fluctuations have been studied for a century, with reports dating back to 1914. By 2006 all but 30 of the park's 150 ice fields had melted since 1850, with the cold slivers that remain estimated to disappear about 2050 at the current rate of shrinking. Similar findings in midlatitudes are reported from Switzerland, where alpine glaciers have lost as much as half their mass since 1850; the Caucasus Mountains of Russia, where glacial ice has decreased by about 50 percent during the twentieth century; and in New Zealand, where, on average, the 127 glaciers in the Southern Alps have become 38 percent shorter and 25 percent smaller in area than when first studied in the twentieth century. At low latitudes, the largest glacier on Africa's Mount Kenya has lost 92 percent of its mass in the last few decades.

At higher latitudes, Alaskan glaciers are in dramatic retreat, having thinned twice as fast in 2000–2005 than during the preceding years. Using a laser altimeter attached to an airplane, a USGS research team flew over 67 glaciers in Alaskan mountains in order to compare their present surface elevations with those that were mapped in the 1950s. Since

(a)

(b)

◆ **FIGURE 11.26** Earth's two continental glaciers. (a) The largest glacier complex covers practically all of Antarctica, a continent that is more than half again as large as the 48 states. The ice sheet's thickness averages about 2,160 meters (7,085 ft), with a maximum of 5,000 meters (16,500 ft). (b) Greenland's ice sheet has a maximum thickness of 3,350 meters (10,988 ft). Elevations are contoured in meters. Vostok, Dome C, GRIP, GISP2, Swiss Camp, Kangerdlussug Glacier, and Jakobshavn Isbre are localities discussed in the text.

◆ FIGURE 11.27 The greenhouse gas (CO_2, CH_4 and NO_2) and deuterium (δD) records for the past 650,000 years from the EPICA Dome C and the Vostok ice cores, Antarctica. δD, a proxy for air temperature, is the deuterium/hydrogen ratio of the ice, expressed as a per mil deviation from the value of an isotope standard—the greater negative values indicate colder conditions; ppb = parts per billion; ppm = parts per million. From Brook, "The Long View", *Science* 310:1285 (11/25/2005). Reprinted with permission from AAAS

the 1950s, most glaciers show several hundred feet of thinning at low elevations, and about 18 meters (60 ft) of thinning at higher elevations. Furthermore, the glaciers were thinning twice as fast between 1997 and 2002 as they did from the 1950s to the mid-1990s. This equates to a rise in sea level of 0.1 millimeter (0.004 in) per year from the mid-1950s to the mid-1990s, making Alaska the largest contributor to rising sea level of any ice-bound region on Earth.

Today's Global Warming

We are clearly seeing the effects of climate change starting to kick in.

—Jay Zwally, NASA glaciologist, referring to the tripling of the rate of melting of parts of Greenland's ice sheet

I'll take ten-to-one-odds against anyone who says global warming is not well underway. And I'll take all the money they care to offer.

—Jerry Mahlman, Director, NOAA Geophysical Fluid Dynamics Laboratory, Princeton University

Evidence of Global Warming

Increasing Temperatures of Earth's Surface and Lower Atmosphere

Temperature records from land areas and oceanic shipping lanes reveal that the average Earth temperature increased about 0.6° C (1.1° F) during the twentieth century, with half of that increase after 1970 (◆ Figure 11.28). The greatest amount of warming occurred at night over land in the higher latitudes. Some areas of Canada, Alaska, and Eurasia warmed as much as 5.5° C (10° F) between 1965 and 2000. These differences may seem small, but such changes in the past have had major consequences. As an example, Earth has warmed by only 3° to 5° C (5°–9° F) since the depths of the last ice age some 20,000 years ago.

Earth's present average temperature is the warmest it has been since 1400, which is as far back as we can go with certainty by direct and indirect evidence. Some authorities believe this may be the warmest period in 1,000 years (◆ Figure 11.29). The warmest years of the last six centuries

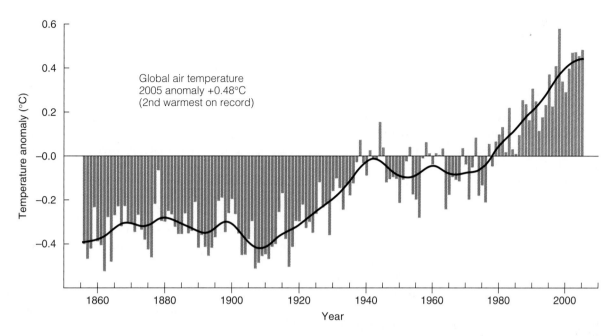

◆ **FIGURE 11.28** Time-series record of the combined global marine and land average surface temperature from 1856 through 2005. The 1990s were the warmest decade in the series. The warmest two years of the series are 1998 and 2005, with the former the warmest at 0.58°C (1.4°F) above the 1961–1990 average; 1998 was the warmest year in 341 years. Data are from proxy climate series (ice cores, corals, tree rings) historical and instrumental records. *Courtesy of Phil Jones and Jean Palutikof, Climatic Research Unit, University of Anglia*

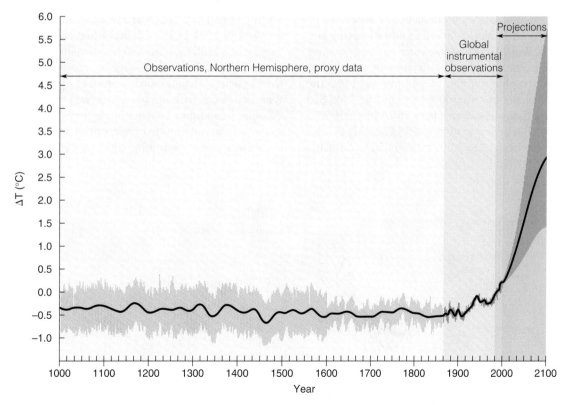

◆ **FIGURE 11.29** The graph known as the "hockey stick" reveals variations of Earth's average surface temperature from AD 1000 to 2100 as determined from proxies and instrumental records. The orange band shows the uncertainty to the 95% level of confidence, which is reduced around 1860 when instrumental records began. ΔT (°C) is the departure scale from the 1990 average temperature value 15°C (59°F). The dark blue region on the right indicates the range of probable temperature projections to 2100 produced by several models. IPCC Third Assessment Report, 2001 were 1998 and 2005 with 1998 the warmest on record, even after correcting for the warming influence due to the active El Niño at the time.

Most temperature reconstructions, such as those shown in Figures 11.27, 11.28, and 11.29, come from temperature proxies, such as tree rings. A temperature history that is totally independent of instrumental or proxy data was constructed from the records of the lengths of 169 glaciers from different regions of the world. The glaciers of the European Alps, where glaciers have been observed and monitored the longest—beginning in 1534 for one Swiss glacier—provided 93 records, northwest America provided 27, with the remaining records from glaciers in Africa, Scandinavia, central Asia, New Zealand, and elsewhere. Unlike biogenic climate proxy data, such as corals and tree rings, glaciers react to climate change in a rather simple manner. By using glacier dynamic theory that treats fluctuations in glacier length as due mainly to precipitation and air temperature, it is possible to calculate the temperature history for any record of glacier length. The temperature record from this reconstruction provides complementary evidence on the timing of the onset of global warming, the magnitude of global warming, and that warming appears to be independent of elevation. The derived temperature record is in general agreement with other temperature reconstructions derived from proxy and instrumental data (◆Figure 11.30).

Alaska's Columbia Glacier moves about 24 meters (80 ft) a day, making it one of North America's fastest moving glaciers. It is the last of Alaska's 51 *tidewater* glaciers—glaciers that terminate in the ocean and waste away by calving—to exhibit a catastrophic retreat. Beginning in 1981 the Columbia Glacier began a drastic retreat and by 2006 had shrunk back 14 kilometers (9 mi) from its former terminus (◆Figure 11.31). It is predicted to shrink back another 14 kilometers within the next 15 to 20 years, eventually to reach a static equilibrium in shallow water near sea level. The rapid disintegration of this glacier is attributed to a complex set of factors dealing with glacier dynamics, not simply the direct result of global warming, although it is believed that the retreat was triggered by warming. The Columbia Glacier is North America's largest contributor to rising sea level.

But mountain glaciers, such as the Columbia, contain only six percent of the world's ice. Of more concern are the enormous continental glaciers of Greenland and Antarctica, which together contain about 90 percent of the world's fresh water. It is estimated that if only 10 percent of the water in these enormous ice sheets were to melt and be added to the ocean, sea level would rise by over six meters (20 feet) and cause coastal devastation worldwide. Based on satellite data, the largest glacier of the West Antarctic Ice Sheet is losing mass at about four gigatons (giga = 1 billion) a year, equivalent to a sea-level rise of 0.01 millimeters (0.0004 in). These glaciers are responding to the higher global temperature between 1977 and 2002, which was 0.4° C (0.7° F) above the 1940–1976 mean.

The Greenland ice sheet is a true remnant of the vast continental glaciers of the last Ice Age. It contains about 2.5 million cubic kilometers or 10 percent of the world's ice—that's enough water to raise the global sea level about 7 meters (23 ft). In the summer of 2002, along with the Arctic sea ice, Greenland's glaciers shrank by a record 400,000 sq mi, the largest decrease ever recorded. This revelation was followed in 2004 by the discovery that since 1997 some of Greenland's outlet glaciers—types of valley glaciers that are nurtured by spillover from large ice cap or continental (ice sheet) glaciers—had thinned as much as 15 meters (49 ft) per year and were melting ten times faster than previously thought. In addition, tongues of ice from several outlet glaciers, each several hundred meters thick and floating several kilometers out to sea, have disintegrated in recent years

◆ **FIGURE 11.30** Figure 11. (a) Temperature reconstruction from glacier length records for various regions. The black curve is an estimated global average temperature value. (b) The best estimate of the global average temperature from glacier length records. The band indicates the estimated standard deviation, with the changing band width reflecting the increasing number of glacier records beginning in the late 19th century. T = temperature; SH = Southern Hemisphere. J. Oerlemans, 2005, Science 308, p. 677.

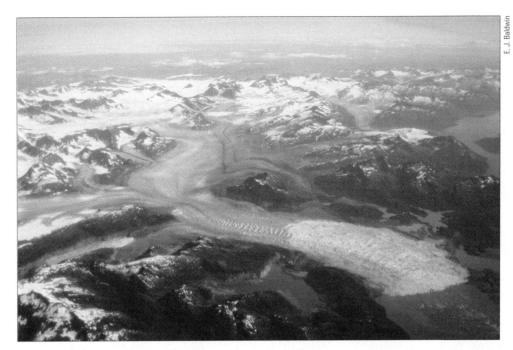

E. J. Baldwin

◆ **FIGURE 11.31** The disintegrating Columbia Glacier, Alaska, in August 1993, about 12 years after beginning its catastrophic retreat. The light-colored lower part of the glacier consists of floating icebergs and slush trapped behind a shallow submerged end moraine. The gray, crevassed part is the active glacier, still in tidewater. By 2006 the terminal end of the glacier had retreated 9 kilometers (5.5 mi) and is expected to retreat an addition 9 kilometers in the next few decades.

reducing the buttress effect holding back the inland ice. That ice is now sliding down channels toward the sea at a pace never before seen. Satellite radar interferometric measurements of ice speed reveal that the flow rates of several of Greenland's glaciers have about doubled since about 2000 (◆Figure 11.32). One glacier, the Kangerdlugssug, has accelerated to an unglacial 14 kilometers (9 mi) per year, nearly tripling its speed since it was last measured in 2002. Combined, the effect has been a greater discharge of meltwater from the Greenland ice sheet as a whole, increasing from about 50 cubic kilometers per year to as much as 239 cubic kilometers a year, more than 200 times the amount of freshwater used each year by the city of Los Angeles (◆Figure 11.33).

The conventional wisdom among geoscientists has long been that in the event of a warming climate, it would take centuries for higher air temperatures to work down through thousands of feet of ice, weaken the ice cap's stability, and turn it to mush and water. In addition, even with a warming climate, a warmer, more humid atmosphere would promote more snowfall at high elevations across the summit of the ice sheet, offsetting the loss due to melting at lower elevations; the ice sheet could thus maintain a kind of dynamic equilibrium for thousands of years. But this is not happening. The movement of Greenland's glaciers occurs in distinct lurches that are recorded by seismographs as microearthquakes and even stronger shakes, one reaching a magnitude of 5.2. The incidence of these ice quakes is seasonal, with five times as many in summer as in water. Such timing suggests that something other than internal glacier dynamics accounts for the increased speeds. The rate of ice quakes has doubled since 1991, beginning about the same time as the increase in surface melting. Evidently, surface meltwater works its way downward through thousands of feet of ice to the rocky base of the Greenland ice sheet. Because of the rough rocky bed, the basal ice moves in a stick-slip manner, lurching downslope only when enough water builds up to raise the hydraulic pressure enough to momentarily lift the glacier over the

Konrad Steffen

◆ **FIGURE 11.32** The Jakobshavn Isbrae, largest of Greenland's outlet glaciers, drains 6.5 percent of the ice sheet. The glacier switched to fast forward in 2004 and now races to the sea at 13 kilometers (8 mi) per year and is rapidly disintegrating where it enters the ocean.

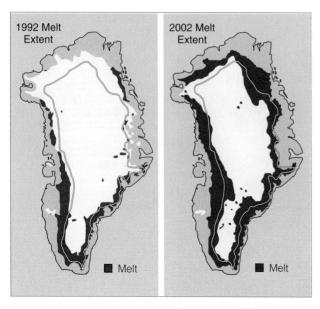

◆ **FIGURE 11.33** Greenland's melting zone, where summer warmth turns ice into slush and ponds of meltwater, has expanded rapidly inland and to higher elevations since the 1990s. The irregular white line marks the 2000 meter (6,500 ft) contour. Konrad Steffen and Russell Huff, CIRES, University of Colorado.

irregularities. The microseisms record these lurching events. Greenland's glaciers are feeling the effects of global warming and, depending on the magnitude of warming, the ice may melt in a far shorter time than centuries, raising sea level much faster than was anticipated as recently as even a few years ago. The contribution of meltwater from Greenland's ice sheet to sea-level rise is a matter of considerable scientific and societal significance.

Consequences of Global warming

Thawing in Boreal and Subarctic Regions

Climate changes in Alaska and the Bering Sea region have already had socioeconomic impacts on Alaskans, most of them negative. For example:

- With less sea ice in the Bering Sea, weather events such as storm surges have increased in frequency and severity, causing increased coastal erosion, inundation, and threats to structures.

- Subsistence lifestyles of the native peoples in the region have been adversely affected by such things as changes in sea-ice conditions. Hunting on the ice, for example, is more dangerous.

- Slope instability, landslides, and erosion are increasingly common in thawing permafrost terrain. This threatens roads and bridges and causes flooding.

- The warmer climate has increased forest-fire frequency and insect outbreaks, reducing timber yields.

- The speed of permafrost thawing has caused major changes in the forest, bog, grassland, and wetland ecosystems that have affected land use.

- Over the past 30 years, the number of days that oil company personnel can travel on Alaska's frozen North Slope to search for oil prospects has shrunk in half—from 200 to 100. The tundra, which must be completely frozen before running vehicles on it, has been freezing later and thawing earlier.

Rising Sea Level

Sea level was about 120 meters (393 ft) lower than the current level during the last glacial maximum, about 20,000 years ago, and its rate of rise has varied. In the nineteenth century it rose about 12 centimeters (5 in), and during the twentieth century it appears to have been about 25 centimeters (10 in). The accelerated rate is due to some combination of the thermal expansion of the oceans and the melting of midlatitude mountain, Alaskan, Greenland, and Antarctic glaciers. Between 1961 and 2003 the melting of glaciers is estimated to have raised sea level at the average rate of 0.51 mm (0.02 in) per year, but for the period of 1994 to 2003 the rate nearly doubled to 0.93 mm (0.034 in) annually. (Sea level raises about 24 centimeters [2.4 in] with each 1° C increase in temperature, with a lag time of about 20 years).

Melting of midlatitude and Greenland glaciers may exert a greater influence on sea level because their meltwater is added directly to the ocean, whereas so much polar and Antarctic ice is floating shelf ice that already displaces its own weight. A factor that may moderate a global rise of sea level is that a warmer atmosphere will hold more water vapor and cause more snow to fall in polar regions.

Biological Response

Observations in North America and Europe reveal that wildlife in various habitats are responding to warming climates, some in alarming ways. Case Study 11.3 on page 345 provides summaries of some research studies.

The Disappearing Polar Ice Cap

Scientists believe that the Arctic Ocean ice cap is displaying a substantial climatic signal. Comparing ice thicknesses measured by submarines between 1958 and 1976 with measurements made in the 1990s revealed that, on average, the ice cap had thinned by 1.3 meters (4.3 ft) and that it had lost 40 percent of its volume in that time. Such a major change in the Arctic could have a significant impact on northern hemisphere weather.

Arctic research was stepped up in the 1990s—a major role in the research was the U.S. Navy's Scientific Ice Expeditions between 1993 and 1997. Their efforts revealed a 1.1° C (2° F) temperature increase in a large part of the Arctic Ocean and recognized that at least part of the increase was due to incursions of warmer water from the Atlantic Ocean. Since 1998 it appears that the torrid pace of thinning of Arctic Ocean ice has slowed. Computer models forecast that Arctic ice will continue to shrink by more than half its 1955 volume by mid-twenty-first century, enough that the thinning and shrinkage will play havoc with Arctic life (see Case Study 11.4) and open a Northwest Passage in summers that may prove useful as a commercial shipping route.

It is uncertain what has caused the decrease in ice—whether it is due to human activities, natural global warming, a natural Arctic climatic fluctuation, or some combination of these factors. A key factor in explaining the retreat of Arctic Ocean ice is the influence of a decades-long atmospheric cycle called the Arctic Oscillation (AO). The AO varies from a cold, still air phase to a warm and windy phase. Normally, the phases shift every ten years or so, but the Arctic has been locked into the warm, windy phase since the 1980s. Some scientists believe that the locked-in warmer mode is due to atmospheric pollutants such as CO_2 enhancing the greenhouse effect and that it forces the decades-long atmospheric swing toward the AO warm, windy phase on which the decadal swings are superposed.

CONSIDER THIS

With what you have learned about the increasing concentration of greenhouse gases in the atmosphere, what changes might you expect over the next 50 years where you live if global temperature should rise by 2° C?

Causes of Today's Global Warming

For every complex problem there is always a simple answer, and it's usually wrong.

H. L. Mencken (1880–1956), American writer

Of the five factors most likely responsible for the large-scale temperature changes presently being experienced, three vary naturally:

- stratospheric volcanic sulfate aerosols,
- climate variability, and
- solar radiation

and two, which have changed decisively, are due to human activity:

- greenhouse gases—mainly CO_2, but also CH_4, NO_x, and CFCs—and
- anthropogenic sulfate aerosols.

A decisive climatic change due to a change in one or more of these factors is called a *forcing*. Some scientists believe that solar forcing may have caused warming in the early 1900s, although natural climate variability and an **anthropogenic** factor (a human factor) cannot be ruled out. But warming from about 1950 to the end of the century, irrespective of any natural forcing, volcanic influence, or increasing solar activity, is most likely attributable to human activity. It was such an analysis that led the United Nations' Intergovernmental Panel on Climate Change (IPCC) in 1995 to recognize that, according to the best estimates from climate models, the climate changes due to human activity add up to just about the amount of expected change. The atmospheric patterns of temperatures match well the increased concentrations of greenhouse gases, sulfate aerosols (mainly from burning fossil fuels), and the reduction in stratospheric ozone from CFCs. In light of this combination of factors, the panel concluded that "the balance of evidence suggests that there is a discernible human influence on global climate."

CONSIDER THIS

If there is a one percent per year increase in greenhouse gases in the atmosphere, how many years does it take for the amount of the gases to double? (Hint: refer to the "rule of 70" in Chapter 1.)

Clouds: A Wild Card in Global Warming

Clouds perform an important role in global temperature control, but scientists are unsure of their exact role. For instance, when Earth is warmer, there is more water vapor in the atmosphere, and consequently there are more clouds. Recognizing this relationship leads to the question, will clouds be the same as we know them today if Earth becomes warmer? Will they be at the same elevation, and will the different types of clouds exist in the same proportion as they do today?

To illustrate some of the uncertainty about the effect of cloud types, consider the global-warming feedback differences between low-altitude clouds and high clouds. Wispy, high cirrus clouds composed of tiny ice crystals are very effective at trapping infrared radiation that is emitted from Earth's surface and thus act to warm the atmosphere; they give positive feedback. On the other hand, the heat-trapping property of low clouds is very poor (negative feedback). In addition, low clouds reflect the sun's radiation back to space, which cools Earth; they give negative feedback in two ways.

The size of the water droplets in clouds is also decisive. Whereas clouds formed of large numbers of small droplets reflect more of the incoming solar radiation away from Earth (giving negative feedback), clouds with larger, fewer droplets give positive feedback, amplifying global warming.

Because of such uncertainties, many scientists have turned away from the debate about whether human-induced global warming is occurring and are now attempting to predict exactly what we can expect to happen in the next century.

◆ FIGURE 11.34 A hypothetical scientist briefs a hypothetical policymaker on the dangers of the emission of greenhouse gases. (After R. Byerly, Jr., "The Policy Dynamics of Global Change," *EarthQuest*, Spring 1989.)

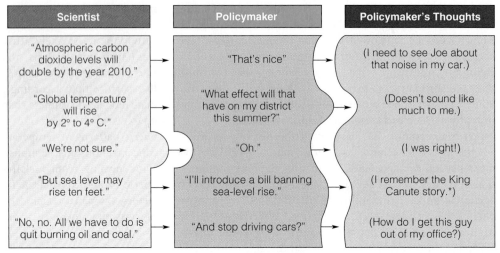

Scientist	Policymaker	Policymaker's Thoughts
"Atmospheric carbon dioxide levels will double by the year 2010."	"That's nice"	(I need to see Joe about that noise in my car.)
"Global temperature will rise by 2° to 4° C."	"What effect will that have on my district this summer?"	(Doesn't sound like much to me.)
"We're not sure."	"Oh."	(I was right!)
"But sea level may rise ten feet."	"I'll introduce a bill banning sea-level rise."	(I remember the King Canute story.*)
"No, no. All we have to do is quit burning oil and coal."	"And stop driving cars?"	(How do I get this guy out of my office?)

*Canute was a king of Denmark, England, and Norway, 1016–1035, who supposedly commanded the oceanic tide to stop rising.

Living with Uncertainty

Atmospheric scientists are still uncertain about why climate changes, and they lack techniques for distinguishing between long-range climate trends and short-term weather events. "The temptation . . . is often to attribute any of these temporal and sometimes local variations to a wider and more pervasive change in climate," note several atmospheric scientists with the National Oceanic and Atmospheric Administration (NOAA). A respected senior climate scientist has shown that U.S. weather has become more extreme since 1980 and has estimated with 80 percent certainty that the extremes are due to human-induced greenhouse warming. In the case of greenhouse warming, built-in delays in Earth's climate system compound the potential dangers of waiting for 100 percent certainty; decades are required to warm or cool the atmosphere and oceans. If the world's policymakers wish to head off the potential for greater climate changes, they must act before the major effects of greenhouse-gas pollution are apparent. Regrettably, global warming has become political, and communication between scientists and policymakers is sometimes difficult (◆ Figure 11.34). If it is due to human activity, we must take measures now to slow or halt it, and enormous up-front costs will be required for mediating the impact. But the determination of certainty must be based on the uncertainty of the past record, and any actions taken may prove to be expensive mistakes if humans are not the primary cause for the apparent climate change.

A few climatologists have been skeptical about global warming, and some of them have doubted that it is occurring. A few feel that warming is indeed happening, but believe that the apocalyptic projections for the future are overblown. Nevertheless, most atmospheric scientists, basing their judgment on a variety of observed changes and studies, express growing confidence that human-induced global warming is occurring. Moreover, computer modeling of the world's climate at NOAA's laboratory throughout the 1990s successfully matched forecasts with actual conditions.

Implications for the Future

It's tough to make predictions, especially about the future.

> Yogi Berra, the all-time great Major League Baseball catcher and manager with the New York Yankees and New York Mets

There can be no genuine security if the planet is ravaged by climate change.

> Tony Blair, Prime Minister of the United Kingdom

Getting a group of scientists to agree on nearly anything, such as forecasting the long-term effects of global warming, is (according to a group of scientists) like trying to herd a bunch of cats. Scientists are especially argumentative when they are thrown a data curveball, as they were in 1999. The curveball was the finding that the rate of greenhouse-gas buildup in the atmosphere had decreased by about 25 percent since 1980. The amount of CO_2 from burning fossil fuels had increased only 0.4 percent in 1998 (despite the emissions from electric power plants increasing by 3.2 percent that year), down from a one percent per year increase on the previous few decades. This does not mean that greenhouse warming had stopped; only that it slowed, thereby giving humankind more time to cope with what many scientists think is inevitable global climate change. The decreasing rate, if it continues, means that the greenhouse-gas buildup will not double by 2050, as many climate forecasters had anticipated; the doubling time has merely been postponed until early in the twenty-second century. Make no mistake, there has been no reduction of greenhouse *emissions,* only in the atmospheric buildup. The reduction in build-up is caused by some unknown process, with the "missing" gases being sequestered in some mysterious manner in oceans, forests, lakes, or wetlands.

In May 2001, President George W. Bush asked the National Academy of Sciences to form a committee to examine what is known and not known about global warming. The Committee on the Science of Climate Change so formed included 11 eminent climate scientists from various U.S. institutions, and their conclusions can be summarized simply: "(1) Earth has become warmer during the past several decades; (2) the warming is likely due to human activities, mainly atmospheric changes caused by the burning of fossil fuels (coal, oil, gas, and wood); (3) Earth will continue to warm, but we are not sure how fast temperatures will rise or how particular regions on Earth will be affected by climate change."[2] The scientists also concluded that it is unlikely that the present warming is caused by natural factors. The scientific data collected indicate that the present warming "is related to an enhancement of the greenhouse effect . . ." and they recognize that the average global temperatures could increase by 1.5° to 5° C (2.7° to 9° F) by 2100.

Most of the scientific community supports global efforts to cut back emissions of greenhouse gases, such as the **Kyoto Protocol,** which set standards for reductions in CO_2. Under conditions of the 1997 Kyoto Protocol, the United States would need to reduce emissions to seven percent below 1990 levels between 2008 and 2012. The Kyoto Protocol has been ratified by some industrialized nations since 1997, but in 2001 the U.S. government, citing economic concerns, withdrew from the agreement. The United States and some other countries favored giving nations credit for CO_2 reductions by considering the amount of CO_2 that is naturally absorbed by forests, plants, and soil. However, those nations that lacked large areas of farmland and forest objected to this idea. Other issues addressed by scientists that remain unresolved are rates of consumption, energy efficiency, and population growth.

A wide range of projections exist on how much warmer it may get, how storm and drought patterns may respond, and what the effects will be on ecosystems, agriculture, and health. Nevertheless, many climate experts say that despite uncertainties, some effects can reasonably be predicted. Let us examine some of the anticipated effects of global warming presented in the Third Assessment Report of the Intergovernmental Panel on Climate Change (IPCC).[3]

- Carbon dioxide concentrations, global surface temperature, and sea level are projected to increase under all IPCC emissions scenarios during the 21st century.

- Globally the average annual precipitation is projected to increase during the 21st century, although at regional levels both increases and decreases are projected ranging from 5 to 20 percent. Locally there will be more intense precipitation events. Increased variability of the Asian summer monsoon.

- Worldwide, glaciers are expected to continue shrinking and retreating during the 21st century.

- Mean sea level is projected to rise by 0.09 to 0.88 meters (3.5 to 35 in) between the years 1990 and 2100, primarily due to the melting of glaciers and ice caps and thermal expansion of the oceans.

- Overall, climate change is projected to increase threats to human health, particularly in lower income populations, principally within tropical and subtropical populations.

- Worldwide, ecological productivity and biodiversity will be altered by climate change and sea-level rise, with an increased risk of extinction of some vulnerable species.

- Climate change will exacerbate water shortages in many water-scarce areas of the world; some areas will experience substantial reductions in available water, while other areas will have increases. Intensified droughts and floods associated with El Niño events in many regions.

- Tens of millions of people who inhabit small islands or low-lying coastal areas such as deltas are at a high risk of severe social and economic effects from sea-level rise and storm surge.

- The impacts of climate change will fall disproportionately upon developing countries and the poor populations of all countries, thereby increasing inequalities in health status, and access to clean water, food, and other resources.

Overall, warming will stress human activities because it will demand rapid adjustment of economic patterns and changes in much of society's infrastructure. There is also a growing indication that the potential effect on human health is no less serious.

In their worst-case scenarios, some global climate models point to the possibility of tens of millions more cases of infectious diseases, as mosquitoes and other pests expand their ranges, and of hundreds of thousands of additional deaths each year due to an increasing incidence of heat waves. Epidemiologists say the most deadly punch of global warming will be delivered to countries of the developing world. Their models predict an increase in such diseases as sleeping sickness, malaria, schistosomiasis, and yellow fever. These diseases already afflict more than 600 million people each year, killing more than two million. Some researchers estimate that global warming would increase the populations of insects and snails that transmit these diseases because cold-blooded insects and invertebrates respond to subtle changes in temperature.

[2]The complete report is available at http://books.nap.edu/books/ 0309075742/html/
[3]The complete report, *Climate Change 2001: Synthesis Report,* is available at www.ipcc.ch/about/about.htm

Changes in rainfall distribution and amounts in some areas would affect river levels and discharge, perhaps causing more flooding. Many high-latitude regions underlain by permafrost (see Chapter 6) would eventually thaw, allowing more bacterial action, and decomposition of organic matter would release methane. The new source of methane, an even more efficient greenhouse gas at absorbing long-wave radiation than CO_2, would add positive feedback to the global warming regime.

What Individuals Can Do

What can we do about global warming? We can do nothing about any of its natural causes, but there are things we can do individually that may help to slow the pace of human-generated global warming that would hardly affect our lifestyles. More than 80 percent of the world's energy and most of the greenhouse-gas emissions comes from burning fossil fuels—oil, coal, and natural gas—and currently we are only getting close to cost-effective alternatives (see Chapter 14). But much can still be done. In the United States there are three main things individuals can do.

⋆TABLE 11.2 Reducing Global Warming Begins at Home	
Action to Take	Estimated Reduction of CO_2, pounds per year
1. Insulate your home, install water-saver shower heads, clean and tune furnace.	2,480
2. Buy a fuel-efficient automobile with a rating of at least 32 mpg to replace your most-used car.	5,600
3. Do not drive your car two days a week.	1,590
4. Recycle all home waste metal, glass, newsprint, packaging, and cardboard.	850
5. Install solar heating to help provide hot water.	720
6. Replace washing machine with low-water-use, low-energy model.	420
7. Buy food and other products with recyclable or reusable packaging.	230
8. Replace refrigerator with a high-efficiency model.	220
9. Use a push lawn mower instead of a power mower.	80
10. Plant two trees.	20

Source: Oregon Energy Office

1. Buy products that reduce energy consumption.
2. Use energy more efficiently.
3. Actively recycle.

⋆ Table 11.2 provides some more specific suggestions. The consequences of our choices and lifestyles are catching up with us, and even small steps will help.

What Industry and Governments Can Do

I find myself increasingly persuaded that a climate effect may be occurring.

Mark Moody-Stuart, CEO, Royal Dutch/Shell Oil Company

There is mounting evidence that the concentration of carbon dioxide in the atmosphere is rising and the temperature of the Earth's surface is increasing.

John Browne, CEO, British Petroleum

In debates about global warming, environmentalists and industrialists have commonly found themselves hollering at each other through clouds of scientific and economic jargon, respectively. This situation began to change in 1998, when several major corporations acknowledged that excess greenhouse gases could well be the cause of global climate change. Among the companies that have made the crossover, warning that "climate change is serious business for all of us," are Boeing, British Petroleum (BP), 3M, United Technologies, Lockheed Martin, and Maytag. Royal Dutch/Shell, for example, announced that it was investing more than half a billion dollars on renewable-energy technology over five years. BP made a new commitment to investment in solar-energy research, and both of these companies backed out of the Global Climate Coalition, an industry lobbying group that opposes the 1997 Kyoto treaty.

> **CONSIDER   THIS**
>
> If you live in the Northeastern United States, determine long-term climate changes in your local area: search out data to show when ponds froze over in the past, and compare with current data. Do the same for the blooming time of dogwoods, the arrival times of hummingbirds in the spring, and when the maple syrup starts to run in the fall.

Ford Motor Company, whose critics point out that it sells more sport utility vehicles (SUVs) and trucks—both major greenhouse-gas emitters—than its competitors, reported that its new minivans and SUVs would qualify as low-emission vehicles. General Motors is experimenting with hybrid electric-power trains that will reduce fuel usage and are currently putting hybrids on the road in mass-transit bus applications, are working on hybrids for personal vehicles, and are investing in a long-term project of developing fuel-cell vehicles. Currently three hybrid personal vehicles are available in the United States that are rated either as Super Ultra Low Emission Vehicles (the cleanest emissions rating after zero emission vehicles) or Ultra Low Emission Vehicles. The Toyota Prius hybrid is rated at

48 miles per gallon and emits about half the CO_2 as the average passenger vehicle on the road today.

Some researchers believe that most of the proposed global emission-reduction plans will do relatively little to slow greenhouse-gas emissions, because they consist mainly of modest, voluntary policies. Furthermore, the industrialized countries' CO_2 emissions may not be the major problem. The United Nations' economic and science advisors on global climate change predict that by 2025 the developing countries and those that are moving away from centrally planned economies (including the former Soviet-bloc countries) will be responsible for nearly 70 percent of all energy-related CO_2 emissions.

A U.S. trade group representing manufacturers, utilities, mining companies, coal and oil producers, and railroads insisted that reducing industrial emissions by 20 percent or more below the 1990 levels, as proposed at the 1995 Intergovernmental Panel on Climate Change (IPCC) conference, would be disastrous for the U.S. economy. They estimated that cuts of this magnitude could cost an average of 600,000 jobs a year for several years.

But the potential costs of doing nothing to curb greenhouse-gas emissions also comes at a price—to the world's economy, agricultural production, and human welfare—but the nature of these costs is beyond the scope of this book.[3]

Offering hope for mitigating CO_2 buildup is a chemical process that combines the gas with materials such as calcium oxide and magnesium oxide to form stable minerals. The

[3]Chapter 25, "Cost, Cost, Cost," in *The Weather Makers* by Tim Flannery (2005), considers the eventual costs of not curbing emissions.

process is viewed as a short-term insurance policy in case political pressure resulting from the threat of global warming forces industry to limit CO_2 emissions. The monetary costs of capturing CO_2 on an industrial scale would be very high. For example, it is estimated that removing the gas from coal-fired electric-power generating plants would double or triple the cost of electricity. Oceanographers have been cautiously exploring the feasibility of dumping finely ground iron particles into the ocean to stimulate the growth of phytoplankton, which, like all plants, metabolize CO_2 by photosynthesis. From initial experiments it is estimated that spreading a half-ton of iron across 100 square kilometers (39 mi^2) of a tropical ocean would stimulate enough plant growth to absorb some 350,000 kilograms (771,800 pounds) of CO_2 from seawater. Performed on a much larger scale, the iron fertilization of sea water could absorb billions of tons of CO_2, offsetting perhaps a third of global CO_2 emissions. The environmental side effects of such large-scale "iron fertilization" are difficult to foresee, but the enhanced bloom of plants could enrich the entire oceanic ecosystem.

In the short term—that is, on the scale of human lifetimes—it appears that there will be global warming. From a long-term, geological perspective, however, the warming is seen as a brief event and a nonrepeatable one because Earth's reserves of fossil fuels will be consumed within the next few hundred years. After reserves are consumed, atmospheric conditions should eventually return to normal. True, human-induced greenhouse warming may last a thousand years, but ultimately the variations in Earth's orbital geometry will change, and Earth will be thrust into yet another ice age.

CASE STUDY 11.1

A Summer on Ice: Research on the Greenland Ice Sheet

by John Maurer, Member, Greenland Climate Network Expedition, 2004

Greenland—Earth's largest island—is mostly covered by an immense sheet of ice, and as thick as 3,000 meters (9,843 feet). As a result, people and animals residing in Greenland mostly live along a thin strip of nearly barren land along the coasts. Greenland's population in 2006 was about 56,000 people and the population of the biggest cities runs about 15,000. As a self-governed Danish territory, a number of Danish people live there, but the population is 88 percent Greenlandic Inuit.

Getting to Greenland involves a flight to Kangerlussuaq, a town of about 500 people along the central west coast at latitude of 68 degrees north, and site of the island's only airport large enough to support jumbo jets. From there, a small utility aircraft, a De Havilland Twin Otter, takes the team and all of their gear and equipment to Swiss Camp (◆Figure 1), a research station on the ice sheet about 300 km (186 mi) north of Kangerlussuaq and 30 km (19 mi) from the ice edge. The camp is strategically located near the *equilibrium line altitude* (ELA) of the

ice sheet—the altitude that divides the regions of negative and positive net annual mass balance. Swiss Camp is so named because Dr. Konrad Steffen, a climatologist, glaciologist, and director of the Cooperative Institute for Research in Environmental Sciences (CIRES) at the University of Colorado at Boulder, and his colleagues from Switzerland built this permanent camp, now serving as a base camp for the Steffen lab on their annual expeditions. The flight to Swiss Camp passes over *Jakobshavn Isbrae* (pronounced "yah-cob-SAH-ven ICE-bray," Danish for Jakobshavn Glacier), Greenland's largest outlet glacier and the fastest moving glacier in the world, which drains into the ocean at a rate of about 13 kilometers (8 mi) per year, or 35 meters (115 ft) per day, or 1.5 meters (5 ft) per hour. Large icebergs calve from its terminus into Disko Bay, to eventually float into Baffin Bay and slowly melt as they travel south into the Labrador Sea. The iceberg that sank the Titanic was likely from Jakobshavn.

CONTINUED

◆ **FIGURE 1** Swiss Camp, which serves as base camp for the Steffen lab's annual expeditions to the Greenland ice sheet for servicing the GC-Net and conducting scientific research.

John Maurer

Though airborne views of Jakobshavn are breathtaking (see text Figure 11.32), the interior of the Greenland ice sheet is flat and as boring as a large parking lot painted white. Summer temperature on the ice sheet usually hovers around 0° C (32° F), plus or minus 3–6° C (5–10° C). But strong winds—often greater than 10 meters per second (22 mph)—create a frigid windchill. Although there can be relatively balmy days in the summer when a single layer of clothing will suffice, the weather often requires wearing thick parkas, hats, and gloves. Because of the strong reflection of sunlight from the snow (and its 24-hour persistence at this far-north latitude), one must wear dark sunglasses and use lots of sunscreen.

Swiss Camp is simply three red tents, each the size of a small room. These serve as kitchen, storage, and laboratory. Power is supplied by a generator, and a propane tank fuels both space heaters and the cookstove. Water for drinking and cooking is from melted snow that is collected in a big bucket. The researchers sleep in their own makeshift tents, held down by bamboo poles so that strong winds don't blow them away in the middle of the night. Snow, which inevitably is dragged into the tent on boots, melts to form puddles of water on the floor, which one must somehow keep from soaking into clothes and gear. Cargo is organized into designated areas outside so that it isn't lost and buried by snowstorms.

Travel to nearby automatic weather stations (AWS) is done via snowmobiles. Although these can cruise along at over 80 kilometers per hour (50 mph), the hopping over gentle hummocks of snow, and hauling heavy sleds of equipment (propane tanks for steam-drilling, extra AWS instruments, etc.) forces them to be operated at slower speeds. Navigation between stations is accomplished using known coordinates and Global Positioning System (GPS) receivers as there are no useful landmarks to follow and because a bad snowstorm or fog can severely limit visibility. Satellite phones are employed for communication (regular cell phones cannot operate that far north). When traveling

into the ablation zone on a snowmobile, the team needs to be especially alert for melt ponds, crevasses, moulins (see Figure 4 in the Gallery), and slushy snow. This requires an experienced eye.

Why do scientists subject themselves to such a hostile environment to study and monitor Greenland's climate? Due to the technical and physical difficulties involved, it is not known yet with much certainty whether Greenland's ice sheet is shrinking or growing. Losses of ice associated with global warming, however, are important to monitor because of the potential for rising sea level. Though continued global warming is not expected to melt the ice sheet entirely, or even very quickly, Greenland's contributions to sea-level rise in the 21st century could still be significant. Rising sea level is an ongoing problem for many coastal regions and islands across the planet, and if this trend continues into the future it could result in large migrations of environmental refugees. Furthermore, meltwater from Greenland could significantly freshen the North Atlantic Ocean (i.e., making it less salty), thereby shutting down or severely weakening oceanic currents that transport heat from the tropics to the Arctic and northern Europe. Should this happen, the Arctic and northern Europe would experience much cooler temperatures, possibly enough to trigger another ice age. For these reasons it is important to monitor Greenland's climate and mass balance—the changes in its total volume of ice and snow.

In order to better understand Greenland's climate, a series of 20 automatic weather stations have been installed since 1995 in order to collect data across Greenland. Sponsored as part of NASA's Program for Arctic Regional Climate Assessment (PARCA), the Greenland Climate Network (GC-Net) provides critical climate information over vast unpopulated regions of the Greenland ice sheet. Dr. Steffen, who manages this network, returns to the ice sheet every summer with the assistance of other scientists and graduate students to maintain and download data from the instruments at the AWS sites and to conduct research.

◆ **FIGURE 2** Servicing a leaning automatic weather station (AWS) on Jakobshavan outlet glacier.

ing near-real-time monitoring of weather conditions on the Greenland ice sheet. The data are available to anyone via the Internet. Servicing the AWS includes downloading all of the measurements stored in its data logger in order to keep the logger from becoming filled and unable to record additional data.

The region of the ice sheet nearest the coast is at lower altitudes where summer warmth can melt the ice sheet's upper layers of snow and ice—this region of the ice sheet is termed the *ablation zone*. Because of the melting, AWS towers in the ablation zone gradually begin to lean as the supporting snow and ice begin to melt. In order to prevent these towers from melting out of the ice and falling over, the towers must be revisited every few years to steam-drill (see text figure 11.3) new, deeper holes in which to reinstall them. In contrast, the interior of Greenland is at higher altitudes and rarely warm enough for snow to melt; this region is called the *dry snow zone*, where winter temperatures often fall below −50° C (−58° F). Consequently, snow accumulates continually in this zone and eventually will bury weather stations there if left unattended. Personnel visit these AWS every few years in order to increase the station's height. This involves lifting the top portion of the tower with a manual crane and inserting an extension to the metal tower. Servicing the necessary AWS towers in this manner is the primary objective of each summer expedition, along with replacing old or broken AWS instruments and downloading all the data.

Digging snow pits is another routine task when visiting an AWS (◆ Figure 3). These provide data for analyzing features in the top several

◆ Figure 2 is an example of an AWS that is part of the GC-Net. Powered by four large batteries and charged by two solar panels, these stations are 5–10 meter- (16–33 ft-) tall metal towers that host a variety of meteorological instruments which are

- anemometers, which measure wind speed and direction;
- barometers, which measure atmospheric pressure;
- hygrometers, which measure relative humidity;
- pyranometers, which measure both incoming and outgoing (reflected) solar radiation;
- thermistors, which measure changes in temperature beneath the surface;
- thermometers, which measure air temperature about two meters above the surface; and
- sonic rangers, which measure changes in the height of snow beneath them (due to accumulation, melt, or redeposition) by sending out pulses of ultrasonic sound and timing the echoes.

Most AWS have duplicate instruments in case one should fail, and the duplicate records serve to validate the data. Data collected are stored digitally year-round in a *data logger* and average measurements are transmitted hourly to a computer in Colorado via satellite, thus provid-

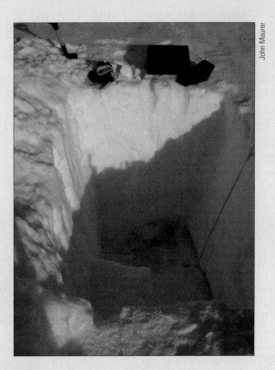

◆ **FIGURE 3** A snow pit near one of the AWS sites, used to analyze subsurface features in the snow for evidence of recent weather events.

CONTINUED

meters of snow that can provide clues to climate events of recent years. Visible bands of slightly blue ice provide evidence of refrozen meltwater. Thin layers of relatively dense snow can be proof of previous storms and strong winds that compacted the snow at what was at one time the surface. Thick, dense layers of relatively large ice crystals, called *hoar frost*, provide evidence of prior summers, and the thickness of snow between two summer layers provides a measurement of net annual snow accumulation at the site. In addition to noting the visual *stratigraphy* of the snow pit, other measurements taken at the site include depth profiles of snow density, temperature, and average grain size of snow crystals. Density is measured by weighing a known volume of snow at different depths along the pit wall, while grain size is measured with a magnifying glass. Together, snow pit measurements help verify, explain, and give a hands-on sense of what the weather instruments at the AWS, have been measuring for the previous few years.

Although satellite-borne remote sensing instruments have become important in studying Greenland because of their frequent and complete coverage of the ice sheet, there are many questions that cannot be answered from space. Despite harsh weather conditions and the difficulty of doing field research on the ice sheet, *in situ* observations remain a critical component in our understanding of Greenland's climate and elsewhere in other data-sparse regions of the remote Arctic. The GC-Net will continue to be useful and important in monitoring climate change and assessing the role of the melting of Greenland's ice sheet in our planet's future.

CASE STUDY 11.2

Climate Data on Ice: The National Ice Core Laboratory

Ice cores from numerous glaciers are stored at the National Ice Core Laboratory (NICL) located on the grounds of the Denver Federal Center in Lakewood, Colorado. The facility currently houses over 14,000 meters (8.7 mi) of ice cores from 100 different bore holes at 34 sites in Greenland, Antarctica, and high mountain glaciers in the western United States. NICL's archived collection of ice cores is kept in the Main Storage area of the lab, which consists of 1,558 cubic meters (55,000 cu ft) of freezer space held at −36° C (−32.8° F) by a computer-controlled refrigeration system (◆ Figure 1). Visiting scientists are able to prepare and measure samples in the 3,050 cubic meter (12,000 cu ft) Exam Room, which is maintained at −25° C (18° F). A cold clean room with filtered air is available for treatment of environmentally sensitive samples. A warm anteroom is provided for suiting up and taking short breaks. The Main Storage collection contains nearly 13,000 tubes of ice samples and contains most of the samples remaining from deep-drilling projects funded by the NSF beginning in 1958, such as Vostock and GISP2.

The NICL provides scientists with the capability of studying ice cores without having to travel to remote field sites, and it preserves the integrity of these core samples for the study of past environmental conditions and global climate change. These cores have been recovered for a variety of scientific investigations, most of which focus on the reconstruction of past climates. By investigating past climate fluctuations, scientists hope to be able to understand the mechanisms by which climate change is accomplished, and in so doing, they hope to develop predictive capabilities for future climate change. Typical data obtained from the cores include age-depth relationships, chemical analyses, oxygen and hydrogen isotope ratios, snow accumulation rates, and pollen analyses. It is the world's most comprehensive ice-core collection available to the scientific community. The NICL is funded by the USGS and the NSF and overseen by a governing board of research scientists, the Ice Core Working Group.

◆ FIGURE 1 The Main Storage area of the National Ice Core Storage Laboratory in Lakewood, Colorado. More than 14,000 meters (8.7 mi) of ice cores are stored in 1,558 cubic meters (55,000 cu ft) of freezer space held at temperature of −36° C (−32.8° F).

CASE STUDY 11.3

Where Are the Wild Things?

Not where they used to be as Earth warms

With the physical evidence of global warming continuing to accumulate, are there indications of global warming in biologic systems? Yes. Studies in the United States and Europe show that some plants and animals are indeed responding to global warming.

As environment changes, plants and animals adjust in two main ways: by moving to more comfortable living quarters and by changing the calendar dates of important event such as migration, breeding, and hibernation. The Edith's checkspot (*Euphydryas editha*), a rather plain brown-, white-, and black-spotted butterfly that is a wide-ranging species in western North America, has extended its range 85 kilometers (55 mi) northward while it is becoming extinct at the southern edge of its range (in Mexico). Furthermore, the rate of extinctions at lower elevations was more than double the rate at elevations above 2,440 meters (8,000 ft). Thus, the butterfly's range is shifting northward and upward. A European study of the ranges of 35 species of butterflies shows similar findings. Two-thirds of the species' habitats shifted northward by 35 to 240 kilometers (21–149 mi) coincidentally with the warming of Europe and only 3 percent had shifted south. In Britain, a 20-year study of 101 bird species found that, coincidentally with the warming trend, most species had extended their northern range by an average of 19 kilometers (30 mi).

The changing of the timing of important life events to accommodate warming is also well documented. Of 677 species studied in North America, two-thirds had advanced important events on their calendar. For example, tree swallows breed about nine days earlier than in the 1950s, and in the Rocky Mountains the yellow-bellied marmot, on average, now emerges from hibernation 23 days earlier than in the 1970s.

In the mountain forests of Monteverde, Costa Rica, 20 of 50 species of frogs and toads disappeared following population "crashes" in 1987. These crashes probably resulted from ecosystem changes that altered the communities of reptiles, amphibians, and birds due to recent warming.

The changes are associated with patterns of dry-season mist frequency, which are related to changes in sea-surface temperatures in the equatorial Pacific since the mid-1970s. The implication is that atmospheric warming has caused the base of the mountaintop cloud bank to raise in elevation and has negatively impacted the mountain forest ecosystem.

Temperature-limited environments in mountains, subarctic, and arctic regions also reveal evidence of warming. In the Swiss and Austrian Alps in the early 1990s, a study compared the plant life on mountain summits exceeding 3,000 meters (9,849 ft) to records collected 70 to 90 years earlier, when the annual temperature averaged 0.7° C (1.26° F) cooler. Altitudinal vegetation belts were found to have shifted to higher elevations by as much as 4 meters (13 ft) per decade, although many belts' shifts were less than 1 meter (3 ft) per decade. A study in Alaska found that **boreal** forests (forests in mountainous and northern regions of North America in which the mean temperature of the hottest season does not exceed 18° C (64.4° F) expanded northward at a rate of 97 kilometers (60 mi) per 1° C (2° F) of temperature increase, and that the length of the growing season increased 20 percent in the last few decades.

Less ice and a longer ice-free season in the Arctic spells trouble for some of its inhabitants. Masses of diatoms, the silica-encased "grass" of the sea, hang from the undersides of floating ice and drop to the sea floor where they are the base of a food chain that extends up to bottom-feeding whales and walruses. Fewer diatoms at the base of the food web means less food for animals higher up the food chain, and research in 1998 shows walruses already to be leaner. On the other hand, disappearance of summer ice could boost the growth of phytoplankton, the floating algae that work up the food web to feed Arctic cod, which in turn become cuisine desired by both seals and humans. For polar bears, however, less Arctic ice spells trouble. Polar bears spend spring to midsummer on ice floes hunting for seals to eat (◆ Figure 1) in order

◆ **FIGURE 1** Walking on thin ice. Between 1976 and 2006 the Arctic Sea ice lost about 40 percent of its volume, thinning by 1.3 meters (4.3 ft) on average. The consequences have already created hard times for polar bears.

CONTINUED

to build energy reserves to get them through the leaner season after ice has melted and they must move onto land. Once on land, they fast, often for months. The warmer temperatures beginning in the 1990s have made for early spring melting and later fall freezing, and seal dinners are now harder to come by. Consequently, polar bears have suffered, their weight dropping by 10 kilograms (22 lbs) for each week that the ice broke up earlier than normal. Furthermore, cub survival is contingent on a well-fed nursing mother and an adequate food supply after weaning. As a result, the polar bear population has dropped 17 percent since 1995, and the U.S. Fish and Wildlife Service is considering adding the polar bear to the endangered species list; the fate of the world's largest carnivore is uncertain should global warming continue.

Sources: Parmesan Camille and Gary Yohe. 2003. A globally coherent fingerprint of climate change impacts across natural systems: *Nature* 421: 37–42; Blaustein, A.R. and Andy Dobson. 2006. A message from the frogs: *Nature* 439: 143–145; Pounds, J. A. and others. 2006. Widespread amphibian extinctions from epidemic disease driven by global warming, *Nature* 439: 161–167; Werner, Gian-Reto and others. 2002. Ecological responses to recent climate change: *Nature* 416, 389; Parmesan, Camille and others. 1999. Poleward shifts in geographical ranges of butterfly species associated with regional warming: *Nature* 399: 579–83; Grabherr, Georg and others. 1994. Climate effects on mountain plants: *Nature* 369, 448.

Wonders of Glaciation

Some of the world's most-visited scenic areas are popular because of the spectacular landscapes that remain as superlative legacies of the work of Pleistocene glaciers. Figures 1 to 5 are a collection of photographs exemplifying the beauties of glaciers and glaciated landscapes.

◆ **FIGURE 1** The Vaughan Lewis Glacier, a valley glacier and an outlet glacier, part of the Juneau Icefield near Juneau, Alaska.

◆ **FIGURE 2** Glaciated landscape including a U-shaped glacial valley, two lakes behind end-moraine dams, three lakes in glacially eroded basins, a small alpine glacier, and a glacial-carved knife-edge ridge. The Arrigetch Peaks area, Gates of the Arctic National Park, Alaska.

◆ **FIGURE 3** A glacial "erratic" that was transported by the Pleistocene valley glacier that occupied Lee Vining Canyon, California. This erratic boulder's location is more than 25 kilometers (15 mi) from the nearest outcropping of the particular bedrock type that could have yielded it.

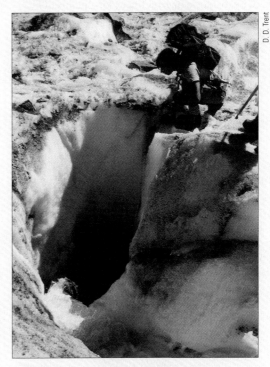

◆ **FIGURE 4** A Moulin (French for mill), or glacier mill, a water-worn pothole formed on a glacier where a surface meltwater stream exploits a weakness in the ice, on the Palisade Glacier, Sierra Nevada, California. Moulins tend to be cylindrical, up to several meters in diameter, and commonly extend downward to the glacier bed.

◆ **FIGURE 5** Striking evidence of ice-sheet erosion, a bedrock surface showing a grooved and polished rock outcrop in New York City's Central Park.

347

Summary

Glaciers

Description

Large masses of ice that form on land where, for a number of years, more snow falls in winter than melts in summer, and which deform and flow due to their own weight because of the force of gravity.

Location

High latitudes and high altitudes.

Classification

Major types are continental (ice sheet), ice field, ice cap, valley (alpine), and piedmont.

Some Important Glacial Features

End moraine—ridge formed at the melting end of a glacier composed of glacially transported rocky debris.
Kettle lakes—water-filled, bowl-shaped depressions formed as glaciers retreated.
U-shaped canyon—remains after a valley glacier melts.
Fjord—U-shaped canyon drowned by the sea.

Effects of Pleistocene Glaciation

1. Some soil conditions, including loess deposits transported by Ice Age winds and some areas of glacial till.
2. Local groundwater conditions.
3. Shoreline configuration due to sea-level changes and isostatic rebound.
4. Human transportation routes.

Climatic Controls

Wind

Movement of air due to unequal heating of Earth's surface. Caused by

1. Variations in the heating of Earth at different latitudes because they receive varying amounts of solar heat energy due to the differing angles of the sun's rays.
2. Due to Earth's rotation, the Coriolis effect deflects winds to the right in the northern hemisphere and to the left in the southern hemisphere.

Air Pressure, Wind, and Climate Belts

Polar highs—polar regions of high pressure; subsiding air produces variable winds and calms.
Westerlies—zones of generally consistent winds lying between 35° and 60° north and south latitudes.
Subtropical highs—zones of high pressure and subsiding air masses lying between 30° and 35° north and south latitudes; have variable winds and calms and, commonly, clear and sunny skies. Often called the *horse latitudes*, these zones are the regions in which most of Earth's deserts are located.

Tradewind—belts of generally consistent easterly winds lying between 5° and 30° north and south latitudes.
Equatorial low and intertropical convergence zone—zone of variable winds and calms lying between latitudes 5° north and 5° south. Sometimes called *the doldrums*.

Heating of Earth

Solar Radiation

Warming Earth by ultraviolet radiation from sun.

Reradiated Energy

Infrared energy from Earth that warms the atmosphere.

Greenhouse Effect

The warming of the atmosphere by an increase in the amount of certain gases in the atmosphere, primarily CO_2 and CH_4, which increase the retention of heat that has been reradiated by Earth.

Greenhouse Gases

Trace amounts of H_2O, CO_2, CH_4, N_2O, and CFCs that trap heat in the atmosphere.

Oceanic Circulation

Description

Each ocean has a characteristic current pattern, the general pattern being clockwise in the northern hemisphere and counterclockwise in the southern hemisphere. The net effect is the movement of cool water from polar regions toward the equator.

Importance

Currents moderate coastal climate and weather, and coastal upwelling brings cool water and nutrients that are important for biologic productivity.

Ice-Age Climate

Description

Temperatures 4° to 10° C cooler than at present.

Causes

A number of interrelated factors contribute to climate changes in ways that are not clearly understood. They include

1. Obliquity of Earth's axis
2. Eccentricity of Earth's orbit
3. Precession of Earth's axis
4. Variations in content of atmospheric gases
5. Changes in greenhouse gases
6. Changes in landmass positions due to plate tectonics
7. Tectonic changes in the elevation of continents
8. Volume and temperature of the oceans

9. Changes in ocean currents
10. Changes in solar radiation
11. Dust and aerosols
12. Oceanic conveyor belt

Some Model-Based Predictions of Climatic Change

1. Globally, average surface temperatures will increase.
2. Globally, average precipitation will increase, but its distribution is uncertain.

3. Northern hemisphere ice will decrease; southern hemisphere ice may increase.
4. Arctic land areas will experience wintertime warming.
5. Sea level will rise at an increasing rate with drowning of low-level coastal plains.
6. Decreasing soil moisture in the northern hemisphere may make farming nearly impossible in much of North America and Europe.
7. Tropical-storm (hurricane) intensity and frequency may increase.
8. Plants and animal ranges will expand in some cases, shrink or disappear altogether in others.

Key Terms

ablate
ablation zone
aerosols
anthropogenic
boreal
calving
chlorofluorocarbons (CFCs)
climate controls
Coriolis effect
dry snow zone
eccentricity

end moraine
esker
firn
fjord
glacial outwash
glacier
global warming
GPS greenhouse effect
greenhouse gases
intertropical convergence zone (ITCZ), "doldrums"

isostatic rebound
kettle lake
Kyoto Protocol
moraine
obliquity
ozone hole
polar front
polar high
precession
proglacial lake
recessional moraine

subpolar low
subtropical highs (horse latitudes)
outlet glacier
till, glacial
upwelling
wind
zone of flowage

Study Questions

1. What makes the wind blow? Why do winds in the northern hemisphere deflect to the right, and winds in the southern hemisphere to the left?
2. Explain the generalization "Glaciers are found at high latitudes and at high altitudes."
3. Glacial ice begins to flow and deform plastically when it reaches a thickness of about 30 meters (100 ft). What is the driving force that causes the ice to flow?
4. Describe the behavior of a glacier in terms of its *budget;* that is, the relationship between accumulation and ablation. How does a glacier behave when it has a balanced budget; a negative budget; a positive budget? What kind of a budget does a surging glacier have?
5. Areas far beyond the limits of the ice sheets were affected by Pleistocene continental glaciation. What are some of the effects? (*Hint:* Consider coastlines, today's arid regions, and modern agricultural regions.)
6. Describe isostatic rebound. What effect has the melting of the great ice sheets had on the crustal regions that were covered

by thick masses of ice until 8,000 to 11,000 years ago? What are the effects of this rebound on society?
7. Describe the greenhouse effect. What causes greenhouse warming?
8. What can be done to modify (or even control) greenhouse warming?
9. What are some potential effects of greenhouse warming on human life?
10. What causes ice ages? Will there be more ice ages? Explain.
11. What is the explanation for the speeding up of Greenland's outlet glaciers?
12. What is desirable about signing the Kyoto Protocol? What is undesirable?
13. What is the effect of clouds and aerosols on global warming? Explain the feedback loops.
14. What causes Greenland's ice quakes?

For Further Information
Books and Periodicals

Brook, E.J. 2005. Tiny bubbles tell all. *Science* 310, 1285–1287.
Cicerone, Ralph. 2003. What we know about global warming. *The American annual, 2002. Yearbook of the Encyclopedia Americana:* 230–239. Grolier.

Dowdeswell, J.A. 2006. The Greenland ice sheet and global sea-level rise. *Science* 311, p. 963–964.
EPIC community members. 2004. Eight glacial cycles from an Antarctic ice core. *Nature* 429, p. 623–628.

Flannery, Tim. 2005. *The weather makers*. New York: Atlantic Monthly Press.

Hambrey, Michael and Jürg Alean. 2004. *Glaciers*, 2nd ed. New York: Cambridge University Press.

Joughin, Ian. 2006. Greenland rumbles louder as glaciers accelerate. *Science* 311, pp. 1719–1720.

Kerr, R.A. 2006. A worrying trend of less ice, higher seas. *Science* 311, pp. 1698–1699.

Monroe, J.S., Reed Wicander, and R.W. Hazlett. 2007. *Physical geology: exploring the earth*, 6th ed. Belmont, Calif.: Brooks/Cole.

Oerlemans, J. 2005. Extracting a climate signal from 169 glacier records. *Science* 308, p. 675–677.

Rignot, Eric and P. Kanagaratnam. 2006. Changes in the velocity structure of the Greenland ice sheet. *Science* 311, p. 986–990.

Singer, S. Fred. 1999. *Hot talk, cold science; global warming's unfinished debate*, 2nd ed., Oakland, Calif.: The Independent Institute.

Internet

Intergovernmental Panel on Climate Change. 2001. *Third assessment report, climate change 2001: Synthesis report, summary for policymakers*. Available at http://www.ipcc.ch/about/about.htm

Science Daily. 2005. Alaska's columbia glacier on disintegrating course. Available at http://www.sciencedailey.com/releases/2005/12/051210120437.htm

Steffen Research Group. 2006. *Melting glaciers and ice sheets contribute to global sea level rise*. Available at http://cires.colorado.edu/steffen/

ThomsonNOW™

Assess your understanding of this chapter's topics with additional comprehensive interactivities at http://www.thomson.com/login, which also has up-to-date web links, additional readings, and exercises.

CHAPTER 12

Arid Lands and Desertification

Deflation Basins, Winds, and the North Africa Campaign of World War II

British War Museum

◆ **FIGURE 1** Northwest Egypt near El Alamein during the North Africa campaign, 1942. A British soldier is watching an approaching dust storm generated by *gibleh* winds.

THE QATTARA DEPRESSION IN NORTHWESTERN EGYPT is an immense, hot wasteland of salt marshes and drifting sand that covers an area of about 18,000 square kilometers (7,200 mi²) at an elevation nearly 135 meters (443 ft) below sea level (◆ Figures 1 and 2). Its origin is partly due to deflation by wind. Wind scour has lowered the land surface to the capillary fringe at the top of the water table. This has led to evaporation of the saline water and crystallization of the salt as a sparkling white crust on the depression floor.

◆ **FIGURE 2** Locations of the Qattara Depression and El Alamein. The decisive battle between the forces of Montgomery and Rommel was fought north of the Qattara Depression.

Mediterranean   Sea

Alexandria

Port Said

El Alamein

Wadi Natrun

Cairo

Suez

Melfa

Qattara

Depression

Gulf of Suez

River Nile

50   100 mi

50   100 km

> Deserts are natural laboratories in which to study the interactions of wind and sometimes of water on the arid surfaces of planets.
>
> A. S. Walker,
> U.S.G.S. geologist

This impressive and forbidding quagmire played a critical role during World War II in a decisive Allied victory in 1942. German Field Marshal Erwin Rommel was a brilliant general who, by turning the flank of his adversary, had been successful in defeating the Allied forces in battles in North Africa. The impassible trough of the Qattara Depression, however, disallowed any flanking maneuvers, thus forcing his *Afrika Korps* into a direct frontal attack against the Eighth Army's heavily fortified positions at El Alamein, a 64-kilometer (40-mi)-wide strip of passable land between the Mediterranean and the hills to the south that mark the edge of the Qattara. Rommel sustained heavy losses in the battle, ran out of supplies, and was forced into retreat. The Allied forces pushed him out of Egypt and eventually westward across Libya. The Allied victory at the Battle of El Alamein proved to be the major turning point in the war between the German and Allied forces.

Throughout the two-year North Africa campaign, the Allied and Axis forces had a common enemy: the *gibleh*, the searing hot winds that blow out of the Sahara. These winds raised temperatures as much as 19° C (35° F) in a few hours and sent sand grains swirling across hundreds of square kilometers. The onslaught of a gibleh dictated the actions of men and machines, preempting military tactics and strategies. Airplanes had to be grounded, and battlefield action stopped for days, as the sun was blotted out and visibility dropped to zero. Soldiers wore tight-fitting goggles to protect their eyes from the clouds of stinging sand and gasped for air through gas masks or makeshift cloth masks. Winds of hurricane strength that tore up camps and turned over vehicles were common. Swirling clouds of sand generated static electricity that rendered useless the magnetic compasses needed for navigating across the desert. Storm-generated static electricity during one gibleh detonated and destroyed an ammunition dump.

Wind as a Geologic Agent in Deserts

Wind erodes by deflation and abrasion. **Deflation** occurs when things are blown away. This produces deflation basins where loose, fine-grained materials are removed, sometimes down to the water table (◆Figure 12.1). **Abrasion** occurs when mineral grains are blown against each other and into other objects. Abrasion by sand can remove paint from vehicles, frost windows, and produce unusual natural features (see the Gallery).

Once fine-grained rock material is eroded it moves, commonly forming migrating dunes—small hills of migrating, wind-blown sand—and drifting sand, which are common in arid regions and can adversely affect desert highways, railroad lines, and even communities (◆Figure 12.2), but they are not limited to arid regions. Strong sea breezes in humid coastal regions coupled with human activities also can cause dune migration (◆Figures 12.3). The problems of migrating sand have been mitigated by building fences, planting windbreaks of wind- and drought-tolerant trees such as tamarisk (◆Figure 12.4), and oiling or paving the areas of migrating sand. Dune stabilization in humid coastal areas of Europe, the eastern United States, and the California coast has been accomplished by planting such wind-tolerant plants as beach grass (*Leymus*) and ice plant "Hottentot fig" (*Carpobrotus*).

Arid Regions, Winds, and Human Health

Each year as much as two billion tons of dust is estimated to be lifted into Earth's atmosphere. Most is stirred up by storms, the most important of which are appropriately named dust storms. A single large dust storm originating in the arid lands of North Africa may drop more than 200 tons of sediment in the Northern Amazon Basin of South America (◆Figure 12.5). North African dust storms routinely affect the air quality in the Middle East and Europe; a fine layer of African dust on snow in Western Europe is not uncommon. Carried along with the dust are pollutants such

D. D. Trent

◆ **FIGURE 12.1** The Devil's Cornfield, a deflation basin that has been lowered to the capillary fringe at the top of the water table; Death Valley National Park, California. The rugged plants growing here—arrow weed, which resemble shocks of corn—are able to tolerate heat and saline soil, and their roots can withstand the effects of exposure to episodic sandblasting.

◆ **FIGURE 12.2** A migrating dune system encroaches on Mauritania's capital city, Novakcott, on Africa's northwest coast. On the left, the mobile sands are threatening a mosque.

◆ **FIGURE 12.3** Coastal dune field near Pismo Beach, California. In the 1960s these dunes began migrating leeward onto agricultural lands due to the destruction of stabilizing plant cover by uncontrolled off-road vehicle use in the dune field.

◆ **FIGURE 12.5** Giant dust storm in February 2001, originating in northwestern Africa and blowing out into the Canary Islands. In addition to dust, such storms appear to carry toxic chemicals, viruses, and other infectious microbes that are now believed to pose a significant hazard to the Caribbean and other regions of the Americas. The image was taken by the Sea-viewing Wide Field-of-view Sensor (SeaWiFS) on the OrbView-2 satellite, which has recorded such storms every year since its launch in 1997.

◆ **FIGURE 12.4** Windbreaks of salt-tolerant *tamarisk* (salt cedar) keep drifting sand from burying railroad tracks; Palm Springs area, California.

as pesticides, herbicides, and microorganisms as well as viruses, bacteria, and fungi. Microbes detected in Caribbean air during African dust events include about 25 percent that are plant pathogens and about 10 percent that are opportunistic human pathogens, organisms that may infect humans. Evidence suggests that fallout has direct consequences on the health of coral communities and may be responsible for high rates of asthma in the Caribbean—a 17-fold increase in asthma cases in Barbados since 1973 corresponds with the period of increased African dust associated with the drought in the Sahel (see ■ Case Study 12.1). Furthermore, African dust events are connected to the meningococcal meningitis pathogen as outbreaks of meningitis in sub-Saharan Africa that often follow Saharan dust storms.

Arid lands in Asia are also a significant source of airborne sediments to the northern hemisphere during the spring. According to the U.S. National Aeronautics and Space Administration, dust from a March 2001 "Yellow Dragon" sandstorm in China (see Case Study 12.1 on page 363) traveled across the Pacific Ocean causing hazy skies in California, and a dust event in April 2002 sullied the skies over Colorado. Some 4,000 tons of sediment per hour may fall in the Arctic during a large dust storm in Asia, and fallout of herbicides and pesticides into the Arctic is common from storms originating in China's semiarid farmlands. These chemicals are found in animal tissues and human breast milk among people living in the Arctic.

Recognition that airborne sediments from one continent can be carried over great distances and affect air quality thousands of miles from their source raises several important but unanswered questions that demonstrate the depth of our ignorance: Can pathogens transported in airborne dust cause outbreaks of disease? Can harmful chemicals transported halfway around the world impact the well-being of ecosystems and human health? What kinds of microorganisms can survive long-range transport in the atmosphere, and can they successfully compete with the indigenous microbial community at a new location?

Deserts

The term *desert* means different things to different people. For some, a desert is a dry barren region of sand dunes; for others, it is a desolate region of bare, rocky outcrops and cactus; for still others, it is a treasure trove of scenic wonders, unique plants, and animals. Regardless of how they are perceived, deserts compose about one-third of Earth's surface and are characterized by meager rainfall, scanty vegetation, a distinct landscape, and a limited population of people and animals. In deserts, the effects of running water, tectonic forces, and wind are clearly apparent. Because these factors combine in different ways in different places, the appearance of various desert landscapes differ as well. Deserts may be hot or cold. They may be mountainous and rocky, or vast, flat sand sheets, and some are covered with gravel. But all deserts are dry. Although deserts appear harsh and rugged, they are enormously fragile, and the misuse of arid lands is a serious problem in many parts of the world (◆Figure 12.6).

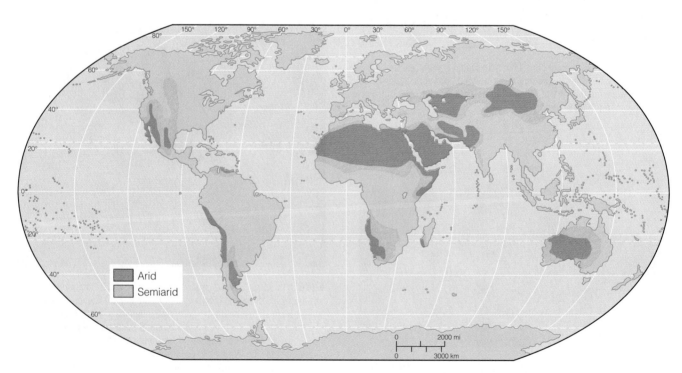

◆ **FIGURE 12.6** Distribution of Earth's arid and semiarid regions.

Kinds of Deserts

A **desert** (Latin *desertus*, "deserted, barren") is defined as a region with mean annual precipitation of less than 25 centimeters (10 in), with a potential to evaporate more water than falls as precipitation, and with so little vegetation that it is incapable of supporting abundant life. Notice that high temperatures are not necessary for a region to be called a desert; only low precipitation, a dry climate, and limited biological productivity. On this basis we can identify four kinds of desert regions: polar, subtropical, midlatitude, and coastal (✴ Table 12.1).

- **Polar deserts** are marked by perpetual snow cover, low precipitation, and intense cold. The most desertlike polar areas are the ice-free dry valleys of Antarctica. The Antarctic continent and the interior of Greenland are true deserts. They are very dry, even though most of the fresh water there is in the form of ice.

- **Subtropical deserts** (also called *tradewind deserts*) are Earth's largest dry expanses. They lie in the regions of subsiding high-pressure air masses in the western and central portions of continents. They receive almost no precipitation and have large daily temperature variation. The Saharan, Arabian, Kalahari, and Australian deserts are of this type.

- **Midlatitude deserts,** at higher latitudes than the subtropical deserts, exist primarily because they are positioned deep within the interior of continents, separated from the tempering influence of oceans by distance or a topographic barrier. The Gobi Desert of China and Mongolia, characterized by scant rainfall and high temperatures, is an example. Marginal to many middle-latitude deserts are **semiarid grasslands,** extensive treeless grassland regions. Drier than prairies, they are especially sensitive to human intervention. In North America and Asia the midlatitude and subtropical arid

regions merge to form nearly unbroken regions of moisture deficiency. Also in the midlatitudes are mountain ranges that act as barriers to the passage of moisture-laden winds from the ocean, a situation leading to the formation of **rain-shadow deserts.** As water-laden maritime air is drawn across a continent, it is forced to rise over a mountain barrier. This causes the air to cool and to lose its moisture as rain or snow on the windward side of the mountains. By the time the air descends on the mountains' leeward side, it has lost most of its moisture, and there we find desert conditions (◆ Figure 12.7). The Mojave Desert and the Great Basin, leeward of the high Sierra Nevada, are examples

✴TABLE 12.1	Classification of Deserts	
Type	Characteristic Location	Examples*
Polar	region of cold, dry, descending air with little precipitation	ice-free, dry valleys of Antarctica
Subtropical	a belt of dry, descending air at 20°–30° north or south latitude	Sahara, Arabian, Kalahari, Australia's Great Sandy and Simpson
Mid-latitude	deep within continental interior remote from the influence of an ocean	Gobi, Takla Makan, Turkestan
Coastal	coastal area in middle latitudes where a cold, upwelling oceanic current chills the shore (Figure 12.8)	Atacama, Namib
Rain-shadow	leeward of a mountain barrier that traps moist ocean air (Figure 12.7)	Mojave, Great Basin

*Figure 12.6 shows the locations of these deserts.

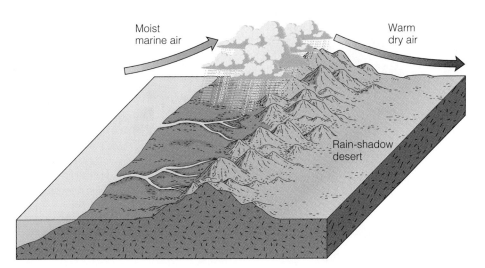

Moist marine air

Warm dry air

Rain-shadow desert

◆ **FIGURE 12.7** The origin of rain-shadow deserts in middle- and high-latitude regions. Moist marine air moving landward is forced upward on the windward side of mountains, where cooling causes clouds to form and precipitation to fall. The drier air descending on the leeward side warms, producing cloudless skies and a rain-shadow desert.

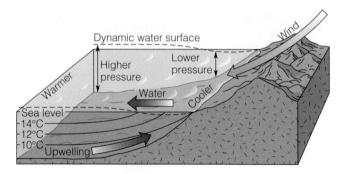

◆ **FIGURE 12.8** The mechanics of wind-driven upwelling of cool water from depth along a coastline. Upwelling delivers nutrients such as phosphates and nitrates to surface waters, where they promote plant plankton blooms and more marine life.

of rain-shadow deserts. Death Valley, the lowest and driest place in North America, is in the rain shadow of the Sierra Nevada. The Sierra Nevada receives heavy precipitation, and Mount Whitney, its highest point and the highest point in the conterminous 48 states, is a scant 100 kilometers (60 mi) from arid Death Valley.

■ **Coastal deserts** lie on the coastal side of a large land mass and are tempered by cold, **upwelling** oceanic currents (◆Figure 12.8). Their seaward margins are perpetually enshrouded in gray coastal fog, but inland, where the air temperatures are higher, the fog evaporates in the warmer dry air. The Atacama Desert in Chile, which may

be the driest area on Earth, is a rain-shadow desert as well as a coastal desert. The Andes on the east block the flow of easterly winds, and air from the Pacific Ocean on the west is chilled and stabilized by the Humboldt Current, the ocean's most prominent cold-water current.

Collectively, midlatitude deserts and semiarid grasslands cover about 41 percent of Earth's land area and constitute the most widespread of Earth's geographic realms.

CONSIDER THIS

Why are the major deserts of the world located at low latitudes?

Desertification

Deluges of blowing sand, such as the one in the North African Desert described in the chapter opener, are common in many arid regions. In the past, sandstorms have been rare in semiarid grasslands marginal to middle-latitude deserts, but this has changed. Across the globe we now see deserts expanding into formerly productive arid, semiarid grasslands and subhumid areas. Such degradation of these drylands is called **desertification,** and it is occurring at alarming rates, especially in countries that can least afford to lose productive land (◆Figure 12.9).

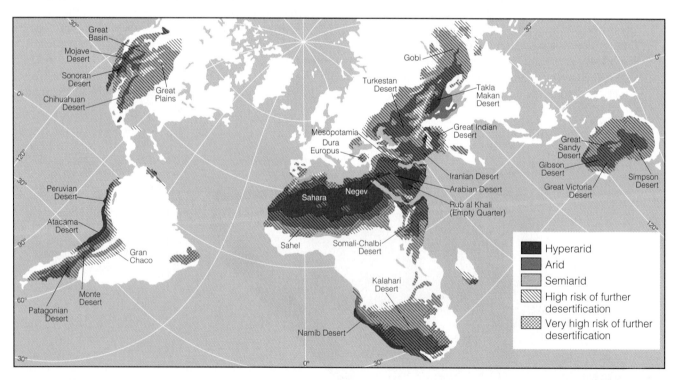

◆ **FIGURE 12.9** Arid and semiarid regions of the world currently experiencing desertification.

Desertification of Earth's arid lands has been going on for at least a thousand years. Until the 20th century, however, even when recognized, it was often seen as a local problem affecting only a few people, and the problem was ignored because new lands were always available. Currently, desertification is devouring more than 60,000 sq km (23,000 sq mi) of Earth's arid grasslands each year—an area about the size of Connecticut, Massachusetts, and Vermont combined—and putting another 181,300 sq km (70,000 sq mi) at risk. Over 250 million people are directly affected by desertification, and perhaps one million others in over 100 countries are at risk.

Understanding the causes of this class of deserts is important, because much of mankind's future in many parts of the world depends on proper and careful use of arid and semiarid lands. Deserts are expanding onto grazing lands and agriculturally productive lands on all continents except Antarctica. The result is that tens of millions of people are dying of starvation or having to migrate, in many cases to areas where more hunger and malnutrition await them.

Desertification does not refer to the expansion of existing deserts. It is the process of altering dryland ecosystems, which cover about a third of Earth's land area, because of the abuse by man. The process breaks down ecosystems by reducing the productivity of desirable plants, undesirably altering the flora and fauna, accelerating soil loss, and undesirably altering the biomass. A common misunderstanding about desertification is that it begins in a nearby desert. However, the existence of a core desert may have no direct influence on desertification. It may start in a cultivated field or a watering hole in semiarid grassland and spread outward if no remedial action is taken.

The expansion of deserts is generally attributed more to human abuse than to climate. Overgrazing of sparse vegetation (◆ Figure 12.10), trampling and compacting soil by livestock,

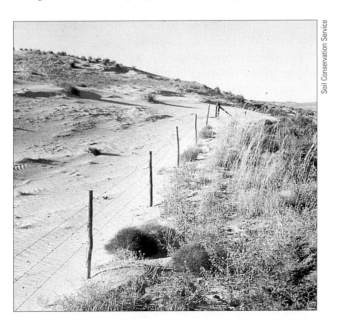

◆ **FIGURE 12.10** Desertification in progress: intensely overgrazed rangeland (left) and lightly grazed (right).

clearing land of trees and brush for fuel without reforesting, rapid growth of large desert cities such as Phoenix and Las Vegas in the southwestern United States and other examples in countries such as Egypt and Saudi Arabia, depletion of groundwater for desert irrigation and urban growth, replacement of native vegetation in arid and semiarid regions with cultivated crops, and soil salinization due to evaporation of irrigation water have all been attributed to root causes of desertification. Even inappropriate economic policies such as practiced in the United States with agricultural subsidies that amounted to $300 million in 2002 are cited as a cause. Such policies result in increased production for export, which encourages placing more land under cultivation, resulting in corresponding increases in erosion and soil loss.

Drylands experience occasional drought. When rainfall in these regions is sufficient, the cultivation or grazing of drylands presents no problems. But once the region is hit by even a modest drought, the crop plants die; few native plants remain that are naturally adapted to survival under drought conditions, and winds carry away what little topsoil exists. Thus a combination of even wise use of the land and drought can be responsible for the expansion of desert regions. Misuse of the land, obviously, will exacerbate the situation. Generally, droughts have tended to be short-term phenomena of a year or two, and the land recovers after the rains return. But in the past decade some regions of the world experiencing desertification have little or no prospect of returning rain. Instead, what appears to be happening is a shift to a new drier climate. True, human changes in land use may be an important element, but attributing human use as the sole cause of desertification is no longer adequate. What other factors are involved?

It was desertification of Africa's sub-Saharan **Sahel** region that first brought the world's attention to the problem that prompted thorough analyses by several climate specialists. The Sahel is a belt of semiarid lands along the southern edge of North Africa's Sahara Desert that stretches from the Atlantic Ocean on the west to the high mountains of Ethiopia on the east, and is 300 to 1,500 kilometers (180–940 mi) wide, (◆ Figure 12.11) in which a large and rapidly expanding population resides; in 1980 the population was 30 million, but by 2000 the population was estimated to be 50 million.

Typically the region has dry winters and wet summers, when the intertropical convergence zone (a rather weak trough of low atmospheric pressure near the equator where the tradewinds converge) moves into the region, bringing rain. Rainfall amounts in the past have varied from year to year, averaging 10 to 20 centimeters (4–8 in), but in some years it has been as much as 50 centimeters (20 in) in the southern part where the Sahel blends into the belt of humid savannah grasslands (◆ Figure 12.12; Figure ◆ 12.13). In 1968 the summer rains began decreasing, exacerbating the man-induced vegetation changes and initiating drought conditions that captured the world's attention with grim images of skeletal mothers and starving children with bloated bellies.

◆ **FIGURE 12.11** North Africa's semiarid Sahel is bordered by grasslands on the south and by the Sahara Desert on the north. From *Meteorology Today: Introduction to Weather, Climate and the Environment,* 4th edition by Ahrens. 1991. Reprinted with permission of Brooks/Cole, a division of Thomson Learning: www.thomsonrights.com. Fax 800 730-2215.

Before the return of a brief rainy period in the 1990s, 250,000 people and 12 million head of livestock died in one of the world's most devastating famines. Many more would have perished had it not been for the massive influx of outside aid. But the region is still experiencing a rainfall deficit and the drought has extended to the Horn of Africa—Somalia, northern Kenya, and the lowland area of eastern Ethiopia (◆Figure 12.14)—where there has been only one year of good rain in the region since 1999. Even if the rains return, it is expected that 80 percent of the cattle in Somalia's Gedo region will die.

The conventional wisdom has been that human use or misuse of dry lands, triggered by a drought, is responsible

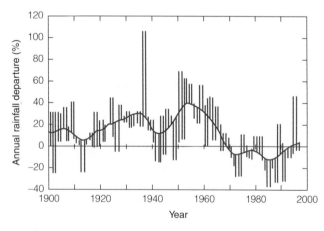

◆ **FIGURE 12.12** Average rainfall departures, by percentage, from the 1961–1990 average for the African Sahel, 10°N to 20°N latitude. The smoothed curve plots the ten-year overlapping means. Mike Hume, Climatic Research Unit, Univ. of East Anglia, England

for desertification. But was such the case for the Sahel disaster? In 2003, climate specialists analyzed the historical record of Indian Ocean sea surface temperatures (SSTs) using computer modeling to simulate rainfall in the Sahel from 1930 to 2000. Surprisingly, the analysis showed that land-use changes in the region were insufficient to cause a climate shift. Instead, the extended drought resulted from rising SSTs in the Indian Ocean, Earth's most rapidly warming ocean. As the ocean transferred heat to the atmosphere, the atmospheric conditions governing the Sahel's monsoon system of wet summers and dry winters were weakened, the consequence of increasing greenhouse gases.

The effect of the weakened monsoon was amplified by land-atmosphere interaction, producing a positive feedback to the drying tendency initiated by changes in the global SSTs. The land-atmosphere interaction began with the loss of cultivated and native vegetation cover, because of the rainfall deficit and firewood gathering. Combined, these produced a second feedback mechanism, increased albedo (reflectance of solar energy hitting Earth) and reduced evaporation, factors similar to that attributed to human land-use changes. Once vegetation cover was reduced, little was left to protect the soil from winds, and the region became even further degraded (◆Figure 12.15). Thus, human land-management practices may have played a part, but large-scale external processes were the underlying cause of desertification.

Another aspect of drought in arid and semiarid regions is dust, and dust originating from the Sahel during wet periods was markedly less than during the drought. Because dusts originating from the Sahel's windstorms are now known to account for about half of the world's total dust load,

© Steve McCurry/Magnum

◆ **FIGURE 12.13** A sharp line marks the boundary between natural pasture and a dune encroaching from the Sahara in the west African country of Mali; a graphic example of desertification. The Sahara Desert is creeping southward into the semiarid Sahel region, and the Sahel, in turn, is expanding into the grasslands to the south of it.

and dust causes global dimming, a phenomenon that decreases the amount of solar energy hitting Earth's surface, the drought in the Sahel may have an unexpected and widespread influence on Earth's climate.

In the United States overgrazing has left an imprint on the arid lands of the west, with salinization and water logging common in many irrigated valleys. By the mid-1800s overgrazing in the southwest was already a problem, but when the railroads arrived in the 1880s, the explosion of cattle grazing

that followed resulted in the carrying capacity of the land being exceeded, accompanied by increased erosion and arroyo (gully) deepening. Consequently, an area of the United States that is a textbook example illustrating the conversion of productive arid land to desert is the Rio Puerco

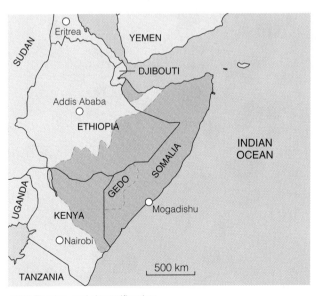

Famine and desertification or threat of it

◆ **FIGURE 12.14** The Horn of Africa, an area threatened by desertification.

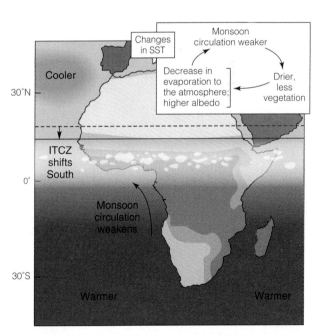

◆ **FIGURE 12.15** The Sahel drought since the 1960s was likely initiated by a change in global ocean temperatures, which reduced the strength of the African monsoon, and exacerbated by land-atmosphere feedbacks through loss of natural vegetation and land cover change. Land use by humans may have played an important role. (SST = sea surface temperature; ITCZ = intertropical convergence zone). Adapted from Zeng 2003, *Science* 302, p.1000

Basin of central New Mexico, one of the most severely eroded regions of western United States (see Case Study 12.2).

As of this writing, much of the west is in its eighth year of drought; such dry conditions in the region have not been experienced for about 700 years. Furthermore, the temperature increase throughout the West since the 1950s has reduced the spring snow pack (◆Figure 12.16a) and has produced an earlier snowmelt (◆Figure 12.16b). And because the 1990s have been the warmest decade in the last 100 years or more, a connection between high temperatures and a rainfall deficit is suggested. As with the Sahel, the link seems to be connected to rising ocean temperatures. Between 1998 and 2002 the central western Pacific Ocean was far warmer than normal and the eastern tropical Pacific was cooler. These conditions forced the path of the jet stream causing storms that would normally move eastward across Oregon and into the central United States to shift northward. Southwest Asia and southern Europe experienced droughts during the same period, and it appears that the changes in the Pacific Ocean SSTs, coincident with the warming of the Indian Ocean, acted in concert to contribute to widespread midlatitude drying. The warmth of the west Pacific and Indian oceans was unprecedented and consistent with forcing by increased greenhouse gases in the atmosphere.

In the southern hemisphere, Australia, the desert continent, is experiencing unprecedented drought, especially in the continent's southwest. During the first 150 years of European settlement in the southwest, winter rainfall was reliable. Now, however, the region experiences a rainfall deficit that is credited to a combination of global warming and the destruction of the ozone layer. Reduction of ozone has cooled the stratosphere over Antarctica, which has drawn Australia's zone of southern rainfall further south. This region of former winter wheat farming in southwest Australia is now turning to desert with the condition exacerbated by increasing summer rainfall. Because of the historically erratic nature of the summer rains, the farmers have never raised summer crops, so the rain now falls on vacant wheat fields, and the water percolates down to the water table where it encounters salt that the prevailing westerly winds have been blowing in from the Indian Ocean for millennia. Under natural conditions, the native plants utilized the summer rains and the salt remained untouched. Currently, however, as the rains fall on bare fields, evaporation draws salty water upward to the surface, poisoning all the plants that it touches. The former wheat-growing region is the world's worst case of dryland salinization, and it comes at a cost of billions of dollars in losses. In addition to the lost

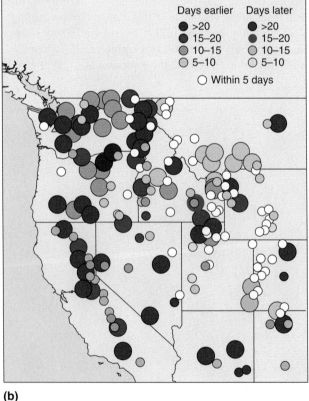

(a)   (b)

◆ **FIGURE 12.16** A modest temperature increase in the western United States from 1950 to 2000 has (a) reduced the snow-water equivalent of the winter snowpacks, and (b) shifted the peak snowmelt to earlier in the summer. From Robert F. Service 2004, *Science* 303, p.1125. Reprinted with permission from AAAS

◆ **FIGURE 12.17** Off-highway vehicle damage to the desert. Jawbone Canyon in California is an example of how human activities contribute to desertification. Because the vehicles compact and alter the surface, they cause reductions in vegetation and permeability, which reduces soil moisture content and thus affects local biological systems. Desert rains have eroded the tracks down the slope, transforming them into gullies, which increases runoff and significantly increases soil loss in the delicate arid environment of the United States west of the 100th meridian. With the simple passage of a few vehicles, soil that required hundreds of years to develop can be destroyed.

agricultural production, houses, roads, and railroads are being damaged by the salt. There appears to be no solution to the salinization.

Scientists are still uncertain whether desertification, as part of global climate change, is permanent or how it can be reversed or halted, but there is some evidence the process can be reversible. An example of reversing desertification occurred in parts of the Great Plains of the United States, which became well known in the 1930s when a combination of poor farming practices and drought turned much of the region into the Dust Bowl. Vastly improved methods of land and water management and farming methods have prevented the Dust Bowl disaster from recurring. Nevertheless, desertification still affects hundreds of millions of people on nearly every continent.

Desertification is a complex and subtle process of deterioration that often may be reversible, but disturbed desert and marginal grassland ecosystems are slow to recover. This is because those ecosystems are characterized by slow plant growth, little bacterial activity in the soil for recycling nutrients, little species diversity, and little water. Already sparse vegetation that has been destroyed by overgrazing (see Figure 12.10) or off highway vehicle use (◆Figure 12.17) may require decades (◆Figure 12.18), perhaps even centuries, to be restored to its natural state. The best program for reversing the trend is to halt exploitation immediately

◆ **FIGURE 12.18** An illustration of the fragile nature of desert ecosystems: annual plants, lichen crust, and surface texture have not recovered in tracks left by a single pass of an Army tank in maneuvers in the Mojave Desert in 1942–43. Photograph taken in 1986.

◆ **FIGURE 12.19** Reclaimed farm land lost to desertification at a farm in Niger, on the southern edge of the Sahel. (a) The farm after one year's participation in a desert reclamation program. (b) The farmer and his farm after seven years of participation in the reclamation program. The young trees are drought tolerant perennials that will eventually provide a market crop and form a wind break to stabilize the soil in this region of nearly persistent drought. Millet stalks remain following the farm's annual harvest.

(a)

(b)

and to adopt measures such as planting drought-tolerant trees (◆Figure 12.19), developing drip irrigation systems for effective water use, establishing protective screens—grass belts or strips of trees—as windbreaks that will help reestablish natural ecosystems, building sand fences, keeping grazing stock moving, and covering drifting sand dunes with boulders or oil or paving areas to interrupt the force of wind near the face of dunes to prevent sand from moving. In areas marginal to Mongolia's Gobi and China's Tengger Deserts, (see ■ Case Study 12.1 on page 363), efforts are being made to reclaim absued marginal lands that have become desert. At a research station along the margin of the Gobi Desert, Chinese scientists, in partnership with others from Japan and Israel,

experiment with techniques for halting desertification. Their research is directed at finding drought- and salt-tolerant grasses, trees, and shrubs, and utilizing drip irrigation for raising such crops as apples, onions, squash, and watermelons in hope of recovering lands lost to desert dust, turning them into once again productive farmland. On a larger scale, a "Green Wall," which eventually will stretch more than 5,700 km (3,540 miles), much longer than China's famous Great Wall, is being planted in northeastern China to protect sandy deserts that are considered to have been created by human misuse.

A good example of natural recovery is seen in Kuwait in an unexpected consequence of the 1991 Gulf War. Thousands of unexploded land mines and bombs are scattered across the desert in the western part of the country. These have discouraged off-road driving by sport hunters of the region's animals. The native vegetation is reestablishing, and the desert now resembles a U.S. prairie. The number of birds in the area is much greater than before the war.

Recognizing the need for an innovative approach in combating desertification, 191 governments joined the United Nations Convention to Combat Desertification in September 2005. The treaty recognizes the complexity of the causes of desertification and that the struggle to reclaim and protect drylands will be difficult—there will be no quick fix.

CONSIDER THIS

In the marginal lands in China, the Sahel and the Horn of Africa that are threatened by desertification, how would you go about convincing local farmers that they should invest money and effort in planting windbreaks and installing drip irrigation?

CASE STUDY 12.1

Is Desertification Swallowing China?

In the People's Republic of China, Longbaoshan, a farming area about 65 kilometers (40 mi) northwest of Beijing, is at the leading edge of China's war against desertification. The advancing desert is driven by a combination of drought, poor land management, overpopulation, and overgrazing. In the 1990s China was hit with more than 20 sandstorms a year, up from eight in the 1960s. Between 1994 and 2000, desert lands in China grew by nearly 53,000 square kilometers (20,300 sq mi)—an area more than the combined area of New Hampshire and Vermont. In the country's driest regions, such as Inner Mongolia (◆ Figure 1), drifting sands smother grasslands in scenes reminiscent of the Dust Bowl days of the 1930s in the midwestern United States (see Chapter 6). China, a quarter of which is arid land, has 20 percent of the world's population but only 2 percent of the world's arable land. China's current desertification causes financial losses of $6.7 billion a year, affects the lives of 400 million people, and threatens farmers and herders. China will experience an unprecedented ecological and human disaster if the marching sands are not halted.

In March 2002 the worst sandstorm in a decade, known as a Yellow Dragon, turned Beijing's sky yellow, blinded its residents by cutting visibility to less than 90 meters (300 ft), and dumped 30,000 tons of sand on the city. Yellow Dragon sandstorms sometimes merge with rain clouds to inundate the city with mud.

The government is trying to halt the moving sands by planting green buffer zones in critical regions. A project intended to protect Beijing, and prepare the region for the 2008 summer Olympic Games, requires reclaiming a large area recently lost to desertification. In Xuanhua County, about 150 kilometers (90 mi) northwest of Beijing, 250,000 soldiers are trying to stop an adjacent desert in a 10-year project of planting pine trees and poplars around the Yanghe Reservoir. Officials are also encouraging farmers to plant trees in dry fields where they once grew crops, paying the peasants with grain and money if 80 percent of the trees survive the first year. Raising trees in this barren mountainous moonscape is arduous because water must be hauled, in some cases up to several kilometers, by oxcart or backpack.

◆ **FIGURE 1** China and Mongolia index map.

CONTINUED

Another strategy for halting drifting sands has been successful in stabilizing windblown sand that had regularly buried the tracks of a main railroad line in China's Tengger Desert on the edge of Inner Mongolia. Inexpensive, low-tech straw mats placed along the railroad right-of-way stabilize the dunes and give desert-adapted plants the time to become established (◆Figure 2).

Water, which is in short supply in China, is the most important weapon against desertifi-cation. The demands of rising living standards and heavy industry have created water short-ages and caused rivers to dry. The lower Huang He (Yellow River), China's "mother" river, ran dry for 225 days in 1997, and for most of the year the river failed to reach the Yellow Sea. A similar disappearance of once raging rivers is repeated elsewhere in the country. For example, in Beijing is a twelfth-century stone bridge made famous by Marco Polo, the thirteenth-century Venetian explorer.

It stretches 300 meters (900 ft) across what was once the Yongding River (◆Figure 3). As recently as the 1970s people fished in the waters and swam in the river beneath the bridge, but today it is nothing but gravel, dust, and weeds.

◆ **FIGURE 2** Straw barrier mats being placed along the railroad line in the Tengger Desert region of China's Inner Mongolia stabilize the desert's drifting sands and give desert plants time to become established.

© George Steinmetz, *National Geographic*

◆ **FIGURE 3** Southwest of Beijing an abandoned paddleboat sits on the dry bed over which the Yongding River once flowed. The 12th century bridge in the background was publicized by Marco Polo after his visit to China in the 13th century.

Frank Langfitt, Sunsource/The Baltimore Sun

CASE STUDY 12.2

Arroyo Cutting and Environmental Change in the Western United States: Climate or Overgrazing?

In the late 19th century and early 20th century, the incision of arroyos made dramatic changes in the landscape of semiarid southwestern United States. Arroyos, common features of the region, are flat-floored, steep-walled stream channels that develop in cohesive, fine-grained material in valley floors. They are complex stream systems and among the most dynamic features of the semiarid landscape, especially in New Mexico and Arizona. Arroyos may be as deep as 20 meters (65 feet) and as wide as 50 meters (165 feet). The deepening and widening of arroyos has been a costly and major nuisance in the West since settlers arrived in the mid-1800s. A striking feature of arroyos is their alternation between periods of aggradation (backfilling) an incision. The most recent period of **arroyo incision,** from about 1865 to 1915, was merely the most recent cycle of cutting, others occurring about 2000 years ago and about 700 years ago. Areas subject to arroyo formation are illustrated in ◆Figure 1, and a record of the arroyo dynamics of the San Pedro River, near Benson, Arizona from 1900 to 1970, is shown in ◆Figure 2.

Arroyo formation may be attributed to three factors, but the relative importance of each is difficult to determine. (1) Climate change producing some years with periods of intense rainfall and other years of virtually no rain is probably a major factor in the arroyo cycle, but the precise role of climate change is unclear; (2) misuse of the land, such as overgrazing and compaction of soils that leaves the land susceptible to erosion, has been blamed for arroyo deepening during the most recent period of erosion (1865–1915); and (3) a natural cycle of erosion and deposition due to internal adjustments within the channel system. It is likely that some combination of these three factors explains the arroyo cycle of alternate incision and backfilling.

In the case of the Rio Puerco in central New Mexico (◆Figure 3), the reports of the Spanish explorers in the 17th and 18th centuries cite the river as draining a grassy basin with cottonwood trees lining the banks (◆Figure 4). Observations of arroyos elsewhere in the southwest include descriptions of *cienegas* (riverbed marshes) that contained beaver and fish, and tall grasses nourished by high water tables. No cottonwoods now line the Rio Puerco, and elsewhere the marshes have been drained by arroyo incision. Such arroyo cutting can destroy agricultural efforts, such as the incision cuts below the water table, causing water tables to drop and wells to run dry. Consequently, agricultural use of the land ends, and farms, even towns, are abandoned, and the once-productive lands become desert.

Erosion also increases the stream's sediment load, causing downstream flooding and burial of agriculturally productive soils, damage to bridges, roads, railroads, and irrigation works. The Rio Puerco carries one of the highest loads of suspended sediment in the world, with an average sediment load of about 400,000 ppm. Or, to put it in other terms, on average, every ten gallons of river water contains four gallons of dirt.

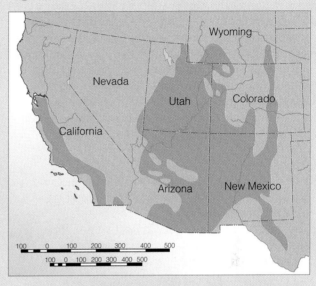

◆ **FIGURE 1** Approximate extent of arroyo development in the southwestern United States. Modified from Cooke and Reeves, 1976

--- Profile c:1900   --- Profile 24/4/28   —— Profile 5/11/70

◆ **FIGURE 2** Incision of the San Pedro Arroyo at the Benson, Arizona railroad bridge. The arroyo was estimated to be only one meter (3 ft) deep and 49 meters (160 ft) wide in 1900. A flash flood destroyed the bridge in 1926 when the channel was deepened nearly 3 meters (10 ft). By 1930 it had entrenched 9 meters (30 ft) below the base of the rail. In 1970, the date of the last available measurement, the floor of the arroyo was 13 meters (42 ft) below the rail, and much of the sediment composing the bank material between the abutments in 1928 had been removed. Entrenchment at the bridge site is not necessarily typical of the entire arroyo because the flow of the San Pedro River is artificially concentrated at this site where severe erosion would be anticipated. Nevertheless, the historical record provides a first order estimate of the rate of arroyo incision. "Incision of the San Pedro Arryo at the Benson, Arizona railroad bridge" from "Arroyos and Environmental Change in the American Southwest" by Cooke, Ronald and Reeves, Richard (1976). By permission of Oxford University Press

CONTINUED

Attempts to control the damage from arroyo cutting began in the 1930s with the reduction of grazing livestock and the construction of control structures. Ranchers, even though acutely aware of the erosion menace, and loss of productive land, were generally unconvinced that grazing livestock was responsible for erosion. Studies of isolated tracts of land near arroyos that were fenced to keep out livestock in order to promote revegetation proved inconclusive—some areas experienced significant recovery in stabilizing arroyo walls, but recovery in other areas was insignificant. Experiments, including placing debris into arroyo channels to slow stream flow, planting trees along banks, and construction of silt-trapping structures, have been tried, but such controls are expensive. It appears there is no known economically viable solution to the arroyo problem in this region.

◆ **FIGURE 3** The meandering Rio Puerco in central New Mexico.

Sources:

Aby, S., A. Gellis, and M. Pavich. 2004. The Rio Puerco arroyo cycle and the history of landscape changes. http//:geochange.er.usgs.gov/sw/impacts/geology/puerco1/

Bauer, P.W., R.P. Lozinsky, C.J. Condie, and L.G. Geer. 2003. Albuquerque, a guide to its geology and culture: Socorro, New Mexico Bureau of Geology and Mineral Resources.

Cooke, R.U. and R. W. Reeves. 1976. Arroyos and environmental change: Oxford University Press, New York.

Vogt, B.J. 2003. The arroyo problem in the southwestern United States. http//:geochange.er.usgs.gov/sw/impacts/geology/arroyos/

(a)

(b)

◆ **FIGURE 4** (a) The Rio Puerco near Cabezon, New Mexico in 1885 before incision of the arroyo. Notice the cottonwood trees along the river and the numerous small trees in the gullies on the distant mesa. (b) The Rio Puerco in 1977 from the same site as photo (a) with several meters of incision. Note the high caving banks, which add to the sediment load of the river; no cottonwood trees remain, and there are fewer small trees in the distant gullies after 92 years of arroyo incision and lowering of the water table.

Desert Oddities

Arid regions, too, have unique and spectacular characteristics that are distinct from other climatic realms.

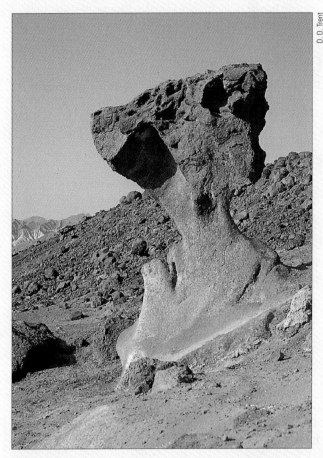

◆ **FIGURE 1** Mushroom rock, Death Valley National Park, California. Rigorous wind erosion in the abrasion zone just above the ground surface can produce unusual landforms such as this.

◆ **FIGURE 2** Remnants of a 1920s plank road, an early attempt to maintain a road in a region of drifting sand; Algodones dune field between El Centro, California and Yuma, Arizona.

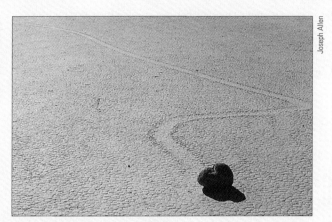

◆ **FIGURE 3** Playa lake scraper; Racetrack Playa, Death Valley National Park, California. The boulder's track is preserved on the mud-cracked surface. The boulder, 25 cm (11 in) at its widest, moved or was moved during a winter wet period due to just the right combination of rain-soaked mud and gusty high wind.

◆ **FIGURE 4** Devil's Golf Course, Death Valley National Park, California, the lowest elevation in the western hemisphere. The salt-encrusted surface has formed at the capillary fringe on the top of the underlying water table.

367

Summary

Deserts

Description

Regions where annual precipitation averages less than 25 centimeters (10 in) and that are so lacking in vegetation as to be incapable of supporting abundant life.

Causes

1. High-pressure belts of subsiding, warming air that absorbs water and precludes cloud formation.
2. Isolation from moist maritime air masses by position in deep continental interior.
3. Windward mountain barrier that blocks passage of maritime air.

Classification

May be classified into four categories determined by climate belts.

Types

1. *Polar deserts,* regions of perpetual cold and low precipitation.
2. *Midlatitude deserts* are found within the interior of continents in the middle latitudes, remote in distance from the influence of oceans.
3. *Subtropical deserts,* Earth's largest realm of arid regions, lie in and on the equatorial side of subtropical zones of subsiding high-pressure air masses in the western and central portions of continents.
4. *Coastal deserts* occur on the coastal side of a land or mountain barrier in subtropical latitudes. Because they are bordered by ocean, they are cool, humid, and often foggy.

Desertification

The expansion of deserts into formerly productive lands because of complex natural and man-induced factors.

Wind as a Geologic Agent

Erosion

1. *Deflation*—earth materials are lifted up and blown away.
2. *Abrasion*—mineral grains are blown against each other and into other objects.

Control of Migrating Sand

Accomplished with sand fences, paving, windbreaks, and stabilizing plants.

Key Terms

abrasion	desert	rain-shadow desert	Sahel
arroyo incision	desertification	semiarid grassland	upwelling
coastal desert	midlatitude desert	subtropical desert	
deflation	polar desert		

Study Questions

1. Explain why the world's largest deserts are located on or near the horse latitudes.
2. What factors other than drought are responsible for the desertification that has resulted in starvation in Africa and elsewhere? (*Hint:* Consider carrying capacity, as discussed in Chapter 1.)
3. Explain why groundwater can be found only a few centimeters to a meter (3 ft) or so below the salt-encrusted surface in some of the driest places in the world—for example, the Devil's Golf Course, at about 75 meters (250 ft) below sea level in Death Valley and the Qattara Depression, at about 135 meters (443 ft) below sea level in the Sahara Desert.
4. List measures that can be taken to halt sand-dune migration.
5. List agricultural practices in arid and semiarid regions of the United States (such as California's Coachella Valley and western Nebraska) that increase the likelihood of desertification.
6. List measures that can be taken to halt desertification.
7. How does the land-atmosphere interaction cause changes in rainfall?
8. Does "global dimming" from excess atmospheric dust produce a positive or negative feedback loop to global warming?

For Further Information

Books and Periodicals

Ahrens, C.D.. 2000. Global climate (pp. 470–502). *Meteorology today*, 5th ed. Pacific Grove, Calif.: Brooks/Cole.

Cook, E.R. et al. 2004. Long-term aridity changes in the western United States. *Science* 306: pp. 1015–1018.

Cooke, U. and R. W. Reeves. 1976. *Arroyos and environmental change in the American south-west*. London: Oxford University Press, 213 p.

Cooke, R.U., A. Warren, and A. Goudie. 1993. *Desert geomorphology*. London: UCL Press.

Ellis, W.S. 1987. Africa's Sahel: the stricken land. *National geographic* 172, no. 2: pp. 140–179.

Flannery, Tim. 2005. Liquid gold: changes in rainfall (pp. 123–134). *The weather makers*. New York: Atlantic Monthly Press.

Gianni, A., R. Saravanan, and P. Chang. 2003. Oceanic forcing of Sahel rainfall on interannual and interdecadal timescales. *Science* 302, p. 1027–1030.

Griffen, D.W., C.A. Kellog, V.H. Garrison, and E.A. Shin. 2002. The global transport of dust. *American scientist* 90, no. 3: pp. 228–235.

Hoerling, M. and A. Kumar. 2003. The perfect ocean for drought. *Science* 299, pp. 691–694.

Karoly, D.J. 2003. Ozone and climate change. *Science* 302, pp. 236–237.

Monroe, J.S., R. Wicander, and R. Hazlett. 2007. The work of wind and deserts (pp. 566–595). *Physical geology, exploring the Earth*, 6th ed. Pacific Grove, Calif.: Brooks/Cole.

Prospero, J.M. and P.J. Lamb. 2003. African droughts and dust transport to the Caribbean: climate change implications, *Science* 302, pp. 236–237.

Reisner, Marc. 1987. *Cadillac desert*. New York: Penguin Books.

Walker, A.S. 1996. *Deserts: geology and resources*. Denver: U.S. Geological Survey.

Webster, D. and G. Steinmetz. 2002. China's unknown Gobi. *National Geographic* 201, no. 1: 48–75.

Zeng, N. 2003. Drought in the Sahel. *Science* 302, pp. 999–1000.

CHAPTER 13

Mineral Resources and Society

Nevada's New Bonanza

We are currently in the midst of the biggest gold-mining boom in U.S. history. The bonanza is the Carlin Trend, a 50 by 5 kilometer (80 by 8 mi) line of enormous low-grade gold deposits in north-central Nevada. In 2002 the Trend poured its 50 millionth ounce of gold since its discovery in 1962, making it the third location in the world to achieve that milestone.

About 20 major mines and several smaller ones, most of them open-pit cyanide heap-leach operations, were mining the Trend in the early twenty-first century. The Trend is a valuable asset to Nevada's economy, producing nearly 4 million ounces of gold per year, contributing $1.8 billion to Nevada's economy. It is estimated that there are another 50 million ounces of gold reserves and resources on the Carlin Trend.

The Gold Quarry Mine, the largest of Newmont Gold Company's several open-pit mines, is representative of the large mines on the Carlin Trend (◆Figure 1). Newmont began operations on the Trend in 1965, and the combined 2001 production of its three open-pit mines exceeded

D. D. Trent

◆ **FIGURE 1** Newmont's Gold Quarry Mine, Carlin, Nevada. Shown are the open pit and mill and concentrator works in the distance.

1.5 million ounces. The cost of recovering gold from Newmont's mines runs about $240 per ounce. An additional cost is reclamation bond money, about $1 for each ounce of gold produced that is set aside to meet the eventual costs of reclamation.

After mining ends, which is estimated to be in 2030, the pits will be closed off with berms and fences, and the waste-rock dumps will be encapsulated with a 4-foot cover of topsoil and planted with native plants in accordance with the mine's operating permits. A network of drainage ditches is designed to collect and divert surface flow from the waste piles. It should be noted that the protective berms will be only a few feet high, and the fences must be maintained forever for reasons of public safety because the berms could create attractive jumps for ATV riders.

Some Nevadans warn that the true cost of mining the Trend is being externalized on the Humboldt River drainage basin. Approximately 18 mines in the region are working below the water table, which requires massive pumping of groundwater. Between 1997 and 2000 the five largest dewatering mines pumped nearly 800,000 acre-feet just to keep the mine pits dry. Such a withdrawal is believed to be creating a water deficit in the basin. Some predictions suggest that when mining ends it would require all of the flow of the Humboldt River at Winnemucca for 32 years to fill the anticipated 5,000,000 acre-foot deficit. It seems highly unlikely that the river will go dry for decades, but it illustrates the concern of some that recharging the deficit may deplete ranchers' wells and many of the normal groundwater discharges including springs.

At the end of mining, the remaining leach heaps, some covering hundreds of acres, become waste products. Abandoned heaps contain water, which may drain out for many years, and rainwater may seep out forever, even in Nevada's arid climate. Because the heaps contain tons of cyanide, mercury, salt, and selenium, drainage water at times may be hazardous. Such hazardous waste could threaten water quality over much of northern Nevada.

Every material used in modern industrial society is either grown in or derived from Earth's natural mineral resources, which are usually classified as either metallic or nonmetallic, as shown in ⋇ Table 13.1. Production and distribution of the thousands of manufactured products and the food we eat is dependent upon the utilization of metallic and nonmetallic mineral resources. The per capita U.S. consumption of mineral resources used directly or indirectly in providing shelter, transportation, energy, and clothing is enormous (◆ Figure 13.1), and the amount of minerals, metals, and fuels estimated by the Minerals Information Institute to be needed during the lifetime of a child born in 2006 is staggering (◆ Figure 13.2). The availability and cost of mineral and rock products influences our nation's standard of living, domestic national product, and position in the world.

With the value of nonfuel minerals produced in the United States in 2005 running about $52 billion, a 13 percent increase over 2004, and the values of materials produced from minerals in 2005 estimated at $47.8 billion (about five percent of the domestic national product) it is amazing that the general public has relatively little knowledge of where these minerals naturally occur, the methods by which they are mined and processed, and the extent to which we depend on them. It is important that the public recognize that exploitable mineral resources occur only in particular places, having formed there due to unique geologic conditions, and

⋇TABLE 13.1 Classification of Mineral Resources	
Metallic Mineral Resources	Nonmetallic Mineral Resources
Abundant Metals	**Minerals for Industrial and Agricultural Use**
iron, aluminum, manganese, magnesium, titanium	phosphates, nitrates, carbonates, sodium chloride, fluorite, sulfur, borax
Scarce Metals	**Construction Materials**
copper, lead, zinc, tin, gold, silver, platinum-group metals, molybdenum, uranium, mercury, tungsten, bismuth, chromium, nickel, cobalt, columbium	sand, gravel, clay, gypsum, building stone, shale, and limestone (for cement)
	Ceramics and Abrasives
	feldspar, quartz, clay, corundum, garnet, pumice, diamond

Source: James R. Craig, David L. Vaughan, and Brian J. Skinner, *Resources of the Earth* (Englewood Cliffs, N.J.: Prentice Hall, 1988).

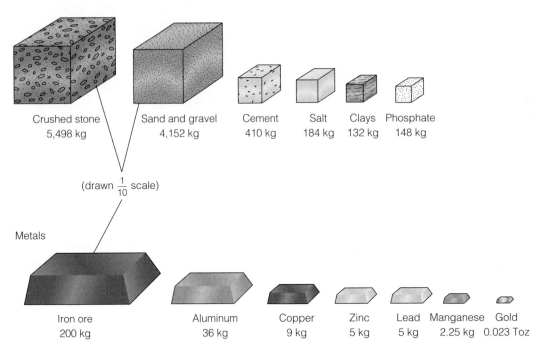

Nonmetallics

Crushed stone
5,498 kg

Sand and gravel
4,152 kg

Cement
410 kg

Salt
184 kg

Clays
132 kg

Phosphate
148 kg

(drawn $\frac{1}{10}$ scale)

Metals

Iron ore
200 kg

Aluminum
36 kg

Copper
9 kg

Zinc
5 kg

Lead
5 kg

Manganese
2.25 kg

Gold
0.023 Toz

◆ **FIGURE 13.1** Approximate annual per capita consumption of nonfuel mineral resources in the United States in 2004. Nonmetallic resources constitute about 94 percent of the mineral use by weight. (A kilogram equals 2.2 pounds.)
Data from Mineral Information Institute

that all deposits are exhaustible. Furthermore, development and exploitation of mineral resources is capital-intensive, requiring substantial long-term investment, and has environmental effects.

Understanding the origins, economics, and methods of mining and processing of mineral resources enables an individual to understand many of the difficult resource-related issues that currently face all levels of government. Increased land-use competition among the interests of mining, housing, wilderness preservation, agriculture, logging, recreation,

31,040 lbs.
Salt

21,418 lbs.
Clays

776 lbs.
Zinc

1.71 million lbs.
Stone, Sand, & Gravel

1,319 lbs.
Copper

83,296 gallons
Petroleum

1,648 Troy oz.
Gold

854 lbs.
Lead

23,435 lbs.
Phosphate Rock

+66,891 lbs.
Other Minerals
& Metals

588,906 lbs.
Coal

5,975 lbs.
Bauxite
(Aluminum)

32,980 lbs.
Iron Ore

72,994 lbs.
Cement

5.78 million cu. ft.
Natural Gas

◆ **FIGURE 13.2** Every American born this year will need 3.6 million pounds of metals, minerals, and fuels in his/her lifetime. Mineral Information Institute

wetlands preservation, and industrial development is forcing our government officials to make decisions that affect mineral-resource development and management and, thus, all of our lives.

Mineral Abundances and Distribution
Economic Mineral Concentration

The elements forming the minerals that make up Earth's crust exist in many forms in a great variety of rocks. The higher the abundance, the richer the deposit and the more economically feasible it is to extract and process the desired element. Locally rich concentrations of minerals are called **mineral deposits.** If they are sufficiently enriched, they may be **mineral reserves,** deposits of earth materials from which useful commodities are economically and legally recoverable with existing technology. Reserves of metallic minerals are called **ores,** and the minerals composing the deposits are referred to as **ore minerals.**

A particular ore deposit may be described in terms of its **concentration factor,** its enrichment expressed as the ratio of the element's abundance in the deposit to its average continental-crustal abundance. ⋆ Table 13.2 illustrates that the minimum concentration factors for profitable mining

★TABLE 13.2   Concentration Factors for Profitable Mining of Selected Metals

Metal	Percentage Abundance		Concentration Factor
	Average in Earth's Crust	In Ore Deposit	
Aluminum	8.0	24 to 32	3 to 4
Iron	5.8	35 to 41	6 to 7
Titanium	0.86	22 to 86	25 to 100
Zinc	0.00829	2.5	300
Copper	0.0058	0.6 to 1.2	100 to 200
Silver	0.00000896	0.00896	1000
Platinum	0.000000596	0.00036	600
Uranium	0.00016	0.08 to 0.16	500 to 1000
Gold	0.000000296	0.0012 to 0.0015	4000 to 5000

Source: Earth Sciences Australia, http://earthsci.org/education/teacher/basicgeol/resource.html

vary widely for eight metallic elements. Note in the table that aluminum, one of the most common elements in Earth's crust, has an average crustal abundance of 8 percent. A "good" aluminum-ore deposit is defined at this time as one that contains about 35 percent aluminum; thus, the present concentration factor for profitable mining of aluminum ore is about 4. In contrast, deposits of some rare elements such as uranium, lead, gold, and mercury must have concentration factors in the thousands in order to be considered mineral *resources*.

A basic tenet of mineral commodity economics is that it is unlikely that we will ever run out of a useful substance, because there are always deposits of any substance that have lower concentrations than are currently economical to mine. If the supply of currently economic deposits is reduced, market forces will cause the price to increase and the concentration factor to increase. Some people see a problem with this rationale. This topic will be explored later in the chapter.

Some elements are extremely common. In fact, 97 percent of Earth's crust is composed of only eight elements: oxygen, silicon, aluminum, iron, sodium, calcium, potassium, and magnesium. For most elements, the **average crustal abundance,** the amount of a particular element present in the continental crust, is only a fraction of a percent (see Table 13.2). Copper, for example, is rather rare; its average crustal abundance is only 0.0063 percent. In some localities, however, natural geochemical processes have concentrated it in mineral deposits that are 2 to 4 percent copper. A deposit with a high concentration of a desired element is called a **high-grade deposit.** A deposit in which the mineral content is minimal but still exploitable is called a **low-grade deposit.** For either grade of deposit, localities where desirable elements are concentrated sufficiently for economic extraction are relatively few.

Factors That Change Reserves

Reserves are not static, because they are defined by the current economics and technology as well as by the amount of a mineral that exists. Reserves fluctuate due to several factors: changing demand, discoveries of new deposits, and changing technology. In a free economy, a mineral deposit will not be developed at an economic loss, and prices will rise with demand. Consequently, low-grade deposits that are marginal or submarginal in today's economic climate may, if demand and prices rise, eventually become profitable to exploit. Advancements in technology also may increase reserves by lowering the cost of development or processing.

For example, the exploitable reserves of gold increased dramatically in the United States in the late 1960s due to a combination of changes in government policies and advances in technology. In 1968, when the price of gold was $35 per troy ounce, the Treasury Department suspended gold purchases to back the dollar and began allowing the metal to be traded on the open market. (A troy ounce equals 31.103 grams, whereas the avoirdupois ounce of U.S. daily life equals 28.330 grams.) Then in the 1970s the federal government removed restrictions prohibiting private ownership of gold bullion. In 1980 the gold price rose to more than $800 an ounce, and by 2006 it had settled at about $550 to $600 an ounce. Thus in a period of about 38 years the price of gold increased by about 1700 percent, meaning that many submarginal mining claims became economically profitable mines in that time. Furthermore, gold exploitation became more cost-efficient in the 1980s with the development of the new technology of cyanide heap-leaching, by which disseminated gold is dissolved from low-grade deposits and then recovered from the solution. A combination of changing economics and the new heap-leach technology initiated a new gold rush in the West beginning in the 1980s (see the chapter opener).

Other factors may reduce reserves, because extracting Earth's riches almost always requires the trade-off of aesthetic and environmental consequences (★ Table 13.3 provides some examples). For example, large low-grade mineral deposits can be mined only by open-pit methods. Not only do these methods devastate the landscape, their excavations also may reach below the water table, which can lead to groundwater contamination, and they produce enormous amounts of waste rock and tailings that can pollute surface-water runoff. **Smelters,** large industrial plants that process ore concentrates and extract the desired elements, produce more air pollution, in the form of flue dust, than any other single industrial activity. Smelters also produce slag, a solid residue that can contain thousands of times the natural levels of lead, zinc, arsenic, copper, and cadmium.

The real and perceived negative environmental impacts that serve to rule out exploitation and development of known deposits also reduce reserves. In recent years there have been several widely publicized instances of wildlife and wilderness values being judged more important than exploitation of mineral or petroleum deposits. Examples include

■ the extraordinary agreement reached between President Clinton and Crown Butte Mines in 1996 that halted proposed mining activity on the doorstep of Yellowstone National Park;

■ the two-year moratorium on hard-rock mining along a 100-mile-long region of Montana's Rocky Mountain Front, one of the nation's most important wildlife areas; and

★TABLE 13.3   Some Negative Environmental Consequences of Mineral Extraction and Processing Operations

Location	Type of Operation	Consequences
Questa, New Mexico	molybdenum mining	Drainage from waste rock from an abandoned molybdenum mine in upper Rio Grande Valley has contaminated watersheds, destroyed wildlife habitat, killed fish, polluted irrigation ditches and water wells, affected agricultural production, and caused illness to area residents. Estimated cleanup cost $129–$368 million.
Baia Mare, Romania	gold mining	A spill of about 1,000,000 m^3 (3.5 million cu ft) in January 2000 of cyanide-laced tailings operations ravaged a 250-mi stretch of the river, killing all aquatic life including thousands of fish.
North-central Montana	gold mining	The Zortman–Landusky open-pit, large-scale cyanide heap-leach gold mine suffered cyanide leaks and spills, causing surface and groundwater contamination, and bird and wildlife fatalities. When faced with cleanup costs, the mining company declared bankruptcy in 1998, forfeiting its cleanup bond, which is estimated to be $8.5 million short of cleanup costs.
Summitville, San Juan Mountains, Colorado	gold mining	Leaking leach pad, contaminated with cyanide and toxic metals, poisoned 27 km (17 mi) of the Alamosa River, on which the region's agriculture depends. When cleanup costs exceeded the posted bond, the Canadian mining company and its parent declared bankruptcy. Estimated cleanup will cost U.S. taxpayers $232 million.
Guyana, South America	gold mining	Cyanide spill from the Omai Mine—backed by the same investors as Colorado's Summitville Mine—released 860 million gallons of cyanide-laced tailings into one of Guyana's largest rivers. The spill killed fish, causing a panic in Guyana's seafood markets.
Sudbury, Ontario, Canada	nickel-copper mining and smelting	This was one of the world's best-known environmental "dead zones." Little vegetation survived in 10,400-hectare (40-mi^2) area around the smelter. Acid fallout destroyed fish populations in lakes within 65 km (40 mi). Conditions improved after completion of $530 million SO_2 smelter-abatement project and construction of the world's tallest smokestack; the city has a successful landscape reclamation program, but there is still significant SO_2 damage downwind of Sudbury.
Pará State, Brazil	Grande Carajas iron ore project	Wood requirements for smelting ore will require cutting 50,000 hectares (193 mi^2) of tropical forest annually during the 250-year life of the project.
Amazon basin, Brazil	gold mining	The region has been invaded by hundreds of thousands of miners digging for gold, clogging rivers with sediment, and releasing some 100 tons of mercury into the ecosystem annually.
Ilo-Locumbacoua area, Peru	copper mining and smelting	Each year, the Ilo smelter emits 600,000 tons of sulfur compounds, and nearly 40 million cubic meters (523 million yd^3) of tailings containing lead, zinc, copper, aluminum, and traces of cyanide are dumped into the ocean, poisoning marine life in a 20,000-hectare (77-mi^2) area. Nearly 800,000 tons of slag are dumped in the sea yearly.

■ the decision by the Office of Surface Mining and Reclamation not to allow surface mining of coal in the watershed of Fern Lake in Kentucky because it would be incompatible with Cumberland National Historic Park's land-use plan, would destroy historic and natural systems, and would damage the region's water quality.

We can expect that controversies over land use will be increasingly common in the future as more and more lower-grade deposits will need to be exploited when higher-grade deposits become exhausted.

Political factors may be related to the economics of mineral resources. The United States imports substantial amounts of mineral resources from other countries. (This is discussed in detail later in the chapter.) Some geopolitical authorities estimate that about a quarter of the roughly 50 wars and armed conflicts in 2001 had a strong "resource dimension." Exploitation of diamonds by Angolan rebels in 1992–2001 resulted in an estimated income of about $4 billion, and emeralds and lapis lazuli from the mid-1990s to 2001 netted Afghan groups (Taliban and the Northern Alliance) $90–100 million per year. Furthermore, resource availability may affect diplomatic policy. In spite of the general trade sanctions the United States enacted in the 1980s against South Africa to protest its apartheid policy, ten minerals the United States imports from South Africa were exempted because of their importance to the United States.

Distribution of Mineral Resources

The global distribution of mineral resources has no relationship to the locations of political boundaries or technological capability. Some mineral deposits, like those of iron, lead, zinc, and copper, originate by such a variety of igneous, sedimentary, and metamorphic processes that they are widely distributed, though in varying abundance. On the other hand, bauxite, essentially the only ore mineral of aluminum (one of the most common elements in Earth's crust), is concentrated by only one geochemical process: deep chemical weathering in a humid tropical climate. For this reason, economically exploitable deposits of bauxite and other such minerals are unequally distributed and restricted to a few highly localized geologic and geographic sites. Such localization of mineral deposits means that desired mineral resources do not occur in all countries. When this unequal supply pattern results in the scarcity of particular mineral resources that are crucial to a nation's economy, those minerals become critical or even strategic in the event of a national emergency. What constitutes "critical" minerals changes from time to time, mainly due to technological advances in mining or processing technologies.

Throughout history, nations' domestic mineral-resource bases and their needs for minerals unavailable within their borders have dictated international relations. Empires and kingdoms have risen and fallen due to the availability or scarcity of critical mineral resources. Two classic examples are those of the Greek and Roman empires. Silver mined by the Greeks near Athens financed the building of their naval fleet that defeated the Persians at the Bay of Salamis in 480 B.C. A century later, Greek gold supported the ambitious conquests of Alexander the Great. The Romans helped finance their vast empire by mining tin in Britain, mercury in Spain, and copper in Cyprus. In the twentieth century the efforts of Japan and Germany to secure mineral and fuel resources lacking within their borders were major factors leading to World War II, and the Soviet Union's annexation of the Karelian highlands of Finland following World War II provided the Soviets with new reserves of copper and nickel. More recently Morocco acquired valuable phosphate deposits when it occupied part of the Spanish Sahara in 1975.

Origins of Mineral Deposits

Specific geological processes must occur in order to concentrate minerals or native elements in a mineral deposit. A simple classification of mineral deposits is based on their concentrating processes (✳ Table 13.4). The geologic processes responsible for many mineral deposits may be understood in terms of plate tectonics, as illustrated in ◆ Figure 13.3, with mineral concentrations occurring in distinct tectonic regimes. For example, the great porphyry copper deposits of the western hemisphere were formed by igneous processes at convergent plate margins at the sites of former volcanic island arcs. On the other hand, deposits of tungsten, tin, some iron ore, gold, silver, and molybdenum originated by hydrothermal activity or by contact metamorphism accompanying the emplacement of granitic plutons (batholiths) within continental lithospheric plates near convergent boundaries.

Igneous Processes
Intrusive Deposits

Pegmatites are small, tabular-shaped, very coarse-grained, intrusive igneous bodies that may be important sources of mica, quartz, feldspar, beryllium, lithium, and gemstones. Reserves of pegmatites in the western hemisphere occur in the Black Hills of South Dakota; at Dunton, Maine; at Minas Gerais, Brazil; and in the tin-spodumene deposits of North Carolina (◆ Figures 13.4 and 13.5).

Crystal settling within a cooling magma chamber of ultramafic composition appears to be responsible for forming layers according to density, with the densest and earliest formed on the bottom and the less-dense and later-to-crystallize above or toward the top (◆ Figure 13.6), although alternate ideas for the layering have been proposed. Examples are the layered deposits of chromite at Red Mountain, Alaska

★TABLE 13.4 Genetic Classification of Mineral Deposits

Genetic Type	Example of Mineral(s) Formed	Location
Igneous Processes		
Pegmatite	tourmaline beryl	Oxford County, Maine; San Diego County, California Minas Gerais, Brazil
Crystal settling	chromite–magnetite–platinum	Bushveld complex, South Africa
Disseminated	copper–molybdenum porphyries diamonds	western North and South America kimberlite pipes in South Africa, Canada, and Australia
Hydrothermal	gold–quartz veins lead–zinc deposits in carbonate rocks	Mother Lode belt, California Mississippi River valley; Leadville, Colorado
Volcanogenic	massive copper sulfide deposits	Wrangell Mountains, Alaska
Sedimentary Processes		
Chemical precipitates in shallow marine basins	banded-iron formation	Lake Superior region
Marine evaporites	potassium salts	Carlsbad, New Mexico
Nonmarine evaporites	carbonates and borax minerals	Searles Lake, Trona, California
Deep-ocean precipitates	iron–manganese nodules	ocean floor, worldwide
Placer deposits	gold	Yukon Territory, Canada
Weathering Processes		
Lateritic weathering	bauxite	Weipa, Australia; Jamaica
Secondary enrichment	copper minerals	Miami, Arizona
Metamorphic Processes		
Contact-metamorphic	tungsten and molybdenum minerals	eastern Sierra Nevada, California
Regional metamorphic	asbestos	Quebec, Canada

and the Bushveld Complex in the Republic of South Africa, the largest single igneous mass on Earth (roughly the size of Maine). Chromium, nickel, vanadium, and platinum are obtained from this source. Some layered nickel-copper-cobalt deposits also are important sources of platinum-group elements.

Disseminated Deposits

Disseminated (scattered) **deposits** occur when a multitude of mineralized veinlets develop near or at the top of a large igneous intrusion (see Chapter 2). Probably the most common of these are the **porphyry copper** deposits (◆Figure 13.7), in which the ore minerals are widely distributed throughout

◆ **FIGURE 13.3** Relationships between metallic ore deposits and tectonic processes.

	Mid-ocean ridge	Oceanic crust	Subduction zone	Volcanic arc basin	Volcanic island arc	Marginal basin	Granitic intrusions (batholiths)
Metals	Copper and zinc as metallic oxides and sulfides	Manganese, cobalt, nickel	Chromium	Copper, lead, zinc	Copper, molybdenum, gold, silver, lead, mercury, tin	Copper, zinc, gold, chromium (petroleum)	Copper, tungsten, tin, iron (Kiruna type), gold, silver, molybdenum
Deposit type	Volcanogenic massive sulfide	Sea-floor nodules	Chromite in serpentine rock (high-pressure, low-temp., metamorphic)	Stratabound	Porphyry copper; hydrothermal veins	Volcanogenic massive sulfide; evaporites	Contact-metamorphic; hydrothermal veins

◆ **FIGURE 13.4** Granitic pegmatite, a very coarse-grained igneous rock. The grains in this sample have lengths up to 3 centimeters.

◆ **FIGURE 13.5** Tourmaline crystals from Dunton, Maine. Tourmaline is commonly found as an accessory mineral in granitic pegmatites.

a large volume of granitic rocks that have been emplaced in regions of current or past plate convergence. The world's largest open-pit mine, at Bingham Canyon, Utah, has extracted more than $6 billion worth of copper and associated minerals from a porphyry copper body (◆ Figure 13.8).

Hydrothermal Deposits

Hydrothermal (hot water) **deposits** originate from hot, mineral-rich fluids that are squeezed from cooling magma bodies during crystallization. Solidifying crystals force the liquids into cracks, fissures, and pores in both the magmatic rocks and the adjacent, "country" rocks (see Figure 13.7). Hydrothermal fluids also may be of metamorphic origin, or they may form from subsurface waters that are heated when they circulate near a cooling magma. Regardless of their origin, the heated waters may dissolve, concentrate, and remove valuable minerals and redeposit them elsewhere. When the fluids cool, minerals crystallize and create hydrothermal **vein**

◆ **FIGURE 13.6** Layered mineral deposit; Red Mountain, Alaska. The black layers are chromite ($FeCr_2O_4$); the light layers are granitic rocks.

deposits, which miners often refer to as **lodes.** The specific minerals formed will vary with the composition and temperature of the particular hydrothermal fluids, but they commonly include such suites (associations) of elements as gold-quartz and lead-zinc-silver.

Volcanogenic Deposits

When volcanic activity vents fluids to the surface, sometimes associated with ocean-floor hot-spring **black smoker** activity, **volcanogenic deposits** are formed (◆ Figure 13.9). These deposits are so named because they occur in marine sedimentary rocks that are associated with basalt flows or other volcanic rocks, and the ore bodies they produce are called **massive sulfides.** The rich copper deposits of the island of Cyprus, which have supplied all or part of the world's needs of copper for more than 3,000 years, are of this type. (The word *copper* is derived from Latin *Cyprium,* "Cyprian metal.") Cyprus's copper sulfide ore formed millions of years ago adjacent to hydrothermal vents near a sea-floor spreading center. Warping of the copper-rich sea floor due to convergence of the European and African plates brought the deposits to the surface when the island formed.

Sedimentary Processes
Surficial Precipitation

Very large, rich mineral deposits may result from evaporation and direct **precipitation** (the process of a solid forming from a solution) of salts in ocean water, usually in shallow marine basins. Minerals formed this way are called **evaporites.** They may be grouped into two types: marine evaporites, which are primarily salts of sodium and potassium, gypsum, anhydrite, and bedded phosphates; and nonmarine evaporites, which are mainly calcium and sodium carbonate, nitrate, sulfate, and borate compounds. Other important

◆ **FIGURE 13.7** A disseminated porphyry copper deposit. Reprinted from Alaska's Oil/Gas & Mineral Industry, © 1982, with permission of Graphic Arts Center Publishing Company.

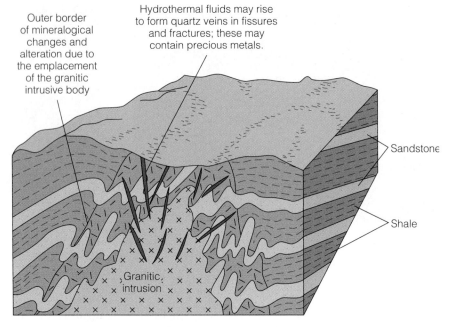

Outer border of mineralogical changes and alteration due to the emplacement of the granitic intrusive body

Hydrothermal fluids may rise to form quartz veins in fissures and fractures; these may contain precious metals.

Sandstone

Shale

Granitic intrusion

Disseminated deposits of copper form when mineralized solutions invade permeable zones and small cracks.

Kennecott Corp.

◆ **FIGURE 13.8** Kennecott Corporation's Bingham Canyon mine south of Salt Lake City, Utah is the world's largest open-pit mine and the largest human-made excavation. By 2006 the pit was more than 800 meters (½ mi) deep and 4 kilometers (2½ mi) wide, with tailings ponds covering about 9,000 acres—more than half the area of New York's Manhattan Island. In 2006 the company began an expansion operation that is expected to extend the life of the mine to at least 2018.

◆ **FIGURE 13.9** A "black smoker" hydrothermal rent on the East Pacific rise at a depth of 2800 meters. The "smoke" is hot water saturated with dissolved metallic-sulfide minerals, which precipitate into black particles upon contact with the cold seawater.

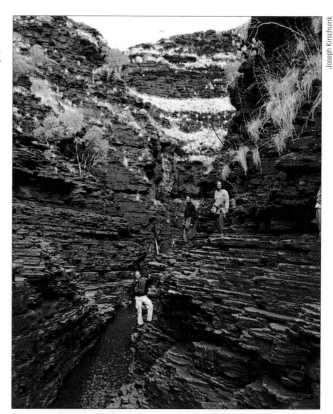

◆ **FIGURE 13.10** Western Australia has extensive areas of banded-iron formation. Some individual layers can be traced for more than 300 kilometers (186 mi). The dark layers are iron oxides; the red layers are chert with fine-grained iron oxides.

sedimentary mineral deposits are the **banded-iron formation** ores (◆Figure 13.10). These deposits formed in Precambrian time, more than a billion years ago, when Earth's atmosphere lacked free oxygen. Without free oxygen, the iron that dissolved in surface water could be carried in solution by rivers from the continents to the oceans, where it precipitated with silica to form immense deposits of red chert and iron ore. Banded-iron deposits are found in the Great Lakes region, northwestern Australia, Brazil, and elsewhere, and they are enormous; they provide two hundred years or more of reserves even without substantial conservation measures.

Deep-Ocean Precipitation

Manganese nodules (◆Figure 13.11) are formed by precipitation on the deep ocean floor. The nodules are mixtures of manganese and iron oxides and hydroxides, with small amounts of cobalt, copper, nickel, and zinc, that grow in onionlike concentric layers by direct precipitation from ocean waters. Any commercial recovery of this resource appears to be many decades away because of technological, economic, international political, and environmental limitations, but eventually it may be necessary to exploit the deposits.

◆ **FIGURE 13.11** Manganese nodules, an example of deep-ocean precipitation. The nodules consist mainly of manganese and iron, with lesser amounts of nickel, copper, cobalt, and zinc.

Placer Deposits

Mineral deposits concentrated by moving water are called **placer deposits** (Spanish *placer*, "reef"; pronounced "plass-er"). Dense, erosion-resistant minerals such as gold, platinum, diamonds, and tin are readily concentrated in placers by the washing action of moving water. The less-dense grains of sand and clay are carried away, leaving gold or other heavy minerals concentrated at the bottom of the stream channel. Such deposits formed by the action of rivers are referred to as **alluvial placers;** ancient river deposits that are now elevated as stream terraces above the modern channels are called **bench placers** (◆Figures 13.12 and 13.13).

(a) Ancient river pattern

(b) Modern river pattern

◆ **FIGURE 13.12** The origin of gold placer deposits. (a) An ancient landscape with an eroding gold-quartz vein shedding small amounts of gold and other mineral grains that eventually become stream sediments. The gold particles, being heavier, settle to the bottom of the sediments in the channel. (b) The same region in modern time. Streams have eroded and changed the landscape and now follow new courses. The original placer deposits of the ancient stream channels are now elevated above the modern river valley as "bench" placers. Reprinted from Alaska's Oil/Gas & Mineral Industry, © 1982, with permission of Graphic Arts Center Publishing Company.

◆ **FIGURE 13.13** Gold nugget weighing 41.3 troy ounces, mined from a placer deposit in the Brooks Range, Alaska.

Considerable uranium is mined from Precambrian placer deposits in southern Africa. The deposits formed under the unique conditions existing on Earth's surface before free oxygen was present in the atmosphere. Some placer deposits occur on beaches, the classic example being the gold beach placers at Nome, Alaska.

Sand and gravel concentrated by rivers into alluvial deposits are important sources of aggregate for concrete. River deposits formed by **glacial outwash**—resulting from the runoff of glacial meltwater—are another type of placer deposit.

Weathering Processes

The deep chemical weathering of rock in hot, humid, tropical climates promotes mineral enrichment, because the solution and removal of more soluble materials leaves a residual soil of less-soluble minerals. Because iron and aluminum are relatively insoluble under these conditions, they tend to remain behind in *laterite*, a highly weathered red subsoil or material that is rich in oxides of iron and aluminum and lacking in silicates. When the iron content of the parent rock is low or absent, however, this lateritic weathering produces rich deposits of **bauxite** (◆Figure 13.14), the principal ore mineral of aluminum (see Chapter 6, Figure 6.16b).

Groundwater moving downward through a disseminated sulfide deposit may dissolve the dispersed metals from above the water table to produce an enriched deposit below the water table by **secondary enrichment** (◆Figure 13.15). At Miami, Arizona, for example, the primary disseminated copper-ore body is of marginal to submarginal grade, containing

◆ **FIGURE 13.14** Bauxite, the ore of aluminum, forms in horizon B of laterites derived from aluminum-rich parent materials.

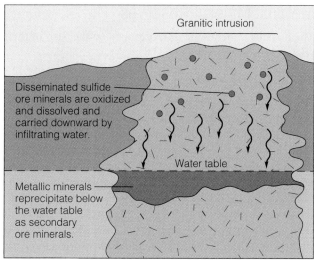

◆ **FIGURE 13.15** The development of ores by secondary enrichment. Descending groundwater oxidizes and dissolves soluble sulfide minerals, carrying them downward and leaving a brightly colored residue of limonite and hematite. Below the water table new metallic minerals are precipitated as secondary ore minerals.

less than one percent copper, but secondary enrichment has improved the grade to more than three percent.

Metamorphic Processes

The high temperatures, high pressures, and ion-rich fluids that accompany the emplacement of intrusive igneous rocks produce a distinct metamorphic halo around the intrusive body. The result, in concert with the accompanying hydrothermal mineralization, is known as a **contact-metamorphic deposit.** If, for example, granite intrudes limestone, a diverse and colorful group of contact-metamorphic minerals may be produced, such as a tungsten-molybdenum deposit (◆Figure 13.16). Asbestos and talc originate by **regional metamorphism,** metamorphism that affects an entire region.

◆ **FIGURE 13.16** The relationship of limestone and a granitic intrusion in the origin of contact-metamorphic mineral deposits. Reprinted from Alaska's Oil/Gas & Mineral Industry, © 1982, with permission of Graphic Arts Center Publishing Company.

Hydrothermal fluids may vent to the surface as geysers or hot springs.

Low-temperature (<200° C) hydrothermal fluids migrate along bedding planes, forming veins.

Sandstone and shale

Granitic intrusion

Limestone

Copper, tin, zinc, or tungsten contact-metamorphic deposits

Low-temperature (<200° C) hydrothermal fluids rise through fractures and migrate along bedding planes to form flat-lying lead–zinc–silver limestone-replacement deposits.

High-temperature (>200° C) hydrothermal fluids rise to form gold, silver, or base-metal–quartz veins in fractures and fissures.

Metallic Mineral Reserves

The metallic minerals are often grouped on the basis of their relative crustal abundance.

The Abundant Metals

The geochemically abundant metals—aluminum, iron, magnesium, manganese, and titanium—have abundances in excess of 0.1 percent by weight of the average continental crust. Economically valuable ore bodies of the abundant metals, such as iron and aluminum, for example, need only comparatively small concentration factors for profitable mining (see Table 13.2) and are recovered mainly from ore minerals that are oxides and hydroxides. Even though they are abundant, these metals require large amounts of energy for production. Because of this, it is not surprising that the world's industrialized nations are the greatest consumers of these metals.

The Scarce Metals

The scarce metals are those whose crustal abundances are less than 0.1 percent by weight of average continental crust. Most of these metals are concentrated in sulfide deposits, but the rarest occur more commonly, or even solely, in rare rock types. Included within this category are copper, lead, zinc, and nickel—which are widely known and used, but nevertheless scarce—along with the more obvious gold and platinum-group minerals. U.S. deposits of chromium, manganese, nickel, tin, and platinum-group metals are scarce or of submarginal grade. Important, less-well-known scarce metals include cobalt, columbium, tantalum, and cadmium, which are important in space-age ferroalloys; antimony, which is used as a pigment and as a fire retardant; and gallium, which is essential in the manufacture of solid-state electronic components. The United States has all of these critical metals in the National Defense Stockpile, a supply of about 100 critical mineral materials valued at about $4 billion that could supply the nation's needs for three years in a national emergency.

Nonmetallic Mineral Reserves

The yearly per capita consumption of nonfuel mineral resources in North America exceeds 10 tons, 94 percent of which is nonmetallic, with the major bulk being construction materials (see Figure 13.1). The nonmetallic minerals are subdivided for convenience into three groups based on their use in industry, agriculture, and construction. The number and diversity of nonmetallic mineral resources is so great that it is impossible to treat the entire subject in a book of this sort. Thus, this subsection discusses only those nonmetallic resources generally considered most important.

Industrial Minerals

Industrial minerals include those that contain specific elements or compounds that are used in the chemical industry—sulfur and halite, for example—and those that have important physical properties, such as the materials used in ceramics manufacture, and the abrasives, such as diamond and corundum. Sulfur, one of the most widely used and most important industrial chemicals, is obtained as a by-product of petroleum refining (◆ Figure 13.17) and from the tops of salt domes in the central Gulf Coast states, where it is associated with anhydrite ($CaSO_4$) or gypsum ($CaSO_4 \cdot 2H_2O$). Salt domes originate from evaporite beds that are compressed by overlying sedimentary rock layers, causing the salt to be mobilized into a dome, which rises, piercing the overlying rocks and concentrating sulfur, gypsum, and anhydrite at the top. Superheated water is pumped into the sulfur-bearing caprock to melt the sulfur, which is then piped to a processing plant. More than 80 percent of domestic U.S. sulfur is used to make sulfuric acid, the most important use for which is the manufacture of

◆ **FIGURE 13.17** Sulfur awaiting shipment to Asia at Vancouver, British Columbia. The sulfur originated as a contaminant in natural gas produced from gas fields in Alberta. Processing plants have separated the sulfur from the natural gas in order to produce a gas whose combustion products meet environmental air-quality standards. The sulfur is a useful by-product of the process.

D. D. Trent

phosphate fertilizers. Salt domes are also important sources of nearly pure halite (NaCl), common salt, and many domes have oil fields on their flanks (see Chapter 14).

In addition to being mined from salt domes, halite is mined from flat-lying evaporite beds in New Mexico, Kansas, and Michigan. The most important use of halite is for manufacturing sodium hydroxide and chlorine gas; about 15 percent of halite production is used for de-icing highways, and significant amounts are used in food products and in the manufacture of steel and aluminum.

Diamond is by far the most important industrial abrasive, although corundum, emery (an impure variety of corundum), and garnet also are used. Traditionally, natural diamonds have been important both as gemstones and as industrial abrasives, but artificial diamonds manufactured from graphite now hold about 70 percent of the market for diamond-grit abrasives. The major source of natural diamonds is kimberlite (named for Kimberley, South Africa), a rare and unique ultramafic rock that forms in pipelike bodies. Not only are kimberlite pipes rare, but most of them lack diamonds. The important diamond-bearing kimberlites are in South Africa, Ghana, the Republic of Zaire, Botswana, Australia, Belarus (formerly Belorussia of the USSR), Yakutia (the largest republic of the Russian Federation), and in Canada's Northwest Territories, where North America's first diamond mine began operations in 1998 (◆Figure 13.18).

The metamorphic minerals corundum and emery, natural abrasives for which U.S. reserves are scarce or nonexistent, have largely been replaced by synthetic abrasives such as carbides, manufactured alumina, and nitrides. The United States still imports limited amounts of corundum from South Africa.

◆ **FIGURE 13.18** The Ekati Diamond Mine™, Canada's first diamond mine, located in a remote Arctic tundra region known as the Barrenlands, is about 300 kilometers (180 mi) northeast of Yellowknife, Northwest Territories. The mine, with a potential life of about 25 years, is developed in kimberlite pipes similar to the famous diamond pipes of South Africa. Development of the property includes consultation with the leadership of the Aboriginal residents of the region and minimizing the impact on the environment. Remediation of disturbed lands is continually ongoing.

Agricultural Minerals

With the world's human population passing the 6 billion mark in September 1999, it seems obvious that food production and the corresponding need for fertilizers and agricultural chemicals also will continue to expand. Therefore, nitrate, potassium, and phosphate compounds will continue to be in great demand. Whereas nearly all agricultural nitrate is derived from the atmosphere, phosphate and potassium come only from Earth's crust. Phosphate reserves occur in many parts of the world, but the major sources are in the United States, Morocco, Turkmenistan, and Buryat (the latter two are republics of the former Soviet Union). The primary sources of phosphate in the United States are marine sedimentary rocks in North Carolina and Florida (see Figure 13.32, later in the chapter), and there are other valuable deposits in Idaho, Montana, Wyoming, and Utah. The main U.S. supply of potassium comes from widespread nonmarine evaporite beds beneath New Mexico, Oklahoma, Kansas, and Texas, with the richest beds being in New Mexico. Canada also has large reserves of potassium salts.

Construction Materials

About two-thirds of the value of industrial minerals mined in the United States are construction materials, with aggregates (crushed stone, sand, and gravel) valued at $13.5 billion and cement (made from limestone and shale) valued at $6.5 billion. Eighty percent of the aggregate is used in road building. Other major construction materials are clay, for bricks and tile, and gypsum, the primary component of plaster and wallboard. It is the mining of aggregate that is probably the most familiar to urban dwellers, because quarries customarily are sited near cities, the major market for the product, in order to minimize transportation costs. The quantity of aggregate needed to build a 1,500-square-foot house is impressive: 67 cubic yards are required, each cubic yard consisting of one ton of rock and gravel and 0.7 ton of sand. This amounts to 114 tons of rock, sand, and gravel per dwelling, including the garage, sidewalks, curbings, and gutters. Thus, it is no wonder that aggregate has the greatest commercial value of all mineral products mined in most states, ranking second only in those states that produce natural gas and petroleum. The annual per capita production of sand, gravel, and crushed stone in the United States amounts to about six tons, the total value of which exceeds $13 billion. The principal sources of aggregate are open-pit quarries in modern and ancient floodplains, river channels, and alluvial fans. In areas of former glaciation, aggregate is mined from glacial outwash and other deposits of sand and gravel that remained after the retreat of the great Pleistocene ice sheets in the northern United States, Canada, and Northern Europe (see Chapter 11).

CONSIDER THIS

How does the nation's need for mineral materials affect U.S. foreign policy?

⋆TABLE 13.5   U.S. Consumption and Production of Selected Metallic Minerals

Mineral	Consumption, Thousands of Metric Tons	Primary Production, Thousands of Metric Tons*	Primary Production as Percentage of Consumption**
Aluminum	7,300	3,300	45.2
Chromium	387	0	0
Cobalt	7.2	0	0
Copper	2,800	1,840	65.7
Iron ore	69,300	57,000	82.3
Lead	1,500	365	24.3
Manganese	695	0	0
Nickel	131	0	0
Tin	46	negligible	0
Zinc	1,220	540	44.3
Platinum-group metals, metric tons	127	8.3	16.3

*Primary production is production from new ore.
**Primary production divided by consumption and rounded to the appropriate number of significant figures.
Source: *Mineral Commodity Summaries,* U.S. Bureau of Mines, 1995.

Mineral Resources for the Future

Just as the world's fossil-fuel reserves are finite (Chapter 14), so are its mineral reserves. Earth has been well-explored, and fairly reliable estimates exist on the reserves of many important minerals. It was estimated in the early 1970s that reserves of some minerals would be exhausted by some time early in the twenty-first century. Obviously, that is not happening, at least not yet, and part of the reason is that precise estimates are subject to the vacillations of several factors that are difficult to foresee: the rate of recycling; new discoveries in unexpected places; new technological breakthroughs in processing; changing costs of energy for extracting, transporting, and processing; political factors; and changes in mineral economics due to increasing demands that may elevate submarginal grades to profitable grades. For example, the commodity values of copper, iron, and tungsten have shot up significantly since 2004 due to the greater needs of China and India as their manufacturing capabilities increase. Consequently, the mining of previously uneconomic ores that provide those metals has become profitable.

U.S. consumption and production data for selected metallic and nonmetallic mineral resources appear in ⋆ Tables 13.5 and 13.6, respectively. Notice in Table 13.5 that we consume

⋆TABLE 13.6   U.S. Consumption and Production of Selected Nonmetallic Minerals

Mineral	Consumption, Thousands of Metric Tons	Primary Production, Thousands of Metric Tons*	Primary Production as Percentage of Consumption**
Clay	37,900	42,300	112
Gypsum	26,000	17,300	66.5
Potash	5,390	1,425	26.4
Salt	47,400	39,500	83.3
Sulfur	13,450	11,300	84
Sand and gravel	922,000	922,000	100
Crushed stone	1,198,000	1,195,000	95.7

*Primary production is production from new ore.
**Primary production divided by consumption and rounded to the appropriate number of significant figures.
Source: *Mineral Commodity Summaries,* U.S. Bureau of Mines, 1995.

Mineral Resources		Important Sources, 1996–1997	Percent
Graphite		China, Mexico, Canada	100
Manganese		South Africa, Mexico, Australia, Gabon	100
Strontium (celestite)		Mexico, Germany	100
Bauxite and alumina		Australia, Guinea, Jamaica, Brazil	100
Vanadium		Czech Republic, Canada, So. Africa, Swaziland	100
Platinum-group metals		South Africa, U.K., Russia, Germany	91
Potash		Canada, Russia, Belarus, Germany	80
Tantalum		Japan, Australia, Thailand, China	91
Tin		Brazil, China, Indonesia, Bolivia, Peru	93
Cobalt		Zambia, Canada, Norway, Finland	78
Tungsten		China, Russia	70
Chromium		South Africa, Russia, Turkey, Zimbabwe, Kazakhstan	69
Zinc		Canada, Mexico, Kazakhistan	52
Nickel		Canada, Norway, Australia, Russia	54
Antimony		China, Mexico, South Africa, Belgium	82
Magnesium compounds		China, Canada, Austria, Australia	56
Diamond (industrial)		Ireland, China, Ukraine	43
Iron and steel		European Union (EU), Japan, Canada, Mexico	15
Iron ore		Canada, Brazil, Venezuela, Australia	4

◆ **FIGURE 13.19** U.S. net import figures for selected nonfuel materials during 2005. L. McCarten, D.E. Morse, S.F. Sibley, and P.A. Plunkert, U.S. Geological Survey. 2005. The United States 2006 Annual Review, *Mining Engineering* 56, no. 5, p. 27.

greater amounts of many metallic mineral commodities than we produce. In the cases of chromium, cobalt, manganese, nickel, tin, and platinum-group metals, all or virtually all of those materials must be imported. The extent of U.S. import reliance for these and other mineral resources is shown in ◆ Figure 13.19. Thus, the United States is far from self-sustaining. By the turn of the twenty-first century, the United States imported an estimated $60 billion worth of raw and processed mineral materials annually. If nothing else, the data constitute a clear case against isolationism if we hope to sustain our present lifestyle.

A brighter forecast is shown by the data in Table 13.6. Note in the table that the United States was self-sustaining in its consumption of domestic nonmetallic and rock resources as of 1995 and that it was producing a surplus of one mineral commodity. There are some apparent disagreements between these tables and Figure 13.19. The lack of imported lead shown in Figure 13.19, for example, does not seem to agree with the value shown in Table 13.5. The discrepancy results from extensive recycling of lead in the United States. Further, the high domestic production of aluminum reported in Table 13.5 results from a high reliance on imported bauxite (reported in Figure 13.19), because domestic sources of bauxite are insignificant.

As the richer deposits of some resources diminish in the coming decades, we can expect shortages of some minerals that presently are common. In many cases technological advances will develop substitute materials that will suffice, but in other cases, we will have to do without. Some minerals will become sufficiently scarce that deposits now classed as "submarginal" will be upgraded to "low-grade" and will be economically exploitable due to market forces.

The need for mineral resources may require exploration and exploitation in more remote regions and more hostile environments. Coal has been mined for more than a half-century well north of the Arctic Circle on Norway's island of Spitsbergen (Svalbard), for example, and sources of fuels and minerals are currently being sought and exploited in the harsh climates of Canada's Northwest Territories and Arctic Islands (see Figure 13.18). Exploration by drilling cores has been done at a lead-zinc-silver prospect in western North Greenland. The Red Dog zinc-lead-silver mine, North America's largest zinc producer, on the lands of the Inupiat Eskimos north of the Arctic Circle in Alaska went into full production in 1991. Even environmentally sensitive Antarctica, which is known to have extensive deposits of coal and iron, may be the target of future exploitation as more is learned about that continent's mineral wealth. Deeper parts of the continents and the sea floor may also be targeted for exploration and exploitation as geophysical innovations and technological advances open up these presently inaccessible regions.

In the future we will experience more recycling of critical metals, such as has been done with gold for thousands of years. The gold in the crown on your tooth, for example, may have been in jewelry during the age of Pericles in Ancient Greece. Such metals as lead, aluminum, iron, and copper have been recycled for years. In many cities the large-scale recycling of metals, especially lead and aluminum, as well as of paper, glass, and plastics, is being conducted successfully as part of municipal trash collection (see Chapter 15; ✻ Table 13.7).

★TABLE 13.7	U.S. Recycling Statistics for Selected Metals	
Metal	Recycled (from Old and New Scrap (Metric Tons)	Amount Obtained by Recycling
aluminum	3,450,000	36%
copper	1,310,000	32%
iron and steel	74,000,000	55%
lead	1,120,000	63%
tin	15,100	29%
titanium	18,500	50%
zinc	436,000	27%

Source: U.S. Geological Survey Circular 1221, 2002.

The recycling rates in 2000 for steel-containing materials were 95 percent for automobiles that had reached the end of their useful life, 84 percent for appliances, and 58.4 percent for steel cans; 62 percent of all aluminum beverage cans were recycled. Collectively, the value of recycled metal and mineral scrap amounted to about 30 percent of the nation's mineral production.

Despite recycling, mining will continue—it is essential for our way of living—but it cannot continue forever. As we explore and develop in more remote areas, more energy is required. We are caught in a twin dilemma: declining richness and remoteness of ores requires an increasingly greater input of energy, and the era of cheap fuels is also in decline.

Mining and Its Environmental Impacts

. . . when the ores are washed, the water which has been used poisons the brooks and streams, and either destroys the fish or drives them away.

Georgius Agricola, *De Re Metallica*, 1550

The General Mining Law of 1872 was important legislation that helped establish the mining industry as a fundamental element in the U.S. economy. At the same time, the law was the ultimate in laissez-faire regulation, as it allowed miners to exploit, to take profits at public expense, to pay little in return for the privilege of mining on federal land, and to walk away from the scars and waste materials remaining when they abandoned their mines. The original nineteenth-century law allowed miners to stake a claim on potentially profitable public land and, should the claim prove to contain valuable minerals, to obtain a patent (legal title) for $2.50 an acre, and reap the profits. This law helped "win" the West by

enticing thousands of prospectors to seek their fortunes in gold, silver, and other valuable commodities.

Since 1872 the law has allowed approximately $245 billion worth of the public's hardrock minerals to be developed by private corporations with no consideration whatever for the environmental consequences of mining for about a century until NEPA, SMCRA, and CERCLA laws and regulations were enacted. The law is staunchly defended today by some public officials and the mining industry who claim that it does a good job of providing the country with valuable minerals, employment, and economic development. The same law exists today, but it has been much modified over the years by more than 50 amendments, so that today's body of mining law fills six volumes. Two examples of the changes are (1) the Mineral Lands Leasing Act of 1920, by which the government retains title to all federal lands possessing energy resources (oil, gas, and coal) and assesses royalties on the profits from the lands leased by developers; and (2) beginning in 1992, a claim maintenance fee of $100 per claim per year that must be paid on claims staked under the 1872 law in order for the claims to remain valid. (This is the only return taxpayers receive for hardrock minerals taken from public lands, which amounts to $25 to $30 million per year, and the funds collected are used to enforce surface mining regulations.) In addition, environmental restrictions added in the 1970s and 1980s dictate that modern mining must be conducted within a different policy framework than the simply drafted law of 1872. Although interest in environmental protection and reclamation in coal mining districts began to develop in the 1930s, serious efforts at regulation and reclamation did not begin until the late 1960s due to the increasing amounts of unreclaimed land, and water pollution and problems arising from the lack of uniform standards among state mining programs. Consequently, the Surface Mining Control and Reclamation Act (**SMCRA**) was passed in 1977. This act established coordination of federal and state efforts to regulate the coal industry in order to prevent the abuses that had prevailed in the past. SMCRA regulations apply to all lands—private, state, and federal. SMCRA established a special fee that is charged on coal production and generates funds for reclaiming abandoned coal-mine lands. SMCRA also provides for state primacy once a state's coal-mine reclamation laws and policies have been approved by the Secretary of the Interior. This gives state regulators primary SMCRA-enforcement jurisdiction as long as the state programs meet federal standards.

Federal reclamation standards and other safeguards established by SMCRA for the coal-mining industry have no counterpart for noncoal-underground and surface-mineral mining on state or private lands. Although there are federal regulations for noncoal mining on federal lands, it is left to the individual state governments to codify safeguards and enforce noncoal-mine-reclamation requirements.

Mining on federal lands must comply with the regulations of the *National Environmental Policy Act* (NEPA) of

1969 (see Chapter 10). A mining company must file an operating plan and an *Environmental Impact Report* (EIR), and conduct public hearings before the administrating agency can approve an operating permit. Even though an applicant may spend several million dollars complying with the NEPA permit-application requirements, there is no assurance that an application will be approved.

There is no specific fund for cleaning up abandoned noncoal mines on state and private lands, nor are there uniform regulatory requirements for these lands. Action is left to the states and the mining companies. However, once any state with coal production has implemented safeguards and standards for coal mining, it may use the SMCRA abandoned-mine fund to address reclamation of abandoned mines that exploited other commodities. For example, Utah's abandoned-mine reclamation program uses SMCRA funds to reclaim metals mines.

Environmental-pollution abatement has become a major concern of domestic gold producers in some states, especially in Alaska, where there are many small placer mines. Reclamation of mined land has become an integral part of an increasing number of gold-mine operating plans. Abandoned mine sites, as well as other contaminated industrial sites that are deemed to pose serious threats to health or safety, may be cleaned up under the Comprehensive Environmental Response, Compensation and Liability Act (**CERCLA**) of 1980, which is overseen by the Environmental Protection Agency (EPA). For example, the Forest Service, a branch of the United States Department of Agriculture, has CERCLA authority to clean up contaminated mines on National Forest System lands. It was CERCLA that established the so-called Superfund to clean up the worst toxic or hazardous waste sites that have been assigned to the National Priorities List (see Chapter 15).

Some states have enacted State Environmental Policy Acts (SEPAs) that are patterned after NEPA, while other states may have little regulation. The differences in the various states' permit procedures, their mining and reclamation standards, and their enforcement of underground- and surface-mining laws can be illustrated by comparing the laws of three states, each of which has over a century of mining activity: Colorado, Arizona, and Michigan. Colorado has strong regulatory provisions relating to mine operation, environmental protection, reclamation bonding, inspections, emergency response by the state, and even the authority over mine operation. In contrast, Arizona, the only state in the country without a mine-reclamation law until 1994, allows companies to self-bond their reclamation fund, to wait as long as 17 years after mining has stopped to begin reclamation, and to set their own reclamation standards. Furthermore, there is an escape clause that may allow companies a variance from any of the law's provisions. Michigan, which ranks sixth among all states in the production value of nonfuel minerals, has no comprehensive mining law. No financial bond is required to ensure that a mine site will be properly closed and reclaimed

if the company abandons the project or declares bankruptcy. No permit is needed to open a mine except a local zoning permit and a federal water-discharge permit—permits that are required of *every* industrial operation. Reportedly, there is no enforcement of the state's voluntary reclamation law.

As we consider the environmental impacts of mining in the United States in this section, it is important to distinguish between (1) the legacy of careless exploitation that is obvious at long-abandoned mines with their residual scars and toxic wastes and (2) the current mining scene, in which, depending upon the particular state and whether the site is on state-owned land, land administered by the U.S. Forest Service or the Bureau of Land Management, more than 30 different permits may by needed in order to develop and operate a mine legally. Many mine owners consider the current permitting requirements to be excessive, and they question whether they will be able to continue to operate in the United States at all if the regulations become more restrictive.

Mining in the past was conducted largely by underground methods with a surface plant for milling and processing and for hoisting workers, ore, and equipment (◆Figure 13.20). Surface-mining methods, typified by vast open-pit excavations such as the Bingham Canyon mine (see Figure 13.8), have now largely replaced underground methods. The surface plant remains much the same, however, although it usually operates on a much larger scale than in the past. Both surface and underground mining create significant environmental impacts on the land and air and on biological and water resources. In addition, the needs for housing and services in mining areas have social impacts.

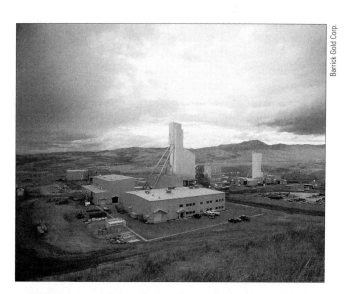

◆ **FIGURE 13.20** A large underground mining operation, the Barrick Goldstrike Meikle Mine on the Carlin Trend near Elko, Nevada. The mine, with 712,688 ounces of gold produced in 2001, had the highest production of any gold mine in the United States.

◆ **FIGURE 13.21** The steps in conventional large-scale underground bituminous-coal mining.

(a)   (b)

(c)   (d)

Impacts of Coal Mining

Much of the coal now mined in the United States is extracted by surface operations, which involve removing rock and soil that overlie the coal beds. Compared with underground mining (◆Figure 13.21), surface mining is generally less expensive, safer for miners, and facilitates more complete recovery of coal. Surface mining, however, causes more extensive disturbances to the land surface and has the potential for serious environmental consequences unless the land is carefully reclaimed. The three major methods of surface mining of coal are contour mining, area mining, and mountaintop-removal mining. Each of these is explained here.

Contour mining is typical in the hilly areas of the eastern United States, where coal beds occur in outcrops along hillsides. Mining is accomplished by cutting into the hillside to expose the coal and then following the coal seam around the perimeter of the hill. Successive, roughly horizontal strips are cut, enlarging each strip around the hillside until the thickness of the overburden is so great that further exposure of the coal bed would not be cost-effective. At each level of mining is a *highwall,* a clifflike, excavated face of exposed overburden and coal that remains after mining is completed. Augers (giant drill bits) are used to extract coal from the areas beneath the highwall. The SMCRA requires that the sites must be reclaimed, that is, returned to the original contour, and highwalls must be covered and stabilized after contour mining is completed. This is accomplished by backfilling **spoil,** the broken fragments of waste rock removed in order to mine the coal, against the highwall, and spreading and compacting as necessary to stabilize the reclaimed hillside. *Hydroseeding,* spraying seeds mixed with water, mulch, fertilizer, and lime onto regraded soil, is used on steep reclaimed slopes to aid in establishing vegetation that will help prevent soil erosion (see ■ Case Study 13.3).

Area mining is commonly used to mine coal in flat and gently rolling terrain, principally in the midwestern and western states. Because the pits of active area mines may be several kilometers long, enormous equipment is used to remove the overburden, mine the coal, and reclaim the land. Topsoil is stockpiled in special areas and put back in place when the mining is completed. After replacing, it is tilled with traditional farming methods to reestablish it as crop or pastureland. Often, the land is more productive after reclamation than before mining.

Mountaintop-removal mining is used primarily in the eastern United States to recover coal that underlies the tops of mountains. After the coal is removed, the mined area is returned to its approximately original shape or left as flat terrain. (◆Figure 13.22). Mountaintop-removal mining involves removal and disposal of all rock and soil materials above a coal bed and allows nearly complete removal of the coal bed. A major environmental problem with mountaintop-removal mining is disposal of the waste rock, which includes carcinogenic chemicals used to wash the coal for market and toxic metals such as mercury and arsenic. Commonly, the waste is simply dumped in hollows and valleys; in West Virginia and Kentucky more than 1,200 miles of streams and rivers have been destroyed, ecosystems have been devastated, whole valleys simply eliminated, and residents have been subjected to health hazards (◆Figure 13.23). In some instances, whole communities and the people whose families have lived for generations along the now-nonexistent stream banks are displaced with little or no financial compensation. Consequently, legal action charged that waste-disposal practices in mountaintop-removal coal mining violates the Clean Water Act and various mining regulations that prohibit unnecessary and undue degradation of the public's land and water. To counter this charge, a final clarification rule was issued by the federal government in 2002 that a company can

◆ **FIGURE 13.22** A massive dragline (on the right) looks like a child's toy when compared with the huge scale of a mountaintop-removal coal-mining operation near Kayford Mountain, West Virginia.

apply to the Corps of Engineers to put virtually anything labeled as fill into U.S. waters (streams, rivers, and lakes) so long as it either turns a portion or all of a water body into dry land or changes the bottom elevation of U.S. waters. This final rule is astounding because it redefines fill and appears to violate both the stated goals of the Clean Water Act and mining regulations. Furthermore, the final rule applies broadly to all mining and industrial wastes including those that are hazardous to the environment and human health, and it may apply to many sites that would qualify as Superfund sites. A federal judge has reminded the administration that only Congress can rewrite federal law, and the issue is progressing through the courts. In 2006 several groups filed litigation challenging the U.S. Army Corps of Engineers' decision to permit three new mountain-removal mining sites

in West Virginia. A temporary restraining order was issued to limit mining on the sites and to refrain from destroying undisturbed areas before the case can be heard in federal court.

Impacts of Underground Mining

The most far-reaching effects of underground mining are ground subsidence (see Chapter 7), the collapse of the overburden into mined-out areas (◆ Figure 13.24), and **acid mine drainage (AMD),** the drainage of acidic water from mine sites. AMD is generally considered to be the most serious environmental problem facing the mining industry today, as some acid drainage may continue for hundreds of years. AMD can result when high-sulfur coal or metallic-sulfide ore bodies are

◆ **FIGURE 13.23** Waste from mountaintop removal coal mining forms an enormous valley fill in the Birchton Curve Valley, West Virginia. Such valley fills have buried many miles of streams, eliminating aquatic vegetation, fish, and other wildlife habitat, as well as entire communities and their residents who have lived for generations along now-buried valleys in West Virginia.

◆ **FIGURE 13.24** Store-building subsiding into an abandoned underground coal mine south of Pittsburgh, Pennsylvania.

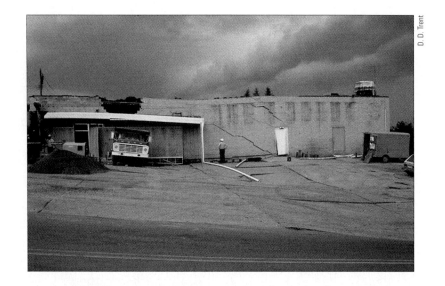

mined. In both cases, pyrite (FeS_2) and other metallic-sulfide minerals are prevalent in the walls of underground mines and open pits; in the **tailings,** finely ground, sand-sized waste material from the milling process that remains after the desired minerals have been extracted; and in other mine waste. The reaction of pyrite or other sulfide minerals with oxygen-rich water produces sulfur dioxide (SO_2), which, facilitated by bacterial decomposition, reacts with water to form sulfuric acid (◆ Figure 13.25 and ■ Case Study 13.1 on page 400).

This not only acidifies surface and underground waters, but it also expedites the leaching, release, and dispersal of iron, zinc, copper, and other toxic metals into the environment. Such substances kill aquatic life and erode human-made structures such as concrete drains, bridge piers, sewer pipes, and well casings. (Zinc concentrations as low as 0.06 mg/L and copper concentrations as low as 0.0015 mg/L are lethal to

some species of fish.) Estimates are that between 8,000 and 16,000 kilometers (5,000 and 10,000 mi) of U.S. streams have been ruined by acid drainage. The oxidized iron in AMD colors some polluted streams rust-red (◆ Figure 13.26). Where polluted water is used for livestock or irrigation water, it may diminish the productive value of the affected land. Although expensive to implement, technologies do exist for preventing and controlling AMD (see ■ Case Study 13.2 on page 401). The subject of surface- and groundwater protection is addressed later in the chapter.

> **CONSIDER THIS**
>
> Pyrite (fool's gold) is common in deposits of gold, lead, zinc, silver, and copper. Why is a conspicuous rusty-colored outcropping often a clue to the existence of buried ore?

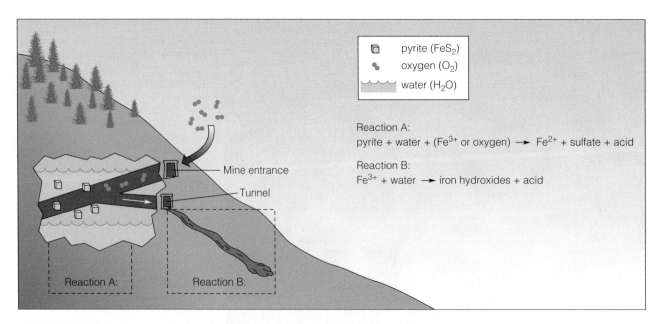

▥	pyrite (FeS_2)
✎	oxygen (O_2)
〜	water (H_2O)

Reaction A:
pyrite + water + (Fe^{3+} or oxygen) ⟶ Fe^{2+} + sulfate + acid

Reaction B:
Fe^{3+} + water ⟶ iron hydroxides + acid

Mine entrance
Tunnel
Reaction A:
Reaction B:

◆ **FIGURE 13.25** Pyrite reacts with air and water to produce sulfuric acid. Based on USGS data

◆ **FIGURE 13.26** Rust-red sludge of acid mine drainage from West Virginia coal mines that were abandoned in the 1960s. The acidic water has eaten away at the Portland-cement-based concrete retaining wall, and the bridge supports will soon share that fate. Problems such as this are rarely caused by modern surface mines, because current mining and reclamation practices eliminate or minimize acid mine drainage.

Impacts of Surface Mining

A variety of surface-mining operations contribute to environmental problems. Hydraulic mining is largely an activity of the past, but **dredging**—scooping up earth material below a body of water from a barge or raft equipped to process or transport materials—continues in the twenty-first century (◆Figure 13.27). Much of the current U.S. production of sand and gravel is accomplished by dredging rivers, and large dredges are used to mine placer tin deposits in southeast Asia. Dredging causes significant disruption to the landscape; it washes away soil, leaves a trail of boulders, and severely damages biological systems. Scarification remains from former dredging in river bottoms in many western

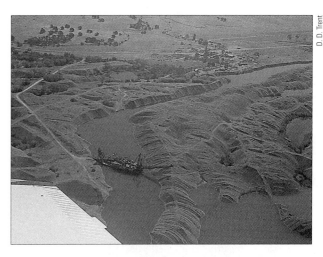

◆ **FIGURE 13.28** Scarified landscape from waste-rock remaining after dredging for gold along the Yuba River, California.

states and elsewhere in the world (◆Figure 13.28). Few gold-dredge areas have been reclaimed, but an outstanding example of what can be accomplished appears in ◆Figure 13.29. Another example is a 73-square-kilometer (28-mi^2) dredge-scarified area near Folsom, California. The area was reclaimed by reshaping the waste piles, covering the surface with topsoil, and then building a subdivision of homes on it. Landscaped with trees and grasses, no evidence remains of the once scarified surface.

In **hydraulic mining,** or *hydraulicking,* a high-pressure jet of water is blasted through a nozzle, called a *monitor,* against hillsides of ancient alluvial deposits (◆Figure 13.30). Hydraulicking requires the construction of ditches, reservoirs, a penstock (vertical pipe), and pipelines. Once constructed, it is possible to wash thousands of cubic yards of gold-bearing gravel per day. The gold is recovered in sluice

◆ **FIGURE 13.27** Placer mining with a bucket-conveyer dredge near Platinum, Alaska, 1958. The dredge operated from the early 1930s until the late 1970s, during which time it was the major producer of platinum-group metals in North America.

◆ **FIGURE 13.29** Reclaimed dredge-mined site, a former placer gold mine; Fox Creek, Fairbanks District, Alaska. The State of Alaska awarded a certificate of commendation for the reclamation work.

◆ **FIGURE 13.30** Hydraulicking a bench placer deposit.

boxes (long open-ended boxes with transverse slats on the bottom over which the slurry of muddy water flows) where mercury (the liquid metal that dissolves gold and silver to form an amalgam) may be added to aid recovery at low cost. Hydraulicking is efficient but highly destructive to the land (◆ Figure 13.31). Because nineteenth-century hydraulicking was found to create river sediment that increased downstream flooding, clogged irrigation systems, and ruined farmlands, court injunctions stopped most hydraulic mining in the United States before 1900 (although its use continued in California's Klamath-Trinity Mountains until the 1950s). Hydraulicking is still being used in Russia's Baltic region for mining amber, and hydraulicking and mercury amalgamation is used to extract placer gold in remote areas of Brazil's Amazon basin. It is estimated that 100 tons of mercury is working its way into the ecosystem of the Amazon basin each year. The danger of using mercury is that when it escapes from mining activity it takes on different geochemical forms, including a suite of organic compounds, the most important being methylmercury, which is readily incorporated into biological tissues and is the most toxic to humans. In California's Mother Lode region, where hundreds of hydraulic placer gold mines operated from the 1860s through the early 1900s, the mercury loss to the environment from these operations

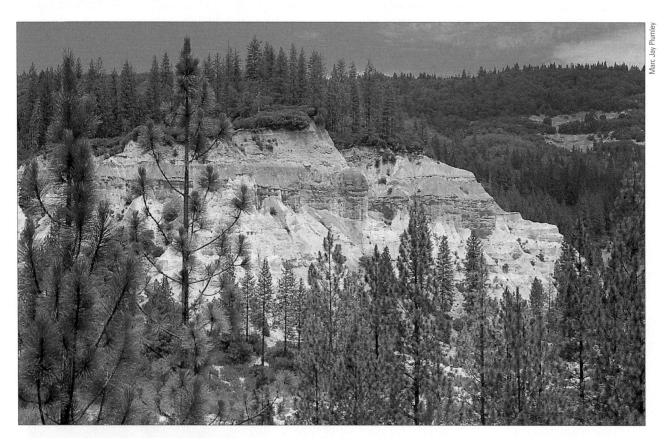

◆ **FIGURE 13.31** A monument to the destructive force of hydraulic mining of bench placer deposits; Malakoff Diggins State Park, Nevada County, California. When the hydraulic mining operations here ended in 1884, Malakoff Diggins was the largest and richest hydraulic gold mine in the world, with a total output of about $3.5 million. More than 41 million cubic yards of earth had been excavated to obtain gold. The site is now marked by colorful, eroded cliffs along the sides of an open pit that is some 7,000 feet long, 300 feet wide, and as much as 600 feet deep.

◆ **FIGURE 13.32** A rich phosphate bed in Florida is strip-mined by a mammoth dragline dredge. The bucket, swinging from a 100-meter boom (that's longer than a football field), can scoop up nearly 100 tons of phosphate at a time. The phosphate is then piped as a slurry to a plant for processing. Fine-grained gypsum, a by-product of processing, is pumped to a settling pond (*upper left*), where it becomes concentrated by evaporation.

is estimated to have been 3 to 8 million pounds, and it still remains in the ecosystem.

Strip-mining is used most commonly when the resource lies parallel and close to the surface. The phosphate deposits of North Carolina and Florida are strip-mined by excavating the shallow, horizontal beds to a depth of about 8 meters (26 ft) (◆Figure 13.32). After the phosphate beds are removed, the excavated area is backfilled to return the surface to its original form.

Open-pit mining is the only practical way to extract many minerals when they occur in a very large low-grade-ore body near the surface. The process requires processing enormous amounts of material and is devastating to the landscape. The epitome of open-pit mining is the Bingham Canyon copper mine in Utah, where about 3.3 billion tons of material—seven times the volume moved in constructing the Panama Canal—have been removed since 1906 (see Figure 13.8). Now a half-mile deep, the pit is the largest human excavation in the world, and the waste-rock piles literally form mountains.

The environmental consequences of open-pit mining are several. The mine itself disrupts the landscape, and the increased surface area of the broken and crushed rocks from mining and milling sets the stage for erosion and the leaching of toxic metals to the environment. This is especially true of sulfide-ore bodies. They produce AMD, because the waste rocks and tailings are highly susceptible to chemical weathering.

Impacts of Mineral Processing

Except for some industrial minerals, excavating and removing raw ore are only the first steps in producing a marketable product. Once metallic ores are removed from the ground,

they are processed at a mill to produce an enriched ore, referred to as a *concentrate*. The concentrate is then sent to a smelter for refining into a valuable commodity.

Concentration and smelting are complex processes, and a thorough discussion of them is well beyond the scope of this book. Briefly, the concentration process requires

1. crushing the ore to a fine powder,
2. classifying the crushed materials by particle size by passing them through various mechanical devices and passing on those particles of a certain size to the next step, and
3. separating the desired mineral components from the noneconomic minerals by a flotation, gravity, or chemical method.

These means of separation are discussed individually here.

Flotation

The **flotation** separation process is widely used, especially for recovering sulfide-ore minerals such as lead, zinc, and copper sulfides from host rock. The process is based on the principles of wettability of mineral particles and surface tension of fluids. After crushing and concentration, the wettability of the *undesired* mineral particles is increased by treating the crushed ore chemically—usually with liquid hydrocarbons—to ensure that the undesired minerals will sink. Air is then bubbled into the slurry of crushed ore and water, forming a froth that collects the *desired* mineral particles of low wettability. The froth, with the attached desirable mineral particles, is skimmed off the top of the flotation tank and dried; this is the concentrate. The undesired mineral particles, the tailings, sink to the bottom of the flotation tank.

They are drawn off and piped to the tailings pond. Although they are usually environmentally undesirable, tailings are an unavoidable waste product of mining.

Gravity Separation

Gravity separation methods are used in recovering high-density ore minerals such as gold, platinum-group metals, tungsten, and tin. By this process, mineral particles mixed with water are caused to flow across a series of riffles placed in a trough. The riffles trap the desired high-density particles, and water carries away the undesired low-density minerals, the tailings.

Chemical Methods

For minerals whose physical properties make them unsuitable for separation by flotation or gravity methods, chemical processes are used, the major ones being leaching and cyanidation. *Leaching* is often used in treating copper-oxide ores. Sulfuric acid is added to crushed ore to dissolve the copper and produce a solution of copper sulfate. The dissolved copper is then recovered by placing scrap iron in the copper sulfate solution; the copper plates out onto the iron. The acidic waste materials are chemically neutralized by treating them with lime. Among the other potential toxic contaminants used in mineral processing are ammonia, benzene, bromine, chlorine, cyanide compounds, cyclohexane, ethybenzene, glycol, ethers, hydrazine, hydrochloric acid, naphthalene, nitric acid, phenol, propylene, sulfuric acid, thiourea, toluene, and xylene. It is beyond the scope of this book to elaborate on the use of these chemicals, but because of cyanide's widespread and controversial use in gold recovery, its use will be explained.

Cyanidation

Cyanidation, used to recover gold and silver since 1890, makes use of the special property of cyanide to dissolve gold and silver. An innovation of cyanide recovery, **cyanide heap-leaching,** began to be widely used in the United States in the 1980s. By the turn of the twenty-first century, about 100 heap-leach operations were active in the western United States and South Carolina. Although heap-leaching is efficient, it is controversial in environmental circles because the open-pit mining, waste-rock dumps, and tailings piles are destructive to the landscape. Furthermore, cyanide is perceived as a hazard to wildlife and a contaminant to ground and surface waters. In Montana alone, 51 cyanide releases were documented between 1982 and 1999. The use of cyanide is illustrated in ◆ Figure 13.33. Ore from an open-pit excavation is pulverized, spread out in piles over an impervious clay or high density polyethylene liner, and sprayed with a dilute cyanide solution, commonly about 200 parts per million (0.02%) (◆ Figure 13.34). The solution dissolves gold and silver (and several other metals) present in small amounts in the ore as it works its way through the heap to the pregnant pond (◆ Figure 13.35). The gold and silver are recovered from the resulting "pregnant" solution by adsorption on activated charcoal, and the barren cyanide solution is recycled to the leach heap. The precious metals are removed from the charcoal by chemical and electrical techniques, melted in a furnace, and poured into molds to form ingots.

Monitoring wells are placed downslope from leach pads and ponds containing cyanide for detecting possible leakage. Maintaining the low concentrations of cyanide required by state regulations requires regular monitoring of the solution. The cyanide solution is kept highly alkaline by additions of sodium hydroxide, a strong base, in order to inhibit the formation of lethal cyanide gas. No measurable cyanide gas has

◆ **FIGURE 13.33** The major components of cyanide heap-leach gold recovery.

◆ **FIGURE 13.35** A typical "pregnant pond" for collecting the cyanide solution containing dissolved gold from a leach heap. The face of the leach heap is at the upper right of the photograph. The pipes on the far side of the pond drain the "pregnant" solution from beneath the leach heap. The pond is lined with two layers of high-density polyethylene underlain by a layer of sand and a leakage detection system of perforated PVC pipe. In the rare chance that leakage should occur, it is trapped in the pregnant pond, and appropriate repairs are made. The pond is covered with fine-mesh netting to keep birds from the toxic solution.

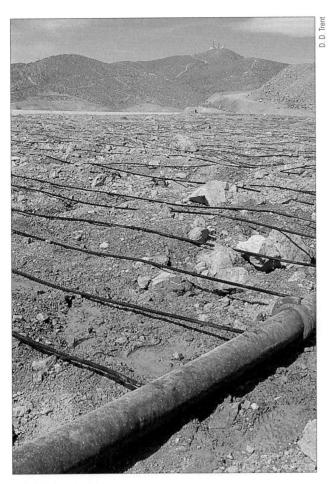

◆ **FIGURE 13.34** Cyanide drip lines on a leach heap. The cyanide concentration is 200 parts per million (one five-thousandth of one percent), and the solution is kept highly alkaline to prohibit cyanide gas from forming.

been detected above leach heaps where instrumental testing for escaping gas has been carried out. Unforeseen peculiarities of the ore chemistry and unusual weather have caused unexpected increases in cyanide values at some mines. This has required an occasional shutdown of operations until the chemistry of the solution could be corrected to the established standards. In a few cases, stiff fines have been assessed where cyanide levels exceeded the limits of the operator's permit. Upon abandonment of a leach-extraction operation, federal and state regulations require flushing and detoxification of any residual cyanide from the leach pile. Regular sampling and testing at groundwater-monitoring wells also may be required for several years following abandonment.

Securing the open cyanide ponds to keep wildlife from drinking the lethal poison is an environmental concern at several operations. After 900 birds died on the cyanide-tainted tailings pond at a mine in Nevada in 1989–1990, the company pleaded guilty to misdemeanor charges, paid a $250,000 fine, and contributed an additional $250,000 to the Nature Conservancy for preservation of a migratory bird habitat.

Various techniques for discouraging wildlife from visiting cyanide-extraction operations have been tried: stringing lines of flags across leach ponds in an effort to frighten birds away, covering pregnant ponds with plastic sheeting, and blasting recorded heavy-metal rock music from loudspeakers. At one mine, the heavy-metal recordings were effective in keeping migratory waterfowl away, but resident birdlife adjusted to the din and remained in the area. One wonders what effect the blasting of recordings by Dragon Force, Mars Volta, or Fear Factory might have. The current standard practice is to enclose the operations with chain-link fencing to keep out the larger animals and to stretch netting completely across the ponds to protect birds (see Figure 13.35). The fences and netting have been successful in some 20 active heap-leach operations in the western states; for example, bird losses have been reduced to only 50 to 60 a year in cyanide ponds. The number is less than trivial when compared with the thousands of birds killed in the western states each year when they fly into building windows, roof-mounted television antennas and the paths of automobiles.

Smelting

Historically, smelters have had bad reputations for causing extensive damage to the environment. Sulfurous fumes emitted as by-products of smelting processes have polluted the air, and toxic substances from smelting operations have contaminated soils and destroyed vegetation. Because water was necessary for operating early-day smelters, they were located near streams. The accepted practice at the time was to discharge mill wastes and tailings into streams or settling ponds, which commonly spilled over into streams. Improved smelting technologies are now eliminating these problems. For example, Kennecott's former smelter at the Bingham Canyon, Utah copper mine released 2,136 kilograms (4,700 lbs) of sulfur dioxide (SO_2) per hour to the atmosphere. Kennecott's new smelter, designed to meet or exceed all existing and anticipated future federal and state emission standards, was put into service in 1995. SO_2 emissions were cut by 96 percent to only 91 kilograms (200 lbs) per hour, less than the rate for what were formerly the world's cleanest smelters, operating in Japan.

Mine-Land Reclamation

The volume of coal-mine spoil and hardrock-mining waste rock is usually greater than the volume occupied by the rock before mining. SMCRA requires that coal-mine spoil be disposed of in fills, usually in the upper reaches of valleys near the mine site. Because some settlement of this material can be expected over time, construction on these reclaimed sites may be risky. Waste rock from hardrock mining is usually deposited in great mesa-like piles near the mines. In recent years, many of these piles have been contoured to break up their unnatural, flat-topped appearance. In both cases the features are engineered and structured for stability with terraces and diversion ditches for controlling surface-water flow and preventing erosion, and then they are landscaped. Groundwater within the fills is commonly channeled through subsurface drains.

Surface- and Groundwater Protection

High-quality, reliable water is critical for domestic, industrial, and agricultural activities, and it is especially precious in arid and semiarid regions. SMCRA requires that a surface coal-mining operation be conducted in a way that will maintain hydrologic balance and ensure the availability of an adequate water supply for postmining use. In the early 1990s nearly 1,500 abandoned U.S. coal mines had been identified as having water problems. Of these, about 500 have been reclaimed or have been funded to begin reclamation.

During surface coal mining all of the runoff water that collects in the pit is required to be collected and treated. Because surface mining destroys the original plant cover and exposes the soil to erosion, mitigation of erosion and sediment loss is needed during mining and reclamation. AMD problems have arisen from the hardrock mining of sulfide ores in the western states, with more than 100,000 abandoned hardrock mines in the west that may pose AMD problems (see ■ Case Studies 13.2 and 13.4), in many areas of Canada, and from coal mining in West Virginia, Maryland, Ohio, and Pennsylvania.

Pennsylvania, recognizing the scars of 200 years of mining, has adopted a new initiative, *Reclaim PA*. Abandoned mine lands in the state—more than 250,000 acres of abandoned surface mines, 2,400 miles of streams polluted with mine drainage (see Figure 13.26), widespread subsidence problems (see Figure 13.24), over 7,000 abandoned gas and oil wells, numerous hazardous mine openings, and affected water supplies—represent as much as one-third of the total problem nationally. Beginning in the 1960s, Pennsylvania became a national leader in establishing regulations and laws to ensure plugging and reclamation are completed after active, operations close down. *Reclaim PA* includes policy and management objectives and legislative initiatives designed to enhance the reclamation efforts of the Pennsylvania Department of Environmental Protection, volunteers, and mine operators. The price tag for correcting Pennsylvania's problems is estimated at $15 billion.

At the federal level, SMCRA requires coal-mine operators to treat water from their mines before releasing it into streams and rivers. Control measures for AMD include

- Holding mine drainage water in entrapment ponds and neutralizing it by adding alkaline materials from other industries such as kiln dust, slag, alkaline fly ash, or limestone before releasing it from the mine-permit area.

- Grading and covering acid-forming materials to promote surface-water runoff and inhibit infiltration.

- Backfilling underground mines with alkaline fly ash, which absorbs water and turns into weak concrete, in order to minimize the flow of water from the mine and reduce the amount of oxygen in the mine. Filling is done by pumping a slurry down several boreholes to reduce AMD and stabilize the ground surface of many communities built over mined-out areas.

- Using wetlands to treat AMD issuing from both operating and abandoned coal mines. Cattails and other wetland plants have been found to be effective in removing some toxic metals and other substances from water. One such Pennsylvania wetland has saved an electric power company $50,000 in water-treatment costs each year since it was built in 1985.

Wastewater from hardrock mines and from processed ore tailings is another source of contamination. These waters are usually treated by chemical or physical processes before disposal. When those processes proved unsuitable at the Homestake Gold Mine at Lead, South Dakota, the company developed a biological treatment. The bacterial bioxidation process breaks down residual cyanide from the mill's wastewater into harmless components that are environmentally compatible with the disposal creek's ecosystem. The creek now supports a viable trout fishery for the first time in over a century.

At some unprotected mine properties, siltation clogs streams and increases the threat of flooding. This problem

John E. Gray, USGS Bulletin 2156

◆ **FIGURE 13.36** A placer gold mining operation near Fairbanks, Alaska. A downstream settling pond traps placer tailings from the mine.

(a)

E. Frank Schnitzer, Oreg. Dept. of Geology and Mineral Industries

(b)

E. Frank Schnitzer, Oreg. Dept. of Geology and Mineral Industries

◆ **FIGURE 13.37** (a) Site of a sand- and gravel-mining operation along the Molalla River in Oregon before restoration, and (b) after reclamation. Not only is the site more attractive, but the pit also has been modified to decrease erosion, shallow ponds have been created to provide habitat suitable for migrating and spawning salmon, and the overall setting is improved for the general benefit of wildlife.

may be mitigated by constructing settling ponds for trapping the sediment downstream from the source (◆Figure 13.36).

Of all mining operations, sand and gravel mining are the most widespread and the most obvious to urban dwellers—especially when the operations are along or within rivers. Such modification to rivers results in a variety of consequences: increased erosion to channels and riverbanks, degradation of water quality, disconnection of links between terrestrial and aquatic ecosystems, and creation of unacceptable habitats for spawning fish such as anadromous (migrating) salmonids (◆Figure 13.37). Fortunately, disrupted river channels can be restored, and more states are requiring restoration elements in mines' operating plans.

Mill and Smelter Waste Contamination

As ore is milled to produce concentrate, about 90 percent of the mined material is discarded as tailings. Smelters that process metallic sulfide concentrates release waste products

that can contain thousands of times the natural levels of heavy metals such as lead, arsenic, zinc, cadmium, and beryllium. These contaminants remain in smelter slag (rendered inert by the smelting process so that it is not bioavailable) and in flue dust that commonly remains around former smelter sites long after smelting has ended. The primary concerns with such contamination are the environmental impact of stormwater runoff into nearby streams or lakes and the risks to human health that result when people unwittingly inhale or ingest the heavy metals. If the site is on the EPA's Superfund list, the cleanup will take one of two directions—either removal or in-place remediation such as enclosing or encapsulating the heavy-metal sources—determined by which one is considered appropriate for preventing human contact. At one Superfund site the discovery of elevated levels of arsenic in the hair and blood of children in a small community built on contaminated soil resulted in the EPA's moving the entire community of about 30 families and

◆ **FIGURE 13.38** Removal of mill tailings at a Superfund site at Butte, Montana. Immense amounts of material must be removed from some Superfund sites.

◆ **FIGURE 13.39** Preparation of a repository site for contaminated smelter-flue dust near Anaconda, Montana. The pit will have a heavy polyethylene liner.

destroying the houses. If a contaminated Superfund area is populated, the EPA may require an ongoing blood-testing program to monitor residents' blood levels of heavy metals. Contaminated stormwater runoff may require construction of a stormwater management system with engineered drainage channels, ponds, and artificial wetlands.

The EPA procedure for remediating contaminated smelter slag, flue dust, and tailings that pose a threat to surfacewater or groundwater is to remove the material and deposit it in specially constructed repository sites (◆Figure 13.38). Commonly these are pits underlain with heavy plastic liners (◆Figure 13.39) into which the contaminated waste is placed and covered with crushed limestone, sealed with topsoil, and revegetated. To eliminate leaching of the material by rainwater or snowmelt, a subsoil drainage system collects excess water and disposes of it in such a way that it poses no threat to human health or the environment. (Disposal of toxic wastes is discussed thoroughly in Chapter 15.)

CONSIDER   THIS
Why does mining that exposes limestone or marble as it removes ore not have AMD problems?

Revegetation and Wildlife Restoration

SMCRA regulations for coal mining and most state reclamation regulations for hardrock mining require healthy vegetation to be reestablished once mining has ended. Permanent vegetation is the principal means of minimizing erosion and reducing stream siltation. The types of vegetation that are to be used in reclamation are stipulated in the original mine permit, based on premining vegetation and intended postmining uses. Commonly, a straw mulch or chemical soil stabilizer is applied after seeding to inhibit erosion and retain

moisture. Mine operators are responsible for maintaining the new plant cover until it is successfully reestablished; the SMCRA minimum is five years in the East and Midwest and ten years in the semiarid West.

Wildlife habitat is one of the most common uses of postmined land. Among the techniques the mining industry uses to meet the EPA, SMCRA, and state regulations for attracting and supporting desirable species of wildlife are contouring the land, introducing plant species that will support browsing and foraging, creating wetland habitats, and stocking ponds for sport fishing.

The Future of Mining

Concern about the future reserves of mineral resources has led to the obvious question: Are we running out? Numerous studies have been conducted over the years to determine reserves, and the answer to the question seems to be: Not yet. The question of availability is probably not the important one, however. Increasing needs for resources will require mining lower and lower grades of minerals. This will require improved technologies and larger, more powerful machines, which in turn will produce greater quantities of waste material. This will impose more stress on environmental systems. Because of these factors, the question that *should* be asked is: Can we afford the environmental and human costs required to satisfy our increasing need for minerals?

Today, we residents of industrialized countries enjoy living in comfortable homes, traveling by automobile, and having labor-saving appliances, all of which provide us with lifestyles that only 100 years ago would have been considered luxurious. These lifestyles are possible only because of the availability of inexpensive raw materials for manufacturing the products to which we have grown accustomed. Few of Earth's people realize that today's prices of mineral commodities typically reflect only the short-term, tangible costs of wages, equipment, fuel, financing, and transportation—just as they have since mining began in ancient times. Worldwide, much of the *real cost* of exploiting mineral and fossil-fuel resources is intangible, and it has been externalized. Historically, the environment has borne a great deal of the cost of extracting raw materials; the consumer has paid only part of the real cost. Even in the United States, where regulations designed to protect the environment are imposed, mining and processing still cause substantial damage.

Worldwide, poor mining and mineral-processing practices contribute significantly to soil erosion, water contamination, air pollution, and deforestation, especially in developing nations, as illustrated by the examples in Table 13.3. Fortunately, the negative environmental impacts of mining and mineral processing are gaining more attention in the developing nations. For example, Mexico adopted new mining and environmental laws in 1992 before encouraging mining by privatizing that industry. And in 1994 Tanzania and Guinea began requiring environmental-impact assessments to be submitted along with applications for mining licenses.

Mining generates twice as much solid waste as all other industries and cities combined, and most mining wastes in the United States are currently unregulated by federal law. In addition, the mineral industry is one of the greatest consumers of energy and a contributor to air pollution and global warming. It is estimated, for example, that the processing of bauxite into aluminum alone consumes about one percent of the world's total energy budget. Miners admit that mines leave holes in the ground, but they go on to point out that when they abandon their currently active mines in the United States, they will be restoring the site to as near a natural appearance as is reasonable, except for the open pits.

In evaluating mining and its impact on the environment, we must recognize that the only way not to disturb the landscape is *not to mine*. This would mean not having the raw materials to build automobiles, houses, farm machinery, airplanes, radios, television sets—virtually all of the objects we view as essential to a modern society. The question thus becomes: What must be done to minimize the impacts?

CONSIDER THIS

What is meant by the statement that the true cost of mining is externalized?

Mining Legislation in the United States

In the 1970s some genuinely important concerns related to mining and processing mineral materials became obvious in the United States and many other countries, and laws began being written to address these concerns. Consequently, in the United States, the EPA now administers a number of acts regulating water quality and toxic wastes, and the Fish and Wildlife Service requires noninterference with rare and endangered species. Beginning in 2001, however, federal regulations dealing with some environmental laws and policies began changing, including regulations dealing with mining. Various constraints are imposed by numerous state and local laws requiring that mining operations meet certain air-quality standards. Many states will not issue a permit for an operation to begin without prior approval of an adequately funded reclamation plan specifying that the waste and tailings piles will be restored to resemble the surrounding topography to the extent that it is possible, that the disturbed ground and the tailings will be replanted with native species, that all buildings and equipment will be removed, and that the open pits will be fenced and posted with warning signs. Most states require that mining companies be bonded to ensure that funds will be available for reclamation in the event of bankruptcy or abandonment of their operation before remediation is completed (see ■ Case Study 13.5).

In 2003 California's State Mining and Geology Board approved permanent regulations requiring new open-pit metallic mines to backfill open pits and recontour their mine sites upon completion of mining. Subsequent to the new regulation, a Canadian mining company is filing suit against the U.S. government under the provisions of the North American Free Trade Act (NAFTA). NAFTA allows foreign investors to sue signatory governments for recovery of real or perceived financial losses caused by policies that foreign investors feel violate their rights. At issue is a group of mining claims in California's Mojave Desert on land that is held sacred to an Indian tribe and that the Canadian corporation would like to develop. However, because of the additional costs required by the new back-fill regulation, open-pit mining of the property is now uneconomic.

It is claimed by some that enforcement of federal regulations pertaining to mining has been weak. Initially, the EPA did little to regulate mining wastes. Further, Congress specifically exempted hardrock-mining wastes and tailings from regulation as hazardous wastes in the Resource Conservation and Recovery Act (1976). Complicating the issues is the fact that instead of the federal government, it is the individual states that play the role of regulator on state and private lands.

Further reform of the Mining Law of 1872 may occur. Beginning in the 1980s public concern grew over the problems of protecting nonmineral values on public lands, the lack of meaningful federal reclamation standards, limited environmental protection, and the lack of royalty collection for exploited public land—issues of public-resource management that are not addressed in the current mining law. Bills revising the mining law have been introduced in nearly every session of Congress since the early 1990s. A point of contention in revising the mining law has been the imposition of royalties on mining income with the funds so generated earmarked for reclamation of some 100,000 abandoned hardrock mines in the western states, much as is already done by SMCRA with abandoned coal mines using the Abandoned Mine Fund. Some critics of mining-law reform believe that charging royalties for hardrock operations on federal lands will close down U.S. mining and drive more mineral production to foreign countries. Nevertheless, efforts at reform are expected to continue.

The future may also bring some changes in the basic attitudes and assumptions that underlie our capitalistic society. The economic assumption that prosperity is synonymous with mineral production is now being questioned. Environmental deterioration from today's unprecedented rate of mineral production will, if continued, eventually overwhelm the benefits gained from increased mineral supplies. If, by 2050, everyone lives as the developed world does at present, mineral production would need to be 3 to 15 times current levels, energy production would need to be some 5 times the current level, and about 45 percent of the water cycle would be needed. It is possible that the use of marginal mineral resources could meet the necessary resource demands, but the energy demands for extraction and processing would increase exponentially as the grade declines. It is imperative that by the middle of the twenty-first century, when the world population has reached 10 to 15 billion (see Chapter 1), new technologies and economic strategies must be in place. The goals of protecting and managing the environment while at the same time exploiting and expanding the mineral resource base in an environmentally responsible manner are not necessarily mutually exclusive. But how can both goals be achieved? Society must recognize the need for sustainable development to replace the current materials-intensive, high-value, planned-obsolescent manufacturing processes that reduce our resource base. Sustainable development will occur only by using raw materials and fuels more efficiently, generating little or no waste, recycling what waste is generated, and developing inexpensive and widely available alternative energy sources. In the long run, sustainability is critical in maintaining the viability of the biosphere. Economists often opine that there is no problem of shortages and that market forces will dictate needed changes, but it is Earth scientists who perhaps have the best understanding of the natural-resource base; however, they are not unified in their view of the future and resource depletion. Some focus on the identification, further exploration, exploitation, and use of resources, while others focus on the limits of resource availability, and overall future of society, and raise ethical questions about the inequality of lifestyles and resource-related wealth. Whether attitudes and technology can modernize fast enough to conserve natural resources at the same time that the world's wealth is increasing is the big question. This is the formidable challenge that must be faced jointly by industry, governments, and society.

> **CONSIDER THIS**
>
> Growth in consumption of natural (nonrenewable) resources increases exponentially, at a faster rate than the growth of Earth's population (which doubled twice during the twentieth century). How long can this continue?

CASE STUDY 13.1

Acid Mine Drainage and Earth Systems

The origin of acid mine drainage (AMD) is an excellent example of the interaction of four of the spheres of the Earth System. When sulfide ore bodies (components of the *lithosphere*) are mined, the surface area of the sulfide minerals in the underground workings, ore piles, waste heaps, and mill tailings is increased (due to their being broken). This increased exposure to chemical processes speeds up the minerals' reactions with both oxygen (an *atmosphere* component) and underground and surface water (components of the *hydrosphere*). The chemical interaction of components of these three Earth spheres produces sulfuric acid and liberates free metallic ions such as those of iron, lead, zinc, copper, and manganese (see Figure 13.25). Additionally, certain bacteria (components of the *biosphere*) thrive in this acidic environment, deriving energy from the conversion of one type of iron (ferrous, Fe^{+2}) to another ferric, Fe^{+3}). In so doing, these bacteria cause a "cascading" effect in the conversion of Fe^{+2} to Fe^{+3}, increasing the rate by as much as a million times what it would be if the bacteria were absent. As the water moves away from a mine site, additional chemical reactions may generate more acid, causing red, orange, and yellow iron-rich precipitates to settle on aquatic plant life and stream bottoms. Heat generated by the chemical and biochemical activity provides positive feedback to the entire process, further speeding up the reactions. The acidic water that is produced by the reaction interacts with other components of the biosphere—aquatic life in streams and rivers and land plants and animals, including humans, that utilize the water—often with injurious effects.

CASE STUDY 13.2

Cleaning Up a Century of Hardrock Mining: The Abandoned Mine Lands Initiative

The challenges of cleaning up abandoned mining lands (AMLs) are well illustrated by ongoing activities in Colorado and Montana, where contaminated mine drainage is a serious environmental problem. Several thousands of miles of these state's streams are contaminated with heavy metals from mine drainage. The water emitted from the mines, acid mine drainage (AMD), is commonly more acidic than lemon juice (citric acid) or vinegar (acetic acid)—often with a pH of less than 4—and contains concentrations of dissolved metals that often exceed the limits of state and federal standards. The high metal concentrations are due to acid dissolution of the country rock and to oxidation of metallic sulfide minerals. These chemical reactions can produce harmful concentrations of such elements as iron, manganese, zinc, lead, copper, arsenic, and cadmium in the waters (see Case Study 13.1). Streams near AMLs can contain metal concentrations and (or) be so acidic that aquatic insects and fish cannot live in them.

From 1997 through 2001 the U.S. Geological Survey (USGS) conducted a program, the Abandoned Mine Lands (AML) Initiative, to provide technical assistance to support Federal Land Management Agency (FLMA) actions to remediate contamination associated with abandoned hardrock mining. The strategy employed a watershed approach in which contaminated sites were identified and remediated based on their impact on the surface waters and ecosystems within the watershed. The initiative began with two pilot projects in the Upper Animas River basin in southwestern Colorado and the Boulder River basin in southwestern Montana.

Upper Animas River Watershed, Colorado

In the area of Silverton, in the San Juan Mountains, many millions of dollars' worth of lead, zinc, silver, and gold were produced between 1874 and 1991. By the late 1990s most of the 1,500 mines in the watershed had been abandoned (◆ Figure 1), and metals-laden AMD issuing from the old mines affected the river's aquatic life and water quality for more than 100 miles downstream. Heavy metals such as cadmium, copper, lead, and zinc, from both mining activity and natural sources are a threat to the environment and possibly human health. Contamination of the watershed is mainly from water discharged from some of the 1,500 inactive mines in the basin, although some of the contamination is from natural weathering of the region's highly sulfide-mineralized rock, such contaminated water being termed **acid rock drainage** (ARD). Part of the assessment of an area is to determine the environmental conditions and natural ARD that existed prior to the beginning of mining in order to establish realistic cleanup goals for an area.

In response to the Colorado Water Control Division's upgrading of water quality standards for the Upper Animas River Basin, the Animas River Stakeholders Group (ARSG) was formed in 1994. The ARSG is a coalition of elected officials, mining companies, environmental groups,

◆ **FIGURE 1** Longfellow Mine, at Red Mountain Pass, one of an estimated 1,500 abandoned mines in the Animas River watershed near Silverton, Colorado.

local, state and federal government agencies, and local interest groups. The ARSG has become part of the AML strategy of the U.S. Department of the Interior and the U.S. Department of Agriculture to clean up federal lands. The AML watershed approach to cleaning up the surface waters is a three-step process: monitoring, feasibility and site characterization, and implementation.

Monitoring consists of studying the mines in the areas, sampling and analyzing any waters draining from the mines. These studies showed that about 350 days a year zinc levels in the upper Animas River exceeded the standards proposed by the Colorado Water Standards Control Division. Feasibility and site characterization consists of determining remediation processes that work best in the area and prioritizing those sites for possible cleanup on the basis of

- the contaminating site's level of environmental impact; that is the relative "metal-loading" contributions to the watershed from a mine site's AMD, and ARD from natural sources;
- identifying the pathways of the toxic contaminants;
- the feasibility of treatment;
- cost-effectiveness;
- the preservation of the area's historic, natural, and cultural values.

Of the 300 or so abandoned mines in the Animas watershed recognized by the ARSG as sources of AMD, 67 were found to contribute over 90 percent of all the metals loading to the Animas watershed. Implementation of remediation at those sites became the Group's highest priority. Technology necessary for remediation, funding, and

CONTINUED

(a)

(b)

◆ **FIGURE 2** (a) An early stage in the remedial work at the Pride of the West (POW) mine in the Animas River basin. Steel I-beams are lowered into place by a helicopter (out of view) over two open stopes. Motion and placement of the beams is controlled by workers using tag lines. (b) A late stage in the remediation of the POW mine. Steel plates are welded, torch cut, and pulled into place over the stopes. The finished project covered the stopes and diverted snow melt water runoff from entering the stopes. Notice the steep terrain, requiring workers to be belayed from above for safety.

access to mine sites on private property were the critical factors in deciding which sites should be restored and in what order. Funding the remediation comes from various state, federal and local sources.

Implementation in the Animas watershed has included plugging and flooding AMD-producing mines and capping or diverting drainage water around mine waste dumps. Perhaps the most complex and interesting remediation is that completed in 2005 to the Pride of the West Mine northeast of Silverton. The mine began working a polymineralic ore body in the late 1870s and continued to be worked sporadically until the 1970s. AMD from the mine was recognized by the ARSG as an important source of contamination to a major tributary of the Animas River.

The Pride of the West Mine is located on extremely steep terrain at an elevation of about 11,000 feet. Implementation consisted of covering two large open stopes—large vertical openings that were excavated upward from underground workings that broke through to the surface. For decades before remediation meltwater streams coursed into these openings, dropped through approximately 700 feet of mine workings, eventually to discharge the toxic cocktail it had acquired into a creek and ultimately into the Animas River. Remediation included constructing a massive complex of steel beams supporting steel plates that were airlifted by helicopter to the site and fixed in place in the steep terrain by a construction crew. Working conditions on the precarious slopes required workers to use technical rock climbing techniques, including wearing a climbing harness and being belayed with climbing ropes (◆ Figure 2). The steel plates, welded in place, now covering the stope's openings, prevent snow, surface water runoff, and avalanche deposits from entering the stopes that previously caused much of the AMD metal loading emerging from the mine's entrance portal at lower elevation. The underground mine workings, which for

decades have been largely filled with ice, will be entered once the ice melts, in order to plug any drill holes that are issuing water.

It is anticipated that these measures will greatly reduce the metals loading from the mine, improve the physical and chemical quality of water in the creek, and enhance the aquatic productivity of the Animas River watershed.

Boulder River Basin, Montana

Lands in the Boulder River Watershed in Montana have been mined since the late nineteenth century. Metals extracted from the area included gold, lead, silver, and zinc. Environmental degradation resulting from a century of mining in the watershed drew together a cooperative partnership of more than 20 landowners, local communities, and several state and federal governmental agencies in an effort to clean up the messes left behind. A textbook example of the massive restoration effort in the mining area is represented by remediation efforts on High Ore Creek, an area with 26 inactive or abandoned mining sites.

The major contributor of contaminants to High Ore Creek has been the Comet Mine and Mill at Comet, Montana, about five miles northeast of the town of Basin. Mining at Comet began about 1800 (◆ Figure 3). Several mines were active in the district, but the Comet Mine was the key player and a major producer of gold, silver, lead, zinc, and copper between 1904 and 1950. By the 1950s its operations had been shut down, and the mill dismantled, but it left behind an abandoned open pit and a legacy of toxic heavy metals contained in a vast tailings dump.

For nearly a century High Ore Creek wound its way through the 3.7-mile flood plain composed of mining wastes and mill tailings from the Comet Mine (◆ Figure 4A). In the process, the creek carried the heavy metals-loaded waters downstream to the Boulder River at Basin. Sediment samples collected along High Ore Creek had metal

Montana Historical Society, Helena

◆ **FIGURE 3** Comet Mine and Mill, 1918. Notice the huge pile of waste rock and tailings, to right of center.

concentrations greater than three times the natural background for arsenic, cadmium, copper, lead, manganese, mercury, silver, and zinc. Elevated levels of arsenic were detected in streambank tailings deposits as far as Basin, where soil samples collected at the school playground exceeded the cancer-risk level. At its best, fish could not survive in High Ore Creek's toxic cocktail of dissolved metals.

From 1997 to 2001 a cooperative effort of the Bureau of Land Management (BLM), the Montana Department of Environmental Quality (MDEQ), and the Montana Bureau of Mines and Geology restored the abandoned mine lands at Comet. The BLM took the clean-up effort an additional step by selecting it as one of two pilot projects of the Abandoned Mine Lands Initiative (AML). The remediation proved to be a classic example of what can be done to improve water quality and restore abandoned mines scattered across the west (◆ Figure 4B). Reclamation consisted of three basic steps: isolate, encapsulate, and keep dry.

The effort, focused on the extensive Comet Mine and Mill site, consisted of removing 229,500 cubic meters (300,000 cu yd) of tailings and waste rock that were disposed of in the abandoned open pit; constructing runoff diversion channels to keep the site dry and protect the excavated areas from erosion; removing 30,600 cubic meters (40,000 cu yd) of tailings and placing them in a nearby repository where they were

David Nimick/USGS

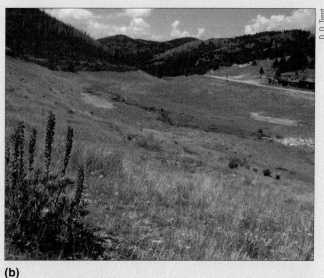

D. D. Trent

(a)

(b)

◆ **FIGURE 4** High Ore Creek Valley, Montana, in (a) 1997, when the creek had eroded through a century's accumulation of metals-loaded tailings from the Comet Mine and Mill, washing them downstream six miles to the Boulder River and enriching the water with heavy-metal concentrations, some of which were toxic and accumulating in the aquatic food chain, and (b) 2006, the valley restored by removal of toxic mine waste, regrading, adding topsoil, revegetation and rebuilding the channel of High Ore Creek. The pollutants have been substantially reduced, and trout are returning to the creek after an absence of many decades.

CONTINUED

isolated from the environment; rebuilding large portions of High Ore Creek that flowed through the area of the former mine dump; removal of 62,000 cu yd of streamside tailings and waste rock along a four-mile length of the stream channel; grading waste-rock slopes to natural contours; amending the soil on the reclaimed area with a mix of compost and lime; seeding with native plants; covering the area with erosion control nets; and construction of toxic sediment settling ponds (◆ Figure 5). Cost for the project totaled $3.5 million, which was funded by a 35-cent tax on each ton of coal mined in the west.

Postreclamation water analyses reveal that heavy-metal concentrations are substantially lower than before reclamation, and by 2006 the area was well on its way to recovery with willows sprouting along the streambanks and grass and wildflowers growing on the reclaimed tailings site (Figure 4b) where before restoration it had been a bare and sterile landscape; and a trout fishery has now returned to High Ore Creek after an absence of almost a century.

State officials have identified 270 other abandoned mine sites in southwestern Montana that are threatening the environment or human health. The successful restoration techniques utilized at Comet will be important in the remediation of other AMLs in the state.

◆ **FIGURE 5** High Ore Creek Valley in 2006 as viewed from the Rumley Mine at Comet, Montana. The grass-covered valley bottom is the area of the remediated tailings dump. In the distance are the toxic sediment settling ponds.

CASE STUDY 13.3

Reclamation of Open Pit Coal Mines

The five steps in reclaiming abandoned coal mine lands are (1) drainage control to eliminate acid mine drainage; (2) stabilization of landforms (◆ Figure 1); (3) revegetation (◆ Figures 2 and 3): (4) ongoing monitoring; and (3) returning the land to use (Figure 4). The reclamation work pictured in Figures 1, 2, and 3 was carried out near Beckley, West Virginia. The site in Figure 4 in near Harding, West Virginia.

◆ **FIGURE 1** Drainage control and diversion at the disturbed area. Spreading and compacting of waste rock, subsoil, and soil against the highwall stabilizes slopes and buries reactive sulfide minerals.

◆ **FIGURE 2** Immediate seeding, here done with a hydroseeder, follows emplacement of topsoil in order to establish vegetation quickly. A biodegradable green dye is added to the seed to help the operator determine the coverage.

◆ **FIGURE 3** A fast-growing, temporary cover crop such as rye grass prevents soil erosion and adds organic matter to the soil. The cover crop is selected carefully in order to avoid using a plant that may be undesirably dominant or persistent.

◆ **FIGURE 4** After the cover crop has died back, permanent legumes and grasses take over. They eventually restore the disturbed land to meadow or pasture so that it can be used for wildlife habitat, recreation, or livestock grazing. Trees eventually may return the site to forest. Reclamation of this site eliminated more than a mile of highwall and sealed four hazardous abandoned mine openings. An underdrain was placed along the length of the highwall to collect drainage from the site. Today the site bears no resemblance to its appearance before reclamation.

CASE STUDY 13.4

A Wounded Mountain Spews Poison

The Little Rocky Mountains in north-central Montana on the southern edge of the Fort Belknap Reservation, homeland to the Assiniboine and Gros Ventre Tribes, is the site of the Zortman-Landusky (Z-L) gold mine. The mine is in an area of the Little Rocky Mountains known to the tribes as the "Island Mountains." Historically, the mountains were used by the tribes for hunting and ceremonial purposes, but they also serve as the major source of the tribes' drinking water. However, when gold was discovered in the mountains in the 1880s, federal commissioners from Washington persuaded the tribes to return the mineralized land to the United States, assuring them that no harm would come to their water supply. They sold 40,000 acres for $36,000 and lived to see the 19th century miners recover over $1 million in gold from their former land.

Large-scale 20th century mining began in 1979, with the Z-L mine, a combination of two mining areas and several open pits, the first major open-pit cyanide heap-leach gold-mining operation in the United States. What followed was a multilayered environmental disaster involving bad science, regulatory gaps, and bankruptcy. The Z-L became the poster child illustrating the inadequacy of state and federal mining regulations of the time. The mine proved to be a failure due to some combination of inexperience with the process by the mining company and state regulators, lack of adequate state regulations, and an ambitious production schedule by the mine's Canadian owner. A bonus package of more than $5 million awarded to the company's top executives, announced shortly before the company filed for bankruptcy protection in 1998, did not help. In just two decades the Canadian company produced $300 million in gold but left Montana with a $33 million cleanup bill, plus maintenance and treatment costs of nearly $800,000 each year through at least 2017.

The science of what happened at Z-L is that the leach pads were built on top of rock that contained sulfide minerals, resulting in the generation of acid mine drainage (AMD) that created a toxic cocktail including high levels of cadmium, copper, lead, and zinc that polluted

CONTINUED

◆ **FIGURE 1** Swift Gulch Creek on the Fort Belknap Reservation, Montana, in October 2003. The creek is reddish-brown from AMD from the Zortman-Landusky mining complex. The water has a pH of 3.4 and contains high amounts of zinc, nickel, manganese iron and sulfate.

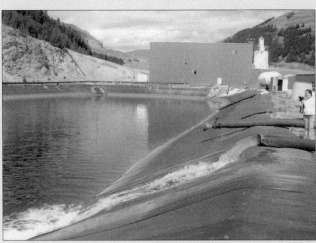

◆ **FIGURE 2** One of three water-treatment plants and holding ponds that clean up contaminated AMD water at the abandoned Zortman-Landusky mine complex. These plants will need to treat the contaminated drainage water in perpetuity.

the area's streams (◆ Figure 1), the company thus operating in violation of federal clean-water standards. Over time, improper management of cyanide resulted in six spills and leaks that contaminated groundwater and polluted local drinking water sources and streams in the area. By the late 1980s health-care workers recognized that something was clearly wrong as they noted more and more cases of lead poisoning and cancer among Fort Belknap residents.

After mining ended in 1996 the company officials issued public comments during the following year that they were responsible corporate citizens and would clean up the property. But the price of gold had fallen, by then below $280 an ounce, the company went bankrupt, and Z-L became one of the worst pollution cases in Montana, leaving the taxpayers with tens of millions of dollars in cleanup costs.

The company was taken to court in 1996, eventually agreeing to pay $32.3 million, mostly to upgrade and expand water treatment. Reclamation was carried out by the Montana Department of Environmental Quality (MDEQ) and the Bureau of Land Management (BLM). Some of the costs were covered by the mining company's surety bond, but the MDEQ and BLM had to contribute an additional

$33 million. Three water-treatment plants (◆ Figure 2) now remove much of the pollutants, but the treated water still does not meet state standards of water quality, elevated levels of arsenic, cadmium, copper, lead, and zinc being the main concerns. Furthermore, the pH of the drainage water is going down, that is, becoming more acidic. The state determined that pollution generated by the mine is so severe that the water-treatment plants will need to operate in perpetuity, with the annual cost for reclamation maintenance, heap-solution management and water treatment totaling almost $770,000. In 2005 Montana's legislature created a special fund for Z-L water treatment for the next 120 years, at a cost of more than $19 million.

In addition to the drainage-water-treatment plants, remediation included isolation and encapsulation of the waste rock; backfilling sulfide-bearing rock in lined disposal pits that are covered with soil and revegetated; and diversion of surface runoff away from the depository sites. But AMD from waste-rock drainage is only part of the problem. Fracturing of the underlying bedrock by mining and blasting has altered the pattern of groundwater flow resulting in contamination of springs in the area. Total remediation appears problematic.

The Legacy of Mines and Mining

The collection of photographs in this gallery illustrates some aspects of past and present mining districts (◆ Figures 1–5).

◆ **FIGURE 1** The Lucky Friday mine in the Coeur d'Alene Mining District near Mullan, Idaho. The mine works a silver-lead-zinc vein. The mine is unique for two reasons: (1) It has been one of Hecla Mining Company's mainstay properties for over 40 years, producing nearly 130 million ounces of silver during its operation, and (2) once ore is removed from along the trend of the veins, the workings are backfilled with cemented tailings thus reducing potential impacts to the environment.

Hecla Mining Company and Idaho Geological Survey

D. D. Trent

◆ **FIGURE 2** Humans can be exposed to waters carrying high concentrations of toxic metals, even in undisturbed natural settings. Several thousands of people living in and near the Brooks Range of northern Alaska rely on subsistence fishing and hunting for food. Massive metallic sulfide deposits in the region pose a potential hazard to all life there if acid-rock drainage (ARD) from these deposits enters streams and rivers. In this photo a scientist is collecting water samples downstream from the Drenchwater massive sulfide deposit in the northwestern part of the range. Water bodies' pH and concentrations of various metals are monitored in order to evaluate the health hazard of this lead-zinc-silver deposit.

John Burghardt/National Park Service, U.S. Dept. of Interior

◆ **FIGURE 3** Even some national parks are not free of contamination from abandoned mining activity. An example is the Mariscal Mercury Mine in Big Bend National Park, Texas. Intermittently between 1900 and 1943 it produced mercury (quicksilver) from cinnabar ore. A detailed site investigation conducted in 1995 by the U.S. Bureau of Mines reports that minimal contamination remains in only a few isolated spots on-site, and there is minimal to no risk for short-term visitors and transient workers at the site.

◆ **FIGURE 4** Creek near an open-pit copper mine at Morenci, Arizona. The water's distinct blue color reveals a high concentration of dissolved copper leached from mine wastes.

◆ **FIGURE 5** The *entire* landscape visible in this photo is productive land reclaimed following extensive surface coal mining carried out in the 1960s and 1970s; near Cologne, Germany.

Summary

Mineral Abundances, Definitions

Mineral Deposit
Locally rich concentration of minerals.

Ore
Metallic mineral resources that can be economically and legally extracted at the time.

Mineral Reserves
Known deposits of earth materials from which useful commodities are economically and legally recoverable with existing technology.

Factors That Change Reserves

Technology Changes
Affect costs of extraction and processing.

Economic Changes
Affect price of the commodity and costs of extraction.

Political Changes
Cut off or open up sources of important mineral materials.

Aesthetic and Environmental Factors
May reduce reserves.

Description of Mineral Resources

Description
Mineral deposits are highly localized; they are neither uniformly nor randomly distributed.

Cause
Concentrations of valuable mineral deposits are due to special, sometimes unique, geochemical processes.

Origins of Mineral Deposits

Igneous Deposits
1. *Intrusive*—occur (a) as a pegmatite, an exceptionally coarse-grained igneous rock with interlocking crystals, usually found as irregular dikes, lenses, or veins, especially at the margins of batholiths; and (b) by crystal settling, the sinking of crystals in a magma due to their greater density, sometimes aided by magmatic convection.
2. *Disseminated*—a mineral deposit, especially of a metal, in which the minerals occur as scattered particles in the rock but in sufficient quantity to make the deposit a worthwhile ore.
3. *Hydrothermal*—a mineral deposit precipitated from a hot aqueous solution with or without evidence of igneous processes.
4. *Volcanogenic*—of volcanic origin, e.g., volcanogenic sediments.

Sedimentary Deposits
Mineral deposits resulting from the accumulation or precipitation of sediment. These include

1. Surficial marine and nonmarine precipitation.
2. Deep-ocean precipitation.
3. Placer deposits.

Weathering Deposits
1. *Lateritic weathering*—concentrations of minerals due to the gradual chemical and physical breakdown of rocks in response to exposure at or near Earth's surface.
2. *Secondary enrichment*—mineral development that occurred later than that of the enclosing rock, usually at the expense of earlier primary minerals by chemical weathering.

Metamorphic Deposits
Concentrations of minerals, such as gem or ore minerals, in metamorphic rocks or from metamorphic processes.

Categories of Mineral Reserves

Abundant Metals
Average continental crustal abundances are in excess of 0.1 percent.

Scarce Metals
Average continental crustal abundances are less than 0.1 percent.

Nonmetallic Minerals
Minerals that do not have metallic properties include industrial minerals, agricultural minerals, and construction materials.

Environmental Impacts of Mining
1. Surface coal mining and land reclamation is regulated by federal law, the Surface Mining Control and Reclamation Act (SMCRA). No similar federal law regulates hardrock mining and land reclamation.
2. SMCRA requires surface coal-mine pits to be backfilled with the mine waste (spoil) and then covered with topsoil and landscaped. Some states in which hardrock mining is conducted require similar handling of waste rock and tailings at currently operating mines.
3. Ground subsidence due to underground coal mining is less common than in the past because of the required backfilling. Surface collapse from hardrock (underground) mining is not common, and stabilization may be expensive.
4. Acid mine drainage (AMD) may be a problem at active and abandoned coal and sulfide-ore mines. Pit water in surface coal mines is required to be held and treated before it is released to streams or rivers. Sealing abandoned mines, covering waste rock with soil and landscaping, and installing drainage courses to direct surface drainage off tailings and waste-rock piles are some methods of controlling AMD formation. Wells are installed below waste-rock and tailings dumps to monitor water quality.

5. Scarified ground, despoiled landscapes, and disrupted drainage that remain after dredging and hydraulic mining can be reclaimed by reshaping, adding topsoil, and landscaping.

6. Abandoned open pits with oversteepened side walls despoil the landscape and may pollute hydrologic systems. They are difficult or impossible to reclaim. The public is protected by surrounding the pits with chain-link fencing and posting warning signs. The pit floor may be partially backfilled and sealed with impermeable clay to protect groundwater from pollution.

7. Cyanide heap-leach gold-extraction methods normally cause minimal environmental problems because they are strictly regulated by state and federal agencies. There are occasional leaks of cyanide into the environment, however. Wildlife losses have been mitigated by placing nets over the lethal ponds. Surface waters and groundwaters are monitored by sampling and monitoring wells, respectively.

8. The main concerns associated with heavy-metal contaminated mill and smelter waste are the environmental impacts resulting from stormwater runoff into nearby surface waters and the human health problems caused by inhaling or ingesting the heavy metals in dust. Superfund cleanups require either removal or in-place remediation by encapsulating the heavy-metal sources. Wetlands with appropriate plantlife may be constructed, or water treatment plants constructed, to clean toxins from surface runoff.

The Future of Mining

Worldwide

Mining and processing of mineral commodities are contributing to soil erosion, water contamination, air pollution, and deforestation.

The United States

Mining and processing of mineral commodities must meet standards of air and water quality set by the EPA and other government agencies. The Mining Law of 1872, although much amended, is being criticized and evaluated in light of current economics, domestic needs, and conflicting land uses.

Key Terms

acid-rock drainage (ARD)	contour mining	lode	porphyry copper
acid mine drainage (AMD)	crystal settling	low-grade deposit	precipitation
alluvial placer	cyanide heap-leaching	manganese nodule	regional metamorphism
area mining	disseminated deposit	massive sulfide deposit	secondary enrichment
average crustal abundance	dredging	mineral deposit	SMCRA
banded-iron formation	evaporite	mineral reserves	smelter
bauxite	flotation	mountaintop-removal mining	spoil
bench placer	glacial outwash	open-pit mining	strip-mining
black smoker	gravity separation	ore	tailings
CERCLA	high-grade deposit	ore mineral	vein deposit
concentration factor	hydraulic mining	pegmatite	volcanogenic deposit
contact-metamorphic deposit	hydrothermal deposit	placer deposit	

Study Questions

1. Distinguish between mineral deposits, ores, and reserves.

2. Why do some metals, such as gold, require concentration factors in the thousands, while others, such as iron, require only single-digit concentration factors?

3. Of which metals does the United States have ample reserves? How do we obtain the scarce mineral resources we need but lack within our borders?

4. How do you expect domestic and foreign supplies of critical mineral resources to change in the next 25 years?

5. What would cause currently marginal or submarginal mineral deposits to become important mineral reserves?

6. Where are the major deposits of porphyry copper and porphyry copper-molybdenum deposits located? How do these deposits relate to plate-tectonic theory?

7. What steps are involved in the origin of a placer gold deposit? Of a bench placer deposit?

8. What minerals may eventually be harvested from the deep-ocean floor? What might be the environmental consequences of such mining?

9. Explain why you wouldn't go to the Hawaiian Islands to prospect for gold.

10. What is hydrothermal activity? What metallic mineral deposits are commonly associated with hydrothermal action?

11. Contrast the gold mining and extraction techniques of the nineteenth century with those of today. What are the environmental legacies of the nineteenth-century mining methods? What environmental concerns accompany modern gold-extraction technology?

12. Contrast the environmental hazards and mitigation procedures of underground, open-pit, and surface mining.

13. Why are mercury and cyanide, very dangerous poisons if they are mishandled, used in gold extraction?

14. Briefly describe the cyanide heap-leach gold-extraction process.

15. It has been suggested that as society exhausts Earth's reserves of critical minerals, lower-grade mineral deposits will be mined, and supply-and-demand economics will dictate prices and costs. This rationale could be extended to a scenario in which average rock would eventually be mined for critical materials. Is there a fallacy to such a rationale? Explain.

16. Discuss the ethics of changing the General Mining Law of 1872 to allow the federal government to collect royalties from current mine operations to be used for the cleanup of historic mines that were abandoned by companies that no longer exist.

For Further Information

Books and Periodicals

Alpers, Charles N. and Michael P. Hunerlach. 2000. *Mercury contamination from historic mining in California.* USGS fact sheet FS-061-00.

Baum, Dan and Margaret L. Knox. 1992. In Butte, Montana, A is for arsenic, Z is for zinc. *Smithsonian* 23, no. 8: 46–56.

Drew, Lawrence and Brian K. Fowler. 1999. The megaquarry: A conversation on the state of the aggregate industry. *Geotimes* 44, no. 6: 17–22.

Dunn, James, Carol Russell, and Art Morrissey. 1999. Remediating historic mine sites in Colorado. *Mining engineering* 51, no. 8: 32–35.

Ernst, W. G., G. Heiken, Susan M. Landon, P. Patrick Leahy, and Eldrige Moores (co-convenors). 2003. The role of the Earth sciences in fostering global equity and stability: *Report of Pardee Symposium K4,* 2002 GSA Annual Meeting, Denver, Colorado, October 28, 2002. *GSA Today,* March, pp. 27–28.

Feiler, J. F. 2006. Mine stope coverage cuts acid mine drainage. *Mining engineering* 58, no. 4: 15–19.

Gray, J. E. and R. F. Sanzolone, Eds. 1996. *Environmental studies on mineral deposits in Alaska.* U.S. Geological Survey Bulletin 2156. Washington, D.C.: Government Printing Office.

James, Patrick M. 1999. The miner and sustainable development. *Mining engineering* 51, no. 6: 89–92.

Kesler, S. E. 1994. *Mineral resources, economics and the environment.* New York: McMillan College Publishing Co.

King, Trude V. V., Ed. 1995. *Environmental considerations of active and abandoned mine lands: lessons from Summitville, Colorado.* U.S. Geological Survey bulletin 2220. Washington, D.C.: Government Printing Office.

National Research Council. 1999. *Hardrock mining on federal lands.* Washington, D.C.: National Academy Press.

Office of Surface Mining Reclamation and Enforcement, Department of the Interior. 1992. *Surface coal mining reclamation: 15 years of progress, 1977–1992, Part 1.* Washington, D.C.: Government Printing Office.

Silva, Michael A. 1988. Cyanide heap leaching in California. *California geology* 41, no. 7: 147–156.

Stewart, K. C. and R. C. Severson, Eds. 1994. *Guidebook on the geology, history, and surface-water contamination and remediation in the area from Denver to Idaho Springs, Colorado.* U.S. Geological Survey circular 1097. Washington, D.C.: Government Printing Office.

Tilton, J. E. 1996. Exhaustible resources and sustainable development—two different paradigms: *Resources Policy,* vol. 22, no. 1/2, pp. 91–97.

Wagner, Lorie A. 2002. *Materials in the economy—material flows, scarcity, and the environment.* US. Geological Survey circular 1221. Washington D.C.: Government Printing Office.

Wheeler, Gregory R. 1999. Teaching mineral resources as an aid to understanding international policy issues. *Journal of geoscience education* 47: 464–468.

Wilshire, Howard, Jane Nielson, and Richard W. Hazlett. In press. *Losing the West: a sourcebook for salvaging America's western lands.* New York, Oxford University Press.

Videos

Hydraulic gold mining. California Department of Parks and Recreation, Publications Section, P.O. Box 942896, Sacramento, CA 94296-0001

The magic of Homestake gold from the discovery of gold to mining today. Homestake Mining Tours, Lead, SD 57754

Mining: discoveries for progress. American Mining Congress, Communications and Education Department, 1920 N Street, NW, Suite 300, Washington, D.C. 20036-1662

Poison in the Rockies. 1992. NOVA. WGBH, P. O. Box 2284, South Burlington, VT 05407-2284; 800-255-9424

Public lands, private profits. 1994. Overview of the controversy surrounding the Mining Law of 1872. Frontline, May 24. PBS Video, 1320 Braddock Place, Alexandria, VA 22314; 800-328-PBS1

ThomsonNOW™

Assess your understanding of this chapter's topics with additional comprehensive interactivities at http://www.thomson.com/login, which also has up-to-date web links, additional readings, and exercises.

CHAPTER 14

Energy and the Environment

> It is difficult for people living now, who have become accustomed to the steady exponential growth in the consumption of energy from the fossil fuels, to realize how transitory the fossil-fuel epoch will eventually prove to be when it is viewed over a longer span of human history.
>
> M. King Hubbert, 1971

Flaming Ice, Energy, and the Greenhouse!

SETTING ICE BALLS ON FIRE IS U.S. GEOLOGICAL SURVEY OCEANOGRAPHER Bill Dillon's idea of fun, and it never fails to amaze his visitors. It is not ordinary ice that flames. Dillon uses hydrated methane (CH_4) recovered from sea-floor sediments deep below the ocean surface. This flame has become a focus of the energy-hungry nations of the world (◆Figure 1). What actually burns is methane gas released from a crystalline solid of methane molecules encased in a "cage" of ice (◆Figure 2). Methane is the gas that constitutes the bulk of the "natural gas" that is piped to your home. Methane hydrates are so extensive in deep-sea sediments that they have the potential to supply a share

USGS

◆ **FIGURE 1** A flame from ignited synthetic methane hydrate.

◆ **FIGURE 2** Crystalline structure of methane hydrate. Methane gas (CH_4) generated by bacterial digestion of organic matter in sea-floor sediments is sometimes trapped in "cages" of frozen H_2O (the large polygons) to form methane hydrate. Peter McCabe and others, 1993, USGS circular 115, p. 46

of the world's future fuel needs, *when and if* practical mining techniques can be developed. India and Japan, at present energy poor, are most interested in developing methane hydrates as an energy source. Experts agree that marine gas hydrates harbor twice the carbon contained in all known natural gas, petroleum, and coal deposits on Earth—about 10,000 gigatons, or 10^{13} tons, of carbon. Extensive gas-hydrate deposits are currently known in hundreds of localities. Particularly interesting for potential development are those of offshore Oregon, Costa Rica, New Jersey, Japan, and Florida (◆ Figure 3). Also intriguing are the significant deposits that have been encountered in oil drilling through Arctic permafrost areas in Canada, Alaska, and Siberia (see Chapter 6).

Gas hydrates in marine sediments have been known for several decades, but their full extent and potential were not realized until the 1990s (◆ Figure 4). Conditions necessary for their formation are high water pressure (water depth >530 m in low latitudes and >250 m in high latitudes) and low ambient temperatures (<7° C) at the water–sediment interface. These conditions are met on the sea floor's continental slope and rise. The exact origin of the gas is not known, but it is strongly suspected that bottom bacteria consume organic-rich detritus and generate methane as a waste product. Under particular conditions, the gas becomes trapped in ice in the sediment instead of being released to the overlying water column.

The bad news is that these hydrated molecular structures can release their caged methane into the atmosphere if there is a slight decrease in pressure (if sea level is lowered, for instance) or a slight warming of the surrounding seawater. Because methane is a powerful "greenhouse" gas linked to global warming (it is about 10 times as effective as carbon dioxide), melting of the hydrates and release of methane could have a drastic impact on Earth's surface temperature (see Chapter 11). One model suggests that as sea levels rose toward the end of the last ice age, the waters covered land that was underlain by permafrost containing the methane hydrates. As the warmer water temperature melted the permafrost ice, the caged greenhouse gas was released, increasing the global warming and the melting of glaciers.

Gas hydrates may also be a geologic hazard and may occupy much of the pore space in bottom sediments. When the hydrate-bearing sediment becomes deeply buried, the temperature may increase to the point at which gas hydrates are no longer stable. When a solid–gas mixture becomes a liquid–gas mixture, high pore pressure and unstable slopes result (see Chapter 7). This presents a danger to offshore drilling platforms, pipelines, communication cables, and other offshore structures. Current interest in methane hydrate is focused on it as an energy source and as a factor in global climate change.

◆ **FIGURE 3** Location of the world's known methane hydrate deposits, 1999. Dots are marine deposits; squares are permafrost deposits.

◆ **FIGURE 4** Methane hydrate nodule in marine sediment from the Blake Ridge off the Florida coast.

From the simplest algal scum to the most complex ecosystem, energy is essential to all life. Derived from the Greek word *energia,* meaning "in work," *energy* is defined as the capacity to do work. The units of energy are the same as those for work, and the energy of a system is diminished only by the amount of work that it does.

Prosperity and quality of life in an industrialized society such as ours depend in large part on the society's energy resources and its ability to use them productively. We may illustrate this in a semiquantitative fashion with the equation

$$L = \frac{R + E + I}{\text{population}}$$

where *L* represents quality of life, or "standard of living," *R* represents the raw materials that are consumed, *E* represents the energy that is consumed, and *I* represents an intangible we shall call *ingenuity.* As the equation expresses, when high levels of raw materials, energy, and ingenuity are shared by a small population, a high material quality of life results. If, on the other hand, a large population must share low levels of resources and energy, a low standard of living would be expected. Some highly ingenious societies with few natural resources and little energy can and do enjoy a high quality of life. Japan is a prime example. Some other countries that are self-sufficient in resources and energy, such as Argentina, are having difficult times. Thus we see that ingenuity, which is reflected in a country's political system, technologies, skills, and education, is heavily weighted in the equation, and can cancel out a lack of resources and a large population.

To a physicist there is no energy shortage, because she or he knows that energy is neither created nor destroyed; it is simply converted from one form to another, such as from nuclear energy to heat energy. Fuels of all kinds are warehouses of energy, which can be tapped by some means and applied in some way to do work. Coal and oil, for example, are fossil fuels that have been storing solar energy in the lithosphere for millions of years (◆ Figure 14.1).

Some forms of energy are **renewable,** that is, they are replenished at a rate equal to or greater than the rate at which they are used. Examples include solar, water, wood, wind, ocean and lake thermal gradients, geothermal, and tidal energy. The energy in all of these resources except for geothermal and tidal (gravitational) energy was originally derived from the sun. Renewable resources are dependable only if they are consumed at a rate less than or equal to their rate of renewal. If they are overexploited, some period of time will be required to replenish them. Peat, a fuel used extensively for space heating and cooking in Ireland and Russia, is estimated to accumulate at a remarkable 3 metric tons per hectare per year (1.3 tons/acre/year). Nonetheless, the conversion from plant litter to peat may take a hundred years. Wood energy may renew in a matter of a few decades, and water and wind are renewed continuously.

Nonrenewable resources are not replenished as fast as they are utilized, and once consumed, they are gone forever. Crude oil, oil shales, tar sands, coal, and fissionable elements are nonrenewable energy resources. Their quantities are finite. Supplies of crude oil, for example, are within a few human generations of exhaustion. Oil underground was discovered almost fifty years before the first automobile was operational. Prior to then, gasoline was a minor by-product of refining oil for kerosene lamps. In 1885 Germans Gottlieb Daimler and Karl Benz independently developed gasoline engines, and in 1893 Massachusetts bicycle makers Charles and Frank Duryea built the first successful U.S. gasoline-powered automobile. By the turn of the century, production automobiles were hitting the roads, horses were being put out to pasture, and refineries were stepping up production to satisfy an increasing demand for gasoline. The transportation revolution to automobiles spawned the largest private enterprise on Earth: the exploration and production of petroleum. This has led to major geopolitical and economic problems, because the nations that consume the most do not produce in comparable amounts.

Petroleum

Although the carbon content of Earth's crust is less than 0.1 percent by weight, carbon is one of the most important elements to Earth's people. It is indispensable to life, and it is the principal source of energy and the principal raw material of many manufactured products. Crude oil, or petroleum (Latin *petra,* "rock," and *oleum,* "oil"), is composed of many **hydrocarbon compounds,** simple and complex combinations of hydrogen and carbon (⋇ Table 14.1). Petroleum occurs beneath Earth's surface in liquid and gaseous forms and at the surface as oil seeps, tar sands, solid bitumen (gilsonite), and oil shales. In addition to its use as a fuel, hydrocarbon compounds derived from petroleum are used in producing paints, plastics, fertilizers, insecticides, soaps, synthetic fibers (nylon and acrylics, for example), and synthetic rubber. Carbon combines chemically with itself and with hydrogen in

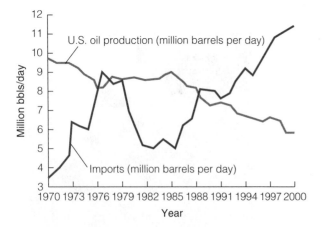

◆ **FIGURE 14.1** Graph illustrating the relationship between oil production in the United States and the amount of oil imported by the United States. Adapted from Larry Fellows, Arizona Geological Survey

★TABLE 14.1   Hydrocarbon Compounds Typically Found in Crude Oil

Name	Molecular Type General Formula	Hydrocarbon Compound		Percentage of Weight in Medium-Grade Crude Oil
Paraffins	C_nH_{2n+2}	methane, CH_4	lighter	25
		ethane, C_2H_6		
		propane, C_3H_8		
		butane, C_4H_{10}*		
		pentane, C_5H_{12}**		
Aromatics	C_nH_{2n-6}***	benzene, C_6H_6		17
Naphthenes	C_nH_{2n}	asphalt		50
Asphaltenes	(solid hydrocarbons)	gilsonite	heavier	8
				100

* Butane gives gasoline quick-starting capability.
** Pentane gives smooth engine warm-up.
*** Aromatics improve mileage and "knock" resistance.

an infinite variety of bonding schemes; some two million hydrocarbon molecules have been identified to date. The manufacturing process of separating crude oil into its various components is known as *refining*, or *cracking*.

Origin and Accumulation of Hydrocarbon Deposits

Carbon and hydrogen did not combine directly to form petroleum; they were chemical components of living organisms before their transformation to complex hydrocarbons in crude oil. Porphyrin compounds found in petroleum are derived either from chlorophyll, the green coloring in plants, or from hemin, the red coloring matter in blood, and their presence is solid evidence for an organic origin for crude oil. The fact that large quantities of oil are not found in igneous or metamorphic rocks also rules out an inorganic source for oil.

Four conditions are necessary for the formation and accumulation of an exploitable petroleum deposit in nature:

- a source rock for oil,
- a reservoir rock in which it can be stored,
- a caprock to confine it, and
- a geologic structure or favorable strata to "trap" the oil.

Even where these geologic conditions are met, the human elements of exploration, location, and discovery still remain. Oil companies utilize the skills of geologists to interpret surface and subsurface geology, to locate the potential oil-bearing structure or stratum, and to specify the optimal location for a discovery well. Until a well is drilled, the geologists' interpretation remains in doubt, much like a medical doctor's diagnosis of an ailment subject to surgery; the diagnosis is tentative until the patient is opened up.

A **source rock** is any volume of rock that is capable of generating and expelling commercial quantities of oil or gas.

Source rocks are sedimentary rocks, mostly shales or limestones, usually of marine (ocean) origin and sometimes of *lacustrine* (lake) origin. The biological productivity (biomass) of surface waters must have been high enough to generate a settling "rain" of dead organisms, and the bottom waters must have been low enough in oxygen to prevent the deposited organic matter from being oxidized or consumed by scavengers. Almost all source rocks are dark-colored, indicative of high organic-matter content, and some of them carry a fetid or rotten-egg odor.

Favorable marine environments are rich in microscopic single-celled plants known as *diatoms* (phytoplankton), which form the largest biomass in the sea. Where there are diatoms, we also find zooplankton—tiny protozoans and larvae of large animals. These together with diatoms provide the molecules that make up crude oil. As the rocks are buried, they are heated. The conversion from organic matter to petroleum takes place mostly between 50° C and 200° C. Thus a proper thermal history, ideally between 100° C and 120° C, is necessary to form liquid petroleum—too cool, and oil does not form; too hot, and the hydrocarbons "boil" away.

After petroleum has formed in a source bed, it is squeezed out and migrates through a simple or complex plumbing system into a **reservoir rock.** This migration is a critical element in the formation of an economically exploitable accumulation of oil. Reservoir rocks are porous and permeable (see Chapter 8). Commonly they are sandstones, porous limestones, or in some cases, fractured shales. Reservoir porosities range from 20 to 50 percent, meaning that for each cubic foot of reservoir rock we will find 1 to 4 gallons of oil. The unit of oil volume is the barrel (equal to 42 gallons), and a so-called giant field, such as the north slope of Alaska, will yield a billion barrels of oil in its lifetime. Using standard recovery techniques, however, as much as 40 to 80 percent of the oil may be left in pore spaces and as films on mineral grains.

An impermeable **caprock** prevents oil from seeping upward to form tar pits at the surface or dissipate into other rocks. Such seals are analogous to aquicludes in groundwater systems and are most commonly clay shales or limestones of low permeability. Our discussion of the fourth requirement, a suitable geologic structure for trapping the oil, requires a separate subsection.

Geologic Traps—Oil and Gas Stop Here
Structural Traps

An **anticline** is an ideal structure for trapping gas and oil. It is a convex-upward fold in stratified rock (◆ Figure 14.2a). Analogous to a teacup inverted in a pan of water that traps a layer of air inside it, an anticline holds a reservoir of gas and oil.

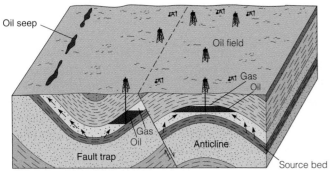
(a) Anticline and fault trap

(b) Salt dome

(c) Stratigraphic traps

◆ **FIGURE 14.2** (a and b) Common structural oil traps. (c) Stratigraphic oil traps.

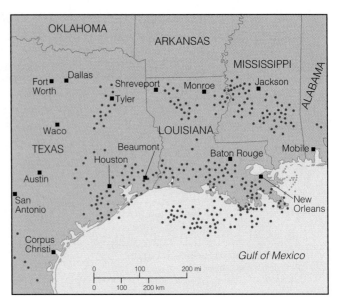

◆ **FIGURE 14.3** Locations of salt domes of the U.S. Gulf Coast. More than 500 domes have been discovered on land and in the shallow parts of the Gulf of Mexico, and more are known to be in deep water offshore.

This occurs because crude oil floats on water and natural gas rises to the top of the reservoir. The anticlinal theory of oil accumulation was not developed until 1900, forty-one years after oil was discovered. Strata dip away from the central axis of an anticline at the ground surface, and most anticlines with surface geologic expression have been drilled. Today the search for oil is more difficult, because less obvious and geologically more complex traps need to be discovered. Many times faults form impermeable barriers to hydrocarbon migration, and oil becomes trapped against them (see Figure 14.2a). Faulted and folded stratified rocks in a single oil field may thus contain many isolated oil reservoirs.

Salt domes are of much interest to geologists (◆ Figure 14.2b). Not only do they create oil traps, but they are also valuable sources of salt and sulfur and may be potential underground storage sites for petroleum and hazardous waste. More than 500 salt domes have been located along the U.S. Gulf Coast, both offshore and on land (◆ Figure 14.3). They rise as flowing fingers of salt, literally puncturing their way through the overlying rocks and buckling the overlying shallow strata into a dome (◆ Figure 14.4). Some fingers rise as high as 13 kilometers (8 mi) above the "mother" salt bed,

◆ **FIGURE 14.4** Ancient salt deposits are buried deeply, and because salt is less dense than the overlying sediments, it rises buoyantly as pillars of salt, creating salt domes.

the Louann salt, and would be taller than Mount Everest if they were at the surface of Earth. Because the salt is considerably less dense than the overlying rock, buoyancy forces drive the salt upward—much as a blob of oil will rise through water. Brittle solids, such as salt or ice, will flow over long periods of time; many salt domes are still rising measurably. The "mother" salt was deposited in Jurassic time by evaporation of seawater when the embryonic Gulf Coast was connected to the open ocean by a shallow opening. The opening allowed seawater to enter the basin but did not allow the denser salt brines at the bottom to escape. Thus the brine became concentrated to the point of saturation, and the great thickness of salt that now underlies the entire Gulf Coast was deposited. Oil accumulates against the salt column and also in the dome overlying the salt. "Old Spindletop," a salt dome near Beaumont, Texas, that was discovered in 1901, is perhaps the most famous U.S. oil field. Soon after its discovery it was producing more oil than the rest of the world combined, and the price of oil plummeted to two cents a barrel.

Stratigraphic Traps

Any change in sedimentary rock lithology (its physical character) that causes oil to accumulate is known as a **stratigraphic trap** (in contrast to anticlines and salt domes, which are structural traps). Thus, if a stratum changes laterally from a permeable sandstone to an impermeable shale or mudstone, oil may be trapped in the stratum (◆ Figure 14.2c).

Ancient coral reefs are ideal reservoirs, because they are porous and were biologically productive when they were living. Oil may be trapped in the porous, permeable debris on the flanks of the reef; production from such fields can be measured in thousands of barrels per day (bbl/d). Many oil fields of the Middle East are of this type, and their production potential is tremendous. A comparison of reef production with that of sandstone reservoirs such as those of California or Texas, which typically yield only a few hundred barrels per day, explains why the Middle East can control oil production and therefore price.

Oil Production

The first successful oil well was drilled in Titusville, Pennsylvania, in 1859 (■ Case Study 14.1 on page 438). In modern jargon, this well would be called a **wildcat well,** because it was the discovery well of a new field. There is 1 chance in 50 of a wildcat well being successful—less favorable odds than those of winning at roulette. The probability improves when we consider all wells drilled, including those in known oil fields. Between 1970 and 2003, 1 well in every 4 drilled was successful. Independent oil entrepreneurs take considerable risks; it is not a business for the faint of heart.

Most successful wells require pumping. If gas and water pressure are sufficient, however, oil may simply flow to the ground surface. High reservoir pressures develop from water pressing upward (buoyancy) beneath the oil and gas pressure

◆ **FIGURE 14.5** Oil in an anticline is driven by gas pressure from above and by buoyant water pressure from below.

pushing downward on the oil (◆ Figure 14.5). In some cases dissolved gases "drag" the oil along with them as they spew forth, as though from a bottle of champagne. If high pressures are not controlled, rocks, gas, oil, and even drill pipe may shoot into the air as a "gusher." High-pressure wells—749 in all—were set afire by Iraqi soldiers in Kuwait during Operation Desert Storm (◆ Figure 14.6). Fewer than a dozen wells were set ablaze in the 2003 battle to free Iraq. Professional oil-fire-fighting firms such as the well-known Red Adair Company and Boots and Coots were called in. With the help of Kuwaiti *roughnecks* (the nickname applied to drilling-rig workers), the fires were extinguished in nine months, three months earlier than the most optimistic estimate.

It is possible to drill a well so that the drill hole slants from the vertical to penetrate reservoir rocks far from the drilling site. This is desirable where the oil structure is offshore and must be "slant-drilled" from land or from a drilling platform. **Slant drilling** is also employed for tapping reservoirs beneath developed land, such as in Beverly Hills, where a large number of oil wells are slant-drilled under fashionable commercial areas. Modern methods use "smart" drill bits that are remotely controlled. Producers can thus withdraw oil from below a large area more economically and at the same time minimize the visual blight of drilling towers.

The ultimate drilling technology of the 1990s was horizontal drilling, a technique by which the drill bit and pipe follow gently inclined reservoir sands and limestones. By this means a single borehole can provide access to reservoirs beneath a much larger area than provided by vertical drilling or slant drilling. This method is now superseded by multilateral drilling, which enables operators to reach multiple oil-bearing reservoirs by means of lateral extensions from one

◆ **FIGURE 14.6** The Kuwaiti night skies were illuminated by 749 blazing oil wells set afire by Iraqi troops during the 1991 Gulf War. The fires continued for nine months and burned off approximately 6 billion barrels of petroleum.

well (◆Figure 14.7). It is worth noting that some offshore drilling platforms are in water more than a mile deep and have strings of drill pipe dangling below them 8.5 kilometers (5 mi), about the height of Mount Everest. There are plans to drill exploratory holes in water depths greater than 3,100 meters (10,000 ft). (See ■ Case Study 14.2).

Secondary Recovery

Secondary recovery methods extract oil that remains in the reservoir rock after normal withdrawal methods have ceased to be productive. As much as 75 percent of the total oil may remain. Secondary recovery methods can be grouped into three categories: thermal, chemical, and fluid-mixing (miscible) methods (◆Figure 14.8). All of these methods require *injection* wells for injecting a fluid or gas and *extraction* wells for removing the remobilized oil.

Thermal methods include steam injection, which makes the adhering oil less viscous and thus more free to flow, and fire flooding, in which air is injected into the reservoir in order to set fire to the oil and thus produce gases and heat that will increase the flow of oil. Water injection is a chemical method that utilizes large-molecule compounds, which when added to water, thicken it and increase its ability to wash or sweep the adhering oil films and globules toward an extraction well. Fluids that mix with oil, that are **miscible,** are very effective in removing "stuck" oil from the reservoir. Miscible recovery methods use mixtures of water with propane or ethane extracted from natural gas or mixtures of CO_2 and water. Even after the use of these secondary recovery methods, as much as a fifth of the total oil may remain in the reservoir.

CONSIDER   THIS

An acquaintance has offered you a share in a sure-shot wildcat oil-drilling venture in the Sierra Nevada. How should you respond to the offer?

◆ **FIGURE 14.7** Multilateral drilling from an offshore platform allows many oil-producing zones to be tapped from one platform. In this illustration, four zones are tapped by lateral horizontal pipes.

◆ **FIGURE 14.8** Secondary recovery. Steam, air, carbon dioxide, or chemicals dissolved in water are injected into a sluggishly producing formation in order to stimulate the flow of oil to extraction wells.

★TABLE 14.2	Typical Composition of an A.P.I. Medium-Grade Crude Oil	
Common Name	Number of Carbon Atoms*	Percentage of Crude-Oil Weight
Gasoline	5–10	27
Kerosene	11–13	13
Diesel fuel	14–18	12
Heavy gas oil	19–25	10
Lubricating oil	26–40	20
Heavy fractions (tars, asphalt)	>40	18
		100

* Volatility decreases as the number of carbon atoms increases, C_3 to C_{40}.

Quality and Price

The price of a barrel of crude (unrefined) oil varies with its grade—its quality—and with market demand at the time. Light oils bring higher prices, because they contain large proportions of paraffins and aromatic hydrocarbons, which are desirable for gasoline and bottled gases. Heavy crudes contain lower proportions of those components and greater proportions of the heavy, less valuable asphalts and tars (see Table 14.1). A scale of crude-oil quality has been established by the American Petroleum Institute based upon its weight. Light crude oil is very fluid and yields a high percentage of gasoline and diesel fuel. Heavy crude, on the other hand, is about the consistency of molasses. The percentages of fuels and lubricating oils yielded by a barrel of medium-weight crude oil are shown in ⋆ Table 14.2.

Reserves and the Future for Oil

The time when we could count on cheap oil and even cheaper natural gas is clearly ending.

—Dave O'Reilly, Chairman, Chevron-Texaco, February, 2005

The United States has about 5 percent of the world's population, yet consumes 28 percent of the world's energy supplies. Daily, Americans use some 3,000 products, including such things as gasoline, lubricating oil, jet and other fuels, fertilizer, makeup, synthetic fabrics, and pharmaceuticals, which are derived from petroleum. Even with conservation efforts, our consumption of petroleum in 2005 was up 6 percent from 2000, averaging 21.11 million barrels a day out of some 80 million barrels a day used each year worldwide (◆ Figures 14.1 and 14.10). (One barrel equals 42 gallons.) To put our oil consumption in a different context, of those 21.11 million barrels a day, about 12 million barrels are imported. Assuming a price of $50 per barrel, $600 million *each day* goes to other countries to pay for our thirst for oil. Thus, it's not surprising that the United States as a net importer must concern itself actively with global issues that affect the long-term oil-reserve outlook for energy supply and demand.

On a global scale, petroleum reserves in 2005 were estimated to be 1,200 billion barrels of oil (◆ Figures 14.9 and 14.10; ⋆ Table 14.3). (**Reserves** are defined as the amount of oil and gas that can be extracted at a profit. But to muddy the waters, there are several kinds of reserves: proved, probable, possible, developed, and undeveloped, and the use of these various terms is not universally consistent.) The 1,200 billion barrels may mean little to us until we realize that approximately two-thirds of the proved reserves are located in just six countries, and about 70 percent of reserves are in predominantly Islamic states (◆ Figure 14.11; Table 14.3). Of these, Saudi Arabia has about one-third of the total, and Iran, Iraq, Kuwait, and the United Arab Emirates have about 100 billion barrels each of proved reserves. The world discovers less than one barrel of oil for every four consumed, and it's been running on deficit since 1981.

Let us look more closely at the significance of the reserve figures in Table 14.3. Most people overlook the margins of uncertainty concerning the actual size of proved reserves. For example, for apparent political reasons, some nations do not allow audits of their oil fields. This is especially true for nations that belonged to the former USSR and for the eleven

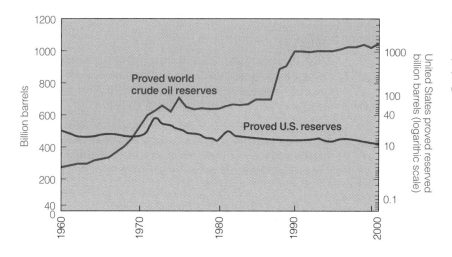

◆ **FIGURE 14.9** World and U.S. proved petroleum reserves. Note the scale change for U.S. reserves and that proved world reserves increased from 1970 to 1990 and then leveled off from 1990 to 2000. In contrast, U. S. reserves have decreased overall since 1970.

◆ **FIGURE 14.10** World energy consumption.
Colorado Geological survey

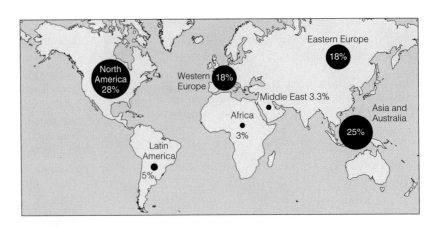

★TABLE 14.3 Global proved reserves, 2002		
Country	Proved Reserves (Billion Barrels)	Percentage of Total World
Saudi Arabia*◆	264	22.0
Iran*◆	137.5	11.5
Iraq*◆	115	9.6
United Arab Emirates*◆	97.8	8.1
Kuwait*◆	101.5	8.5
Venezuela◆	79.7	6.6
Russian Federation	74.4	6.2
Kazakhstan*	39.6	3.3
Libya*◆	39.1	3.3
Nigeria◆	35.9	3.0
United States	29.3	2.4
Canada	16.5	1.4
China	16.5	1.4
Qatar*◆	15.2	1.3
Mexico	13.7	4.1
Algeria*◆	12.2	1.0
Brazil	11.8	1.0
Norway	9.7	0.8
Angola	9.0	0.8
Oman*	5.6	0.5
India	5.9	0.5
Malaysia*	4.2	0.3
Indonesia*◆	4.3	0.4
United Kingdom	4.0	0.3
Yemen*	2.9	0.2
Rest of world	55.9	4.6
Total world	1,200.7	100.0
Total OPEC	838.9	70.0
Total for dominantly Islamic nations	577.5	48.0

* Dominantly Islamic nation
◆ OPEC nation
Source: British Petroleum Statistical Review of World Energy, 2006

members of OPEC. The quantity of oil exported from OPEC member countries is based on the portion of the country's remaining reserves, thus giving these countries an incentive to manipulate data. For example, in 1985 Kuwait increased the estimated reserves of their oil fields by 50 percent, and yet there were no new discoveries of consequence. This raised Kuwait's oil export quota. The other OPEC members quickly followed suit, and because reserves in these nations are state secrets, their official reserve reports are highly suspect. To quote Colin Campbell, an international petroleum-exploration geologist and former president of the Association for the Study of Peak Oil,

> It is noteworthy that Saudi Arabia reported 170 Gb [170,000 million barrels] in 1989, before the country had reason to inflate the number to 258 Gb in the following year to protect itself in the "OPEC quota wars." Engineers familiar with the [Saudi oil] fields think that a reasonable estimate of the oil-in-place is 600 Gb compared with the official estimate of 716 Gb. Applying a fairly generous recovery factor of 45 percent yields about 270 Gb recoverable, of which 104 Gb have been produced. It suggests that Saudi Arabia is reporting *original* and not *remaining* reserves [italics added for emphasis].

The reserve figure for Saudi Arabia shown on ★ Table 14.3 is the value used by British Petroleum in their 2006 annual summary of world reserves. All of the reserve estimates from the OPEC states are open to question.

The United States is the most energy-deficient of the largest oil-producing countries (Figure 14.11; ★ Tables 14.3 and 14.4). Overall U.S. production dropped 4.6 percent in 2005, the largest decline in 50 years. Production in 2005 from the nation's largest oil field at Prudhoe Bay dropped to about 75 percent of its peak in 1987. We imported approximately 60 percent of the 6.5 billion barrels of crude oil and natural gas condensates consumed in 2005. (Condensates are natural gas liquids that form when the gas depressurizes at Earth's surface.) At the current rate of production, the U.S. reserves are expected to last about 10 years. U.S. natural gas production is also declining at five percent per year despite frenetic drilling; and adding to the problem is that half of our nation's homes are heated with natural gas, and all electric power plants built after 1980 are designed to be fueled by gas.

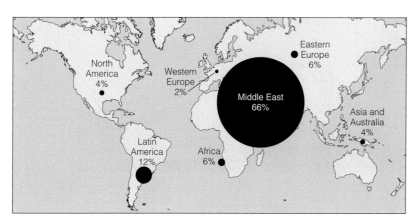

◆ **FIGURE 14.11** World and U.S. proven petroleum reserves. Notice the scale change for U.S. reserves. Colorado Geological survey

What about "all the oil" in the Arctic National Wildlife Refuge (ANWR)? In 2002 the U.S. Geological Survey estimated that there are between 5.7 and 16 billion barrels of probable and possible reserves oil in ANWR. The average of these estimates gives a median value of 10.4 barrels, a value that has been widely quoted in the media. The number, however, is a statistical fiction that represents the median value between a very large amount with only a five percent chance of being found and a more likely small amount with a 95 percent chance of being found. The very high (very low chance) estimate unduly pumps up the median, a figure that the uncritical public may not recognize. It should be noted that even if the refuge were opened tomorrow, it would be at least seven years before a single barrel reaches the lower 48 states. Even if 10.4 billion barrels

exist, with our present thirst for oil amounting to 6 to 7 billion barrels a year, that amount of oil is equal to only about 1.5 year's supply. Some significant facts that should be kept in mind when evaluating annual per capita energy consumption are that each individual in the United States consumes

- 4 tons of oil
- 2.5 tons of coal
- 2+ tons of natural gas, and
- the individual's weight in oil—every 7 days.

Even though domestic and worldwide production rates will continue to decline, new reserves, such as the recent deepwater discoveries in the Gulf of Mexico (■ Case Study 14.2), may be discovered, and there will not be an abrupt end to the nation's production. Nevertheless, worldwide production of oil and gas liquids is on the declining limb of bell-shaped production curve (◆Figure 14.12), and the gap between petroleum discovery and production continues to grow (◆Figure 14.13). The future is not so bleak when we factor U.S. ingenuity into the energy equation. Some oil remains to be discovered using current exploration techniques, although a crude-oil price of at least $50/barrel may be required to make the expensive searches feasible. In addition, there are nonconventional sources of petroleum such as oil shale, tar sands, and coal from which liquid fuel can be derived; and coal is also an alternate source of fuel-grade natural gas. Complacency, however, is not warranted, because the availability of energy from these sources comes with a steep price tag for it takes considerable energy to process these alternate sources of oil.

TABLE 14.4   2002 U.S. Oil Production

State	Thousand Barrels/Day	Million Barrels/Yr	Percentage
Louisiana	1,513	552	25.7
Texas	1,400	511	23.8
Alaska	1,050	383	17.9
California	857	313	14.6
Oklahoma	193	70	3.3
New Mexico	176	64	3.0
Wyoming	167	61	2.8
North Dakota	90	33	1.5
Kansas	80	29	1.4
Other	355	130	6.0
Total	5,881	2,147	100.0
Offshore U.S. production			
La., Tex., Alaska, Calif.	4,820	1,759	82.0
Gulf of Mexico OCS	1,420	518	24.1

* Not including natural gas liquids
Source: Arizona Geological Survey, American Petroleum Institute (A.P.I.)

CONSIDER THIS

It has been forecast that the last drop of oil will not be pumped until some time beyond your life expectancy. In light of this, do you think we should go on consuming energy as usual, or should the world's peoples and their governments do something to delay the day when that last drop will be used?

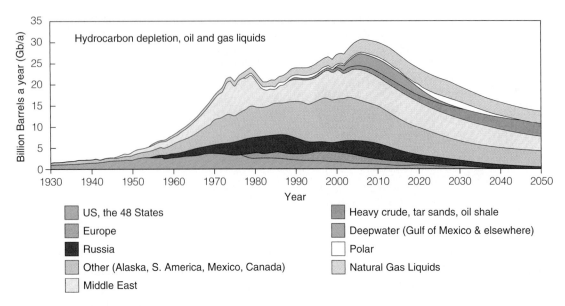

◆ **FIGURE 14.12** Hydrocarbon depletion, oil and gas liquids. Association for the Study of Peak Oil (ASPO)

Energy Gases and the Future

Some experts predict that the decline in the supply of affordable oil will begin as early as 2010, some claim it has already happened, and others say the crunch will not start until 2040 or 2050. They refer to the time as *the end of cheap oil*. When it will happen, and the speculation about when the world will run completely out of oil, is not relevant. What does matter is when production will fall off as demand inexorably continues to rise. In other words, price depends on the well-known supply-and-demand curves of the economists. ◆ Figure 14.14 reflects this. It shows the predicted decline in the use of oil in the twenty-first century and the increasing use of natural gases and alternative energy sources. Natural gas is currently reasonably plentiful, and it burns cleaner than coal, gasoline, or heating oil. It currently accounts for 75 percent of the total U.S. energy used in space heating and cooking, and it is in wide use as fuel for electric power plants. Natural gas is measured as cubic feet of gas at an atmospheric

pressure of 14.7 pounds per square inch and a temperature of 60°F. A trillion cubic feet (Tcf) of gas would fill a cube 2 miles on a side (8 cubic miles), and the United States consumes about 17 Tcf per year. We have proven reserves of 177 Tcf, which suggests that we will "run out" in 10.4 years. However, it is estimated that about 2,400 Tcf of natural gas exists in the United States (see Fisher in the For Further Information section). Many new discoveries will be made, with 40 percent of those at depths greater than 4,500 m (14,500 ft, almost 3 mi). About 300 Tcf will come from coal-bed methane and 500 Tcf will come from the growth of existing fields. Fisher calls the approaching transition period from oil to gas the *methane economy*.

By the 1990s **coal-bed methane** was recognized as a world-class commodity by several states, and there was a 95 percent

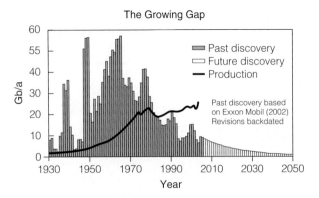

◆ **FIGURE 14.13** The growing gap between petroleum discovery and production. Collin Campbell, ASPO

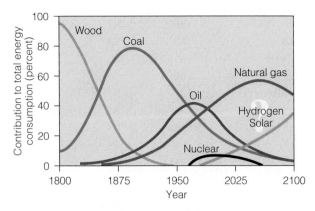

◆ **FIGURE 14.14** Use of energy resources in the United States since 1800, with projections to 2100. The shifts from wood to coal and then from coal to oil and natural gas each took about 50 years. Many analysts believe a new shift, to increased use of solar energy and hydrogen gas, will occur over the next 50 years. Note the natural gas peak at about 2050 and the oil peak at about 1970. Department of Energy

Todd Wilkinson

◆ **FIGURE 14.15** Drilling for coal-bed methane where the deer and the antelope play, near Pinedale, Wyoming.

probability that 30 Tcf could be found in the coal regions of Wyoming, Colorado, Utah, Montana, and New Mexico. Coal-bed methane is easy to extract by a drilled well (◆ Figure 14.15) as opposed to extracting coal, which involves destructive surface mining. But the gas production, as with all the nonconventional fuels, comes at a price, because it requires disruptive wells, a network of roads, disposal of salty water, pipelines, and methane leakage, all of which degrade the environment. An example of the problems involved is the Powder River Basin, a large drainage basin straddling the Montana-Wyoming border, where coal-bed-methane producers pump salty groundwater out of the coal seams to release the gas. The water is discharged into streams, ponds, and dry washes where the salt becomes a threat to irrigated crops and aquatic ecosystems. Ranchers worry that pumping will deplete the groundwater aquifers upon which they depend. In 2006 most of the 24,200 wells in the basin were on the Wyoming side of the border, but energy companies began moving into Montana. Montana government officials recognize the potential economic benefits to their state from the extraction of coal-bed methane, but they view Wyoming's development as uncontrolled and destructive. Thus, Montana will require producers to re-inject the water into the ground or remove the salt and other pollutants before dumping it into surface water bodies in accordance with the EPA's enforcement of the Clean Water Act. Re-injection and water treatment both require an expenditure of energy, which would cut into the profits of the developers, reduce the net amount of energy produced, and reduce the tax revenue to the state. Montana's tough water-quality standards would require rivers draining north from Wyoming into Montana to meet these standards. Wyoming politicians have accused Montana of "targeting" their state's thriving coal-bed-methane industry.

In addition to the two state governments as protagonists, two federal government agencies are also at odds. The EPA wants to enforce the Clean Water Act, but the Department of Energy (DOE) has focused on the potential impact on the national energy supply, stating that re-injection would cut the gas production significantly, resulting in losses of up to $21 billion worth of gas. Montana and the EPA are facing an uphill fight with Wyoming and the DOE; it may be that in this case there is no magic bullet to satisfy both environmental requirements and energy needs.

As we consider methane, don't forget methane hydrates as a potential fuel source (see the chapter opener).

Hydrogen is another gas that has been touted as a potential fuel. Many experts consider it will be the energy of the future as it burns without pollutants, emitting only water vapor. Unfortunately, there are no large reservoirs of hydrogen, and it is not a primary fuel source; it must be manufactured using fossil fuel, which then shifts the burden of pollution to some coal- or gas-fired power plant. It may offer promise as a fuel for airplanes and autos, and it might become economically viable if it can be produced in large quantities using solar, wind, or hydroelectric energy.

Coal

Coal is the carbonaceous residue of plant matter that has been preserved and altered by heat and pressure. Next to oil and oil shales, coal is Earth's most abundant reserve of stored energy. Deposits are known from every geologic period since Devonian time and the appearance of widespread terrestrial plant life some 390 million years ago. Permian coal is found in Antarctica, Australia, and India—pre-continental drift

Gondwanaland (Chapter 3). The large fields of North America, England, and Europe were deposited during the Carboniferous Period, so named because of the extensive coal deposits in rocks of that age. In the United States the Carboniferous Period is divided into the Mississippian and Pennsylvanian Periods, named after the states where the deposits are found. Tertiary coals are found in such diverse locations as Spitsbergen Island in the Arctic Ocean, the western United States, Japan, India, Germany, and Russia.

Coalification and Rank

The first stage in the process of *coalification* is the accumulation of large amounts of plant debris under conditions that will preserve it. This requires high plant production in a low-oxygen depositional environment, the conditions usually found in nonmarine brackish-water swamps. The accumulated plant matter must then be buried to a depth sufficient for the heat and pressure to expel water and volatile matter. The degree of metamorphism (conversion) of plant material to coal is denoted by its **rank.** From lowest to highest rank, the metamorphism of coal follows the sequence *peat,* to *lignite,* to *subbituminous,* to *bituminous,* to *anthracite.* The sequence is accompanied by increasing amounts of fixed carbon and heat (Btu) content, and a decreasing amount of quickly burned volatile material. Once ignited, it is the carbon that burns (oxidizes) and gives off heat, just as wood charcoal does in a barbecue pit.

Bituminous, or soft, coal usually occurs in flat-lying beds at shallow depths that are amenable to surface-mining techniques. Anthracite, the highest rank of coal, is formed when coal-bearing rocks are subjected to intense heat and pressure—a situation that sometimes occurs in areas of plate convergence. In the Appalachian coal basin, high-volatile bituminous coals

★TABLE 14.5 Active U.S. Coal Mines by Region, 1977 and 2000						
	Surface Mines		Underground Mines		Total	
Region	1977	2000	1977	2000	1977	2000
Appalachia*	185	130–175	205	380–500	390	510–675
Midwest	91	95–135	54	120–180	145	215–315
West	141	700–1,005	13	80–110	154	780–1,115

* Encompasses parts of Pennsylvania, eastern Kentucky, West Virginia, Virginia, Maryland, Tennessee, and Ohio.
Source: U.S. Geological Survey

occur in the western part of the basin and increase in rank to low-volatile bituminous coals to the east. Anthracite formed close to the ancient plate-collision zone of North America and Africa (pre-Pangaea), where the coals were more intensely folded and subject to higher levels of heat. Traveling east from the Appalachian Plateau to the folded Ridge and Valley Province, one goes from flat-lying bituminous terrain to folded anthracite terrain. West Virginia, Kentucky, and Pennsylvania are the leading coal producers of the eastern states. The interior coal basins of the Midwest are characterized by high-sulfur bituminous coal, whereas the younger Western deposits are low-sulfur lignite and subbituminous coal. ⋇ Table 14.5 projects the development of coal-mining activity in the United States. The expansion of mining activity will occur mainly in the Western coal basins, because the coal seams there are very thick and easily mined and the coals are low in sulfur. Wyoming, with its low-sulfur coal, was the leading coal producer in 2005 (587 million short tons), followed in order by West Virginia, Kentucky, Pennsylvania, and Illinois (◆ Figure 14.16).

◆ **FIGURE 14.16** Production in million short tons (and percent change from 2004) for each of the coal-producing regions and the total production for the United States. Note the shift in production from the Appalachian region to the Western coal states. Energy Information Administration.

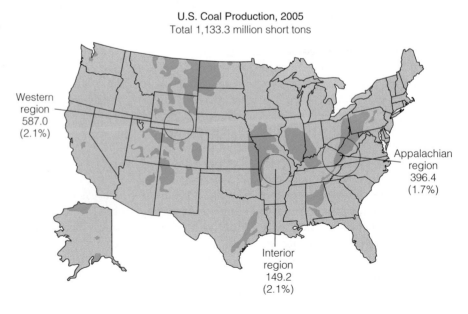

U.S. Coal Production, 2005
Total 1,133.3 million short tons

Western region 587.0 (2.1%)

Appalachian region 396.4 (1.7%)

Interior region 149.2 (2.1%)

Reserves and Production

The future of coal-derived energy in the United States is far more optimistic than the outlook for petroleum. Coal constitutes 80 percent of U.S. energy stores but only 18 percent of present usage. In 1989 electric utilities accounted for 86 percent of the coal consumed, with residential and industrial use accounting for the remainder. It is estimated that there are 84 trillion (84×10^{12}) recoverable tons of coal in the world, the equivalent of 34 trillion barrels of oil. The United States has 283 billion tons of recoverable reserves, which could last 200–300 years at the current rates of production and use. These reserves could meet only 50 years of total U.S. energy demand, however.

It has been estimated that energy demand in the early twenty-first century will be between 100 and 150 quads (a quad is a quadrillion British thermal units, 10^{15} Btu), compared with 73 quads in 1973 and about 80 quads in 1980 (* Table 14.6). Coal production will double to meet the demand, and this increase will be mostly in the Western coal basins, where the relatively inexpensive surface-mining techniques can be used. Underground mining costs more, requires a greater capital investment, and takes more time to get into production. Also, miners who work underground face greater risks than those who work at the surface.

The various methods of mining coal are illustrated in ◆ Figure 14.17. A key element for the economic future of coal may lie in its use as a substitute fuel for oil and gas. The technology is in place to make methane from coal—the product, called *synthesis gas*, has been used on a large scale to manufacture petrochemicals, including methanol (methyl alcohol). Direct liquefaction of coal also shows promise. Using coal- or petroleum-based solvents, coal is dissolved and hydrogenated, resulting in about 75 percent gasoline and the remainder propane and butane. About 5.5 barrels of liquid are derived from a ton of coal at a cost less than the most expensive oil during the Iraq War, $55–$60 a barrel. A major facet of our energy future lies in converting coal to liquid or gaseous **synthetic fuels**, or *synfuels*. This will be discussed further later in the chapter.

★TABLE 14.6	Energy (Power) Units
Unit	Explanation
British thermal unit (Btu)	The amount of heat required to raise the temperature of 1 pound of water 1° F; ≈ energy released by a burning match
Quad (quadrillion)	10^{15} Btu = 172 million bbl/oil
Barrel of oil	5.8 million Btu = 42 gallons
Bituminous coal (average)	25 million Btu/ton
Natural gas	Variable Btu content, measured in cubic feet (cf)
Megawatt (MW)	1,000 kilowatts (kw), or a million watts
Gigawatt (GW)	1,000 megawatts, or a billion watts

CONSIDER THIS

Your Christmas stocking contains nothing but a lump of anthracite coal. Being an optimist, you rejoice in this gift. Why?

◆ **FIGURE 14.17** Schematic cross section illustrating conventional underground and surface coal-mining technology. Adapted from Colorado Geological Survey

Nonconventional Fossil Fuels

Tar Sands

Tar sands contain oil that is too thick to flow at normal temperatures. These deposits, found in Canada, Venezuela, Madagascar, and the United States, are surface mined like coal or drilled using steam to mobilize and recover the oil. Canada's Athabasca sands (◆Figure 14.18) constitute the largest oil field in the world. Canada claims that more than 1.7 trillion barrels of recoverable oil will come from the deposits.

Tar sands that are too deep (500 m) for surface exploitation underlie Alberta's Cold Lake area. Steam at 300° C (575° F) is injected at high pressure and allowed to "soak" for a month. The oil released from the sand is then brought to the land surface by familiar "rocking-horse" pumps. More than 2,000 steam-injection and oil-production wells deliver 130,000 barrels of oil per day. The area is estimated to contain 220 billion barrels of recoverable oil.

At present only the easily exploited deposits are being worked, and the supply of natural gas necessary to refine the oil is declining precipitously. Apparently, the tar-sand operations are facing shortages of equipment, steel, and workers, numbering 20,000 in 2006 but expected to double by 2008. Operations costs are soaring, with the French company TOTAL delaying its production start-up from 2010 to 2013 and Shell Oil announcing its planned expansion could cost nearly $13 billion, double the original estimate. Clearly, substitutes for conventional oil do not come cheap; nevertheless, production is expected to grow, especially when the world price of crude oil stands at $50 or greater per barrel. Production is expected to reach 30 days of current U.S. consumption by 2030. Currently Canada's tar sands produce less than five percent of what is consumed in the United States, and it is unlikely that it will ever be able to satisfy all of the U.S. demand.

Oil Shales

Oil shales are sedimentary rocks that yield petroleum when they are heated. Found on all continents, including Antarctica, they were originally deposited in lakes, marshes, or the ocean. The original rock oil used in kerosene lamps was produced from black oil shales. The most extensive U.S. deposits, the Green River shales, were formed during Eocene time in huge freshwater lakes in the present-day states of Wyoming, Colorado, and Utah. They are not oily like tar sands, but when heated to 500° C (900° F) they yield oil (◆Figure 14.19). The source of oil in the rock is **kerogen,** a solid bituminous substance; a ton of oil shale may yield 10–150 gallons of good-quality oil. Potential deposits of economic interest yield 25–50 gallons per ton, and the U.S. Geological Survey includes 3 trillion barrels of oil from shale in their estimates of reserves. Kerogen-rich lake deposits are also found in China, Yugoslavia, and Brazil.

When oil and gas prices were low, even the most accessible oil shale was not economical to mine. Richer deposits are buried under hundreds of feet of barren rock, which would require even more energy to mine. As the end of cheap conventional oil approaches, it is questionable whether exploiting oil shale will ever become economical. Water, too, is a

(a)

© Visuals Unlimited

(b)

◆ **FIGURE 14.18** (a) Locations of Alberta's tar sands: Athabasca, Cold Lake, and Peace River. (b) After extraction by huge machinery, the sands are washed with hot water to extract the oil adhering to the grains. Cleaned sand is then returned to the open pit, and the land is restored to its original contours.

◆ **FIGURE 14.19** Oil shale from the Green River Formation in Wyoming and a beaker of the heavy oil that can be extracted from it.

limiting factor, because processing the shale requires water volumes 3 to 4 times greater than that of the oil extracted. Furthermore, the extraction process destroys the natural landscape, and some of the richest shales are in scenic wilderness areas. At this time the oil-shale industry cannot compete economically in the energy market.

Problems of Fossil Fuel Combustion

Air Pollution

Obtaining energy by burning fossil fuels creates environmental problems of global proportions. It produces oxides of carbon, sulfur, and nitrogen and fine-particulate ash. Carbon monoxide (CO), an oxide produced by combustion of all fossil and plant fuels, is converted to carbon dioxide (CO_2), which contributes to global warming. Burning coal also releases sulfur oxides (SO_x) to the atmosphere, where they form environmentally deleterious compounds. Nitrogen oxides (NO_x), mostly NO and NO_2, are products of combustion in auto engines and are the precursors of the photochemical oxidants, ozone, and peroxyacetyl nitrate (PAN), which we associate with smog. Water and oxygen in the atmosphere combine with SO_2 and NO_2 to form sulfuric acid (H_2SO_4) and nitric acid (HNO_3), the main components of **acid rain**—rain with increased acidity due to environmental factors such as atmospheric pollutants (■ Case Study 14.3 on page 440).

The Clean Air Act of 1963 as amended in 1970 and 1990 specifies standards for pollutant oxides and hydrocarbon emissions. By 1980 new cars were 90 percent cleaner than their 1970 counterparts. The Clean Air Act Amendments of 1990 (CAAA) set goals and timetables that are affecting how and what we drive. Beginning in 1992 fuel suppliers were required to sell only reformulated gasoline in 39 areas where

winter air quality was a problem. Reformulations using methyl tertiary butyl ether (MTBE) add as much as 2.5 percent oxygen to the fuel, causing it to burn cleaner and create less ozone, at a cost of about 10 cents more per gallon. Unfortunately, reformulated gasoline (RFG) is stored in underground tanks that sometimes leak and pollute groundwater. As a result, a Blue Ribbon Panel appointed by EPA administrator Barbara Browner has recommended the following:

- Remove the Clean Air Act requirement for 2 percent oxygen in RFG.
- Enhance underground storage tanks, thus improving protection of the nation's drinking water.
- Reduce the use of MTBE nationwide, maintaining current air quality benefits.

So much for MTBE and reformulated fuels.

> **CONSIDER THIS**
>
> Historically, Pennsylvania crude oil (such brands as Quaker State and Pennzoil) has been known for its superior lubricating properties compared with, say, heavier California or Texas crude oils. Why do you suppose this is so? (Table 14.1 can help you deduce a reasonable answer.)

Sulfur Emissions and Acid Rain

Sulfur occurs in coal as tiny particles of iron sulfide, most of which is the mineral pyrite, or "fool's gold" (◆ Figure 14.20). Coal also contains organic sulfur originally contained in the

◆ **FIGURE 14.20** Small pyrite masses in a bituminous coal matrix (gray). The light-gray material is the cell walls of the original plant material, and the darker gray is the solid material that was contained within the cell cavities. Earth pressures compacted the plant material, squeezed out any water, and collapsed the cavities. That pyrite formed within the coal before completion of compaction is evidenced by plant materials bent around solid pyrite masses. The pyrite "blebs" are about 50 microns across.

◆ **FIGURE 14.21** Atmospheric concentration of sulfate for a 26-quad U.S. coal-use scenario in 1990. The point is that the heaviest concentrations are in the Northeast, where most coal is burned. After A. C. Stern, ed., *Air Pollution*, Vol. 1, San Diego, Academic Press.

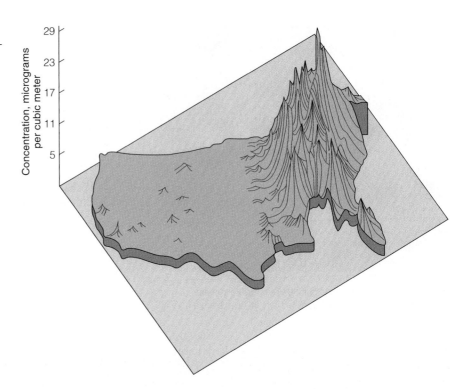

coal-forming vegetation. Upon combustion, mostly in coal-burning electrical generating plants, the sulfide is oxidized to sulfur dioxide (SO_2) and carried out through smokestacks into the environment. Emissions of SO_2 are known to have a negative impact on human health, particularly lung problems. Although most coal-burning in the United States occurs in the Midwest and the East, significant volumes of SO_x can travel 1,000 kilometers (600 mi) or more from their source. ◆ Figure 14.21 shows typical U.S. SO_2 emission densities, which reflect the pattern of coal usage very closely. Mobile sources using petroleum fuels emit less than 4 percent of the total.

Sulfur dioxide emitted from a smokestack may be deposited dry near the facility, where it will damage plant life and pose a health threat to animals. If the gas plume from the smokestack is transported away from the facility, its SO_2 will react with the atmosphere and eventually fall to Earth as acid rain. Acid rain can damage crops; acidify soils; corrode rocks, buildings, and monuments; and contaminate streams, lakes, and drinking water. Meanwhile, it is estimated that annual U.S. emissions of sulfur gases will increase almost 30 percent from 1990 levels by 2010.

Sulfur oxides can be removed from combustion gases in smokestacks by using a device called a *scrubber*, which selectively reacts with SO_2 and absorbs or neutralizes it. Many coal-burning facilities are switching to a process known as fluidized-bed combustion. Coal and pulverized limestone are burned together, and the heat of combustion converts the limestone into calcium oxide (CaO) and CO_2. CO_2 is emitted, and the CaO combines with sulfur and oxygen to form calcium sulfate ($CaSO_4$, a gypsumlike substance) as a solid waste product. Sulfur emissions are reduced, but CO_2 emissions increase. It is thus a tradeoff between the health benefits of reduced atmospheric sulfur and the environmental effects of increased contributions to global warming.

Nitrogen Oxides and Smog

Nitrogen oxide emissions (NO_x) are significant from both stationary (coal-burning) and mobile (vehicular) sources. Mobile sources are the most difficult to control, and their contribution to total NO_x is increasing as the number of automobiles increases. NO_x forms when engine combustion causes nitrogen in air to oxidize to NO and NO_2, which then react with oxygen, free radicals (incomplete molecules that are highly reactive), and unburned hydrocarbons to produce **photochemical smog.** Photochemical smog requires sunlight for its formation. Although the word smog is a contraction of the words *smoke* and *fog,* the air pollution in Los Angeles, Mexico City, and Denver has little direct relationship to either smoke or fog.

Both NO_2 and ozone (O_3) are reactive oxidants and cause respiratory problems. A level of only 6 parts per million (ppm) of ozone can kill laboratory animals by pulmonary edema (water in the lungs) and hemorrhage within four hours. In humans, alcohol consumption, exercise, and high temperatures have been found to increase adverse reaction to ozone, whereas vitamin C and previous exposure seem to lessen the reaction. One investigator noted that the person most likely to succumb to ozone would be "an alcoholic with a 'snootful' arriving at LAX for the first time on a hot, smoggy day and jogging all the way to Beverly Hills." Such a scenario may not be all that unlikely in southern California.

Energy-efficient cars and new fuels have gone a long way toward decreasing NO_x emissions. Exhaust-system catalytic conversion of nitrogen oxides, carbon monoxide, and hydrocarbons into carbon dioxide, nitrogen, and water are mandatory automotive equipment on new cars in most states.

Domestic Coal Burning

China is the world's largest producer of coal, accounting for 25 percent of global output. It currently produces 10 percent of the global emissions of CO_2, and it is estimated that by 2025 it will emit more CO_2 than the United States, Canada, and Japan combined. Coal provides 76 percent of the huge country's commercial energy, and it is the only fuel millions of people use.

In a typical home coal is burned in unvented stoves for cooking, space heating, and heating water. In many areas, foods are brought indoors in the fall for drying with coal fires, as the climate is too cool and damp to dry them outdoors. At least 3,000 people in Guizhou Province in southwest China suffer from severe arsenic poisoning caused by consuming chili peppers dried over high-arsenic coal fires (◆ Figure 14.22). Although fresh chili peppers have less than 1 ppm arsenic, chili peppers dried over high-arsenic coal have up to 500 ppm arsenic. More than ten million people in the same province suffer dental and skeletal fluorosis due to eating corn that has been cooked over coal containing large amounts of fluorine. About 3.5 billion people worldwide are exposed to toxic fumes indoors caused by coal burning. Each year, an estimated 178,000 people die prematurely due to indoor air pollution in China alone. To combat these health hazards, Chinese and U.S. Geological Survey geologists are working together to identify coal deposits with high toxic-element concentrations that make them unsuitable for domestic use.

Mine Collapse

Whenever coal is extracted from shallow underground seams, there is a risk of collapse of the overburden into the mine opening. Lignite and bituminous (soft) coals are most susceptible to collapse because they are exploited from near-horizontal beds at relatively shallow depths. The "room and pillar" method recovers about 50 percent of the coal, leaving the remainder as pillars for supporting the "roof" of the mine. As a mine is being abandoned, the pillars are sometimes removed or reduced in size, increasing the yield from the mine but also increasing the possibility of subsidence at some time in the future. Even when the pillars are left, failure is possible. The weight of the overlying strata can cause the pillars to rupture, and sometimes it physically drives the pillars into the underlying shale beds. Subsidence has been documented in Pittsburgh, Scranton, Wilkes-Barre, and many other areas in Pennsylvania (see Figure 13.24). In 1982

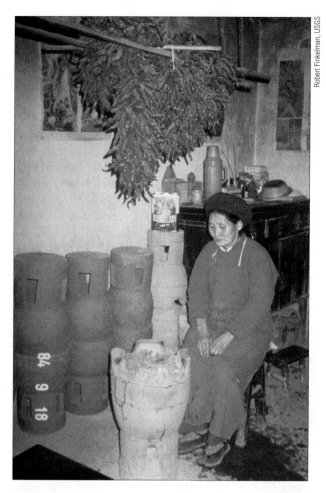

◆ **FIGURE 14.22** Drying chili peppers over a coal fire that emits arsenic fumes increases the arsenic content of the chilies up to 500 times, and eating them causes arsenic poisoning. Also, as families gather about coal fires at night, they are exposed to polycyclic aromatic hydrocarbons from incomplete combustion of the coal. Breathing these substances can lead to lung and esophageal cancer.

an entire parking lot disappeared into a hole above a mined-out coal seam 88 meters (290 ft) below the surface. Wyoming, Montana, South Dakota, and other western "lignite" states are pockmarked with subsidence features, but human activities and human lives are less likely to be affected by subsidence, or collapse, in those areas.

Energy for the Future

Our oil-based economy is "mature," and certainly the energy scenario of the twenty-first century will be different and not carbon-based as it is now. The primary energy source will be, as always, the Sun. The primary fuel may very well be hydrogen, the most common element in the universe and one that burns readily. This section examines the alternative energy sources that are available to us at this time.

Beyond Petroleum—Alternatives for the Future

The race is on to find a suitable alternative for gasoline for use in automobiles. The contenders are **ethanol, methanol, biodiesel,** electricity, hydrogen, **liquefied natural gas,** and **compressed natural gas.**

Leading the **biofuel** pack is ethanol (ethyl alcohol) derived from corn. Biofuels are any fuels derived from **biomass** (straw; agricultural waste; sugar cane; food leftovers; waste from the wood, paper and forestry industrial sectors; corn; switchgrass; any organic waste; cow manure; etc.). Ethanol made from sugar cane has been used in Brazil for many years as an auto fuel, and at one time almost 90 percent of the cars there burned it.

As with petroleum and coal, biomass is a form of stored solar energy that has been captured by growing plants by the process of photosynthesis. Ethanol derived from corn has received the most attention, the costs being closely competitive to gasoline. A big plus is that as a high percentage blend in automobile fuel, it releases less CO_2 than gasoline, but only in high percentage blends; when used as a low percent additive in a blend with gasoline it worsens CO_2 emissions. Ethanol fuel cuts ozone-forming gases, and it is a safe substitute for the gasoline additive MTBE. A drawback is that ethanol has only about 67 percent of the energy content of an equal volume of gasoline. One reason it is competitive is that the corn-ethanol industry is subsidized by the federal government as a result of policies promoted by the politically powerful corn-growing states. Corn ethanol has three major problems:

- It takes considerable energy to make corn ethanol, and that energy from coal-fired ethanol plants would completely undermine the reduced greenhouse gas emission of ethanol. Furthermore, it requires energy to plant, fertilize, harvest, and transport the corn, all of which produces considerable greenhouse gases that outweigh the advantages.

- The supply problem. If the entire U.S. corn production were devoted to producing E85 (a blend of 85 percent ethanol and 15 percent unleaded gasoline), it would meet only about 12 percent of the nation's current demands. Consequently, for ethanol to win the race, it will need feedstock other than corn.

- It is corrosive, thus not suitable for sending through pipelines. Instead it must be shipped in tank cars constructed of special materials.

The complex question of energy consumed in converting corn to ethanol compared with the energy content of the ethanol has created controversy with estimates ranging widely from a net loss of energy of 20 to 29 percent to a net gain of 67 percent. The range of estimates is due to differences in energy input values, changes in ethanol production processes, and accreditation of the energy value of production by-products (which are used mainly as animal feed). In 2006 the United States had 100 ethanol plants in operation. An additional 200 more are under construction or in the planning stage, which may use coal for power because coal is much less expensive than their current fuel, natural gas. As mentioned above, using coal would offset the greenhouse gains of ethanol.

Methanol (methyl alcohol), running a close second, uses natural gas (methane) as a feedstock, but the United States has vast coal reserves that can be used as feedstock. One company, Norcal Waste Systems in San Francisco, California, is even developing a process for making methane feedstock from dog droppings. (For many years, San Francisco has been a major producer of the stuff, wastefully compelling visitors to the city to carry it away stuck to their shoes.) West Virginia and Montana are developing systems for making coal-derived methanol. Pennsylvania already has a system that turns coal waste into diesel fuel. Methanol can be used directly as fuel; Indy race cars and model airplanes have used it for years. Methanol is an interesting fuel: its combustion generates little nitric oxide (NO) and ozone and it has a high octane number—about 110, which has made it attractive for race cars and high-compression engines. Although it has lower heat (Btu) content than gasoline, it has only about 50 percent of the energy content of an equal volume of gasoline in contrast to ethanol's 67 percent, and it burns more efficiently, which may even things out. On the negative side, methanol releases greater emissions of CO_2. Methanol can also be used in the process of making biodiesel, although biodiesel is currently manufactured from soybeans and other feedstocks, with its use amounting to 75 million gallons in 2005. A challenge facing all the biofuel contenders in the race is the ability to cost-effectively store, collect, and transport biomass feedstocks, and the development of a sustainable and safe supply system.

Direct Solar Energy

Although the amount of solar energy that reaches Earth far exceeds all human energy needs, it is very diffuse. For example, the amount that strikes the atmosphere above the British Isles is 80 times Great Britain's energy needs; it averages about 1 kilowatt per square meter. Cloud cover reduces the amount by 80 percent, but there is still more than enough. So why aren't there solar-electrical plants in every city and hamlet? The reason is cost. The current technology requires a great deal of space, which makes installations expensive. There are essentially two ways to put the sun to work for us:

1. Solar-thermal methods utilize panels or "collectors" to warm a fluid, which is then used for heating or for generating electricity.

2. Photovoltaic cells use the second most common element on Earth, silicon, to convert light directly into electricity.

★TABLE 14.7 Cost of Electricity by Energy Source	
Energy Source	Cost, cents/kwh
Sun	15.8*
Geothermal	13.3*
Biomass	13.0*
Wind	7.5**
Oil	4.4[†]
Gas	2.9[†]
Coal	1.2[†]
Nuclear	0.93[†]

* The rates that Southern California Edison Company was paying for purchased and manufactured energy in December 1995.
** 1998 value.
[†] The rates that Southern California Edison Company was paying for purchased and manufactured energy in December 1991 (more recent data not available).

In 1995 the electricity produced from photovoltaic cells cost about 16 cents per kilowatt hour (kwh), many times that produced by fossil fuels (★ Table 14.7). However, it is estimated that photovoltaic electricity will soon cost less than 10 cents per kilowatt hour and will compete with conventional electrical generation in this century.

Solar-thermal facilities called *power towers* illustrate a creative use of solar energy. The "Solar One" station in the Mojave Desert near Barstow, California, generated electricity between 1982 and 1988 for the Southern California Edison Company. It employed 1,818 suntracking mirrors focused on a water-filled receiver atop a tower where temperatures reached 900° C (◆ Figure 14.23). The super-heated water was transferred to a plant where it flashed to steam and drove turbines that operated an electrical generator. Because of the success of Solar One, a 10-megawatt facility was built on the same site and began operating in mid-1996. Solar Two uses molten nitrate salt as the heat-transfer medium. Molten salt has excellent heat-storing properties; the heat can be used immediately to generate steam, or it can be stored and used later, during cloudy periods or after sundown. Solar Two generated enough power for 10,000 homes and operated from 1996 to 2000, when government funding ended. San Francisco has installed a $5.2 million solar energy project at the Moscone Convention Center. It was dedicated in late 2002, and it is estimated that it will cut energy costs as much as 38 percent and, after debt service, save the taxpayers $200,000.

Photovoltaic cells (PV cells) absorb pulses of light energy on semiconductor materials and turn that energy into an electric current. They are used widely as a power source for satellites, calculators, watches, and remote communication and instrumentation systems. In recent years the cost of PV cells has been reduced by 80 percent, and it is now possible to apply thin films of these materials to shingles, tiles, and window glass, enabling buildings to generate their own electricity. Costs need to fall another 50–75 percent to make them competitive with fossil-fuel generating plants. Several U.S. utility companies have installed PV systems to supply small users in out-of-the-way places without building costly power-line extensions.

Indirect Solar Energy

Wind Energy

Wind power is the biggest success story in renewable energy. It is the fastest growing energy segment in the world, and it has been for the past 25 years. During the same time interval, the cost of wind power has dropped approximately 90 percent, but the present production pales in comparison to what electrical wind generation will be in 20 years. Costs depend on the wind velocity, turbine design and the diameter of the propeller. First, the energy that can be tapped from the wind

◆ **FIGURE 14.23** Solar One, a direct solar-energy power conversion facility in the Mojave Desert near Barstow, California. The heliostat (reflector) field directs sunlight to the central tower.

is proportional to the cube of the wind velocity. For this reason a slight increase in the wind speed results in a large increase in the electricity produced. For instance, an increase of the wind speed from 14 to 16 miles/hour results in an increase in electrical generation of nearly 50 percent. Second, a larger blade size requiring a taller tower yields a good increase in production. Increasing the blade diameter from 10 meters (1980s technology) to 50 meters (2004 technology) gives a 55-fold increase in yearly electrical production. Part of this is because a taller tower is required, and wind speeds normally increase with distance from the ground. Finally, a bigger wind farm is less costly to operate than a small one and thus the electricity is cheaper. Nearly forty percent is the difference between a small 3-MW installation (0.059 ¢/kwh) and a larger 51-MW plant (0.036 ¢/kwh).

California leads the nation in wind power and produces enough electricity to light a city the size of San Francisco. Ninety-five percent of California wind turbines are in three locations: Tehachapi Pass southeast of Bakersfield, Altamont Pass east of San Jose, and Banning Pass near Palm Springs (◆ Figure 14.24). These narrow passes through the mountains separate hot, desert-like valleys from areas with cooler maritime climates. As the heated air rises in the valleys, cooler air from the maritime regions is drawn through the narrow passes to replace it. Modern, "smart" windmills with larger props and programmed turbines produce electricity at a price competitive with other sources (✳ Table 14.8).

The wind potential of the lower 48 states is shown in ◆ Figure 14.25. One of the most attractive features of wind is that it can produce electricity during peak demand periods, on hot summer days and early in the evening in winter, thus avoiding construction of additional fossil-fuel plants to meet the need. There are environmental problems that accompany wind generation, such as noise, land acquisition, TV interference, and most important, visual blight. Modern generators have largely solved the problem of noise and TV reception, but a couple of hundred windmills are hard to ignore. The feeling

✱TABLE 14.8	Electrical Capacities of Selected U.S. Geothermal Fields	
State	Field	Electrical Capacity, MW
California	The Geysers*	1,970[1]
	Coso	256[2]
	Salton Sea area*	214[2]
	East Mesa	10[3]
	Long Valley	43[3]
Hawaii	Puna	25[2]
Nevada	Dixie Valley	50[2]
	Steamboat Springs	18[2,3]
Utah	Cove Fort	13[2,3]

* 1993 data.
[1] Steam is piped directly to a power plant.
[2] Flash wells produce a mixture of steam and water that must be separated.
[3] Binary wells produce hot water that is piped to a power plant, where heat is transferred to another fluid.
Source: U.S. Geological Survey circular 1125, 1994.

is that they destroy the visual aesthetics of a region. On the other hand, ranchers at Altamont love the windmills. They can still graze their cattle and at the same time receive land use royalties that have increased their prewindmill land value.

Europe is the leader in wind-energy development with its wind farms producing almost 35,000 megawatts (MW) (the equivalent of 35 coal-fired power plants) in 2005. One MW is enough electricity to power 250 to 300 homes. The United States, with 2,750 operable wind turbines, generated just over 7,000 MW, and Denmark produced over 3,000 MW. It is estimated that more than 90,000 MW of new wind-generating capacity will be installed annually around the

◆ FIGURE 14.24 Wind "farm" in San Gorgonio Pass near Palm Springs, California. The San Jacinto Mountains are in the background.

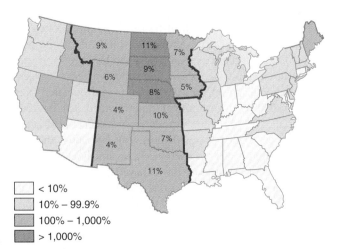

◆ FIGURE 14.25 Wind-electric potential of the 48 contiguous states as a percentage of each state's energy need. Twelve states in the central part of the country could provide about 90 percent of the total U.S. need.
From "Energy from the Sun," by C. J. Weinberg and R. Williams, *Scientific American,* 1990.

world by about 2015. Five countries are anticipated to set the pace for adding new capacity through 2007: the United States, 5,285 MW; Spain, 5,200 MW; Germany, 5,000 MW; China, 4,725 MW; and India, 4,000 MW. The Global Wind Energy Council estimates that 12 percent of the world's energy could be provided by wind energy by 2030, resulting in the reduction of 1,832 million tons of CO_2 emissions.

Hydroelectric Energy

Falling water, our largest renewable resource next to wood, has been used as an energy source for thousands of years. First used to generate electricity about 100 years ago on the Fox River near Appleton, Wisconsin, today it provides a fourth of the world's electricity. In Norway 99 percent of the country's electricity and 50 percent of its total energy is produced by falling water. The principle is relatively simple: impound water with a dam and then cause the water to fall through a system of turbines and generators to produce electricity. Because of this simplicity, electricity coming from existing facilities is also the cheapest source of this power. Aitupu Dam on the Parana River between Paraguay and Brazil, completed in 1982, is the largest producing electrical complex in the world; its potential is 12,600 megawatts. It provides much more electricity than the present demand in this part of South America.

Because of land costs and environmental considerations, it is doubtful that any more large dams will be built in the United States (see Chapter 9, also Case Study 9.4). Therefore, dams that were built for other purposes have become attractive for retrofitting with generators. Hydroelectrical facilities are particularly useful for providing power during times of peak demand in areas where coal, oil, or nuclear generation provides the base load. Hydroelectricity can be turned on or off at will to provide peak power, and many utilities have built pumped-water-storage facilities for just that reason. During off-peak hours, when plenty of power is available, water is pumped from an aqueduct or other source to a reservoir at a higher level. Then during peak demand the water is allowed to fall to its original level, fulfilling the temporary need for added electricity.

Although hydroelectric energy is clean, dams and reservoirs change natural ecological systems into ones that require extensive management. One of the social consequences of dam building is displaced persons. This displacement is unacceptable in most societies today. Also unacceptable are recurring attempts to dam areas of great aesthetic value, such as the Grand Canyon. Finally, dam failures—most often geological failures of dams' foundations—result in floods that can take enormous human and economic tolls.

Geothermal Energy

Earth's interior is an enormous reservoir of heat produced by the decay of small amounts of naturally radioactive elements that occur in all rocks. When the deep heat rises to shallow

depths, this **geothermal energy** can be tapped for human use. Furthermore, this natural heat is cleaner than many other energy sources, and there are fewer negative environmental consequences of using it. Not surprisingly, the prospects for using geothermal energy are best at or near plate boundaries where active volcanoes and high heat flow are found. The Pacific Rim (Ring of Fire), Iceland on the Mid-Atlantic Ridge, and the Mediterranean belt offer the most promise. Today the United States, Japan, New Zealand, Mexico, and countries of the former USSR are utilizing energy from Earth heat. Iceland uses geothermal energy directly for space heating (one geothermal well there actually began spewing lava), and many other countries have geothermal potential. The versatility of Earth heat ranges from using it to grow mushrooms to driving steam-turbine generators (◆ Figure 14.26).

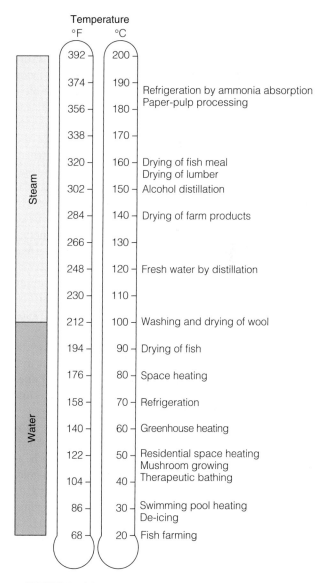

◆ **FIGURE 14.26** Some established commercial uses of geothermal energy.

B. Pipkin

◆ **FIGURE 14.27** The Geysers geothermal field in Sonoma County, California, is steam-dominated. It is the largest geothermal-energy producer in the world.

Geothermal energy fields may be found and exploited where magma exists at shallow depths and where there is sufficient underground water to form steam. Geothermal fields are classified as either *steam-dominated* systems or *hot-water-dominated* systems. Larderello, Italy, and The Geysers near Napa Valley in northern California (◆Figure 14.27) are examples of steam-dominated fields. Such fields are the rarest and most efficient energy producers. They occur where water temperatures are high and discharge is low so that steam forms. They are much like an oil reservoir in that porous rocks that hold steam or very hot water are overlain by an impermeable layer that prevents the upward escape of the steam or water. ⋇ Table 14.8 shows the electrical generating and direct-use capacities of selected U.S. geothermal fields. The Geysers is the largest producer of geothermal power in the world; its production is sufficient to supply electricity to a city of over one million people. More than 600 wells have been drilled there, some of them as deep as 3.2 kilometers (10,400 ft).

Geothermal energy is clean. The amount of CO_2 it emits is about one-tenth of the CO_2 emitted by coal-burning plants per megawatt of electricity produced, and about one-sixth of relatively clean-burning natural gas. Similar contrasts exist for emissions of sulfur and sulfur oxides.

The problems associated with geothermal energy production are related to water withdrawal and water quality. Some geothermal waters contain toxic elements such as arsenic and selenium and heavy metals such as silver, gold, and copper. Technology is in place to transfer the heat of the toxic brine deep within the wells to a clean, working fluid that can be brought safely to the surface. In some geothermal areas removal of underground water can cause surface subsidence and perhaps even earthquakes. At The Geysers, subsidence of 13 centimeters (5 in) has been measured without noticeable impact. Reinjecting the cooled water back into the geothermal reservoir decreases the subsidence risk and helps

ensure a continued supply of steam to the electrical generators. All geothermal fields in California are being monitored for possible seismic activity related to steam production. Small quakes have been reported from The Geysers, but none of significant magnitude.

The future for geothermal energy looks good. About 20 geothermal fields in the United States are generating electricity, and direct-use hydrothermal systems are being developed at more than 30 sites. Electricity was first produced from geothermal energy in 1904. By 2004 the production had grown to about 8,000 megawatts in 21 countries around the world. The United States alone produces 2,700 megawatts of electricity from geothermal energy, equivalent to burning 60 million barrels of oil each year to produce the same amount of electricity.

Nuclear Energy

At one time nuclear energy was considered *the* solution to the world's future energy needs—being clean, no CO_2 emissions, no blots on the landscape other than an occasional cooling tower and containment dome, and the power generated "too cheap to meter." More than 400 nuclear power plants were built worldwide, 109 of them in the United States (five U.S. nuclear plants are now shut down).

Globally, there are now 318 operating nuclear plants generating 16% of the planet's electrical power (◆Figure 14.28). The United States currently gets 20 percent of its electricity from 104 operating nuclear plants. Some countries have gone heavily into nuclear: France with 59 reactors obtains 79 percent of its power from nuclear fission, and China, facing a shortage of electric power, is building new reactors at a rapid pace—one or two a year.

But the allure of nuclear power began to tarnish with the Chernobyl accident in April 1986, following the 1979 Three Mile Island event in the United States. In addition, the challenge of radioactive waste disposal, and the poor economics compared with fossil-fuel-powered plants, helped reinforce people's anxieties regarding nuclear power. Collectively, these concerns resulted in the cancellation of all orders for new "nuke" plants in the United States. The current threat of terrorist attacks has added to those fears.

Nuclear reactors and fossil-fuel plants generate electricity by similar processes. Both heat a fluid, which then directly or indirectly makes steam that spins turbine blades that drive an electrical generator. Uranium is the fuel of atomic reactors, because its nuclei are so packed with protons and neutrons that they are capable of sustained nuclear reactions. All uranium nuclei have 92 protons and between 142 and 146 neutrons. The common isotope uranium-238 (^{238}U) has 146 neutrons and is barely stable. The next most common isotope, ^{235}U, is so unstable that a stray so-called slow neutron penetrating its nucleus can cause it to split apart completely, a process known as **fission**—a term particle physicists borrowed from the biological sciences. Nuclei that are split

Nuclear Reactors in Selected Countries

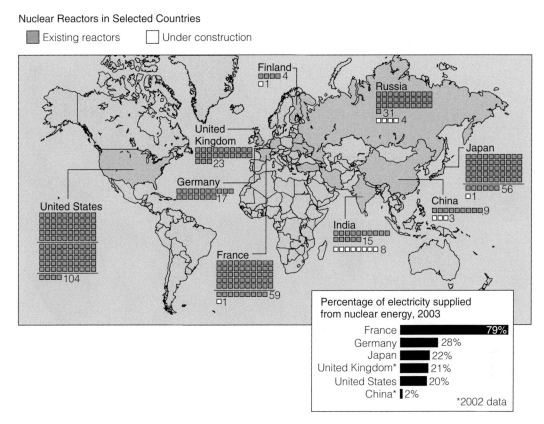

◆ **FIGURE 14.28** The percentage of electricity supplied by nuclear reactors and the number of reactors for selected countries, 2003. Note France is the world's most nuclear energy dependent nation with 59 reactors generating nearly 80 percent of its electricity needs. International Energy Agency

easily, such as those of ^{235}U, ^{233}U, and plutonium-239 (^{239}Pu), are called **fissile isotopes.** Fission occurs when a fissile nucleus absorbs a neutron and splits into lighter elements, called *fission products,* while at the same time emitting several "fast" neutrons and energy, 90 percent of which is heat (◆Figure 14.29). The lighter fission products are elements that recoil from the split nucleus at high speeds. This energy of motion and subsequent collisions with other atoms and molecules creates heat, which raises the temperature of the surrounding medium.

Meanwhile, the stray fast neutrons collide with other nuclei, repeating the process in what is called a **chain reaction.** A controlled chain reaction occurs when one free neutron (on average) from each fission event goes on to split another nucleus. If more than one nucleus is split by each emitted neutron (on average), the rate of reaction increases rapidly, and the reaction eventually goes out of control. Because ^{235}U makes up only 0.7 percent of all naturally occurring uranium, the rest being ^{238}U, it must be "enriched" for use in commercial nuclear reactors.

The major risk associated with nuclear energy is that of contamination during processing, transportation, and disposal of ^{235}U and high-level nuclear waste products. The locations of these risks in the nuclear fuel cycle are apparent in ◆Figure 14.30.

Geological Considerations

One of the many criteria in the siting of nuclear reactors is geologic stability. The selected site must be free from landsliding, tsunamis, volcanic activity, flooding, and the like. The Nuclear Regulatory Commission (NRC), the federal

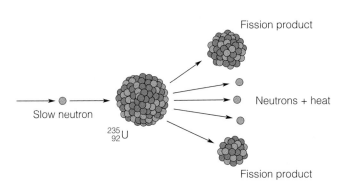

◆ **FIGURE 14.29** Nuclear fission. A slow neutron penetrates the nucleus of a U-235 atom, creating fission products (also called *daughter isotopes*), 2 or 3 fast neutrons, and heat.

◆ **FIGURE 14.30** The nuclear fuel cycle. The steps include mining, enrichment, transportation, power generation, reclamation, and disposal.

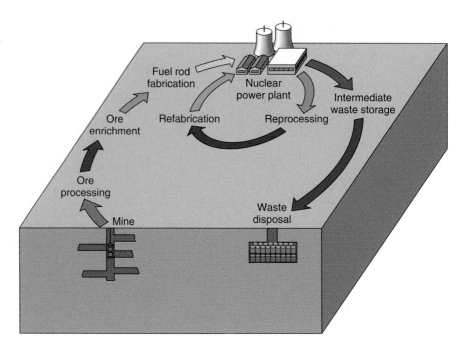

government body that licenses nuclear reactors for public utilities, requires that all active and potentially active faults within a distance of 320 kilometers (200 mi) of a nuclear power plant be located and described. Reactors must be built a distance from an active fault determined by the fault's earthquake-generating potential. Further, the NRC defines an active fault as one that has moved once within the last 30,000 years or twice in 500,000 years. This is a very strict definition, and sites that meet these criteria are difficult to find along active continental margins. To provide additional safety and allow for geological uncertainty, reactors are programmed to shut down immediately at a seismic acceleration of 0.05 *g*. This is conservative indeed, and the shutdown would prevent overheating or meltdown should the earthquake be a damaging one.

And finally, another geological consideration is that nuclear power is far from renewable, because the readily mineable uranium mineral deposits won't last much more than 50 years.

Energy from the Sea
Ocean Thermal Energy Conversion

Ocean thermal energy conversion (OTEC) utilizes the temperature difference between warm surface water and colder deep waters, at least 22° C (72° F), to vaporize a low-boiling-point fluid and operate a generator. A potential OTEC site must be in a coastal area where water depth increases rapidly enough to obtain the needed temperature differential and close enough to shore for power transmission. The Island of Oahu in Hawaii has the population, need, and oceanographic conditions for this form of energy conversion. A

mini-OTEC of about 50 kilowatts was operated in Hawaii in the 1980s. The electricity produced was not transmitted to the shore, but a continuously burning lightbulb on a float near the village of Mokapu testified to OTEC capability.

Wave Energy

Capturing energy and converting it to electricity is not a new idea, but until recently its practicality has been little improved since 1900. Research in wave-powered technology by a renewable-energy company based in New Jersey has resulted in their PowerBuoy system that appears successful at extracting the energy of ocean waves. Ocean trials have successfully captured wave energy and converted it to electricity, and the firm now has 40kW-rated PowerBuoys in service in New Jersey and Hawaii. Beginning in 2006 the company began installation of a 1.25-MW PowerBuoy wave "farm" off the northern coast of Spain. An application is pending for placing one of its generating buoys off Gardiner, Oregon, and a full-size demonstration plant of 10 MW capacity is planned for installation in waters of the United Kingdom.

ThomsonNOW™
Click **Geology Interactive** to work through activities on Wave Properties, Wave Progression, and Wind–Wave Relationships through Waves, Tides, and Currents.

Tidal Currents

Tidal currents have been used by coastal dwellers to power mills for at least a thousand years. Restored working tidal mills in New England and Europe are popular tourist attractions. Both flood (landward-moving) and ebb (seaward-moving) tidal currents are used. Modern designs utilize basins that fill with seawater at high tide and empty at low tide, generating electricity in the process. A potential site must have a large tidal range—the height difference between high and low tides—and adequate area for storing the elevated water. It is estimated that there are more than 100 suitable sites in the world that, together, are capable of generating 5 percent of the world's present generating capacity.

The first and best-known large-scale tidal power plant is on the Rance River near St. Malo on the English Channel in northwest France. The tidal range here varies from 9 to 14 meters (30–46 ft), and the power output is a reversible operation; that is, the plant generates power at both flood and ebb tides. Because the hydrostatic head (water drop) is only a few meters, 24 small 10-MW generators with a total capacity of 240 MW are used. On balance, the operation has been successful.

Annapolis Royal in Nova Scotia, Canada, is the only modern tidal-generating plant in North America (◆Figure 14.31). It generates over 30 million kilowatts per year, enough electricity to support 4,500 homes. An island in the mouth of the Annapolis River was selected as the site for the powerhouse that opened in 1984 after four years of construction (◆Figure 14.32). It is an ideal location because the Bay of Fundy has the highest tides in the world, and there was an existing causeway on the river with sluice gates that dammed a pond in the river. On the incoming tide the sluice gates are opened and the incoming seawater fills the pond. The sluice gates are then closed, which traps the seawater in the pond upstream of the generating turbine. As the tide recedes, the level of the water below the pond drops and a hydraulic head develops. When the difference is 1.6 meters or more the gates are opened and water flows through the turbine to generate

◆ **FIGURE 14.31** Annapolis Royal tidal electricity-generating station in Nova Scotia, Canada, the only modern tidal generator in North America. The plant generates more than 30 million kilowatts per year, enough electricity to support 4,500 homes.

electricity. Tidal power is clean and renewable, and in Canada, what started as a demonstration project turned into a successful power-generating facility.

CONSIDER THIS

What nonfossil-fuel energy sources are likely to be expanded in the United States in the coming century? In other words, if you wanted to make a long-term investment in one of them, which one would you choose?

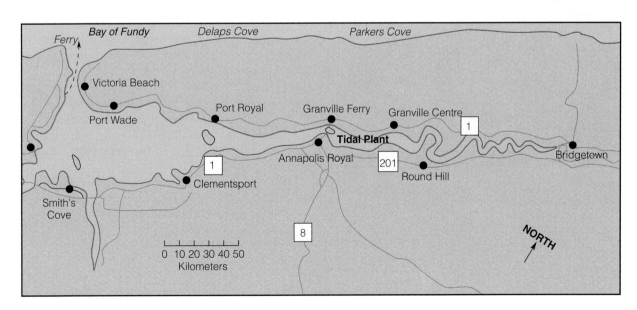

◆ **FIGURE 14.32** Map of the site of the Annapolis Royal, Canada, tidal generating station. The Bay of Fundy has the highest tides in the world, which are put to work at the station to generate electricity. Nova Scotia Power, Inc.

CASE STUDY 14.1

Rock Oil and the Colonel

The history of the petroleum industry is full of interesting characters, and probably none was more charismatic than the self-styled Colonel of Titusville, Pennsylvania, Edwin L. Drake (◆ Figure 1). In the 1840s the demand for whale oil and lard had outstripped the supply and was being supplemented by "rock oil" from seeps and tar pits. The oil on northwest Pennsylvania's Oil Creek, so-named because oil bubbled to its surface, had long been skimmed by the Seneca Indians and other Native Americans and used to waterproof their homes and boats. Later, Europeans skimmed it for use as lamp oil, paraffin, liniments, and lubrication.

Drake was a railway conductor in New Haven, Connecticut, who had an interest in petroleum exploration but no experience. There are several versions of why Drake went to Titusville. The most credible one

is that he had bought some shares in the Seneca Oil Company in New Haven and was sent by one of its founders, a friend of his, to stimulate the seepage at Oil Creek, which the company had leased from the Pennsylvania Rock Oil Company. Drake had a "Lincolnesque" appearance, and he frequently wore a knee-length topcoat and stovepipe hat. The company bestowed upon him the honorary title of *Colonel* to enhance his credibility in Pennsylvania.

Colonel Drake tried digging trenches to stimulate the flow, and he installed a series of skimmers to collect the oil. The process was so inefficient that he persuaded the company to lease the land and attempt drilling. Drake enlisted the help of local "salt borers," who drilled for brine from which salt was extracted. Often these drillers had struck oil instead of water, and they had been run out of town because of the terrible mess it created. The Colonel finally found an experienced driller named Uncle Billy Smith, who used percussion tools featuring a chisel on a cable to chip the rock and a bailer to remove the cuttings. Trouble with cave-ins ensued, and Drake ingeniously drove a large-diameter pipe into the caving zone and drilled the hole through it. On Friday, August 27, 1859, they struck oil, although they didn't know it until they checked the well on Sunday. A black goo had filled the 21-meter (69-ft)-deep hole, and the world had its first successful oil well.

Drake's well produced 10–35 barrels per day, almost doubling the previous world output of rock oil. The oil price jumped to $20/bbl, and a thousand oil pits sprang up around Titusville. Within a year the price had dropped to $0.20/bbl, and the Seneca Oil Company sold the Drake Well. Nearby towns such as Pithole City flourished for a few years and then became ghost towns. At Oil City a few miles south of Titusville, a Cleveland hay and grain dealer named John D. Rockefeller built the first commercial oil refinery in 1863. Seven years later he established the Standard (now Exxon/Mobil) Oil Company.

Because Edwin Drake had filed no patents and established no lease claims, he did not benefit from his vision and labor. He later lost his money speculating on oil stocks and became impoverished. He was forced to live on the generosity of friends. Learning of his dire need in 1873, Titusville citizens took up a collection for him. Three years later the Pennsylvania legislature voted to give him an annual income of $1,500. Drake was buried in Bethlehem, Pennsylvania, in 1880, but his body was reinterred in Titusville in 1901, ironically, the same year that a gusher in Texas, "Old Spindletop," drastically changed the oil supply of the world.

Today, Oil Creek between Titusville and Oil City is the site of the Oil Creek State Park. The ghost town of Pithole is just east of the park, and Drake Well Memorial Park is at the park's northern boundary.

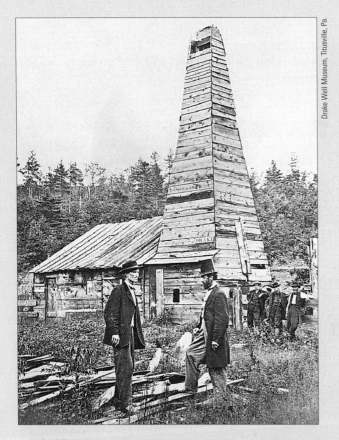

Drake Well Museum, Titusville, Pa.

◆ **FIGURE 1** Colonel Edwin L. Drake (right) in front of his well in 1861 with his friend, Titusville druggist Peter Wilson. The men in the background are probably drillers.

CASE STUDY 14.2

Industry Cracks Open a New Oil Source in the Gulf of Mexico

In what could become the biggest new source of domestic oil in the United States since the discovery of Alaska's North Slope in the 1970s, the first successful oil production from a part of the Gulf of Mexico that lies in very deepwater was announced in September, 2006. The Jack field, 435 kilometers (270 mi) southwest of New Orleans, and a dozen comparable discoveries in the same region, may hold as much as 15 billion barrels of oil and gas reserves (◆ Figure 1)—a barrel of oil is 42 gallons. If successfully exploited, it would boost the U.S. reserves by about 50 percent to more than 29 billion barrels. Production from these deep-water discoveries may well exceed the output of Alaska's giant Prudhoe Bay field, the largest of all U.S. oil fields. True, the new discoveries are sizable, but the Gulf's deep water oil doesn't come close to Mexico's huge Cantarell oil field, or the enormous fields in the Middle East.

The Jack well, one of the world's deepest producing wells at a total depth of five miles, taps a reservoir in rocks of Early Tertiary age. The well was drilled at an estimated cost of more than $100 million. Further development will cost several billion dollars for building platforms (◆ Figure 2), drilling, and laying pipelines to the mainland. Such deep-water discoveries are now possible by advances in seismic exploration and by today's large floating drilling platforms. These technological innovations have made it possible for geologists to search out and drill below the massive salt beds that typically overlie and obscure petroleum reservoirs in these deep-water Early Tertiary sedimentary rocks.

A consortium of three oil companies discovered the Jack field, which lies under 7,000 feet of water, by drilling two wells from a floating platform, the *Cajun Express*. The first well was completed in 2004 at the incredible depth of 29,066 feet, and the second, in 2005, reached a depth of 28,175 feet. The oil produced is light and sweet; that is, low in sulfur, the kind of petroleum that is in demand and realizes the best prices. Nevertheless, the discovery is somewhat provocative as stated by international oil expert Colin Campbell: the discovery "represents a remarkable technological achievement but at the same time reflects the extreme desperation of the industry, evidently having little easier [remaining] to test."

Courtesy of Shell Oil Company

◆ **FIGURE 1** Shell Oil Company's tension-leg semisubmersible platform *Ursa* in the Gulf of Mexico, about 265 kilometers (164 mi) south of New Orleans, anchored in water with a depth of 1160 meters (3805 ft). One platform such as this may drill and provide for as many as 30 wells. It is designed to withstand waves up to 22 meters (72 ft) high and hurricane winds up to 225 km/hour (139 mi/hour).

CONTINUED

◆ **FIGURE 2** Ultradeep water discoveries in the Gulf of Mexico. Oil companies drilling in waters up to 3 kilometers (2 mi) deep have made some significant discoveries. The first test of a well in Chevron's Jack field, which is under 2.1 kilometers (7,000 ft) of water, was drilled in 2004 to a total depth of 8.7 kilometers (28,543 ft or 5.4 mi), and was successful. Ten other ultradeep prospects in the Gulf offer promise. Department of the Interior, Minerals Management Service

CASE STUDY 14.3

Baking Soda, Vinegar, and Acid Rain

The term *acid rain* refers to the atmospheric deposition of acidic substances including rain, snow, fog, dew, particles, and certain gases. Although volcanic activity (see Chapter 5) is the greatest source of materials that may form acids—sulfur, carbon dioxide, and chlorine—sulfur and nitrogen oxides introduced by human activities are approaching the amount of nature's contributions. Combustion of fossil fuels and the refining of sulfide ores are the major human sources of these contaminants. Acids form when these gases come in contact with water in the atmosphere or on the ground.

Whereas carbon dioxide forms carbonic acid, a weak acid (see Chapter 6), chloride ion and the oxides of sulfur and nitrogen form the strong hydrochloric, sulfuric, and nitric acids, respectively.

The acidity or basicity (the chemical opposite of acidity) of an aqueous solution is referenced to the pH scale (◆ Figure 1), a measure of the solution's hydrogen-ion activity. A neutral solution will have a pH value of 7.0. The more hydrogen ions floating around in the solution, the more acidic it is, and the lower its

pH will be. Note that the scale is reversed, so to speak; a solution with a pH below 7.0 is acidic, and one with a pH above 7.0 is basic, or "alkaline." Acid-rain events with acidities below pH 2.8, the pH of vinegar, have been reported in large cities and heavily industrialized areas. In contrast, lakes without outlets, such as Lake Natron in Africa, may become extremely alkaline and have pHs greater than 11.0—well in excess of the pH of a concentrated solution of baking soda and water.

◆ **FIGURE 1** The pH scale. A neutral solution has a pH of 7.0. A solution whose pH is less than 7.0 is acidic, and a solution whose pH is above 7.0 is basic, or alkaline.

Energy Is Where You Find It

Humans devote a great deal of mental and physical energy to harnessing Earth's energy. Energy, like fresh water, is invaluable, and when it is in short supply, a family, a tribe, or a country will do almost anything to obtain it. The four photos in this gallery illustrate some of Earth's nonconventional energy sources and some relics of fossil energy. Keep in mind that all these energy resources derive from our Sun.

◆ **FIGURE 1** A community gathers around its solar-cell-powered television set; the Republic of Niger. More than likely they are watching a cricket or soccer match, not MTV or *Desperate Housewives*.

John ChiAsson/Gamma Liaison

Peter Bentham, BP Exploration

◆ **FIGURE 2** This could be a scene in West Texas, Oklahoma, or Tampico, Mexico, in the 1920s and 1930s. Little regulation of the impact of oil production on the environment existed at the time. In reality, this is the Balakhany Oil Field in Northern Baku, Azerbaijan, in 2003.

◆ **FIGURE 3** Three versions of a new vertical-axis wind turbine (VAWT) that went into commercial deployment in 2006. The inner blades, each shaped as a half-cylinder, rotate around a central vertical axis, while the outer blades, shaped like airplane wings, are fixed. The result is that the VAWTs are 43–45 percent efficient in contrast to conventional propeller-type turbines with only 25–40 percent efficiencies. The VAWTs can function at wind speeds up to 110 kilometers per hour (68 mph) that would shut down conventional turbines. Furthermore, in eight years of experience, the VAWT have proven to be bird and bat friendly.

◆ **FIGURE 4** The Blue Lagoon, a great hot-water pool 40 kilometers (25 mi) from Reykjavík, Iceland. It uses geothermal power-plant outlet water, which is salty and grows algae, giving it its blue color. Open every day, the lagoon attracts about 100,000 visitors annually.

Summary

Energy

Defined

Capacity or ability to do work. A society's quality of life depends in large part on the availability of energy.

Types

1. Renewable energy is replaced at least as fast as it is consumed; e.g., solar, wind, and hydrologic energy.
2. Nonrenewable energy is replenished much more slowly than it is utilized; e.g., energy derived from coal, oil, and natural gas (fossil fuels).

Petroleum

Defined

Volatile hydrocarbons composed mostly of hydrogen and carbon. Crude oil contains many different hydrocarbon compounds.

Origin and Accumulation

The necessary conditions for an oil field:

1. Source rock—origin as organic matter;
2. Reservoir rock—porous and permeable;
3. Caprock—impermeable overlying stratum; and
4. Geologic trap—such as an anticline, faulted anticline, reef, or stratigraphic trap.

Production

Drilled wells are either pumped or they flow if under gas and water pressure. Even with the best drilling and producing techniques, primary production may recover only half the oil.

Secondary Recovery

Oil remaining in pore spaces underground is stimulated to flow to a recovery well by injecting water, chemicals, steam, or CO_2. Much of the "stuck" oil can be stimulated to flow to the extraction well by these methods.

Value

Varies with weight. Light crude oil is the most valuable.

Reserves

The world's oil production may peak as early as 2010—the exact date is unknown. Alternate energy sources will become increasingly important.

Energy Gases

May be the fuel of the first half of the twenty-first century.

1. Methane hydrates, ice balls of natural gas
2. Natural gas from unconventional sources
3. Hydrogen gas

Coal

Defined

Carbonaceous residue of plants that has been preserved and altered by heat and pressure.

Rank

As coal matures, it increases in heat content and decreases in the amount of water and volatile matter it contains. The sequence is plant matter to peat, to lignite, to subbituminous, to bituminous, to anthracite.

Reserves

The United States may have enough coal to last 200–300 years.

Synfuels

The manufacture of combustible gas, alcohol, and gasoline from coal has a promising future.

Other Fossil Fuels

Tar Sands

Sands containing oil that is too thick to flow and that can be surface-mined. Oil is then washed from the sand. One place the sands are mined is the Athabasca Field in Alberta, Canada.

Oil Shale

Eocene lake deposits containing light kerogen oil that can be removed by heating. Deposits are found in Wyoming, Utah, and Colorado.

Problems with Fossil-Fuel Combustion

Air Pollution

Products of combustion contribute to global warming, smog, and acid rain. Acid rain is a hazard in the U.S. East and Southeast and in eastern Canada, which receives some of the U.S. emissions. This is a major international air-pollution problem.

Mitigation

Sulfur content must be reduced below 1 percent. Methods include fluidized-bed combustion, neutralizing sulfur dioxide in smokestacks with limestone scrubbers, cleaning coals by gravity separation, and chemical leaching methods.

Subsidence and Collapse

Areas underlain by shallow lignite are subject to subsidence.

Alternative Energy Sources

Direct Solar

1. Solar heat collectors warm a fluid, which is then put to work.
2. Photovoltaic cells convert light directly into electricity.

Indirect Solar

Wind is produced by unequal heating of Earth's surface.

Synfuel

A fuel manufactured from organic materials, corn, farm waste, or coal.

Geothermal

Facilities for generating electricity with geothermal energy currently are in place and may supply as much as 2 percent of U.S. electrical energy needs. Geothermal heat is also used worldwide for heating interior spaces, keeping sidewalks free of winter snow and ice, etc.

Hydroelectric

Hydroelectric dams harness the power of water distributed over Earth by the hydrologic cycle.

Oceans

The energy in waves, currents, and tides can be converted to do work for humans. Ocean thermal energy conversion (OTEC) shows some promise, but little has been done with waves and currents. Tidal power is being used successfully only at the Rance River, France, and in Nova Scotia, Canada, at present.

Fuel Cells

Fuel cells generate electricity fueled by hydrogen. Many think this is the fuel–motor combination of the future.

Nuclear Energy

Provides 16 percent of world and 20 percent of U.S. energy needs. Heat generated by fission of uranium isotopes and their daughter-isotopes such as plutonium is converted to electricity. There are 104 commercial nuclear power plants operating in the United States.

1. *Problems*—Mining, transportation, and disposal of high-level nuclear materials are the most dangerous aspects of the nuclear energy cycle. If the chain reaction runs out of control, the heat generated may lead to a central-core meltdown such as occurred at Chernobyl.

2. *Geological considerations*—Very careful geological site studies and investigations are performed to assess hazards from earthquakes, mass-wasting, subsidence, and coastal and riverine floods.

Key Terms

acid rain	fissile isotopes	oil shale	slant drilling
anticline	fission	photochemical smog	source rock
biodiesel	geothermal energy	rank (coal)	stratigraphic trap
biomass fuel	hydrocarbon compound	renewable resource	synthetic fuels (synfuels)
caprock	kerogen	reserves	tar sands
chain reaction	methanol	reservoir rock	wildcat well
coal-bed gas	miscible	salt dome	
ethanol	nonrenewable resource	secondary recovery	

Study Questions

1. What four conditions are required for an oil deposit to form?

2. What oceanographic conditions favor the formation of a good source rock for oil?

3. Draw a geologic cross section that shows an anticline and a faulted anticline. Assume your cross section is looking north. What are the directions of the dips and strikes of the two limbs of the anticline? Dip and strike determination is explained in Appendix 3.

4. What nonrenewable energy resources exist in the United States, and which one is most abundant?

5. Describe atomic fission. How does it create heat for electrical generation?

6. What are methane hydrates, and what is their potential as fuel for the twenty-first century?

7. What are the environmental consequences of burning fossil fuels? What will be the impact upon the global environment of continued dependence upon fossil fuels?

8. How can solar energy be collected and used for heating, generating electricity, and producing fuels?

9. What sector of the U.S. economy uses the most fossil fuel, and what international problem is connected with this use?

10. Explain the meaning of renewable energy. Which renewable energy sources have been developed, and which undeveloped renewable sources show the most promise?

For Further Information

Fact sheets may be obtained from the USGS free of charge. Write to U.S. Geological Survey (Information Services), P. O. Box 25286, Denver Federal Center, Denver, CO 80225.

Books and Periodicals

Collett, T. S. 2004. Gas hydrates as a future energy resource. *Geotimes 49,* no. 11 November: 24–27.

Cooper, G. A. 1994. Directional drilling. *Scientific American*, May: 82–87.

Deffeyes, Kenneth S. 2003 (Rev. ed.). *Hubbert's Peak: The impending world oil shortage.* Princeton Univ. Press.

Duffield, W. A., J. H. Sass, and M. Sorrey. 1994. *Tapping the Earth's natural heat.* U.S. Geological Survey circular 1125.

Fellows, Larry D. 2001. Energy resources in Arizona. *Arizona geology 31*, no. 2.

Finch, Warren I. 1997. Uranium, its impact on the national and global energy mix. U.S. Geological Survey circular 1141.

Fisher, William L. 2002. The coming methane economy. *Geotimes 47*, no. 11, November.

Goldstein, David. 2004. *Out of Gas: The end of the age of oil.* New York. W. W. Norton and Company.

Haq, Bilal U. 1998. Gas hydrates: Greenhouse nightmare? Energy panacea or pipe dream? *GSA today 8*, no. 11, November.

Heinberg, Richard. 2003. *The party's over: Oil, war and the fate of industrial societies.* Gabriola Island, British Columbia. New Society Publishers.

Hirsch, Robert L. 1987. Impending United States energy crisis. *Science 235*:1467–1473.

Hubbard, N. King. 1971. The energy resources of the Earth. *Scientific American 225*, no. 3, p. 60–70.

McCabe, Peter J., and others. 1993. *The future of energy gases.* U.S. Geological Survey circular 1115, Public issues in Earth science series.

Mossop, Grant D. 1980. Geology of the Athabasca oil sands. *Science 207*, p. 145.

Reese, April. 1999. Bad air days. *E: The environmental magazine,* November–December: 28–35.

Ross, David. 1987. *Energy from waves* (2nd ed.). New York: Pergamon Press.

Schmandt, Jurgen, J. Clarkson, and Hilliard Roderick (Eds.) 1988. *Acid rain and friendly neighbors: The policy dispute between Canada and the United States.* Durham, N.C.: Duke University Press.

Scientific American. 1990. Energy for planet Earth. *Scientific American* special issue, September.

Spencer, Jon E., and Steven L. Rauzi. 2001. Crude oil supply and demand: Long-term trends. *Arizona geology 31*, no. 4.

Sperling, Daniel. 1996. The case for electric vehicles. *Scientific American,* November: 54–59.

Suess, Erwin, Gerhard Bohrmann, Jens Greinert, and Erwin Lausch. 1999. Flammable ice. *Scientific American,* November: 76–83.

U.S. Geological Survey. 1998. Arctic National Wildlife Refuge (ANWR), 1002 Area, petroleum assessment 1998. Fact sheet FS-040-98, May.

U.S. Geological Survey. 2000. USGS world petroleum assessment 2000. Fact sheet FS-070-00, April.

U.S. Geological Survey. 2001. Coal-bed gas resources of the Rocky Mountain region. Fact sheet FS-110-01, November.

U.S. Geological Survey. 2002. Natural gas production in the United States. Fact sheet FS-113-01, January.

ThomsonNOW™

Assess your understanding of this chapter's topics with additional comprehensive interactivities at http://www.thomson.com/login, which also has up-to-date web links, additional readings, and exercises.

Waste Management and Geology

CHAPTER 15

Trash Talk

A WASTE-DISPOSAL SITE'S ABILITY TO isolate solid and liquid waste is determined almost entirely by its geologic and hydrologic conditions. The primary goal in site selection is to protect the local water supply. Surface and underground water become polluted when rainwater percolates through solid wastes. Geologists assess a potential site's suitability through field observation, soil tests for percolation and strength, drill-hole sampling of underground rock materials, and evaluations of the region's underground water conditions based on tests of nearby wells. In addition, an environmental impact report must be submitted that addresses potential problems related to the local biology, air quality, traffic congestion, and visual blight.

Wrangell, Alaska, is a town of 2,000-some people on Wrangell Island in the state's beautiful southern panhandle. In 1999 the town's open trash dump was deemed unacceptable and was sealed (◆ Figure 1). It was determined that

> We aren't going to solve world peace if we can't figure out what to do with garbage.
>
> Willie Brown, Mayor of San Francisco

B. Pipkin

◆ **FIGURE 1** Wrangell's open trash dump before it was closed and sealed in 1999.

the island has no geologically suitable landfill site, and that the town's solid waste must be transferred by ocean barge to acceptable sites in the lower 48 states, hundreds of kilometers away. Much of the town's small budget now goes to pay for this new means of waste disposal.

In sharp contrast to the picture at Wrangell is an engineered sanitary landfill being manufactured in Southern California (◆Figure 2). Graded slopes are designed to provide stability, and a plastic liner has been placed beneath a compacted, impermeable clay layer. The clay-layer "seal" will prevent liquids from migrating out of the fill into the groundwater environment. Yes, geology is very important in the world of trash.

◆ **FIGURE 2** An engineered solid-waste landfill; Southern California. Note the black plastic liner and tractor at the base of the slope.

Getting rid of trash is a major environmental problem in industrialized nations. Growing populations of consumers have created an explosion of solid, liquid, and hazardous wastes, much of which requires special handling. At risk due to careless waste disposal are groundwater and surface-water purity, air quality, public health, and less threatening but still important, scenic beauty and land-surface integrity. Municipal solid waste generated in the United States in 2003 (the most recent year for which data are available) amounted to 236 million tons, which amounts to about 2 kilograms (4.4 lbs) per person per day. This category of waste includes yard cuttings, garbage, construction materials, paper products, metal cans, plastics, and glass (◆Figure 15.1). It does not include wastes from agriculture, industry, utilities, or mining, which

account for more than 96 percent of the solid waste generated in the United States (◆Figure 15.2). After incineration and recovery for recycling and composting, 57 percent went to a landfill. Just one day's total U.S. waste would cover 15 square kilometers (almost 6 mi²) to a depth of 3 meters (10 ft). If it were loaded into ten-ton trucks lined up bumper to bumper, the trucks would stretch around the world 20 times. Those trucks containing only the day's *municipal solid waste* would circle Earth almost 3 times. The spectrum of solid-waste disposal problems ranges from the need to isolate highly dangerous nuclear waste to the challenge of dismantling and scrapping an astounding number of cars every year, estimated at 15 million in the United States alone. (One year 60,000 cars were abandoned on the streets of New York City.)

(a)   **(b)**

◆ **FIGURE 15.1** Components of urban solid waste (a) by sector and (b) by material for total waste generated in 2003 (236 million tons before recycling). EPA

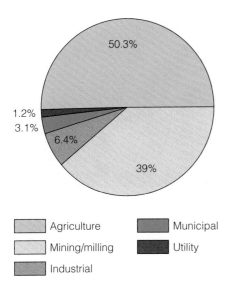

50.3%

1.2%
3.1%

6.4%

39%

Agriculture   Municipal

Mining/milling   Utility

Industrial

◆ **FIGURE 15.2** Estimated relative contributions to total U.S. solid waste, 1992. The ratios had not changed appreciably by 2005. EPA

The amount of trash a country or governmental entity generates *per unit of land area* is just as important as the *total* amount it generates. If small countries with limited disposal sites generate large quantities of trash, major problems are created. Although the United States generates the highest total amount of waste in the world, the tiny city-state of Singapore generates the most trash per unit area of land, almost 2,500 tons per square kilometer per year. This is in comparison with less than 2 tons per square kilometer for Canada and 20 tons per square kilometer for the United States. Poland generates the most *industrial* waste per unit area, followed by Japan; and Hungary produces the most *toxic* waste per unit area, followed by the United States.

The impetus to develop environmentally safe trash disposal sites, known as *landfills*, was the passage of two important laws, the National Environmental Policy Act of 1969 (**NEPA**) and the Resource Conservation and Recovery Act of 1976 (**RCRA**). The NEPA requires an in-depth field study and issuance of an Environmental Impact Statement on the consequences of all projects on federal land. The RCRA mandates federal regulation of waste products and encourages solid-waste planning by the states. The RCRA addresses the problems of hazardous waste and its impact upon surface-water and groundwater quality, and it created the framework for regulating hazardous wastes. These laws sent the message that the then-prevailing "out of sight, out of mind" approach to disposing of wastes of all kinds, hazardous and benign, was no longer acceptable. The laws mandated "cradle to the grave" systems for impounding wastes and monitoring them to ensure their low potential for migrating into freshwater supplies. The Environmental Protection Agency (**EPA**) is charged with monitoring and policing the provisions of these and subsequent laws and amendments intended to prevent pollution of natural systems (■ Case Study 15.1 on page 466).

Disposing of solid and liquid wastes, regardless of how they are generated, falls into two main categories:

- **isolation,** encapsulating, burying, or in some other way removing waste from the environment; and
- **attenuation,** diluting, incinerating, or spreading trash or a pollutant so thinly that it has little impact.

Attenuation (dilution) is effective with sewage, some waste chemicals, and certain gaseous pollutants. About 10 percent of our waste, including sewage sludge, is incinerated in large, modern incinerators, usually found where land-disposal sites are not available. Historically, most of our solid waste has been isolated in dumps. Open dumps, the local "garbage dumps" of small towns such as the one pictured in the chapter opener, are no longer acceptable because of their attendant insect, vermin, odor, and air-pollution problems. By 2003 more than 70 percent of U.S. trash was being disposed of in 3,091 landfills, down from 7,900 landfills in 1988. Most landfill closures occurred because they had reached their capacity, but many others could not meet the stringent EPA standards for protecting groundwater. Deep wells are used successfully for isolating hazardous liquid wastes, although the tremendous volume of used motor oil remains a problem. Today, good **waste management** consists not only of waste disposal, but also of reducing the amount of waste at its sources and promoting waste recovery and recycling programs.

Municipal Waste Disposal
Municipal Waste Disposal Methods
Sanitary Landfills

In 1912 the first solid-waste sanitary landfill was established in Great Britain. Known as "controlled tipping," this method of isolating wastes expanded rapidly and was adopted by thousands of municipalities by the 1940s. The city of Fresno, California, claims to be the first city in the United States to employ a sanitary landfill for waste disposal. A **sanitary landfill** differs from an open dump in that each day's trash is covered with a layer of soil to isolate it from the rest of the environment. Although this sounds simple, the method involves spreading trash in thin layers, compacting it to the smallest practical volume with heavy machinery, and then covering the day's accumulation with at least 15 centimeters (6 in) of soil (◆ Figure 15.3). When finished, a landfill is sealed by 50 centimeters (20 in) of compacted soil and is graded so that water will drain off the finished surface. This prevents water infiltration and the production of potentially toxic fluids within the fill (◆ Figure 15.4). **Leachate** refers to the water that filters down through a landfill, acquiring (leaching out) dissolved chemical compounds and fine-grained solid and microbial contaminants as it goes. Protecting the local environment from leachate is a major consideration in designing and operating waste-disposal

(a)

(b)

◆ **FIGURE 15.3** (a) Method of dump and cover employed in a sanitary landfill. (b) An urban sanitary landfill in action; Palos Verdes, California.

◆ **FIGURE 15.4** (a) Local-government landfill specifications for cells, final cover, and leachate-collection system. Note the barrier for reducing the visual blight of the landfill. (b) A full, graded landfill before planting; Puente Hills, Los Angeles County, California. Final grades and slope benches for intercepting runoff are visible in the photo.

(a)

(b)

*TABLE 15.1   Classifications of Disposal Sites and Waste Groups

Geology of Disposal Sites

Class I	No possibility of discharge of leachate to usable waters. Inundation and washout must not occur. The underlying lining material, whether soil or synthetic, must be essentially impermeable; that is, it must have a permeability less than 0.3 cm/year. All waste groups may be received (Figure 15.5, part a).
Class II	Site overlies or is adjacent to usable groundwater. Artificial barriers may be used for both vertical and lateral leachate migration. Geologic formation or artificially constructed liners or barriers should have a permeability of less than 30 cm/year. Groups 2 and 3 waste may be accepted (Figure 15.5, part b).
Class III	Inadequate protection of underground- or surface-water quality. Includes filling of areas that contain water, such as marshy areas, pits, and quarries. Only inert Group 3 wastes can be accepted (Figure 15.5, part c).

Constituents of Waste Groups

Group 1	Consists of but not limited to toxic substances that could impair water quality. Examples are saline fluids, toxic chemicals, toilet wastes, brines from food processing, pesticides, chemical fertilizers, toxic compounds of arsenic, and chemical-warfare agents.
Group 2	Household and commercial garbage, tin cans, metals, paper products, glass, cloth, wood, yard clippings, small dead animals, and hair, hide, and bones.
Group 3	Non-water-soluble, nondecomposable inert solids such as concrete, asphalt, plasterboard, rubber products, steel-mill slag, clay products, glass, and asbestos shingles.

sites. The dump-and-cover procedure carried out at sanitary landfills is known as the "cell" method, because it isolates waste from the environment in rhomb-shaped compartments, or cells. A well-operated sanitary landfill is relatively free of odors, blowing dust, and debris (■ Case Study 15.2 on page 466).

Landfills and individual disposal sites within a given landfill are classified on the basis of their underlying geology and the potential impact that leachate could have upon local ground or surface water. Each of the three classes is certified to accept specific wastes of differing degrees of reactivity (see ✳ Table 15.1 and ◆Figure 15.5). Some landfill sites encompass all three classifications within their boundaries.

Incineration

Burning is the only proven way to significantly reduce the volume of garbage, sometimes by as much as 90 percent. In addition to reducing volume, combustors, when properly equipped, can convert water into steam to generate electricity or fuel heating systems. Recycling also can be accommodated at incineration facilities. Over one-fifth of the U.S. municipal waste incinerators use refuge-derived fuel, which is the combustible fraction remaining after recovery of recyclables (metals, glass, cans, etc.). Scrubbers, devices that neutralize acid gases, and filters, devices that remove tiny ash particles, significantly reduce gases or other pollutants emitted to the atmosphere. All combustion ash and air emissions must meet with the applicable federal and state regulations. The use of **incineration** is highest in areas with high population density, little open land, or high water tables. Massachusetts, New Jersey, Connecticut, Maine, Delaware, and Maryland, for instance, burn more than 20 percent of their waste.

New York City is a leader in trash incineration, burning about 720,000 tons per year, or 11 percent of all its waste.

(a) Class I landfill

(b) Class II landfill

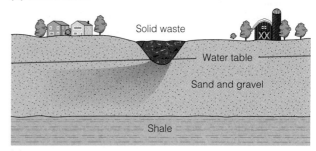

(c) Class III landfill

◆ **FIGURE 15.5** Geology of the three classes of landfills. Note that a Class I fill offers maximum protection to underground water and that a Class III fill offers no protection.

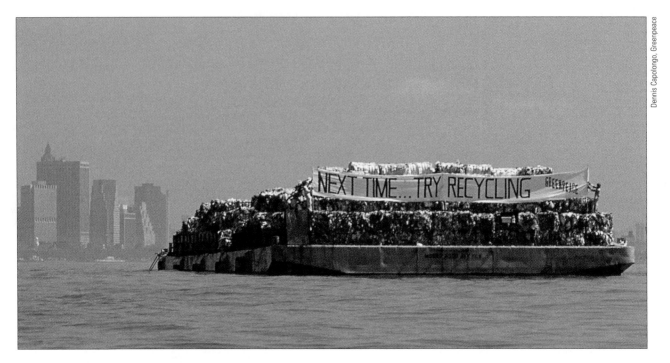

◆ **FIGURE 15.6** Greenpeace hung a protest banner on this loaded garbage barge in New York Harbor. In the past trash such as this was destined for sea burial. Disposal of solid waste is a problem in urban areas in all parts of the world.

Wastes must be burned at very high temperatures, and incinerator exhausts are fitted with sophisticated scrubbers that remove dioxins and other toxic air pollutants. Incinerator ash presents another problem, because it is in itself a hazardous waste, containing high ratios of heavy metals that are chemically active (see Case Study 15.2).

The City of Philadelphia operates trash incinerators but lacks landfills for isolating the ash. In desperation, in the mid-1980s 14,500 metric tons (16,000 tons) of the ash from two of its incinerators was loaded onto the steamship *Khian Sea* and sent to sea (◆Figure 15.6). Like the sailor in Coleridge's "Rime of the Ancient Mariner," the *Khian Sea* sailed "alone, alone on a wide, wide sea" for two years, seeking a place to offload its unwanted cargo, with port after port refusing. In 1988 a miracle must have occurred, as the ship sailed into Singapore empty. No explanation has ever been given.

Incineration has fallen into disfavor, only 112 plants remaining in 2003 from the 186 in use in 1990. Reasons for the reduction include more stringent federal and state emission requirements, public opposition, and expense; disposal of municipal solid waste in landfills is less expensive than disposal of the residual ash.

Ocean Dumping

Greek mythology relates how Herakles (Latin *Hercules*) was given the task of cleaning King Augeas's stables, which contained 30 years' accumulation of filth from 3,000 head of cattle. Inasmuch as one cow produces roughly 18 wet tons of manure per year, Herakles was up to his ears in 1.6 million tons of you-know-what, about the amount of sewage sludge that New York City generates in four months. Because Herakles was to perform the cleanup in a day, he ingeniously diverted the courses of two rivers to make them flow through the stables and wash the filth into an estuary. Had an environmental impact statement been required, it would have noted that a huge mass of solid sludge would cover a large area of the wetlands and bury bottom-dwelling organisms. In addition, phosphates and nitrates in the effluent would promote explosive algal blooms at the expense of other organisms, and dissolved oxygen in the water would decrease to the point of mass mortality of swimming and bottom-dwelling organisms.

Historically, all coastal countries have used the sea for waste disposal. This practice is based on the *assimilative capacity* approach to waste disposal; that is, the assumption that a body of seawater can hold a certain amount of material without adverse biological impact. No U.S. municipality has dumped garbage in the sea since New York City stopped the practice in 1934.

Ocean pollution is governed by the Marine Protection Reserve and Sanctuary Act of 1972, better known as the *Ocean Dumping Act*. This act requires anyone dumping waste into the ocean to have an EPA permit and to provide proof that the dumped material will not degrade the marine environment or endanger human health. Hazardous substances entering the sea from the land (⁕ Table 15.2) are contained in sewage sludge (the solid part of sewage), dredged materials, industrial effluents, and natural runoff. Sludge and other particulate matter have been found to create a biological imbalance in the ocean in three ways:

TABLE 15.2 Examples of Recognized Seawater Pollutants from Human and Natural Sources

Organic Pollutants	
PCBs	polychlorinated biphenyls
PCDFs	polychlorinated dibenzofurans
PCDDs	polychlorinated dioxins
DDT	chlorinated hydrocarbon pesticide

Inorganic Pollutants	
Cd	cadmium
Pb	lead
Co	cobalt
Hg	mercury
Zn	zinc

* Pollutants originating in sludge, materials dredged from harbors or estuaries, and sewage-treatment and industrial wastewater that are known to pose health hazards.
Source: EPA (adapted).

■ they are consumed by marine life as a food source,

■ they introduce heavy-metal and chlorinated organic compounds when they are attached to the particles, and

■ they inhibit light in the water column.

These findings led to the Ocean Dumping Ban of 1988 that required total cessation of ocean dumping by 1991. Coastal cities that once ocean-dumped were forced to begin dewatering sludge and exporting it as a soil additive or depositing it in landfills. In the west Texas town of Sierra Blanca, instead of "Home on the Range," they now sing "sludge on the range." Two hundred and fifty tons a week of wet sludge is brought to Sierra Blanca to be sprayed on 78,500 acres of the contractor's (Merco) "sludge ranch." As an EPA employee and sludge critic said, "The fish in New York are being protected. The people in New York are being protected. The people of Texas are being poisoned." The feeling is that the odors coming off the application area are not just a nuisance and trespass, they are a health hazard. However, the EPA says the spreading is environmentally safe. Time will tell.

CONSIDER THIS

Incinerating all our waste would go a long way toward solving the landfill capacity problem, and the heat that would be generated could be put to use. Some negative aspects of burning trash must be considered, however. What are they?

Problems of Municipal Waste Isolation

Organic refuse in landfills ultimately decomposes. As it does, the ground surface settles; methane, carbon dioxide, and other gases are generated; and noxious or even toxic leachate from it may seep into the water table or bordering streams. Thus, a landfill's *pollution potential* depends upon the change in volume that accompanies decomposition, the waste's reactivity (which determines the chemistry of the leachate), the local geology, and the climate. Organic matter decomposes more slowly in cold, dry climates than in warm, wet ones.

Stabilization

Landfills continue to settle as decomposition goes on for many decades after burial. Typically, settlement is rapid at first and diminishes to a much slower rate after about ten years (◆Figure 15.7). The rate of subsidence depends upon many factors, including the climate, the kind of waste, and the amount of compaction during filling. Thirty-ton tractors left on a fill over a weekend have been known to settle as much as a meter into the trash, and total settlement of as much as 30 percent has been measured in landfills. Variation

(a)

(b)

◆ FIGURE 15.7 (a) Graph of landfill settlement over time. The percentage of settlement is calculated by dividing the amount of settlement (ΔL) by the original thickness of the landfill (L) and multiplying by 100. The settlement values here are for illustration only and are not real values. (b) Landfill weigh station on the Palos Verdes Peninsula, California, built on trash-filled land. The station eventually collapsed, requiring that a new structure and scale be established at a different location.

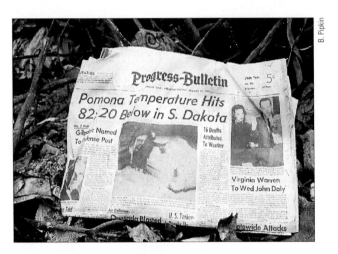

◆ **FIGURE 15.8** Underground newspaper—still readable after at least ten years' burial in a Pomona, California, landfill.

◆ **FIGURE 15.9** Methane-extraction well and drill rig. The extracted gas is conveyed to a central location for conversion to electricity.

is great. A 6-meter-thick landfill in Seattle settled 23 percent in its first year, whereas a 23-meter-thick fill in Los Angeles settled only 1 percent per year in its first three years. Settlement is a problem, because it results in cracks, fissures, and infestation by vermin. It is monitored to ensure that water does not pond and percolate downward, creating a high volume of polluting leachate.

As microorganisms break down organic material (*biodegradation*), they release heat, methane (natural gas), and other gases, including hydrogen sulfide, carbon dioxide, and oxygen. Research at the University of Arizona and elsewhere has shown that biodegradation can be surprisingly slow, as illustrated by exhumed garbage containing virtually unblemished 10- to 20-year-old newspapers (◆Figure 15.8), a 14-year-old mound of recognizable guacamole, and positively ancient hot dogs (testimony to the effectiveness of sausage preservatives). The most efficient decomposers are the voracious oxygen-using aerobic bacteria, such as those that quickly turn grass cuttings into compost for our gardens. Most landfills are sealed off from the atmosphere, however, giving rise to anaerobic (no oxygen) microorganisms that manufacture methane and hydrogen sulfide in the slow process of decomposing cellulose. Pumping air into a fill, a procedure known as **composting,** stimulates aerobes, accelerates decomposition and settlement, and creates more space for trash.

Gas Generation

Methane (CH_4), a gaseous hydrocarbon, is the principal component of natural gas. Also known as *marsh gas,* it bubbles forth from stagnant ponds and swamps, the result of complex chemical fermentation of plant material by bacteria. It is the same gas that causes the explosions in coal mines that have taken innumerable lives. Methane is explosive when present in air at concentrations between 5 and 15 percent. Although enormous volumes of methane are generated by anaerobic

microorganisms in a landfill, there is little danger of the fill exploding because no oxygen is present. Being lighter than air, methane migrates upward in a fill. Methane leaking through the cover of a landfill converted to a golf course near Bel Air, California, was known to "pop" from ignition when cigarettes were dropped on its greens. Methane can also migrate laterally, and it did so several hundred yards into the wall spaces of structures near a landfill south of Los Angeles. Fortunately, the potentially explosive situation was discovered, and wells were drilled to intercept and extract the gas (◆Figure 15.9). One strategy for handling the large volumes of methane generated at large landfills is to extract it through perforated plastic pipes, remove the impurities (mostly CO_2), and use it as fuel—the so-called refuse-derived fuel, *RDF.* This can be accomplished either by piping the gas away via pipelines or by using it on the site to generate electricity. Because the gas may be as much as 50 percent CO_2, it is more expedient to use the fuel directly to generate electricity than to clean out the impurities and put it into pipelines. The Los Angeles County (California) Sanitation District extracts landfill methane and generates sufficient electricity to supply up to 45,000 homes.

Leachate

The compositions of leachates ("garbage juice") in and leaving landfills are highly variable, but they are dangerous to the environment until established otherwise (◆Figure 15.10). A leachate may be such that a receiving body of water can assimilate it without any impairment in water quality. Some purification of a leachate occurs as it filters through clayey soils, and some purification also occurs when contained organic pollutants are oxidized. Groundwater-quality measurements taken in the vicinity of a landfill, at the fill, and downstream from the fill are shown in ✴ Table 15.3. Note that the leachate was causing deterioration of groundwater quality in the vicinity of the monitoring well. To correct this, the leachate must be intercepted by wells or a barrier must be installed between the

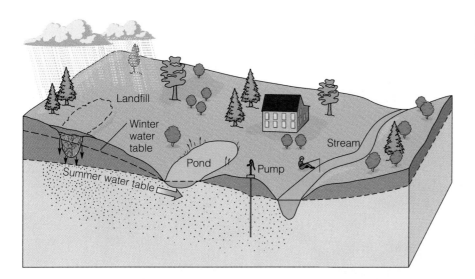

◆ **FIGURE 15.10** The flow of leachate from a landfill can contaminate underground water, ponds, and streams.

leachate and the water table. Under existing regulations, a landfill that is in a geologic setting where leachate threatens local water bodies may accept only inert (Group 3) wastes.

The Completed Landfill

A completed state-of-the-art landfill is illustrated in ◆Figure 15.11. It is designed to collect leachate above the bottom liner and to recover methane for use in power generation. Note the inclusion of leachate- and gas-monitoring wells in the design. Double-lined landfills have been required in the United States since 1996. These landfills are designed to accept waste for 10–40 years, and owners are required to monitor the fills for at least 30 years after closure. If they begin to leak after that period, the contamination problem belongs to whomever is living in the area at the time.

*TABLE 15.3   Groundwater Quality Measured Near One Landfill

Water Characteristics	Measurement Site		
	Local Groundwater	Fill Leachate	Monitoring Well
Total dissolved solids, ppm	636	6,712	1,506
BOD, mg/L	20	1,863	71
Hardness, ppm	570	4,960	820
Sodium content, ppm	30	806	316
Chloride content, ppm	18	1,710	248

*Biological oxygen demand: the amount of oxygen per unit volume of water required for total aerobic decomposition of organic matter by microorganisms.
Source: D. R. Brunner and D. J. Keller, 1992, see For further Information.

Recycling

Resource recovery—the removal of certain materials from the waste "stream" for the purpose of recycling or composting them—not only saves materials, it saves energy. Recycled aluminum cuts energy use 96 percent over processing aluminum ore. For recycled steel the saving is 74 percent, and for copper 87 percent. In 2002, 120 million tons of material were being recycled in the United States, which saved energy equal to 4 months electrical demand. Remanufacturing—the process of disassembling a worn-out product, cleaning and replacing its own parts, then reassembling it—is estimated to save 85 percent of the energy required to make the product new from raw materials. Remanufacturing is estimated worldwide to be equal to the electricity generated by five nuclear power plants, and saves enough raw materials to fill 155,000 railroad cars, forming a train 1,100 miles long. The industrial nations are the "Saudi Arabias" of trash, and all have the same problems—dwindling resources and dwindling space for solid waste.

Until recently, **recycling** held little appeal; that is, it cost more to separate, sort, and recycle trash than to landfill it. Recycling is now mandated in many states, however, because existing landfills are filling, and acceptable sites for new ones are difficult to find. An effective way to extend the lifetimes of landfills and natural resources is to recycle municipal wastes. The consuming public is "thinking green" these days, and manufacturers are realizing favorable marketing results by using recycled materials in packaging their products. Because of a growing awareness that mineral and other resources are finite, recycling increased from 10 percent to 30 percent of municipal waste between 1985 and 2003 (◆Figure 15.12). One indicator of the anticipated value of trash is that glass and high-grade plastics have joined corn and pork bellies as commodities bought and sold on the Chicago Board of Trade. Trash futures?

◆ FIGURE 15.11 State-of-the-art landfills are designed to eliminate the problems of toxic leachate and methane escaping into the environment. Note the double lining (clay and plastic layers) to prevent leakage. Unfortunately, 85 percent of U.S. sanitary landfills are unlined.

◆ FIGURE 15.12 Recycling rates of selected materials recovered from the waste stream for 2003 as a percentage of the total weight recovered. EPA data.

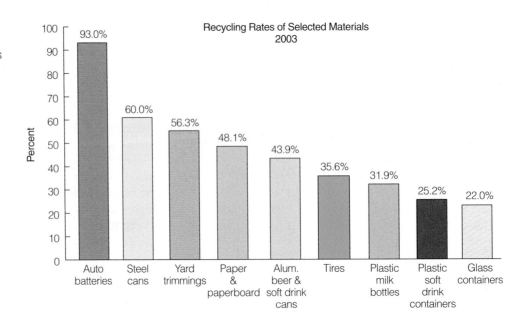

Curbside recycling programs have grown enormously as of 1988. Since then the national recycling rate (including composting) has increased to 30 percent, with hundreds of communities reporting levels above 50 percent and several exceeding 60 percent. Many communities use a "pay as you throw" program, which bases collection charges on the amount of true waste that is added to a landfill; materials sorted out for recycling are collected free of charge. Many communities require separation of glass, metal, paper products, and plastics from other trash materials. Plastic recycling is difficult to handle and expensive, because there are seven kinds of plastic that must be separated by hand. Only 2 percent of waste plastic was recycled in 1995. Ingenuity pays, however. A small Massachusetts company grew into a $1.3 million business by recycling spent plastic ink-jet-printer cartridges. It sells refurbished cartridges to consumers and the worn plastic and metal components to recyclers.

The newest thing entering the waste stream is electronic waste, or "e-waste." Computers, printers, fax machines, and cellular phones have short lives. The National Safety Council estimates that the life span of a cell phone is about 18 months, with PCs being replaced every two years on average. It is estimated that between 1997 and 2007 a half billion computers will be obsolete and become e-waste. And where do the outmoded electronic gadgets and discarded computers end up? Stored by their owners in garages, basements, storerooms or left on the curb to end up as toxic waste in landfills? Because older computer monitors may contain over 100 chemicals, including toxic metals such as cadmium, mercury, and lead, these devices need to be removed from the waste stream.

Because more than 100 million cellular phones and 250 million personal computers are thrown away each year, several computer manufactures such as Dell, HP, Intel, and Apple offer "e-cycling" programs to their customers. Most manufacturers' recycling programs require their customers to buy a new computer in order to recycle the old one free. Most large cities have commercial recycling firms that accept e-waste.

Beginning in 2002 the European Union required European manufactures to pay for the entire cost of e-cycling their products—everything from laptops to stereos to computers. In the United States, grassroots computer-recycling nonprofits, like Free Geek in Portland, Oregon, are springing up. E-cycling is catching on with some more aggressive states, including Maine, California, Minnesota, and Massachusetts, banning such electronics as cathode ray tubes, the bulky picture tubes in older computer monitors and TVs, from landfills for fear that toxic materials could leak into groundwater. By 2009 Washington State will require manufacturers to be responsible for both collecting and recycling their products.

Not easily solvable is the problem of what to do with old automobile tires. There are at least 3 billion used tires stockpiled in the United States, a stockpile that is being added to at a rate of 250 million per year. When placed in landfills they tend to rise in the fill, a fact that caused 33 states to ban them

there. In 2000 the nation used 32 million scrap tires (California alone contributes this many) in civil engineering projects, an increase of 23 percent of 1999. The incidental uses of old tires are construction of small dams, erosion control, houses (New Mexico is the leader), fencing, rifle ranges, playgrounds (◆Figure 15.13), and grain-storage structures. Used tires are being used experimentally as bedding for livestock corrals, as a replacement for stone in septic systems, and as reinforcement in flood-control structures. Because old tires are such an enormous environmental problem, many engineers and scientists are working on a technological "fix" that will rid us of this blight.

As more curbside separation of garbage for recycling is mandated, and as more states enact container-bill legislation encouraging the return of beverage containers, the flow of recyclables increases. The "champion" states (percentage recycled) in the United States are Minnesota (41%), New Jersey (39%), and Washington (35%). Taiwan is the world champion paper recycler; 98 percent of the paper used in that almost treeless country is recycled.

◆ **FIGURE 15.13** Three thousand tires were recycled as children's playground equipment and landscaping material at this park in Japan.

◆ **FIGURE 15.14** Multiple land use, a cycle that can benefit everyone.

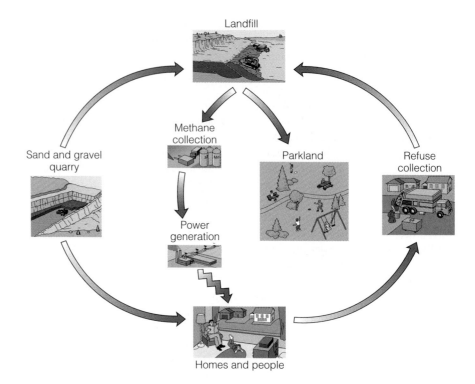

Composting

When decomposed by bacteria, biodegradable wastes, the so-called green garbage, can be used as a fertilizer and soil amendment. Yard cuttings, most kitchen wastes, and organic wastes from commercial operations are acceptable compost material. Because yard wastes are second only to paper in landfill tonnage, many states and municipalities have mandated separate collection for them. As a result, the number of composting facilities in the United States grew dramatically from 651 facilities in 1988 to nearly 4000 in 2006.

CONSIDER   THIS

Composting is a "win–win" process, yet we have barely scratched the surface of its potential. What are the benefits of small-scale and large-scale composting to individuals, cities, and states?

Multiple Land-Use Strategies

Land, like trash, can be recycled. Where the local geology is amenable to it, abandoned rock quarries as well as sand and gravel pits have been converted to sanitary landfills. Population pressure and the need to conserve resources in the twenty-first century will require that we not only dispose of our waste efficiently, but also that we gain some benefit from the stored trash and the disposal site. The average new home requires about 65 cubic meters of concrete in its construction, and its inhabitants will generate about a ton of trash a year. Thus, it *makes sense* to place the household's trash in an opening created to build the house. After a landfill is completed, methane gas can be recovered from it and converted to energy, and the land may be reshaped into a golf course, athletic field, public garden, or the like. An ideal, beneficial cycle of multiple land uses is shown in ◆Figure 15.14.

As explained earlier, structures placed directly on a landfill are subject to settlement and to methane emanations. A restaurant and shops built upon a thin landfill (<8 meters thick) south of Los Angeles were placed on piles driven through the fill to keep them from settling. The walkways around the buildings were not, however, and after a few years they settled and had to be built up to the base of the structures (◆Figure 15.15). In the same commercial development, methane is extracted and used to illuminate exterior gas lanterns.

◆ **FIGURE 15.15** Commercial development built on a landfill. Whereas the buildings are founded on piles through the fill to bedrock, the pavement was placed directly on the fill. The lanterns are fueled by methane from the fill.

As cities expand and coalesce—such as in the New York-to-Boston corridor and the strip between Los Angeles and San Diego—waste-disposal-site selection must become very creative.

CONSIDER THIS

During the past few decades in the United States, recycling waste has evolved from a concept to a major component of waste management for many communities. Why do some environmental groups object to waste-problem solutions that emphasize recycling?

Hazardous Waste Disposal

Hazardous wastes are primarily such industrial products as sludges, solvents, acids, pesticides, PCBs (polychlorinated biphenyls; highly toxic organic fluids used in plastics and electrical insulation), and nuclear waste. The EPA estimates that U.S. industries generate 260 million metric tons of hazardous waste per year. A typical rate at which liquid hazardous waste was generated in the early 1980s was 150 million metric tons per year, which can be thought of as 40 billion gallons. If that amount could be placed in 55-gallon drums placed end to end, they would encircle Earth 16 times (◆Figure 15.16). By 2005 this amount increased almost 30 times. Examples of hazardous wastes that individuals introduce into the environment include drain cleaners, paint products, used crankcase oil, and discarded fingernail polish (not trivial).

Hazardous-Waste Disposal Methods

Secure landfills are designed to totally isolate the received waste from the environment. Wastes are packaged and placed in an underground vault surrounded by a clay barrier, thick plastic liners, and a leachate removal system. Unfortunately, few of the nation's existing 75,000 industrial landfills have plastic liners, clay barriers, or leachate drains. Many older fills will either have to be retrofitted with modern environmental-protection systems or shut down. Additional protection is provided by existing regulations that mandate groundwater monitoring at disposal sites. An ideal secure landfill for hazardous waste would be a site in a dry climate with a very low water table. In humid climates where water tables are high, alternative means of safe disposal must be found.

Deep-well injection into permeable rocks far below freshwater aquifers is another method of isolating toxic and other hazardous liquid substances (◆Figure 15.17). Before such a well is approved, thorough studies of subsurface geology must be made in order to determine the location of faults, the state of rock stresses at depth, and the impact of fluid pressures on the receiving formations (■ Case Study 15.3 on page 467). The injection boreholes are lined with steel casing to prevent the hazardous fluids from leaking into freshwater zones above the injection depth.

Disposal of hazardous wastes, both liquid and solid, is regulated by the Resource Conservation and Recovery Act of 1976 (RCRA). Exempt from the requirements of this act are businesses that generate less than a metric ton of waste per month. According to EPA estimates, about 700,000 of these small firms generate 90 percent of our hazardous waste. Consequently, most of these wastes end up in sanitary landfills.

Discharge into sealed pits is the least expensive way to dispose of large amounts of water containing relatively small amounts of hazardous substances. If the pit is well sealed and evaporation of water equals or exceeds the input of contaminated water, the pit may receive and hold hazardous waste almost indefinitely. Problems can arise from leaky seals and overflow of holding ponds during heavy storms or floods.

Superfund

What about the thousands of old and mostly unrecorded sites where hazardous waste has been dumped improperly in the past? Hazardous substances have been disposed of

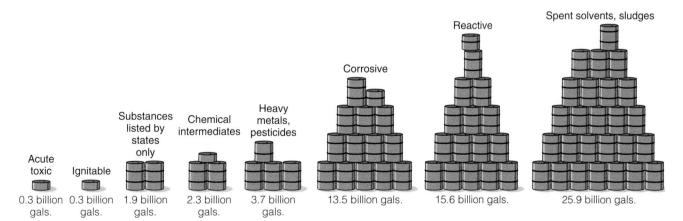

◆ FIGURE 15.16 Breakdown by category of the 40 billion gallons of toxic waste U.S. industries generated in 1981; by 2005 this amount had increased almost 30 times. Note: the total of all categories is greater than 40 billion because of overlap; for example, a fluid may be both corrosive and reactive.

◆ **FIGURE 15.17** Deep-well injection of hazardous waste. This method presumes that wastes injected into strata of porous rock deep within the ground are isolated from the environment forever. What could go wrong? (1) Toxic spills may occur at the ground surface. (2) Corrosion of the casing may allow injected waste to leak into an aquifer. (3) Waste may migrate upward through rock fractures into the groundwater. Data from AIPG

⋆TABLE 15.4	Top Ten States on the National Priority List (Superfund), 2006	
State	Number of Sites
New Jersey	115
Pennsylvania	94
California	93
New York	86
Michigan	66
Florida	49
Washington	47
Illinois	42
Wisconsin	37
Massachusetts	32

Source: EPA Final National Priority List Sites—by State, 2006

CONSIDER THIS

Perhaps no other recent environmental legislation has received as much public attention as the act with the catchy nickname "Superfund." What is Superfund? Who manages it, and what legislation is behind it? From an environmental standpoint, what is its main problem?

indiscriminately since the eighteenth century in the United States. **Superfund,** the Comprehensive Environmental Response, Compensation, and Liability Act (CERCLA), was passed in 1980 to rectify past and present abuses from toxic-waste dumping. It authorizes the EPA to clean up a spill and send the bill to the responsible party. CERCLA also empowered the EPA to establish a National Priorities List (NPL) for cleaning up the worst of the 40,000 identified abandoned toxic and hazardous waste sites now known as *Superfund sites,* some of which date back many decades (■ see Case Study 15.4). By 2006, 1,305 sites had been designated or were pending. New Jersey has the dubious distinction of harboring six of the worst 15 Superfund sites as ranked by impact on the environment—five landfills and one industrial site. ⋆ Table 15.4 lists the top 10 states with Superfund sites.

Although the cost of cleaning them up is staggering, toxic dump sites do not just "go away" on their own. They need to be cleaned up. Some problems with Superfund also need to be cleaned up. The Superfund concept was well intended, but the program has been poorly executed. As a result, 40 percent of its funding has gone to litigation expenses. Superfund has become a "lawyers' money pit," as one journalist put it.

Nuclear Waste Disposal

There is probably no more sensitive and emotional issue in geology today than the need to provide for safe disposal of the tons upon tons of radioactive materials that have accumulated over many decades. These wastes are the largest deterrent to further development of nuclear energy, as they present a legitimate hazard to humans, their offspring, and generations yet to come. Nuclear-waste products must be isolated because they emit high-energy radiation that kills cells, causes cancer and genetic mutations, and causes death to individuals exposed to large doses. The need to develop the means for safe, permanent disposal led Congress to pass the Nuclear Waste Policy Act in 1982 (NWPA). This law gave the Department of Energy (DOE) responsibility for locating a fail-safe underground disposal facility, a **geological repository,** for high-level nuclear waste and designated nine locations in six states as potential sites. Based upon preliminary studies, President Reagan approved three of the sites for intensive scientific study (known as *site characterization*): Hanford, Washington; Deaf Smith County, Texas; and Yucca Mountain, Nevada. In 1987 Congress passed the Nuclear Waste Policy Amendments Act, which directed DOE to study only the Yucca Mountain site (◆Figure 15.18). Yucca Mountain in Nevada finally received approval to store over 70,000 metric tons of high-level nuclear waste, over the objection of and veto by Nevada's Governor Kenny Guinn. In

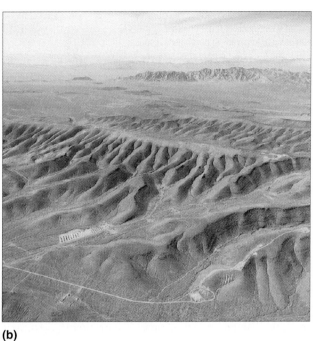

(b)

◆ **FIGURE 15.18** (a) Location of the proposed Yucca Mountain nuclear repository. (b) Aerial view of the Yucca Mountain study area. The structures are at the site of the proposed nuclear-waste repository. DOE data.

(a)

July 2002 the U.S. Senate approved the site, which had received approval overwhelmingly by the House with President Bush's blessing. The DOE had spent over 20 years and $6.7 billion studying various ways and sites at which to store nuclear waste safely. Even if this site passes further legal objections by the State of Nevada, 2010 is the soonest that shipments could be sent there. This site is discussed further later in the chapter.

Types of Nuclear Waste

High-Level Wastes

High-level wastes, by-products of nuclear power generation and military uses, are the most intensely radioactive and dangerous. About once a year, a third of a reactor's fuel rods are removed and replaced with fresh rods. Replacement is necessary because, as the fissionable uranium in a reactor is consumed, the fission products capture more neutrons than the remaining uranium produces. This causes the chain reaction to slow, and eventually it would stop. The radioactive rods, called *spent fuel,* are the major form of high-level nuclear waste. Currently they are stored in water-filled pools at the individual reactor sites, supposedly a temporary measure until a final grave is prepared for them. More than 63,000 MTHM of spent fuel is stored across the country, and at many of the reactors, pool storage capacity is nearly filled (◆Figure 15.19). Quantities of spent nuclear fuel are usually expressed in terms of metric tons of heavy metal (MTHM), mostly uranium. The number does not include other materials such as the tubes that contain the fuel and structural materials. One metric ton is 1,000 kilograms or 2,200 pounds. Two major concerns about pool storage are that an unintended nuclear reaction might start in the pool and that the rods might deteriorate and release fuel pellets. It should be noted that although the fuel removed from a reactor every year weighs about 31,000 kilograms (65,000 lbs), because of its high density, it is only about the size of an automobile.

Alternatively, the rods are chopped up and *reprocessed* to recover unused uranium-235 and plutonium-239. However, the liquid waste remaining after reprocessing contains more than 50 radioactive isotopes, such as strontium (^{90}Sr) and iodine (^{131}I), that pose significant health hazards. In 1992 the Department of Energy (DOE) decided to phase out reprocessing of spent fuel. Unfortunately, the volume of existing reprocessed waste in temporary storage would cover a football field to a depth of 60 meters (200 ft). These wastes are currently stored in metal tanks at four U.S. sites. The oldest site, the one at Hanford, Washington, originally stored wastes in single-walled steel tanks. In 1956 a tank leak was detected, and since then, 750,000 gallons of high-level waste have

◆ **FIGURE 15.19** Location of temporarily stored spent nuclear fuel and other high-level nuclear waste awaiting permanent disposal, 2000. The symbols do not reflect precise locations. DOE data.

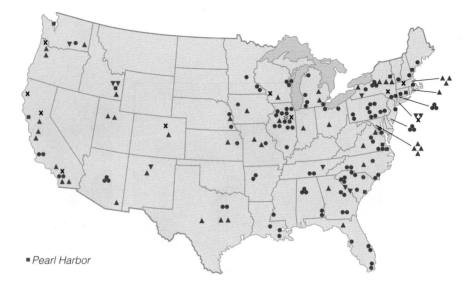

■ *Pearl Harbor*

leaked underground from 60 of 149 storage tanks. It is said by some that "radioactive waste was invented here." Cleanup at Hanford may be the costliest environmental cleanup in world history; the cost has been estimated to be at least $57 billion.

Low-Level Wastes

Low-level waste, by NCR definition, is anything that is not high-level waste or transuranic waste. Low-level wastes are created in research labs, hospitals, and industry as well as in reactors. Ocean dumping of these wastes in 55-gallon drums was a common practice between 1946 and 1970. Since then, shallow land burial has been the preferred disposal method, but many sites have been found to leak.

Mill Tailings

Uranium-mill tailings, the finely ground residue that remains after uranium ore is processed, are typically found in mountainous piles outside the mill facility. Large volumes of tailings exist that still contain low concentrations of radioactive materials, including thorium (^{230}Th) and radium (^{226}Ra), both of which produce radioactive radon gas (^{222}Rn), the so-called hidden killer (■ Case Study 15.5 on page 469). Most of the abandoned tailings piles are in sparsely settled areas of the West. A former Atomic Energy Commission policy permitted the use of uranium-mill tailings in the manufacture of building materials such as concrete blocks and cement. For almost twenty years, 30,000 citizens of Grand Junction, Colorado, lived in homes whose radon levels were up to seven times the maximum allowed for uranium miners. Uranium tailings were used in building materials in Durango, Rifle, and Riverton, Colorado; Lowman, Idaho; Shiprock, New Mexico; and Salt Lake City, Utah.

The Uranium Mill Tailings Radiation Control Act (1978) makes the DOE responsible for 24 inactive sites in 10 states left from uranium operations. The act specifies that the federal government will pay 90 percent of the cleanup cost, with the respective state to pay the remainder. Uranium-mill

tailings could become a serious problem, because they contain the largest volume of radioactive waste in the country.

Isolation of Nuclear Waste

Scientists agree that nuclear waste must be isolated from contact with all biological systems for at least 250,000 years in order for radioactive materials—particularly plutonium-239, whose half-life is 24,000 years—to decay to harmless levels. Should the ban on plutonium recovery be rescinded, the conditions for high-level-waste disposal may change. Several methods of storing wastes have been proposed, but any method must meet these conditions:

- Safe isolation for at least 250,000 years,
- Safe from terrorists or accidental entry,
- Safe from natural disasters (hurricanes, landslides, floods, etc.),
- Noncontaminating to any nearby natural resources,
- Geologically stable site (no volcanic activity, earthquakes, etc.), and
- Fail-safe handling and transport mechanisms.

A number of disposal methods have been proposed. The more serious ones are discussed here.

1. *Continue the present tank storage.* This is not a permanent solution because the tanks have limited lifetimes and leakage has already occurred.

2. *Dispose of waste in a convergent plate boundary (subduction zone).* The feasibility of this very imaginative proposal has not been demonstrated, because the rate of plate movement is very slow.

3. *Place containerized waste on the ice sheets of Antarctica or Greenland.* Radioactive heat would cause the containers to melt downward to the ice-bedrock contact surface, which could place the radioactive waste two miles

beneath ice in either Greenland or Antarctica. This proposal assumes that long-term global warming will not occur in the 250,000-year period. This is unsound, however, because the last ice sheet of the Pleistocene melted back to Greenland in less than 10,000 years.

4. *Geologic repository: salt mines or domes.* Salt is dry, flows readily, and is self-healing. Because it is a good conductor of heat, temperatures in the repository rocks would not become excessive. Salt is subject to underground solution, however, and some hydrated minerals in salt beds give up their water when heated. Salt beds and salt domes occur in geologically stable regions such as Texas, Louisiana, and Mississippi.

5. *Geologic repository: deep chambers in granite, volcanic rocks, or some other very competent, relatively dry rock formation.* This would require detailed site analysis to ensure that all geologic criteria are met.

Yucca Mountain Geologic Repository

The DOE's Civilian Radioactive Waste Management Program has been conducting a site characterization of Yucca Mountain, Nevada, as a high-level-nuclear-waste repository since the early 1980s. This is the site approved by the Congress and president in 2003. The 7-square-kilometer (2.7-mi^2) repository at Yucca Mountain is in pyroclastic rocks (tuffs, some welded, see Chapter 2), and would be placed more than 200 meters (650 ft) below the ground surface. The zone of aeration or vadose zone and the natural system operating there are shown in ◆Figure 15.20. All geologic studies indicate that the proposed repository is an acceptable site, although there are detractors. The DOE delivered its licensing application to the Nuclear Regulatory Commission in late 2004, and the agency is expected to take several years to review the request. The earliest that radioactive waste could find a permanent home at the repository is 2010. In the meantime, high-level nuclear waste will continue to grow and present a hazard to the public.

Waste Isolation Pilot Plant

In 1999 the U.S. Department of Energy (DOE) opened the Waste Isolation Pilot Plant (**WIPP**), the nation's first operating underground repository for defense-generated transuranic waste. Transuranic waste includes tools, residues, clothing, and other such items contaminated with small amounts of radioactive elements, mainly plutonium. These radioactive elements have an atomic number greater than uranium—hence transuranic (beyond uranium)—and are manmade. Located in southeastern New Mexico, near Carlsbad, the site covers 41 square kilometers (16 sq mi). WIPP is a project designed to demonstrate safe, cost-effective, and environmentally sound storage of defense-related radioactive waste. Elsewhere, transuranic wastes are stored at five major DOE sites and 18 other locations across the United States.

The concerns of WIPP are comprehensive, including safe transportation in containers certified by the Nuclear Regulatory Commission in special WIPP trucks driven by highly trained drivers, notification of states and tribal

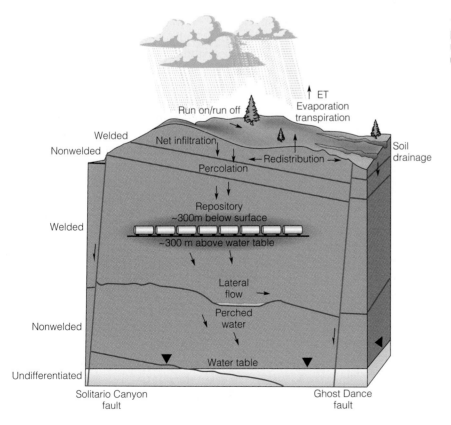

◆ **FIGURE 15.20** Block diagram showing processes acting within proposed vadose (unsaturated) zone repository at Yucca Mountain. Office of Civilian Radioactive Waste Management, 1998.

authorities when materials will be passing through their jurisdictions, and monitoring the location of each shipment by a satellite tracking system while in transit. Oversight of the WIPP program is provided by numerous state and federal agencies and the Environmental Evaluation Group, an independent group that participates in, and comments on, the various WIPP activities.

Storage of the radioactive materials is in excavated rooms 655 meters (2,150 feet—nearly one-half mile) underground in an ancient, stable salt bed. The 610-meter (2,000-ft)-thick salt deposit was chosen as the site because of very little earthquake activity, the absence of flowing water that could move waste to the surface, and because salt readily heals its own fractures due to its plastic character. Furthermore, the salt will slowly flow into and fill the mined areas, safely isolating the waste from the environment.

A system of permanent markers was designed to tell our descendants that the area of the WIPP is not in its natural state, and that it has been marked for good reason. The site must remain inviolate for 10,000 years, and the warning components include a 9-meter-high (30-ft) berm, an information center, monuments along the perimeter, and a summary in six languages printed on archival paper with warnings that it must be preserved for the 10,000-year regulatory period.

Health and Safety Standards for Nuclear Waste

There is general agreement that any nuclear-waste repository will leak radiation over the course of the next 10,000 years. Nuclear waste emits three types of radiation:

1. Alpha (α) particles, the most energetic but least penetrating type of radiation (they can be stopped by a piece of paper). If α emitters are inhaled or ingested, alpha radiation can attack lung and body tissue.

2. Beta (β^-) radiation, penetrating but most harmful when a β^- emitter is inhaled or ingested. For example, strontium-90 is a β^- emitter that behaves exactly like calcium (builds bone) in the food chain.

3. Gamma (γ) rays, nuclear X rays that can penetrate deeply into tissue and damage human organs (◆Figure 15.21).

Nuclear-waste policy limits the radioactivity that may be emitted from a repository, as measured by cancer deaths directly attributable to leaking radiation. The mortality limit is 10 deaths per 100 years, and for this reason the maximum allowable radiation dose per year per individual in the proximity of a repository is set at 25 millirems. The *rem* is the unit used for measuring the amounts of ionizing radiation that affect human tissue, and a millirem (mrem) is 0.001 rem. Doses on the order of 10 rems can cause weakness, redden the skin, and reduce blood-cell counts. A dose of 500 rems would kill half of the people exposed. Rem units take into account the type of radiation—alpha, beta, or gamma—and the amount

◆ **FIGURE 15.21** Penetrating abilities of alpha, beta, and gamma radiation, the three types of radiant energy emitted by nuclear wastes.

of radioactivity deposited in body tissue. ◆Figure 15.22 shows how the average annual dose of 208 mrems is partitioned for U.S. citizens and common sources of radiation. (Case Study 15.5 explains the hazards of high levels of radon gas in the home and methods for testing and mitigating them.) It is estimated that a person living within 5 kilometers (3 mi) of the Yucca Mountain repository would receive less than 1 mrem per year as a result of nuclear waste being stored there (currently no one lives that close to the site). The 25-mrem standard for maximum annual dosage is equal to the radiation a person would receive in 2 or 3 medical X rays.

Is There a Future for Nuclear Energy?

Nuclear reactors are very complex; a typical U.S. reactor may have 40,000 valves, whereas a coal-fired plant of the same size has only 4,000. This fact alone makes reactors relatively unforgiving of errors in operation, construction, or design. A newer generation of "standard" reactors is now under consideration. These use natural forces such as gravity and convection instead of the network of pumps and valves currently required. For example, if the core of one of these new reactors should overheat, a deluge of water stored in tanks above the reactor would inundate the core. In addition, design would be standardized in the new reactors, which would greatly simplify construction, maintenance, and repair.

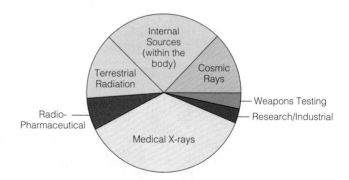

◆ **FIGURE 15.22** The typical American receives 208 millirems of radiation per year from the various sources. Some medical, research, and industrial workers' exposures may exceed the 208-millirem average.
National Academy of Sciences, NRC.

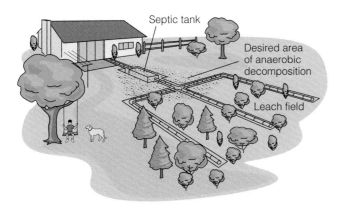

◆ **FIGURE 15.23** A septic tank near the house drains into a leach field of drain tiles that are laid in trenches and covered with filter gravel and soil.

Standardization would also facilitate better operator training and would eliminate the possibility of some human errors.

The ultimate clean nuclear-energy source is released by **fusion,** whereby two nuclei merge to form a heavier nucleus and in the process give off tremendous amounts of heat. Deuterium ($^2_1$H) is a heavy isotope of hydrogen that at very high temperatures fuses to form helium ($^4_2$He). This is the very same nuclear process that energizes our Sun. The fuel is inexhaustible, the reaction cannot run out of control, and it is environmentally nonpolluting.

Private Sewage Disposal

Modern household sewage-disposal systems utilize a septic tank, which separates solids from the effluent, and leach lines, which disseminate the liquids into the surrounding soil or rock (◆Figure 15.23). A septic tank is constructed in such a way that all solid material stays within the tank and only liquid passes on into the leach field. A leach field consists of rows of tile pipe surrounded by a gravel filter through which

the effluent percolates prior to seeping into the soil or underlying rock. Sewage is broken down by *anaerobic* bacteria in the septic tank and the first few feet of the leach lines. As the effluent percolates into the soil or bedrock, it is filtered and oxidized, and aerobic conditions are established. Studies have shown that the movement of effluent through a few feet of unsaturated fine-grained soil under aerobic conditions reduces bacterial counts to almost nil. Fine-grained soils have been found to be the best filters of harmful pathogens, whereas coarse-grained soils allow pathogenic organisms and viruses to disperse over greater distances.

Under the best of conditions, leach lines have a life expectancy of 10–12 years. Factors that reduce infiltration rates and thus limit the life of a septic system are dispersion of clay particles by transfer of sodium ions (Na^+) in sewage to clay particles in the soil, plugging by solids, physical breakdown of the soil by wetting and drying, and biological "plugging." This plugging occurs when the leach system becomes overloaded with sewage and anaerobic conditions invade the leach lines, resulting in a growth of organisms that plug the filter materials.

After passing through the leach field, the effluent must be kept underground until oxidation and bacteria can purify it. The geologic condition that most commonly causes a private sewage-disposal system to fail is a high water table that intersects or is immediately beneath the leach lines (◆Figure 15.24a). This condition initiates the anaerobic growth that plugs filter materials and tile drains. Water tables may rise due to prolonged heavy precipitation or due to the addition of a number of septic tanks in a small area. One way to avoid exceeding the soil's ability to accept effluent is to design leach fields on the basis of percolation tests performed during wet periods. If necessary, a system's lifetime can be extended by constructing multiple leach fields whose use can be rotated regularly by switching a valve. Another problem is the improper placement of leach lines. This results in effluent seepage on hill slopes or stream-valley walls (◆Figure 15.24b). Although

(a)   **(b)**

◆ **FIGURE 15.24** Conditions under which raw effluent can seep into the ground. (a) A drain tile and filter material intersect a high water table. When this occurs sewage rises, and the growth of anaerobic bacteria is promoted in the leach field. This leads to biological plugging of the filter material. (b) A leach line is underlain by low-permeability layers adjacent to a steep slope.

typical plumbing codes specify a minimum of 5 meters (16 ft) horizontal distance from a hill face, this may not be sufficient if the vertical permeability is low and the hill slope is steep.

Nitrates in sewage effluent pose a **eutrophication** problem if households are built near a lake or pond (see Chapter 8). Cultural (human-caused) eutrophication accelerates the process and can convert an attractive, "real-estate" lake into a weed-choked bog in a short time. Nutrients from sewage systems and fertilized lawns must not be allowed to flow unchecked into bodies of water. Solving this problem requires the help of such experts as aquatic biologists and hydrogeologists.

CASE STUDY 15.1

The Sociology of Waste Disposal

The EPA is charged with the Herculean tasks of monitoring existing land and ocean dump sites, approving new hazardouswaste disposal sites, and supervising the cleanup of historic toxic sites and accidental spills and leaks. In carrying out these responsibilities, EPA personnel have encountered the spectrum of political and public attitudes about waste disposal. A wall poster at EPA headquarters in Washington, D.C., provides the following acronyms for those attitudes:

NIMBY	Not In My Back Yard
NIMFYE	Not In My Front Yard Either
PIITBY	Put It In Their Back Yard
NIMEY	Not In My Election Year
NIMTOO	Not In My Term Of Office
LULU	Locally Unavailable Land Use
NOPE	Not On Planet Earth

CASE STUDY 15.2

The Highest Point between Maine and Florida

Fresh Kills landfill on Staten Island, New York, can claim fame for two reasons: it stands 165 meters (500 ft) above seal level, the highest elevation on the eastern shore of the United States, and before closure it was the world's largest landfill, with 25 times the volume of the Great Pyramid of Giza, Egypt (◆ Figure 1). Fresh Kills (Dutch *kil*, "stream") served the five boroughs of New York City, its suburbs, and parts of New Jersey. The fill was established in 1948 on a salt marsh with no provisions for constraining leachate. For over five decades more than 175,000 tons of municipal waste per week ended up at the site, and up to 4.2 million liters (1 million gallons) of leachate leaked into the marsh and nearby waters each day.

Included in the waste stream to the fill was ash residue from the three active trash incinerators operated by New York City. Because the ash contained toxic metals, specially-designed ash-only fill areas were constructed, each with a double liner and a double leachate-collection system to keep toxic substances within the fill. A clay slurry "wall" was excavated around the fill to further confine leachate if there were leaks. Methane was extracted and used for heating and cooking in nearby homes, and construction debris was recycled.

The landfill was scheduled for closure in March, 2001 due to public pressure and the support of the EPA. However, following the attacks

Great Pyramid of Giza   Fresh Kills landfill

(a)

B. Pipkin

(b)

◆ **FIGURE 1** (a) Comparison of the volumes of the Great Pyramid of Giza and the Fresh Kills landfill. (b) The Great Pyramid (right) built by King Cheops at Giza on the west bank of the Nile River in the third century B.C. The length of each side at the base averages 756 feet, and its present height is 451 feet (original height, 481 feet). The smaller pyramid was built by Chephren, a later king. The automobiles give an idea of the immensity of these structures.

on the World Trade Center on September 11, 2001, the landfill was reopened to accommodate disposal of debris from the destruction.

Most of the debris ended up being sold for scrap and recycled, and the site was officially closed in 2003. In 2006 the site was in the process of being converted into a complex of landscaped public parklands and reclaimed marshlands.

Closure of the Fresh Kills landfill and the other five landfills that had reached their capacity in 2001 solved one problem for the city, but created another: how to dispose of thousands of tons of waste per day without landfilling and incineration. The city was left with one option: exportation.

The 8 million residents and thousands of businesses in the city's five boroughs generate 26,000 tons of waste per day (TPD). The New York City Department of Sanitation is responsible for disposal of about 13,000 TPD, the remainder is handled by commercial waste-handling companies. The 13,000 TPD is shipped to facilities out of the city, mostly in Virginia, Pennsylvania and Ohio. The commercial waste-handling companies also export to facilities outside the city. As a consequence of recent state controls on accepting waste from other states, exporting cannot last forever. New technologies for waste disposal that are being investigated by New York City are plasma pyrolysis, which not only destroys the waste but generates energy and by-products that can be sold; and anaerobic digestion (see the reference to the Solid Waste Alternative Technology Team in the For Further Information section.).

◆ **FIGURE 2** Fresh Kills landfill on Staten Island.

CASE STUDY 15.3

Deep-Well Injection and Human-Caused Earthquakes

The U.S. Army's Rocky Mountain Arsenal in suburban Denver drilled a 3,764-meter (2⅓-mi)-deep well for disposing of chemical-warfare wastes in 1961. The Tertiary and Cretaceous sedimentary rocks into which the well was drilled were cased off, and the lower 23 meters (75 ft) were open in Precambrian granite. About 40 kilometers (25 mi) to the west of the arsenal is the frontal fault system of the Rocky Mountains (◆ Figure 1).

Injection began in 1962 at a rate of about 700 cubic meters per day (176,000 g/day). Soon after injection began, numerous earthquakes were felt in the Denver area. The earthquake epicenters lay within 8 kilometers (5 mi) of the arsenal and plotted along a line northwest of the well. A local geologist attributed the quakes to the fluid injection at the arsenal.

◆ **FIGURE 1** Relationship between the Rocky Mountain Arsenal and the Rocky Mountain frontal fault system.

Although the army denied any cause-and-effect relationship, a graph of injection rates versus the number of earthquakes showed an almost direct correlation—especially during the quiet period when fluid injection was stopped (◆ Figure 2).

The fractured granite into which the fluid was being injected was in a stressed condition,

CONTINUED

and the high fluid pressures at the bottom of the hole decreased the frictional resistance on the fracture surfaces. Earthquakes were generated along a fracture propagating northwest of the well as the rocks adjusted to relieve internal stresses.

Thus earthquakes *can* be "triggered" by human activities, and the Denver earthquakes initiated research into the possibility of modifying fault behavior by fluid injection; that is, relieving fault stresses by producing a large number of small earthquakes. Seismic studies conducted during a water-injection (see Chapter 14) program at the nearby Rangely Oil Field confirmed that earthquakes *could* be turned on or off at will, so to speak, in areas of geologic stress. To date no group or government entity has assumed responsibility for triggering earthquakes by fluid injection, for obvious reasons.

◆ **FIGURE 2** Correlation of fluid waste injection and the number of earthquakes per month in the Denver area, 1962–1965.

CASE STUDY 15.4

Love Canal—A Precedent in Human-Caused Environmental Pollution

Love Canal, in the honeymoon city of Niagara Falls, New York, may sound very romantic, but it's not. Excavated by William T. Love in the 1890s but never finished, the canal is 1,000 meters long and 25 meters wide (3,300 ft × 80 ft). Unused and drained, Love Canal was bought by Hooker Chemical and Plastics Corporation in 1942 for use as a waste dump. In the next 11 years Hooker dumped 21,800 tons of toxic waste into the canal, which was believed to be impermeable and thus an ideal "grave" for hazardous substances.

After the canal was filled and covered with a clay cap, Hooker sold it to the Niagara Falls School Board for one dollar. The company inserted in the deed a disclaimer denying legal liability for any injury caused by the wastes. In 1957 Hooker warned the school board not to disturb the clay cap because of the possible danger from leakage of toxic chemicals. A school was built on the landfill, and hundreds of homes and all the infrastructure needed to support a suburban community were built nearby.

In the early 1970s, after several years of heavy rainfall, water leaked through the "impermeable" clay cap and into basements and yards in the Love Canal area, and also into the local sewer system. Soon the new community was experiencing high rates of miscarriages, birth defects, liver cancer, and seizure-inducing diseases among children. Residents complained that toxic chemicals in the water were causing these adverse health effects.

In 1978 the New York State Health Commissioner requested the EPA's assistance in investigating the chemistry of fluids that were leaking into a few houses around the canal. The study revealed the presence of 82 toxic chemicals including benzene, chlorinated hydrocarbons, and dioxin. Five days later then President Carter declared it a federal disaster area, the first human-caused environmental problem to be so designated in the United States. The recommendation that pregnant women and children under the age of two be evacuated from the area followed, and New York State appropriated $22 million to buy the homes and repair the leaks. In all, a thousand families were relocated (◆ Figure 1).

Love Canal was a precedent-setting case, because it spurred Congress to enact CERCLA, which provides federal money for toxic

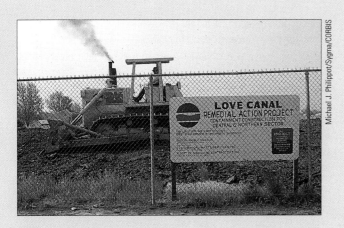

cleanup without long appeals. It also authorizes the EPA to sue polluters for the costs of cleanup and relocation of victims. Although Love Canal has been essentially contained, some chemicals still infect a nearby stream and schoolyard, and maintenance costs amount to a half-million dollars annually. The EPA no longer ranks Love Canal high among the nation's most dangerous waste sites, and the New York State Health Commissioner has announced that recent federal-state studies found four of the seven polluted Love Canal areas to be habitable. In spite of the commissioner's statement, there has been no stampede to reinhabit the area.

After 16 years of litigation, the legal battles over Love Canal ended in 1995. Occidental Chemical Corporation, which purchased Hooker Chemical in 1968, agreed to pay Superfund $102 million, and the Federal Emergency Management Agency (FEMA) agreed to pay $27 million. The State of New York made a $98 million settlement with the EPA in 1994. The cleanup is estimated to have cost $275 million.

◆ **FIGURE 1** Where the honeymoon ended and the nightmares began; Love Canal, Niagara Falls, New York.

CASE STUDY 15.5

Radon and Indoor Air Pollution

Radon (^{222}Rn) is a radioactive gas formed by the natural disintegration of uranium as it transmutes step by radioactive step to form stable lead. The immediate parent element of radon is radium (^{226}Ra), which emits an alpha particle (^{4}He) to form ^{222}Rn. Radon-222 has a half-life of only 3.8 days, but it in turn breaks down into other elements that emit dangerous radionuclides. *Emroation* is sometimes used to describe the behavior of this element, and concern has been growing about the health hazard posed by radon emanating from rocks and soils and seeping into homes. The EPA estimates that between 5,000 and 20,000 people die every year of lung cancer because they have inhaled radon and its decay products.

Radon is a problem only in areas underlain by rocks whose uranium concentrations are greater than 10 ppm—three times the average amount found in granite. For comparison, uranium ore contains more than 1,000 ppm of uranium. As radon disintegrates in the top few meters of rock and soil, it seeps upward into the atmosphere, or into homes through cracks in concrete slabs or around openings in pipes. The measure of radon activity is *picocuries per liter (pCi/L)*—the number of nuclear decays per minute per liter of air. One pCi per liter represents 2.2 potentially cell-damaging disintegrations per minute. In as much as the average human inhales between 7,000 and 12,000 liters (2,000–3,000 gal) of air per day, high radon concentrations in household air can be a significant health hazard.

Cancer due to bombardment of lung tissue by breathing radon-222 or its decay products is a major concern of health scientists. The EPA has established 4 pCi/L as the maximum allowable indoor radon level. This is equivalent to smoking a half-pack of cigarettes per day or having 300 chest X rays in a year. ◆ Figure 1 vividly illustrates the dangers of inhaling indoor radon (and of smoking). Such cancer is rarely apparent before 5–7 years of exposure, and its incidence is rare in individuals under the age of 40.

Widespread interest in radon pollution first appeared in the 1980s with the discovery of high radon levels in houses in Pennsylvania, New Jersey, and New York. The discovery was made accidentally when a nuclear-plant worker set off the radiation monitoring alarm when he arrived at work one day. Since his radioactivity was at a safe level, he did not worry about it. Returning to work after a weekend at home, he once again triggered the alarm. An investigation of his home revealed very high levels of radon. This was the first time radon was recognized as a public health hazard.

There are currently two types of radon "detectors." One is a charcoal canister that is placed in the household air for a week and then returned to the manufacturer for analysis. The other is a plastic-film alpha-track detector that is placed in the home for 2–4 weeks. It is recommended that the less-expensive canister type be used first, and that if a high radon level is indicated, a follow-up measurement with

CONTINUED

pCi/L	Comparable Exposure Level	Comparable Risk *
200	1,000 times average outdoor level	More than 75 times nonsmoker risk of dying from lung cancer
100	100 times average indoor level	4-pack/day smoker 10,000 chest X rays per year
40		30 times nonsmoker risk of dying from lung cancer
20	100 times average outdoor level	2-pack/day smoker
10	10 times average indoor level	1-pack/day smoker
4		3 times nonsmoker risk of dying from lung cancer
2	10 times average outdoor level	200 chest X rays per year
1	Average indoor level	Nonsmoker risk of dying from lung cancer
0.2	Average outdoor level	

* Based on lifetime exposure

◆ **FIGURE 1** Lung cancer risk due to radon exposure, smoking, and X-ray exposure. A few houses have been found with radon radiation levels greater than 100 pCi/L, and one in Pennsylvania had a level of 2,000 pCi/L.

a plastic-film detector be made. Any reading above 4 pCi/L requires follow-up measurements. If the reading is between 20 and 200 pCi/L, one should consider taking measures to reduce radon levels in the home. Common methods are increasing the natural ventilation below the house in the basement or crawlspace, using forced air to circulate subfloor gases, and intercepting radon before it enters the house by installing gravel-packed plastic pipes below the floor slabs. For houses with marginal radon pollution, sealing all openings from beneath the house that go through the floor or the walls is usually effective.

Waste Disposal Then and Now

All humans generate solid waste, and disposing of it has always been a societal challenge. Safely disposing of containers of all kinds, old tires, large and small appliances, and just plain trash presents major problems today. As individuals we must recycle, demand recycled and recyclable containers, and actively assist in reducing the volume of waste (◆Figure 1). Historians point out that Ancient Rome was a filthy city; its cobblestones were noisy, its air was polluted from thousands of wood fires, and municipal sewage disposal was nonexistent. Medieval castles, monasteries, and convents had primitive waste-disposal systems, most of which were unhealthy and emanated noxious odors (◆Figure 2). Conditions are not much better in some parts of rural America today (◆Figure 3). And it should be pointed out that sanitary landfills are not all work and no play (◆Figure 4).

Robert Rathe

◆ **FIGURE 1** Norris McDonald organized a major cleanup of the Anacostia River in Washington D.C., and adjacent Maryland.

Joe Halbig, Univ. of Hawaii-Hilo

◆ **FIGURE 3** An all-too-common method of private sewage disposal in the rural United States.

B. Pipkin

GREAT DRAIN
RIVER WATER WAS CHANNELLED ALONG HERE TO FLUSH AWAY WASTE FROM THE KITCHEN AND TOILETS. LATER IN THE ABBEY'S HISTORY, THE WATER POWERED THE ABBEY MILL AND THIS CHANNEL SERVED AS A MILL – LADE UP UNTIL 1960.

◆ **FIGURE 2** An adjacent stream was diverted to this medieval abbey in Scotland to create what was called a "great drain." All of the abbey's wastes went into the drain, which carried them to the stream, thus polluting its water for downstream users. Little wonder that lifespans were so short in those days; diseases such as cholera, typhoid fever, and dysentery and pestilence caused by the lack of sanitation took their toll. The correlation between stream pollution and disease was not widely recognized until the 1800s.

B. Pipkin

◆ **FIGURE 4** Caterpillar tractor operators play "king of the mountain" at a landfill. The 25-ton "Cats" are used to compact and flatten the debris to reduce its volume.

Summary

Waste Management

Management Components

Geology must be considered in all components:
1. Waste disposal
2. Source reduction
3. Waste recovery
4. Recycling

Rationale

Extending the lifetimes of landfills and natural resources.

Categories of Waste-Disposal Methods

Isolation and attenuation.

Municipal Waste Disposal

Sanitary Landfill

Trash is covered with clean soil each day.

Ocean Dumping

Favored in the past for disposal of sewage, sludge, dredgings, and canistered nuclear wastes. Now regulated by Marine Protection Reserve and Sanctuary Act (Ocean Dumping Act).

Landfill Problems

Leachate, settlement, gas generation, visual blight.

Resource Recovery

Amount of waste delivered to landfills can be reduced through recycling programs, composting, and implementing waste-reduction strategies.

Multiple Land-Use Concept

A mine or quarry becomes a landfill, which when full may be converted to a park or other recreational area. Although some shallow landfills have been built upon, settlement is always a problem.

Hazardous-Waste Disposal

Secure Landfill

Lined with plastic and impermeable clay seal. Built with leachate drains.

Deep-Well Injection

Into dry permeable rock body sealed from aquifers above and below. Has triggered earthquakes in Denver area.

Superfund

Comprehensive Environmental Response, Compensation, and Liability Act (CERCLA) created in 1980 to correct and stop abuses from irresponsible toxic-waste dumping.

Private Sewage Disposal

Requires permeability and porosity and can lead to local pollution.

Radioactive Waste Disposal

High-Level Wastes

High-level nuclear waste from reactors (spent fuel rods), and 63,000 MTHM, is currently kept at individual reactors in pools of water. This is not a good situation. Yucca Mountain as the final geologic respository received approval in early 2003. But licensing by the Nuclear Regulatory Commission will take several years, and it will be at least 2010 before any waste is delivered to the site.

Low-Level Wastes

These are disposed of by shallow burial.

Mill Tailings

There are 24 inactive sites in 10 states, many of which are being cleaned up with the government paying 90 percent of the costs.

Health and Safety Standards

The standard for radiation that a person may receive is 25 mrem per year, about equal to the dosage that a person would receive from 2 or 3 medical X rays.

The Future

There is a future for nuclear energy and it lies in new technology and training.

Key Terms

attenuation (waste disposal)	geological repository	NEPA	secure landfill
composting	high-level wastes	RCRA	Superfund
deep-well injection	isolation (waste disposal)	recycling	waste management
EPA	leachate	resource recovery	WIPP
eutrophication	incineration	radon	
fusion	low-level waste	sanitary landfill	

Study Questions

1. Explain the federal legislation known as NEPA and RCRA and describe their impacts on the environmental safety of landfills.

2. What is leachate, and what methods are used to prevent landfill leachates from entering bodies of water?

3. Explain the "cell" method of placing trash in a landfill.

4. How much solid waste does the average American generate each day in kilograms? In pounds?

5. What problems are associated with operating a sanitary landfill?

6. What resources are found in a landfill, and how can they be recovered? What can individuals do to assist in recovering and extending the lifetimes of certain limited natural resources?

7. Describe two common methods of isolating hazardous wastes from the environment. Explain the steps that are taken to keep these wastes from polluting underground water.

8. What constitutes a good geological repository, and do you think Yucca Mountain is a good choice? (See Figures 15.19 to 15.21 to help you answer this one.)

9. What are some of the health hazards connected with exposure to radiation, and how are dosages measured?

10. Transuranic waste must be contained and remain inviolate for 10,000 years. Is this possible?

For Further Information

Books and Periodicals

Alexander, J. H. 1993. *In defense of garbage*. New York: Praeger.

Barber, D. A. 2002. *Building with tires*. University of Arizona, Report on Research. Tucson: University Publications.

Brown, Lester, and others. 1999. *State of the world*. New York: Worldwatch Institute and W. W. Norton.

Brunner, D. R., and D. K. Keller. 1972. *Sanitary landfill design and operations*. Washington, D.C.: U.S. Environmental Protection Agency.

Crowley, Kevin D., and John F. Ahearne. 2002. Managing the environmental legacy of U.S. nuclear weapons production. *American scientist* 90, November–December.

Environmental Protection Agency. 2006. *2004 toxic release inventory (TRI) public data release report. EPA 260-R-06-00.* Washington, D.C.: U.S. Environmental Protection Agency.

Grove, Noel. 1994. Recycling. *National geographic 186*, no. 1 (July).

Lewin, David. 1991. Solid waste: Bury, burn, or reuse. *Mechanical engineering*, August: 75.

McKinney, Michael. 2003. *Environmental science*. (3rd edition). Boston: Jones and Bartlett.

Miller, G. Tyler. 2004. *Environmental science*. Belmont, California; Thomson-Brooks/Cole.

Rathje, William L. 1991. Once and future landfills. *National geographic*, May: 114–134.

Rathje, William L., and Cullen Murphy. 1992. *Rubbish! The archeology of garbage*. New York: Harper Collins.

Solid Waste Alternative Technology (SWAT) Team. 2004. *Solid waste alternative technologies for New York City's waste disposal*. New York: School of International and Public Affairs, Columbia University.

U.S. Department of Energy, Office of Civilian Radioactive Waste Management. 2002. Final Environmental Impact Statement for a Geologic Repository for the Disposal of Spent Nuclear Fuel and High-Level Radioactive Waste at Yucca Mountain, Nye County, Nevada. DOE/EIS-0250F, February.

U.S. Environmental Protection Agency. 1992. *Characterization of municipal solid waste in the United States: Final report.*

White, Peter T. 1983. The wonderful world of trash. *National geographic*, April.

ThomsonNOW™

Assess your understanding of this chapter's topics with additional comprehensive interactivities at http://www.thomson.com/login, which also has up-to-date web links, additional readings, and exercises.

Periodic Table of the Elements

Noble Gases

Period	IA													IIA	IVA	VA	VIA	VIIA	

Atomic Number — 1
Symbol of Element — H
Atomic Mass — 1.008 (rounded to four significant figures)

Period 1
- 1 **H** 1.008 (IA)
- IIA
- 2 **He** 4.003

Period 2
- 3 **Li** 6.941
- 4 **Be** 9.012
- 5 **B** 10.81
- 6 **C** 12.01
- 7 **N** 14.01
- 8 **O** 16.00
- 9 **F** 19.00
- 10 **Ne** 20.18

Period 3
- 11 **Na** 22.99
- 12 **Mg** 24.31
- IIIB IVB VB VIB VIIB — VIII — IB IIB
- 13 **Al** 26.98
- 14 **Si** 28.09
- 15 **P** 30.97
- 16 **S** 32.06
- 17 **Cl** 35.45
- 18 **Ar** 39.95

Period 4
- 19 **K** 39.10
- 20 **Ca** 40.08
- 21 **Sc** 44.96
- 22 **Ti** 47.90
- 23 **V** 50.94
- 24 **Cr** 52.00
- 25 **Mn** 54.94
- 26 **Fe** 55.85
- 27 **Co** 58.93
- 28 **Ni** 58.71
- 29 **Cu** 63.85
- 30 **Zn** 65.37
- 31 **Ga** 69.72
- 32 **Ge** 72.59
- 33 **As** 74.92
- 34 **Se** 78.96
- 35 **Br** 79.90
- 36 **Kr** 83.80

Period 5
- 37 **Rb** 85.47
- 38 **Sr** 87.62
- 39 **Y** 88.91
- 40 **Zr** 91.22
- 41 **Nb** 92.91
- 42 **Mo** 95.94
- 43 **Tc**^{x} 98.91
- 44 **Ru** 101.1
- 45 **Rh** 102.9
- 46 **Pd** 106.4
- 47 **Ag** 107.9
- 48 **Cd** 112.4
- 49 **In** 114.8
- 50 **Sn** 118.7
- 51 **Sb** 121.8
- 52 **Te** 127.6
- 53 **I** 126.9
- 54 **Xe** 131.3

Period 6
- 55 **Cs** 132.9
- 56 **Ba** 137.3
- 57 **La** 138.9
- 72 **Hf** 178.5
- 73 **Ta** 180.9
- 74 **W** 183.9
- 75 **Re** 186.2
- 76 **Os** 190.2
- 77 **Ir** 192.2
- 78 **Pt** 195.1
- 79 **Au** 197.0
- 80 **Hg** 200.6
- 81 **Tl** 204.4
- 82 **Pb** 207.2
- 83 **Bi** 209.0
- 84 **Po**^{x} (210)
- 85 **At**^{x} (210)
- 86 **Rn**^{x} (222)

Period 7
- 87 **Fr**^{x} (223)
- 88 **Ra**^{x} 226.0
- 89 **Ac**^{x} (227)
- 104 **Unq**^{x} (261)
- 105 **Unp**^{x} (262)
- 106 **Unh**^{x} (263)
- 107 **Uns**^{x} (262)
- 108 **Uno**^{x} (265)
- 109 **Une**^{x} (266)

● Lanthanide series

■ Actinide series

Lanthanide series
- 58 **Ce** 140.1
- 59 **Pr** 140.9
- 60 **Nd** 144.2
- 61 **Pm**^{x} (147)
- 62 **Sm** 150.4
- 63 **Eu** 152.0
- 64 **Gd** 157.3
- 65 **Tb** 158.9
- 66 **Dy** 162.5
- 67 **Ho** 164.9
- 68 **Er** 167.3
- 69 **Tm** 168.9
- 70 **Yb** 173.0
- 71 **Lu** 175.0

Actinide series
- 90 **Th**^{x} 232.0
- 91 **Pa**^{x} 231.0
- 92 **U**^{x} 238.0
- 93 **Np**^{x} 237.0
- 94 **Pu**^{x} (244)
- 95 **Am**^{x} (243)
- 96 **Cm**^{x} (247)
- 97 **Bk**^{x} (247)
- 98 **Cf**^{x} (251)
- 99 **Es**^{x} (254)
- 100 **Fm**^{x} (257)
- 101 **Md**^{x} (258)
- 102 **No**^{x} (255)
- 103 **Lr**^{x} (256)

x: All isotopes are radioactive.

() indicates mass number of isotope with longest known half-life.

Some Important Minerals

Mineral	Chemical Composition	Color	Hardness	Other Characteristics	Primary Rock Occurrence
1. amphibole (e.g., hornblende) (hydrous)	Na, Ca, Mg, Fe, Al silicate	green, blue brown, black	5 to 6	often forms needlelike crystals; two good cleavages forming 60°–120° angle crystals hexagonal in cross section	igneous and metamorphic; minor amounts in all types
2. apatite	$Ca_5(PO_4)_3$ (F, Cl, OH)	blue-green	5	crystals hexagonal in cross section	minor amounts, all types
3. biotite (a mica)	hydrous K, Mg, Fe silicate	brown to black	2½–3	excellent cleavage into thin sheets	all types
4. calcite	$CaCO_3$	variable; colorless if pure	3	effervesces in weak acid	sedimentary and metamorphic
5. dolomite	$CaMg(CO_3)_2$	white or pink	3½ to 4	powdered mineral effervesces in acid	sedimentary
6. galena	PbS	silver-gray	2½	metallic luster; cubic cleavage; heavy	sulfide veins
7. garnet	Ca, Mg, Fe, Al silicate	variable; often dark red	7	glassy luster	metamorphic
8. graphite	C	dark gray	1 to 2	streaks like pencil lead	metamorphic
9. gypsum	$CaSO_4 \cdot 2H2O$	colorless	2	2 directions of cleavage	sedimentary
10. halite	NaCl	colorless	2½	salty taste; cleaves into cubes	sedimentary
11. hematite	Fe_2O_3	red or dark gray	5½ to 6½	red-brown streak regardless of color	oxidation of iron-bearing minerals
12. limonite	$Fe_2O_3 \cdot 3H_2O$	yellow-brown	2 to 3	earthy luster; yellow-brown streak	hydration of iron oxides
13. magnetite	Fe_3O_4	black	6	strongly magnetic	minor amounts, all types
14. muscovite (mica)	K, Al, Si, silicate	colorless to light brown	2 to 2½	excellent basal cleavage	all types
15. olivine	Fe, Mg silicate	yellow-green	6½ to 7	glassy luster	igneous and metamorphic
16. plagioclase feldspar	Na, Ca, Al silicate	white to gray	6	2 cleavages at 90°, striations on cleavage surfaces	all types
17. orthoclase feldspar	K, Al silicate	white; or colored pink or aqua	6	two good cleavages forming 90° angle; no striations	all types
18. pyrite	FeS_2	brassy yellow	6 to 6½	metallic luster; black streak	all types
19. pyroxene (e.g., augite)	Na, Ca, Mg, Fe, Al silicate	usually green or black	5 to 7	two good cleavages forming 90° angle	igneous and metamorphic
20. quartz	SiO_2	variable; commonly colorless or white	7	glassy luster; conchoidal fracture; hexagonal crystals	all types

The Elements

Element	Symbol	Atomic Number	Element	Symbol	Atomic Number
Actinium	Ac	89	Mercury	Hg	80
Aluminum	Al	13	Molybdenum	Mo	42
Americium	Am	95	Neodymium	Nd	60
Antimony	Sb	51	Neon	Ne	10
Argon	Ar	18	Neptunium	Np	93
Arsenic	As	33	Nickel	Ni	28
Astatine	At	85	Niobium	Nb	41
Barium	Ba	56	Nitrogen	N	7
Berkelium	Bk	97	Nobelium	No	102
Beryllium	Be	4	Osmium	Os	76
Bismuth	Bi	83	Oxygen	O	8
Boron	B	5	Palladium	Pd	46
Bromine	Br	35	Phosphorus	P	15
Cadmium	Cd	48	Platinum	Pt	78
Calcium	Ca	20	Plutonium	Pu	94
Californium	Cf	98	Polonium	Po	84
Carbon	C	6	Potassium	K	19
Cerium	Ce	58	Praseodymium	Pr	59
Cesium	Cs	55	Promethium	Pm	61
Chlorine	Cl	17	Protactinium	Pa	91
Chromium	Cr	24	Radium	Ra	88
Cobalt	Co	27	Radon	Rn	86
Copper	Cu	29	Rhenium	Re	75
Curium	Cm	96	Rhodium	Rh	45
Dysprosium	Dy	66	Rubidium	Rb	37
Einsteinium	Es	99	Ruthenium	Ru	44
Erbium	Er	68	Samarium	Sm	62
Europium	Eu	63	Scandium	Sc	21
Fermium	Fm	100	Selenium	Se	34
Fluorine	F	9	Silicon	Si	14
Francium	Fr	87	Silver	Ag	47
Gadolinium	Gd	64	Sodium	Na	11
Gallium	Ga	31	Strontium	Sr	38
Germanium	Ge	32	Sulfur	S	16
Gold	Au	79	Tantalum	Ta	73
Hafnium	Hf	72	Technetium	Tc	43
Helium	He	2	Tellurium	Te	52
Holmium	Ho	67	Terbium	Tb	65
Hydrogen	H	1	Thallium	Tl	81
Indium	In	49	Thorium	Th	90
Iodine	I	53	Thulium	Tm	69
Iridium	Ir	77	Tin	Sn	50
Iron	Fe	26	Titanium	Ti	22
Krypton	Kr	36	Tungsten	W	74
Lanthanum	La	57	Uranium	U	92
Lawrencium	Lr	103	Vanadium	V	23
Lead	Pb	82	Xenon	Xe	54
Lithium	Li	3	Ytterbium	Yb	70
Lutetium	Lu	71	Yttrium	Y	39
Magnesium	Mg	12	Zinc	Zn	30
Manganese	Mn	25	Zirconium	Zr	40
Mendelevium	Md	101			

Planes in Space: Dip and Strike

Geologists describe the orientation of a plane surface by the plane's "strike" and "dip." Geologists measure such tangible planes as those made by sedimentary strata, foliation, and faults, because it allows them to anticipate hazards during excavations for such things as tunnels, dam foundations, and roadcuts. Accurate surface measurements of planes also enable geologists to predict the underground locations of valuable resources such as oil reservoirs, ore deposits, and water-bearing strata.

Strike is the direction of the trace of an inclined plane on the horizontal plane, and the direction is referenced to north. In the illustrated example, the strike is 30° west of north. In geologic notation, this is written *N30° W.*

Dip is the vertical angle that the same inclined plane makes with the horizontal plane. Dip is assessed perpendicular to the strike, because any other angle will give an "apparent dip" that is less than the true dip. Because a plane that strikes northwest may be inclined to either the southwest or the northeast, the general direction of dip must be indicated. In our example, the dip is 60° to the northeast, which is notated *60° NE.*

Thus, a geologist's notes for the bedding planes in this example would describe their orientation as "strike N30° W, dip 60° NE." All other geologists would understand that the plane has a strike that is 30° west of north and a dip that is 60° to the northeast.

Block diagram showing sedimentary rock that is striking N30° W and dipping 60° northeast. The apparent dip is shown on the north–south cross section at the lower front of the diagram.

Modified Mercalli Scale

The Rossi–Forel intensity scale was the first scale developed for evaluating the effects of an earthquake on structures and humans. It was developed in Europe in 1878 and assigned Roman numerals from *I* (for *barely felt*) to *X* (for *total destruction*) for varying levels of intensity. This scale was first modified by Father Giuseppi Mercalli in Italy and later in 1931 by Frank Neumann and Harry O. Wood in the United States. The Modified Mercalli scale is the scale most widely used today for evaluating the effects of earthquakes in the field. An abbreviated version is given here.

I. Not felt except by a very few persons under especially favorable circumstances.

II. Felt by a few persons at rest, especially by persons on upper floors of multistory buildings, and by nervous or sensitive persons on lower floors.

III. Felt quite noticeably indoors, especially on upper floors, but many people do not recognize it as an earthquake; vibrations resemble those made by a passing truck.

IV. Felt indoors by many persons and outdoors by only a few. Dishes, windows, and doors are disturbed, and walls make creaking sounds as though a heavy truck had struck the building. Standing cars are rocked noticeably.

V. Felt by nearly everyone. Many sleeping people are awakened. Some dishes and windows are broken, and some plaster is cracked. Disturbances of trees, poles, and other tall objects may be noticed. Some persons run outdoors.

VI. Felt by all. Many people are frightened and run outdoors. Some heavy furniture is moved, and some plaster and chimneys fall. Damage is slight, but humans are disturbed.

VII. General fright and alarm. Everyone runs outdoors. Damage is negligible in buildings of good design and construction, considerable in those that are poorly built. Noticeable in moving cars.

VIII. General fright approaching panic. Damage is slight in specially designed structures; considerable in ordinary buildings, with partial collapse; great in older or poorly built structures. Chimneys, smokestacks, columns, and walls fall. Sand and mud are ejected from ground openings (liquefaction).

IX. General panic. Damage is considerable in specially designed structures, well-designed frame structures being deformed; great in substantial buildings, with partial collapse. Ground is cracked; underground pipes are broken.

X. General panic. Some well-built wooden structures and most masonry and frame structures are destroyed. Ground is badly cracked; railway rails are bent; underground pipes are torn apart. Considerable landsliding on riverbanks and steep slopes.

XI. General panic. Ground is greatly disturbed, with cracks and landslides common. Sea waves of significant height may be seen. Few if any structures remain standing; bridges are destroyed.

XII. Total panic. Total damage to human engineering works. Waves seen on the ground surface. Lines of sight and level are distorted. Objects are thrown upward into the air.

Glossary

aa A basaltic lava that has a rough, blocky surface.

ablation All processes by which snow or ice is lost from a glacier, floating ice, or snow cover. These processes include melting, evaporation, and calving.

ablation zone The part of a glacier or a snowfield in which ablation exceeds accumulation over a year's time; the region below the firn line.

abrasion The mechanical grinding, scraping, wearing, or rubbing away of rock surfaces by friction or impact. Abrasion agents include wind, running water, waves, and ice.

absolute age dating Assigning units of time, usually years, to fossils, rocks, and geologic features or events. The method utilizes mostly the decay of radioactive elements, but ages may also be obtained by counting tree rings or annual sedimentary layers.

accretion The mechanism by which the earth is believed to have formed from a small nucleus by additions of solid bodies, such as meteorites, asteroids, or planetesimals. Also used in plate tectonics to indicate the addition of terranes to a continent.

accumulation zone The part of a glacier or snowfield in which build-up of snow and ice exceeds ablation over a year's time; the region above the firn line. Also the B-horizon of a soil.

acid mine drainage (AMD) The acid runoff from a mine or mine waste.

acid rain Corrosive precipitation due to the solution of atmospheric sulfuric acid in rain, which makes it acidic. Although it is generally considered human-caused, it can also be natural, as from volcanic activity.

acid rock drainage The natural background of spring or stream runoff from a mineralized rock mass.

active layer The zone in permafrost that is subject to seasonal freezing and thawing.

active sea cliff A cliff whose formation is dominated by wave erosion.

adsorption The attraction of ions or molecules to the surface of particles, in contrast to *absorption,* the process by which a substance is taken into a clay-mineral structure.

aerosol A suspension of very fine, liquid and solid particles in the atmosphere.

alluvial fan A gently sloping, fan-shaped mass of alluvium deposited in arid or semiarid regions where a stream flows from a narrow canyon onto a plain or valley floor.

alluvial placer A placer deposit that is concentrated in a streambed.

alluvium Stream-deposited sediment.

alpha decay The transformation that occurs when the nucleus of an atom spontaneously emits a helium atom, reducing its atomic mass by 4 units and its atomic number by 2; for example, $^{238}_{92}U \rightarrow ^{234}_{90}Th + ^{4}_{2}a$.

amorphous Descriptive term applied to glasses and other substances that lack an orderly internal crystal structure.

andesite line The petrographic boundary between basalts and andesites. It runs roughly around the Pacific basin margin. It also marks the boundary between continental (explosive) and oceanic (Hawaiian-type) volcanoes in the Pacific Ocean.

angle of repose The maximum stable slope angle that granular, cohesionless material can assume. For dry sand this is about 34°.

anomaly A deviation from the average or expected value. In paleomagnetism, a "positive" anomaly is a stronger-than-average magnetic field at the earth's surface.

Anthropocene The informal term given for the period of geologic time in which the human species has been a major player in shaping landscape change on Earth's surface.

anthropogenic Relating to or resulting from the influence of humans on nature.

anticline A generally convex-upward fold that has older rocks in its core. (*Contrast with* syncline.)

aphanitic texture A fine-grained igneous-rock texture resulting from rapid cooling. Aphanites are fine-grained igneous rocks.

A.P.I. gravity (American Petroleum Institute) The weight of crude oil arbitrarily compared to that of water at 60° F, which is assigned a value of 10°. Most crude oils range from 5° to 30° A.P.I.

aquiclude A layer of low-permeability rock that hampers groundwater movement. Often applied to the confining bed in a confined aquifer.

aquifer A water-bearing body of rock or sediment that will yield water to a well or spring in usable quantities.

area mining The mining of coal in flat terrain (strip mining).

arroyo incision Erosional deepening of arroyos, desert gullies that may contain water only a few hours or days a year.

artesian pressure surface An imaginary surface defined by the level to which water will rise in an artesian well.

artificial levee An embankment constructed to contain a stream at flood stage. *See* levee.

ash Very fine, gritty volcanic dust: particles are less than 4 mm in diameter.

ash fall A "rain" of airborne volcanic ash.

asthenosphere The *plastic* layer of the earth, at whose upper boundary the brittle overlying lithosphere is detached from the underlying mantle.

atom The smallest particle of an element that can exist either alone or in combination with similar particles of the same or a different element.

atomic mass The sum of the number of protons and neutrons (uncharged particles) in the nucleus of an atom.

atomic number The number of protons (positively-charged particles) in an atomic nucleus. Atoms with the same atomic number belong to the same chemical element.

attenuation (waste disposal) To dilute or spread out the waste material.

average crustal abundance The percentage of a particular element in the composition of the earth's crust.

a-zone The upper soil horizon (topsoil) capped by a layer of organic matter. It is the zone of leaching of soluble soil salts.

back slope The gentler slope of a dune, scarp, or fault block.

ball mill A large rotating drum containing steel balls that grinds ore to a fine powder. Batteries of ball mills are used in modern milling operations.

banded-iron formation An iron deposit consisting essentially of iron oxides and chert occurring in prominent layers or bands of brown or red and black.

barchan dune An isolated, moving, crescent-shaped sand dune lying transverse to the direction of the prevailing wind. A gently sloping, convex side faces the wind, and the horns of the crescent point downwind.

barrier beach (barrier island) A narrow sand ridge rising slightly above hightide level that is oriented generally parallel with the coast and separated from the coast by a lagoon or a tidal marsh.

basalt A dark-colored, fine-grained volcanic rock that is commonly called *lava*. Basaltic lavas are quite fluid.

base isolation Building design option using a movable base under the building that allows the ground to move but minimizes building vibration and sway.

base level The level below which a stream cannot erode its bed. The ultimate base level is sea level.

base shear Due to a rapid horizontal ground acceleration during an earthquake. It can cause a building to part from its foundation, thus the term.

batholith A large, discordant intrusive body greater than 100 km² (40 mi²) in surface area with no known bottom. Batholiths are granitic in composition.

bauxite An off-white, grayish, brown, or reddish brown rock composed of a mixture of various hydrous aluminum oxides and aluminum hydroxides.

beach cusps A series of regularly spaced points of beach sand or gravel separated by crescent-shaped troughs.

bedding *See* stratification.

bedding planes The divisions or surfaces that separate successive layers of sedimentary rocks from the layers above and below them.

bench placer Remnant of an ancient alluvial placer deposit that was concentrated beneath a former stream and that is now preserved as a bench on a hillside.

Benioff–Wadati zone A zone of earthquake epicenters beneath oceanic trenches that extends from near the surface to a depth of 700 km (430 mi). The zone is named after Hugo Benioff and is thought to indicate active subduction.

bentonite A soft, plastic, light-colored clay that swells to many times its volume when placed in water. Named for outcrops near Fort Benton, Wyoming, bentonite is formed by chemical alteration of volcanic ash.

beta decay The radioactive emission of a nuclear electron (beta ray, ß⁻) that converts a neutron to a proton. The element is changed to the element of next-highest atomic number; for example, $^{14}_{6}C \rightarrow ^{14}_{7}N + ß^{-}$.

biodiesel A diesel-fuel equivalent derived from plant or animal sources.

biogenic sedimentary rock Rocks resulting directly from the activities of living organisms, such as a coral reef, shell limestone, or coal.

biological oxygen demand (B.O.D.) Indicator of organic pollutants (microbial) in an effluent measured as the amount of oxygen required to support them. The greater the B.O.D. (ppm or mg/liter) the greater the pollution and less oxygen available for higher aquatic organisms.

biomass fuels Fuels that are manufactured from plant materials; for example, grain alcohol (ethanol) is made from corn.

bioremediation Use of bacteria to degrade petroleum-based pollutants. Used primarily for remediating soil contamination.

black smoker A submarine hydrothermal vent associated with a mid-oceanic spreading center that has emitted or is emitting a "smoke" of metallic sulfide particles.

block (volcanology) A mass of cold country rock greater than 32 mm (1¼ in) in size that is ripped from the vent and ejected from a volcano.

block glide (translational slide) A landslide in which movement occurs along a well-defined plane surface or surfaces, such as bedding planes, foliation planes, or faults.

body wave Earthquake waves that travel through the body of the earth.

bolide A large meteor that explodes as it passes through the earth's atmosphere.

bomb (volcanology) A molten mass greater than 32 mm (1¼ in) in diameter that is ejected from a volcano and cools sufficiently before striking the ground to retain a rounded, streamlined shape.

boreal The northern and mountainous regions of the Northern Hemisphere in which the average temperature of the hottest season does not exceed 18° C (64.4° F).

breakwater An offshore rock or concrete structure, attached at one end or parallel to the shoreline, intended to create quiet water for boat anchorage purposes.

breeder reactor A reactor that produces more fissile (splittable) nuclei than it consumes.

British thermal unit (Btu) The amount of heat, in calories, needed to raise the temperature of 1 pound of water 1° F.

caldera Large crater caused by explosive eruption and/or subsidence of the cone into the magma chamber, usually more than 1.5 km (1 mi) in diameter.

caliche In arid regions, a sediment or soil that is cemented by calcium carbonate ($CaCO_3$).

calving The breaking away of a block of ice, usually from the front of a tidewater glacier, that produces an iceberg.

caprock An impermeable stratum that caps an oil reservoir and prevents oil and gas from escaping to the ground surface.

capillary fringe The moist zone in an aquifer above the water table. The water is held in it by capillary action.

capillary water Water that is held in tiny openings in rock or soil by capillary forces.

carrying capacity The number of creatures a given tract of land can adequately support with food, water, and other necessities of life.

CERCLA The Comprehensive Environmental Response, Compensation and Liability Act of 1980. *See* Superfund.

chain reaction A self-sustaining nuclear reaction that occurs when atomic nuclei undergo fission. Free neutrons are released that split other nuclei, causing more fissions and the release of more neutrons, which split other nuclei, and so on.

chemical sedimentary rock Rock resulting from precipitation of chemical compounds from a water solution. *See* evaporite.

chlorofluorocarbons (CFCs) A group of compounds that, on escape to the atmosphere, break down, releasing chlorine atoms that destroy ozone molecules; for example, Freon, which is widely used in refrigeration, air-conditioning, and formerly was a propellant in aerosol-spray cans.

cinder cone A small, straight-sided volcanic cone consisting mostly of pyroclastic material (usually basaltic).

cinders Glassy and vesicular (containing gas holes) volcanic fragments, only a few centimeters across, that are thrown from a volcano.

clastic Describing rock or sediment composed primarily of detritus of preexisting rocks or minerals.

clastic sedimentary rock Rock composed of fragments of minerals or other rock materials.

clay minerals Hydrous aluminum silicates that have a layered atomic structure. They are very fine grained and become plastic (moldable) when wet. Most belong to one of three clay groups: kaolinite, illite, and smectite, the last of which are expansive when they absorb water between layers.

claypan A dense, relatively impervious subsoil layer that owes its character to a high clay-mineral content due to concentration by downward-percolating waters.

cleavage The breaking of minerals along certain crystallographic planes of weakness that reflects their internal structure.

climate controls The relatively constant factors that dictate a region's climate.

climax avalanche Deep, thick avalanches that tend to occur in late spring when the snowpack has warmed and weakened.

coal-bed gas Methane gas obtained by drilling into coal beds.

coastal desert A desert on the western edge of continents in tropical latitudes; for example, near the Tropic of Capricorn or Cancer. The daily and annual temperature fluctuations are much less than in inland tropical deserts.

cohesion The tendency of a material to stick to itself; the strength a material has when no normal force is applied.

columnar jointing Vertically oriented polygonal columns in a solid lava flow or shallow intrusion formed by contraction upon cooling. They are usually formed in basaltic lavas.

compaction The reduction in bulk volume of fine-grained sediments due to increased overburden weight or to tighter packing of grains. Clay is more compressible than sand and therefore compacts more.

complex landslide When both rotational and translational sliding are found within one landslide mass.

compound growth equation An equation quantifying how rapidly a certain quantity will grow at a fixed rate of increase (given, for example, as a percentage per year).

composting Bacterial recycling of organic material.

concentrate Enriched ore, often obtained by flotation, produced at a mill.

concentration factor The enrichment of a deposit of an element, expressed as the ratio of the element's abundance in the deposit to its average crustal abundance.

cone of depression The cone shape formed by the water table around a pumping well when pumping exceeds the flow of water to the well.

confined aquifer A water-bearing formation bounded above and below by impermeable beds or beds of distinctly lower permeability.

contact metamorphism A change in the mineral composition of rocks in contact with an invading magma from which fluid constituents are carried out to combine with some of the country-rock constituents to form a new suite of minerals.

continental drift The term applied by American geologists to Wegener's hypothesis of long-distance horizontal movement of continents he called "continental displacement."

contour mining The mining of coal by cutting into and following the coal seam around the perimeter of the hill.

convection The circulatory movement within a body of nonuniformly heated fluid. Warmer material rises in the center, and cooler material sinks at the outer boundaries. It has been proposed as the mechanism of plate motion in plate tectonic theory.

convergent boundary Tectonic boundary where two plates collide. Where a tectonic plate sinks beneath another plate and is destroyed, this boundary is known as a *subduction zone*. Subduction zones are marked by deep-focus seismic activity, strong earthquakes, and violent volcanic eruptions.

core Center of the earth, consisting of dense, metallic, iron-rich material.

Coriolis effect A condition peculiar to motion on a rotating body such as the Earth. It appears to deflect moving objects in the Northern Hemisphere to the right and objects in the Southern Hemisphere to the left, to an observer on the rotating body.

craton A part of the earth's continental crust that has attained stability—that has not been deformed for a long period of time. The term is restricted to continents and includes their most stable areas, the continental shields.

creep (soil) The imperceptibly slow downslope movement of rock and soil particles by gravity.

cross-bedding Arrangement of strata, greater than 1 cm thick, inclined at an angle to the main stratification.

crust A thin "skin" of aluminum and alkali-rich silicate rocks that surrounds the earth's mantle; it is still evolving.

crystal settling In a magma, the sinking of crystals because of their greater density, sometimes aided by magmatic convection. (*See* gravity separation).

cubic feet per second (cfs) Unit of water flow or stream discharge. One cubic foot per second is 7.48 gallons passing a given point in one second.

cutoff A new channel that is formed when a stream cuts through a very tight meander. (*See* oxbow lake).

cyanide heap leaching A process of using cyanide to dissolve and recover gold and silver from ore.

c-zone Soil zone of weathered parent material leading downward to fresh bedrock.

Darcy's Law A derived formula for the flow of fluids in a porous medium.

debris avalanche A sudden, rapid movement of a water–soil–rock mixture down a steep slope.

debris flow A moving mass of a water, soil, and rock mixture. More than half of the soil and rock particles are coarser than sand, and the mass has the consistency of wet concrete.

deep-well injection A liquid waste disposal process that pumps liquids hundreds of feet underground into aquifers that have no potential to contaminate potential or existing potential potable water aquifers.

deflation The lifting and removal of loose, dry, fine-grained particles by the action of wind.

delta The nearly flat land formed where a stream empties into a body of standing water, such as a lake or the ocean.

desert An arid region of low rainfall, usually less than 25 cm (10 in) annually, and of high evaporation or extreme cold. Deserts are generally unsuited for human occupation under natural conditions.

desert pavement An interlocking cobble mosaic that remains on the earth surface in a dry region after winds have removed all fine-grained sediments.

desertification The process by which semiarid grasslands are converted to desert.

detrital *See* clastic.

dip The angle that an inclined geological planar surface (sedimentary bedding plane, fault, joint) makes with the horizontal plane.

discharge (Q) The volume of water, usually expressed in cfs, that passes a given point within a given period of time.

disseminated deposit A mineral deposit, especially of a metal, in which the minerals occur as scattered particles in the rock, but in sufficient quantity to make the deposit a commercially worthwhile ore.

divergent boundary Found at mid-ocean ridge or spreading center where new crust is created as plates move apart. For this reason they are sometimes referred to as *constructive* boundaries and are the sites of weak shallow-focus earthquakes and volcanic action.

doldrums The area of warm rising air, calm winds, and heavy precipitation between 5° north latitude and 5° south latitude. It is where the northeast and southeast tradewinds meet.

doubling time The number of years required for a population to double in size.

drainage basin The tract of land that contributes water to a particular stream, lake, reservoir, or other body of surface water.

drainage divide The boundary between two drainage basins.

drawdown The lowering of the water table immediately adjacent to a pumping well.

dredging The excavation of earth material from the bottom of a body of water by a floating barge or raft equipped to scoop up, discharge by conveyors, and process or transport materials.

drift A general term for all rock material that is transported and deposited by a glacier or by running water emanating from a glacier.

driving force (landslide) Gravity.

dry snow zone The area of a snow field that is rarely warm enough for snow to melt.

dune A mound, bank, ridge, or hill of loose, windblown granular material (generally sand), either bare or covered with vegetation. It is capable of movement, but maintains its characteristic shape.

Dust Veil Index (DVI) A measure of the impact of a volcanic eruption on incoming solar radiation and climate.

eccentricity The deviation of the Earth's path around the sun from a perfect circle.

ecological overshoot The condition in which a population of organisms reaches a level above and beyond the capacity of needed natural resources to support it.

effective stress The average normal force per unit area (stress) that is transmitted directly across grain-to-grain boundaries in a sediment or rock mass.

elastic Said of a body in which strains are totally recoverable, as in a rubber band. (*Contrast with* plastic).

elastic rebound theory The theory that movement along a fault and the resulting seismicity is the result of an abrupt release of stored elastic strain energy between two rock masses on either side of the fault.

element A substance that cannot be separated into different substances by usual chemical means.

end moraine (terminal moraine) A moraine that is produced at the front of an actively flowing glacier; a moraine that has been deposited at the lower end of a glacier.

engineering geology The application of the science of geology to human engineering works.

ENSO Abbreviation for the periodic meteorological event known as El Niño–Southern Oscillation.

environmental geology The relationship between humans and their geological environment.

eolian Of, produced by, or carried by wind.

EPA The Environmental Protection Agency.

epicenter The point at the surface of earth directly above the focus of an earthquake.

erosion The weathering and transportation of the materials of the earth's surface.

erratic A rock fragment that has been carried by glacial ice or floating ice and deposited when the ice melted at some distance from the outcrop from which it was derived.

esker A long sinuous ridge winding across a landscape that has been formed by sediment deposited on the bed of a subglacial or englacial river that flowed in ice tunnels in or beneath a retreating glacier.

estuary A semienclosed coastal body where outflowing river water meets tidal sea water.

ethanol A colorless liquid chemical compound commonly called grain alcohol with the formula CH_3CH_2OH.

eutrophication The increase in nitrogen, phosphorous, and other plant nutrients in the aging of an aquatic system. Blooms of algae develop, preventing light penetration and causing reduction of oxygen needed in a healthy system.

evaporite A nonclastic sedimentary rock composed primarily of minerals produced when a saline solution becomes concentrated by evaporation of the water; especially a deposit of salt that precipitated from a restricted or enclosed body of sea water or from the water of a salt lake.

evapotranspiration That portion of precipitation that is returned to the air through evaporation and transpiration, the latter being the escape of water from the leaves of plants.

exfoliation The process whereby slabs of rock bounded by sheet joints peel off the host rock, usually a granite or sandstone.

exfoliation dome A large rounded dome resulting from exfoliation; e.g., Half Dome in Yosemite National Park.

exotic terranes Fault-bounded bodies of rock that have been transported some distance from their place of origin and that are unrelated to adjacent rock bodies or terranes.

expansive soils Clayey soils that expand when they absorb water and shrink when they dry out.

extrusive rocks Igneous rocks that formed at or near the surface of the earth. Because they cooled rapidly, they generally have an *aphanitic* texture.

factor of safety The balance between driving and resisting forces in a landslide. Failure occurs when the factor of safety is less than one.

fault Fracture in the earth along which there has been displacement.

fault creep (tectonic) The gradual slip or motion along a fault without an earthquake.

felsic Descriptive of magma or rock with abundant light-colored minerals and a high silica content. The term is derived from *fel*dspar + *si*lica + *c*.

fetch The unobstructed stretch of sea over which the wind blows to create wind waves.

fiord (fjord) A narrow, steep-walled inlet of the sea between cliffs or steep slopes, formed by the passage of a glacier. A drowned glacial valley.

firn A transitional material between snow and glacial ice, being older and denser than snow, but not yet transformed into glacial ice. Snow becomes firn after surviving one summer melt season; firn becomes ice when its permeability to liquid water becomes zero.

fissile isotopes Isotopes with nuclei that are capable of being split into other elements (*see* fission).

fission The rupture of the nucleus of an element into lighter elements (fission products) and free neutrons spontaneously or by absorption of a neutron.

fjord *See* fiord.

flood frequency The average time interval between floods that are equal to or greater than a specified discharge.

floodplain The portion of a river valley adjacent to the channel that is built of sediments deposited during times when the river overflows its banks at flood stage.

floodwall A heavily reinforced wall designed to contain a stream at flood stage.

floodway Floodplain area under federal regulation for flood insurance purposes.

flotation The process of concentrating minerals with distinct non-wettable properties by floating them in liquids containing soapy frothing agents such as pine oil.

fluidization The process whereby granular solids (corn, wheat, volcanic ash and lapilli) under high gas pressures become fluid-like and flow downslope or can be pumped.

fluvial Pertaining to rivers.

focus (hypocenter) Point within the earth where an earthquake originates.

foliation The planar or wavy structure that results from the flattened growth of minerals in a metamorphic rock.

forecast Evaluation of the probability of an earthquake occurring during a given time period.

foreshore slope The zone of a beach that is regularly covered and uncovered by the tide.

fossil fuels Coal, oil, natural gas, and all other solid or liquid hydrocarbon fuels.

fracture Break in a rock caused by tensional, compressional, or shearing forces (*see also* joints).

frictional strength The strength of a material that is proportional to the normal force applied

frost wedging The opening of joints and cracks by the freezing and thawing of water.

fusion The combination of two nuclei to form a single heavier nucleus accompanied by a loss of some mass that is converted to heat.

Gaia The controversial hypothesis that proposes that life has a controlling influence on the oceans and atmosphere. It states that the earth is a giant self-regulating body with close connections between living and nonliving components.

gaining stream A stream that receives water from the zone of saturation.

geologic agents All geologic processes—for example, wind, running water, glaciers, waves, mass wasting—that erode, move, and deposit earth materials.

geological repository (nuclear waste) An underground vault in terrane area free from geologic hazards. Repositories in salt mines, granite, and welded tuff have been studied.

geothermal energy Energy derived from circulating hot water and steam; usually associated with cooling magma or hot rocks.

gigawatt (GW) A thousand million (a billion) watts; 1,000 megawatts.

glacial outwash Deposits of stratified sand, gravel, and silt that have been removed from a glacier by meltwater streams.

glacier A large mass of ice formed, at least in part, on land by the compaction and recrystallization of snow. It moves slowly downslope by creep or outward in all directions due to the stress of its weight, and it survives from year to year.

global warming The general term for the steady rise in the average global temperatures over the last 100 years.

Gondwana succession The fossil assemblage used by Alfred Wegener and others to discern the past existence of southern Pangaea.

GPS Global Positioning System, a navigational system of coded satellite signals that can be processed in a GPS electronic receiver, enabling the receiver to compute position, elevation, and velocity.

graben An elongate flat-floored valley bounded by faults on each side.

graded stream A stream that is in equilibrium, showing a balance of erosion, transporting capacity, and material supplied to it. Graded streams have a smooth profile.

gradient (stream) The slope of a streambed usually expressed as the amount of drop per horizontal distance in meters per kilometer (m/km) or in feet per mile (ft/mi).

granular material A material with no cohesion between grains.

gravity separation *See* crystal settling.

greenhouse effect The warming of the atmosphere by an increase in the amount of certain gases in the atmosphere, primarily CO_2, CH_4 and H_2O, that increase the retention of heat that has been radiated by the earth.

greenhouse gases *see* greenhouse effect.

groin A structure of rock, wood, or concrete built roughly perpendicular to a beach to trap sand.

ground water That part of subsurface water that is in the zone of saturation (below the water table).

gullying The cutting of channels into the landscape by running water. When extreme, it renders farmland useless.

half-life The period of time during which one-half of a given number of atoms of a radioactive element or isotope will disintegrate.

hard rock (a) A term loosely used for an igneous or metamorphic rock, as distinguished from a sedimentary rock. (b) In mining, a rock that requires drilling and blasting for economical removal.

hardpan Impervious layer just below the land surface produced by calcium carbonate ($CaCO_3$) in the B horizon (*see* claypan).

high-grade deposit A mineral deposit with a high concentration of a desired element.

high-level nuclear waste Mostly radioactive elements in spent fuel with long half lives.

horse latitudes Oceanic regions in the *subtropical highs* about 30° north and south of the equator that are characterized by light winds or calms, heat, and dryness.

hot spot A point (or area) on the lithosphere over a plume of lava rising from the mantle.

human carrying capacity The size of human population that can be indefinitely supported by essential natural resources.

hydration A process whereby anhydrous minerals combine with water.

hydraulic conductivity A ground-water unit expressed as the volume of water that will move in a unit of time through a unit of area measured perpendicular to the flow direction. Commonly called permeability, it is expressed as the particular aquifer's $m^3/day/m^2$ (or m/day) or $ft^3/day/ft^2$ (or ft/day).

hydraulic gradient The slope or vertical change (ft/ft or m/m) in water-pressure head with horizontal distance in an aquifer.

hydraulic mining, hydraulicking A mining technique by which high-pressure jets of water are used to dislodge unconsolidated rock or sediment so that it can be processed.

hydrocarbon One of the many chemical compounds solely of hydrogen and carbon atoms; may be solid, liquid, or gaseous.

hydrocompaction The compaction of dry, low-density soils due to the heavy application of water.

hydrogeologist A person who studies the geology and management of underground and related aspects of surface waters.

hydrograph A graph of the stage (height), discharge, velocity, or some other characteristic of a body of water over time.

hydrologic cycle (water cycle) The constant circulation of water from the sea to the atmosphere, to the land, and eventually back to the sea. The cycle is driven by solar energy.

hydrology The study of liquid and solid water on, under, and above the earth's surface, including economic and environmental aspects.

hydrolysis The chemical reaction between hydrogen ions in water with a mineral, commonly a silicate, usually forming clay minerals.

hydrothermal Of or pertaining to heated water, the action of heated water, or a product of the action of heated water—such as a mineral deposit that precipitated from a hot aqueous solution.

hypocenter See focus.

hypothesis A scientifically reasonable idea that requires further testing or observations to verify as a theory or fact.

ice crusts Ice layer on top or within a snow pack.

igneous rocks Rocks that crystallize from molten material at the surface of the earth (volcanic) or within the earth (plutonic).

illuviation Movement of clay through a soil profile by the action of water.

inactive sea cliff A cliff whose erosion is dominated by subaerial processes rather than wave action.

Incineration A waste treatment process that involves the combustion of waste at high temperatures and converts the waste into heat (that can be used to generate electricity), emits gases to the atmosphere, and makes residual ash.

indicated reserves The hydrocarbons that can only be recovered by secondary recovery techniques such as fluid injection. These reserves are in addition to the reserves directly recoverable from a known reservoir.

intensity scale An earthquake rating scale (I–XII) based upon subjective reports of human reactions to ground shaking and upon the damage caused by an earthquake.

Intertropical Convergence Zone (ITCZ) *see* doldrums.

intrusive rocks Igneous rocks that have "intruded" into the crust, hence they are slowly cooled and generally have phaneritic texture.

inundation Flooding by water.

ion An atom with a positive or negative electrical charge because it has gained or lost one or more electrons.

IPAT equation A relationship describing how human environmental impact is a result of population, affluence, and choice of technology.

isolation (waste disposal) Buried or otherwise sequestered waste.

isoseismals Lines on a map that enclose areas of equal earthquake shaking based upon an intensity scale.

isostatic rebound Uplift of the crust of the earth that results from unloading such as results from the melting of ice sheets.

isotope One of two or more forms of an element that have the same atomic number but different atomic masses.

J-curve The shape of a graphing of geometric (exponential) growth. Growth is slow at first, and the rate of growth increases with time.

jetties Structures built perpendicular to the shoreline to improve harbor inlets or river outlets.

joint Separation or parting in a rock that has not been displaced. Joints usually occur in groups ("sets"), the members of a set having a common orientation.

karst topography, karst terrane Area underlain by soluble limestone or dolomite and riddled with caves, caverns, sinkholes, lakes, and disappearing streams.

kerogen A carbonaceous residue in sediments that has survived bacterial metabolism. It consists of large molecules from which hydrocarbons and other compounds are released on heating.

kettle A bowl-shaped depression without surface drainage in glacial-drift deposits, often containing a lake, believed to have formed by the melting of a large detached block of stagnant ice left behind by a retreating glacier.

Kyoto Protocol 1997 agreement by which participating countries would reduce CO_2 emissions.

lahar A debris flow or mudflow consisting of volcanic material.

landslide The downslope movement of rock and/or soil as a semi-coherent mass on a discrete slide surface or plane (*see also* mass wasting).

lapilli (cinders) Fragments only a few centimeters in size that are ejected from a volcano.

lateral spreading The horizontal movement on nearly level slopes of soil and mineral particles due to liquefaction of quick clays.

laterite A highly weathered brick-red soil characteristic of tropical and subtropical rainy climates. Laterites are rich in oxides or iron and aluminum and have some clay minerals and silica. Bauxite is an Al-rich deposit of a similar origin.

lava Molten material at the surface of the earth.

lava dome (volcanic dome) Steep-sided protrusion of viscous, glassy lava, sometimes within the crater of a larger volcano (e.g., Mount St. Helens) and sometimes free-standing (e.g., Mono Craters).

lava plateau A broad elevated tableland, thousands of square kilometers in extent, underlain by a thick sequence of lava flows.

leachate The noxious fluids that percolate through sanitary landfills. If released to the surface or underground environment, leachate can pollute surface and underground water.

levees (natural) Embankments of sand or silt built by a stream along both banks of its channel. They are deposited during floods, when waters overflowing the stream banks are forced to deposit sediment.

liquefaction *See* spontaneous liquefaction.

lithification The conversion of sediment into solid rock through processes of compaction, cementation, and crystallization.

lithified Changed into stone, as in the transformation of loose sand to sandstone.

lithosphere The rigid outer layer from the earth's surface down to the asthenosphere. It includes the crust and part of the upper mantle and is of the order of 100 km (60 mi) thick. The "plates" in plate tectonic theory.

littoral drift Sediment (sand, gravel, silt) that is moved parallel to the shore by longshore currents.

lode A mineral deposit consisting of a zone of veins in consolidated rock, as opposed to a *placer deposit.*

loess A blanket deposit of buff-colored calcareous silt that is porous and shows little or no stratification. It covers wide areas in Europe, eastern China, and the Mississippi valley. It is generally considered to be windblown dust of Pleistocene age.

longitudinal wave (P-wave) A type of seismic wave involving particle motion that is alternating expansion and compression in the direction of wave propagation. Also known as *compressional waves,* they resemble sound waves in their motion.

longshore current (littoral current) The current adjacent and parallel to a shoreline that is generated by waves striking the shoreline at an angle.

longshore drift The movement of sand along a beach caused by longshore currents.

losing stream A stream or reach of a stream that contributes water to the zone of saturation.

low-grade deposit A mineral deposit in which the mineral content is minimal but still exploitable at a profit.

low-level nuclear wastes Wastes generated in research labs, hospitals, and industry. Shallow burial in containers is sufficient to sequester this waste.

luster The manner in which a mineral reflects light using such terms as metallic, resinous, silky, and glassy.

M-discontinuity (Moho) The contact between the earth's crust and the mantle. There is a sharp increase in earthquake P-wave velocity across this boundary.

maar A low-relief, broad volcanic crater formed by multiple shallow explosive eruptions. Maars commonly contain a lake and are surrounded by a low rampart or ring of ejected material. They typically form from *phreatic eruptions.*

mafic Descriptive of a magma or rock rich in iron and magnesium. The mnemonic term is derived from *ma*gnesium + *f*erric + *ic.*

magma Molten material within the earth that is capable of intrusion or extrusion and from which igneous rocks form.

magnetic polarity A property indicating the position of Earth's magnetic poles relative to a rock during its formation, as expressed by the alignment of tiny iron-bearing grains contained within the rock.

magnitude (earthquake) A measure of the strength or the strain energy released by an earthquake at its source. (*See* moment magnitude, Richter magnitude.)

manganese nodule A small irregular black to brown, laminated concretionary mass consisting primarily of manganese minerals with some iron oxides and traces of other metallic minerals, abundant on the floors of the world's oceans.

mantle A thick shell of magnesium-silicate matter that surrounds the earth's core.

mantle lid Part of the earth's rigid outer shell that also includes the crust.

marine trenches Steep-walled abyssal valleys that fringe some ocean floors.

mass wasting A general term for all downslope movements of soil and rock material under the direct influence of gravity.

massive sulfide deposit Usually volcanogenic, often rich in zinc and sometimes in lead.

maximum contaminant level (MCL) The highest level of a contaminant that is allowed in drinking water. MCLs are set as close to the MCLGs as feasible using the best available treatment technology.

maximum contaminant level goal (MCLG) The level of a contaminant in drinking water below which there is no known or expected risk to health. MCLGs allow for a margin of safety.

meander One of a series of sinuous curves in the course of a stream.

megawatt (MW) A million watts; 1,000 kilowatts.

meltdown *See* central-core meltdown.

metamorphic rocks Preexisting rocks that have been altered by heat, pressure, or chemically active fluids.

methanol A colorless liquid chemical compound commonly called wood alcohol that is volatile, flammable, and poisonous, with the chemical formula CH_3OH.

mid-latitude desert A desert area occurring within latitudes 30°–50° north and south of the equator in the deep interior of a continent, usually on the lee side of a mountain range that blocks the path of prevailing winds, and commonly characterized by a cold, dry climate (*see* rain-shadow desert).

mid-ocean ridges Belts of broad volcanic highlands that bisect the sea floor worldwide.

millirem A measure of radioactive emissions in the environment.

mineral Naturally occurring crystalline substance with well-defined physical properties and a definite range of chemical composition.

mineral deposit A localized concentration of naturally occurring mineral material (e.g., a metallic ore or a nonmetallic mineral), usually of economic value, without regard to its mode of origin.

mineral reserves Known mineral deposits that are recoverable under present conditions but as yet undeveloped. The term excludes *potential ore.*

mineral resources The valuable minerals of an area that are presently legally recoverable or that may be so in the future; include both the known ore bodies (*mineral reserves*) and the *potential ores* of a region.

miscible Soluble; capable of mixing.

modified Mercalli scale Earthquake intensity scale from I (not felt) to XII (total destruction) based upon damage and reports of human reactions.

Mohs hardness scale A scale that indicates the relative hardness of minerals on a scale of 1 (talc, very soft) to 10 (diamond, very hard).

moment magnitude (M_w or M) A scale of seismic energy released by an earthquake based on the product of the rock rigidity along the fault, the area of rupture on the fault plane, and the amount of slip.

moraine A mound, ridge, hill, or other distinct accumulation of unsorted, unstratified glacial drift, predominantly till, deposited chiefly by direct action of glacial ice in a variety of landforms.

mother lode (a) A main mineralized unit that may not be economically valuable in itself but to which workable deposits are related; e.g., the Mother Lode of California. (b) An ore deposit from which a placer is derived; the *mother rock* of a placer.

mountaintop-removal mining The mining of coal that underlies the tops of mountains.

natural levee *See* levee.

negative anomaly Magnetization in ancient rocks caused by a magnetic field oriented opposite to the one existing at present; that is, the northern magnetic pole existed in the south, and the southern one existed in the north.

NEPA The National Environmental Policy Act of 1969.

neutron An electronically neutral particle (zero charge) of an atomic nucleus with an atomic mass of approximately 1.

nonrenewable resource An energy or material resource that once used is not available for reuse in human time spans. Coal, oil, and metallic minerals are examples.

normal force The force applied perpendicular to the failure plane of a landslide.

nucleus The positively charged central core of an atom containing protons and neutrons that provide its mass.

nuée ardenté (pyroclastic flow) French for "glowing cloud," it is a highly heated, almost incandescent cloud of volcanic gases and pyroclastic material that travels with great velocity down the slopes of a volcano. Produced by the explosive disintegration of viscous lava in a vent.

NWPA Nuclear Waste Policy Act of 1982 mandating selection of a repository for nuclear waste.

obliquity The tilt of the earth's axis.

oil shale A group of fine-grained sedimentary rocks rich enough in organic material (kerogen) that will yield petroleum upon distillation.

open-pit mining Mining from open excavations, most commonly for low-grade copper and iron deposits, and coal.

ore A volume of rock containing useful minerals in concentrations that can be profitably mined, transported, and processed.

ore deposit The same as a *mineral reserve* except that it refers only to a metal-bearing deposit.

ore mineral The part of an ore, usually metallic, that is economically desirable.

outgassing The release of gases and water vapor from molten rocks, leading to the formation of the earth's atmosphere and oceans.

outlet glacier A tongue-shaped glacier that originates from an ice sheet or mountain ice-field.

overturn Process by which stagnant bottom waters in a lake come to the surface and are refreshed with oxygen.

oxbow lake A crescent-shaped lake formed along a stream course when a tight meander is cut off and abandoned.

ozone hole An area in the atmospheric ozone layer that is thin or absent.

pahoehoe Basaltic lava typified by smooth, billowy, or ropy surfaces.

paleoseismicity The rock record of past earthquake events in displaced beds and liquefaction features in trenches or natural outcrops.

Pangaea A supercontinent that existed from about 300–200 Ma, which included all the continents we know today.

passive margins Coastlines such as the Eastern Seaboard of the U.S. that are no longer active in terms of volcanism and mountain building.

pedalfer Soil of humid regions characterized by an organic-rich A horizon and clays and iron oxides in the B horizon.

pedocal Soil of arid or semiarid regions that is rich in calcium carbonate.

pedologist (Greek *pedo*, "soil," and *logos*, "knowledge") A person who studies soils.

pedology The study of soils.

pegmatite An exceptionally coarse-grained igneous rock with interlocking crystals, usually found as irregular dikes, lenses, or veins, especially at the margins of batholiths.

perched water table The upper surface of a body of ground water held up by a discontinuous impermeable layer above the static water table.

permafrost Permanently frozen ground, with or without water, occurring in arctic, subarctic, and alpine regions.

permafrost table The upper limit of permafrost.

permeability The degree of ease with which fluids flow through a porous medium (*see* hydraulic conductivity).

phaneritic texture A coarse-grained igneous-rock texture resulting from slow cooling. Phanerites are coarse-grained igneous rocks.

photochemical smog Atmospheric haze that forms when automobile-exhaust emissions are activated by ultraviolet radiation from the sun to produce highly reactive oxidants known to be health hazards.

phreatic eruption Volcanic eruption, mostly steam, caused by the interaction of hot magma with underground water, lakes, or seawater. Where significant amounts of new (magmatic) material are ejected in addition to steam, the eruptions are described as *phreatomagmatic*.

phytoremediation The use of plants to remove soil contaminants, particularly excess salt.

piping Subsurface erosion in sandy materials caused by the percolation of water under pressure. A somewhat similar effect is obtained by placing a garden-hose nozzle in a sandbox and jetting an opening through the sand.

placer deposit (pronounced "plass-er") A surficial mineral deposit formed by settling from streams of mineral particles from weathered debris. (*See also* lode.)

plastic Capable of being deformed continuously and permanently in any direction without rupture.

plate Broad region of the earth's crust that is structurally distinctive.

plate tectonics View of the structure and movement of the earth's outermost skin and landforms such as mountains and valleys.

Pleistocene The geologic Epoch of the Quaternary Period known as the Ice Age, falling by definition between 1.6 million and 12,000 years ago. Extensive glaciation is known as far back as the Pliocene Epoch 2.5 million years ago. The exact boundaries shift in time as new data are revealed.

Plinian column A steady, turbulent, nearly vertical column of ash and steam released from a vent at high velocity in an explosive eruption.

plutonic Pertaining to rock formed by any process at depth, usually with a phaneritic texture.

point bar A deposit of sand and gravel found on the inside curve of a *meander*.

polar desert The bitterly cold, arid region centered at the south pole that receives very little precipitation.

polar front The boundary in the atmosphere where cold polar surface air and mild-temperature surface air converge.

polar high The region of cold, high-density air that exists in the polar regions.

population dynamics The study of how populations grow.

population growth rate The number of live births less deaths per 1,000 people, usually expressed as a percentage; a growth rate of 40 would represent 4.0% growth.

pore pressure The stress exerted by the fluids that fill the voids between particles of rock or soil.

porosity A material's ability to contain fluid. The ratio of the volume of pore spaces in a rock or sediment to its total volume, usually expressed as a percentage.

porphyry copper A copper deposit, usually of low grade, in which the copper-bearing minerals occur in disseminated grains and/or in veinlets through a large volume of rock.

positive anomaly Magnetization in ancient rocks caused by a magnetic field oriented much as at present ("positive" pole in the north and "negative" pole in the south).

potable water Water that is suitable for drinking.

potential ore As yet undiscovered mineral deposits and also known mineral deposits for which recovery is not yet economically feasible.

potentiometric surface The hydrostatic head of ground water and the level to which the water will rise in a well. The water table is the potentiometric surface in an unconfined aquifer. Also called *piezometric surface*.

powder snow avalanche Avalanche of dry, recently fallen snow that has little cohesion

precession The slow gyration of the Earth's axis, analogous to that of a spinning top, which causes the slow change in the orientation of the Earth's axis relative to the sun that accounts for the reversal of the seasons of winter and summer in the Northern and Southern Hemispheres every 11,500 years.

precipitation The separation of a solid substance from a solution by a chemical reaction.

precursors (of earthquakes) Observable phenomena that occur before an earthquake and indicate that an event is soon to occur.

pregnant pond A catchment basin that holds a gold- and silver-bearing cyanide solution.

proglacial lake An ice-marginal lake formed just beyond the frontal moraine of a retreating glacier and generally in direct contact with the ice.

proton A particle in an atomic nucleus with a positive electrical charge and an atomic mass of approximately one.

protostar A star in the process of formation that has entered the slow gravitational contraction phase.

pumice Frothy-appearing rock composed of natural glass ejected from high-silica, gas-charged magmas. It is the only rock that floats.

P-wave *See* longitudinal wave.

pyroclastic ("fire broken") Descriptive of the fragmental material, ash, cinders, blocks, and bombs ejected from a volcano. (*See also* tephra.)

quad A quadrillion British thermal units (10^{15} Btu).

quick clay (sensitive clay) A clay possessing a "house-of-cards" sedimentary structure that collapses when it is disturbed by an earthquake or other shock.

radioactivity The property possessed by certain elements that spontaneously emit energy as the nucleus of the atom changes its proton-to-neutron ratio.

radiometric dating *See* absolute age dating.

radon A radioactive gas emitted in the breakdown of uranium.

rain-shadow desert A desert on the lee side of a mountain or a mountain range (*see* mid-latitude desert).

rank (coal) A coal's carbon content depending upon its degree of metamorphism.

RCRA The Resource Conservation and Recovery Act of 1976.

recessional moraine One of a series of nested end moraines that record the stepwise retreat of a glacier at the end of an ice age.

recrystallization The formation in the solid state of new mineral grains in a metamorphic rock. The new grains are generally larger than the original mineral grains.

recycling Reprocessing of materials into new products.

recurrence interval The return period of an event, such as a flood or earthquake, of a given magnitude. For flooding, it is the average interval of time within which a given flood will be equalled or exceeded by the annual maximum discharge.

regional metamorphism A general term for metamorphism that affects an extensive area.

regolith Unconsolidated rock and mineral fragments at the surface of the earth.

Regulatory Floodplain The part of a floodplain that is subject to federal government regulation for insurance purposes.

relative age dating The chronologic ordering of geologic strata, features, fossils, or events with respect to the geological time scale without reference to their absolute age.

renewable resource An energy or material resource that continually renews itself as it is being consumed. Timber, solar energy, wind, and water are examples.

replacement rate The birth rate at which just enough offsprings are born to replace their parents.

reserves Those portions of an identified resource that can be recovered economically.

reservoir rock A permeable, porous geologic formation that will yield oil or natural gas.

residence time The average length of time a substance (atom, ion, molecule) remains in a given reservoir.

residual soil Soil formed in place by decomposition of the rocks upon which it lies.

resisting force (landslide) Friction along the slide plane and normal forces across the plane.

resonance The tendency of a system (a structure) to vibrate with maximum amplitude when the frequency of the applied force (seismic waves) is the same as the vibrating body's natural frequency.

resource recovery The removal of certain materials from the waste stream for the purpose of recycling or composting.

revetment A rock or concrete structure built landward of a beach to protect coastal property.

Richter magnitude scale (earthquakes) The logarithm of the maximum trace amplitude of a particular seismic wave on a seismogram, corrected for distance to epicenter and type of seismometer. A measure of the energy released by an earthquake.

rift zone (volcanology) A linear zone of weakness on the flank of a shield volcano that is the site of frequent flank eruptions.

rill erosion The carving of small channels, up to 25 cm (10 in) deep, in soil by running water.

riparian Pertaining to or situated on the bank of a body of water, especially of a river.

rip current A local, focused current that returns water from the beach zone to deeper water.

rock cycle The cycle or sequence of events involving the formation, alteration, destruction, and reformation of rocks as a result of processes such as erosion, transportation, lithification, magmatism, and metamorphism.

rocks Aggregates of minerals or rock fragments.

rotational landslide (slump) A slope failure in which sliding occurs on a well-defined, concave-upward, curved surface, producing a backward rotation of the slide mass.

runoff That part of precipitation falling on land that runs into surface streams.

runup The elevation to which a wind wave or tsunami advances onto the land.

Sahel Belt of populated semiarid lands along the southern edge of North Africa's Sahara Desert.

salt dome A column or plug of rock salt that rises from depth because of its low density and pierces overlying sediments.

sanitary landfill A method of burying waste where each day's dumping is covered with soil to protect the surrounding area. This is also monitored to ensure protection of local underground water.

sea-floor spreading A hypothesis that oceanic crust forms by convective upwelling of lava at mid-ocean ridges and moves laterally to trenches where it is destroyed.

seawall A rock or concrete structure built landward of a beach to protect the land from wave action. (*See also* revetment.)

secondary enrichment Processes of near-surface mineral deposition, in which oxidation produces acidic solutions that leach metals, carry them downward, and reprecipitate them, thus enriching sulfide minerals already present.

secondary recovery Production of oil or gas by artificially stimulating a depleted reservoir with water, steam, or other fluids in order to mobilize the remaining hydrocarbons.

secure landfill A landfill that totally isolates the received waste from the environment.

sedimentary rock A layer of rock deposited from water, ice, or air and subsequently lithified to form a coherent rock.

seif (longitudinal) dune A very large, sharp-crested, tapering chain of sand dunes; commonly found in the Arabian Desert.

seismogram The recording from a seismograph.

seismograph An instrument used to measure and record seismic waves from earthquakes.

semiarid grasslands Extensive treeless grassland regions that are marginal to many mid-latitude deserts.

sensitive clay *See* quick clay.

settlement This occurs when the applied load of a structure's foundation is greater than the bearing strength of the foundation material (soil or rock).

sheet erosion The removal of thin layers of surface rock or soil from an area of gently sloping land by broad continuous sheets of running water (sheet flow), rather than by channelized streams.

sheet joints (*See* joint) Cracks more or less parallel to the ground surface that result from expansion due to deep erosion and the unloading of overburden pressure.

shield volcano (cone) The largest type of volcanoes, composed of piles of lava in a convex-upward slope. Found mainly in Hawaii and Iceland.

sinkhole Circular depression formed by the collapse of a shallow cavern in limestone.

slab avalanche A coherent block of snow that fails as a slide and then moves downslope in chunks

slant-drilling (whipstocking) Purposely deflecting a drill hole from the vertical in order to tap a reservoir not directly below the drill site. The deflecting tool is a whipstock.

slide plane (slip plane) A curved or planar surface along which a landslide moves.

slip face The steeper, lee side of a dune, standing at or near the angle of repose of loose sand and advancing downwind by a succession of slides whenever that angle is exceeded.

slump *See* rotational landslide.

smelter An industrial plant that mechanically and chemically produces metals from their ores.

SMCRA The Surface Mining Control and Reclamation Act of 1977.

soil (a) Loose material at the surface of the earth that supports the growth of plants (pedological definition). (b) All loose surficial earth material resting on coherent bedrock (engineering definition).

soil horizon A layer of soil that is distinguishable from adjacent layers by properties such as color, texture, structure, or chemical composition.

soil order A means by which major soil types can be classified.

soil profile A vertical section of soil that exposes all of its horizons or zones.

solution (weathering) The dissolving of rocks and minerals by natural acids or water.

source rock The geologic formation in which oil and/or gas originate.

specific yield The ratio of the volume of water drained from an aquifer by gravity to the total volume considered.

speleology The study of caves and caverns.

spheroidal weathering Weathering of rock surfaces that creates a rounded or spherical shape as the corners of the rock mass are weathered faster than its flat faces.

spit A narrow stretch of sand that extend out from the coast line often formed by longshore drift

spoil Refuse rock material that result from mining, excavation or dredging.

spontaneous liquefaction Process whereby water-saturated sands, clays, or artificial fill suddenly become fluid upon shaking, as in an earthquake.

stage The height of flood waters in feet or meters above an established datum plane.

stalactites Deposits of calcium carbonate precipitated from solution and building down from the top of a cave.

stalagmites Deposits of calcium carbonate precipitated from solution and building up from the bottom of a cave.

steppe An extensive treeless grassland in the semiarid mid-latitudes of Asia and southeastern Europe. It is drier than the prairie that develops in the mid-latitudes of the United States.

storm surge The sudden rise of sea level on an open coast due to a storm. Storm surge is caused by strong onshore winds and results in water being piled up against the shore. It may be enhanced by high tides and low atmospheric pressure.

strain Deformation resulting from an applied stress (=force per unit area). It may be elastic (recoverable) or ductile (nonreversible).

stratification (bedding) The arrangement of sedimentary rocks in strata or layers.

stratigraphic trap An accumulation of oil that results from a change in the character (permeability) of the reservoir rock, rather than from structural deformation.

stratovolcano A large volcano that is shaped slightly concave upward and is composed of layers of ash and lava.

stress The force applied on an object per unit area, expressed in pounds per square foot (lb/ft^2) or kilograms per square meter (kg/m^2).

strike The direction west or east of north of the trace of the inclined plane (sedimentary bedding plane, fault, or joint surface) on the horizontal plane.

strip-mining Surficial mining, in which the resource is exposed by removing the overburden.

subduction The sinking of one lithospheric plate beneath another at a convergent plate margin. (*See* convergent boundary.)

subpolar low A region of low atmospheric pressure located at about latitudes 60° north and 60° south.

subsidence Sinking or downward settling of the earth's surface due to solution, compaction, withdrawal of underground fluids, or to cooling of the hot lithosphere or to loading with sediment or ice.

subtropical desert A hot, dry desert occurring between latitudes 15°–30° north and south of the equator where subtropical air masses prevail. (*See* trade-wind desert.)

subtropical highs The climatic belts at latitudes of approximately 30°–35° north and south of the equator characterized by semipermanent high-pressure air masses, moderate seasonal rainfall, summer heat, dryness, and generally clear skies.

Superfund A spinoff of CERCLA insuring financial accountability for environmental polluters.

surcharge Weight added to the top of a natural or artificial slope by sedimentation or by artificial fill.

surface hoar Deposit of ice directly from water vapor onto the top of the snow pack. Forms a very weak layer upon which avalanches run.

surface wave Seismic waves that travel the surface of the earth. They are generated by the unreflected energy of P- and S-waves striking the earth's surface. They are the most damaging of earthquake waves.

surging glacier A glacier that alternates periodically between brief periods (usually 1–4 years) of very rapid flow, called *surges,* and longer periods (usually 10–100 years) of near-stagnation.

suspension (a) A mode of sediment transport in which the upward currents in eddies of turbulent flow are capable of supporting the weight of sediment particles and keeping them held indefinitely in the surrounding fluid (as silt in water or dust in air). (b) The state of a substance in such a mode of transport.

sustainable society A population capable of maintaining itself while leaving sufficient resources for future generations.

sustained yield (hydrology) The amount of water an aquifer can yield on a daily basis over a long period of time.

S-wave *See* transverse wave.

syncline A concave-upward fold that contains younger rocks in its core. (*Contrast with* anticline.)

synthetic fuels (synfuels) A manufactured fuel; for example, a fuel derived by liquefaction or gasification of coal.

tailings The worthless rock material discarded from mining operations.

talus Coarse angular rock fragments lying at the base of a cliff or steep slope from which they were derived.

tar sand A sand body that is large enough to hold a commercial reserve of asphalt or other thick oil. It is usually surface excavated to remove the thick hydrocarbons.

tectonism (adj. tectonic) Deformation of the earth's crust by natural processes leading to the formation of ocean basins, continents, mountain systems, and other earth features.

tephra A collective term for all *pyroclastic* material ejected from a volcano.

terrain anchors Surface roughness such as trees or rocks which prevent avalanches from releasing by holding back snow.

terranes (*See* exotic terranes.)

texture The size, shape, and arrangement of the component particles or crystals in a rock.

till Unsorted and unstratified drift, generally unconsolidated, that is deposited directly by and beneath a glacier without subsequent reworking by water from the glacier.

tombolo A sandbar that connects an island with the mainland or another island.

total fertility rate Average number of children born to women of child-bearing age.

trace element An element that occurs in minute quantities in rocks or plant or animal tissue. Some are essential for human health.

trade winds Steady winds blowing from areas of high pressure at 30° north and south latitudes toward the area of lower pressure at the equator. This pressure differential produces the northeast and southeast trade winds in the Northern and Southern Hemispheres, respectively.

trade wind desert *See* subtropical desert.

transform boundaries Plate boundaries with mostly horizontal (lateral) movement that connect spreading centers to each other or to subduction zones.

translational slide *See* block glide.

transported soils Soil developed on *regolith* transported and deposited by a geological agent. Hence the term *glacial* soils, alluvial soils, *eolian* soils, *volcanic* soils, and so forth.

transuranic elements Radioactive elements that have an atomic number greater than uranium and are man made.

transverse dune A strongly asymmetrical sand dune that is elongated perpendicularly to the direction of the prevailing winds. It has a gentle windward slope and a steep leeward slope that stands at or near the angle of repose of sand.

transverse wave (S-wave) A seismic wave propagated by a shearing motion that involves oscillation perpendicular to the direction of travel. It travels only in solids.

troposphere That part of the atmosphere next to the earth's surface, in which temperature generally decreases rapidly with altitude and clouds and convection are active. Where the weather occurs.

tsunami Large sea wave produced by a submarine earthquake, a volcanic eruption, or a landslide. Incorrectly known as a tidal wave.

tuff A coherent rock formed from volcanic ash, cinders, or other *pyroclastic* material.

tundra (soil) A treeless plain characteristic of arctic regions with organic rich, poorly drained tundra soils and permanently frozen ground.

unconfined aquifer Underground body of water that has a free (static) water table; that is, water that is not confined under pressure beneath an aquiclude.

upwelling A process whereby cold, nutrient-rich water is brought to the surface. Coastal upwelling occurs mostly in trade-wind belts.

vapor extraction The use of vacuum pumps placed in shallow bore holes to remove vaporized organic contaminants in the soil, such as gasoline or TCE.

vein deposit A thin, sheetlike igneous intrusion into a crevice.

ventifact Any stone or pebble that has been shaped, worn, faceted, cut, or polished by the abrasive or sandblast action of wind-blown sand, generally under arid conditions.

Volcanic Explosivity Index (VEI) A scale for rating volcanic eruptions according to the volume of the ejecta, the height to which the ejecta rise, and the duration of the eruption.

volcanogenic deposit Of volcanic origin; for example, volcanogenic sediments or ore deposits.

waste management A complex of processes including waste disposal, reducing the amount of waste at its sources, waste recovery and recycling.

water cycle *See* hydrologic cycle.

water table The contact between the zone of aeration and the zone of saturation.

wave base The depth at which water waves no longer move sediment, equal to approximately half the wavelength.

wavelength The distance between two equivalent points on two consecutive waves; for example, crest to crest or trough to trough.

wave of oscillation A water wave in which water particles follow a circular path with little forward motion.

wave of translation A water wave in which the individual particles of water move in the direction of wave travel, as in broken waves (surf).

wave period (T) The time (in seconds) between passage of equivalent points on two consecutive waveforms.

wave refraction The bending of wave crests as they move into shallow water.

weathering The physical and chemical breakdown of materials of the earth's crust by interaction with the atmosphere and biosphere.

welded tuff A glassy pyroclastic rock that has been made hard by the welding together of its particles under the action of retained heat.

wetted perimeter (stream) The length of stream bed and bank that are in contact with running water in the stream in a given cross section.

wildcat well An oil well drilled in a region not known to be an oil field.

Wilson cycle An evolutionary sequence for oceans that identifies five stages in their birth and death; named for J. Tuzo Wilson.

wind The movement of air from one place to another.

WIPP Waste Isolation Pilot Plant; sequesters defense-related transuranic waste.

zero population growth A population growth rate of 0; that is, the number of deaths in a population is equal to the number of live births on average.

zone of aeration (vadose zone) The zone of soil or rock through which water infiltrates by gravity to the water table. Pore spaces between rock and mineral grains in this zone are filled with air; hence the name.

zone of flowage The lower part of a glacier that deforms due to the glacier's own weight.

zone of saturation The ground-water zone where voids in rock or sediment are filled with water.

Credits

This page constitutes an extension of the copyright page. We have made every effort to trace the ownership of all copyrighted material and to secure permission from copyright holders. In the event of any question arising as to the use of any material, we will be pleased to make the necessary corrections in future printings. Thanks are due to the following authors, publishers, and agents for permission to use the material indicated.

Chapter 1. 1: Richard Hazlett **5:** Fig 1.3: © CORBIS **6:** Fig. 1.4: © Eastcott Momatiuk/Getty Images **6:** Fig. 1.5: © Bettmann/CORBIS **6:** Fig. 1.6: © Hulton-Deutsch Collection/CORBIS **7:** Fig. 1.7: © Chuck Keeler/Getty Images **7:** Fig 1.8: © John Maier Jr/Getty Images **8:** Fig. 1.9: © Alessandro Della Bella/epa/CORBIS **9:** Fig. 1.10: Richard Hazlett **12:** Fig. 1: B. Pipkin **12:** Fig. 2: (a) © Owen Franken/Sygma/CORBIS **12:** Fig. 2: (b) © Owen Franken/Sygma/CORBIS **12:** Fig. 3: NO CREDIT

Chapter 2. 15: Fig. 1: NASA/JPL/Cornell **16:** Fig. 2: NASA/JPL/Cornell **17:** Fig: 2.1: D. D. Trent **21:** Fig. 2.6: (a), USGS **21:** Fig. 2.6: (b-d), © Paul Silverman, Fundamental Photographs **22:** Fig 2.7: top right and bottom left, Sue Monroe **22:** Fig 2.8: all, Sue Monroe **22:** Fig. 2.7: bottom right, © Paul Silverman, Fundamental Photographs **22:** Fig. 2.7: top left, © Michael Dalton, Fundamental Photographs **25:** Fig 2.12: B. Pipkin **26:** Fig 2.13: all, Sue Monroe **27:** Fig. 2.14: all, B. Pipkin **28:** Fig. 2.16: all, B. Pipkin **29:** Fig: 2.17: D. D. Trent **29:** Fig: 2.18: D. D. Trent **30:** Fig. 2.20: all, B. Pipkin **30:** Fig 2.21: all, Sue Monroe **31:** Fig: 2.22: D. D. Trent **37:** Fig. 1: Janet Blabaum, Highland Geotechnical, AIPG **37:** Fig. 2: Janet Blabaum, Highland Geotechnical, AIPG **39:** Fig 1: (a) B. Pipkin **39:** Fig. 1: (b) © Martin Land, Science Photo Library/Photo Researchers **39:** Fig. 1: (c) © Carl Frank/Photo Researchers **40:** Fig. 1: © 1994 Margaret Millar/The National Audubon Society Collection/Photo Researchers **40:** Fig. 3: (a) © Smithsonian Institute **40:** Fig 3: (b-e) Sue Monroe **41:** Fig. 1: (a) Reed Wicander **41:** Fig. 1: (b) Reed Wicander **42:** Fig. 2: From Monroe and R. Wicander, The Changing Earth, Brooks/Cole, 1997 **42:** Fig. 3: Theodore Roosevelt Collection, Harvard College Library **42:** Fig. 4: B. Pipkin

Chapter 3. 45: Fig. 1: © 1969–2006 MDA Federal Inc. All Rights Reserved. (Formerly Earth Satellite Corporation), **46:** Fig. 4: (a) Richard Hazlett **46:** Fig. 4: (b) Richard Hazlett **47:** Fig. 3.1: (a) Patricia Gensel, University of N. Carolina **48:** Fig. 3.2: (c) Scott Katz **55:** Fig. 3.11: (b) © Photo Researchers, Inc. **55:** Fig. 3.11: © USGS **56:** Fig. 3.12: Richard Hazlett **66:** Fig. 1: Bildarchiv Preussischer Kulturbesitz **66:** Fig. 2: Rodney Supple **67:** Fig. 3: (a) © Woods Hole Oceanographic Institution **67:** Fig. 3: (b) © Woods Hole Oceanographic Institution **67:** Fig. 3: (c) © Woods Hole Oceanographic Institution

Chapter 4. 71: Fig. 4.1: (b) Wendy Van Norden, Harvard Westlake School **71:** Fig. 4.1: (d) D. Trent **71:** Fig. 4.1: (f) USGS **72:** Fig. 4.2: (e) USGS **74:** Fig. 4.5: B. Pipkin **74:** Fig. 4.6: Trustees of the Science Museum, London **77:** Fig: 4.10: (b) USGS, **80:** Fig 4.12: (d) Dennis

Fox **80:** Fig. 4.12: (b) Dorothy Stout, Cypress College **81:** Fig. 4.13: James C. Anderson, USC **82:** Fig. 4.15: B. Pipkin **82:** Fig. 4.16: (a) NOAA **82:** Fig 4.16: (b) NOAA/NGDC 97 **82:** Fig: 4.18: Dave Johnson **84:** Fig. 4.19: Metropolitan Museum of Art, H. O. Havemeyer Collection (JP 1847) **86:** Fig 4.20: (a) EOS-American Geophysical Union **86:** Fig 4.20: (b) USGS **87:** Fig. 4.21: (b) Courtesy of Rod Combellick, Div. of Geological and Geophysical Surveys, State of Alaska **88:** Fig 4.22: USGS **88:** Fig. 4.23: Kerry Sieh, Cal Tech **90:** Fig. 4.26: (a) Greg Davis, USC **90:** Fig: 4.26: (b) Greg Davis, USC **90:** Fig. 4.26: (c) Greg Davis, USC **91:** Fig. 4.27: Dennis Fox **93:** Fig. 4.30: (b) USGS Fact Sheet 168–95, **96:** Fig. 4.34: USGS, MODIFIED AND UPDATED **98:** Fig: 4.37: Kerry L. Sieh, Seismological Laboratory, California Institute of Technology **99:** Fig. 4.40: D. D. Trent **99:** Fig. 4.41: D. D. Trent **102:** Fig. 1: Southern California Earthquake Center (SCEC) **103:** Fig. 1: B. Pipkin **104:** Fig. 1: B. Pipkin **105:** Fig. 2: San Francisco Chronicle/Frederick Larson **105:** Fig. 3: B. Pipkin **106:** Fig. 4: Yi-Ben Tsai, National Central University, Taiwan **106:** Fig. 5: Ted Reeves, Chaffey High School, Upland, CA **107:** Fig. 1: B. Pipkin **107:** Fig. 3: B. Pipkin **107:** Fig.2: Frederick Larson, San Francisco Chronicle **108:** Fig. 4: Yi-Ben Tsai, National Central University, Taiwan **108:** Fig. 5: Ted Reeves, Chaffey High School, Upland, California

Chapter 5. 109: Fig. 1: Joyce M. Warren and USGS **110:** Fig. 2: (b) NASA **110:** Fig. 3: (a) USGS **116:** Fig. 5.7: B. Pipkin **116:** Fig. 5.8: (a) USGS/Eros Data Center **117:** Fig. 5.10: (a) USGS **117:** Fig. 5.10: (b) J. D. Griggs/USGS **117:** Fig: 5.10: (c) J. D. Griggs/USGS, **118:** Fig. 5.11: J. B. Stokes, USGS **118:** Fig. 5.12 (a) Pele, goddess of Hawaii's volcanoes, by artist Herb Kawainui Kane **118:** Fig. 5.12: (b) B. Pipkin **118:** Fig. 5.13: (b) B. Pipkin **119:** Fig. 5.14: (a) Richard Hazlett **119:** Fig. 5.14: (b) Arturo Aburto Quesada **120:** Fig: 5.15: B. Pipkin **120:** Fig. 5.16: B. Pipkin **121:** Fig. 5.17: (a) B. Pipkin **121:** Fig. 5.18: USGS **122:** Fig. 5.19: B. Pipkin **124:** Fig. 5.21: (a) B. Pipkin **124:** Fig. 5.21: (b) NOAA, National Geophysical Data Center, Boulder, Colo. **124:** Fig. 5.22: NOAA, National Geophysical Data Center, Boulder, Colo. **125:** Fig. 5.23: NOAA, National Geophysical Data Center, Boulder, Colo. **125:** Fig. 5.24: (a) Keith Ronnholm **125:** Fig. 5.24: (b) B. Pipkin **126:** Fig. 5.25: (a) Richard Hazlett **126:** Fig. 5.25: (b) Richard Hazlett, **126:** Fig. 5.25: (c) Richard Hazlett **126:** Fig. 5.25: (d) Richard Hazlett **127:** Fig. 5.26 (a) B. Pipkin **128:** Fig. 5.28: B. Pipkin **131:** Fig. 5.30: USGS **132:** Fig. 5.33: (a) USGS **132:** Fig. 5.33: (b) Richard Hazlett **132:** Fig. 5.33 (c): USGS **132:** Fig.5.33: (d) Richard Hazlett **136:** Fig. 1: (b) David M. Bailey, Grant, CO. Airport, Moses Lake, Wash. **137:** Fig. 2: (a) NOAA, **137:** Fig. 2: (b) NOAA, **138:** Fig. 1: Simon R. Young, Montserrat Volcano Observatory **140:** Fig. 2: (b) John Rogie **140:** Fig. 3: B. Pipkin **141:** Fig. 4: Jason D. Opliger, Inyo National Forest **142:** Fig. 1: (B) T. Orban, Sygma/CORBIS **142:** Fig. 1: (a) Mike Tuttle, USGS **142:** Fig. 2: (a) John Rogie **143:** Fig. 1: John Mead/Science Photo Library/Photo Researchers **143:** Fig. 2: Jack Green, Calif. State Univ., Long Beach **144:** Fig. 3: J. D. Griggs, Hawaiian Volcano Observatory,

USGS **144:** Fig. 4: Jim Mori, USGS **144:** Fig. 5: B. Pipkin **144:** Fig. 6: J. D. Griggs, Hawaiian Volcano Observatory, USGS

Chapter 6. 148: Fig. 1: © UPI/Bettmann/CORBIS **149:** Fig. 2: © CORBIS, **151:** Fig. 6.3: (a) P. Bierman **151:** Fig. 6.3: (b) P. Bierman **151:** Fig. 6.3: (c) P. Bierman **151:** Fig. 6.3: (d) D. D. Trent **152:** Fig. 6.4: (a) John Shelton, **152:** Fig. 6.4: (b) John Shelton, **154:** Fig. 6.6: (a) B. Pipkin **154:** Fig: 6.6: (b) B. Pipkin, **154:** Fig. 6.7: (a) Courtesy Lawrence Livermore National Laboratory **154:** Fig. 6.7: (b) P. Bierman **155:** Fig. 6.8: (a) B. Pipkin **155:** Fig. 6.8: (b) D. D. Trent **156:** Fig. 6.10: D. D. Trent **157:** Fig. 6.11: B. Pipkin, **158:** Fig. 6.13: N0 CREDIT **161:** Fig. 6.16: (a) © Walt Anderson, Visuals Unlimited **161:** Fig. 6.17: Photo courtesy of Paul McDaniel, University of Idaho **162:** Fig. 6.19: (a) Stew Monroe **162:** Fig. 6.19: (b) USDA **164:** Fig. 6.21: USGS **165:** Fig. 6.24: Doug Burbank, Univ. of Calif., Santa Barbaraa **166:** Fig. 6.25: Edward P. Nuhfer and AIPG **167:** Fig. 6.28: Troy L. Pewe, USGS **167:** Fig. 6.29: Troy L. Pewe, USGS **168:** Fig. 6.30: Larry Hinzman, Univ. of Alaska **168:** Fig. 6.31: (a) © Bryan & Cherry Alexander Photography/Alamy **168:** Fig. 6.31: (b) B. Pipkin **169:** Fig. 6.32: (a) ARCO **169:** Fig. 6.32: (b) © Danita Delimont/Alamy **170:** Fig. 6.33: © Dennis Hallinan/Alamy **170:** Fig. 6.34: Douglas J. Hathwell, Cornell Univ. **171:** Fig. 6.35: (a) P. Bierman **171:** Fig. 6.35: (b) P. Bierman **172:** Fig. 1: © Visuals Unlimited **173:** Fig. 1: © Bettmann/CORBIS, **173:** Fig. 2: P. Bierman **173:** Fig. 3: P. Bierman **174:** Fig. 1: (a) Al Robb III **174:** Fig. 1: (b) Al Robb III **175:** Fig. 1: Bierman, P., Lini, A., Davis, P. T., Southon, J., Baldwin, L., Church, A., and Zehfuss, P., 1997, Post-glacial ponds and alluvial fans: recorders of Holocene landscape history: GSA Today, v. 7, p. 1–8. Reprinted with permission of Paul Bierman and GSA Today. **175:** Fig. 2: Robert Thayer, Projections

Chapter 7. 178: Fig. 1: B. Pipkin **181:** Fig. 7.3: (b) P. Bierman **181:** Fig. 7.3: (c) B. Pipkin **182:** Fig. 7.4: (a) Kevin Lamb **182:** Fig. 7.4: (b) P. Bierman **183:** © Chris Gulker **183:** Fig. 7.8: (a) Los Angeles County Fire Department **185:** Fig. 7.10: (b) B. Pipkin **185:** Fig. 7.10: (c) B. Pipkin **186:** Fig. 7.11: B. Pipkin **188:** Fig. 7.13: USGS **188:** Fig. 7.14: © AP/Wide World Photos **189:** Fig. 7.15: NGDC **192:** Fig. 7.19 (b) Siang Tan, CDMG **192:** Fig. 7.19 (a): Pam Irvine, CDMG **193:** Fig. 7.20: (b) B. Pipkin **193:** Fig. 7.21: (b) B. Pipkin **195:** Fig. 7.23: (a) Bob Hollingsworth **195:** Fig. 7.23: (b) USGS **196:** Fig. 7.24: (a) NPS Geologic Resources Division **196:** Fig. 7.24: (c) P. Bierman **196:** Fig. 7.24: (d) P. Bierman **199:** Fig. 7.26: (a) Robinson, G. M., and Peterson, D. E., 1962, Notes on earth fissures in southern Arizona: U.S. Geological Survey Circular 466, 7 p. Photo by Ray Harris/Arizona Geological Survey **199:** Fig. 7.27: USGS/Office of Ground Water **200:** Fig. 7.28: (b) James L. Ruhle & Associates **201:** Fig. 1: B. Pipkin **201:** Fig. 2: B. Pipkin **202:** Fig. 1: Robert Schuster, USGS **204:** Fig. 1: Ronny Jacques, Photo Researchers **205:** Fig. 1: EROS/USGS **206:** Fig. 1: B. Pipkin **207:** Fig. 1: P. Bierman **207:** Fig. 2: Vermont Historical Society **208:** Fig. 1: University of Vermont, Special Collections, Bailey Howe Library. **208:** Fig. 2: R. V. Dietrich **209:** Fig. 3: NASA/JPL

Chapter 8. 213: Fig. 1: © L. Lefkowitz/Taxi/Getty **219:** Fig. 8.8: NO CREDIT **219:** Fig. 8.9: © Bettmann/CORBIS **221:** Fig. 8.12: (b) © BBC Photo Library **221:** Fig. 8.12: (c) © BBC Photo Library **225:** Fig. 8.19: D. D. Trent **230:** Fig. 8.27: (a) Frank Kujawa, Univ. of Central Florida **230:** Fig. 8.27: (b) B. Pipkin **236:** Fig. 2: © VYACH-ESLAV OSELEDKO/AFP/Getty Images **239:** Fig. 2: (a) B. Pipkin **239:** Fig. 2: (b) Texas Geological Society **241:** Fig. 3: Nassau County

Dept. of Public Works **242:** Fig. 2: Scott Fee, Am. Speleological Society **242:** Fig. 3: Reed Wicander **242:** Fig. 3: Visuals Unlimited **Chapter 9. 246:** Fig. 1: B. Pipkin **247:** Fig. 2: (a) B. Pipkin **247:** Fig. 2: (b) B. Pipkin **249:** Fig. 9.3: Vermont Historical Society **250:** Fig. 9.4: left, USGS **250:** Fig. 9.4: right, © Alex Jones Photography **251:** Fig. 9.5: (a) NOAA **251:** Fig. 9.5: (b) Courtesy Susquehanna River Basin Commission, PA **251:** Fig. 9.5: (c) Water Resources Archive, Colorado State University Library **252:** Fig. 9.6: (a) USGS **252:** Fig. 9.6: (b) © Frank Owens, www.owensstudios.com **253:** Fig. 9.7: left, USGS **253:** Fig. 9.7: right, USGS **253:** Fig. 9.8: (a) P. Bierman **253:** Fig. 9.8: (b) P. Bierman **255:** Fig. 9.11: P. Bierman **256:** Fig. 9.13: (b) Victor Baker, University of Arizona **262:** Fig. 9.23: (a) B. Pipkin **263:** Fig. 9.24: (a) B. Pipkin **264:** Fig.1: P. Bierman **264:** Fig. 2: The Art Archive/Bibliothèque des Arts Décoratifs Paris/Dagli Orti **265:** Fig. 1: New Orleans Sewerage & Water Board **266:** Fig. 2: NOAA **267:** Fig. 1: University of Vermont, Bailey-Howe Library, Special Collections **267:** Fig. 2: U.S. Army Corps of Engineers **268:** Fig. 1: Lloyd Olson **269:** Fig. 1: Fairbanks Museum and Planetarium, St. Johnsburg, VT **269:** Fig. 2: Fletcher Free Library, Burlington, VT **270:** Fig. 3: Anders Noren **270:** Fig. 4: Sarah Brown **271:** Fig. 2: P. Bierman **272:** Fig. 1: National Park Service **273:** Fig. 2: (a) Security Pacific National Bank Historical Collection, Los Angeles County Library **273:** Fig. 2: (b) Security Pacific National Bank Historical Collection, Los Angeles County Library **273:** Fig. 3: E. Olson

Chapter 10. 276: Fig. 1: B. Pipkin **277:** Fig. 2: Karl and Jill Wallin/Getty Images **279:** Fig. 10.3: (a) Tom Servais, Surfer magazine **279:** Fig. 10.3: (b) Tom Servais, Surfer magazine **279:** Fig. 10.4: (b) B. Pipkin **280:** Fig.10.6: B. Pipkin **280:** Fig. 10.7: John S. Shelton **281:** Fig. 10.9: B. Pipkin **285:** Fig. 10.15: (a) EERC Library. Copyright © 2005 the Regents of the University of California. Jan Kozak Collection: KZ84 **285:** Fig. 10.15: (b) © 1995 Matematisk Institutt, Universitetet i Oslo **285:** Fig. 10.15: (c) Professor Neal Driscoll/ Scripps Institution of Oceanography. Driscoll, Weissel, and Goff, Geology, May 2000, v. 28, no. 5, p. 407#410. **287:** Fig. 10.17: (b) © JimWark@AirPhotoNA.com **288:** Fig. 10.18: (a) B. Pipkin **288:** Fig. 10.19: (b) B. Pipkin **290:** Fig. 10.21: (b) Maryland Geological Survey **290:** Fig. 10.21: (c) Rutgers University/Institute of Marine and Geological Sciences **290:** Fig. 10.22: B. Pipkin **292:** Fig. 10.23: (a) Jim Falls, Calif. Dept. of Mines and Geology **292:** Fig. 10.23: (b) Geophoto Pub. Co. **292:** Fig. 10.24: B. Pipkin **293:** Fig. 10.25: U.S. Army Corps of Engineers **293:** Fig. 10.26: NOAA **294:** Fig. 10.27: NOAA/Ethan Gibney **295:** 10.30: © Mike Theiss/ultimatechase.com **295:** 10.31: © Mike Theiss/ultimatechase.com **297:** Fig. 10.35: (a) New Haven Railroad Historical and Technical Association, Inc./ Bill Reidy Collection **297:** Fig. 10.35: (b) Hartford Historical Society **299:** Fig. 10.36: (a) NOAA **299:** Fig. 10.37: (a) NOAA **302:** Fig. 2: B. Pipkin **302:** Fig. 3: USN **303:** Fig. 1: NASA **303:** Fig. 2: all, Mike Booher **304:** Fig. 1: Illinoisphotos.com **304:** Fig. 2: Illinoisphotos.com **304:** Fig. 3: Illinoisphotos.com **306:** Fig. 1: Illinoisphotos.com/U.S. Navy photo by Photographer's Mate 2nd Class Philip A. McDaniel **307:** Fig. 1: NOAA **307:** Fig. 2: B. Pipkin **307:** Fig. 3: Ruth Flanagan, copyright 1993, Earth magazine, Kalmbach Publishing Co.

Chapter 11. 311: Fig. 1: (a) Stantion, Glacier National Park Archives **311:** Fig. 1: (b) Lisa Mckeon, USGS **312:** Fig. 2: © Reuters/CORBIS **314:** Fig. 11.3: Wilfried Haeberli **315:** Fig. 11.5: John S. Shelton **316:** Fig. 11.6: Richard P. Jacobs, JLM Visuals **316:** Fig. 11.8: D. D. Trent **317:** Fig. 11.9: D. D. Trent **317:** Fig. 11.10: B. Pipkin **318:** Fig. 11.11: C. Hillaire-Marcel **320:** Fig. 11.14: Rolf A. Larsson **321:** Fig. 11.16:

D. D. Trent **322:** Fig. 11.17: D. D. Trent **322:** Fig. 11.18: John S. Shelton **335:** Fig. 11.31: E. J. Baldwin **335:** Fig. 11.32: Konrad Steffen **342:** Fig. 1: John Maurer **343:** Fig. 2: John Maurer **343:** Fig. 3: John Maurer **344:** Fig. 1: © Roger Ressmeyer/CORBIS **345:** Fig. 1: © Dan Guravich, National Audubon Society Collection, Photo Researchers **347:** Fig. 1: D. D. Trent **347:** Fig. 2: Barislav Bosnjak **347:** Fig. 3: D. D. Trent **347:** Fig. 4: D. D. Trent **347:** Fig. 5: D. D. Trent

Chapter 12. 351: Fig. 1: British War Museum **352:** Fig. 12.1: D. D. Trent **353:** Fig. 12.2: © Georg Gerster/Photo Researchers **353:** Fig. 12.3: D. D. Trent **353:** Fig. 12.4: D. D. Trent **353:** Fig. 12.5: SeaWIFS Project, NASA Goddard Space Flight Center and Orbimage **357:** Fig. 12.10: Soil Conservation Service **359:** Fig. 12.13: © Steve McCurry/Magnum **361:** Fig. 12.17: Howard G. Wilshire, USGS **361:** Fig. 12.18: Howard G. Wilshire, USGS **362:** Fig. 12.19: (a) Eden Foundation **362:** Fig. 12.19: (b) Eden Foundation **364:** Fig. 2: © George Steinmetz, National Geographic **364:** Fig. 3: Frank Langfitt/SunSource/The Baltimore Sun **366:** Fig. 3: Richard Lozinski **366:** Fig. 4: (a) USGS **366:** Fig. 4: (b) USGS **367:** Fig. 1: D. D. Trent **367:** Fig. 2: D. D. Trent **367:** Fig. 3: Joseph Allen **367:** Fig. 4: D. D. Trent

Chapter 13. 370: Fig. 1: D. D. Trent **377:** Fig. 13.4: B. Pipkin **377:** Fig. 13.5: Wendell E. Wilson **377:** Fig. 13.6: Clifford Taylor, USGS Bulletin 2156 **378:** Fig. 13.8: Kennecott Corp. **379:** Fig. 13.9: Woods Hole Oceanographic Institute **379:** Fig. 13.10: Joseph Kirschuink **379:** Fig. 13.11: Bruce Heezen, Scripps Institute of Oceanography **380:** Fig. 13.13: T. K. Buntzen, Silverado Mines U.S., Inc. **381:** Fig. 13.14: Sue Monroe **382:** Fig. 13.17: D. D. Trent **383:** Fig. 13.18: Jiri Hermann/BHP Billiton Diamonds, Inc. **387:** Fig. 13.20: Barrick Gold Corp. **389:** Fig. 13.22: Vivian Stockman **389:** Fig. 13.23: Vivian Stockman **390:** Fig. 13.24: D. D. Trent **391:** Fig. 13.26: W. Virginia Geological and Economic Survey **391:** Fig. 13.27: D. D. Trent **391:** Fig. 13.28: D. D. Trent **391:** Fig. 13.29: T. K. Buntzen **392:** Fig. 13.30: Donald B. Sayner Collection **392:** Fig. 13.31: Marc Jay Plumley **393:** Fig. 13.32: IMC Fertilizer, Inc. **395:** Fig. 13.34: D. D. Trent **395:** Fig. 13.35: D. D. Trent **397:** Fig. 13.36: John E. Gray, USGS bulletin 2156 **397:** Fig. 13.37: (a) E. Frank Schnitzer, Oregon Dept. of Geology

and Mineral Industries **397:** Fig. 13.37: (b) E. Frank Schnitzer, Oregon Dept. of Geology and Mineral Industries **398:** Fig. 13.38: ARCO **398:** Fig. 13.39: ARCO **401:** Fig. 1: D. D. Trent **402:** Fig. 2: (b) Daniel Hinds, Frontier Environmental Services **402:** Fig. 2: (a) Daniel Hinds, Frontier Environmental Services **403:** Fig. 3: Montana Historical Society, Helena **403:** Fig. 4: (a) David Nimick/USGS **403:** Fig. 4: (b) David Nimick/USGS **404:** Fig. 1: Ed Nuhfer, The Citizens Guide to Geologic Hazards **404:** Fig. 2: Ed Nuhfer **404:** Fig. 5: D. D. Trent **405:** Fig. 3: Ed Nuhfer **405:** Fig. 4: Chuck Meyers, Office of Surface Mining, Reclamation, and Enforcement **406:** Fig. 1: Dean Stiffarm, Fort Belknap Environmental Control Office **406:** Fig. 2: Dean Stiffarm, Fort Belknap Environmental Control Office **407:** Fig. 1: Hecla Mining Company and Idaho Geological Survey **407:** Fig. 2: D. D. Trent **407:** Fig. 3: John Burghardt, National Park Service, U.S. Dept. of Interior **408:** Fig. 4: D. D. Trent **408:** Fig. 5: D. D. Trent

Chapter 14. 412: Fig. 1: USGS **413:** Fig. 4: Dillon, USGS **418:** Fig. 14.6: Steve Dutch, Univ. of Wisconsin, Green Bay **423:** Fig. 14.15: Todd Wilkinson **426:** Fig. 14.18: (b) © Visuals Unlimited **427:** Fig. 14.19: Department of Energy (DOE) **429:** Fig. 14.22: Robert Finkelman, USGS **431:** Fig. 14.23: Richard Keeler, So. Cal. Edison Company **432:** Fig. 14.24: D. D. Trent **434:** Fig. 14.27: B. Pipkin **437:** Fig. 14.31: D. D. Trent **438:** Fig. 1: Drake Well Museum, Titusville, Pennsylvania **439:** Fig. 1: Courtesy of Shell Oil Company **442:** Fig. 1: John Chiasson/Gamma Liaison **442:** Fig: 2: Peter Bentham, BP Exploration **443:** Fig. 3: B. Pipkin **443:** Fig. 4: D. D. Trent

Chapter 15. 447: Fig. 1: B. Pipkin **448:** Fig. 2: B. Pipkin **450:** Fig. 15.3: (b) B. Pipkin **450:** Fig. 15.4: (b) B. Pipkin **452:** Fig. 15.6: Dennis Capolongo, Greenpeace **453:** Fig. 15.7 (b) B. Pipkin **454:** Fig. 15.8: B. Pipkin **454:** Fig. 15.9: B. Pipkin **457:** Fig. 15.13: Mitsuhiro Wada/Gamma Liaison **458:** Fig. 15.15: B. Pipkin **461:** Fig. 15.18: (b) Department of Energy **466:** Fig. 1: (b) B. Pipkin **469:** Fig. 1: Michael J. Philippot/Sygma/CORBIS **471:** Fig. 1: Robert Rathe **471:** Fig. 2: B. Pipkin **471:** Fig. 3: Joe Halbig, University of Hawaii-Hilo **471:** Fig. 4: B. Pipkin

Index

A

aa (lava), 124
Abandoned Mines Lands Initiative (AMLI), 401–404
ablation, zone of, 313
abrasion, 352, 368
absolute-age dating, 31, 43
abundant metals, 382
Acasta Gneiss, 35
acceleration of gravity, 79
acid mine drainage (AMD), 389–390, 400
acid rain, 152, 427–428, 440–441
acid rock drainage (ARD), 401
acids, 440–441
active sea cliffs, 291
active volcanoes, 134
adsorption, 166
aeration, zone of, 220, 243
aerosols, 329–330
Africa
    desertification in, 357–358
    soil degradation in, 5
aftershocks, 101–102
agricultural minerals, 383
aircraft, effect of airborne ash on, 109
air pollution, 427
    acid rain, 427–428
    coal burning, 429
    definition of, 444
    nitrogen oxides, 428–429
    smog, 428–429
    sulfur emissions, 427–428
air routes, 110
Alaska
    earthquakes in, 77, 86–87, 91
    glaciers, 331–332
    terranes in, 64
Alaskan oil pipeline, 169
Alaskan Volcano Observatory, 110–111, 131
Aleutian Islands, 110
alkalinity, 441
All-American Canal, 172
alluvial placers, 380
alluvial soils, 156
alluvium, 274
alpha decay, 33
alpha particles, 464
alpine glaciers, 186–187, 314
Alquist-Priolo Special Study Zones Act, 83
amorphous solids, 19
amphiboles, 21–22
Anak Krakatoa volcano, Indonesia, 128

Anatolia fault, Turkey, 70
andesite line, 115
Angkor Wat, Cambodia, 170
animal behavior, 104
anion, 19
Antelope Valley, California, 198
anticline, 198, 416
Aqaba, Jordan, 46
aqua alta flooding, 204
aquicludes, 220, 243
aquifers, 220, 243
Aral Sea, 235–236
Archbishop Ussher, 34–35
Archean Eon, 32
Arctic Oscillation, 337
area mining, 388
arid lands, 352–354
Arkansas River, Colorado, 254
arroyos, 365–366
arsenic, 232
artesian pressure, 223–224
artesian wells, 223–224, 243
artificial levees, 256–257, 262–263
artificial recharge, 227
A Sand County Almanac (book), 5
asbestos minerals, 37–38
ash clouds, 110–111
ash falls, 124–127, 145
Asia, soil degradation in, 5
Askole, Pakistan, 158
astenosphere, 57–58
Aswan High Dam, 265
Atacama Desert, 356
Atlantic Ocean, 282
atmosphere, 16, 323
atmospheric carbon dioxide (CO_2), 2, 327
atmospheric pressure, 299
atomic mass, 19
atomic number, 19
atoms, 18–19
Attleboro, Massachusetts, 175
augite, 21–22
Augustine volcano, Alaska, 125
Australia, desertification in, 360
avalanches, 195–197
average crustal abundance, 373
Ayers Rock, 41
Aztec civilization, 63

B

backwash, 279
Balcones Escarpment, Texas, 248

Banda Ache, Indonesia, 305–306
banded-iron formation, 379
Bangladesh, coastal flooding in, 255
bank-full stage, 258
bar-formed estuaries, 308
barium, 232
barrier islands, 287
basal cleavage, 22
basalt flows, 124
base isolation, 98–99
base level, 254, 274
base shear, 79, 98
batholith, 25
bauxite, 380–381
beach drifting, 279
beaches, 286–287
    barrier islands, 287
    definition of, 308
    erosion of, 288–291, 308
    longshore current, 279–281
    longshore drift, 279
    protective barriers, 292–293
    rip currents, 281
bench placers, 380
Benioff, Hugo, 49
Benioff-Wadati zones, 49
bentonite, 40, 185
benzene, 234
Bering bridge, 317
beta decay, 33
beta radiation, 464
Big Stone Lake, 322
Bingham Canyon mine, 378
biodegradation, 454
biogenic sedimentary rocks, 25, 28
biomass, 430
bioremediation, 174, 233
biosphere, 16
biota, 150
biotite, 22
bituminous coal, 424
black smokers, 67
blind thrusts, 89
block glides, 185–186
blue asbestos, 37
blue baby syndrome, 231
Blue Ridge Mountains, 184
Boca Raton, Florida, 280
body waves, 73
bolides, 286
Boltwood, Bertram, 33, 35
bombs (lava), 121–122

Bonnevile Salt Flats, 319
boron, 232
bottomland, 254
boulder fences, 175
Boulder River Basin, Montana, 402–404
brackish water, 227–228
breakers, 278, 308
breakwaters, 289, 292–293
Browning, Iben, 93
building codes, 98, 191–192
buttress fills, 192–193

C
cadmium, 232
Calavaeras fault, 79
calderas, 120, 139
caliche, 156
California, earthquakes in, 91
calving, 314
Cambrian Period, 21, 32
cancer, 37
Cape Hatteras Lighthouse, 302–303
Cape May, New Jersey, 280
capillary fringe, 220
caprock, 416
Carbon-14, 33–34
carbonate minerals, 20
carbon dioxide emissions, 129, 139, 340–341
carbonic acid, 152
Carboniferous Period, 21
carcinogenic minerals, 37–38
carrying capacity, 5–7, 13
Cascadia subduction zone, 93–94, 111–112
case histories, 9
Cathedral Peak Granite, 42
cation, 19
cat litter, 40
caving, 242
Cenozoic Era, 32
Central America, soil degradation in, 5
chain reaction, 436
chalcopyrite, 20
Charleston, South Carolina, 91
Chaucer, Geoffrey, 2
Chehalis River, Washington, 260–261
Chelungu fault, Taiwan, 106
chemical sedimentary rocks, 25, 28
chemical weathering, 151–153
    See also weathering
        definition of, 176
        hydration, 152
        hydrolysis, 153
        oxidation, 152
        solution, 152
Chesapeake Bay, 252
Chicxulub crater, 286
China
    desertification in, 363–364
    loess deposits in, 157
    one-child policy in, 12

Chinese civilization, 63
chlorine, 19
chlorofluorocarbons, 328–329
chromium, 232
chrysotile, 37
cinder cones, 121–122, 145
civilizations, and tectonic setting, 63
clastic sedimentary rocks, 25, 28
clasts, 25
clay, 158–159
clay minerals, 22, 153
clearcutting, 4, 206–208
cleavage, 22–23
climate, 323
    and Earth's surface, 323
    oceanic circulation, 325–326
    winds, 323–325
climate change, 326–330
    causes of, 326–330
        atmospheric carbon dioxide, 327
        dust and aerosols, 329–330
        greenhouse gases, 327–329
        ocean currents, 330
        plate tectonics, 327
        solar radiation, 327
        variations in Earth's orbit,
            326–327
    evidence of, 330–332
    and flooding, 251–252
    and glaciation, 322–323
    model-based predictions of, 349
    and volcanic eruptions, 128–129
    and water balance in lakes, 217
climax avalanches, 195–196
clouds, 337
coal, 423–424
coal-bed methane, 422–423
coal mines and mining,
            423–424
    collapse, 429
    impacts of, 388–389
    by region, 424
    reserves and production, 425
coastal deserts, 355–356
coastal flooding, 255, 309
coastal-plain estuaries, 308
Coccidioides immitis, 101
coccidioidomycosis, 101
Colima, Mexico, 86–88
collective behavior, 3
Colorado, landslides in, 202–203
Colorado brown stain, 232
Colorado Desert, 83
Columbia Glacier, 334–335
Columbia River, 201
columnar jointing, 143
Community Internet Intensity Maps
            (CIIM), 76
compaction, 170–173
complex landslides, 186

composite cones, 119–120
composting, 454, 458
compound growth equation, 11
Comprehensive Environmental Response,
            Compensation and Liability Act
            (CERCLA), 386–387
Comprehensive Test Ban Treaty, 79
compression, 54
concentrates, 393
concentration factors, 372–373
cone of depression, 221–222
confined aquifers, 223–224
conservation-tillage, 165
construction materials, 383
constructive plate boundaries, 55
contact-metamorphic deposit, 381
contamination, 174, 177
continental crust, 57
continental drift, 47–51
    description of, 68
    evidence of, 68
continental flood basalts, 117–119,
            145
continental glaciers, 314
contour maps, 9–10
contour mining, 388
Contra Costa County, California, 191
Control of Nature (book),
            182–183
convergent boundaries, 54, 62
copper, 232
coral reefs, 276–277
core, 57
Coriolis effect, 323–325
Coriolis force, 293
correlative-rights doctrine, 238
Corriente del Niño, 300
corundum, 383
cosmogenic isotopes, 154
cracking, 415
Crater Lake, Oregon, 120
cratons, 64–65
creep, 180
Cretaceous Period, 21
crocidolite, 37
Croll, John, 326
cropland losses, 163–165
crop rotation, 165
cross-bedding, 26
crust, 43, 57
crystals, shapes of, 23
crystal settling, 375–376
Cullinan diamond, 38
cultural eutrophication, 219
cutoff, 256, 274
cyanidation, 394–395
cyanide, 234
cyanide heap-leaching, 394
cyclones, 293
Cyprus, 62, 377

D

dams, 268
    See also floods
    controlling floods with, 261–262
    failure of, 250–251, 272–273
    and soil erosion, 164
Darcy's Law, 224, 237
Darwin, Charles, 71, 150
Dead Sea, 45–46
Death Valley, 217, 319
debris flows, 180
    See also mass wasting; subsidence
    causes of, 180–184
    and deforestation, 206–208
    intensity and duration of, 181–182
    mitigating, 194
    speed of, 181
    susceptibility to, 182–184
Deccan Traps, 119
decomposed granite, 156
deep earthquakes, 94
deep-ocean precipitation, 379
Deep Sea Drilling Project, 61
deep subsidence, 198–199, 211
deep-well injection, 459, 467–468
deflation, 352, 368
deflecting devices, 210
deflecting walls, 194
deforestation, 7, 206–208
deltas, 254–255, 274
depth hoar, 195
derivative maps, 9–10
desertification, 356–363
deserts, 354–356
    causes of, 368
    definition of, 368
    landscapes, 367
    types of, 355–356, 368
desert soils, 170–171
destructive plate boundaries, 55
developed countries, 11
developing countries, 11
Devil's Tower National Monument, 143–144
Devonian Period, 21
Dhaulagiri, Nepal, 66
diamonds, 38–39
    in Great Lakes region, 39
    hardness of, 20, 23
    major producers of, 39
    mining of, 383
diatoms, 415
dichloro-diphenyl-trichloroethane (DDT),
    235
dieldrin, 234
differential subsidence, 205–206
dilution, 174
dioxin, 234
dips, 29
dip slope, 186
disasters, and environmental changes, 1–2

discharge, 253, 274
disease outbreaks, 101
disposal sites, 449–451
disseminated deposits, 376–377, 409
dissolved substances, 229–232
distributaries, 254
divergent boundaries, 51–54
divining rods, 218
docking, 64
doldrums, 323
dormant volcanoes, 134
doubling time, 11
dowsers, 218–219
drainage basins, 257, 274
drainage divides, 257, 274
Drake, Edwin, 438–439
drawdown, 221
dredging, 391
Drift Creek Wilderness area, 181
dripstone, 242
driving force, 188–190
dust, 329–330
Dust Bowl, 148–149, 162–163
Dust Veil Index (DVI), 129
dust veils, 129

E

Earthquake Fault Zones Act, 83
earthquake-resistant designs, 79–81, 97–99,
    102–103
earthquakes, 71–74
    aftershocks, 101–102
    and animal behavior, 104
    body waves of, 73–74
    damages to cars, 105
    damages to freeways, 102–103
    and deep-well injection, 467–468
    and disease outbreaks, 101
    epicenter of, 72, 74–75
    focus of, 72
    intraplate, 91–93
    measurement of, 75–78, 107
        intensity scales, 75–76
        moment magnitudes, 77–78
        Richter magnitude scale, 76
    mitigation, 97–99, 107
    prediction of, 94–97
        forecasts, 95, 107
        geological methods, 95–97, 107
        statistical methods, 95, 107
    site effects of, 79–84
        fires, 84
        floods, 251
        ground failure, 82–83
        ground rupture, 82–83
        ground shaking, 79–81
        landslides, 82
        tsunamis, 84, 282–283
    with strong magnitudes, 84–90
        Alaska (2002), 86–87

Colima, Mexico (2003), 86
Gujarat, India (2001), 85–86
Northridge, California (1994), 88–90
significant earthquakes (1900–2005),
    85
Sumatra, Indonesia (2004), 87–88
    survival tips, 99–100
    waves, 72–74
Earth system, 16–18
    and acid mine drainage, 400
    age of, 34–36
    composition of, 43
    energy sources, 17
    internal structure of, 57
    materials, 17–30
        minerals, 19–23
        oldest known, 35
        rocks, 23–30
    orbit, 326–327
    surface of, 17–18
    water in, 214
earthworms, 150
Eastern Sierra Nevada, 139
East Pacific Rise, 56
echo sounding, 49
ecological overshoot, 6
Edwards Air Force Base, 198
Edwards aquifer, 239
Edwards Dam, 262
Edwards Plateau, Texas, 248
effusive eruptions, 115–117
Egyptian civilization, 63
elastic rebound theory, 72
elastic waves, 72
electronic waste, 457
elements, 18–19
elevation maps, 9
El Niño, 182, 298–299, 300–301
El Niño-Southern Oscillation (ENSO),
    300–301, 309
Elwha Dam, 262
emerald, 39
emroation, 469
end moraines, 314, 348
endrin, 234
energy, 414
    alternative sources of, 430–431
        geothermal, 433–434
        hydroelectric, 433
        illustrations, 442–443
        nuclear, 434–436
        ocean thermal energy conversion, 436
        solar, 431–432
        tidal currents, 437–438
        wave, 436–437
        wind, 432–433
    coal, 423–425
    definition of, 444
    of Earth system, 17
    natural gases, 422–423

nonconventional fossil fuels, 426–427
   nonrenewable sources of, 414
   petroleum, 415–421
   renewable sources of, 414
energy gases, 416–417, 422–423, 444
Energy Star appliances, 234
enivironment, 2
environmental geologists, 8–9
   case histories, 9–10
   tools of, 9
environmental geology, 2–3, 13
environmentalism, 2
environmentalists, 2
environmental laws, 386–387
Eocene Epoch, 21
eolian soils, 156
epicenter, 72, 74–75
Erebus Crater (Mars), 16
erosion, 161–164
   of beaches, 287–290, 308
   causes of, 163
   and cropland loss, 163–165
   and deforestation, 206–208
   mitigation of, 165–166
   by State, 163
   by streams, 274
   types of, 161–163, 176
eruption forecasting, 131–134
eskers, 319–320
estuaries, 308–309
ethanol, 430
Europe, soil degradation in, 5
European Project for Ice Coring in
      Antarctica (EPICA), 331
eutrophication, 219, 466
eutrophic lakes, 217–218
evaporites, 377
evapotranspiration, 215
excavation, 192–193
exfoliation domes, 155
expansive soils, 166, 176
exponential growth, 11
extinct volcanoes, 134
extrusive rock, 25

F
factor of safety, 190
falls, 186–187, 210
fans, 254–257
fault-block estuaries, 308
faults, 71
   See also earthquakes
   creep, 79
   in crustal rocks, 29
   scarp, 106
feldspar, 20–22, 153
felsic magmas, 115, 145
felsic rock, 25
Fernandina volcano, Galapagos Island,
      116

ferromagnesian minerals, 153
ferromagnesian silicates, 20
fertilizers, 6
fiords, 308
fires, 84, 150
firn, 313
fissile isotopes, 435
fission, 435
fission products, 435
fissures, 116
fjords, 348
flash floods, 257
flood basalts, 117–119, 145
floodplains, 254, 263, 274
floods, 250–252
   causes of, 257–258
   coastal, 255, 309
   in Europe and Russia (2002), 246–247
   flash, 257
   frequency of, 258–261
   ice-jam, 266–267
   impacts of, 252–257
      inundation, 252
      river systems, 252–254
      streams, 254–257
   measurement of, 258
   mitigation, 261–264
      artificial levees, 262–263
      dams, 261–262
      floodplain management, 263
      floodproofing, 263
      insurance, 263, 274
   and precipitation, 248
   probability of, 274
   types of, 250–252
   in the United States, 259
   and urban development, 270–271, 274
flood stage, 258
floodwalls, 263
flotation, 393–394
flowage, zone of, 313
flows, 180–184, 210
fluidized bed, 135
fluoride, 232
fluorite, 23
foliation, 29
forcing, 337
forensic geologists, 26
forests, conservation of, 3–4
Fossil Succession, Law of, 31–32
foundation failure, 82–83
Franklin, Benjamin, 128
Fresh Kills landfill, 466–467
fresh-water resources, 218–229
      groundwater, 219
      lakes, 218
      rivers, 216
      underground, 218–219
      usage trends, 228–229
frictional strength, 190

frost wedging, 150
fully developed sea, 278
fumarole, 132, 143–144
fusion, 465

G
gabbro, 25
gaining streams, 221–222
Galapagos Rift, 67
galena, 20
gamma rays, 464
Ganges-Brahmaputra delta, Bangladesh,
      254–255
gas chromatographs, 132
gems, 38–40
General Mining Law of 1872, 386
geographic information systems (GIS), 9
geological repositories, 460, 463–464
geologic contacts, 9
geologic maps, 9–10
geologic time, 30–35, 43
geologic traps, 416–417
geologists, 8–9
geothermal energy, 122, 145, 433–434, 445
geysers, 141, 434
Ghyben-Herzberg lens, 227
giant tube worms, 67
gibleh, 352
glacial drift, 157
glacial outwash, 317, 380
glacial soils, 156
glacial till, 314
glaciation, 312–313
   and climate change, 322–323
   and groundwater resources, 317
   and human transportation routes,
      318–319
   landscapes, 347
   Pleistocene lakes, 319–322
   and sea-level changes, 317
   and soil distribution, 317
Glacier Bay National Park, 314
glaciers, 311–313
   budget, 313–314
   classification of, 314
   and climate change, 331–332
   collapse of, 186–187
   definition of, 348
   features of, 314–316
   and global warming, 334–335
   and isostatic rebound, 318
   origin and distribution of, 313
glassy obsidian, 27
global population growth, 11
global positioning systems (GPS), 9, 134
global warming, 332–341
   See also climate change
   biological responses to, 345–346
   causes of, 337
   consequences of, 1, 336–337

global warming (*continued*)
  emission-reductions plans, 340–341
  evidence of, 332–336
  implications of, 338–340
  reducing, 340
Glossopteris, 47
gneiss, 31
Gobi desert, 16
gold mines, 370–371
golf courses, 178–179
Gondwana Succession, 47
Gould, Stephen J., 35
graben, 45
graded stream, 274
gradient, 253
grain size, 158–159
Grand Banks earthquake (1929), 284–285
granite, 22
graphite, 38
gravimeters, 133
gravity separation, 394
Gray, William, 298–299
Great Man-Made River Project (Libya),
    220–221
Great Plains, 148
Great Rift Valley, 55
Great Salt Lake, 319
Greco-Minoan civilization, 63
greenhouse gases, 327–329
Greenland, 334–336, 341–344
Grinell glacier, 311
groins, 280, 292
ground failure, 82–83
ground level, changes in, 83
ground rupture, 83
groundwater, 218–230
    See also water
  definition of, 243
  geologic work by, 229–230
  and glaciation, 317
  interaction with saltwater, 227–228
  interaction with surface water, 228–229,
      244
  laws, 238
  location and distribution of, 220–224
      pressurized underground water,
          223–224
      static water table, 220–223
  mining of, 214, 226–227
  pollution, 232–234, 396–397
  pressurized, 223–224
  and rock formations, 242
  solution by, 244
  storage and management of, 224–226, 243
  supply, 219
  sustained yield, 226, 243
  usage trends, 228–229
  withdrawal of, 198
  zone of aeration, 243
  zone of saturation, 243

growth rate, 11
Guadalupe River, Texas, 250
Gujarat, India, 85–86
Gulf of Aden, 55
Gulf of Aqaba, 46
Gulf of Mexico, oil drilling in, 439–440
gullying, 162
Gutenberg, Beno, 76

H
Haber, Fritz, 6
halite, 20
Halloween storm of 1991, 299–300
Harappan civilization, 63
hardness scale, 20, 23
hard water, 232
Hawaiian Islands, 116
    hot spots in, 62
    lava-flow hazard zones, 132
    volcanic gases, 129
Hawaiian Volcano Observatory, 131
Hayward fault, 79
hazardous waste disposal, 459–460, 472
heap-leaching, 394
Hector Mine earthquake, 106
Heimaey Island, Iceland, 131
helium, 19
herbicides, 7
Hess, Harry, 49
high-grade deposit, 373
high-level nuclear wastes, 461–462, 472
High Plains aquifer, 214, 226
highwalls, 388
Hilo, Hawai, 301–302
Hog Island, Virginia, 287
Holmes, Arthur, 48–49
Holocene Epoch, 21, 35
Home Plate (Mars), 16
Homo sapiens, 35
honeycomb weathering, 153–154
Honolulu, Hawaii, 56
horizontal water table, 220–223
hornblende, 21–22
horsebacks, 319
horse latitudes, 323, 348
Horseshoe Lake, 140
hot spots, 61, 112
hot-water dominated geothermal energy, 434
Huang Ho River, China, 157
human-earth interaction, 4
human-induced subsidence, 197
humans, and geological environment, 3
humus, 155
Huntington, Vermont, 175
Hurricane Camille, 307
Hurricane Gilbert, 294
Hurricane Katrina, 1, 205, 304–305
hurricanes, 293–297
    circulation patterns within, 293
    definition of, 309

examples of, 297–298
prediction of, 298–299, 309
Saffir-Simpson scale, 297–298
storm surges by, 295–296, 309
tracks of, 295–296
winds, 293–295
Hurricane Wilma, 1
hydrated methane, 412–413
hydration, 152
hydrauger, 192
hydraulic conductivity, 220, 237
hydraulic gradient, 237
hydraulic head, 223–224
hydraulicking, 391–393
hydraulic mining, 391–393
hydrocarbons, 414–415
hydrocompaction, 199–200
hydroelectric energy, 433, 445
hydrogen, atomic structure of, 19
hydrogeologists, 219
hydrograph, 257–258, 274
hydrologic cycle, 215, 243
hydrologists, 247
hydrolysis, 153
hydroseeding, 388
hydrosphere, 16
hydrothermal deposits, 377, 409
hyperaccumulator plants, 174
hypothesis, 8–9

I
Ice Age, 322, 348
ice cap, 336–337
ice crusts, 195
ice-field glaciers, 314
ice-jam floods, 266–267
ice-sheet glaciers, 314
Idaho, earthquakes in, 91
igneous rocks, 24–25
    classification of, 26
    definition of, 43
    extrusive, 27
illuviation, 159
Imperial Valley, California, 71, 172
impulsely generated waves. *See* tsunamis
inactive sea cliffs, 291
Incan civilization, 63
inceptisol, 175
incineration, 451–452
Indiana Dunes National Lakeshore, 288
Indonesian tsunami (2004), 87–88,
    305–306
indoor pollution, 469–470
industrial minerals, 382–383
infantile methemoglobinemia, 231
infiltration tests, 171
infrared radiation, 323
inselberg, 41
intensity scale, 75–76
interferometry, 133

Intergovernmental Panel of Climate Change (IPCC), 337
intertropical convergence zone (ITCZ), 323–325
intraplate earthquakes, 91–93
intrusive deposits, 375–376, 409
intrusive rock, 25
inundation, 252
ions, 19
IPAT equation, 3–4, 13
ironstone, 170
irrigation, 172
isoseismals, 75–76
isostatic rebound, 318
isothermal temperature, 217
isotopes, 19
    in age-dating, 33–34
    cosmogenic, 154
Isua Greenstone Belt, Greenbelt, 35

J

Jakobshavn Isbrae glacier, 335
Java, Indonesia, 62
Jawbone Canyon, California, 163–165
Jericho, 45
Jet Propulsion Laboratory, 15–16
jetties, 289, 291
joints, 29
Jordan River, 45–46
Jovian planets, 15
Jurassic Period, 21

K

Kamchatka Peninsula, 110
Kangerdlugssug glacier, 335
Kars limestone plateau, Yugoslavia, 229
karstified flow system, 239
karst terrane, 229, 242
Katrina (hurricane), 1, 205
Kelvin waves, 300
Kennebec River, Maine, 261–262
kerogen, 426
kettle lakes, 315–316, 348
Khian Sea (ship), 451–452
Kilauea volcano, Hawaii, 116–117, 129, 131
kimberlites, 383
Kingman, Arizona, 71
Krakatoa volcano, 127, 136

L

lahars, 127, 145
Lake Fissure, Iceland, 128
Lake Fork River, Colorado, 202–203
Lake George, New York, 322
Lake Magadati, Kenya, 55
Lake Manix, 217
Lake Nyos, Cameroon, 141–142
lakes, 216–218
    definition of, 243
    fountaining, 141–142

nutrient cycle, 217–218
overturning, 217–218
Pleistocene, 319–322
Lake San Cristobal, Colorado, 203
Lake Taupo, New Zealand, 135
Lake Victoria, 55
land bridges, 317
Landers earthquake (1992), 83
landfills, 449–451
landslides, 184–186
    See also mass wasting
    block glides, 185–186
    classification of, 180
    control and stabilization, 192–194
        excavation and redistribution, 192, 210
        retaining devices, 193–194, 210
        water drainage, 192, 210
    definition of, 210
    and deforestation, 206–208
    and disease outbreaks, 101
    driving force in, 188–190
    earthquake-triggered, 82
    hazard-zone maps, 190–191
    on Mars, 209
    normal force in, 189
    resisting force in, 188–190
    severity of, 179
    slumps, 184–185
    submarine, 284–286
    from submarine volcanic action, 285–286
lateral spreading, 187–188
laterite, 160, 170–171, 380, 409
Laurasia, 53
lavas, 25
    See also volcanoes
    domes, 120–121, 145
    flows, 49, 123–124, 145
    fountains, 117–118
    types of, 145
Law of Fossil Succession, 31–32
Lawrence Livermore Laboratory, 154
leachate, 454–455
leaching, 394
leaching, zone of, 155–156
lead, 232
Leaning Tower of Pisa, 169–170
Leopold, Alfred, 5
lesser developed countries, IPAT equation for, 4
levees, 205, 256–257, 262–263
lighthouses, 302–303
limestone, 20, 30
lindane, 234
Linz, Victor, 47
liquefaction, 82–83
Lisbon tsunami (1755), 284–285
lithification, 27
lithified sediments, 25, 27
lithosphere, 16, 57–58
littoral drift, rates of, 290

loam, 158–159
lodes, 377
loess, 157–158
Loihi volcano, Hawaii, 116
Loma Prieta earthquake (1989), 82, 89, 97
Lone Pine Canyon, California, 17
Long Island, water supply in, 240–241
longitudinal waves, 73–74
longshore current, 279–280
longshore drift, 279–280, 308
Long Valley caldera, 139
Los Angeles City, water supply in, 139
losing streams, 221
Love Canal, 468–469
Lovell, Wyoming, 40
Love waves, 74
low-emission vehicles, 340–341
low-grade deposit, 373
lowland floods, 257, 274
low-level nuclear wastes, 462, 472
Lumpkin, Georgia, 162
luster, 23

M

maar, 141
Madagascar, 161
Madison County, Virginia, 182, 184
Madison River, Montana, 82
mafic magmas, 115, 145
mafic rock, 25
magma, 24, 115
magnetic cycle, 327
magnetic epoch, 52
magnetic field, 50–52
magnetic polarities, 49–50
magnetic poles, reversal of, 50–52
magnetometer, 49, 132
Malthus, Thomas, 6
Mammoth Mountain, California, 129, 139–140
Manaus, Brazil, 12
manganese nodules, 379
mantle lid, 57–58
marble, 20, 31
Marine Protection Reserve and Sanctuary Act of 1972, 452–453
marine trenches, 49
Mars, 15–16
Mars Exploration Rovers, 15–16
marsh gas, 454
Martian landscape, 15–16
Martian landslide, 209
massive sulfides, 377
mass wasting, 179
    classification of, 179–180
    control and stabilization, 192–194
        debris flow mitigation, 194
        excavation and redistribution, 192
        retaining devices, 193–194
        water drainage, 192

mass wasting (*continued*)
  definition of, 210
  falls, 186–187, 210
  flows, 180–184, 210
  landslides. *See* landslides
  lateral spreading, 187–188
  on Mars, 209
  reducing losses from, 190–192
    building codes, 191–192
    hazard-zone maps, 190–191
  snow avalanches, 195–197
  subsidence, 197–200
Matthews, Drummond, 51
Mauna Kea volcano, Hawaii, 115–116
Mauna Loa volcano, Hawaii, 115–116
Maunder minimum, 327
maximum contaminant level (MCL), 231
maximum contaminant level goals
    (MCLGs), 231
McPhee, John, 182–183
meanders, 254–255, 274
Mediterranean Sea, salt deposits in, 61
Meinesz, Vening, 51
Mendeleyev, Dmitri, 18
mercury, 232
Mesosarus, 47
mesotrophic lakes, 218
Mesozoic Era, 32
metallic minerals, 382
  See also nonmetallic minerals
  abundant, 383
  concentrates, 393
  consumption and production of, 384
  processing of, 393–396
    chemical methods, 394
    cyanidation, 394–395
    flotation, 393–394
    gravity separation, 394
    smelting, 395–396
  recycling of, 386
  scarce, 383
metamorphic rocks, 29–31, 43
metamorphism, 30
meteorites, 286
methane, 328, 412–413, 454
methane economy, 422
methanol, 430
Mexico, soil degradation in, 5
Mexico City, 198–199
Meyer, Lothar, 18
micas, 21–22, 153
microcontinents, 64
microplates, 64
Mid-Atlantic Ridge, 56
midlatitude deserts, 355, 368
mid-ocean ridges, 49, 58–59
Midwest earthquake zone, 92
mill tailings, 462, 472
mineral deposits, 372
  deep-ocean precipitation, 379

definition of, 409
disseminated, 376–377
hydrothermal, 377
intrusive deposits, 375–376
origins of, 375–381, 409
  igneous processes, 375–377, 409
  metamorphic processes, 381
  sedimentary processes, 377–380, 409
  weathering processes, 380–381, 409
placer, 380
surficial precipitation, 377
volcanogenic, 377
mineral reserves, 372
  categories of, 382–383, 409–410
  factors, 409
  metallic, 382
  nonmetallic, 382–383
    agricultural, 383
    construction materials, 383
    industrial, 382–383
mineral resources, 371–372
  classification of, 371
  concentration factors, 372–373
  consumption and production of,
      384–386
  definition of, 409
  distribution of, 375
  factors, 373–375
  reserves, 373–375
minerals, 19–20
  carcinogenic, 37–38
  crystal shapes of, 23
  definition of, 43
  groups, 20
  hardness of, 20
  identification of, 20–23
  rock-forming silicates, 20–21
Minhasa, Celebes, 143
minimum-till farming, 165
mining, 386–400
  abandoned mines, 401–404
  coal, 388–389
  contaminants, 39708
  environmental impacts of, 386–387
  future of, 398–399, 410
  land reclamation, 396
  laws, 399–400
  legacy of, 407–408
  and revegetation, 398
  surface, 391–393
  surface- and groundwater protection in,
      396–397
  underground, 389–390
  and wildlife restoration, 398
Mining Law of 1872, 399
Miocene Epoch, 21
Mississippian Period, 21
Mississippi River, 197, 205, 248, 254–255,
    263
Mobil Oil Co., 174

modified Mercalli Scale (MM), 75–76
Mohs, Friedrich, 20
Mohs hardness scale, 20, 23
Mojave Desert, 106
moment magnitudes (M_w), 77–78
Mono-Inyo Craters, California, 120, 139
Montserrat, 138
moraines, 314
Morgan Hill, California, 98–99
Morley, Lawrence, 51
Motagua fault, 56
mountaintop-removal mining, 388–389
Mount Erebus, 111
Mount Etna, Italy, 123
Mount Fujiyama, Japan, 119
Mount Katmai, Alaska, 125
Mount Kliuchevskoi, Russia, 110
Mount Mazama, Oregon, 120
Mount Pelée, Martinique, 125–126
Mount Pinatubo, Philippines, 110, 124
Mount Rainier, Washington, 127–128
Mount Ruapehu, New Zealand, 134
Mount Rushmore, South Dakota, 42
Mount Shasta, California, 119
Mount Spurr, Alaska, 110
Mount St. Helens, Washington, 121, 125,
    129, 136
Mount Vesuvius, Italy, 119, 126–127, 136
Mount Whitney, California, 25
mud cracks, 26
mud volcano, 144
Muir, John, 42
multiple land-use strategies, 472
municipal waste disposal, 448–449
  See also waste disposal
  incineration, 451–452
  multiple land-use strategies, 458–459,
      472
  ocean dumping, 452–453, 472
  problems in, 453–455
  recycling, 455–458, 472
  sanitary landfills, 449–451, 472
muscovite, 21

N

National Environmental Policy Act (NEPA),
    386–387
National Flood Insurance Act of 1968, 263,
    274
National Forest Service, 3
National Hurricane Center, 299
National Ice Core Laboratory (NICL), 344
National Primary Drinking Water
    Regulations (NPDWRs), 231
National Weather Service, 299
native elements, 19
natural gases, 416–417, 422–423, 444
natural levees, 256–257
natural subsidence, 197–198
negative anomaly, 51

Neogene Period, 21
Neolithic ice man, 312
Nevada
    earthquakes in, 91
    gold mining in, 370–371
Nevado del Ruiz volcano, Colombia, 127
New England flood of 1927, 269–270
New Madrid earthquakes (1811-2), 91–93
New Orleans, Louisiana, 205, 265–266
New Zealand, volcanoes in, 135–138
Niigata, Japan, 82
Nile River, 172, 254–255, 264–265
Nilometers, 264–265
nitrates, 232
nitrogen oxide, 328–329, 428–429
nonmetallic minerals, 382–383
    agricultural, 383
    construction materials, 383
    consumption and production of, 384
    industrial, 382–383
nor'easters, 250, 299
Norris glacier, 320
North America
    earthquake zones in, 91–92
    soil degradation in, 5
    terranes of, 64
North Pacific Ocean, 16–17
Northridge earthquake (1994), 75, 88–90
no-til farming, 165
Nubian Sandstone, 220
nuclear energy, 434–436, 445, 464–465
nuclear fission, 435
nuclear wastes, 460–465
    See also waste disposal
    disposal of, 462–463
    geological repositories, 463–464
    health and safety standards for, 464, 472
    high-level, 461–462, 472
    isolation of, 462–463
    low-level, 462, 472
    mill tailings, 462, 472
nucleus, 19
nuée ardente, 120

O
obsidian, 27
Ocean City, Maryland, 289–290
ocean dumping, 452–453, 472
Ocean Dumping Act of 1972, 452–453
Ocean Dumping Ban of 1988, 452–453
oceanic circulation, 325–326, 348
oceanic crust, 57
oceans, 58
    changes in currents, 330
    evolutionary stages of, 58
    surface currents, 325–326, 348
ocean thermal energy conversion, 436
Ocean Trails Golf Course, 178–179
offshore winds, 326
Ogallala Sandstone, 226

oil. See petroleum
Oil Creek, 438–439
oil pipelines, 169
oil shales, 426–427, 444
Old Faithful (geyser), 226
Olgas, 41
Oligocene Epoch, 21
oligotrophic lakes, 217–218
olivine, 21–22
one-child policy, 12
opal, 38
open-pit mining, 393, 404–405
Opportunity Rover (spacecraft), 15–16
orbit, 326–327
Ordovician Period, 21
Oregon, debris flows in, 201
ore minerals, 372
ores, 372
organic pollutants, 234
Origin of Continents and Oceans, The
    (book), 48
orographic effect, 248
orthoclase, 22
oscillation, waves of, 308
outlet glaciers, 314
overpopulation, 4, 12
overturn, 141–142, 217–218
Owens Valley, California, 151
oxbow lake, 256, 274
oxidation, 152
oxide minerals, 20
oxisols, 170–171
oxygen, atomic structure of, 19
ozone layer, 328–329

P
Pacific Northwest earthquake zones, 93–94
Pacific Ocean, 282
Pacific plate, 54
Pahala ash, 156
pahoehoe, 124
Paleocene Epoch, 21
Paleogene Period, 21
Paleozoic Era, 32
Pangaea, 47, 53, 60
Panthalassa Ocean, 53
paper, annual consumption of, 4
Papua, New Guinea, 282–283
Paricutin volcano, Mexico, 121
passive margins, 60–63
Patton, George S., 172–173
peak discharge, 258
Pecos River, Texas, 248
pedologists, 159
pegmatites, 375
Pele's hair, 117
Pennsylvanian Period, 21
perched water table, 220
periodic table, 18–19
permafrost, 166–169, 176

permafrost table, 167
permeability, 220, 237, 243
Permian Period, 21
persistent pollutants, 231
pesticides, 7
petroleum, 414–415
    consumption and production of,
        420–421
    definition of, 444
    geologic traps, 416–417
    origin and accumulation of, 415–416,
        444
    production of, 417–418, 444
    quality and price of, 419
    reserves, 419–420, 444
    secondary recovery of, 418, 444
phaneritic texture, 24
Phanerozoic Eon, 32
phenols, 234
phosphates, 383
photochemical smog, 428–429
phreatic eruptions, 135, 141
physical weathering, 150, 176
phytoremediation, 174
piedmont glaciers, 314
piezometric surface, 223–224
Pinchot, Gifford, 3
pingo, 167
placer deposits, 380
plagioclase, 22
planets, 15
plastic flow, 313
plate, 51
plateaus, 117–119
plate tectonics, 51–56
    See also earthquakes
    cause of, 68
    and climate change, 327
    convergent boundaries, 54
    description of, 68
    divergent boundaries, 51–54
    drift rate, 56
    and environment, 61
    evidence of, 56–58, 68
    hot spots, 61–62
    and human environment, 61–63
    model of, 56
    and rock cycle, 61
    and supercontinent formation, 58–60
    transform boundaries, 54–55
playas, 216–217, 243
Pleistocene Epoch, 21, 35
Pleistocene lakes, 319–322
Plinian columns, 124
Pliocene Epoch, 21
plow zones, 175
plug flow, 202
plunging breakers, 278
plutons, 25
point bar, 256

Point Fermin landslide, 185–186
polar deserts, 355, 368
polar front, 325
polar high, 323, 348
pollutants, 232–234, 244
polychlorinated biphenyls (PCBs), 234
Pompeii, 126–127
Ponce, Puerto Rico, 185–186
population, growth rate of, 11
population density, 7–8
porewater pressure, 198
porosity, 237, 243
porphry copper, 376–377
positive anomaly, 51
potable water, standards for, 230–232
potassium, 17, 383
Potassium-40, 34
Potomac River, stage and discharge for, 260
powdersnow avalanches, 196
power towers, 431
Precambrian Period, 32
precipitation, 248, 250
precursors, 94
predators, populations of, 6
prediction, 131
pressurized underground water, 223–224
preys, populations of, 6
primary waves (P-waves), 73–74
prior-appropriation doctrine, 238
proglacial lakes, 319–322
Proterozoic Eon, 32
Prudhoe Bay, Alaska, 168
pumice, 27, 237
pyrite, 20, 390
pyroclastic ejecta, 121
pyroclastic flows, 135, 145
pyroxenes, 21–22

Q
Qattara Depression, Egypt, 351–352
Quake Lake, Montana, 82
quartz, 21–22, 39–40, 153
quartzite, 30–31
Quaternary Period, 32, 35
Queen Creek, Arizona, 199
Queensland, Australia, lava flows in, 123
quick clays, 82–83, 187–188

R
radiation, 323
radicals, 19
radioactive minerals, 37
radiogenic decay, 17, 33–34
radiometric dating, 33
radon, 469–470
rain-shadow deserts, 355–356
Rayleigh waves, 74
reasonable-use doctrine, 238
recessional moraines, 314
recharge areas, 220, 225

recharge mound, 221
recontouring, 192
recrystallization, 29
recurrence interval, 95, 258, 274
recycling, 455–458, 472
Red Mountain, Montana, 82
Red River, North Dakota, 260
Red Sea, 55
Reelfoot Rift, 92
refining, 415
refuse-derived fuel, 454
regional metamorphism, 381
regolith, 155
Regulatory Floodplain, 263
Reid, Harold F., 72
relative-age dating, 31, 43
remediation, 174
reservoir rock, 415
residence time, 233, 244
residual soils, 156, 176
resisting force, 188–190
resonance, 81
Resource Conservation and Recovery Act of
      1976, 399, 459
resource inequities, 4
resource recovery, 455–458, 472
retaining devices, 193–194
revegetation, 398
reversed magnetic field, 52
reverse fault, 71
Richter, Charles, 76
Richter magnitude scale, 76
right-lateral strike-slip fault, 71–72
Rilito Creek, Arizona, 256
rill erosion, 162, 176
Ring of Fire, 112
Rio Grande River, 258, 260
Rio Negro, Brazil, 12
riparian doctrine, 238
rip current, 280
ripple marks, 26–29
riverine floods, 257
rivers, 216
    discharges, 274
    drainage basins, 274
    flooding, 252–254
    stream velocity if, 274
rock bolts, 194, 210
rock climbing, 29
rock cycle, 24, 43, 61
Rockefeller, John D., 439
rockfalls, 186–187
rock-forming silicates, 20–21
rock oil, 438–439
rocks, 23–30
    defects, 29
    definition of, 43
    igneous, 24–25
    metamorphic, 29
    porosity of, 220, 237

sedimentary, 25–29
    weathering, 149–155
        chemical, 151–153
        physical, 150
Rocky Mountain Arsenal, 467–468
Rodinia, 60
Roman civilization, 63
Roosevelt, Theodore, 3, 42
rotational landslides, 184, 210
Rubidium-87, 34
rural-to-urban transformation, 7–8,
      11, 13

S
Sacramento River, California, 254
Saffir-Simpson scale, 297–298
Sahara Desert, 357–358
Sahel region, Africa, 357–358
salinization, 172
salt, 20
salt-crystal growth, 150–151
salt domes, 382–383, 416–417
Salt Lake City and County Building,
      98–99
Salton Sea, 172
saltwater, 227–228
saltwater encroachment, 227–228
San Andreas fault, 79
    historic seismic activity of, 97
    marsh and lake deposits in, 98
    similarities with Anatolia fault, 70
sand, 158–159
San Fernando Valley, California, 89
San Francisco Bay region, earthquake
      probability in, 96
sanitary landfills, 449–451, 472
San Joaquin Valley, California, 199–200, 238
Santa Ana winds, 101
Santa Barbara, California, 289–291
Santa Clara Valley, California, 227
Santa Cruz Mountains, California, 97
Santa Susana Mountains, 101
satellite interferometry, 133
saturation, zone of, 220, 243
scarce metals, 382
schist, 31
schistosomiasis, 265
scientific method, 8–9
scrubbers, 428
sea cliffs, 291–293, 308
sea-floor spreading, 49–51, 68
sea level, 317, 336
seawater encroachment, 227–228, 244
seaways, 46, 54
secondary enrichment, 380–381, 409
secondary recovery, 418, 444
secondary waves (S-waves), 73–74
sedimentary rocks, 25–29
    See also rocks
    biogenic, 25

chemical, 25
classification of, 28
clastic, 25
definition of, 43
on Mars, 16
seismic design factors, 79–84
See also earthquakes
earthquake resistance, 98–99, 102–103
fires, 84
ground failure, 82–83
ground rupture, 82–83
ground shaking, 79–81
importance of, 90–91
landslides, 82
tsunamis, 84
seismic gaps, 96
seismic joints, 81
seismic records, forensic use of, 79
seismogram, 74
seismograph, 74
selenium, 232
semiarid grasslands, 355
Seneca Oil Co., 438–439
sensitive clays, 187–188
Sequoia National Park, California, 17
seracs, 313
settlement, 169–170, 176
sewage disposal, 465–466. *See also* waste
disposal
shallow earthquakes, 94
shallow subsidence, 199–200, 211
shear, 54
shear walls, 81
shear waves, 74
sheet erosion, 161–162, 176
sheet joints, 155
shield volcanoes, 115–117
shingle beaches, 286
shorelines, 286
short-wave radiation, 323
shotcrete, 194
Sieh, Kerry, 96
Sierra Nevada, California, 25, 120
silica, 25
silicates, 20
silica tetrahedron, model of, 21
silt, 158–159
Silurian Period, 21
silver, 232
Sina Peninsula, 55
sinkholes, 229–230
site characterization, 460
slab avalanches, 195
slant drilling, 417
slate, 31
Slide Mountain, Nevada, 184
slide planes, 179, 185
slow earthquakes, 283
Slumgullion landslide, Colorado,
202–203

smectite, 40
smelters, 374
smelting, 395–396
smog, 428–429
snow avalanches, 195–197, 211
sodium, 19, 232
soils, 149
classification of, 159–160
color of, 157–158
compaction of, 170–173
composition of, 149
contamination of, 174
definition of, 176
degradation, 5, 162
erosion, 7
causes of, 163
mitigation of, 165–166
types of, 161–163
in the United States, 163
formation of, 17, 155
grain size, 158–159
horizons, 155–156
liquefaction, 82–83
minerals in, 157–158
problems, 161–171, 176
crop losses, 164–165
erosion, 161–164
expansive soils, 166, 176
permafrost, 166–169, 176
settlement, 169–170, 176
profile, 155–157
residual soils, 156
transported soils, 156–157
as records of history, 175
remediation, 174
salinization, 172
texture of, 158–159
from weathering of rock, 149–155
solar energy, 431–432, 444–445
Solar One station, 431
solar radiation, 327
solar system, 43
solid waste disposal, 448–449
solution, 152
Soufrière Hills volcano, Montserrat, 138
source rock, 415
South America, soil degradation in, 5
southern oscillation, 300–301
specific retention, 225, 243
specific yield, 225, 243
speleology, 242
spelunking, 242
spent fuel, 461
sphalerite, 23
spheres, 43
spheroidal weathering, 154–155
spilling breakers, 279
Spirit Rover (spacecraft), 15–16
spodsol, 161
spontaneous liquefaction, 82–83

spreading centers, 54
springs, 224
stage hydrograph, 258
stalactites, 242
stalagmites, 242
static water table, 220–223
steam-dominated geothermal energy, 434
steering winds, 293–295
St. Francis Dam, failure of, 272–273
Stone Forest, China, 242
Storegga submarine landslide, 284–285
storm surges, 295–296, 309
strain, 72
Strait of Gibraltar, 61
stratification, 26
stratigraphic traps, 417
stratovolcanoes, 119–120, 145
streams, 254–257, 274
stress, 72
strikes, 29
strip-cropping, 165
strip-mining, 391–393
Stromboli volcano, 111
structural traps, 416–417
subduction, 49–51
subduction earthquakes, 94
submarine landslides, 284–286
submarine volcanoes, 145, 285–286
subpolar low, 325
subSaharan Africa, paper consumption in, 4
subsidence, 197–200
See also mass wasting
causes of, 211
classification of, 198–200
deep, 198–199, 211
shallow, 199–200, 211
in coal mines, 429
definition of, 211
differential, 205–206
earthquakes, 94
human-induced, 197
in major cities, 197
mitigation of, 200, 211
natural, 197–198
vs. settlement, 197
subtropical deserts, 355, 368
subtropical highs, 323, 348
sulfates, 20
sulfide minerals, 20
sulfur, 382
sulfur dioxide, 427–428
sulfur emissions, 427–428
Sumatra, Indonesia, 87–88
Sumerian civilization, 63
sun, 17
sunspots, 327
supercontinent, 47, 58–60
Superfund, 397–398, 459–460
surface hoar, 195
surface mining, 391–393

Surface Mining Control and Reclamation
    Act (SMCRA), 386–387
surface water, 216–218, 228–229, 396–397
surface waves, 73
surficial precipitation, 377–379
surging, 314
sustained yield, 226, 243
swash, 279
swell, 278
Swiss Alps, 187
syncline, 186
synthetic fuels, 425
system, 17

T
tailings, 390
Taka Makan desert, 16
Taku glacier, 320
talik, 167
talus slopes, 186, 188
Tambora volcano, Indonesia, 128–129
tar sands, 426, 444
Taupo Volcanic Zone, 135–136
tension, 54
tephra, 121
Terminal Island, 198
terminal moraines, 314
terracing, 165
terrain anchors, 195
terranes, 64
terrestrial planets, 15
Tertiary Period, 21
Teton Dam, failure of, 272–273
Texas, floods in, 250
Texas Gulf Coast, subsidence in, 197
thermocline, 217
thermotectonic arch, 60
Thinking Like a Mountain (essay), 5
Thomson, William, 35
thorium, 17
Three Gorges Dam, 268
Throrium-232, 34
thrust fault, 88
tidal currents, 437–438
tidal wave. *See* tsunamis
tidewater glaciers, 334
tiltmeter, 132
toe, 202
toluene, 234
tombolo, 293
Tongariro National Park, New Zealand, 135
topographic maps, 9–10
total dissolved solids, 231
Toutle River, 127
tower karst, 242
Toxic Substance Control Act of 1972, 38
tradewind deserts, 355
translation, waves of, 308
translational slides, 185–186, 210
transportation system, 17

transported soils, 156–157, 176
transverse waves, 74
traps, 118
tremor, 133
triangulation, 75–76
Triassic Period, 21
tricholoroethylene (TCE), 234
Trimble, Stan, 164
tropospheric winds, 298
troughs. *See* tsunamis
tsunamis, 281–284
    See also earthquakes
    causes of, 282–286
        bolide impacts, 286
        earthquakes, 84, 282–283
        submarine landslides, 284–286
        submarine volcanic action, 127–128,
            145, 285–286
    definition of, 308
    Indonesia (2004), 87–88, 305–306
    mitigation of damages, 301–302
    monitoring system, 305–306
    velocities of, 282
    warning system, 283–284
tuff, 27
Tumult Creek debris flow (Oregon), 201
tundra, 167
Turnagain Heights, Alaska, 82, 188–189
typhoons, 293

U
Ukraine, soil fertility in, 157
Uluru National Park, Australia, 41
unconfined aquifers, 220–221, 243
underground mining, 389–390
underground water. *See* groundwater
undertow, 279
Uniform Building Code, 98, 191–192
upland floods, 257, 274
upwelling, 326
uranium, 19, 33–34
Uranium-235, 19, 34
Uranium-238, 19, 34
Uranium Mill Tailings Radiation Control
    Act of 1978, 462
urban population, 7–8

V
Vaiont Dam landslide (Italy), 186–187
valence, 19
valley fever, 101
valley glaciers, 186–187, 314
vapor extraction, 174
Venice, Italy, 204
ventification, 150
vertisol, 166
Vesuvius Volcano Observatory, 131
Vienna Convention for the Protection of
    Ozone Layer, 329
Vine, Fred, 51

viscosity, 145
volcanic ash, 156–157
Volcanic Explosivity Index (VEI), 113, 130
volcanic gases, 129, 145
volcanic soils, 156
volcanic tremor, 133
volcanoes, 111–114
    activity of, 134
    ash clouds from, 109–111
    benefits of, 122, 145
    cones, 115
        cinder, 121–122
        lava domes, 120–121
        shield, 115–117
        stratovolcanoes, 119–120
    in continental United States, 113
    definition of, 145
    distribution of, 145
    diversion of lava, 131
    dust veils, 129
    eruptions, 113–115
        comparison of, 130
        effusive, 115
        explosive, 119–120
        survival tips, 134
    geothermal energy from, 122
    hazards, 123–129, 145
        ash falls, 124–127, 145
        gases, 129
        lahars, 127, 145
        lava flows, 123–124, 145
        tsunamis, 127–128, 145
        on weather and climate, 128–129
    mitigation and prediction, 130–134, 146
        diversion of lava flows, 130
        eruption forecasting, 131–134
        hazard-zone maps, 130–131
    at plate boundaries and hotspots, 112
    submarine, 285–286
volcanogenic deposits, 377, 409
Volcán San Cristóbal, Nicaragua, 119

W
Wadati, Kiyoo, 49
Wailuku River, 301–302
Wasatch Plateau, Utah, 71
Washington, earthquakes in, 91
waste disposal, 448–449
    hazardous wastes, 459–460, 472
    in history, 471
    municipal wastes, 449–459, 472
    nuclear wastes, 460–465, 472
    private sewage, 465–466
    sociology of, 466
Waste Isolation Pilot Plant (WIPP),
    463–464
water, 215
    alternative sources of, 234, 244
    conflicts over, 213–214
    conservation of, 234, 244

consumption rate, 221
drainage, 192
hardness scale, 232
pollution, 232–234
quality of, 230–234
  definition of, 244
  dissolved substances,
    230–232
  standards for, 244
softener, 232
spreading, 227
surface, 216–218
sustained yield, 226
tables, 220–223, 243
use of, 243
waterlogging, 172
water witches, 218
wave base, 278
wave period, 81
wave refraction, 279–281, 308
waves, 277–279
  as energy source, 436–437
  factors of size, 308
  impulsely generated. *See* tsunamis
  orthogonals, 280
  of oscillation, 278, 308

of translation, 278, 308
wind, 277–279
weather, effect of volcanic eruptions on,
    128–129
weathering, 149–155
  chemical, 151–153, 176
  definition of, 150, 176
  deposits, 380–381, 409
  geologic features of, 154–155
  physical, 150, 176
  rate of, 153–154, 176
Wegener, Alfred, 47–48, 66
West Antarctic Ice Sheet, 334
westerlies, 348
Westhampton, New York, 307
Whakapapa Skifield, New Zealand, 137
wildcat wells, 417
Wilma (hurricane), 1
Wilmington oil field, 198
Wilson, J. Tuzo, 51, 58–60
Wilson cycle, 58–60
wind erosion losses, 163
winds, 323–325
  definition of, 348
  as energy source, 432–433
  as geologic agent, 352, 368

wind waves, 277–281
Winter Park, Florida, 229–230
women, empowerment of, 11
Wrangelia terrane, 64–65
Wrangell Island, Australia, 447–448

X
xylene, 234

Y
Yellow River, China, 157
Yellowstone National Park, calderas in, 120
Yorkshire, England, sandstone wall in, 42
Yucca Mountain Geologic Repository, 463

Z
Zion National Park, Utah, 29
zircon, 35
zone of ablation, 313
zone of accumulation, 156
zone of aeration, 220, 243
zone of flowage, 313
zone of leaching, 156
zone of saturation, 220, 243
zooplanktons, 415
Zortman-Landusky gold mine, 405–406